8th Workshop on Noisy User-generated Text (W-NUT 2022)

Gyeongju, South Korea
12-17 October 2022

ISBN: 978-1-7138-6200-0

Printed from e-media with permission by:

Curran Associates, Inc.
57 Morehouse Lane
Red Hook, NY 12571

Some format issues inherent in the e-media version may also appear in this print version.

Printed with permission by Curran Associates, Inc. (2023)

For permission requests, please contact the Association for Computational Linguistics at the address below.

Association for Computational Linguistics
209 N. Eighth Street
Stroudsburg, Pennsylvania 18360

Phone: 1-570-476-8006
Fax: 1-570-476-0860

acl@aclweb.org

Additional copies of this publication are available from:

Curran Associates, Inc.
57 Morehouse Lane
Red Hook, NY 12571 USA
Phone: 845-758-0400
Fax: 845-758-2633
Email: curran@proceedings.com
Web: www.proceedings.com

COLING

International Conference on Computational Linguistics

Proceedings of the Conference and Workshops

COLING

Volume 29 (2022), No. 4

Proceedings of 8th Workshop on Noisy User-generated Text (W-NUT 2022)

The 29th International Conference on Computational Linguistics

October 12 - 17, 2022
Gyeongju, Republic of Korea

Introduction

The W-NUT 2022 workshop focuses on a core set of natural language processing tasks on top of noisy user-generated text, such as that found on social media, web forums and online reviews. Recent years have seen a significant increase of interest in these areas. The internet has democratized content creation leading to an explosion of informal user-generated text, publicly available in electronic format, motivating the need for NLP on noisy text to enable new data analytics applications.

We have received 39 main workshop submissions (22 long and 17 short papers). The workshop will be held in hybrid in-person and virtual modes. We have two invited speakers Yulia Tsvetkov (University of Washington) and David Jurgens (University of Michigan) who will talk about their work. We're very thankful to have them in our workshop.

We have the best paper award(s) sponsored by Megagon Labs this year, for which we are thankful. We would like to thank the Program Committee members who reviewed the papers. We would also like to thank the workshop participants.

Wei Xu, Alan Ritter, Tim Baldwin and Afshin Rahimi
Co-Organizers

Organizers:

Wei Xu, Ohio State University
Alan Ritter, Ohio State University
Tim Baldwin, University of Melbourne
Afshin Rahimi, University of Queensland

Program Committee:

Muhammad Abdul-Mageed (University of British Columbia)
Željko Agić (Corti)
Sweta Agrawal (University of Maryland)
Gustavo Aguilar (Amazon)
Hamed Alhoori (Northern Illinois University)
Emily Allaway (Columbia University)
Hadi Amiri (University of Massachusetts, Lowell)
Antonios Anastasopoulos (George Mason University)
Maria Antoniak (Cornell University)
Rahul Aralikatte (University of Copenhagen)
Eiji Aramaki (NAIST)
Pepa Atanasova (University of Copenhagen)
Ashutosh Baheti (Georgia Institute of Technology)
JinYeong Bak (SungKyunKwan University)
Kalika Bali (Microsoft Research)
Francesco Barbieri (Snap)
Elisa Bassignana (IT University of Copenhagen)
Adrian Benton (JHU)
Eduardo Blanco (University of North Texas)
Marcel Bollmann (Jönköping University)
Marco Brambilla (Politecnico di Milano)
Julian Brooke (University of British Columbia)
Cornelia Caragea (University of Illinois at Chicago)
Tuhin Chakrabarty (Columbia University)
Tanmoy Chakraborty (Indraprastha Institute of Information Technology, Delhi)
Ilias Chalkidis (University of Copenhagen)
Sihao Chen (University of Pennsylvania)
Colin Cherry (Google)
Dhivya Chinnappa (Thomson Reuters)
Monojit Choudhury (Microsoft Research)
Zewei Chu (University of Chicago)
Manuel R. Ciosici (IT University of Copenhagen)
Çağrı Çöltekin (University of Tübingen)
Danilo Croce (University of Rome)
Marina Danilevsky (IBM Research)
Pradipto Das (Rakuten Institute of Technology)
A. Seza Doğruöz (Universiteit Gent)
Xinya Du (Cornell University)
Heba Elfardy (Amazon)
Mai ElSherief (University of California, San Diego)

Micha Elsner (Ohio State University)
Alexander Fabbri (Yale University)
Manaal Faruqui (Google)
Song Feng (IBM Research)
Yansong Feng (Peking University)
Francis Ferraro (University of Maryland, Baltimore Countys)
Catherine Finegan-Dollak (IBM Research)
Lucie Flek (University of Marburg)
Lisheng Fu (Amazon)
Yoshinari Fujinuma (University of Colorado, Boulder)
Wei Gao (Singapore Management University)
Sahil Garg (University of Southern California)
Dan Garrette (Google)
Spandana Gella (Amazon)
Tirthankar Ghosal (Charles University)
Dan Goldwasser (Purdue University)
Amit Goyal (Amazon)
Yvette Graham (Dublin City University)
Chulaka Gunasekara (IBM Research)
Cathal Gurrin (Dublin City University)
Xiaochuang Han (Carnegie Mellon University)
Jonathan Herzig (Tel-Aviv University)
Jack Hessel (AI2)
Md Mosharaf Hossain (University of North Texas)
Diana Inkpen (University of Ottawa)
Kokil Jaidka (National University of Singapore)
Yangfeng Ji (University of Virginia)
Jing Jiang (Singapore Management University)
Nanjiang Jiang (Ohio State University)
Chao Jiang (Georgia Institute of Technology)
Lifeng Jin (Ohio State University)
Ishan Jindal (IBM Research)
Kristen Johnson (Michigan State University)
Gareth Jones (Dublin City University)
David Jurgens (University of Michigan)
Preethi Jyothi (IIT Bombay)
Katharina Kann (University of Colorado, Boulder)
Ashkan Kazemi (University of Michigan)
Ashique KhudaBukhsh (Carnegie Mellon University)
Gunhee Kim (Seoul National University)
Bennett Kleinberg (Tilburg University)
Roman Klinger (University of Stuttgart)
Zornitsa Kozareva (Facebook)
Reno Kriz (University of Pennsylvania)
Vivek Kulkarni (Stanford University)
Jonathan Kummerfeld (University of Michigan)
Tsung-Ting Kuo (University of California, San Diego)
Vasileios Lampos (University College London)
Wuwei Lan (Ohio State University)
Jiwei Li (ShannonAI)
Jessy Junyi Li (University of Texas Austin)

Jing Li (Hong Kong Polytechnic University)
Yitong Li (University of Melbourne)
Kwan Hui Lim (Singapore University of Technology and Design)
Nut Limsopatham (Microsoft Research)
Lucy Lin (University of Washington)
Fei Liu (University of Melbourne)
Yiqun Liu (Tsinghua University)
Nikola Ljubešić (Jožef Stefan Institute)
Mounica Maddela (Georgia Institute of Technology)
Bodhisattwa Prasad Majumder (University of California, San Diego)
David Mimno (Cornell University)
Shachar Mirkin (Digimind)
Yasuhide Miura (Fuji/Xerox)
Manuel Montes (National Institute of Astrophysics, Mexico)
Ahmed Mourad (RMIT University)
Maximilian Mozes (University College London)
Hamdy Mubarak (Qatar Computing Research Institute)
Graham Mueller (Leidos)
Animesh Mukherjee (IIT Kharagpur)
Maria Nadejde (Grammarly)
Preslav Nakov (Qatar Computing Research Institute)
Guenter Neumann (German Research Center for Artificial Intelligence)
Vincent Ng (University of Texas at Dallas)
Thien Huu Nguyen (University of Oregon)
Dat Quoc Nguyen (VinAI Research)
Eric Nichols (Honda Research Institute)
Brendan O'Connor (University of Massachusetts, Amherst)
Alice Oh (KAIST)
Naoaki Okazaki (Tohoku University)
Naoki Otani (CMU)
Symeon Papadopoulos (CERTH-ITI)
Yuval Pinter (Georgia Tech)
Barbara Plank (IT University of Copenhagen)
Matt Post (Johns Hopkins University)
Vinodkumar Prabhakaran (Stanford University)
Daniel Preoţiuc-Pietro (Bloomberg)
Dianna Radpour (University of Colorado Boulder)
Preethi Raghavan (IBM Research)
Afshin Rahimi (University of Queensland)
Sudha Rao (Microsoft Research)
Hannah Rashkin (Google)
Sravana Reddy (ASAPP)
Roi Reichart (Technion - Israel Institute of Technology.)
Adithya Renduchintala (Facebook AI)
Anthony Rios (The University of Texas at San Antonio)
Paolo Rosso (Universitat Politècnica de València)
Alla Rozovskaya (City University of New York)
Mirco Schoenfeld (University of Bayreuth)
Djamé Seddah (University Paris-Sorbonne)
Ori Shapira (Bar-Ilan University)
Ashish Sharma (University of Washington)

Dan Simonson (BlackBoiler)
Kevin Small (Amazon)
Xingyi Song (University of Sheffield)
Andreas Spitz (University of Konstanz)
Richard Sproat (Google)
Gabriel Stanovsky (Allen Institute for Artificial Intelligence)
Ian Stewart (University of Michigan)
Sara Stymne (Uppsala University)
Danae Sánchez Villegas (University of Sheffield)
Zeerak Talat (University of Sheffield)
Zhiyang Teng (Westlake University)
James Thorne (University of Cambridge)
Marc Tomlinson (Language Computer Corporation)
Sara Tonelli (FBK)
Rob van der Goot (University of Groningen)
Vasudeva Varma (IIIT Hyderabad)
Daniel Varab (IT University of Copenhagen)
Olga Vechtomova (University of Waterloo)
Rob Voigt (Northwestern University)
Soroush Vosoughi (Dartmouth University)
Thanh Vu (Oracle)
Xiaojun Wan (Peking University)
Hong Wei (University of Maryland)
Zhongyu Wei (Fudan University)
Roman Yangarber (University of Helsinki)
Ziyu Yao (George Mason University)
Ning Yu (Leidos)
Nasser Zalmout (Amazon)
Marcos Zampieri (Rochester Institute of Technology)
Vicky Zayats (University of Washington)
Chiyu Zhang (University of British Columbia)
Xiao Cosmo Zhang (Amazon)
Mike Zhang (IT University of Copenhagen)
Ayah Zirikly (Johns Hopkins University)
Shi Zong (Nanjing University)
Hamid Beigy (Sharif University of Technology)
Soroush Vosoughi (Dartmouth College)

Invited Speakers:

Yulia Tsvetkov (University of Washington)
David Jurgens (University of Michigan)

Table of Contents

Conference Program

Saturday 16 October 2022

9:00 **AM–11:19 AM Morning Session**

Welcome

Invited Talk 1

Changes in Tweet Geolocation over Time: A Study with Carmen 2.0
Jingyu Zhang, Alexandra DeLucia and Mark Dredze

Extracting Mathematical Concepts from Text
Jacob Collard, Valeria de Paiva, Brendan Fong and Eswaran Subrahmanian

Data-driven Approach to Differentiating between Depression and Dementia from Noisy Speech and Language Data
Malikeh Ehghaghi, Frank Rudzicz and Jekaterina Novikova

Cross-Dialect Social Media Dependency Parsing for Social Scientific Entity Attribute Analysis
Chloe Eggleston and Brendan O'Connor

Impact of Environmental Noise on Alzheimer's Disease Detection from Speech: Should You Let a Baby Cry?
Jekaterina Novikova

Exploring Multimodal Features and Fusion Strategies for Analyzing Disaster Tweets
Raj Pranesh

NTULM: Enriching Social Media Text Representations with Non-Textual Units
Jinning Li, Shubhanshu Mishra, Ahmed El-Kishky, Sneha Mehta and Vivek Kulkarni

Robust Candidate Generation for Entity Linking on Short Social Media Texts
Liam Hebert, Raheleh Makki, Shubhanshu Mishra, Hamidreza Saghir, Anusha Kamath and Yuval Merhav

TransPOS: Transformers for Consolidating Different POS Tagset Datasets
Alex Li, Ilyas Bankole-Hameed, Ranadeep Singh, Gabriel Ng and Akshat Gupta

An Effective, Performant Named Entity Recognition System for Noisy Business Telephone Conversation Transcripts
Xue-Yong Fu, Cheng Chen, Md Tahmid Rahman Laskar, Shashi Bhushan TN and Simon Corston-Oliver

Gather.Town social event

12:20 PM–3:40 PM Afternoon Session

Invited Talk 2

Leveraging Semantic and Sentiment Knowledge for User-Generated Text Sentiment Classification
Jawad Khan, Niaz Ahmad, Aftab Alam and Youngmoon Lee

An Emotional Journey: Detecting Emotion Trajectories in Dutch Customer Service Dialogues
Sofie Labat, Amir Hadifar, Thomas Demeester and Veronique Hoste

Supervised and Unsupervised Evaluation of Synthetic Code-Switching
Evgeny Orlov and Ekaterina Artemova

ArabGend: Gender Analysis and Inference on Arabic Twitter
Hamdy Mubarak, Shammur Absar Chowdhury and Firoj Alam

Automatic Identification of 5C Vaccine Behaviour on Social Media
Ajay Hemanth Sampath Kumar, Aminath Shausan, Gianluca Demartini and Afshin Rahimi

Automatic Extraction of Structured Mineral Drillhole Results from Unstructured Mining Company Reports
Adam Dimeski and Afshin Rahimi

"Kanglish alli names!" Named Entity Recognition for Kannada-English Code-Mixed Social Media Data
Sumukh S and Manish Shrivastava

Gather.Town social event

Span Extraction Aided Improved Code-mixed Sentiment Classification
Ramaneswaran S, Sean Benhur and Sreyan Ghosh

AdBERT: An Effective Few Shot Learning Framework for Aligning Tweets to Superbowl Advertisements
Debarati Das, Roopana Chenchu, Maral Abdollahi, Jisu Huh and Jaideep Srivastava

Increasing Robustness for Cross-domain Dialogue Act Classification on Social Media Data
Marcus Vielsted, Nikolaj Wallenius and Rob van der Goot

Disfluency Detection for Vietnamese
Mai Dao, Thinh Hung Truong and Dat Quoc Nguyen

A multi-level approach for hierarchical Ticket Classification
Matteo Marcuzzo, Alessandro Zangari, Michele Schiavinato, Lorenzo Giudice, Andrea Gasparetto and Andrea Albarelli

Towards better structured and less noisy Web data: Oscar with Register annotations
Veronika Laippala, Anna Salmela, Samuel Rönnqvist, Alham Fikri Aji, Li-Hsin Chang, Asma Dhifallah, Larissa Goulart, Henna Kortelainen, Marc Pàmies, Deise Prina Dutra, Valtteri Skantsi, Lintang Sutawika and Sampo Pyysalo

True or False? Detecting False Information on Social Media Using Graph Neural Networks
Samyo Rode-Hasinger, Anna Kruspe and Xiao Xiang Zhu

Analyzing the Real Vulnerability of Hate Speech Detection Systems against Targeted Intentional Noise
Piush Aggarwal and Torsten Zesch

Gather.Town social event

Best paper award and closing

Changes in Tweet Geolocation over Time: A Study with Carmen 2.0

Jingyu Zhang and **Alexandra DeLucia** and **Mark Dredze**
Department of Computer Science
Johns Hopkins University
{jzhan237, aadelucia, mdredze}@jhu.edu

Abstract

Researchers across disciplines use Twitter geolocation tools to filter data for desired locations. These tools have largely been trained and tested on English tweets, often originating in the United States from almost a decade ago. Despite the importance of these tools for data curation, the impact of tweet language, country of origin, and creation date on tool performance remains largely unknown. We explore these issues with Carmen, a popular tool for Twitter geolocation. To support this study we introduce Carmen 2.0, a major update which includes the incorporation of GeoNames, a gazetteer that provides much broader coverage of locations. We evaluate using two new Twitter datasets, one for multilingual, multiyear geolocation evaluation, and another for usage trends over time. We found that language, country origin, and time does impact geolocation tool performance.

https://github.com/AADeLucia/carmen-wnut22-submission

1 Introduction

Demographic studies leverage location-specific social media posts to track impactful events such as civil unrest (Sech et al., 2020; Chinta et al., 2021; Alsaedi et al., 2017; Littman, 2018), natural disasters (Wang et al., 2015), and disease spread (Xu et al., 2020). For social media posts from Twitter, researchers either collect posts from locations of interest in real-time with the Twitter API, or use third-party *Twitter geolocation* tools to identify tweet locations on an existing dataset. In Han et al. (2016), the authors distinguish between *user* and *tweet* geolocation. We focus on tweet geolocation in this work. These tools identify the location of a user or tweet based on tweet metadata (Dredze et al., 2013), tweet content (Alsaedi et al., 2017; Rahimi et al., 2016; Han et al., 2014; Wu and Gerber, 2018; Izbicki et al., 2019), and social networks (Rout et al., 2013; Jurgens, 2013).

While widely used, geolocation tools tend to be English-centric and are often not evaluated for global coverage or performance across time and language. These factors are important to study, since available user metadata, Twitter policies, and content patterns on which the tools depend on can change significantly over time.

In this work, we assess how the following factors impact geolocation tools:

1. **Language:** Is there a performance difference between languages, specifically between English and non-English tweets?
2. **Country:** Is there a performance difference between countries, specifically inside and outside the US?
3. **Time:** How does geolocation performance change over a large span of time? What differences in the data contribute to this performance change?

We measure performance in geolocation by coverage, i.e. the number of tweets that can be mapped to a location, and accuracy, the correctness of the assigned locations. When evaluated together, these metrics provide analogues to recall and precision, respectively.

To answer the above research questions, we analyze the performance of Twitter geolocation tool Carmen (Dredze et al., 2013), across time, language, and country of origin. In order to study performance across these factors, we introduce TWITTER-GLOBAL, a new geocoded multilingual and multiyear dataset (2013–2021) of 15.3M tweets. We created this dataset to fill a gap in other geolocation evaluation datasets that are either English-only (Han et al., 2012), or multilingual but restricted to short periods of time (Izbicki et al., 2019). We focus on Carmen since it is a rule-based tool that can be run quickly on large collections of tweets.

Since Carmen was built for English tweet

Proceedings of the 2022 COLING Workshop: The 8th Workshop on Noisy User-generated Text (W-NUT 2022), pages 1–14

datasets from 2013, we update the tool and introduce Carmen 2.0. This updated version relies on GeoNames,[1] an open-source geographical dictionary, or gazetteer. In contrast to Carmen's US and English-centric database, GeoNames provides global coverage in many languages. Through comparisons of GeoNames-augmented Carmen 2.0 with the original Carmen location database, we can study the effects of incorporating more non-US and non-English locations on geolocation performance.

In addition to studying Carmen 2.0's performance with regard to different factors, we also include a longitudinal study of Twitter demographics over time from 2013–2021, with respect popularity across different countries, languages, and geolocation metadata. This study is on a collection of 5.7M tweets sampled from the 1% Twitter stream, which we refer to as TWITTER-RANDOM. The demographic and metadata analysis provides statistics to support design decisions for researchers developing their own geolocation tools.

We contribute the following:

1. Analysis of the effects of time, language, and country origin on Twitter geolocation tool performance.
2. Longitudinal study of user geolocation metadata availability and changes in frequency of tweets from different countries and languages.
3. Carmen 2.0, an improved version of the popular geolocation tool.
4. TWITTER-RANDOM, a randomly (1% based) sampled 5.7M Twitter dataset to support analysis of metadata and user trends over time (2013–2021).
5. TWITTER-GLOBAL, a geocoded multilingual, multiyear 15.3M Twitter dataset to support temporal and global geolocation evaluation.

All experiment code and data (tweet IDs) are released on in the GitHub code repository.

2 Related Work

Most work in Twitter geolocation focuses solely on tool development and performance, usually on English-centric datasets published years ago. In this paper we question how those tools would perform on Twitter datasets today, but focus on a single tool, Carmen.

[1]https://www.geonames.org/

Geolocation Analysis Kruspe et al. (2021) analyze the impact of Twitter policy changes on research. The authors study tweet metadata availability over time, such as exact coordinate availability and granularity of place objects. Most importantly, the authors discuss the impact of the 2019 Twitter policy change to remove precise locations from tweets (starting from 2019), and how that affects geolocation tools and researchers who depend on the coordinates. Their work limits their study to tweets from 2020–2021, and in our work we study these metadata patterns over a larger span of time, 2013–2021, in addition to the impact of other factors, such as language and country of origin, on geolocation tool performance. We compare our multi-year trend analysis to theirs in Section 6. This multi-year analysis is useful for researchers geolocating tweets in older Twitter datasets.

Geolocation Tools Most approaches for social media geolocation use tweet/user-level metadata (Dredze et al., 2013), tweet content, including hashtags, (Alsaedi et al., 2017; Rahimi et al., 2016; Han et al., 2014; Wu and Gerber, 2018; Halterman, 2017; Izbicki et al., 2019), and social networks (Rout et al., 2013; Jurgens, 2013). The UnicodeCNN geolocation tool (Izbicki et al., 2019) is notable because it is not English- or US-centric, and can infer location from multilingual tweet content.[2] Izbicki et al. (2019) also introduced a large, global geotagged dataset of 900M tweets across 100 languages, but this dataset is not appropriate for our temporal evaluation since it only includes tweets from 2017 to 2018. The authors did not provide a trend analysis on the dataset for comparison to our analysis in Section 6. Huang and Carley (2019) use a combination of all these features, and Ribeiro and Pappa (2017) create an ensemble classifier to combine existing methods, improving accuracy and coverage. Geolocation approaches for other social media platforms, such as Reddit, use similar methods (Harrigian, 2018).

There are a few ways to ascertain the location of a user or tweet: (1) use the coordinates embedded in one or more of the user's tweets, (2) use the embedded place metadata, (3) use the user's location string in their profile, (4) infer a location from the tweet content, and (5) leverage social network information. Methods (1) and (2) are most accurate, but less than 2% of tweets contain location

[2]The UnicodeCNN model is unavailable for comparison at time of writing.

metadata (Kruspe et al., 2021). Method (4) is common (see tools above that use tweet content), but requires building more sophisticated language models as opposed to examining the metadata. Method (5) also performs well, but requires access to significantly more tweets in order to build the social network structure (Jurgens, 2013).

3 Carmen 2.0

In this paper we present Carmen 2.0, an updated version of geolocation tool Carmen. We aim to increase the coverage and robustness of Carmen to language and countries by using a open-source database, GeoNames.

In addition to a new location database, we include other performance improvements, such as compatibility with Twitter API v2 (see Appendix §B). Since Carmen 2.0 does not change the core functionality, we focus on the construction and use of the internal location database, and we direct the reader to Appendix §A for a review of the location resolvers or Dredze et al. (2013) for more details.

3.1 Carmen: A Review

Carmen, introduced by Dredze et al. (2013), uses tweet and user profile metadata for geolocation.[3] Carmen has three "resolvers" which use different information from the tweet: (1) embedded coordinates in the `geo` object,[4] (2) matching the Place object to the internal locations database, and (3) mapping the user profile location string to the internal location database.

3.1.1 Original Location Database

The tweet location is resolved to an entry in an internal database of 7041 places.[5] Locations are stored in JSON form, where each location object has city, county, state/province, country, coordinates, and "aliases."

The original database was developed from tweets available at the time that Carmen was released in 2013, specifically 10K tweets sampled from the Bergsma et al. (2013) dataset. This dataset consists of roughly 4 billion tweets between May 2009 and August 2012, in addition to 80 million tweets from users who follow specific feeds for locations and

[3]The Python version of the tool is available at `https://github.com/mdredze/carmen-python`.

[4]According to Kruspe et al. (2021), Twitter stopped including coordinates in 2019.

[5]The original paper says 4K locations, but the database was expanded by the authors between 2013 and 2022.

	Original		GeoNames	
	Count	Percent	Count	Percent
City	4401	62.51%	24568	33.24%
County	1995	28.33%	45154	61.08%
State	461	6.55%	3947	5.34%
Country	184	2.61%	252	0.34%
Total	7041		73921	

Table 1: The statistics of city, county, state, and country-level locations in the original Carmen location database and the new GeoNames database versions developed for Carmen 2.0. The GeoNames-augmented databases have more than 10 times the number of location entries than `Original`. Percentage refers to portion of the database dedicated to each granularity.

languages. The internal location database was constructed from the geotagged places in the development set, and then augmented through manual and automatic collection of **aliases**, or alternate names. The motivation for including aliases stemmed from inconsistent names for Twitter places, mostly due to location references in different languages, e.g., "polnia" and "poland." Aliases also include colloquial names for a place, such as "the big apple" for New York City, which could be found in a user profile location string. Place information was included as much as possible (i.e., province) by obtaining full location information from Yahoo's PlaceFinder API.[6]

Thus, because of the origin of its location database, which was built from tweets between 2009–2012, Carmen's database is biased towards common locations and languages in tweets before 2012, primarily English tweets from the US. Further, the database does not align with an external knowledge base, so Carmen locations cannot be directly matched against other place information. These limitations prompted our updates, without which we would be unable to answer the questions of this paper.

3.2 Expanded Database: GeoNames

The original Carmen location database was crafted from a Twitter sample (see §3.1.1). This decision biased Carmen towards locations popular with Twitter users from 2009–2012, which is not representative of today's users. Further, the location identifiers were unique to Carmen, and thus could not be meaningfully shared for external analysis or easily augmented with other place information.

[6]This API is no longer available.

To remedy both issues, we augmented the internal Carmen database with GeoNames, an open source geographical database that covers all countries and millions of place names.

GeoNames Structure GeoNames has a hierarchical structure, where every entry has a link to its parent. For example, Austin (`city`) has a link to Texas (`admin1`), which in turn has a link to United States (US, `country`). Sometimes `admin2` is also present, which refers to a county in the US. All counties, administrative regions (i.e., state or province), and countries were also added to the database.

Similar to Carmen's aliases, GeoNames contains a list of "alternate names" of each entry. While Carmen's methods were geared towards colloquial names, GeoNames contains the name of each entry in many languages, in addition to a few colloquial names.

Database Merging While GeoNames contains cities from all over the world, we only include cities with a population over 15K. This is to ensure a more efficient location resolution process, since tweets are more likely to originate from highly populated places. Also, only including more populated locations is important for user privacy, since a user can remain more anonymous when aggregated in a large group. We discuss more ethical concerns surrounding geolocation, such as privacy, in Section 7. We use GeoNames to create two versions of a new Carmen location database: (1) GeoNames only and (2) a merged GeoNames and Carmen database. The **GeoNames-only** database, (1), converts the GeoNames format for cities, states/provinces, and countries to Carmen-formatted JSON objects.

The **GeoNames-combined** database, (2), required matching Carmen database entries to GeoNames entries. We matched locations based on string similarity of location name, the distance between coordinates, and country name. To maintain accuracy of mapped locations, our mapping criteria was strict and 4,467 out of 7,041 (63.44%) Carmen locations were successfully mapped to GeoNames. We then added the alternate names of each location in Carmen to the new GeoNames backed location entries. The merged version also contains all county, state/province, and country entries as (1). The remaining entries in Carmen were that were unable to be matched were disregarded. A spot-check on these unmatched locations confirmed they were

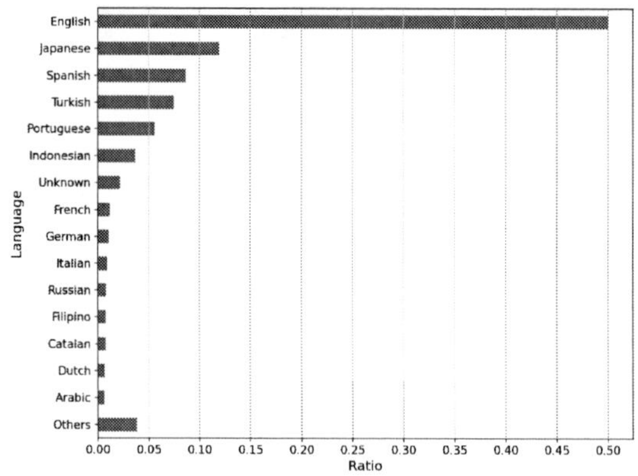

Figure 1: Language distribution for tweets in TWITTER-GLOBAL. Only the top 15 languages are shown. Languages are identified by tweet metadata

cities with population less than 15K or contained errors, such as incorrect county or province information.

Both **GeoNames-only** and **GeoNames-combined** contain 73921 entries. The number of entries is the same since they differ only in alias lists. Database details are in Table 1.

4 Geolocation Evaluation

Through comparing Carmen's original database (see §3.1.1) with the new GeoNames based database (see §3.2), we can answer our research questions from Section 1 to see how geolocation tool coverage and accuracy change with respect to language, country of origin, and time. The performance is evaluated with similar metrics of other geolocation tools mentioned in §2. In addition to updating Carmen, we also created two datasets to support our analysis.

4.1 Ground Truth Data

There are a handful of "standardized" datasets for Twitter tweet geolocation evaluation (Han et al., 2012, 2016), but they often are not global, multilingual, or recent. In this work we introduce two datasets, TWITTER-GLOBAL and TWITTER-RANDOM. Despite the temporal (2011–2012) and language (English only) limitations of the popular `TWITTER-WORLD` (Han et al., 2012) geolocation evaluation dataset, we include Carmen's performance in Appendix §D so others can refer to it for comparison.

Twitter-Global This new geolocation evaluation dataset is collected from multiple geolocation filtering Twitter streams that are designed to cover the world.[7] The data from these streams was collected from 2013 to 2021 for a total of 15.3M tweets, balanced over the years. Due to the nature of the stream, all tweets are "geotagged" with Twitter Place objects. The ground truth for tweets are the place names and coordinates in the Place metadata. We follow previous work in using geotagged tweets as ground truth, although we note the bias introduced by only evaluating on geotagged data (Pavalanathan and Eisenstein, 2015).

Unlike popular geolocation evaluation dataset `TWITTER-WORLD`, our dataset is multilingual. While Han et al. (2012) removed non-English tweets in order to not make it "easy" on the tool, we want to ensure the geolocation tools work in a multilingual setting. Language distribution is in Figure 1. Since TWITTER-GLOBAL includes samples from North America, we omit evaluation on another popular evaluation dataset, `TWITTER-US` (Han et al., 2012). Izbicki et al. (2019) introduced a larger, global geotagged dataset of 900M tweets across 100 languages, but is not appropriate for our temporal evaluation since it only includes tweets from 2017 to 2018.

Twitter-Random In addition to the new geolocation evaluation dataset, we introduce a multiyear random sample. This sample is useful for analyzing shifts in usage patterns across the world with respect to metadata inclusion, language, etc.

We created this dataset by sampling 100K tweets per month from the Twitter Streaming API between 2013 and 2021, resulting in 5.7M tweets.

4.2 Evaluation Metrics

Evaluating geotagging performance is grouped into two categories: (1) *coverage*, or percentage of the data our method successfully found a location, and (2) *accuracy*, or how well the proposed locations compare to the ground truth. We use metrics similar to other work on Twitter geolocation. Formulas are provided in Appendix §C.

4.2.1 Coverage

Given a tweet, Carmen resolves it to an entry in the internal database if such mapping can be found. Since Carmen only uses information from tweet and user profile metadata, we define **coverage** as the fraction of resolved tweets among all tweets that have location information (i.e. has a Twitter Place object). Coverage is similar to *recall* and *sensitivity*, but does not incorporate whether the prediction is correct.

4.2.2 Accuracy

Coverage gives us a good metric of Carmen's sensitivity to locations contained in tweets. However, it does not evaluate the *correctness* of the mapped results. We measure the location mapping accuracy by string comparison (country, state/province, city) and by geographical distance. These metrics are referred to as **match ratio** and **distance**.

Match Ratio A predicted location can be accurate on different levels of granularity, such as a correct state or province prediction, but incorrect city prediction. The **match ratio** metric awards partial credit for correct identification of a country or state even if another portion of the prediction is incorrect, such as the city. Match ratio on level L, denoted mr_L, where $L \in \{\text{country}, \text{admin}, \text{city}\}$, is the ratio of the number of resolved tweets where the prediction is correct on level L over the total number of tweets where L is available in the ground truth. We restrict the denominator to tweets where the level is available, since it is unfair to penalize the model for an "incorrect" city prediction when the city is not available in the ground truth.

Distance We also use geographical distance to measure accuracy. This metric is inspired by Eisenstein et al. (2010) and Cheng et al. (2010) and their calculation of regression performance, or mean and median distance between proposed location coordinates and ground truth.

Distance, d, is measured as the geodesic distance, calculated with `geopy`, between the resolved location and the ground-truth tweet coordinates. We calculate distance at the dataset level, which is the average distance over all tweets, where 0 is best. In addition to the average distance, we also consider "accuracy at K", or Acc@K, the ratio of resolved tweets such that the distance error does not exceed K miles (Ribeiro and Pappa, 2017; Han et al., 2014). This metric is less influenced by outliers than d.

5 Experiments

As enumerated in §1, we are interested in how the following factors impact geolocation tool performance: **language**, **country**, and **time**.

[7]While streams are meant to cover the entire world, there are gaps due to Twitter API restrictions.

To answer these questions we perform an ablation study over Carmen location databases (see §3.2) and different subsets of TWITTER-GLOBAL (see §4.1).

5.1 Performance across Language

Many geolocation tools (and even evaluation datasets (Han et al., 2012)) focus on English tweets. We can analyze the performance difference of English-biased tools by comparing the performance of Carmen's original English-centric database with the GeoNames-augmented ones on multilingual data. Since TWITTER-GLOBAL is multilingual, we create two subsets of English and Non-English data, as identified by the tweet language metadata. Tweets with "unknown" language tag are omitted. Since the GeoNames-only and GeoNames-combined location databases contain translations for location names, we expect Carmen to perform better with these over the original database, as corroborated in Table 2.

Overall, Carmen has better coverage for English tweets than on non-English with all location databases (roughly 49% compared to 32-41%). While the coverage on the English data is the same for the three databases (less than 2% difference), there is a large difference in coverage for non-English tweets. Both GeoNames-based databases were able to provide predictions for 42% of tweets and the Original database only provided matching 32% of tweets. Accuracy also differs between databases and language splits, but only at the higher granularities of admin (state/province) and city level, where the match ratio drops from 95% on English data to 66-75% for non-English at the admin level and from 48% to 14-20% at the city level across databases. Country-level accuracy remains stable at a 99% match ratio. The decrease in accuracy at the admin and city levels is also apparent through the distance metrics, where average distance is higher for non-English than English tweets. The high distance error for the GeoNames-only database can be attributed to different coordinates between the GeoNames and Twitter places gazetteer entries, and prediction error within large countries, such as the US and India, which can be detrimental.

In summary, using a multilingual geolocation tool can increase geolocated data for studies, with highest accuracy at the country level.

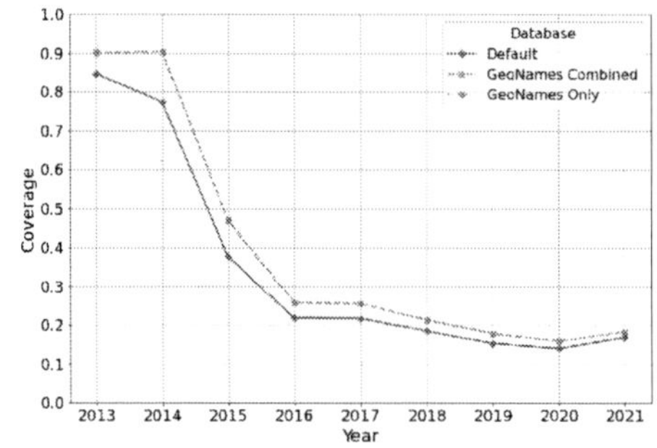

Figure 2: Ablation over Carmen location database and performance over data from different years of Twitter data, 2013-2021. Evaluated on TWITTER-GLOBAL. Metric is coverage, where higher score is better.

5.2 Performance across Countries

Similar to concerns with language bias, geolocation tools can also be US-centric. In order to analyze difference in performance across countries, we simplify the study to inside and outside of the US. We split TWITTER-GLOBAL into "US" and "non-US" categories for the evaluation. Similar to the language performance, we expect the GeoNames-augmented databases to provide an advantage over the original location database, due to the alternate names list. The results are shown in Table 3.

There is a similar trend between US/non-US split and English/non-English split. Overall, all databases have higher coverage of locations inside the US (50%) than outside of the US (32-42%), possibly confounded by differences in language. However, using a multilingual non-US based database helps with coverage significantly, as shown in the difference between GeoNames-augmented databases (42%) and the Original database (32%).

Accuracy is also better inside the US, as seen with the match ratio at the state/province (99% vs 60-66%) and city levels (54% vs 11-19%). Average distance is also higher for non-US locations, except for GeoNames-only which is most likely due to difference in coordinates for large countries.

5.3 Performance over Time

Carmen's performance over time degrades significantly between 2015 and 2021, as shown in Figure 2. In 2013–2014, Carmen has 80-90% coverage with all databases, but this coverage drops to 40-50% in 2015 and below 20% after 2018. This drop is most likely due to Carmen's heavy reliance on

Language	Database	Coverage	$mr_{country}$	mr_{admin}	mr_{city}	d	Acc@10	Acc@100	Acc@1000
English	GeoNames-Only	49.58%	99.42%	95.63%	47.49%	853.9	0.81	0.85	0.86
	GeoNames-combined	49.63%	99.43%	94.36%	47.69%	58.7	0.81	0.91	0.99
	Original	48.14%	99.35%	94.94%	48.90%	46.4	0.78	0.91	1.00
Non-English	GeoNames-Only	41.77%	99.36%	66.50%	20.13%	482.3	0.84	0.88	0.88
	GeoNames-combined	41.78%	99.35%	66.83%	20.27%	105.3	0.84	0.90	0.99
	Original	32.27%	98.95%	75.61%	14.22%	106.2	0.67	0.87	0.99

Table 2: Ablation over Carmen location database and performance on English and non-English tweets. Evaluated on TWITTER-GLOBAL. "Acc@K" represents the ratio of tweets predicted within K miles of the ground truth. Higher values are best for all metrics except distance (d).

Origin	Database	Coverage	$mr_{country}$	mr_{admin}	mr_{city}	d	Acc@10	Acc@100	Acc@1000
US	GeoNames-only	50.56%	99.37%	99.87%	53.66%	994.2	0.79	0.84	0.84
	GeoNames-combined	50.60%	99.37%	99.87%	53.81%	23.6	0.79	0.91	1.00
	Original	51.03%	99.93%	99.96%	55.33%	23.7	0.79	0.91	1.00
non-US	GeoNames-only	42.63%	99.37%	61.51%	18.73%	439.3	0.84	0.89	0.89
	GeoNames-combined	42.65%	99.37%	60.81%	18.88%	121.2	0.84	0.90	0.98
	Original	32.89%	98.45%	66.11%	11.10%	118.0	0.67	0.87	0.99

Table 3: Ablation over Carmen location database and performance on tweets originating from and outside of the United States (US). Evaluated on TWITTER-GLOBAL. "Acc@K" represents the ratio of tweets predicted within K miles of the ground truth. Higher values are best for all metrics except distance (d).

tweet metadata as opposed to tweet content or other features, which has decreased over time. We discuss the impact of metadata availability further in Section 6.3.

6 Longitudinal Analysis of Twitter User Location

We have seen how using a less biased geolocation tool offers better performance with respect to coverage and accuracy. However, despite the overall better performance with the GeoNames-combined location database, coverage still varied greatly when evaluated over time, as in Section 5.3. To better understand this performance difference and to provide insights for other geolocation researchers, we present a longitudinal study of trends in location metadata availability and user demographics. All metadata and demographic statistics are gathered from TWITTER-RANDOM (see §4.1).

6.1 Location Metadata Availability

As discussed in §2, Twitter geolocation tools make use of tweet/user-level metadata, tweet text, and social network information. Tools that exclusively use tweet and/or user metadata are most at the mercy of changes to Twitter API or policy.

As shown in Figure 3, the rate of tweets in the random stream with tagged Places increased slightly from 2013 to 2014 and then decreased from 2% to 0.5% from 2014 to 2021. This 75% decrease

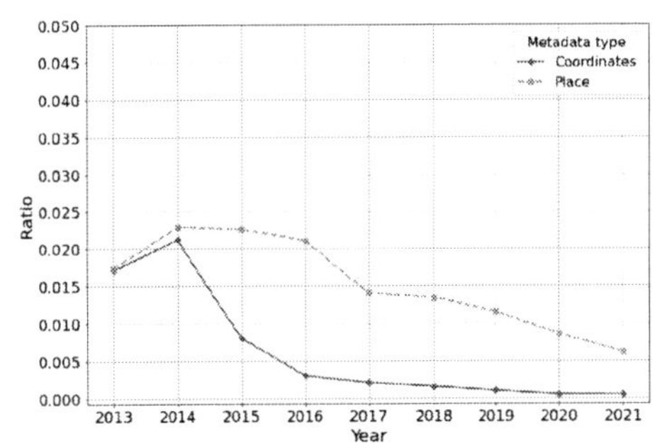

Figure 3: Prevalence of tweet metadata over time in TWITTER-RANDOM. We limit to metadata commonly used in geolocation of users or tweets. Note scale is from 0-5%.

represents millions of tweets. While inclusion of place information has declined, the rate of place types has remained the same. High-granularity types like points of interests (POIs) and neighborhoods are largely unused (less than 1% of Place objects), followed by country- and state/province-level tags (5% and 11%). The most common type by far is at the city level, comprising 83% of tagged place types.

The number of tweets with embedded coordinates has decreased even more than tagged places starting in 2015, even before the 2019 Twitter policy that removed coordinates. This decrease is most likely due to another Twitter policy enacted April 2015 which changed the default "precise location" setting from enabled to disabled.[8] The only metadata that has stayed consistent since 2013 is the user profile location field, which is available in 60% of tweets.

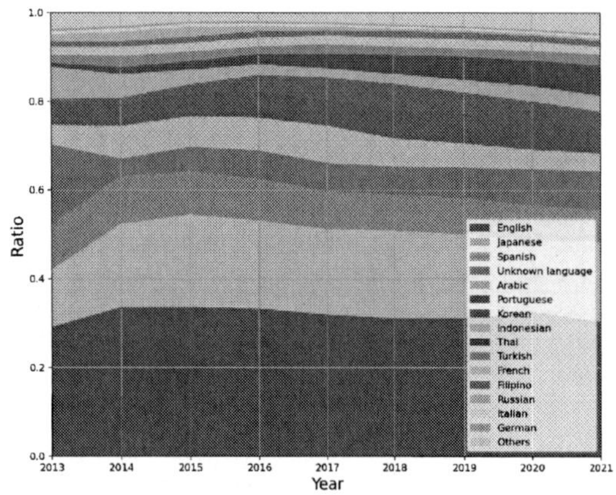

Figure 4: Language distribution for tweets in TWITTER-RANDOM over time. Languages are identified by tweet metadata

6.2 Twitter Demographics

In addition to changes in metadata availability, we also analyzed the change in countries and languages present in the random stream. No geolocation is needed for the language analysis, as it is included in tweet metadata, but we are limited by tweets that can be geotagged by Carmen 2.0 (GeoNames-combined database) for the country analysis. While this geotagging biases the sample to tweets with location information, this is representative of the distribution other researchers can expect from geotagged tweets in the random stream. Carmen was able to identify locations for 21% of the data, or 1.2M tweets.

Country The top 10 countries in the dataset are (in descending order): United States (US), United Kingdom (UK), Brazil, Indonesia, Japan, Argentina, India, France, Philippines, and Thailand. The US has a significantly larger share of tweets, roughly 30%. In comparison, tweets from the UK are only 6% of all tweets. The share of every country in the dataset is shown in Figure 5. The overall numbers can often hide year-specific trends. Within the top countries, Indonesia decreases from 11% in 2013 to less than 5% after 2015. Inversely, India starts with very few tweets and steadily grows to roughly 9% of tweets. The other countries remain largely stable over the years.

Language The top languages follow the languages spoken in the top countries very closely, as shown in Figure 4. English comprises about 30% of all languages, followed by Japanese, Spanish, Arabic, Portuguese, Korean, Indonesian, Thai, and Turkish. Following the decrease in tweets from Indonesia, Indonesian tweets also decreased from 7% in 2013 to 4% in 2021. In the same time frame, tweets in Hindi follow the pattern of tweets from India, increasing from 0% to 1% of all languages. While not in the top languages or countries, there is also a decrease in tweets from Russia and in Russian from 2015 (2.5%) to 2021 (0.5%).

The Twitter language identification system likely changed between 2013 and 2014, as "unknown" languages dropped from 18% to 4%. This rate of unknown languages steadily increases to 8% in 2021, possibly due to increase of users tweeting in languages not officially supported by Twitter.

6.3 Impact on Geolocation Tools

Researchers applying existing tools to their own datasets should consider the locations and languages best represented by the tools, in addition to which metadata (if any) the tool relies on. Due to the large distribution of languages, it is important for geolocation tools to have multilingual support to increase coverage and accuracy. Further, the metadata trends in Section 6.1 suggest that geolocation tools should be frequently checked for API and policy compatibility.

Carmen's performance analyzed over time in Section 5.3 is a prime example of how Twitter policy changes can affect geolocation tools. Carmen relies heavily on tweet metadata, specifically the presence of coordinates and place objects, but the prevalence of this information has decreased since 2015. A tool less reliant on metadata and more based on content or other signals, could be more temporally robust.

Ensuring a geolocation tool is temporally robust, i.e., has the same performance over time, is important for identifying tools that need to be periodically updated with new data (Dredze et al., 2016). This is especially important for tools that use features that can be subject to distribution shift, such as social networks, tweet content, and metadata availability.

[8] https://www.wired.com/story/twitter-location-data-gps-privacy/

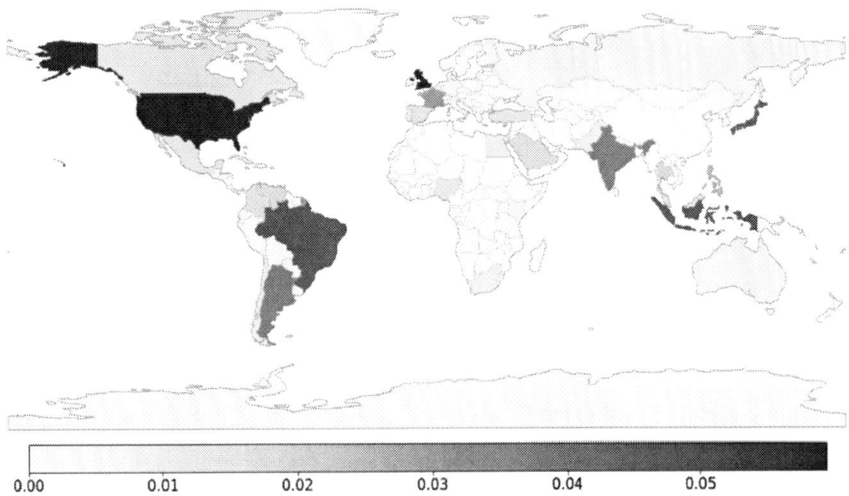

Figure 5: Distribution of country origin of tweets in TWITTER-RANDOM, a subset of the public Twitter API stream from 2013-2021. Locations are identified by Carmen. Scale is from 0 to 0.06 to show more detail. The United States represents 30% of tweets (0.3) and is capped to 0.06 for visualization purposes.

7 Ethical Concerns

Two issues that arise when geolocating users on social media: (1) privacy concerns and (2) consequences of incorrect predictions.

The privacy concerns are related to surveillance and revealing sensitive locations of users, such as their home address. Since Carmen only uses metadata provided by the user in the form of tagged places, coordinates, and profile location, it only infers locations readily shared by users. Kruspe et al. (2021) provide a helpful discussion of applications that require differing levels of location granularity, such as disaster relief or disease spread requiring more precise information (high granularity) versus marketing campaigns or opinion tracking (low granularity).

An issue with low granularity arises in high-risk applications where low precision is not helpful, such as tracking disease spread within a country. A possible solution for balancing higher granularity and user privacy is to map a user's location to the largest city closest to the user. Carmen 2.0 does this automatically since the database only contains cities with population greater than 15000.

There can be negative consequences to using incorrectly inferred locations, such as in tracking high-risk emergencies like disease spread and civil unrest. Geolocation tool performance ablation over granularity, language, and country, is important for researchers to make informed decisions about location accuracy.

8 Conclusion

Geolocation tweets is useful for researchers that need to filter tweets to those originating in specific locations to study health, opinions, etc, by demographic. In this work we study and discuss the impact the factors of language, country origin, and time, can have on tweet geolocation.

To support our study we introduced Carmen 2.0, an updated version of geolocation tool Carmen (Dredze et al., 2013) backed by an open-source database, GeoNames. In addition to the tool, we introduced two datasets: (1) TWITTER-GLOBAL, a Twitter geolocation evaluation dataset for language, country, and time ablation studies, and (2) TWITTER-RANDOM, a sample of the worldwide Twitter stream from 2013-2021 for studying general country and language demographics and metadata availability over time.

We found a significant difference in performance in the ablation, with higher performance for English and US-based tweets. Also, we provided trends in metadata availability from 2013 to 2021, and discuss reasons for the decline in coordinates and place metadata. For future work in Twitter tweet geolocation, we encourage the use of content and metadata fields, such as user profile location. Focus on these consistently available metadata can make a tool robust to policy changes. Also, we encourage evaluating the geolocation model across language, time, and countries to ensure fair performance.

Acknowledgment

We thank Arya McCarthy, Nathaniel Weir, and the anonymous reviewers for their time, helpful edits, and suggestions.

References

Nasser Alsaedi, Pete Burnap, and Omer Rana. 2017. Can We Predict a Riot? Disruptive Event Detection Using Twitter. *ACM Transactions on Internet Technology*, 17(2):18:1–18:26.

Shane Bergsma, Mark Dredze, Benjamin Van Durme, Theresa Wilson, and David Yarowsky. 2013. Broadly Improving User Classification via Communication-Based Name and Location Clustering on Twitter. In *Proceedings of the 2013 Conference of the North American Chapter of the Association for Computational Linguistics: Human Language Technologies*, pages 1010–1019, Atlanta, Georgia. Association for Computational Linguistics.

Zhiyuan Cheng, James Caverlee, and Kyumin Lee. 2010. You are where you tweet: A content-based approach to geo-locating twitter users. In *Proceedings of the 19th ACM International Conference on Information and Knowledge Management*, CIKM '10, page 759–768, New York, NY, USA. Association for Computing Machinery.

Abhinav Chinta, Jingyu Zhang, Alexandra DeLucia, Mark Dredze, and Anna L. Buczak. 2021. Study of Manifestation of Civil Unrest on Twitter. In *Proceedings of the Seventh Workshop on Noisy User-generated Text (W-NUT 2021)*, pages 396–409, Online. Association for Computational Linguistics.

Mark Dredze, Miles Osborne, and Prabhanjan Kambadur. 2016. Geolocation for Twitter: Timing Matters. In *Proceedings of the 2016 Conference of the North American Chapter of the Association for Computational Linguistics: Human Language Technologies*, pages 1064–1069, San Diego, California. Association for Computational Linguistics.

Mark Dredze, Michael J. Paul, Shane Bergsma, and Hieu Tran. 2013. Carmen: A Twitter Geolocation System with Applications to Public Health. Association for the Advancement of Artificial Intelligence.

Jacob Eisenstein, Brendan O'Connor, Noah A. Smith, and Eric P. Xing. 2010. A Latent Variable Model for Geographic Lexical Variation. In *Proceedings of the 2010 Conference on Empirical Methods in Natural Language Processing*, pages 1277–1287, Cambridge, MA. Association for Computational Linguistics.

Andrew Halterman. 2017. Mordecai: Full Text Geoparsing and Event Geocoding. *Journal of Open Source Software*, 2(9):91.

B. Han, P. Cook, and T. Baldwin. 2014. Text-Based Twitter User Geolocation Prediction. *Journal of Artificial Intelligence Research*, 49:451–500.

Bo Han, Paul Cook, and Timothy Baldwin. 2012. Geolocation Prediction in Social Media Data by Finding Location Indicative Words. In *Proceedings of COLING 2012*, pages 1045–1062, Mumbai, India. The COLING 2012 Organizing Committee.

Bo Han, Afshin Rahimi, Leon Derczynski, and Timothy Baldwin. 2016. Twitter Geolocation Prediction Shared Task of the 2016 Workshop on Noisy User-generated Text. In *Proceedings of the 2nd Workshop on Noisy User-generated Text (WNUT)*, pages 213–217, Osaka, Japan. The COLING 2016 Organizing Committee.

Keith Harrigian. 2018. Geocoding Without Geotags: A Text-based Approach for reddit. In *Proceedings of the 2018 EMNLP Workshop W-NUT: The 4th Workshop on Noisy User-generated Text*, pages 17–27, Brussels, Belgium. Association for Computational Linguistics.

Brent Hecht, Lichan Hong, Bongwon Suh, and Ed H. Chi. 2011. Tweets from Justin Bieber's heart: the dynamics of the location field in user profiles. In *Proceedings of the SIGCHI Conference on Human Factors in Computing Systems*, pages 237–246. Association for Computing Machinery, New York, NY, USA.

Binxuan Huang and Kathleen Carley. 2019. A Hierarchical Location Prediction Neural Network for Twitter User Geolocation. In *Proceedings of the 2019 Conference on Empirical Methods in Natural Language Processing and the 9th International Joint Conference on Natural Language Processing (EMNLP-IJCNLP)*, pages 4732–4742, Hong Kong, China. Association for Computational Linguistics.

Mike Izbicki, Vagelis Papalexakis, and Vassilis Tsotras. 2019. Geolocating Tweets in any Language at any Location. In *Proceedings of the 28th ACM International Conference on Information and Knowledge Management*, CIKM '19, pages 89–98, New York, NY, USA. Association for Computing Machinery.

David Jurgens. 2013. That's What Friends Are For: Inferring Location in Online Social Media Platforms Based on Social Relationships. *Proceedings of the International AAAI Conference on Web and Social Media*, 7(1):273–282. Number: 1.

Anna Kruspe, Matthias Häberle, Eike J. Hoffmann, Samyo Rode-Hasinger, Karam Abdulahhad, and Xiao Xiang Zhu. 2021. Changes in Twitter geolocations: Insights and suggestions for future usage. In *Proceedings of the Seventh Workshop on Noisy User-generated Text (W-NUT 2021)*, pages 212–221, Online. Association for Computational Linguistics.

Justin Littman. 2018. Charlottesville Tweet Ids. Publisher: Harvard Dataverse type: dataset.

Umashanthi Pavalanathan and Jacob Eisenstein. 2015. Confounds and Consequences in Geotagged Twitter Data. In *Proceedings of the 2015 Conference on*

Empirical Methods in Natural Language Processing, pages 2138–2148, Lisbon, Portugal. Association for Computational Linguistics.

Afshin Rahimi, Trevor Cohn, and Timothy Baldwin. 2016. pigeo: A Python Geotagging Tool. In *Proceedings of ACL-2016 System Demonstrations*, pages 127–132, Berlin, Germany. Association for Computational Linguistics.

S. Ribeiro and G. Pappa. 2017. Strategies for combining Twitter users geo-location methods. *GeoInformatica*.

Dominic Rout, Kalina Bontcheva, Daniel Preoţiuc-Pietro, and Trevor Cohn. 2013. Where's @wally? a classification approach to geolocating users based on their social ties. In *Proceedings of the 24th ACM Conference on Hypertext and Social Media*, HT '13, pages 11–20, New York, NY, USA. Association for Computing Machinery.

Justin Sech, Alexandra DeLucia, Anna L. Buczak, and Mark Dredze. 2020. Civil Unrest on Twitter (CUT): A Dataset of Tweets to Support Research on Civil Unrest. In *Proceedings of the Sixth Workshop on Noisy User-generated Text (W-NUT 2020)*, pages 215–221, Online. Association for Computational Linguistics.

Haoyu Wang, E. Hovy, and Mark Dredze. 2015. The Hurricane Sandy Twitter Corpus. In *AAAI Workshop: WWW and Public Health Intelligence*.

Congyu Wu and Matthew S. Gerber. 2018. Forecasting Civil Unrest Using Social Media and Protest Participation Theory. *IEEE Transactions on Computational Social Systems*, 5(1):82–94. Conference Name: IEEE Transactions on Computational Social Systems.

Paiheng Xu, Mark Dredze, and David A. Broniatowski. 2020. The Twitter Social Mobility Index: Measuring Social Distancing Practices With Geolocated Tweets. *Journal of Medical Internet Research*, 22(12):e21499.

A Carmen Review

A.1 Aliases

The alias list was constructed through two methods: (1) manually filtering resolved user location strings, and (2) using the user clustering method from Bergsma et al. (2013). For (1), common user location strings were resolved with Yahoo's PlaceFinder API and then manually filtered and merged. In (2), users were clustered based on social network, fullnames, and the profile location strings. This process discovered that "balto" is an alias for "Baltimore", based on the frequency that users with "balto" in their profile location communicate with "Baltimore" users.

A.2 Resolvers

Carmen includes three location resolvers to map from the tweet to a location in the internal database. The default settings are to use the resolvers in the following order, but this is user configurable: geocode (coordinates), place, and profile.

Geocode Some tweets (before 2019) contain exact coordinates, and we use these coordinates to find the closest location in our internal database. The distance threshold between our internal location and the coordinates is user configurable.

Place A Twitter Place object is a JSON that is returned with the tweet, but only 2% of tweets contain a place (Kruspe et al., 2021). The object is in a different location in API v2 and must be specifically requested, but the object itself has not significantly changed. The place includes an ID that refers to a Twitter Places database, the place type (neighborhood, city, admin), name, fullname, country code, country name, and a bounding box.[9] Twitter Places are supported by Foursquare and Yelp (Kruspe et al., 2021).

Profile If a tweet does not contain place or coordinate information, the user profile resolver is used. As reported by Kruspe et al. (2021), only 30-40% of tweets contain user profile location information. While more users have their profile location filled in, the information is a free-text field completed by the user and is not restricted, thus some users put jokes or made-up locations (Hecht et al., 2011).

The profile resolver matches the string to the internal database by normalizing it (e.g., removing punctuation), identifying state or country names with regular expressions, and then matching the string, along with the state/country, against the location database.

Twitter introduced similar functionality with their Profile Geo Enrichment in the paid Enterprise API, but not all user location strings can be geocoded.[10]

Like the place object, accessing the user location string is different in API v2, and needs to be requested separately from the tweet object.

B Carmen 2.0 Updates

B.1 Functionality Updates

The Carmen code was updated to be compatible with tweets in Twitter API v2 format. As mentioned in §A, the placement of some metadata has changed in the new API. In Carmen 2.0, besides obtaining coordinates from the "coordinates" field of a Tweet object, we also obtain coordinates from the bounding box coordinates from the place object, if it exists. We use the average of all bounding box coordinates as the coordinates used for the geocode resolver. Although this is less accurate and is not an exact coordinate compared to the "coordinates" field, it still serves as a reliable source of location metadata.

Another improvement is a faster geocode resolver. The algorithm uses coordinates from the internal location database to group the known locations into *cells*. The default cell is size 0.5, which groups location within 0.5 degrees of each other, or 34.5 miles for latitude and 27.3 miles for longitude. For example, a coordinate of $(1.2, 1.3)$ will be mapped to a cell containing all coordinates within the interval $[0.75, 1.25) \times [1.25, 1.75)$ The grouping is performed at Carmen initialization, so inference is a limited linear search over all locations in the database that are in the same cells as the query coordinates. Because different gazetteers might select different coordinate points for the same location, the design of cells gives a margin of error and allow the correct location entry to be mapped even if the coordinates does not match exactly.

[9] `https://developer.twitter.com/en/docs/twitter-api/v1/data-dictionary/object-model/geo`

[10] `https://developer.twitter.com/en/docs/twitter-api/enterprise/enrichments/overview/profile-geo`

	Resolved/s	Tweets/s
Original	263.03	655.41
GeoNames-only	120.14	297.20
GeoNames-combined	140.51	311.13

Table 4: Processing speed for different Carmen 2.0 models. Resolved/s is the average number of resolved tweets per second, and Tweets/s is average number of processed tweets per second.

B.2 Processing Speed

Table 4 shows processing speed of Carmen 2.0 with the different databases. To measure speed we use two metrics: (1) resolved tweets per second, the average number of tweets that Carmen resolves per second, and (2) tweets per second, which is the average number of processed tweets per second. The Original database, with only 7K locations, is faster than the GeoNames-only and GeoNames-combined databases, which have 74K locations. Despite this 10x increase in database size, the speed does not reduce linearly with the number of locations. This sublinear scaling is important for addition of new locations, such as incorporating cities in GeoNames with a population under 15K.

C Evaluation Metric Details

C.1 Coverage

Given Twitter dataset D, coverage is formally defined in Equation (1)

$$coverage(D) = \frac{|\{t \in D \mid t \text{ is resolved}\}|}{|\{t \in D \mid t \text{ is geotagged}\}|} \quad (1)$$

C.2 Accuracy

Match Ratio Match ratio on level L, denoted mr_L, is the number of resolved tweets such that the name matches the ground truth on level L over the number of resolved tweets that have location information on level L, where $L \in \{\text{country}, \text{admin}, \text{city}\}$.

$$D' = \{t \in D \mid t \text{ is resolved}\}$$
$$mr_l(D) = \frac{|\{t \in D' \mid x_L(t) = y_L(t)\}|}{|\{t \in D' \mid y_L(t) \neq \texttt{null}|\}} \quad (2)$$

Distance Using similar notation as Equation (2), let $x_c(t)$ denote the Carmen resolved geo-coordinates of tweet t and $y_c(t)$ denote the ground truth geo-coordinates of tweet t. We define the mapping distance of a tweet, $d(t)$ as the geodesic distance provided in the `geopy` package.[11] The distance accuracy over all tweets in D is the average of mapping distance of all resolved tweet:

$$d(D) = \frac{1}{|D'|} \sum_{t \in D'} d(t) \quad (3)$$

In addition to the average distance (Equation (3)), we also consider Acc@$K(D)$, the ratio of resolved tweets such that the distance error does not exceed K miles. This metric removes outlier influence possibly present in $d(D)$.

$$\text{Acc@}K(D) = \frac{|\{t \in D' \mid d(t) \leq K\}|}{|D'|} \quad (4)$$

Acc@$K(D)$ can be easily retrieved from a percentile plot of the mapping distances.

We exclude other commonly used metrics such as classification accuracy (Eisenstein et al., 2010), since it is relatively weak metric because the proposed method uses either 4-way or 49-way classification, much less granular than the entries in Carmen or GeoNames gazetteer. Cheng et al. (2010) use Acc@K as a ranking metric, which is not applicable to models that only return one prediction, like Carmen.

D Carmen 2.0 Comparison

TWITTER-WORLD This frequently used dataset was collected via the Twitter Streaming API over a span of 5 months (September 21 2011 to February 29 2012). It was filtered to English tweets, non-duplicate tweets, and tweets from users with at least 10 geo-tagged tweets. Locations are assigned on a per-user basis, where the "ground truth" is the city where the majority of a user's tweets originate. Since Carmen does not require training, we only use the test split of 0.45M tweets.[12]

The coverage and accuracy metrics are shown in Table 5. Before performing ablations, we evaluate all versions of Carmen on `TWITTER-WORLD` and TWITTER-GLOBAL.

In general, all versions of Carmen perform significantly better on `TWITTER-WORLD` than TWITTER-GLOBAL. We believe this is

[11] `https://geopy.readthedocs.io`

[12] Available for download from author's website `http://tq010or.github.io/research.html`

Database	Dataset	Coverage	$mr_{country}$	mr_{admin}	mr_{city}	d	Acc@10	Acc@100	Acc@1000
GeoNames-only	TWITTER-WORLD	93.82%	97.42%	73.59%	48.66%	522.6	0.866	0.906	0.907
	TWITTER-GEO-STREAM	45.45%	99.37%	83.87%	32.69%	653.0	0.823	0.867	0.869
GeoNames-combined	TWITTER-WORLD	95.34%	97.73%	56.08%	49.07%	19.2	0.866	0.947	0.999
	TWITTER-GEO-STREAM	45.48%	99.37%	83.30%	32.86%	83.6	0.824	0.902	0.989
Original	TWITTER-WORLD	91.54%	97.45%	49.12%	50.04%	40.3	0.796	0.929	0.995
	TWITTER-GEO-STREAM	39.35%	99.16%	88.75%	32.70%	75.0	0.724	0.890	0.992

Table 5: Ablation over Carmen location database and performance on popular geolocation dataset TWITTER-WORLD and new dataset, TWITTER-GLOBAL. "Acc@K" represents the ratio of tweets predicted within K miles of the ground truth. Higher values are best for all metrics except distance (d).

due to the higher availability of metadata in TWITTER-WORLD, since the data is from 2011-2012. This change in metadata availability is discussed more in §5.3 and §6.

Within each dataset, we see a clear trend in GeoNames-combined performing better than GeoNames-only, and Original, with respect to coverage.

Extracting Mathematical Concepts from Text

Jacob Collard
National Institute of Standards and Technology
jacob.collard@nist.gov

Valeria de Paiva
Topos Institute
valeria@topos.institute

Brendan Fong
Topos Institute
brendan@topos.institute

Eswaran Subrahmanian
National Institute of Standards and Technology
eswaran.subrahmanian@nist.gov

Abstract

We investigate different systems for extracting mathematical entities from English texts in the mathematical field of category theory as a first step for constructing a mathematical knowledge graph. We consider four different term extractors and compare their results. This small experiment showcases some of the issues with the construction and evaluation of terms extracted from noisy domain text. We also make available two open corpora in research mathematics, in particular in category theory: a small corpus of 755 abstracts from the journal *TAC* (3188 sentences), and a larger corpus from the nLab community wiki (15,000 sentences).[1]

1 Introduction

The majority of scientific research is communicated using natural language, often in the form of papers like this one. However, the volume of scientific literature in any given field is too large to be completely understood by any one individual. So how can expert researchers, let alone newcomers or outsiders, come to terms with the breadth of scientific knowledge in their field?

Recently, NLP tools have become stunningly effective at making information that is relevant to everyday concerns more accessible. Tools for search, question answering, and summarization have improved significantly on various general benchmarks. To make research more effective and accessible, similar tools are needed for specialized domains. Some research communities might number only in the thousands of researchers, and have specialized vocabulary and language usage, including heavy use of symbols, diagrams and/or markup

[1]Certain commercial entities, equipment, or materials may be identified in this document in order to describe an experimental procedure or concept adequately. Such identification is not intended to imply recommendation or endorsement by the National Institute of Standards and Technology, nor is it intended to imply that the entities, materials, or equipment are necessarily the best available for the purpose.

> We define the notion of a (torsor) for an (inverse semigroup), which is based on (semigroup actions), and prove that this is precisely the structure classified by the (topos) associated with an (inverse semigroup). Unlike in the (group) case, not all (set-theoretic torsors) are (isomorphic): we shall give a complete description of the (category of torsors)...

Figure 1: An example of extracting terms from a single paragraph of text.

language, as in mathematics. These smaller communities require a general methodology for constructing specialized tools themselves.

Knowledge graphs—networks of concepts and their relations in a particular domain of knowledge—have become the preferred technology for representing, sharing, and adding knowledge to modern AI applications (Ilievski et al., 2020). The construction of such a graph begins with the identification of central concepts in the domain in question. Given a corpus of text, such as a collection of papers, the task of identifying these central concepts is sometimes known as *term extraction*, and there are many generic toolkits for performing this task. In this paper we study four examples: TextRank (Mihalcea and Tarau, 2004), DyGIE++ (Wadden et al., 2019), OpenTapioca (Delpeuch, 2020), and Parmenides (Bhat et al., 2018).

A potential methodology to construct specialized, domain-specific knowledge management tools would begin by running a generic term extractor over a suitable corpus of domain-specific text

Proceedings of the 2022 COLING Workshop: The 8th Workshop on Noisy User-generated Text (W-NUT 2022), pages 15–23

and assuming that it extracts a reliable set of terms. However, each research community may wish to evaluate these terms to test whether they meet the community's specific needs. This evaluation must determine how well the underlying terms reflect important concepts in the domain. Ideally, such an evaluation would be made against a corpus annotated by human experts, which would provide a gold standard reference for a representative sample of the domain. Such a corpus would ideally capture all and only the relevant concepts present in the corpus, allowing evaluation based on both precision and recall.

However, obtaining a hand-annotated reference corpus is not always practical, especially with noisy data. First, hand annotation is time-consuming, and may be infeasible for certain research communities. Second, the specialized nature of the text means that the annotators will need to be experts in the domain. This makes hand annotation potentially very expensive for highly specialized domains. In particular, we are also seeking a methodology that can be undertaken with little to no additional direct effort from domain experts, and hand annotation does not meet this criterion.

What, then, does a methodology for constructing and evaluating extracted terms look like for specialized research domains? In this paper we propose an evaluation methodology that combines information from different 'silver standard' sources. In our case, we study author-selected keywords from paper abstracts, titles from a community-managed wiki, and linguistically identified noun phrases. We argue that, in the case that traditional F_1 scores are not informative enough when drawn from any individual source, the evaluation of several sources nonetheless gives us valuable information about the properties of terms extracted.

We apply this methodology to evaluate lists of terms extracted from text in the mathematical field of category theory. By analyzing the results, we see that generic tools do not have their full efficacy on the specialized domain of category theory, and we have the grounds to infer some reasons why. Nonetheless, this amalgamated evaluation method provides a path forward for constructing and maintaining a high quality list of domain-specific concepts in category theory. A key result of this paper is also the groundwork we lay, including two small corpora and some basic experiments, for understanding how NLP tools can be used to build a knowledge graph for mathematics.

1.1 Related work

Automatic terminology extraction (ATE) is a well-studied task in natural language process that involves the extraction of domain-specific phrases from a corpus. ATE is somewhat distinct from key phrase extraction, which operates at the document level, though the two tasks have some similarities (Zhang et al., 2018). ATE algorithms often rely on two distinct levels: the identification of linguistic units and the ranking of those units to identify the most relevant and distinctive terms. Some algorithms instead identify terms directly, though this usually requires training on an annotated dataset where relevant terms are explicitly identified (Wadden et al., 2019). Work on ATE has been done using large corpora, such as the CiteSeerX library containing millions of scientific documents from many disciplines (Patel et al., 2020). However, we are not aware of any specific work on ATE for mathematics.

We are aware of two ACL-style competitions related to mathematical text processing. Firstly, the Math Tasks in NTCIR-10, 11, and 12 studied the recognition of mathematical formulas (Aizawa and Kohlhase, 2021)[2]. The second competition is the 2017 SemEval Task 10 [3], described in Augenstein et al. (2017). This task was about extracting keyphrases and relations between them from scientific documents: the domains chosen were computer science, material science and physics[4]. Though mathematics itself was not included, all of these disciplines rely on mathematics.

There has also been a great deal of work on technical language processing that is not related to mathematics and does not explicitly involve ATE. For example, Olivetti et al. (2020) reviews the use of NLP for materials science, while Perera et al. (2020) covers biomedical information extraction. The latter is of particular interest due to their use of named entity recognition (NER), which bears some similarity to ATE, and the problems they discuss with recognizing specialized terms. Generalized approaches face challenges in these domains; as a result, these pipelines make use of domain-specific knowledge bases or expert annotations.

[2] https://ntcir-math.nii.ac.jp/

[3] https://alt.qcri.org/semeval2017/task10/

[4] https://scienceie.github.io/resources.html

2 Category theory as a case study

Although we seek to develop a generic methodology, we have chosen to ground these investigations in the specific field of category theory. Category theory is a branch of mathematics focused on relationships and composition. It is often seen as a way to organize mathematics as a whole (Marquis, 2021). While this choice is largely dictated by the interests of the authors, category theory presents a number of features which reflect the challenges and potential of automatically constructing domain-specific knowledge management tools.

Category theory as a field dates back to the 1940s (Eilenberg and MacLane, 1945). While the field is well established, the volume of text available remains small compared to the corpora used in other NLP applications. A leading journal in the field, *Theory and Applications of Categories* (TAC), published 55 papers in 2021, and a total of 845 papers since its first issue in 1995. This is small compared to, for example, the 3.27 million materials science abstracts used to train the NLP backend for the materials science search engine MatScholar (Kim et al., 2017).

Most of category theory research is described in natural language, especially English. However, the language is specialized in ways that may pose challenges to automatic systems:

- Many technical terms in CT redefine common English words. For example, 'category', 'limit', 'group', 'object', and 'natural transformation' all have more specific, formalized meanings in CT that they do not have in everyday English.
- Many technical terms involve vocabulary that is not present in everyday English at all, such as 'groupoid', 'monoidal', and 'colimit'.
- Special symbols and even diagrams are often interspersed with text, such as 'Let $\mathcal{C}$ be a category...'. Often, LaTeX markup is used, and sometimes inconsistent.
- Abbreviations and shortcuts are used which would not be common in everyday text, such as the use of '(co)homology' to refer simultaneously to both homology and cohomology.

Though the category theory community is relatively small, it has a large online presence, which has supported the creation of community-oriented websites and blogs, including the *n*Lab, a wiki for notes, expositions, and collaborative work, with a focus on category theory. The *n*Lab was started in 2008, and as of May 2022, has over 16000 articles.

The authors' own interest and expertise in category theory also allows us to quickly analyze the results of any experiments from the perspective of a potential user.

3 Automatic Term Extraction Algorithms

We run a number of experiments to test four different automatic terminology extraction methods: OpenTapioca (a simple entity linking system designed specifically for category theory), DyGIE++ (a neural NER system that has been trained to extract scientific terms), TextRank (a graph-based algorithm originally designed for key phrase extraction, but adapted to ATE), and Parmenides (a linguistically-motivated phrase extraction system that combines symbolic processing and neural parsing).

OpenTapioca: OpenTapioca (Delpeuch, 2020) is a simple named entity linking system that links phrases of natural language text to entities in WikiData (Vrandečić and Krötzsch, 2014). It cannot identify new concepts—only those already represented in WikiData. OpenTapioca is a simple baseline system that uses basic string matching to identify relevant phrases, built on the recognition that powerful knowledge bases like WikiData has led to recent success in other systems.

OpenTapioca is of particular interest, because it is designed to link entities that are not just locations, dates, or the names of people and organizations, but a variety of technical concepts. OpenTapioca also provides a filter that allows it to limit results to entities that appear in *n*Lab, effectively filtering out concepts that are not related to category theory.

DyGIE++: DyGIE++ (Wadden et al., 2019) is a span-based neural scientific entity extractor. The system builds upon the older DyGIE (Luan et al., 2019). Both systems were developed in collaboration with the Allen Institute for Artificial Intelligence, and use supervised methods to identify relevant spans of text. DyGIE++ has been trained on a variety of different corpora and subtasks, including the identification of chemical compounds, drug names, and mechanisms. Though DyGIE++ has not been trained or tested directly on category theory, the similarities between the domains it has been trained on and CT, as well as its overall strong performance, make it a good candidate to test for extracting CT concepts.

TextRank: TextRank (Mihalcea and Tarau, 2004) is a graph-based ranking algorithm based on PageRank, which has been applied to keyword extraction and text summarization as well as automatic terminology extraction. Though TextRank is a somewhat older algorithm, it is still a common algorithm that has been implemented many times. We use a modern Python implementation, PyTextRank[5].

Parmenides: Parmenides (Bhat et al., 2018) takes a linguistic approach to terminology extraction. It uses spaCy[6] to identify syntactic structures, then normalizes the syntactic structure and identifies phrases for extraction. Parmenides is highly customizable, but is designed primarily for linguistic analysis and not for terminology extraction. Nevertheless, it can be used to identify key linguistic phrases as an initial step for ATE.

4 Test Corpus

Automatic terminology extraction takes a corpus of natural language text and produces a list of relevant terms. To produce a list of terms for category theory, we need to supply a corpus of category theory text.

To create such a corpus, we take abstracts from *Theory and Applications of Categories* (TAC). This is the primary corpus that we use for our experiments. We also provide a second corpus, using a subset of the *n*Lab wiki[7]. These corpora will be made publicly available. We remove markup, section headings, and LaTeX expressions from the text to create a cleaned version of the corpus. Both corpora are written in English.

After cleaning the corpora, we run spaCy to produce automatic annotations in the style of CoNLL-U. SpaCy is a free open-source library for natural language processing in Python distributed since 2015. It features named entity recognition (NER), part-of-speech (POS) tagging, dependency parsing, and word vectors.

Note that these are the first publicly available category theory corpora, and we are not aware of any other cleaned, open-source corpora of mathematics research text.

5 Evaluation Methodology

The ATE systems described in Section 3, combined with the TAC corpus described in 4, allow us to construct candidate lists of category theory concepts, which could be used as the basis for a knowledge graph. We now arrive at the central question of this paper: how do we assess the quality of such lists?

Again, our goal is not to assess the quality of the extraction algorithms as generic tools, but rather to assess the quality of the lists of category theory concepts they produce. This is a key distinction: our goal is not generality, but the evaluation of data in a particular context.

More precisely, the usual methodology (Chuang et al., 2012) would be to construct an expertly annotated corpus, labeling all the category theory concepts contained within it. We could then compare the list of terms produced by the term extractors against the gold standard, to produce standard metrics such as precision, recall, and F_1 score. As described above, this methodology can be expensive and impractical for small, highly technical research communities.

Instead, we seek to evaluate against multiple, imperfect sources of truth to discern different properties of the data. To compensate for the imperfect nature of our reference lists, we must pair each one with a qualitative description of the properties it can reveal. This allows us to use the list to shed light on the nature of the concepts under evaluation, even if a single, representative score cannot be constructed.

The reference lists we consider for this paper are described in Table 1. The properties of each reference list are determined based on how the reference list was constructed. Author-selected keywords are constructed by human experts to capture the most important concepts in a given abstract. As a result, they have high precision: all of these elements will be concepts from the field of category theory. However, they have relatively low recall, because the authors have no incentive to include *all* possible concepts, only the concepts which are new, advanced, or distinctive. Thus, many simpler or more common concepts will be excluded from this list. The page titles from the community wiki, in this case *n*Lab, are similar: they are generally chosen by experts, but will not cover every possi-

[5] `https://pypi.org/project/pytextrank/`
[6] `https://spacy.io`
[7] https://ncatlab.org/nlab/show/HomePage

Reference List	Properties
Author-selected keywords	High precision on advanced, new concepts; poor recall
Page titles from community wiki	High precision on basic concepts; poor recall
Automatically extracted noun phrases	High recall on noun phrases; low precision

Table 1: The different reference lists under consideration and their properties

ble concept. In this case, basic, common concepts will be covered, but more advanced concepts will not. Finally, we extract a list of noun phrases uses a pre-trained spaCy model. This operates under the assumption that many technical terms are noun phrases (Chuang et al., 2012). This will capture many of these technical terms, but will also capture phrases that are not necessarily technical terms or are only meaningful in context, such as 'key results' or 'the aforementioned category'.

While each of these reference lists can give insight on its own, the intersection or union of two or more reference lists can also reveal properties of the extracted terms. For example, concepts that appear in *both* author keywords and wiki page titles can be understood to be central concepts in the field, so for knowledge graphs, we should focus on having high recall in this area. Choosing these reference lists well (i.e., such that their evaluation properties are balanced across desirable properties of our knowledge graph), means we can discover strengths and weaknesses of our extracted term lists.

A key feature of the reference lists that we have chosen is that they incorporate community-maintained, evolving sources. This means that our methodology will be able to improve with increased community effort. This empowers researchers in the domain to take simple actions that will improve the quality of our term extraction system and its evaluations.

Because the terminology extraction algorithms that we use are all extractive, our reference lists have to be extractive as well. To ensure this, we filter the phrases in each reference list by comparing them to the TAC corpus. First, we normalize the phrases using spaCy to remove variations such as morphological inflections and the presence of stop words. This allows us to compare terms in the reference list to strings in the corpus to determine if each is present, and remove the terms that are not found in the corpus.

Given an extractive reference list R, our evaluation process is fairly standard. For each term extractor E describe above, we:

1. Run term extractor E on corpus C.
2. Normalize results using spaCy to get predication list P
3. Produce lists of true positives (appears in both P and R), false positive (appears in P but not R), and false negatives (appears in R but not P).
4. Calculate recall, precision, and F1 scores.

Note that this produces scores for each reference list, and there is no generic score that covers the extractor in the general case.

6 Reference Lists

We now discuss in more detail the properties of the reference lists we have chosen for category theory. Figure 2 shows the overlap of terms found between the three reference lists.

6.1 Author Keywords

Our first reference list contains keywords selected by the authors of articles in the journal TAC.

Authors are experts on their own papers. Author-selected keywords are thus an important, reliable source of truth describing concepts in papers. However, this reference list has a few complications. For example, many of the author-selected keywords never show up in the text as described—they are not always *extractive*, and may be more abstract than the terms actually used in the text. For example, the phrase 'topological quantum field theory' could describe the topic of an abstract, but due to its generality, does not necessarily appear in the abstract. In addition, keywords may contain shortcuts and abbreviations that are easily understood by humans, but not by machines. For example, '(co)homology' may be used to describe an abstract that is about both 'homology' and 'cohomology'. Though the normalization described above accounts for author-selected keywords that never show up in texts, it may filter out relevant terms in some cases, such as

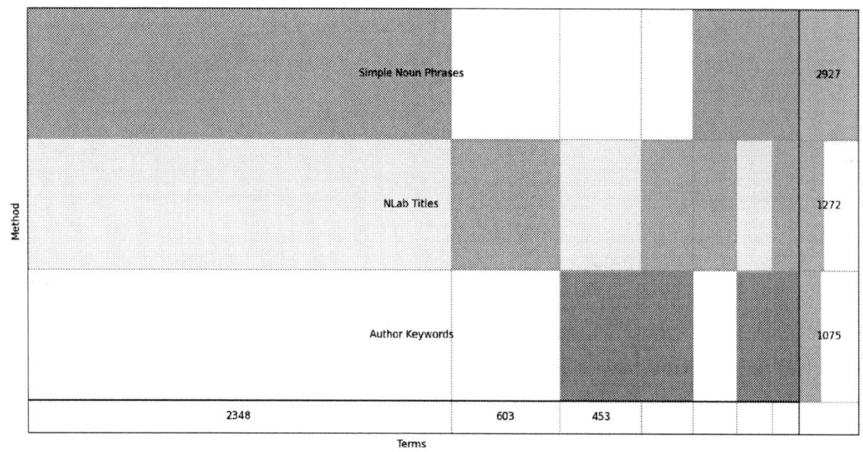

Figure 2: Unique and shared keywords identified by our three reference standards. Each column represents a set of terms; the filled portions of each row represent that the given set of terms was identified by a particular method. For example, the leftmost column shows that 2348 terms were identified only by simple noun phrases. The fourth column shows terms that were identified by both *n*Lab titles and author keywords.

the '(co)homology' example above, which won't be recognized due to the unusual formatting. However, this reference list's property of high precision should be maintained due to the authors' expertise.

One final note is that the author keywords are abstract-specific, while ATE is concerned about the corpus as a whole. Author-selected keywords are still concepts in category theory, but this fact contributes to the lower precision of this reference list: the authors will only select concepts that distinguish their articles from others, and not all concepts that they make reference to.

6.2 nLab page titles

Our second reference list is made using page titles from the *n*Lab, a community wiki for mathematics.

In the ideal case, an encyclopedic community wiki would have an article describing every concept in the field. In practice, this is not the case. First, the wiki may be initially incomplete, and as the field advances, will lag behind changes in the field. Second, there may be pages in the wiki that do not necessarily describe concepts *per se*: titles of books, meta-pages, historical notes, and lists do not necessarily belong in a knowledge graph. Since we make each reference list extractive, this should not be a significant problem.

This reference list is also very precise, but focuses on concepts that are more likely to be fundamental in category theory, as opposed to more advanced or less common concepts. This complements the author keywords well, and shows how well a list of extracted keywords reflects basic concepts in category theory.

6.3 Noun phrases

Our third reference list consists of a noun-noun compounds and adjective-noun phrases extracted from the text by spaCy. These are all two-word phrases as identified by spaCy's part-of-speech tagger, with LaTeX markup automatically removed.

There is a considerable difference between this reference list and the other two. Author keywords and wiki articles are both constructed by experts, and thus clearly belong to the field of category theory. By contrast, automatically-identified noun phrases, even those taken directly from category theory articles, may not necessarily be mathematical concepts.

Chuang et al. (2012) suggests that around 9.04% of all keywords chosen by humans are compounds, so this reference list may identify new concepts that are not picked up by other reference lists, though it certainly contains invalid terms, such as 'future work' and 'next section', as well.

Metric	DyGIE++	OpenTapioca	Parmenides	TextRank
True Positives	391	236	**979**	600
False Positives	1105	**522**	13710	3231
False Negatives	684	839	**96**	475
Precision	0.26	**0.31**	0.07	0.16
Recall	0.36	0.22	**0.91**	0.56
F_1	**0.30**	0.26	0.12	0.24

Table 2: Extracted terminology compared to author-selected keywords

Metric	DyGIE++	OpenTapioca	Parmenides	TextRank
True Positives	399	507	**1160**	684
False Positives	1097	**251**	13529	3147
False Negatives	873	765	**112**	588
Precision	0.27	**0.67**	0.08	0.18
Recall	0.31	0.40	**0.91**	0.54
F_1	0.29	**0.50**	0.15	0.27

Table 3: Extracted terminology compared to *n*Lab page titles

7 Results

Analyses of each corpus, with respect to all three reference lists, can be found in our GitHub repo. Summaries of the results of our experiments are given in Tables 2, 3, and 4. We also evaluate the results against the union of all three reference lists, as shown in Table 5.

Further results are described in our repository[8]. Overall, however, the general ranking of the term lists remains the same, with few exceptions.

8 Discussion

Overall, the F_1 scores presented here are very low when compared to the results of SEMEVAL 2017 (Augenstein et al., 2017). DyGIE++ also reports higher numbers on the datasets it has been trained on (Wadden et al., 2019). Our results are, however, similar to the results of Patel et al. (2020), which considers the problems of terminology extraction using papers indexed in CiteSeerX, which reports F_1 scores of 0.33.

Parmenides always outperforms the other models we consider on recall, but generally performs poorly on precision. Conversely, OpenTapioca has relatively high precision scores, resulting in the highest F_1 score for both author keywords and *n*Lab page titles. Parmenides was designed as a linguistic analysis tool; it extracts all possible phrases, with only limited power to rank those phrases by relevance. As a result, it extracts almost all of the linguistic units that are available, including large amounts of irrelevant text. OpenTapioca, on the other hand, is designed to pull out only category theory concepts, but is limited in its ability to extract novel terms and those not described in *n*Lab.

The terms extracted by DyGIE++ are reasonable in terms of F_1 score. For author-selected keywords, DyGIE++ performs the best, and it has the second-highest F_1 score for *n*Lab page titles.

However, it is not enough to just consider F_1 scores in this case. The reference lists that we consider have limitations, and we cannot rely on them all to be both complete and precise. As described above, the author keywords and *n*Lab titles have limited *recall*—they do not contain all of the possible category theory terms in the text, because they are designed for other purposes. For these reference lists, we can only rely on the recall of the extracted terms. Low recall on the author keywords indicates that a list does not contain many of the advanced concepts from category theory, while low recall on the *n*Lab titles indicates that a list does not contain many of the basic concepts from category theory. Low precision on these, however, may indicate that a list contains terms which may still be valid, but which do not appear in these reference lists.

The proper conclusion, then, should not be that OpenTapioca is the best option because it has the best overall F_1 score. Nor is DyGIE++ necessarily ideal just because of its high performance on author-

[8]https://github.com/ToposInstitute/tac-corpus

Metric	DyGIE++	OpenTapioca	Parmenides	TextRank
True Positives	378	216	**2439**	976
False Positives	1118	**542**	12250	2855
False Negatives	2549	2711	**488**	1951
Precision	0.25	**0.28**	0.17	0.25
Recall	0.13	0.07	**0.83**	0.33
F_1	0.17	0.12	0.28	**0.29**

Table 4: Extracted terminology compared to noun phrases

Metric	DyGIE++	OpenTapioca	Parmenides	TextRank
True Positives	748	547	**3606**	1653
False Positives	748	**211**	11083	2178
False Negatives	3518	3719	**660**	2613
Precision	0.50	**0.72**	0.25	0.43
Recall	0.18	0.13	**0.85**	0.39
F_1	0.26	0.22	0.38	**0.41**

Table 5: Extracted terminology compared to the combined reference lists

selected keywords. OpenTapioca, as shown by low recall on noun phrases, cannot extend well to novel terms. DyGIE++ performs reasonably well overall, but is outperformed by several extractors in recall of *n*Lab page titles and by Parmenides and TextRank on recall of author-selected keywords. Instead, TextRank appears to be the best candidates, having high recall on author-selected keywords and *n*Lab page titles as well as high precision on noun phrases, though a better measure of precision is desirable.

9 Conclusions

We present the first computational work extracting mathematical concepts from abstracts. We investigated four different term extractors, previously described for other domains, and evaluated the results against the limited annotated data we had for category theory. The results are somewhat limited as well, compared to previous results on more generic domains. However, other domain-specific analyses have some of the same problems, which suggests that our results are still promising.

We also provide insight into the evaluation of automatically-generated terminologies for limited-resource domains. The usual F_1 scores are not entirely reliable unless the gold standard can be assumed to include both all and only the relevant terms, but partially-correct 'silver standards' may still provide useful insight into the data.

In our case, we can draw some important conclusions about the terminology lists that we extract. Because author keywords and *n*Lab titles are most reliable for recall, we can determine that tools such as Parmenides and TextRank are able to extract large quantities of both advanced and basic category theory terms. However, the large number of other terms extracted by Parmenides suggests that it may need additional filtering to be useful for automatic terminology extraction for our use-case. Our evaluation can also be further improved. The low relative recall of the noun phrase reference list itself suggests that additional phrase types are common in our data. Adding verb phrases and more complex noun phrases could help us identify high-precision terminologies, as well as high-recall ones.

Another possibility in our case is to continue working toward our use-case. Since we have further downstream uses of the terminology—namely, the creation of a knowledge graph—we can use this to further our evaluation. By extracting relations between terms, we can identify which terms are the most connected and which are isolated, under the assumption that isolated terms are less likely to be part of domain-specific language.

We have also constructed two publicly-available corpora that can be developed into more sophisticated datasets. Though there are still many limitations to both evaluation and ATE in mathematics, we hope that our work provides a basis for future developments in the area, and that our insights on evaluation and domain-specific research can be applied more generally.

References

Akiko Aizawa and Michael Kohlhase. 2021. *Mathematical Information Retrieval*, pages 169–185. Springer Singapore, Singapore.

Isabelle Augenstein, Mrinal Das, Sebastian Riedel, Lakshmi Vikraman, and Andrew McCallum. 2017. SemEval 2017 task 10: ScienceIE - extracting keyphrases and relations from scientific publications. *CoRR*, abs/1704.02853.

Talapady Bhat, John Elliott, Ursula Kattner, Carelyn Campbell, Eswaran Subrahmanian, Ram Sriram, Jacob Collard, and Monarch Ira. 2018. Generating domain terminologies using root- and rule-based terms. (104).

Jason Chuang, Christopher D. Manning, and Jeffrey Heer. 2012. Without the clutter of unimportant words: Descriptive keyphrases for text visualization. *ACM Trans. Comput. Hum. Interact.*, 19:19:1–19:29.

Antonin Delpeuch. 2020. OpenTapioca: Lightweight entity linking for Wikidata.

Samuel Eilenberg and Saunders MacLane. 1945. General theory of natural equivalences. *Transactions of the American Mathematical Society*, 58(2):231–294.

Filip Ilievski, Daniel Garijo, Hans Chalupsky, Naren Teja Divvala, Yixiang Yao, Craig Rogers, Rongpeng Li, Jun Liu, Amandeep Singh, Daniel Schwabe, et al. 2020. KGTK: a toolkit for large knowledge graph manipulation and analysis. In *International Semantic Web Conference*, pages 278–293. Springer.

Edward Kim, Kevin Huang, Adam Saunders, Andrew McCallum, Gerbrand Ceder, and Elsa Olivetti. 2017. Materials synthesis insights from scientific literature via text extraction and machine learning. *Chemistry of Materials*, 29(21):9436–9444.

Yi Luan, David Wadden, Luheng He, Amy Shah, Mari Ostendorf, and Hannaneh Hajishirzi. 2019. A general framework for information extraction using dynamic span graphs. In *NAACL*.

Jean-Pierre Marquis. 2021. Category Theory. In Edward N. Zalta, editor, *The Stanford Encyclopedia of Philosophy*, Fall 2021 edition. Metaphysics Research Lab, Stanford University.

Rada Mihalcea and Paul Tarau. 2004. TextRank: Bringing order into text. In *Proceedings of the 2004 Conference on Empirical Methods in Natural Language Processing*, pages 404–411, Barcelona, Spain. Association for Computational Linguistics.

Elsa A. Olivetti, Jacqueline M. Cole, Edward Kim, Olga Kononova, Gerbrand Ceder, Thomas Yong-Jin Han, and Anna M. Hiszpanski. 2020. Data-driven materials research enabled by natural language processing and information extraction. *Applied Physics Reviews*, 7(4):041317.

Krutarth Patel, Cornelia Caragea, Jian Wu, and C Lee Giles. 2020. Keyphrase extraction in scholarly digital library search engines. In *International Conference on Web Services*, pages 179–196. Springer.

Nadeesha Perera, Matthias Dehmer, and Frank Emmert-Streib. 2020. Named entity recognition and relation detection for biomedical information extraction. *Frontiers in cell and developmental biology*, page 673.

Denny Vrandečić and Markus Krötzsch. 2014. Wikidata: A free collaborative knowledgebase. *Commun. ACM*, 57(10):78–85.

David Wadden, Ulme Wennberg, Yi Luan, and Hannaneh Hajishirzi. 2019. Entity, relation, and event extraction with contextualized span representations. *ArXiv*, abs/1909.03546.

Ziqi Zhang, Johann Petrak, and Diana Maynard. 2018. Adapted textrank for term extraction: A generic method of improving automatic term extraction algorithms. *Procedia Computer Science*, 137:102–108.

Data-driven Approach to Differentiating between Depression and Dementia from Noisy Speech and Language Data

Malikeh Ehghaghi[1,2], **Frank Rudzicz**[1,2,3,4,5], **Jekaterina Novikova**[1]
[1]Winterlight Labs, Toronto, ON
[2]Department of Computer Science, University of Toronto, ON
[3]Vector Institute for Artificial Intelligence, Toronto, ON
[4]Li Ka Shing Knowledge Institute, St Michael's Hospital, Toronto, ON
[5]Surgical Safety Technologies Inc., Toronto, ON
{malikeh, jekaterina}@winterlightlabs.com, {frank}@spoclab.com

Abstract

A significant number of studies apply acoustic and linguistic characteristics of human speech as prominent markers of dementia and depression. However, studies on discriminating depression from dementia are rare. Co-morbid depression is frequent in dementia and these clinical conditions share many overlapping symptoms, but the ability to distinguish between depression and dementia is essential as depression is often curable. In this work, we investigate the ability of clustering approaches in distinguishing between depression and dementia from human speech. We introduce a novel aggregated dataset, which combines narrative speech data from multiple conditions, i.e., Alzheimer's disease, mild cognitive impairment, healthy control, and depression. We compare linear and non-linear clustering approaches and show that non-linear clustering techniques distinguish better between distinct disease clusters. Our interpretability analysis shows that the main differentiating symptoms between dementia and depression are acoustic abnormality, repetitiveness (or circularity) of speech, word finding difficulty, coherence impairment, and differences in lexical complexity and richness.

1 Introduction

Depressive disorder and dementia are clinical conditions that both impose a substantial cost globally in terms of mortality and morbidity and have a significant negative impact on social and economic productivity (Jaeschke et al., 2021). Distinguishing between these conditions has proven to be a challenging task (Murray, 2010) as they frequently co-occur and have many overlapping symptoms such as apathy (Lee and Lyketsos, 2003), changes in sleep patterns (Thorpe, 2009), and concentration issues (Korczyn and Halperin, 2009). However, depression is generally curable by either psychotherapy or medication, while dementia is a neurodegenerative disease, which is caused by irreversible deterioration of the nervous system. It is hence crucial to differentiate between these two conditions (Fraser et al., 2016b).

Previous studies demonstrated that machine learning methods and speech analysis are useful in detecting dementia from depression (Fraser et al., 2016b; Murray, 2010). However, the machine learning methods used in prior studies suffer from three main limitations:

Firstly, the datasets applied in prior literature only comprise Alzheimer's disease (AD), healthy control (HC), and depression (Depr) samples of senior participants with similar demographic distributions and recording environments (Fraser et al., 2016b; Murray, 2010). In real world settings, the datasets are very noisy due to variations in the data collection procedures. Additionally, dementia is not necessarily of the AD type in all cases, and other types of dementia like mild cognitive impairment (MCI) can be included.

Secondly, to the best of our knowledge, previous studies have only used classification approaches to detect AD from HC (Pulido et al., 2020; Balagopalan et al., 2021; Balagopalan and Novikova, 2021), Depr from HC (Wu et al., 2022), or AD from Depr (Fraser et al., 2016b) using speech. This might not be an ideal simulation of the real world diagnosis procedure. In clinical diagnosis, the first step is to detect the symptoms and explore the pattern changes in patient records before diagnosing the disease (Regier et al., 2013), while in classification, we first map the samples to the disease labels and then, apply interpretability methods to explore the differentiating features between the classes (Gordon, 1999).

Lastly, prior studies demonstrated that acoustic

Proceedings of the 2022 COLING Workshop: The 8th Workshop on Noisy User-generated Text (W-NUT 2022), pages 24–37

and linguistic features extracted from spontaneous speech provide valuable indicators of both mental disorders such as depression (Low et al., 2020) and cognitive impairment like AD or MCI (Fraser et al., 2016a; Boschi et al., 2017). However, they did not derive a strong conclusion about the main distinguishing speech-based symptoms in classifying dementia from depression (Fraser et al., 2016b).

To address the first limitation, we generate a novel aggregated dataset, which combines several speech datasets comprising AD, MCI, HC, and Depr labels with a variety of data collection procedures. To address the second and third limitations, we introduce a novel approach, which applies clustering techniques to inspect what data-driven feature categories (symptoms) are the main differentiators between AD, MCI, Depr, and HC samples. We then use the distinguishing symptoms as a feature selection technique to classify AD, MCI, and Depr. Our key findings indicate that 1) the non-linear clustering approaches outperform the linear techniques in terms of separability level of distinct disease clusters; 2) acoustic abnormalities, variations in lexical complexity and richness, repetitiveness (or circularity) of speech, word finding difficulty, and coherence impairment are the main differentiating symptoms to distinguish between different types of dementia (e.g., AD and MCI), and Depr; 3) data-driven differentiators are able to substantially improve performance of classification across diseases.

2 Related Work

There has been a substantial number of studies on detecting either dementia (e.g., MCI or AD) or depression from spontaneous speech. However, little has been done to distinguish dementia from depression using discourse patterns.

To discriminate dementia from depression, Fraser et al. (2016b) applied speech data from the Pitt corpus in the DementiaBank database (Becker et al., 1994), elicited from elderly participants through picture description task, with 'Cookie Theft' (Goodglass et al., 2001) used as a picture. The samples were labeled as either AD or HC based on a personal history and a neuropsychological assessment battery (Iverson et al., 2008). A subset of the samples were labeled as depressed or non-depressed based on the established threshold on Hamilton Depression Rating Scale (HAM-D) test scores (Bagby et al., 2004). To explore the distinguishing discourse patterns between AD and Depr, Murray (2010) collected a speech dataset of elderly participants (with Depr, AD, or HC labels) who completed a picture description task, with Norman Rockwell's painting 'The Soldier' used as a picture. Samples with Depr were diagnosed based on DSM-IV criteria (Frances et al., 1995) and samples with AD met NINCDS-ADRDA criteria (Tierney et al., 1988) for probable AD. The datasets used in these studies didn't include other types of dementia such as MCI, and all of their samples followed the same data collection procedure, while we create an aggregated dataset, which consists of AD, MCI, HC, and Depr samples from different speech datasets with various data collection procedures.

Murray (2010) examined whether elderly individuals with depression can be distinguished from those at early stages of AD through distinct patterns in narrative speech. Based on their findings, individuals with AD generated less informative speech compared to the depressed patients in their picture descriptions, while there were no significant differences in the informativeness of the narratives between HC and Depr samples. Furthermore, quantitative and syntactic measures of discourse did not differ across the three groups. However, Murray (2010) did not attempt to make predictions using the data.

Fraser et al. (2016b) investigated if the automated AD screening tools misclassify cognitively healthy participants with Depr as AD when using narrative speech. They also used linguistic and acoustic features to classify non-depressed AD subjects from those with comorbid depression from speech elicited through picture description task. In their study, they compared logistic regression (LR) with support vector machines (SVM) classification models. Their performance in distinguishing between depressed and non-depressed AD samples was moderate (accuracy = 0.658) due to a wide range of overlapping symptoms. In addition, they only applied classification approaches and they didn't derive the most informative features discriminating between AD patients with and without depression. In the present work, we apply clustering approaches to cluster the diseases based on the similarities in the discourse patterns, and apply interpretability techniques to explore the distinguishing feature categories (symptoms) between distinct diagnosis labels (i.e., HC, AD, MCI, and Depr). We use the differentiating symptoms as a feature selection technique to classify the diseases.

3 Methods

3.1 Dataset

In this paper, we generated an aggregated superset of the datasets listed in Table 1 that contains speech recordings of English-speaking participants describing pictures. All the audio recordings were manually transcribed by trained transcriptionists, using the CHAT protocol and annotations (MacWhinney, 2014).

Dataset	AD	MCI	Depr	HC
DementiaBank (Becker et al., 1994)	178	138	0	229
Healthy Aging	0	214	0	211
ADReSS (Luz et al., 2020)	54	0	0	54
DEPAC+ (Tasnim et al., 2022)	0	0	222	532
AD Clinical Trial	1616	0	0	0
Aggregated dataset	1848	352	222	1026

Table 1: Speech datasets used. For each dataset, the number of samples with each diagnosis label is reported in the following columns.

DementiaBank (Becker et al., 1994) and **ADReSS** (Luz et al., 2020) are the datasets of pathological speech elicited from participants through picture description task, with 'Cookie Theft' (Goodglass et al., 2001) used as a picture. The recordings are labeled as AD, MCI, and HC.

Healthy Aging is the dataset of speech elicited from community volunteers through picture description task, with 'Family in the Kitchen', 'Man in the Living Room', 'Food Market', 'Picnic', 'Grandmother's Birthday', and 'Romantic Dinner' proprietary images. The recordings are labeled as possible HC and MCI. Soft labels are based on the established threshold on Montreal Cognitive Assessment (Nasreddine et al., 2005) screening tool.

DEPAC+ is the extended version of the **DEPAC** (Tasnim et al., 2022) dataset, with more samples collected using the same data collection procedure. This is a dataset of narrative speech elicited from participants through picture description task, with 'Family in the Kitchen' and 'Man Falling' images. The recordings are labeled as HC and Depr. Soft labels are based on the established threshold on Patient Health Questionnaire-9 (PHQ-9) (Kroenke et al., 2001) test scores[1].

AD Clinical Trial is a dataset of speech recordings from the baseline and screening visits of a clinical trial elicited from participants through picture description task, with 'Family in the kitchen', 'Man in the Living Room', 'Grandmother's Birthday', 'Romantic Dinner', and 'Cookie Theft' (Goodglass et al., 2001) images. All the recordings are labeled as AD according to the the National Institute on Aging/Alzheimer's Association citeria (Frisoni et al., 2011).

All images other than 'Cookie Theft' (Goodglass et al., 2001) were designed to match the 'Cookie theft' picture in style and the amount of information content units according to picture design principles described by Patel and Connaghan (2014).

3.2 Feature Extraction

We extracted 220 acoustic features from audio, and 325 linguistic features from the associated transcripts. These features were classified into the following categories (the full list is in Appendix A):

Acoustic: This category includes spectral and voicing-related features (e.g., Mel-Frequency Cepstral Coefficients (MFCC) (Rudzicz et al., 2012), Fundamental frequency (F_0), or statistical functionals of Zero-Crossing Rate (ZCR) (Kulkarni, 2018)) describing the acoustic properties of the sound wave.

Syntactic Complexity: This category comprises variables like the frequencies of various production rules from the constituency parsing tree of the transcripts (Chae and Nenkova, 2009), or Lu's syntactic complexity features (Lu, 2010) enumerating the rate of usage of different syntactic structures.

Discourse Mapping: This category consists of features such as utterance distances, or speech-graph features (Mota et al., 2012) like graph density (Mirheidari et al., 2018) to calculate the repetitiveness or circularity of speech.

Lexical Complexity and Richness: This category accounts for the variables like frequency of words, or measures of vocabulary diversity such as type-token ratio (Richards, 1987) describing the lexical complexity and vocabulary richness of the transcripts.

Information Content Units: This category includes variables such as the number of objects, subjects, locations, and actions used to measure the number of items correctly named in the picture description task previously found to be associated with memory impairment (Croisile et al., 1996).

Sentiment: This category contains features such as valence, arousal, and dominance scores (War-

[1]The participants with a PHQ-9 score ≤ 9 were labeled as HC, and the remaining samples with a PHQ-9 score ≥ 10 met criteria for symptoms of depression.

riner et al., 2013) for all words and word types describing the sentiment of the words used.

Word Finding Difficulty: This category consists of features including speech rate, duration of words, and number of filled (e.g., um, uh) and unfilled pauses as signs of word finding difficulty, which result in less fluid or fluent speech.

Coherence (Global and Local): This category includes variables like average, minimum, and maximum cosine distances (Mirheidari et al., 2018) between subsequent utterances (local coherence) or between utterances and key words (global coherence) using word2vec (Church, 2017) representation of the utterances to calculate their semantic similarity.

4 Proposed Novel Approach: Data-Driven Approach to Detecting Differentiating Speech-based Symptoms between Dementia and Depression

4.1 Dimensionality Reduction and Clustering

We first applied dimensionality reduction techniques to the preprocessed features (see Appendix B). To explore linear dimension reduction approaches, we applied Principal Component Analysis (PCA) (Wold et al., 1987) as well as Linear Discriminant Analysis (LDA) (Izenman, 2013). For non-linear dimensionality reduction techniques, we used Uniform Manifold Approximation and Projection (UMAP) (McInnes et al., 2018) and T-distributed Stochastic Neighbour Embedding (t-SNE) (Van der Maaten and Hinton, 2008) (See details of implementation and hyperparameter setting in Appendix C).

Next, we clustered the low-dimensional data points by K-Means clustering (Mysiak, 2020) to group them in an unsupervised way into distinguishable clusters. Clusters were meant to represent groups associated with data labels - HC, AD, MCI, and Depr.

4.1.1 Performance Metrics

The performance of the clustering methods was measured based on the following metrics:

1. *Optimal number of disease clusters* determined by the elbow method (Yuan and Yang, 2019)) after training K-Means clustering on the feature embeddings resulted from dimension reduction. The ideal case is to derive 4 distinct disease clusters in line with the 4 diagnosis labels in the aggregated dataset (i.e., HC, AD, MCI, and Depr).

2. *Silhouette score* (Rousseeuw, 1987) was used to measure the level of cluster separability. Its value ranges from -1 to 1. '1' means clusters are well apart from each other and clearly distinguished. '0' means that the distance between clusters is not significant. '-1' means clusters are assigned in the wrong way (Bhardwaj, 2020). The results were recorded for K=4 (the number of labels in the dataset), where K is the number of clusters generated by K-Means clustering.

4.2 Analysis of the Differentiating Feature Categories between the Disease Clusters

Analysis of the differentiating feature categories across the disease clusters consists of 3 main steps: LIME-based explanation of the low-dimentional embeddings, analysis of feature contributions to the non-linear components, and feature selection using the differentiating feature categories in classification of AD vs MCI vs Depr.

4.2.1 Local Explanation of the Non-linear Embeddings by LIME

We applied a LIME-for-t-SNE[2] interpretability method developed by Bibal et al., 2020 to find the main differentiating feature categories between AD, Depr, MCI, and HC diagnosis labels. This approach adapts Local Interpretable Model-agnostic Explanations (LIME) (Ribeiro et al., 2016) to locally explain t-SNE components.

4.2.2 Analysis of Feature Contributions to the Non-linear Components

In this experiment, we investigated what feature categories are the main differentiating factors between the distinguishable disease clusters derived by K-Means clustering. As the first step, we randomly selected 10 HC samples from each cluster and applied Lime-for-t-SNE model to explain the local trends in their neighborhood. We also picked 10 Depr and 10[3] AD data points from the associated disease clusters and followed the same procedure to locally explain the low-dimensional components.

[2]Publicly available at `https://github.com/vu-minh/mlteam-lime-for-tsne`

[3]We selected 10 samples from each disease cluster, since each group must contain at least 5 samples for both Kruskal-Wallis H-Test (Lomuscio, 2021) and Mann-Whitney U-Test (Bedre, 2021) explained in 4.2.2.

Dimension reduction method	Is the optimal number of clusters (K) equal to 4?	Silhouette score (K = 4)
PCA (linear)	-	0.2010
LDA (linear)	-	0.4125
t-SNE (non-linear)	x	0.4723
UMAP (non-linear)	x	**0.5580**

Table 2: Summary of the performance of all dimensionality reduction techniques. The second column checks if the optimal number of clusters is equal with the total number of labels (e.g., HC, MCI, AD, and Depr) in the aggregated dataset. 'K' refers to the number of clusters in K-Means clustering applied on the embeddings in the low-dimensional space.

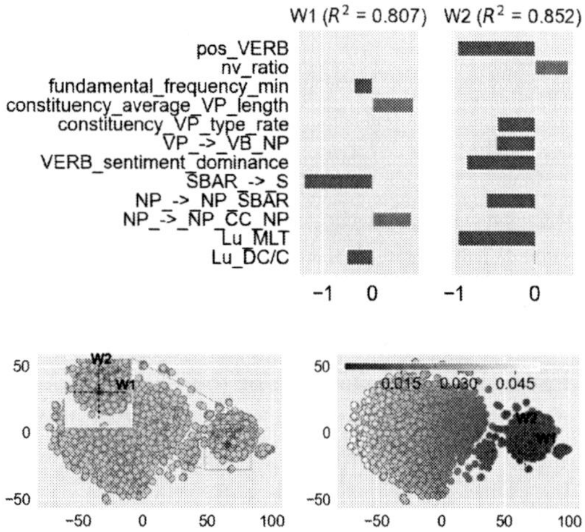

Figure 1: Explanation of the local trends in the t-SNE embeddings for a selected Depr instance. The figure at the top indicates the weights of the highly-contributed features explaining each local dimension (R^2 score indicates how well the local trends are linearly explained per each axis.) The blue transparency in the scatter plot represents the errors of the linear model applied locally on the original instance. The figure at the bottom left is a zoom on the zone of interest for local explanation, with projected samples in red (Bibal et al., 2020)

Figure 1 depicts an example of the local explanation of t-SNE embeddings for a selected Depr instance. For each candidate sample, we generated a vector of length 9 indicating the total number of highly-contributed features explaining either quasi-horizontal (e.g., $W1$ in Figure 1) or quasi-vertical (e.g., $W2$ in Figure 1) trends per each feature category including acoustic, syntactic complexity, discourse mapping, lexical complexity and richness, information content units, sentiment, word finding difficulty, coherence (global and local), and utterance cohesion.

Overall Group Comparison (Kruskal-Wallis H-Test): After calculating the feature frequency vectors of the selected samples, we applied overall group comparison per each feature category to test the overall difference between the feature frequencies across the disease groups. For this purpose, we used Kruskal-Wallis H-test (Kruskal and Wallis, 1952) using the `scipy.stats.kruskal` library in python.

Pairwise Group Comparison (Mann-Whitney U-Test): As a post-hoc comparison method, we then applied pairwise Mann-Whitney U-test (Mann and Whitney, 1947) using the `scipy.stats.mannwhitneyu` python library to determine the distributions of which feature categories are significantly different between each pair of the selected disease groups.

4.2.3 Classification of AD vs Depr vs MCI

After analyzing the feature contributions to the non-linear components, we used the main differentiating feature categories as a feature selection technique to investigate whether they improve the classification performance of AD vs Depr vs MCI. For this purpose, we separately trained Multi-layer Perceptron classifier (MLPClassifier) on the following feature sets:

1. F: All the hand-crafted acoustic and linguistic features
2. F_d: Only the feature categories that are shown to be the main differentiators between AD and Depr based on Mann-Whitney test
3. $F - F_d$: All the hand-crafted features excluding the main distinguishing feature categories

We implemented MLPClassifier by `neural_network.MLPClassifier` package of Scikit-learn (Pedregosa et al., 2011) with all the hyperparameters set to their default parameter settings. We trained the models using grouped 10-fold cross validation to avoid overlapping subjects between the train and test folds and evaluated the performance of the models in terms of macro average accuracy, precision, recall, and F1 scores across the 10 folds.

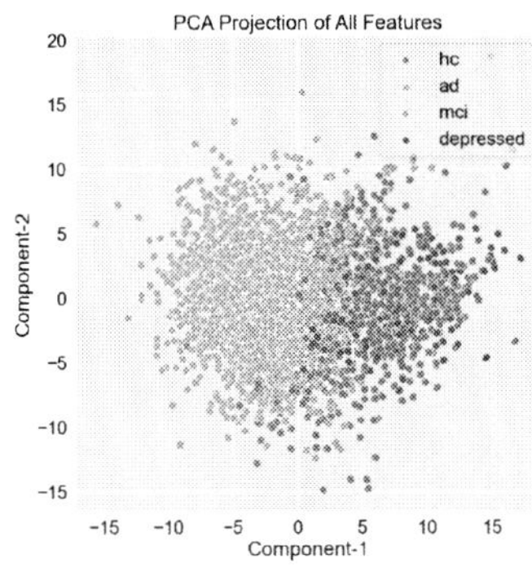

(a) PCA - Disease Clusters

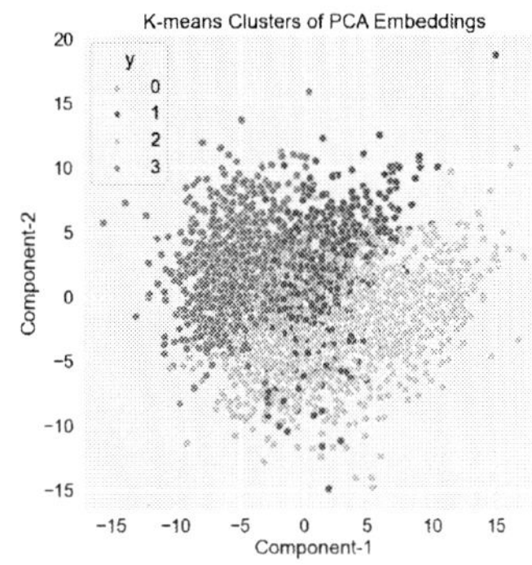

(b) PCA - K-Mean Clusters

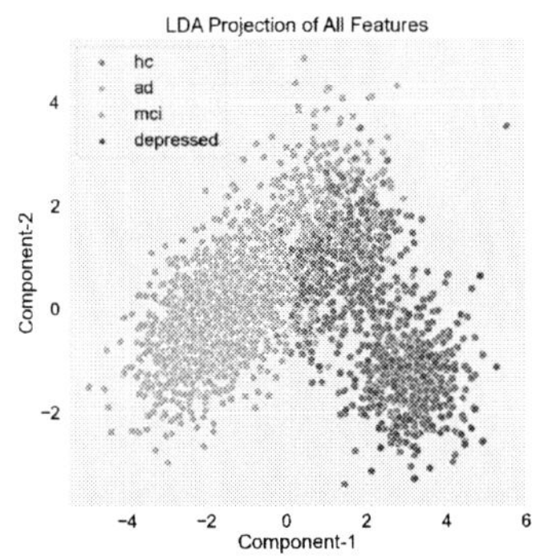

(c) LDA - Disease Clusters

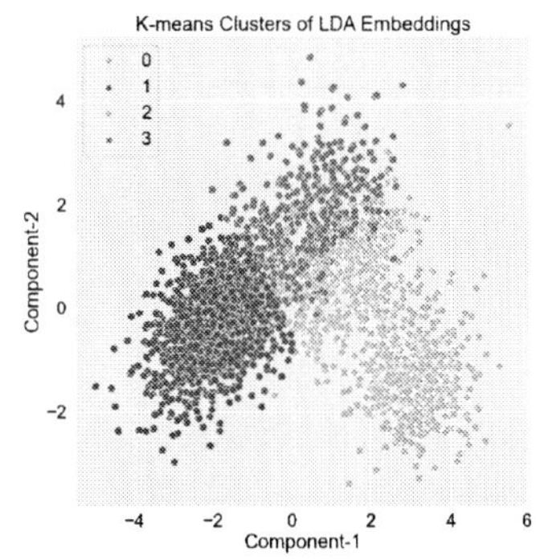

(d) LDA - K-Means Clusters

Figure 2: Pairwise scatter plots of the linear dimensionality reduction techniques (Component-1 vs Component-2). Left figures: 2-D representation of the samples colored based on their diagnosis labels. Right figures: 2-D representation of the samples colored based on the data-driven clusters resulted from K-Means clustering for K=4.

5 Results and Discussion

5.1 Comparison of Linear and Non-linear Dimensionality Reduction Approaches

Table 2 compares how the linear approaches (e.g., PCA, and LDA) perform versus the non-linear techniques (e.g., t-SNE, and UMAP) in distinguishing between distinct diagnosis labels (i.e., AD, MCI, HC, and Depr). Their performance is compared according to their optimal number of K-Means clusters, and Silhouette score. The second column of Table 2 represents whether the optimal number of data-driven disease clusters in K-Means clustering is equal to the total number of diagnosis labels in the aggregated dataset, which is our ideal case.

Between the linear techniques, the Silhouette score obtained by LDA is about twice in value compared to PCA. This can be due to the fact that LDA (Izenman, 2013) is a supervised dimensionality reduction technique which focuses on maximizing the class separability by projecting the data points on a new linear axis, while PCA (Wold et al., 1987) tries to find the directions of maximal variance. Based on Figure 2c and 2d, the clusters of different diseases, as well as the K-Means clusters in LDA, are more visually distinguishable when compared to PCA (See Figure 2a and 2b). It is also interesting to note how the clusters are placed in LDA plots. MCI comes between AD and HC samples, while depressed data points are positioned on the right end of the figure. This visualization creates a spectrum from AD to MCI, to healthy samples and also, well-separated depressed data points from the rest of the samples.

Interestingly, the optimal number of K-Means clusters in t-SNE is exactly equal with 4 (the total number of disease labels in our data set), which is our ideal case. In addition, its Silhouette score is higher than both PCA and LDA methods. Figure 3a illustrates how well the disease clusters are separated in this model.

In Table 2, we observe that UMAP demonstrates

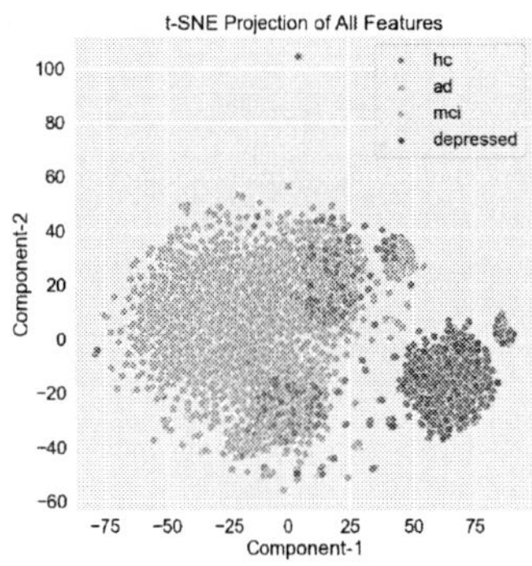

(a) t-SNE - Disease Clusters

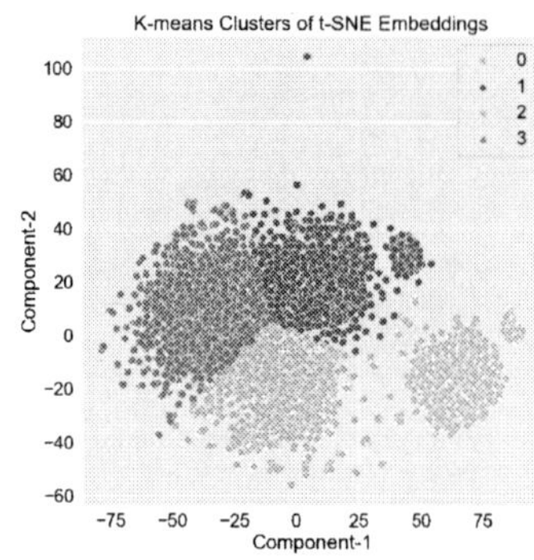

(b) t-SNE - K-Means Clusters

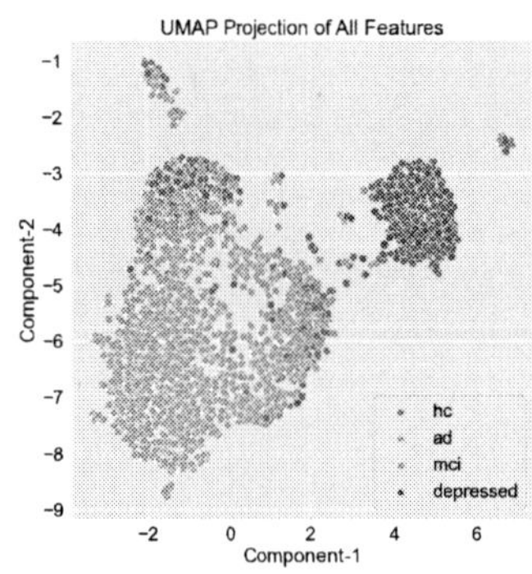

(c) UMAP - Disease Clusters

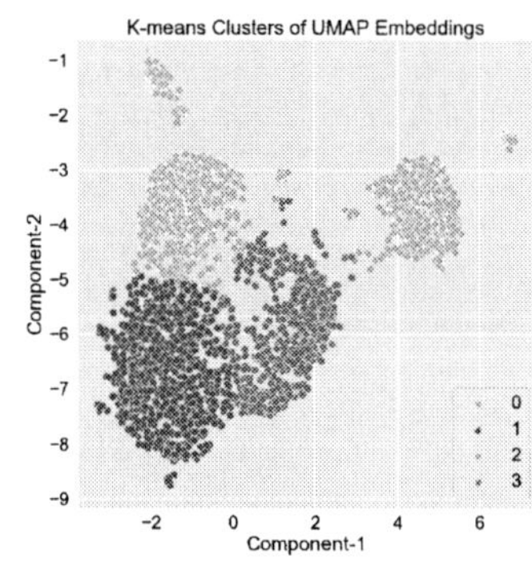

(d) UMAP - K-Means Clusters

Figure 3: Pairwise scatter plots of the non-linear dimensionality reduction techniques (Component-1 vs Component-2). Left figures: 2-D representation of the samples colored based on their diagnosis labels. Right figures: 2-D representation of the samples colored based on the data-driven clusters resulted from K-Means clustering for K=4.

the best performance among all clustering techniques according to its optimal number of K-Means clusters and Silhouette score. Its optimal number of clusters determined by elbow method is exactly the same as the original number of diagnosis labels. In addition, its Silhoutte score is higher than other approaches meaning that the level of separability of the data-driven disease clusters is higher in UMAP. The associated cluster visualizations for UMAP are also depicted in Figure 3c. We see depressed samples are well-separated from AD, and MCI, although AD and MCI themselves are not easily distinguishable.

In summary, linear dimensionality reduction techniques like PCA and LDA transform the data to a low-dimensional space as a linear combination of the original variables, while non-linear techniques are applied when the original high-dimensional data contains non-linear relationships (Sumithra and Surendran, 2015). Consequently, our findings suggest that the linearity assumption might be incorrect for our aggregated dataset and hence, this can be another reason why the non-linear dimensionality reduction techniques outperformed the linear ones.

5.2 Analysis of the Differentiating Feature Categories between the Disease Clusters

As it is illustrated in Figure 3b, K-Means clustering derived four distinct disease clusters in a data-driven way using t-SNE embeddings. Cluster 2 corresponds to the right-most cluster in Figure 3a, which is a mixture of Depr and HC samples. Cluster 3 associates with the AD green clump of points on the left-most side of Figure 3a and clusters 0 and 1 match with the two zones in the middle comprising a combined set of AD, MCI, and HC data points. We randomly selected 10 HC samples from three distinct clusters 0, 1, and 2. We also picked 10 random Depr points from cluster 0 and 10 random AD points from cluster 3. For each instance, we applied LIME-for-t-SNE to explain its local

Compare	Acoustic	Syntactic Complexity	Discourse Mapping	Lexical Complexity and Richness	Information Content Units	Sentiment	Word Finding Difficulty	Coherence (Global and Local)	Utterance Cohesion
AD vs HC	x	-	x	x	x	-	x	x	-
Depr vs HC	x	-	-	x	-	x	-	x	-
HC Variations	x	-	-	x	-	x	-	x	-
AD vs Depr	x	-	x	x	-	-	x	x	-

Table 3: Pairwise Mann-Whitney U-Test on frequency vectors of disease groups. For each pair of disease groups, the feature categories with p-value < 0.05 are marked as differentiating symptoms.

Feature Set	Precision	Recall	F1 Score	Accuracy
F	0.88 ± 0.04	0.86 ± 0.04	0.87 ± 0.04	0.90 ± 0.02
F_d	$\mathbf{0.90 \pm 0.03}$	$\mathbf{0.88 \pm 0.03}$	$\mathbf{0.89 \pm 0.03}$	$\mathbf{0.92 \pm 0.02}$
$F - F_d$	0.74 ± 0.06	0.69 ± 0.07	0.71 ± 0.06	0.82 ± 0.03

Table 4: Performance of AD vs MCI vs Depr classification using different feature sets. Here, F denotes all hand-crafted acoustic and linguistic features. F_d denotes differentiating feature categories between AD and Depr. $F - F_d$ denotes all features excluding differentiating feature categories.

neighbourhood and derive its frequency vector of feature categories (See Section 4.2). Overall group comparison using Kruskal-Wallis H-Test on the frequency vectors represents that the feature categories including acoustic, lexical complexity and richness, and coherence are significantly different (with p-value < 0.05) across the disease groups including AD, Depr, and different variations of HC.

As post-hoc group comparison, we applied pairwise Mann-Whitney U-test on each pair of disease groups to assess what feature categories are the main differentiating symptoms across the disease clusters. As it is shown in Table 3, acoustic, lexical complexity and richness, sentiment, and coherence are significantly different across different variations of HC. These differences show variations within the group of healthy samples that can root in the data origin, and data collection procedures.

Our results indicate that some samples labeled as Depr are similar to HC samples across all the feature categories. This can be due to the distribution of PHQ-9 scores in DEPAC+ dataset with the majority of samples with scores in the range of 5 to 14 from mild to moderate levels of depression severity. Minor levels of depression does not meet the full criteria of major depressive disorder and the symptoms of minor forms of depression are less severe compared to major depressive disorder (Shin et al., 2021). This increases the risk of confusing modest rates of depression with control samples (Cummins et al., 2015).

Acoustic, discourse mapping (repetitiveness or circularity of speech), lexical complexity and richness, word finding difficulty, and coherence are found to be the main differentiating symptoms between AD and Depr disease clusters. To investigate the effectiveness of our results, we used these feature categories as a feature selection method.

5.3 Change in Classification Performance

We reported the performance of classification of AD vs MCI vs Depr in Table 4. According to paired sample t-test, the expected value of the accuracy, precision, recall, and F1 scores across 10 folds are significantly different between each pair of F, F_d, and $F - F_d$ feature sets, with p-value < 0.05. Compared to when using all the features, feature selection using only the differentiating feature categories significantly improved the classification performance in terms of all metrics. Also, excluding the differentiating feature categories significantly worsened the performance of the model in classifying the diseases. These observations support that our proposed method shows a promising avenue toward detecting the data-driven symptoms that can successfully differentiate between Depr, AD, and MCI diseases.

6 Conclusion

In this work, we generate a novel aggregated dataset composed of a number of speech corpora including a combination of different clinical conditions (e.g., AD, MCI, HC, and Depr). We extract a hand-crafted set of acoustic and linguistic features derived from speech data, which are used as model predictors for discriminating between the diagnosis labels and we categorize these features under data-driven feature categories in line with the clinical symptoms of these diseases. We cluster the samples into distinguishable disease clusters and examine what speech symptoms are the main differentiating factors between the diseases. Based on our findings, non-linear clustering approaches outperform the linear ones in terms of distinguishing between distinct disease clusters. Our results signify that acoustic abnormality, repetitiveness, or circularity of speech, word finding difficulty, coherence, and differences in lexical complexity and richness are the main differentiating symptoms between different types of dementia (e.g., MCI and AD), and depression.

References

R Michael Bagby, Andrew G Ryder, Deborah R Schuller, and Margarita B Marshall. 2004. The hamilton depression rating scale: has the gold standard become a lead weight? *American Journal of Psychiatry*, 161(12):2163–2177.

Aparna Balagopalan, Benjamin Eyre, Jessica Robin, Frank Rudzicz, and Jekaterina Novikova. 2021. Comparing pre-trained and feature-based models for prediction of alzheimer's disease based on speech. *Frontiers in aging neuroscience*, 13:635945.

Aparna Balagopalan and Jekaterina Novikova. 2021. Comparing Acoustic-based Approaches for Alzheimer's Disease Detection. *INTERSPEECH 2021*.

James T Becker, François Boiler, Oscar L Lopez, Judith Saxton, and Karen L McGonigle. 1994. The natural history of Alzheimer's disease: description of study cohort and accuracy of diagnosis. *Archives of neurology*, 51(6):585–594.

Renesh Bedre. 2021. Mann-whitney u test (wilcoxon rank sum test) in python [pandas and scipy].

Ashutosh Bhardwaj. 2020. Silhouette coefficient.

Adrien Bibal, Viet Minh Vu, Géraldin Nanfack, and Benoît Frénay. 2020. Explaining t-sne embeddings locally by adapting lime. In *ESANN*, pages 393–398.

Veronica Boschi, Eleonora Catricala, Monica Consonni, Cristiano Chesi, Andrea Moro, and Stefano F Cappa. 2017. Connected speech in neurodegenerative language disorders: a review. *Frontiers in psychology*, 8:269.

Étienne Brunet et al. 1978. *Le vocabulaire de Jean Giraudoux structure et évolution*. Slatkine.

Marc Brysbaert and Boris New. 2009. Moving beyond kučera and francis: A critical evaluation of current word frequency norms and the introduction of a new and improved word frequency measure for american english. *Behavior research methods*, 41(4):977–990.

Simone Centellegher. 2020. How to compute PCA loadings and the loading matrix with scikit-learn.

Jieun Chae and Ani Nenkova. 2009. Predicting the fluency of text with shallow structural features: Case studies of machine tanslation and human-written text. *Association for Computational Linguistics*.

Kenneth Ward Church. 2017. Word2Vec. *Natural Language Engineering*, 23(1):155–162.

Bernard Croisile, Bernadette Ska, Marie-Josee Brabant, Annick Duchene, Yves Lepage, Gilbert Aimard, and Marc Trillet. 1996. Comparative study of oral and written picture description in patients with Alzheimer's disease. *Brain and language*, 53(1):1–19.

Nicholas Cummins, Stefan Scherer, Jarek Krajewski, Sebastian Schnieder, Julien Epps, and Thomas F Quatieri. 2015. A review of depression and suicide risk assessment using speech analysis. *Speech communication*, 71:10–49.

Alexis Dinno. 2009. Implementing Horn's parallel analysis for principal component analysis and factor analysis. *The Stata Journal*, 9(2):291–298.

Allen Frances, Michael B First, and Harold Alan Pincus. 1995. *DSM-IV guidebook*. American Psychiatric Association.

Kathleen C Fraser, Jed A Meltzer, and Frank Rudzicz. 2016a. Linguistic features identify Alzheimer's disease in narrative speech. *Journal of Alzheimer's Disease*, 49(2):407–422.

Kathleen C Fraser, Frank Rudzicz, and Graeme Hirst. 2016b. Detecting late-life depression in alzheimer's disease through analysis of speech and language. In *Proceedings of the Third Workshop on Computational Linguistics and Clinical Psychology*, pages 1–11.

Giovanni B Frisoni, Bengt Winblad, and John T O'Brien. 2011. Revised NIA-AA criteria for the diagnosis of alzheimer's disease: a step forward but not yet ready for widespread clinical use. *International psychogeriatrics*, 23(8):1191–1196.

Harold Goodglass, Edith Kaplan, and Sandra Weintraub. 2001. *BDAE: The Boston Diagnostic Aphasia Examination*. Lippincott Williams & Wilkins Philadelphia, PA.

Allan David Gordon. 1999. *Classification*. CRC Press.

Antony Honoré et al. 1979. Some simple measures of richness of vocabulary. *Association for literary and linguistic computing bulletin*, 7(2):172–177.

Grant L Iverson, Brian L Brooks, Travis White, and Robert A Stern. 2008. Neuropsychological assessment battery: Introduction and advanced interpretation. *The neuropsychology handbook*, pages 279–343.

Alan Julian Izenman. 2013. Linear discriminant analysis. In *Modern multivariate statistical techniques*, pages 237–280. Springer.

Kara Jaeschke, Fahmy Hanna, Suhailah Ali, Neerja Chowdhary, Tarun Dua, and Fiona Charlson. 2021. Global estimates of service coverage for severe mental disorders: findings from the WHO Mental Health Atlas 2017–addendum. *Global Mental Health*, 8.

Amos D Korczyn and Ilan Halperin. 2009. Depression and dementia. *Journal of the neurological sciences*, 283(1-2):139–142.

Kurt Kroenke, Robert L Spitzer, and Janet BW Williams. 2001. The PHQ-9: validity of a brief depression severity measure. *Journal of general internal medicine*, 16(9):606–613.

William H Kruskal and W Allen Wallis. 1952. Use of ranks in one-criterion variance analysis. *Journal of the American statistical Association*, 47(260):583–621.

Nilesh Kulkarni. 2018. Use of complexity based features in diagnosis of mild Alzheimer disease using EEG signals. *International Journal of Information Technology*, 10(1):59–64.

Hochang B Lee and Constantine G Lyketsos. 2003. Depression in alzheimer's disease: heterogeneity and related issues. *Biological psychiatry*, 54(3):353–362.

Samantha Lomuscio. 2021. Getting started with the kruskal-wallis test.

Daniel M Low, Kate H Bentley, and Satrajit S Ghosh. 2020. Automated assessment of psychiatric disorders using speech: A systematic review. *Laryngoscope Investigative Otolaryngology*, 5(1):96–116.

Xiaofei Lu. 2010. Automatic analysis of syntactic complexity in second language writing. *International journal of corpus linguistics*, 15(4):474–496.

Saturnino Luz, Fasih Haider, Sofia de la Fuente, Davida Fromm, and Brian MacWhinney. 2020. Alzheimer's dementia recognition through spontaneous speech: the ADReSS challenge. *arXiv preprint arXiv:2004.06833*.

Brian MacWhinney. 2014. *The CHILDES project: Tools for analyzing talk, Volume II: The database*. Psychology Press.

Henry B Mann and Donald R Whitney. 1947. On a test of whether one of two random variables is stochastically larger than the other. *The annals of mathematical statistics*, pages 50–60.

Leland McInnes, John Healy, and James Melville. 2018. Umap: Uniform manifold approximation and projection for dimension reduction. *arXiv preprint arXiv:1802.03426*.

Tomas Mikolov, Ilya Sutskever, Kai Chen, Greg S Corrado, and Jeff Dean. 2013. Distributed representations of words and phrases and their compositionality. In *Advances in neural information processing systems*, pages 3111–3119.

Bahman Mirheidari, Daniel Blackburn, Traci Walker, Annalena Venneri, Markus Reuber, and Heidi Christensen. 2018. Detecting signs of dementia using word vector representations. In *Interspeech*, pages 1893–1897.

Natalia B Mota, Nivaldo AP Vasconcelos, Nathalia Lemos, Ana C Pieretti, Osame Kinouchi, Guillermo A Cecchi, Mauro Copelli, and Sidarta Ribeiro. 2012. Speech graphs provide a quantitative measure of thought disorder in psychosis. *PloS one*, 7(4):e34928.

Laura L Murray. 2010. Distinguishing clinical depression from early alzheimer's disease in elderly people: can narrative analysis help? *Aphasiology*, 24(6-8):928–939.

Kamil Mysiak. 2020. Explaining k-means clustering.

Ziad S Nasreddine, Natalie A Phillips, Valérie Bédirian, Simon Charbonneau, Victor Whitehead, Isabelle Collin, Jeffrey L Cummings, and Howard Chertkow. 2005. The Montreal Cognitive Assessment, MoCA: a brief screening tool for mild cognitive impairment. *Journal of the American Geriatrics Society*, 53(4):695–699.

Rupal Patel and Kathryn Connaghan. 2014. Park play: A picture description task for assessing childhood motor speech disorders. *International Journal of Speech-Language Pathology*, 16(4):337–343.

F. Pedregosa, G. Varoquaux, A. Gramfort, V. Michel, B. Thirion, O. Grisel, M. Blondel, P. Prettenhofer, R. Weiss, V. Dubourg, J. Vanderplas, A. Passos, D. Cournapeau, M. Brucher, M. Perrot, and E. Duchesnay. 2011. Scikit-learn: Machine learning in Python. *Journal of Machine Learning Research*, 12:2825–2830.

Jeffrey Pennington, Richard Socher, and Christopher D Manning. 2014. Glove: Global vectors for word representation. In *Proceedings of the 2014 conference on empirical methods in natural language processing (EMNLP)*, pages 1532–1543.

Benjamin Pope, Thomas Blass, Aron W Siegman, and Jack Raher. 1970. Anxiety and depression in speech. *Journal of Consulting and Clinical Psychology*, 35(1p1):128.

María Luisa Barragán Pulido, Jesús Bernardino Alonso Hernández, Miguel Ángel Ferrer Ballester, Carlos Manuel Travieso González, Jiří Mekyska, and Zdeněk Smékal. 2020. Alzheimer's disease and automatic speech analysis: a review. *Expert systems with applications*, 150:113213.

Darrel A Regier, Emily A Kuhl, and David J Kupfer. 2013. The dsm-5: Classification and criteria changes. *World psychiatry*, 12(2):92–98.

Marco Tulio Ribeiro, Sameer Singh, and Carlos Guestrin. 2016. " why should i trust you?" explaining the predictions of any classifier. In *Proceedings of the 22nd ACM SIGKDD international conference on knowledge discovery and data mining*, pages 1135–1144.

Brian Richards. 1987. Type/token ratios: What do they really tell us? *Journal of child language*, 14(2):201–209.

Peter J Rousseeuw. 1987. Silhouettes: a graphical aid to the interpretation and validation of cluster analysis. *Journal of computational and applied mathematics*, 20:53–65.

Frank Rudzicz, Graeme Hirst, and Pascal van Lieshout. 2012. Vocal tract representation in the recognition of cerebral palsied speech. *Journal of speech, language, and hearing research : JSLHR*.

Daun Shin, Won Ik Cho, C Hyung Keun Park, Sang Jin Rhee, Min Ji Kim, Hyunju Lee, Nam Soo Kim, and Yong Min Ahn. 2021. Detection of minor and major depression through voice as a biomarker using machine learning. *Journal of Clinical Medicine*, 10(14):3046.

Hans Stadthagen-Gonzalez and Colin J Davis. 2006. The Bristol norms for age of acquisition, imageability, and familiarity. *Behavior research methods*, 38(4):598–605.

V Sumithra and Subu Surendran. 2015. A review of various linear and non linear dimensionality reduction techniques. *Int. J. Comput. Sci. Inf. Technol*, 6(3):2354–2360.

Mashrura Tasnim, Malikeh Ehghaghi, Brian Diep, and Jekaterina Novikova. 2022. Depac: a corpus for depression and anxiety detection from speech. In *Proceedings of the Eighth Workshop on Computational Linguistics and Clinical Psychology*, pages 1–16.

Lilian Thorpe. 2009. Depression vs. dementia: how do we assess. *The Canadian Review of Alzheimer's Disease and Other Dementias*, 12(3):17–21.

Mary C Tierney, Rory H Fisher, Anthony J Lewis, Maria L Zorzitto, W Gary Snow, David W Reid, and Paula Nieuwstraten. 1988. The nincds-adrda work group criteria for the clinical diagnosis of probable alzheimer's disease: A clinicopathologic study of 57 cases. *Neurology*, 38(3):359–359.

Laurens Van der Maaten and Geoffrey Hinton. 2008. Visualizing data using t-SNE. *Journal of machine learning research*, 9(11).

Amy Beth Warriner, Victor Kuperman, and Marc Brysbaert. 2013. Norms of valence, arousal, and dominance for 13,915 english lemmas. *Behavior research methods*, 45(4):1191–1207.

Martin Wattenberg, Fernanda Viégas, and Ian Johnson. 2016. How to use t-SNE effectively. *Distill*.

Haydée F Wertzner, Solange Schreiber, and Luciana Amaro. 2005. Analysis of fundamental frequency, jitter, shimmer and vocal intensity in children with phonological disorders. *Revista Brasileira de Otorrinolaringologia*, 71:582–588.

Svante Wold, Kim Esbensen, and Paul Geladi. 1987. Principal component analysis. *Chemometrics and intelligent laboratory systems*, 2(1-3):37–52.

Pingping Wu, Ruihao Wang, Han Lin, Fanlong Zhang, Juan Tu, and Miao Sun. 2022. Automatic depression recognition by intelligent speech signal processing: A systematic survey. *CAAI Transactions on Intelligence Technology*.

Victor H Yngve. 1960. A model and an hypothesis for language structure. *Proceedings of the American philosophical society*, 104(5):444–466.

Chunhui Yuan and Haitao Yang. 2019. Research on k-value selection method of k-means clustering algorithm. *J*, 2(2):226–235.

A List of the features

Detailed description of the linguistic and acoustic variables in our conventional feature set is represented respectively in Table 5 and Table 6.

B Data Preprocessing

B.1 Standardization

In the data preprocessing step, the features with constant values were removed and then, the feature values were standardized by removing the mean and scaling to unit variance. The standard score of a sample x was calculated as:

$$y = \frac{x - \mu}{\sigma} \tag{1}$$

here μ and σ are the mean and standard deviation of the sample x in all training samples.

B.2 Feature selection

To remove multicollinearity, one of each pair of the features with Pearson correlation higher than 0.9 was removed.

C Implementation and Hyperparameter Setting of the Dimensionality Reduction Models

C.1 Linear Approaches

PCA: PCA was implemented by the `sklearn.decomposition.PCA` package in Scikit-learn (Pedregosa et al., 2011) and its number of components was set to the optimal number of Principal Components (PCs) calculated by Horn's parallel analysis (Dinno, 2009), which was equal to **46**. After sorting the PCs based on their explained variance ratio, the feature loadings (Centellegher, 2020) were calculated to measure the correlation between the features and the low-dimensional components. According to the distribution of the feature loadings, features with absolute value of loadings $\geq$ 0.4 were selected as the highly-correlated features in each PC. The number of components with the largest values of explained variance ratio and at least one highly-correlated feature was chosen as the optimal number of components. As a result, the tuned number of components was equal with **8**. This approach selects the components which explain the most variance in data and include features which are highly-correlated with PCs on a linear scale.

LDA: LDA was implemented by the `LinearDiscriminimumantAnalysis` package of Scikit-learn (Pedregosa et al., 2011) with its default parameter settings. The number of components was set equal to 3 (the maximum allowed value), which is the number of classes-1, to achieve the highest total explained variance ratio. The classes represent the diagnosis labels in our study including HC, AD, Depr, and MCI.

C.2 Non-linear Approaches

t-SNE: t-SNE (Van der Maaten and Hinton, 2008) was implemented by the `sklearn.manifold.TSNE` package of Scikit-learn (Pedregosa et al., 2011). Perplexity was tuned by grid search to obtain the highest Silhouette score (See Section 4.1.1) in K-Means clustering trained on the t-SNE embeddings. The rest of the hyper-parameters were left unchanged with their default values. We used perplexity=30 to preserve both local and global structure of the given data to an adequate level (Wattenberg et al., 2016), in line with the recommended range of perplexity values by Van der Maaten and Hinton (2008). The number of components in t-SNE was manually tuned to 2, which was the best performing one based on the Silhouette score metric (See Section Section 4.1.1).

UMAP: This algorithm was implemented using the original `UMAP`[4] library. Among different combinations of parameter settings, grid search indicated that number of components=2, the number of neighbours=50, and minimum distance=0.1 obtained the highest Silhouette score (See Section 4.1.1) in K-Means clustering trained on the UMAP embeddings. The remaining parameters were set to their default values.

[4]https://umap-learn.readthedocs.io/en/latest/

Linguistic Features

Feature Category	**#Features**	**Brief Description**
Syntactic complexity	143	**Constituency-parsing based features**: Scores based on the parse tree (Chae and Nenkova, 2009) (e.g., the height of the tree, the statistical functions of Yngve depth (a measure of embeddedness) (Yngve, 1960), and the frequencies of various production rules(Chae and Nenkova, 2009)). **Lu's syntactic complexity features**: Metrics of syntactic complexity suggested by Lu (2010) such as the length of sentences, T-units, and clauses, etc. **Utterance length**: Statistical functionals of utterance length.
Lexical complexity and richness	103	**Grammatical constituents**: The constituents of the parse tree represented in a collection of context-free grammar variables. **Vocabulary richness**: Type-token ratios; brunet (Brunet et al., 1978); Honore's statistic (Honoré et al., 1979). **Lexical norm-based**: Average norms across all words, verbs only, and nouns only for imageability, age of acquisition, familiarity (Stadthagen-Gonzalez and Davis, 2006) and frequency (Brysbaert and New, 2009).
Discourse mapping	18	**Utterance distances** quantifying the utterance similarity via distance metrics and **speech-graph** (Mota et al., 2012) features based on the graph representation of the transcripts.
Global coherence	15	Statistical functionals of cosine distance between GloVe (Pennington et al., 2014) word embeddings of each utterance and its nearest content unit centroid utterances.
Local coherence	15	Statistical functionals of the similarity between Word2Vec (Mikolov et al., 2013) embeddings of the successive utterances.
Word finding difficulty	11	**Pauses and fillers**: Variables like hesitation, speech rate, word duration, and number of filled and unfilled pauses as markers of difficulty in finding words resulting in less fluent speech (Pope et al., 1970). **Invalid words**: The proportion of words not in the English dictionary (NID).
Information units	10	The number of information content units including objects, subjects, locations, and actions applied to quantify the number of items correctly named through the picture description task.
Sentiment	9	Valence, arousal, and dominance scores for all words and word types describing the sentiment of the words used (Warriner et al., 2013).
Utterance cohesion	1	Proportion of the number of switches in verb tense across utterances.

Table 5: List of all hand-curated linguistic features derived from transcripts. The number of features in each feature category is indicated in the second column (titled '#Features').

Spectral and Energy Related Features		
Feature	**#Features**	**Brief Description**
Mel-Frequency Cepstral Coefficients (MFCC) 0-12	168	Statistical functionals of 42 MFCC coefficients.
Intensity	8	Statistical functionals of the perceived loudness in dB (auditory model based).
Zero-Crossing Rate (ZCR)	4	Statistical functionals of zero crossing rate across all the voiced frames.
Voicing Related Features		
Harmonic-to-Noise Ratio (HNR)	12	Statistical functionals of the degree of acoustic periodicity in dB using both autocorrelation and cross-correlation methods.
Jitter and Shimmer	11	Jitter indicates the variability or perturbation of fundamental frequency, while shimmer refers to the same perturbation, but it is related to the amplitude of sound wave, or intensity of vocal emission (Wertzner et al., 2005).
Pauses and Fillers	8	Number and duration of short, medium, and long pauses, fillers(um,uh), mean pause duration, and pause-to-speech ratio.
Fundamental Frequency (F_0)	6	Statistical functionals of the fundamental frequency in Hz.
Durational features	2	Total sample and speech duration in the audio record.
Phonation Rate	1	Number of voiced samples over the total number of samples.

Table 6: List of all hand-curated acoustic features derived from audio records. The number of features in each feature category is indicated in the second column (titled '#Features').

Cross-Dialect Social Media Dependency Parsing for Social Scientific Entity Attribute Analysis

Chloe Eggleston
University of Massachusetts Amherst
ceggleston@umass.edu

Brendan O'Connor
University of Massachusetts Amherst
brenocon@cs.umass.edu

Abstract

In this paper, we utilize recent advancements in social media natural language processing to obtain state-of-the-art syntactic dependency parsing results for social media English. We observe performance gains of 3.4 UAS and 4.0 LAS against the previous state-of-the-art as well as less disparity between African-American and Mainstream American English dialects. We demonstrate the computational social scientific utility of this parser for the task of socially embedded entity attribute analysis: for a specified entity, derive its semantic relationships from parses' rich syntax, and accumulate and compare them across social variables. We conduct a case study on politicized views of U.S. official Anthony Fauci during the COVID-19 pandemic.[1]

1 Introduction

Corpora of social media text contain wide ranges of beliefs that researchers may seek to analyze. But numerous studies have found significant challenges in applying natural language processing (NLP) techniques to social media, ranging from inconsistent spelling practices to continuously evolving terminology (Baldwin, 2012; Eisenstein, 2013).

Under the now-ubiquitous modeling paradigm of pretrained transformers (Peters et al., 2018; Devlin et al., 2019; Bender et al., 2021; Bommasani et al., 2021), it is crucial to include social media content in a language model pretraining corpus. BERTweet (Nguyen et al., 2020), a language model trained entirely on English Twitter, has shown state-of-the-art results in classification (Barbieri et al., 2020), part-of-speech (POS) tagging (Nguyen et al., 2020), and named entity recognition (NER) (Jiang et al., 2022) on social media English.

In addition, treebanks have been annotated to cover this specific variety of English. Tweebank v2

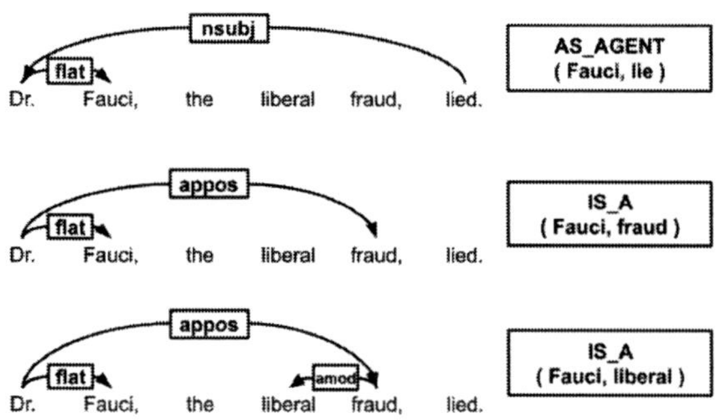

Figure 1: Examples of dependencies and TweetIE's entity attribute extraction system (§4).

(Liu et al., 2018) consists of 3,550 English tweets annotated according to Universal Dependencies (Nivre et al., 2020), and Jiang et al. (2022) add NER tags following the four-class CoNLL 2003 guidelines (Tjong Kim Sang and De Meulder, 2003).

Other work has considered the impact of demographic and dialectical factors on social media NLP. Blodgett et al. (2016, 2018) investigate linguistic variation of African-American English (AAE) on Twitter from aggregate user demographics, developing a small 500 tweet Universal Dependencies corpus half of which consists of tweets heavily using AAE. On this AAE subset, dependency parsers encounter worse performance than on Mainstream American English (MAE), and a similar AAE-MAE dialect disparity is widespread in other areas of NLP (e.g. Koenecke et al., 2020; Ziems et al., 2022).

Social media NLP advances could enable novel techniques in computational social science. Retrieval and representation of the beliefs and opinions of various groups and ideologies is of clear importance to many social sciences, with applications ranging from misinformation studies (Ayoub et al., 2021) to political science and economics (Ash et al., 2021).

With these goals in mind, we train a state-of-

[1]Code for this paper is available at: https://github.com/slanglab/TweetIE_WNUT2022

Proceedings of the 2022 COLING Workshop: The 8th Workshop on Noisy User-generated Text (W-NUT 2022), pages 38–50

the-art social media dependency parser, evaluating social media English performance, as well as AAE dialect disparity, among eleven alternative pretrained models (§3). To illustrate dependency parsing's utility for social media analysis, we implement a rule-based semantic attribute extractor to analyze authors' views toward an entity (Figure 1; §4), and evaluate it in a case study of political narratives surrounding the U.S. official Dr. Anthony Fauci during the COVID-19 pandemic—we compare extractions against the authors' social variable of geolocated election results (§5). We find our TweetIE system has better yield and higher precision for this task, compared to using previous open information extraction systems.

2 Related Work: Social Semantic Extraction

Natural language processing has been used to extract social insight from corpora in humanistic and social scientific study. Archak et al. (2007); Ghose et al. (2007) analyze the economic impact of dependency parse-extracted adjective modification from product reviews and seller feedback, associating perceived attributes with monetary prices. Narrative analysis of fictional characters has used dependency parses to extract attributes associated with character archetypes (Bamman et al., 2013); our semantic relation extractor follows and extends their approach. These dependency-based systems can be viewed as expanding on widely used collocation methods that tabulate words appearing near an entity (Baker, 2006); for example, Blinder and Allen (2016) use words directly before an entity (a rough adjective modifier extractor) to analyze attributes ascribed to immigrants in political discourse.

In the NLP context, outside of computational social science, open information extraction (OIE) is a related semantic approach that extracts relational tuples without a predefined schema, often applied to large heterogenous corpora, such as web data (Banko et al., 2007), typically using off-the-shelf NLP technologies such as part-of-speech (POS) tagging, named entity recognition (NER), semantic role labelling, and dependency parsing (Mausam, 2016). Our TweetIE information extractor uses a rule system working directly from dependency parses, following the approach of argument extraction and normalization systems PropS (Stanovsky et al., 2016) and PredPatt (White et al., 2016); the latter performs well on OIE benchmarks (Zhang et al., 2017). We share PredPatt's motivation to rely on Univerisal Dependencies parses, which have coverage and availability across many language varieties, including social media English here. This contrasts favorably to the domain-dependent limitations of machine-learned semantic role labeling (Carreras and Màrquez, 2005) and semantic dependency parsing (Oepen et al., 2014).

3 Dependency Parsing

3.1 Approach

Dependency parsing is typically performed by either transition-based (Covington, 2001; Nivre, 2003) or graph-based (Eisner, 1996) models, and can utilize representations including word embeddings, recurrent neural networks (Kiperwasser and Goldberg, 2016), and/or transformers (Grünewald et al., 2021). For experiments we use SuPar,[2] a Python library for syntactic and semantic parsing, to implement a graph-based transformer dependency parser using a deep biaffine attention (Dozat and Manning, 2017) layer, fine tuned from a HuggingFace-compatible pretrained transformer language model (Wolf et al., 2020). Due to its comparative performance (§3.3), we select BERTweet-base for the pretrained model for our final parser, fine-tuned[3] on Tweebank v2. Our experiments use the Tweebank v2 splits from its supplied "converted" CoNLL-compatible variant. We use "Twitter-Stanza (TB2)" for tokenization, since it achieves state-of-the-art results on Tweebank v2 tokenization (98.64 F1) (Jiang et al., 2022).[4]

Overall performance results are averaged over three seeds, shown in the last row of Table 1. Our results outperform the BiLSTM baselines featured in (Liu et al., 2018) by 3.4 unlabelled attachment score (UAS) and 4.0 labelled attachment score (LAS), as well as the previous state of the art, spaCy-XLM-RoBERTa, a transition-based parser using the multilingual transformer XLM-R (Conneau et al., 2020).

[2] https://github.com/yzhangcs/parser

[3] Hyperparameters tested (selections underlined): epochs=(50, 75, <u>100</u>), warmup rate=(0.1, <u>0.15</u>, 0.2), lr = (1e-5, 5e-6, <u>1e-4</u>), projective=(false, <u>true</u>)

[4] SuPar provides an option to use either projective (Eisner, 2000; Zhang et al., 2020), or non-projective (matrix tree: Koo et al., 2007; Ma and Hovy, 2017) parsing; we use projective parsing, finding it attains slightly better performance (+0.3 UAS, +0.2 LAS from preliminary experiments), presumably since non-projectivity is rare in English (Peng and Zeldes, 2018).

This software platform easily allows us to compare training treebanks and pretrained language models, which we next explore for their impact on overall social media performance as well as dialect disparity.

System	UAS	LAS
TweeboParser (Kong et al., 2014)	81.4	76.9
Deep Biaffine (Dozat and Manning, 2017)	81.8	77.7
Ensemble Model (Liu et al., 2018)	83.4	79.4
spaCy-XLM-RoBERTa (Jiang et al., 2022)	83.8	79.4
SuPar-BERTweet (this work)	**87.2**	**83.4**

Table 1: Performance (in F1) of systems on Tweebank v2 test set. First four rows are from Liu et al. (2018) and Jiang et al. (2022).

3.2 Impact of Training Treebank

In order to measure the impact of treebanks on performance in this domain, we fine-tune RoBERTa-base (Liu et al., 2020) on three different treebanks, and measure its respective performance on Tweebank v2's test set using the CoNLL evaluation script. In order to ensure compatibility with this script and the ability to evaluate cross-treebanks, we drop the corpora-specific dependency subtypes.

We select the Georgetown University Multilayer Corpus (GUM) (Zeldes, 2017) and English Web Treebank (EWT) (Silveira et al., 2014). These include user-generated content and are 2.5 and 4.5 times larger than Tweebank v2 respectively. Despite their increased size, both see significant performance drops when evaluated on Tweebank v2 (Table 2).

	In-Domain		*Tweebank v2*	
Fine-tuning Corpus	**UAS**	**LAS**	**UAS**	**LAS**
GUM	92.9	90.9	66.6	57.1
EWT	90.7	89.6	70.2	61.5
Tweebank v2	85.7	81.4	**85.7**	**81.4**

Table 2: Performance (in F1) of SuPar-RoBERTa when trained on a given corpus, and its checkpoint with best dev split performance evaluated against the associated (in-domain) test split, as well as Tweebank v2.

3.3 Impact of Pretrained Model Selection

In addition to fine-tuning corpora, we observe a noticeable performance impact with respect to the models used, suggesting that pretraining has a role as well.

We evaluate the performance of eleven transformer models on Tweebank v2. BERT (Devlin et al., 2019), RoBERTa (Liu et al., 2020), ELECTRA (Clark et al., 2020), XLNet (Yang et al., 2019), and DeBERTa v3 (He et al., 2021) are general purpose English transformers. XLM-R (Conneau et al., 2020) adapts RoBERTa to multilingual corpora, and InfoXLM (Chi et al., 2021) improves upon XLM-R with mutual information-improved loss function for cross-lingual context. TimeLMs (Loureiro et al., 2022) fine-tunes RoBERTa, training continually with larger temporal range, yield checkpoints for 2019 and 2019-2021 respectively. BERTweet is a RoBERTa model trained from scratch on Twitter. XLM-T (Barbieri et al., 2022) fine-tunes XLM-R on multilingual Twitter.

Model	UAS	LAS
General Purpose Models		
BERT-base-uncased	85.0	80.8
RoBERTa-base	85.7	81.4
ELECTRA-base	85.6	81.6
XLNet-base-cased	85.8	81.7
DeBERTa-v3-base	87.1	83.2
Multilingual Models		
XLM-R-base	86.2	82.4
InfoXLM-base	86.5	82.7
Social Media Models		
TimeLMs-2019	85.7	81.6
TimeLMs-2021	86.3	82.3
BERTweet-base	**87.2**	**83.4**
Multilingual Social Media Models		
XLM-T-base	86.5	82.0

Table 3: Performance (in F1) of SuPar dependency parsers using various pretrained transformers, fine-tuned and evaluated on the Tweebank v2 train and test splits, with the epoch of the best dev split performance being selected.

Table 3 indicates that stronger performance can be achieved through either better representations in modeling or through more social media pretraining, as seen respectively with DeBERTa v3 and BERTweet, one having the highest GLUE score (Wang et al., 2018; He et al., 2021), and the other trained entirely on Twitter.

3.4 Performance on Non-Majority English

One key challenge of working with social media text is the lack of adherence to any standardized dialect of a language, and the inclusion of significant minority dialects, such as high prevalence of African American English (AAE) (Jones, 2015; Blodgett et al., 2016). AAE dependency parsing includes significant challenges from recognizing null copulas to correctly understanding phonologically

Model	Tweebank v2 MAE	Tweebank v2 AAE	Tweebank v2 R.E.	TwitterAAE Deps MAE	TwitterAAE Deps AAE	TwitterAAE Deps R.E.
General Purpose Models						
BERT	84.03	78.93	1.32	74.24	67.31	1.27
RoBERTa	84.40	78.61	1.37	75.46	67.50	1.32
ELECTRA	84.35	80.73	1.23	74.18	67.31	1.27
XLNet	84.41	79.85	1.29	75.72	69.75	1.25
DeBERTa-v3	**85.63**	82.44	1.22	77.08	71.90	1.23
Multilingual Models						
XLM-R	85.14	81.56	1.24	74.07	68.06	1.23
InfoXLM	85.17	82.11	1.21	74.44	68.19	1.24
Social Media Models						
TLMs19	84.22	81.33	1.18	76.23	72.22	1.17
TLMs21	84.87	82.30	1.17	76.91	72.38	1.20
BERTweet	85.42	**84.38**	**1.07**	**78.10**	**76.55**	**1.07**
Multilingual Social Media Models						
XLM-T	84.86	82.62	1.15	76.14	72.94	1.13

Table 4: MAE/AAE Performance (in LAS F1) and Relative Error of the models from Table 3, trained on Tweebank v2, and evaluated on Tweebank v2 test split and TwitterAAE deps.

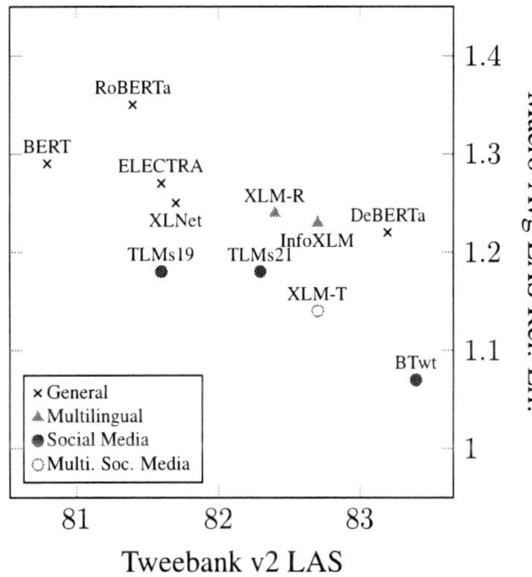

Figure 2: Graph of the performance of the models presented in Table 3 in LAS and macro-average of the relative error on the MAE/AAE split Tweebank v2 test set and TwitterAAE dependencies.

driven alternative spellings (Blodgett et al., 2018).

We evaluate the ability of the previously listed dependency parsing models by using the relative error of their performance on Mainstream American English (MAE) and AAE test sets,

$$\text{LASRelErr} = \frac{1 - \text{LAS}_{\text{AAE}}}{1 - \text{LAS}_{\text{MAE}}} \quad (1)$$

which attains 1 if accuracy is equal across dialects. We have found this to be always greater than 1.0 in our experiments, indicating performance is worse for the minority dialect, AAE.

In order to measure disparity on the fine-tuning source, we measure the relative error of both the TwitterAAE dependencies and use the TwitterAAE demographic dialect inference model to partition the Tweebank v2 test set into splits based on whether there was higher proportion MAE or AAE, yielding 951 and 249 tweets respectively. We also measure this on the TwitterAAE dependencies, which provides 250 tweets of both MAE and AAE respectively.

Table 4 and Figure 2 display the disparities between MAE and AAE performance on Tweebank v2 and TwitterAAE dependencies. This form of demographic evaluation offers insight on a key question that is not visible in the UAS / LAS scores alone: whether the performance gains come from overfitting on the majority dialect or increased performance across dialects.

We observe the social media models to have less LAS relative error than the general purpose models, with BERTweet, the model exposed to the most social media content, having less relative error than any model. As seen in Table 4, its state-of-the-art performance in Tweebank v2 does not suggest that it has the best performance with the syntax of standard English; it actually underperforms DeBERTa-v3, and only outperforms in total due to the 2 LAS difference on AAE. The relative error suggests that BERTweet's performance only adds on average 7% more error to a AAE sample compared to standard English, while general purpose models like DeBERTa v3 and RoBERTa add around 22.5% and 34.5% more, despite being fine-tuned on the same corpora.

The implications suggest that social media transformers capture the syntax not only better than their general purpose counterparts, regardless of architecture improvements, but also do it in a more equitable manner. This is important for applications sensitive to demographic effects.

4 TweetIE: Belief Extraction from Dependencies

A well-performing social media dependency parser, along with pre-existing POS and NER taggers, enable novel applications for computational social science. We apply these technologies for a belief extraction system, which decodes these syntactic structures into simple semantic representations and presents information applicable for computational social scientific purposes, specifically the delineation of beliefs to communities represented by social variables. We call this system **TweetIE**.

4.1 Design Principles

In order to preserve the benefits of the domain-specific dependency parsing system while maintaining a simple overall system, we seek to:

- Infer relations using dependency parses, NER tags, and POS tags, not through lexicons that might only cover standard English.
- Focus on relations regarding a named entity and its attributes.
- Minimize the number of arguments for relations to allow for accumulation and comparison across social variables.

4.2 Target Entities and Pronoun Coreference

We focus our extraction based on the attributes of a single named-entity in a given tweet, through either specifying a name, or using an @ mention of that user's account. In the case of names of persons or organizations, we take into account the specified token, and expand it using the *flat* relation and the span of any BIO NER tags. If the root of this span is a *conj* dependency or if any relevant predicates have *conj* dependencies, we distribute dependency relations over them, as done in the CCprocessed/Enhanced++ variants of Stanford (De Marneffe and Manning, 2008) and Universal (Schuster and Manning, 2016) Dependencies.

In order to capture common forms of anaphora such as possessive pronoun usage, we implement a simple precision-oriented coreference system for binary gendered target entities. The user specifies the target's gender, and the system seeks any personal pronouns with the target as the antecedent. It first determines whether the target's mention(s) are in second person (denoted by the *vocative* relation) or third person (otherwise). It attributes pronouns of the determined person and specified gender to the target if there are no other entities (denoted by "PER" NER tags) mentioned in the text before it that are potentially applicable (as in they agree with regards to grammatical person).

To evaluate this system, we annotated a random sample of 100 tweets for whether their POS-tagged pronouns refer to the target entity of our later case study, Dr. Anthony Fauci (see Section 5). Our system achieved 33/39 (84.6%) precision and 33/52 (63.5%) recall.

4.3 Relations

We limit our focus to the following semantic relations:

4.3.1 IS_A

The IS_A relation covers any nominal or adjectival properties stated to directly pertain to the target entity, represented using the following patterns:[5]

1. target $\xleftrightarrow{\text{nsubj}}$ property$_{nom}$
2. property$_{adj}$ $\xrightarrow{\text{nsubj}}$ target
3. target $\xleftrightarrow{\text{appos}}$ property$_{nom}$
4. target $\xrightarrow{\text{compound}}$ property$_{nom}$
5. target $\xrightarrow{\text{amod}}$ property$_{adj}$
6. target $\xleftrightarrow{\text{nsubj}}$ property$_{nom}$ $\xrightarrow{\text{amod}}$ property$_{adj}$
7. target $\xleftrightarrow{\text{appos}}$ property$_{nom}$ $\xrightarrow{\text{amod}}$ property$_{adj}$

Patterns 1 and 2 detect subject-complement linking through copular clauses, even when explicit copulas are omitted. Pattern 3 detects appositions, and Pattern 4 detects titles that do not make up fully formed appositions (ex: "*President* Obama").

Pattern 5 detects adjective modifiers. Patterns 6 and 7 detect adjective modifiers of previously captured nominal properties, hoping to capture intersective adjectives (ex: "Trump is a *famous* person").

4.3.2 HAS_A

The HAS_A relation pertains to any object possessed the target entity, implemented through possessive modification.

1. object$_{nom}$ $\xrightarrow{\text{nmod:poss}}$ target

4.3.3 AS_AGENT, AS_PATIENT

The AS_AGENT and AS_PATIENT relations pertain to actions performed by the target entity and performed upon the target entity respectively.

1. active verb $\xrightarrow{\text{nsubj}}$ target$_{agent}$
2. active verb $\xrightarrow{\text{obj}}$ target$_{patient}$
3. passive verb $\xrightarrow{\text{nsubj:pass}}$ target$_{patient}$
4. passive verb $\xrightarrow{\text{obl}}$ target$_{agent}$
5. active verb $\xrightarrow{\text{obl}}$ target$_{patient}$ $\xrightarrow{\text{case}}$ prep.

[5] H→D represents a relation from a head H to its dependency D, while X⟷Y indicates a relation in either direction.

Patterns 1 and 2 account for active tense verbs, while 3 and 4 account for passive tense verbs, which are distinguished from active tense by the presence of a *nsubj:pass* dependency.

Pattern 5 consists of when the target acts as an adjunct of the verb using a preposition, and is lexicalized through appending the preposition to the verb (ex: "I *stand with* Obama", "He *listens to* Bill Gates").

4.3.4 AS_CONJUNCT

The AS_CONJUNCT relations pertains to any nominal conjoined with the target entity. If this nominal consists of a named-entity, it is expanded in the same manner as the target entity (through *flat* dependencies and BIO NER spans).

1. target $\overset{\text{conj}}{\longleftrightarrow}$ conjunct

Although this has no explicit semantic meaning, it suggests that the two hold a latent semantic relationship, such as co-hypernymy (Snow et al., 2004).

4.4 Negation

A theoretical concern for this mode of semantic extraction deals with the presence of negative polarity adverbs. Intuitively when comparing these extractions across social variables, this form of negation should not be accumulated in the same case as the original clause.

However, dependency relations describing negative polarity do not exist in the current version of Universal Dependencies, with the *neg* relation being removed in Universal Dependencies v2 (Nivre et al., 2020). In order to account for this, we check previous version of treebanks for user-generated content with this relation: specifically EWT v1.4. In this treebank, the *neg* relation only covers the following tokens: ['no', 'not', 'never', 'nt', 'n't'].

We utilize this list by adding a negative polarity to any relation extracted that is modified by any of those tokens. This is implemented by prepending the extraction's argument with 'not_', an approach used in sentiment analysis (Das and Chen, 2007). A word list in this vein has clear limitations - it does not cover social media variations in spelling, yet it allows us to capture this quality on its most common variants.

4.5 Evaluation

TweetIE can either be evaluated through the accuracy of each component, or qualitatively through how well its outputs model the social variables. On a component level, its accuracy depends foremost upon the performance of its dependency parsing, NER, and POS models.

The performance of the dependency parsing has been described in Section 3. For POS and NER tagging use Jiang et al. (2022)'s state-of-the-art-models: "HuggingFace-BERTweet (TB2+EWT)" for POS (which achieved 95.38 UPOS accuracy on Tweebank v2) and "HuggingFace-BERTweet (TB2+W17)" for NER (which achieved 74.35 F1 on Tweebank-NER).

Finally, we examine externally validity by investigating the model's ability to capture social context in the following case study.

5 Case Study: COVID-19 Polarization

A key source of variation in opinion is with respect to political ideology, and social media is rife with arguments about political figures specifically. In this section, we show TweetIE's ability to capture the ideological attributes of said figures, specifically the attributes social media users ascribe to Dr. Anthony Fauci, director of the National Institute of Allergy and Infectious Diseases, who is a key figure in United States COVID-19 discourse. While TweetIE could be used to study a network of entities and their relations, we find focusing on a single entity is a useful and insightful first step.

5.1 Corpora Design and Configuration

We collect a corpus of tweets from Twitter Decahose with the token 'fauci' spanning from March 1, 2020 to December 31, 2021. We filter to messages with geographic location information: either from a tweet's official API geotag, or from its author having a self-described *user.location* text field consisting of a city and state in postal code notation (e.g. "Minneapolis, MN"). We look up these fields using the US Census Bureau's Place boundary shapefiles,[6] and as a proxy for political valence, each valid place is paired with its county's Biden-Trump margin, the difference of Joe Biden's versus Donald Trump's percentage votes won in the 2020 U.S. presidential election (MIT Election Data & Science Lab, 2018).[7] Additionally, we discard any tweets from verified users or users with over 10,000 followers in order to capture conversational

[6]https://www.census.gov/geographies/mapping-files/time-series/geo/tiger-line-file.2020.html

[7]For Alaska we use the state-level result, since it does not provide county-level results.

Relation	Trump-Leaning ($t < -2$)	Biden-Leaning ($t > 2$)
IS_A(fauci, $property_{\text{nom}}$)	murderer**, joke**, hack*, fraud*, rat*, flip*, idiot, flop, state, prison, fake, jail	nih**, hero, md, director, president
IS_A(fauci, $property_{\text{adj}}$)	fake*, little*, deep, liberal, wrong, corrupt	beloved, optimistic, best
AS_AGENT(fauci, *verb*)	sweat**, force**, need*, help*, read*, lie*, know*, let*, not_fund*, not_understand*, flip, predict, write, make, stick, hold, prove, want, not_say, admit, not_get, demand, issue, laugh, state, put, spread, pull	speak**, join*, warn*, throw, not_recommend, offer, provide, respond, consider, debunk, fail, reveal
AS_PATIENT(fauci, *verb*)	not_trust***, screw, prosecute, grill, keep to, arrest, expose, lock, do to, remove, accord to, look like, mean, blast, read	know*, feature, discredit, threaten, worship, join, insult
HAS_A(fauci, *object*)	friend*, nih*, family, mind, hand, ex-employee, involvement, fraud, mask	guidance, time
AS_CONJUNCT(fauci, *conj.*)	gates***, obama**, bill gates*, biden*, brix, cdc, rest, covid, nih, company, government	director, experts

Table 5: TweetIE extractions with at least 20 unique users with a county-level political valence t-statistic outside of [-2, 2]. Results are reported in decreasing absolute value t-statistic. * $|t| > 3$, ** $|t| > 4$, *** $|t| > 5$.

dialogue rather than statements by reporters and officials.

5.2 Results and Qualitative Evaluation

We obtain 75,325 tweets, which have an electoral margin average of 22.8 and standard deviation of 33.9. TweetIE yields 13,532 unique triples of *relation*(Fauci, *token*), which we call unique extractions. The counts of these sum to 99,633 total extractions overall. In order to improve aggregation, we lowercase and normalize the *token* terms with NLTK's WordNetLemmatizer (Loper and Bird, 2002), and remove stopwords from NLTK's English stopword list.

For each tuple that is expressed by at least 20 unique users, we use a one-sample student's t statistic to determine if the mean author-geography political sentiment of the tuple is significantly different than the corpus population's. We require $|t| > 2$ as a rough filter for traditional statistical significance.[8] This method for term ranking is appropriate for the continuous variable of political sentiment. Since words' frequencies greatly vary, rare terms tend to be sentiment average outliers; the t statistic's normalization by standard error helps control for an expression's sample size.[9]

This results in 110 expressions have test statistics greater than 2 or less than -2, shown in Table 5. These reflect common political narratives concerning Fauci and his COVID-19 response. Political scientific work has found liberal respondents to be more trusting in COVID-19 experts such as Fauci than conservatives (Kerr et al., 2021), as well as more hesitant towards COVID-19 vaccination (Khubchandani et al., 2021), whose development and production Fauci was involved with.

The notable considerations of Fauci as a joke or a fraud, or that he lies or is not trusted, reflect lack of trust in Fauci by the Trump-leaning. Likewise, suggesting that Fauci is a hero or beloved, as well as emphasizing what he says or his warnings show trust in Fauci from the Biden-leaning.

There are elements of COVID-19 related right-wing conspiracism in the Trump-leaning extractions as well. Common antecedents of COVID-19 conspiracism include the notions of a fraudlent pandemic, vaccination as a weapon, suspicions of the government, pharmaceutical industry, Democrats, and Bill Gates (van Mulukom et al., 2022). In our analysis this theme surfaces in Gates' appearance as a frequent conjunct; furthermore, many Trump-leaning extractions indicate Fauci as a murderer for his involvement in vaccination, or as someone who should be prosecuted, arrested, or put in prison. A shortcoming of our token-based approach can be seen with the bigram "deep state", a key narrative element, being split into two separate IS_A statements, which would be better viewed together.

[8] Under the central limit theorem, $|t| > 1.96$ corresponds to p-value < 0.05. Given multiple hypothesis testing issues we do not propose a formal significance test interpretation, though false discovery rate or other methods could be applied (Bamman et al., 2012).

[9] Social science NLP has often ranked terms by analogous confidence measures of term frequency versus a discrete social variable, such as χ^2 (Gentzkow and Shapiro, 2010) or log-odds posterior confidence (Monroe et al., 2008).

5.3 Alternative Systems

To demonstrate TweetIE's value over open information extraction (OIE) systems for this task, we evaluate two other systems against the Fauci corpus. These are ReVerb, a lexical pattern and POS-based system (Fader et al., 2011), and ClausIE, a Stanford Dependencies based system (Del Corro and Gemulla, 2013). ReVerb was selected to represent systems that do not require a parser, while ClausIE is the state-of-the-art system on the BenchIE OIE benchmark (Gashteovski et al., 2022). Like other OIE systems, these extract <Arg1, Relation, Arg2> tuples where relations and arguments are (normalized) strings from the sentence. While some work has sought to use OIE triples for social insight (Ash et al., 2021), we map them to IS_A, AS_AGENT, and AS_PATIENT for comparability.[10]

ReVerb is an OIE system that extracts relations using POS tags, noun phrase chunks, and lexical constraints; its output OIE triples have normalized values. If the relation is normalized to "be", and the target entity is in one of the arguments, we extract the other argument as IS_A. Otherwise if the target entity is in Argument 1, the relation is extracted as AS_AGENT, and if in Argument 2, AS_PATIENT.

ClausIE parses a sentence using Stanford Dependencies, using pattern detectors to eventually arrive at final OIE triples ("propositions"). While the relations are short, unfortunately the arguments can be very long phrases, and cannot be accumulated for counts or social variable aggregates. For a fair and generous comparison, we utilize ClausIE's intermediate representation of "clause" tuples, which are based on one of seven syntactic patterns such as copular clauses (SVC) or monotransitives (SVO); these are tuples of syntactic head words.[11] For IS_A, we take all detected copular clauses with the target entity in the subject or complement role, recording the remaining of the two as an IS_A extraction. For AS_AGENT, we extract the verb argument of any non-copular clause with the target entity in the subject role. We do the same for AS_PATIENT if the target entity is in the complement or object roles. We normalize these outputs in the same way as TweetIE.

As neither ReVerb nor ClausIE use coreference resolution, we present TweetIE with and without coreference enabled for comparison.

The systems share common extractions; the top ten IS_A share *fraud, one, liar, expert, doctor, man*, the top five AS_AGENT share *say* and *tell*, and the top five AS_PATIENT share *fire* and *trust*.

This suggests that they all can capture similar phenomena in the dataset, yet the amount of information they actually extract (total yield) varies significantly. Over these three patterns, ReVerb yields 16,980 total extractions, ClausIE yields 43,097, $\text{TweetIE}_{\text{no-coref}}$ yields 61,484, and TweetIE yields 74,572. TweetIE's superior yield is important, as the statistical inference over social variables is reliant on the ability to extract on a scale large enough to be representative; the smaller yield from ReVerb is likely to be inadequate. This occurs in our social analysis criteria of requiring terms to have at least 20 unique users and a t-statistic outside of [-2,2]. For IS_A, AS_AGENT and AS_PATIENT respectively, ReVerb yields 1/1/2, ClausIE yields 12/22/6, $\text{TweetIE}_{\text{no-coref}}$ yields 23/28/22, and TweetIE yields 26/39/22.

In addition, ClausIE struggled to understand @ mentions, and they appeared as extractions of every variety instead of extraneous vocative mentions (second most common IS_A and AS_AGENT, most common AS_PATIENT). We attribute this to ClausIE's reliance on a parser not trained on a social media domain without the benefit of transformer modeling.

Finally, we perform a precision evaluation to judge which systems' extractions more accurately reflect semantic implications of the text. We randomly sample 250 tweets and annotate whether each semantic tuple from ReVerb, ClausIE, and TweetIE is present in or directly implied by the text. The annotator (first author) was presented with the text of the tweet, along with the outputs of all systems in a random order (with system names hidden). Each output was labelled as implied or not implied; for each system we report the precision and its 95% confidence interval from bootstrapped standard errors, from 100,000 simulations of resampling at the tweet level. This results in ReVerb having a precision of $73.8 \pm 12.5\%$ (31/42), ClausIE having a precision of $66.1 \pm 8.5\%$ (84/129), and TweetIE having the highest precision at $83.5 \pm 4.7\%$

[10]While IS_A requires adaptation from the OIE framework, AS_AGENT and AS_PATIENT relations can be viewed as a Davidsonian-style binarization of an OIE triple: e.g. *<Fauci, hate, us>* is equivalent to *AGENT(hate, Fauci)* $\wedge$ *PATIENT(hate, us)*, at least assuming a Dowty (1991)-style proto-role theory of what OIE Arg1 and Arg2 mean.

[11]A shortcoming of this approach is that ClausIE only applies coordination handling to the final OIE triples; it was not clear to us if it was possible to backport this feature to the clause tuples.

(187/222).

The difference between TweetIE and ClausIE is statistically significant ($p < 0.001$). Thus TweetIE is able to achieve its higher yield but without any cost to precision, presumably due to its modeling and rule improvements.

6 Conclusion and Future Work

The annotations from Tweebank v2 and the performance improvements from BERTweet have lead to significant advancements in social media dependency parsing, with performance gains of 3.4 UAS and 4.0 LAS, as well as significantly lessening how much performance lags for the non-standard language variety of African-American English.

These achievements enable downstream applications of syntactic parsing on social media data, of which we note information extraction as being especially utilizable for computational social scientific means. We outline a process to decode these dependency parses into aggregatable semantic structures, for comparisons with social variables that one may seek to study.

We show how one can model political narratives with respect to named entities with a case study on elements and actions attributed to Dr. Anthony Fauci on social media during the COVID-19 pandemic. Through this, we replicate findings in social scientific literature on the topic, and we have similar extractions to pre-existing open information extraction yet with increased yield, enabling more substantial computational social scientific analyses.

Future work can build upon these foundations by extending these techniques to beliefs spanning multiple entities, by considering additional social variables, or by taking into account temporal effects through timestamps. This could allow for the observation of more complex phenomena, such as actions from an entity towards another entity or the adoption and decline of beliefs over time.

Acknowledgements

We are thankful for feedback from the UMass NLP and AAE groups, as well as comments from the reviewers. This work was supported by National Science Foundation grants 1845576 and 2042939. Any opinions, findings, and conclusions or recommendations expressed in this material are those of the authors and do not necessarily reflect the views of the National Science Foundation.

References

Nikolay Archak, Anindya Ghose, and Panagiotis G. Ipeirotis. 2007. Show me the money!: deriving the pricing power of product features by mining consumer reviews. In *Proceedings of the 13th ACM SIGKDD international conference on Knowledge discovery and data mining*, pages 56–65.

Elliott Ash, Germain Gauthier, and Philine Widmer. 2021. Relatio: Text semantics capture political and economic narratives.

Jackie Ayoub, X. Jessie Yang, and Feng Zhou. 2021. Combat covid-19 infodemic using explainable natural language processing models. *Information Processing & Management*, 58(4):102569.

Paul Baker. 2006. *Using Corpora in Discourse Analysis*. Bloomsbury Discourse. Bloomsbury Academic.

Timothy Baldwin. 2012. Social media: Friend or foe of natural language processing? In *Proceedings of the 26th Pacific Asia Conference on Language, Information, and Computation*, pages 58–59, Bali, Indonesia. Faculty of Computer Science, Universitas Indonesia.

David Bamman, Brendan O'Connor, and Noah A. Smith. 2012. Censorship and deletion practices in Chinese social media. *First Monday*, 17(3).

David Bamman, Brendan O'Connor, and Noah A. Smith. 2013. Learning latent personas of film characters. In *Proceedings of the 51st Annual Meeting of the Association for Computational Linguistics (Volume 1: Long Papers)*, pages 352–361, Sofia, Bulgaria. Association for Computational Linguistics.

Michele Banko, Michael J. Cafarella, Stephen Soderland, Matt Broadhead, and Oren Etzioni. 2007. Open information extraction from the web. In *Proceedings of the 20th International Joint Conference on Artifical Intelligence*, IJCAI'07, page 2670–2676, San Francisco, CA, USA. Morgan Kaufmann Publishers Inc.

Francesco Barbieri, Jose Camacho-Collados, Luis Espinosa Anke, and Leonardo Neves. 2020. TweetEval: Unified benchmark and comparative evaluation for tweet classification. In *Findings of the Association for Computational Linguistics: EMNLP 2020*, pages 1644–1650, Online. Association for Computational Linguistics.

Francesco Barbieri, Luis Espinosa-Anke, and Jose Camacho-Collados. 2022. XLM-T: Multilingual Language Models in Twitter for Sentiment Analysis and Beyond. In *Proceedings of LREC*.

Emily M Bender, Timnit Gebru, Angelina McMillan-Major, and Shmargaret Shmitchell. 2021. On the dangers of stochastic parrots: Can language models be too big? In *Proceedings of the 2021 ACM Conference on Fairness, Accountability, and Transparency*, pages 610–623.

Scott Blinder and William L. Allen. 2016. Constructing immigrants: Portrayals of migrant groups in british national newspapers, 2010–2012. *International Migration Review*, 50(1):3–40.

Su Lin Blodgett, Lisa Green, and Brendan O'Connor. 2016. Demographic dialectal variation in social media: A case study of African-American English. In *Proceedings of the 2016 Conference on Empirical Methods in Natural Language Processing*, pages 1119–1130, Austin, Texas. Association for Computational Linguistics.

Su Lin Blodgett, Johnny Wei, and Brendan O'Connor. 2018. Twitter Universal Dependency parsing for African-American and mainstream American English. In *Proceedings of the 56th Annual Meeting of the Association for Computational Linguistics (Volume 1: Long Papers)*, pages 1415–1425, Melbourne, Australia. Association for Computational Linguistics.

Rishi Bommasani, Drew A Hudson, Ehsan Adeli, Russ Altman, Simran Arora, Sydney von Arx, Michael S Bernstein, Jeannette Bohg, Antoine Bosselut, Emma Brunskill, et al. 2021. On the opportunities and risks of foundation models. *arXiv preprint arXiv:2108.07258*.

Xavier Carreras and Lluís Màrquez. 2005. Introduction to the CoNLL-2005 shared task: Semantic role labeling. In *Proceedings of the Ninth Conference on Computational Natural Language Learning (CoNLL-2005)*, pages 152–164, Ann Arbor, Michigan. Association for Computational Linguistics.

Zewen Chi, Li Dong, Furu Wei, Nan Yang, Saksham Singhal, Wenhui Wang, Xia Song, Xian-Ling Mao, Heyan Huang, and Ming Zhou. 2021. InfoXLM: An information-theoretic framework for cross-lingual language model pre-training. In *Proceedings of the 2021 Conference of the North American Chapter of the Association for Computational Linguistics: Human Language Technologies*, pages 3576–3588, Online. Association for Computational Linguistics.

Kevin Clark, Minh-Thang Luong, Quoc V. Le, and Christopher D. Manning. 2020. ELECTRA: Pre-training text encoders as discriminators rather than generators. In *ICLR*.

Alexis Conneau, Kartikay Khandelwal, Naman Goyal, Vishrav Chaudhary, Guillaume Wenzek, Francisco Guzmán, Edouard Grave, Myle Ott, Luke Zettlemoyer, and Veselin Stoyanov. 2020. Unsupervised cross-lingual representation learning at scale. In *Proceedings of the 58th Annual Meeting of the Association for Computational Linguistics*, pages 8440–8451, Online. Association for Computational Linguistics.

Michael A. Covington. 2001. A fundamental algorithm for dependency parsing. In *In Proceedings of the 39th Annual ACM Southeast Conference*, pages 95–102.

Sanjiv R. Das and Mike Y. Chen. 2007. Yahoo! for amazon: Sentiment extraction from small talk on the web. *Management Science*, 53(9):1375–1388.

Marie-Catherine De Marneffe and Christopher D Manning. 2008. Stanford typed dependencies manual. Technical report, Stanford University.

Luciano Del Corro and Rainer Gemulla. 2013. Clausie: Clause-based open information extraction. In *Proceedings of the 22nd International Conference on World Wide Web*, WWW '13, page 355–366, New York, NY, USA. Association for Computing Machinery.

Jacob Devlin, Ming-Wei Chang, Kenton Lee, and Kristina Toutanova. 2019. BERT: Pre-training of deep bidirectional transformers for language understanding. In *Proceedings of the 2019 Conference of the North American Chapter of the Association for Computational Linguistics: Human Language Technologies, Volume 1 (Long and Short Papers)*, pages 4171–4186, Minneapolis, Minnesota. Association for Computational Linguistics.

David Dowty. 1991. Thematic proto-roles and argument selection. *Language*, 67(3):547–619.

Timothy Dozat and Christopher D. Manning. 2017. Deep biaffine attention for neural dependency parsing. In *International Conference on Learning Representations*.

Jacob Eisenstein. 2013. What to do about bad language on the internet. In *Proceedings of the 2013 Conference of the North American Chapter of the Association for Computational Linguistics: Human Language Technologies*, pages 359–369, Atlanta, Georgia. Association for Computational Linguistics.

Jason Eisner. 2000. *Bilexical Grammars and their Cubic-Time Parsing Algorithms*, pages 29–61. Springer Netherlands, Dordrecht.

Jason M. Eisner. 1996. Three new probabilistic models for dependency parsing: An exploration. In *COLING 1996 Volume 1: The 16th International Conference on Computational Linguistics*.

Anthony Fader, Stephen Soderland, and Oren Etzioni. 2011. Identifying relations for open information extraction. In *Proceedings of the 2011 Conference on Empirical Methods in Natural Language Processing*, pages 1535–1545, Edinburgh, Scotland, UK. Association for Computational Linguistics.

Kiril Gashteovski, Mingying Yu, Bhushan Kotnis, Carolin Lawrence, Mathias Niepert, and Goran Glavaš. 2022. BenchIE: A framework for multi-faceted fact-based open information extraction evaluation. In *Proceedings of the 60th Annual Meeting of the Association for Computational Linguistics (Volume 1: Long Papers)*, pages 4472–4490, Dublin, Ireland. Association for Computational Linguistics.

Matthew Gentzkow and Jesse M. Shapiro. 2010. What drives media slant? Evidence from U.S. daily newspapers. *Econometrica*, 78(1):35–71.

Anindya Ghose, Panagiotis Ipeirotis, and Arun Sundararajan. 2007. Opinion mining using econometrics: A case study on reputation systems. In *Proceedings of the 45th Annual Meeting of the Association of Computational Linguistics*, pages 416–423, Prague, Czech Republic. Association for Computational Linguistics.

Stefan Grünewald, Annemarie Friedrich, and Jonas Kuhn. 2021. Applying occam's razor to transformer-based dependency parsing: What works, what doesn't, and what is really necessary. In *Proceedings of the 17th International Conference on Parsing Technologies and the IWPT 2021 Shared Task on Parsing into Enhanced Universal Dependencies (IWPT 2021)*, pages 131–144, Online. Association for Computational Linguistics.

Pengcheng He, Jianfeng Gao, and Weizhu Chen. 2021. Debertav3: Improving deberta using electra-style pre-training with gradient-disentangled embedding sharing.

Hang Jiang, Yining Hua, Doug Beeferman, and Deb Roy. 2022. Annotating the tweebank corpus on named entity recognition and building nlp models for social media analysis. In *Proceedings of the Language Resources and Evaluation Conference*, pages 7199–7208, Marseille, France. European Language Resources Association.

Taylor Jones. 2015. Toward a Description of African American Vernacular English Dialect Regions Using "Black Twitter". *American Speech*, 90(4):403–440.

John Kerr, Costas Panagopoulos, and Sander van der Linden. 2021. Political polarization on covid-19 pandemic response in the united states. *Personality and Individual Differences*, 179:110892.

Jagdish Khubchandani, Sushil Sharma, James H. Price, Michael J. Wiblishauser, Manoj Sharma, and Fern J. Webb. 2021. Covid-19 vaccination hesitancy in the united states: A rapid national assessment. *Journal of Community Health*, 46(2):270–277.

Eliyahu Kiperwasser and Yoav Goldberg. 2016. Simple and accurate dependency parsing using bidirectional LSTM feature representations. *Transactions of the Association for Computational Linguistics*, 4:313–327.

Allison Koenecke, Andrew Nam, Emily Lake, Joe Nudell, Minnie Quartey, Zion Mengesha, Connor Toups, John R. Rickford, Dan Jurafsky, and Sharad Goel. 2020. Racial disparities in automated speech recognition. *Proceedings of the National Academy of Sciences*, 117(14):7684–7689.

Lingpeng Kong, Nathan Schneider, Swabha Swayamdipta, Archna Bhatia, Chris Dyer, and Noah A. Smith. 2014. A dependency parser for tweets. In *Proceedings of the 2014 Conference on Empirical Methods in Natural Language Processing (EMNLP)*, pages 1001–1012, Doha, Qatar. Association for Computational Linguistics.

Terry Koo, Amir Globerson, Xavier Carreras, and Michael Collins. 2007. Structured prediction models via the matrix-tree theorem. In *Proceedings of the 2007 Joint Conference on Empirical Methods in Natural Language Processing and Computational Natural Language Learning (EMNLP-CoNLL)*, pages 141–150, Prague, Czech Republic. Association for Computational Linguistics.

Yijia Liu, Yi Zhu, Wanxiang Che, Bing Qin, Nathan Schneider, and Noah A. Smith. 2018. Parsing tweets into Universal Dependencies. In *Proceedings of the 2018 Conference of the North American Chapter of the Association for Computational Linguistics: Human Language Technologies, Volume 1 (Long Papers)*, pages 965–975, New Orleans, Louisiana. Association for Computational Linguistics.

Yinhan Liu, Myle Ott, Naman Goyal, Jingfei Du, Mandar Joshi, Danqi Chen, Omer Levy, Mike Lewis, Luke Zettlemoyer, and Veselin Stoyanov. 2020. RoBERTa: A robustly optimized BERT pretraining approach.

Edward Loper and Steven Bird. 2002. NLTK: The natural language toolkit. In *Proceedings of the ACL-02 Workshop on Effective Tools and Methodologies for Teaching Natural Language Processing and Computational Linguistics*, pages 63–70, Philadelphia, Pennsylvania, USA. Association for Computational Linguistics.

Daniel Loureiro, Francesco Barbieri, Leonardo Neves, Luis Espinosa Anke, and Jose Camacho-collados. 2022. TimeLMs: Diachronic language models from Twitter. In *Proceedings of the 60th Annual Meeting of the Association for Computational Linguistics: System Demonstrations*, pages 251–260, Dublin, Ireland. Association for Computational Linguistics.

Xuezhe Ma and Eduard Hovy. 2017. Neural probabilistic model for non-projective MST parsing. In *Proceedings of the Eighth International Joint Conference on Natural Language Processing (Volume 1: Long Papers)*, pages 59–69, Taipei, Taiwan. Asian Federation of Natural Language Processing.

Mausam Mausam. 2016. Open information extraction systems and downstream applications. In *Proceedings of the Twenty-Fifth International Joint Conference on Artificial Intelligence*, IJCAI'16, page 4074–4077. AAAI Press.

MIT Election Data & Science Lab. 2018. County Presidential Election Returns 2000-2020.

Burt L. Monroe, Michael P. Colaresi, and Kevin M. Quinn. 2008. Fightin' Words: Lexical feature selection and evaluation for identifying the con tent of political conflict. *Political Analysis*, 16(4):372.

Dat Quoc Nguyen, Thanh Vu, and Anh Tuan Nguyen. 2020. BERTweet: A pre-trained language model for English tweets. In *Proceedings of the 2020 Conference on Empirical Methods in Natural Language Processing: System Demonstrations*, pages 9–14, Online. Association for Computational Linguistics.

Joakim Nivre. 2003. An efficient algorithm for projective dependency parsing. In *Proceedings of the Eighth International Conference on Parsing Technologies*, pages 149–160, Nancy, France.

Joakim Nivre, Marie-Catherine de Marneffe, Filip Ginter, Jan Hajič, Christopher D. Manning, Sampo Pyysalo, Sebastian Schuster, Francis Tyers, and Daniel Zeman. 2020. Universal Dependencies v2: An evergrowing multilingual treebank collection. In *Proceedings of the 12th Language Resources and Evaluation Conference*, pages 4034–4043, Marseille, France. European Language Resources Association.

Stephan Oepen, Marco Kuhlmann, Yusuke Miyao, Daniel Zeman, Dan Flickinger, Jan Hajič, Angelina Ivanova, and Yi Zhang. 2014. SemEval 2014 task 8: Broad-coverage semantic dependency parsing. In *Proceedings of the 8th International Workshop on Semantic Evaluation (SemEval 2014)*, pages 63–72, Dublin, Ireland. Association for Computational Linguistics.

Siyao Peng and Amir Zeldes. 2018. All roads lead to UD: Converting Stanford and Penn parses to English Universal Dependencies with multilayer annotations. In *Proceedings of the Joint Workshop on Linguistic Annotation, Multiword Expressions and Constructions (LAW-MWE-CxG-2018)*, pages 167–177, Santa Fe, New Mexico, USA. Association for Computational Linguistics.

Matthew E. Peters, Mark Neumann, Mohit Iyyer, Matt Gardner, Christopher Clark, Kenton Lee, and Luke Zettlemoyer. 2018. Deep contextualized word representations. In *Proceedings of the 2018 Conference of the North American Chapter of the Association for Computational Linguistics: Human Language Technologies, Volume 1 (Long Papers)*, pages 2227–2237, New Orleans, Louisiana. Association for Computational Linguistics.

Sebastian Schuster and Christopher D. Manning. 2016. Enhanced English Universal Dependencies: An improved representation for natural language understanding tasks. In *Proceedings of the Tenth International Conference on Language Resources and Evaluation (LREC'16)*, pages 2371–2378, Portorož, Slovenia. European Language Resources Association (ELRA).

Natalia Silveira, Timothy Dozat, Marie-Catherine de Marneffe, Samuel Bowman, Miriam Connor, John Bauer, and Chris Manning. 2014. A gold standard dependency corpus for English. In *Proceedings of the Ninth International Conference on Language Resources and Evaluation (LREC'14)*, pages 2897–2904, Reykjavik, Iceland. European Language Resources Association (ELRA).

Rion Snow, Daniel Jurafsky, and Andrew Ng. 2004. Learning syntactic patterns for automatic hypernym discovery. In *Advances in Neural Information Processing Systems*, volume 17. MIT Press.

Gabriel Stanovsky, Jessica Ficler, Ido Dagan, and Yoav Goldberg. 2016. Getting more out of syntax with props.

Erik F. Tjong Kim Sang and Fien De Meulder. 2003. Introduction to the CoNLL-2003 shared task: Language-independent named entity recognition. In *Proceedings of the Seventh Conference on Natural Language Learning at HLT-NAACL 2003*, pages 142–147.

Valerie van Mulukom, Lotte J. Pummerer, Sinan Alper, Hui Bai, Vladimíra Čavojová, Jessica Farias, Cameron S. Kay, Ljiljana B. Lazarevic, Emilio J.C. Lobato, Gaëlle Marinthe, Irena Pavela Banai, Jakub Šrol, and Iris Žeželj. 2022. Antecedents and consequences of covid-19 conspiracy beliefs: A systematic review. *Social Science & Medicine*, 301:114912.

Alex Wang, Amanpreet Singh, Julian Michael, Felix Hill, Omer Levy, and Samuel Bowman. 2018. GLUE: A multi-task benchmark and analysis platform for natural language understanding. In *Proceedings of the 2018 EMNLP Workshop BlackboxNLP: Analyzing and Interpreting Neural Networks for NLP*, pages 353–355, Brussels, Belgium. Association for Computational Linguistics.

Aaron Steven White, Drew Reisinger, Keisuke Sakaguchi, Tim Vieira, Sheng Zhang, Rachel Rudinger, Kyle Rawlins, and Benjamin Van Durme. 2016. Universal decompositional semantics on Universal Dependencies. In *Proceedings of the 2016 Conference on Empirical Methods in Natural Language Processing*, pages 1713–1723, Austin, Texas. Association for Computational Linguistics.

Thomas Wolf, Lysandre Debut, Victor Sanh, Julien Chaumond, Clement Delangue, Anthony Moi, Pierric Cistac, Tim Rault, Remi Louf, Morgan Funtowicz, Joe Davison, Sam Shleifer, Patrick von Platen, Clara Ma, Yacine Jernite, Julien Plu, Canwen Xu, Teven Le Scao, Sylvain Gugger, Mariama Drame, Quentin Lhoest, and Alexander Rush. 2020. Transformers: State-of-the-art natural language processing. In *Proceedings of the 2020 Conference on Empirical Methods in Natural Language Processing: System Demonstrations*, pages 38–45, Online. Association for Computational Linguistics.

Zhilin Yang, Zihang Dai, Yiming Yang, Jaime G. Carbonell, Ruslan Salakhutdinov, and Quoc V. Le. 2019. Xlnet: Generalized autoregressive pretraining for language understanding. *CoRR*, abs/1906.08237.

Amir Zeldes. 2017. The GUM corpus: Creating multilayer resources in the classroom. *Language Resources and Evaluation*, 51(3):581–612.

Sheng Zhang, Rachel Rudinger, and Benjamin Van Durme. 2017. An evaluation of PredPatt and open IE via stage 1 semantic role labeling. In *IWCS 2017 — 12th International Conference on Computational Semantics — Short papers*.

Yu Zhang, Zhenghua Li, and Min Zhang. 2020. Efficient second-order TreeCRF for neural dependency parsing. In *Proceedings of the 58th Annual Meeting of the Association for Computational Linguistics*, pages 3295–3305, Online. Association for Computational Linguistics.

Caleb Ziems, Jiaao Chen, Camille Harris, Jessica Anderson, and Diyi Yang. 2022. VALUE: Understanding dialect disparity in NLU. In *Proceedings of the 60th Annual Meeting of the Association for Computational Linguistics (Volume 1: Long Papers)*, pages 3701–3720, Dublin, Ireland. Association for Computational Linguistics.

Impact of Environmental Noise on Alzheimer's Disease Detection from Speech: Should You Let a Baby Cry?

Jekaterina Novikova
Winterlight Labs / Toronto, Canada
jekaterina@winterlightlabs.com

Abstract

Research related to automatically detecting Alzheimer's disease (AD) is important, given the high prevalence of AD and the high cost of traditional methods. Since AD significantly affects the acoustics of spontaneous speech, speech processing and machine learning (ML) provide promising techniques for reliably detecting AD. However, speech audio may be affected by different types of background noise and it is important to understand how the noise influences the accuracy of ML models detecting AD from speech. In this paper, we study the effect of fifteen types of environmental noise from five different categories on the performance of four ML models trained with three types of acoustic representations. We perform a thorough analysis showing how ML models and acoustic features are affected by different types of acoustic noise. We show that acoustic noise is not necessarily harmful - certain types of noise are beneficial for AD detection models and help increasing accuracy by up to 4.8%. We provide recommendations on how to utilize acoustic noise in order to achieve the best performance results with the ML models deployed in real world.

1 Introduction

Alzheimer's disease (AD) is a progressive neurodegenerative disease that affects over 40 million people worldwide (Prince et al., 2016). Current forms of diagnosis are both time consuming and expensive (Prabhakaran et al., 2018), which might explain why almost half of those living with AD do not receive a timely diagnosis (Jammeh et al., 2018). Studies have shown that ML methods can be applied to distinguish between speech from healthy and AD participants (Fraser et al., 2016; Balagopalan et al., 2018; Zhu et al., 2019; Eyre et al., 2020). Currently, speech recording for AD-related research typically takes place in a quiet room with a guiding clinician. Given that smartphone technology is rapidly advancing, speech assessments using ML models trained on recordings obtained by smartphones offer a potentially simple-to-administer and inexpensive solution, scalable to the entire population, that can be performed anywhere, including the patient's home (Kourtis et al., 2019; Mc Carthy and Schueler, 2019; Fristed et al., 2021). However, the problem of model robustness to acoustic noise becomes increasingly important when deploying ML models in real world (Robin et al., 2020).

Current popular approaches to dealing with acoustic noise in AD detection models involve: 1) eliminating noise using various audio preprocessing techniques (Luz et al., 2021), 2) selecting features that are resilient to ASR error/noise (Zhou et al., 2016), 3) minimizing the effects of noise with multimodal fusion of features (Rohanian et al., 2021). All these approaches share a common assumption of acoustic noise being definitely harmful for ML models detecting AD from speech. However, in other ML research areas, such as computer vision or NLP, adding a certain level of natural and artificial noise to data is considered a valid and advantageous practice that helps achieving better performance in tasks like image recognition (Koziarski and Cyganek, 2017; Steffens et al., 2019), text generation (Feng et al., 2020) and relation classification (Giridhara et al., 2019), among others. The recent studies in AD classification from transcribed speech show that small levels of linguistic noise do not negatively affect performance of BERT-based models (Novikova, 2021), although there is a difference in predictive power between lexical and syntactic features, when it comes to AD detection from speech (Novikova et al., 2019).

Motivated by the previous work, in this paper we study the effect of acoustic noise on performance of the ML models trained to detect AD from speech. The contributions of this paper are:

Proceedings of the 2022 COLING Workshop: The 8th Workshop on Noisy User-generated Text (W-NUT 2022), pages 51–61

1. we analyze the effect of environmental acoustic noise on the values of acoustic features extracted from speech;

2. we perform a thorough study on the effect of acoustic noise on AD classification performance across ML models, extracted acoustic features and noise categories;

3. we provide recommendation to ML researchers and practitioners on how to utilize acoustic noise in order to achieve the best performance results.

2 Related Work

2.1 Environmental Noise and Speech Quality

Multiple previous studies attempted to investigate the influence of the environment background noise on speech quality. For example, Naderi et al. (2018) conducted a study in which participants rated the quality of speech files first in the laboratory and then in noisy speech collection settings, such as cafeteria and living room. They found that the presence of a "cafeteria" or a "crossroad" background noise would decrease the correlation to speech quality ratings.

Furthermore, multiple studies have addressed the issue of speech intelligibility under certain background noise conditions. To name some, Meyer et al. (2013) tackled the problem of speech recognition accuracy in ecologically valid natural background noise scenarios and showed the relation between the levels of noise and confusion of vowels, lexical identification and perceptual consonant confusion.

Jiménez et al. (2020) investigated the influence of environmental background noise on speech quality, where the quality of speech files was assessed under the influence of two types of background noise at different levels, i.e., street noises and tv-show. The authors found there was a certain threshold of the environment background noise level that impacted the quality of speech, and different types of noise had a different effect on the quality.

Motivated by the previous studies, in this work we analyze fifteen different types of environmental background noise in order to figure out differences in their impact. We also compare the impact of short and continuous noise to follow up on the findings of the impact threshold.

2.2 Alzheimer's Disease Detection in Noisy Settings

Given the number of people with AD is growing and the population is aging fast in many countries (Brookmeyer et al., 2018), it becomes more and more important to have tools to help identify the presence of cognitive impairment relating to AD that can be deployed frequently, and at scale. This need will only increase as effective interventions are developed, requiring the ability to identify patients early in order to facilitate prevention or treatment of disease (Vellas and Aisen, 2021). Most of the current AD screening tools represent a significant burden, requiring invasive procedures, or intensive and costly clinical testing. However, recent shifts toward telemedicine and increased digital literacy of the aging population provide an opportunity for using digital health tools that are ideally poised to meet the needs for novel solutions. Recently, automated tools have been developed that assess speech and can be used on a smartphone or tablet, from one's home (Robin et al., 2021). Digital assessments that can be accessed on a smartphone or tablet, completed from home and periodically repeated, would vastly improve the accessibility of AD screening compared to current clinical standards that require clinical visits, extensive neuropsychological testing or invasive procedures.

The pervasiveness of high-quality microphones in smart devices makes the recording of speech samples straightforward, not requiring additional equipment or sensors. However, there is a lack of control over the participants performing digital assessments in home environment, and often not enough information is collected about their playback system and background environment. Participants might be exposed to different environmental conditions while executing specific tasks, and as such, their recorded speech quality may be disturbed with some background noise.

In the speech community, the active ongoing effort is focused on solving the problem of automated speech enhancement with the methods of noise suppression that are based on machine learning and deep learning (Zhang et al., 2022; Braun et al., 2021; Choi et al., 2018; Odelowo and Anderson, 2017, among many others). However, this problem is not considered to be solved, and the research community continues developing methods for effective noise elimination from audio recordings (Dubey et al., 2022).

These challenges motivate us asking a question whether noise suppression is absolutely necessary when it comes to the specific task of AD detection from speech. In this work, we perform a thorough study on the effect of acoustic background noise, standard for home environments, on AD classification performance across a range of ML models.

2.3 Speech Quality and Alzheimer's Disease Detection

Speech is a promising modality for digital assessments of cognitive abilities. Producing speech samples is a highly ecologically valid task that requires little instruction and at the same time is instrumental to daily functioning. Advances in signal processing and natural language processing have enabled objective analysis of speech samples for their acoustic properties, providing a window into monitoring motor and cognitive abilities. Most importantly, previous research has extensively shown that speech patterns are affected in AD, demonstrating the clinical relevance of speech for detecting cognitive impairment and dementia (Martínez-Nicolás et al., 2021; de la Fuente Garcia et al., 2020; Slegers et al., 2018).

Some of the features employed to describe acoustic characteristics of the voice applied to AD detection, include conventional acoustic features, such as fundamental frequency, jitter and shimmer, as well as pre-trained embeddings from deep neural models for audio representation, such as wav2vec (Balagopalan and Novikova, 2021). Quality of speech, which may be influenced by environmental noise, inevitably affects the values of these acoustic features extracted from speech and as a result may potentially influence the performance of ML models that use these features as internal representations of human speech.

However, in other research areas, such as computer vision or NLP, adding a certain level of natural or artificial noise to data is considered a valid and advantageous practice that helps achieving better performance in tasks like image recognition (Koziarski and Cyganek, 2017; Steffens et al., 2019), text generation (Feng et al., 2020) and relation classification (Giridhara et al., 2019), among others. Moreover, deep neural acoustic models, such as wav2vec, that are used to generate acoustic embeddings used in AD detection, are pre-trained on healthy speech. As such, it is possible that the subparts of the embeddings that are affected by environmental noise are not used for the task of AD detection directly and as a result, they do not influence the performance of such detection.

Figure 1: Cookie Theft picture used to collect speech for the ADReSS*o* dataset.

In this work, we make an attempt to understand how different types of environmental noise are impacting the values of different types of acoustic features extracted from speech, as well as how this affects performance of ML models relying on these features.

3 Methodology

3.1 Dataset

We use the ADReSS*o* Challenge dataset (Luz et al., 2021), which consists of 166 training speech samples from non-AD (N=83) and AD (N=83) English-speaking participants. Speech is elicited from participants through the Cookie Theft picture from the Boston Diagnostic Aphasia exam (Figure 1). In contrast to the other datasets for AD detection such as DementiaBank's English Pitt Corpus, the ADReSS*o* challenge dataset is well balanced in terms of age and gender. In addition, the pre-processing step of ADReSS*o* recordings were acoustically enhanced with stationary noise removal and audio volume normalisation applied across all speech segments to control for variation caused by recording conditions such as microphone placement. Such enhancements make this dataset a great source of the noise-clean audio, which is important for our experiments.

3.2 Feature Extraction

The following groups of features were extracted for the further use in the experiments:

1. **ConvFeat** : We extract 182 acoustic features from the unsegmented speech audio files. Those include several statistics such as mean, std, median, etc. of mel-frequency cepstral coefficients (MFCCs), onset detection, rhythm, spectral and power features, following prior works in AD classification (Fraser et al., 2016; Zhu et al., 2018; Balagopalan et al., 2020).

2. **eGeMAPSv02** : The extended Geneva Minimalistic Acoustic Parameter Set (eGeMAPS) features are a selected standardized set of statistical features that characterize affective physiological changes in voice production. We extracted these features for the entire recording, as this feature set was shown to be usable for atypical speech (Xue et al., 2019) and was successfully used for classifying AD from speech (Gauder et al., 2021; Pappagari et al., 2021).

3. **wav2vec** : In order to create audio representations using this approach, we make use of the huggingface[1] implementation of the wav2vec 2.0 (Baevski et al., 2020) base model *wav2vec2-base-960h*. This base model is pretrained and fine-tuned on 960 hours of Librispeech on 16kHz sampled speech audio. Closely following (Balagopalan and Novikova, 2021) that used these representations for AD classification, we extracted the last hidden state of the wav2vec2 model and used it as an embedded representation of audio.

3.3 Adding Noise

We used the audiomentations[2] library to add two types of audio noise that are common when recording audio with smart devices - 1) background noise, and 2) short noise (Vhaduri et al., 2019; Dibbo et al., 2021). We use a reduced version of the ESC-50 dataset (Piczak, 2015) to generate noisy audio, where we select three classes of noise from all the five presented major categories:

1. **Animal** sounds: dog, cat, crow
2. **Natural** soundscapes: rain, wind, chirping birds
3. **Human** sounds: crying baby, sneezing, coughing
4. **Domestic / interior** sounds: clock ticking, washing machine, vacuum cleaner
5. **Urban / exterior** noises: train, car horn, siren

3.4 Experiments

We first analyze how significantly addition of noise changes the values of acoustic features **ConvFeat** and **eGeMAPSv02** . We calculate the ratio of features that are impacted significantly by noise, with the Mann–Whitney U test used to estimate significance of difference.

Next, we experiment with the effect of noise addition to the performance of AD classification models. Following multiple previous studies on AD classification from speech (Balagopalan et al., 2020, 2021; Balagopalan and Novikova, 2021), we use a set of linear and non-linear ML models: Logistic regression (LR), Support Vector Machines (SVM), Neural Network (NN), and Decision Tree (DT).

We use 10-fold cross-validation approach to evaluate the performance of classifiers, with the F1 score being the main classification performance evaluation metric.

4 Results and Discussion

4.1 Effect of Noise on the Values of Acoustic Features

The results in Table 1 show that different types of noise have very different impact on the acoustic features, where *sneezing* sound introduced several times within recordings for short periods only affects 10% of **ConvFeat** , while continuous background sound of rain significantly changes more than 90% of these features. Unsurprisingly, background noise affects recordings much stronger than short noise. Notably, conventional acoustic features are on average more vulnerable than **eGeMAPSv02** to both short noise (12.5% higher ratio of significantly affected features) and background noise (19.8% higher ratio), with the categories of *natural sounds, domestic/interior* and *urban/exterior* bringing the strongest difference between the **ConvFeat** and **eGeMAPSv02** .

Both **ConvFeat** and **eGeMAPSv02** are quite robust to the *human* non-speech noise, especially the sound of *sneezing*. Out of all the noise types analyzed in this work, *sneezing* is the only one that

[1] https://huggingface.co/models
[2] https://github.com/iver56/audiomentations

Noise category	Subcategory	Features	Ratio of sign diff features: Short noise	Ratio of sign diff features: Background noise
Animals	cat	ConvFeat	32.42%	68.68%
		eGeMAPSv02	32.95%	50.00%
	crow	ConvFeat	55.49%	80.22%
		eGeMAPSv02	45.45%	59.09%
	dog	ConvFeat	23.08%	63.19%
		eGeMAPSv02	23.86%	50.00%
Natural	chirping birds	ConvFeat	69.23%	71.43%
		eGeMAPSv02	44.32%	54.55%
	rain	ConvFeat	67.58%	90.11%
		eGeMAPSv02	32.95%	69.32%
	wind	ConvFeat	48.35%	78.02%
		eGeMAPSv02	42.05%	60.23%
Human	coughing	ConvFeat	37.36%	52.20%
		eGeMAPSv02	27.27%	32.95%
	crying baby	ConvFeat	53.30%	68.68%
		eGeMAPSv02	40.91%	67.05%
	sneezing	ConvFeat	10.44%	41.21%
		eGeMAPSv02	27.27%	25.00%
Domestic/ interior	clock ticking	ConvFeat	48.35%	63.74%
		eGeMAPSv02	23.86%	30.68%
	vacuum cleaner	ConvFeat	63.19%	87.36%
		eGeMAPSv02	42.05%	60.23%
	washing machine	ConvFeat	51.10%	82.97%
		eGeMAPSv02	28.41%	65.91%
Urban/ exterior	car horn	ConvFeat	39.01%	81.32%
		eGeMAPSv02	27.27%	45.45%
	siren	ConvFeat	53.30%	74.73%
		eGeMAPSv02	42.05%	62.50%
	train	ConvFeat	56.04%	83.52%
		eGeMAPSv02	39.77%	57.95%

Table 1: Impact of noise addition on the value of ConvFeat and eGeMAPSv02 . Ratio of sign. diff. features shows the percentage of all the features that is significantly ($p < 0.05$) different from the original values as a result of adding short noise and background noise to original audio samples. Lighter cell color indicates higher than 50% ratio, darker - higher than 80% ratio.

only affects up to 50% of acoustic features, both in a format of short and background noise. *Natural* sounds, such as *rain*, *wind* or *chirping birds*, affect the acoustic features the strongest.

The above results suggest that noise strongly disturbs the quality of audio samples, as represented by both ConvFeat and eGeMAPSv02 . Next, we analyze whether such a disturbance is beneficial or harmful when it comes to AD detection from disturbed speech.

4.2 Effect of Noise on Performance of AD Classification

Four types of ML models (SVM, neural network / NN, logistic regression / LR and decision tree / DT) were trained on noisy and original audio recordings represented using ConvFeat , eGeMAPSv02 and wav2vec . Each set of features was extracted from both original audio recordings and the recordings with added 20 subcategories of noise. Each ML model was evaluated with the F1 score on three different random seeds. As such, it is possible to analyse the mean classification performance level

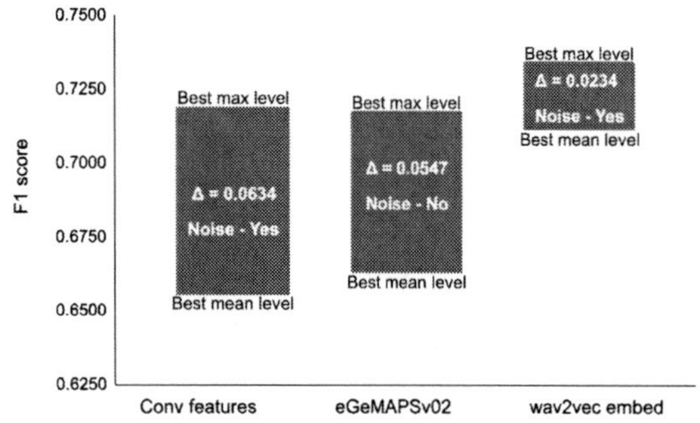

Figure 2: AD classification performance by feature type.

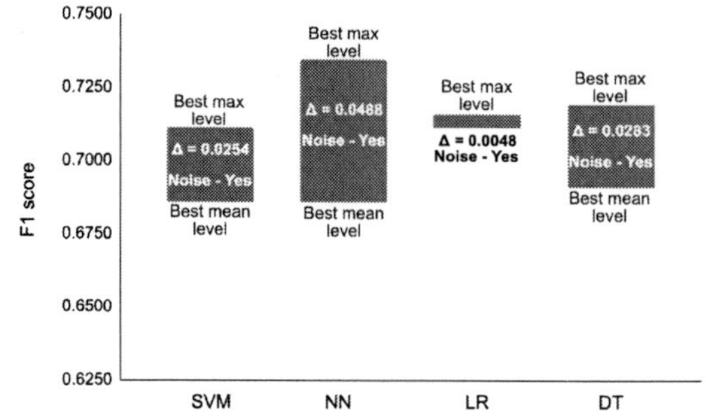

Figure 3: AD classification performance by model.

per feature type, where performance is averaged across all the seeds, for each model, noise subcategory and feature type.

4.2.1 Analysis Per Feature Type

The best mean F1 score represents the model that performs the best on average (across three random seeds) for some specific noise subcategory. Based on the best mean F1 score, the wav2vec -based model outperforms substantially the eGeMAPSv02 -based model, while the ConvFeat -based model achieves the lowest best mean level of performance (see Figure 2). Interestingly in all three cases, the best mean level of performance is achieved by the models trained on the original audio without noise addition.

The best maximum F1 score represents the best possibly achievable performance across all the seeds, i.e. the model that performs the best on a single best seed. The difference between the best mean level and the best maximum level shows the potential of the models to achieve higher level of performance. Figure 2 shows that such a potential is the strongest for the ConvFeat -based models (+6.3%), and there is not that much room for improvement for the wav2vec -based models (+2.3%). However, given the strong starting point, i.e. the strong best mean level, the absolute best maximum level of performance is achieved by the wav2vec -based model. Interestingly, this best maximum level is achieved by the model trained on the noisy data, not the original audio. The same is true for the second-best maximum performance, i.e. of the ConvFeat -based model.

4.2.2 Analysis Per Model Type

The best mean F1 score is achieved by the LR model, while SVM and NN both share the lowest level of the best mean performance (Figure 3). The growth potential of both linear models (LR and SVM) is weaker than that of the non-linear models (DT and NN), with the NN model showing the strongest potential across all model types. Once again, the best mean level of all the models is achieved when training the models on the original noise-free recordings, while the best maximum level is always achieved by training the models on the noisy audio recordings.

To overview, the results strongly suggest that noise has a beneficial effect on performance of AD classifiers, both linear and non-linear and utilizing different sets of features. However, all these performance results are aggregated across different categories and subcategories of noise. Next, we investigate in more detail how each specific noise category affects AD classification model performance.

4.2.3 Analysis Per Noise Type

The results of classification experiments with models trained on the noise-free and noisy audio show that best average classification performance is achieved when models are trained on clean noise-free audio recording (*Best mean F1 w/o noise* and *Mean F1 w/ noise* columns in Table 2). However, the maximum performance is consistently higher for the models trained on the noisy audio (columns *Max F1 w/ noise* vs *Best max F1 w/o noise* in Table 2).

Out of all the noise categories, domestic/interior sounds seem to be the least beneficial for the AD classification models - none of the noise subcategories helps consistently improving classification performance. In the other categories, such as animal sounds, natural sounds, and urban/exterior noise, at least one noise subcategory consistently achieves substantially higher performance with the models trained on the noisy recordings, with all the tested audio features. The human noise is the most

Noise category	Subcategory	Features	Count	Mean F1 w/ noise	Max F1 w/ noise	Best mean F1 w/o noise	Best max F1 w/o noise
Animals	cat	CONVFEAT	24	0.6232	**0.6842***	0.6557	0.6557
		EGEMAPSV02	24	0.6284	**0.6907***	0.6557	0.6557
		WAV2VEC	24	0.6222	0.7006	0.7111	**0.7200**
	crow	CONVFEAT	24	0.6217	**0.6591**	0.6557	0.6557
		EGEMAPSV02	24	0.6345	**0.6800***	0.6557	0.6557
		WAV2VEC	24	0.6400	0.6878	0.7111	**0.7200***
	dog	CONVFEAT	24	0.6255	**0.6704**	0.6557	0.6557
		EGEMAPSV02	24	0.6318	**0.7014***	0.6557	0.6557
Natural	chirping birds	CONVFEAT	24	0.6273	**0.7018***	0.6557	0.6557
		EGEMAPSV02	24	0.6443	**0.6995***	0.6557	0.6557
		WAV2VEC	24	0.6275	0.6966	0.7111	**0.7200***
	rain	CONVFEAT	24	0.6229	**0.6882***	0.6557	0.6557
		EGEMAPSV02	24	0.6506	**0.7135***	0.6557	0.6557
	wind	CONVFEAT	24	0.6156	0.6480	**0.6557**	**0.6557**
		EGEMAPSV02	24	0.6138	**0.7019***	0.6557	0.6557
Human	coughing	CONVFEAT	24	0.6182	**0.6923***	0.6557	0.6557
		EGEMAPSV02	24	0.6387	**0.7120***	0.6557	0.6557
	crying baby	CONVFEAT	24	0.6182	**0.6816***	0.6557	0.6557
		EGEMAPSV02	24	0.6472	**0.7079***	0.6557	0.6557
		WAV2VEC	24	0.6344	***0.7345****	0.7111	0.7200
	sneezing	CONVFEAT	24	0.6071	0.6444	**0.6557**	**0.6557**
		EGEMAPSV02	24	0.6406	**0.6800***	0.6557	0.6557
Domestic/ interior	clock ticking	CONVFEAT	24	0.6013	**0.6557**	**0.6557**	**0.6557**
		EGEMAPSV02	24	0.6284	**0.6990***	0.6557	0.6557
	vacuum cleaner	CONVFEAT	24	0.5775	0.6292	**0.6557**	**0.6557**
		EGEMAPSV02	24	0.5937	**0.6561**	0.6557	0.6557
	washing machine	CONVFEAT	24	0.6254	**0.6919***	0.6557	0.6557
		EGEMAPSV02	24	0.6391	**0.6990***	0.6557	0.6557
		WAV2VEC	24	0.6194	0.6816	0.7111	**0.7200***
Urban/ exterior	car horn	CONVFEAT	24	0.6324	**0.7111***	0.6557	0.6557
		EGEMAPSV02	24	0.5868	**0.6832**	0.6557	0.6557
		WAV2VEC	24	0.6069	0.6631	0.7111	**0.7200***
	siren	CONVFEAT	24	0.6274	**0.7191***	0.6557	0.6557
		EGEMAPSV02	24	0.6098	**0.6919***	0.6557	0.6557
		WAV2VEC	24	0.5961	0.6667	0.7111	**0.7200***
	train	CONVFEAT	24	0.6112	**0.6818***	0.6557	0.6557
		EGEMAPSV02	24	0.6382	**0.6866***	0.6557	0.6557

Table 2: Change in AD classification performance when models are trained on the noisy audio recordings, by noise category, subcategory and feature type. **Bold** denotes best performance per noise subcategory+features, ***bold italic*** denotes best overall performance, green background denotes noise subcategory that has consistently highest performance when models are trained on the noisy recordings. * indicates significant difference of $p < 0.05$ on McNemar's test.

beneficial noise category for getting high AD classification results: 1) the overall best classification performance is achieved by the model trained on the noisy recording of this category (model trained on wav2vec embeddings of the audio with the *crying baby* noise), 2) two out of three noise subcategories (*coughing* and *crying baby*) consistently achieve higher performance level across all the audio features. The best overall performance motivates us to investigate in more detail the classification performance of the models trained on the audio with the *crying baby* noise.

4.2.4 Analysis of the *Crying Baby* Noise

All the CONVFEAT -based models trained on the audio recordings with the sounds of *crying baby* present as short noise, perform better than those

F1	Model	Original noise-free audio			Short noise			Background noise		
		ConvFeat	eGeMAPSv02	wav2vec	ConvFeat	eGeMAPSv02	wav2vec	ConvFeat	eGeMAPSv02	wav2vec
Mean	SVM	0.6557	0.6480	0.6857	0.6816	0.6484	0.6885	0.6096	**0.7079**	0.6067
	LR	0.5698	0.6630	0.7111	0.6441	0.6413	**0.7159**	0.6243	0.6369	0.5914
	NN	0.6289	0.6541	0.6857	0.6355	0.6603	**0.7061**	0.6206	0.6595	0.5901
	DT	0.5882	0.5567	**0.6908**	0.6142	0.6004	0.6113	0.5154	0.6234	0.5653
Max	SVM	0.6557	0.6480	0.6857	0.6816	0.6484	0.6885	0.6096	**0.7079**	0.6067
	LR	0.5698	0.6630	0.7111	0.6441	0.6413	**0.7159**	0.6243	0.6369	0.5914
	NN	0.6519	0.7177	0.7200	0.6705	0.6832	**0.7345**	0.6484	0.6634	0.6034
	DT	0.6250	0.5795	**0.7045**	0.6292	0.6077	0.6328	0.5263	0.6292	0.5843

Table 3: Classification performance of the models trained on the noisy audio recordings with the sounds of crying baby. Mean F1 is averaged across three random seeds. **Bold** denotes the best performance per noise type (*short* and *background*), green background denotes performance that is higher than the analogous one for the model+feature set trained on the original noise-free audio.

same models trained on the original noise-free audio recordings (see Table 3 for details). Same is true for the majority of wav2vec -based models, with wav2vec -based NN achieving the overall best performance.

When it comes to the sound of crying baby to be introduced as a continuous background noise, the overall performance level of wav2vec and ConvFeat -based models decreases substantially. wav2vec -based models are not able anymore to outperform any of noise-free models, and only linear ConvFeat -based models are still able to outperform their noise-free analogues. The eGeMAPSv02 -based SVM model is able to achieve its best performance with this type of noise.

4.3 Recommendations

Based on the results of our analysis, we outline a set of recommendations for the ML researchers and practitioners interested in deploying AD classification models in real world.

First, if acoustic features are extracted using conventional and not deep learning-based features, such as ConvFeat or eGeMAPSv02 , it is important to use the noise removal speech pre-processing techniques to normalize the audio dataset that is used for training ML models. As explained in Section 4.1, even short segments of unwanted noise, such as accidental siren, craw caw or a short vacuum cleaner sound, may significantly change more than 50% of acoustic features. Having the training dataset where otherwise similar datapoints are represented by significantly different acoustic features, introduces many unnecessary challenges in model development.

Second, it is important to make sure the deployed models are not be used in certain types of real world environments where certain noises are common. As explained in Section 4.2, domestic noise, such as washing machine or vacuum cleaner, may decrease classification performance. As such, it is important to recommend the real world users of the AD classification model to avoid this type of noise when recording audio in order to expect better accuracy of the model. Other noises, such as baby cry, cough or dog bark, are not harmful and there is no need to avoid them. This is also important to know because these types of noise are much more difficult to securely avoid in real world scenarios than sounds of a vacuum cleaner or washer.

Third, model developers should expect different effects of noise on the AD classification performance depending on the type of audio representation and model used. Deep features, such as wav2vec , are affected less strongly by the presence of noise comparing to more conventional acoustic features, such as ConvFeat and eGeMAPSv02 , although models utilizing all three types of features may benefit from certain noises in audio. More simplistic linear models, such as SVM and LR, may be impacted positively but not very strongly (up to 2.5%) by the presence of appropriate noise in the recordings. The more complex non-linear models, such as DT and NN, may experience twice stronger positive effect (+4.8%) due to appropriate noise.

5 Conclusions

In this paper, we study the effect of fifteen types of acoustic noise, standard in home environments, on AD classification from speech. We perform a thorough analysis showing how four ML models and three types of acoustic features are affected by different types of acoustic noise. We show that natural environmental noise is not necessarily harmful, with certain types of noise even being beneficial for AD classification performance and helping increase accuracy by up to 4.8%. We provide recommendations on how to utilize acoustic noise in order to achieve the best performance results with the ML models deployed in real world in order to facilitate the use of scalable digital health tools for AD detection from speech. Further research is necessary to investigate the effect of more types of acoustic noise common in real world scenarios.

References

Alexei Baevski, Yuhao Zhou, Abdelrahman Mohamed, and Michael Auli. 2020. wav2vec 2.0: A Framework for Self-Supervised Learning of Speech Representations. *Advances in Neural Information Processing Systems*, 33.

Aparna Balagopalan, Benjamin Eyre, Jessica Robin, Frank Rudzicz, and Jekaterina Novikova. 2021. Comparing pre-trained and feature-based models for prediction of Alzheimer's disease based on speech. *Frontiers in aging neuroscience*, 13:189.

Aparna Balagopalan, Benjamin Eyre, Frank Rudzicz, and Jekaterina Novikova. 2020. To BERT or Not To BERT: Comparing Speech and Language-based Approaches for Alzheimer's Disease Detection. *INTERSPEECH 2020*.

Aparna Balagopalan and Jekaterina Novikova. 2021. Comparing Acoustic-based Approaches for Alzheimer's Disease Detection. *INTERSPEECH 2021*.

Aparna Balagopalan, Jekaterina Novikova, Frank Rudzicz, and Marzyeh Ghassemi. 2018. The Effect of Heterogeneous Data for Alzheimer's Disease Detection from Speech. In *NeurIPS 2018 Workshop Machine Learning for Health (ML4H)*.

Sebastian Braun, Hannes Gamper, Chandan KA Reddy, and Ivan Tashev. 2021. Towards efficient models for real-time deep noise suppression. In *ICASSP 2021-2021 IEEE International Conference on Acoustics, Speech and Signal Processing (ICASSP)*, pages 656–660. IEEE.

Ron Brookmeyer, Nada Abdalla, Claudia H Kawas, and María M Corrada. 2018. Forecasting the prevalence of preclinical and clinical alzheimer's disease in the united states. *Alzheimer's & Dementia*, 14(2):121–129.

Hyeong-Seok Choi, Jang-Hyun Kim, Jaesung Huh, Adrian Kim, Jung-Woo Ha, and Kyogu Lee. 2018. Phase-aware speech enhancement with deep complex u-net. In *International Conference on Learning Representations*.

Sofia de la Fuente Garcia, Craig W Ritchie, and Saturnino Luz. 2020. Artificial intelligence, speech, and language processing approaches to monitoring alzheimer's disease: a systematic review. *Journal of Alzheimer's Disease*, 78(4):1547–1574.

Sayanton V Dibbo, Yugyeong Kim, and Sudip Vhaduri. 2021. Effect of Noise on Generic Cough Models. In *2021 IEEE 17th International Conference on Wearable and Implantable Body Sensor Networks (BSN)*, pages 1–4. IEEE.

Harishchandra Dubey, Vishak Gopal, Ross Cutler, Ashkan Aazami, Sergiy Matusevych, Sebastian Braun, Sefik Emre Eskimez, Manthan Thakker, Takuya Yoshioka, Hannes Gamper, et al. 2022.

Icassp 2022 deep noise suppression challenge. In *ICASSP 2022-2022 IEEE International Conference on Acoustics, Speech and Signal Processing (ICASSP)*, pages 9271–9275. IEEE.

Benjamin Eyre, Aparna Balagopalan, and Jekaterina Novikova. 2020. Fantastic features and where to find them: detecting cognitive impairment with a subsequence classification guided approach. *W-NUT at EMNLP 2020*.

Steven Y Feng, Varun Gangal, Dongyeop Kang, Teruko Mitamura, and Eduard Hovy. 2020. GenAug: Data Augmentation for Finetuning Text Generators. In *Proceedings of Deep Learning Inside Out (DeeLIO): The First Workshop on Knowledge Extraction and Integration for Deep Learning Architectures*, pages 29–42.

Kathleen C Fraser, Jed A Meltzer, and Frank Rudzicz. 2016. Linguistic features identify Alzheimer's disease in narrative speech. *Journal of Alzheimer's Disease*, 49(2):407–422.

Emil Fristed, Caroline Skirrow, Marton Meszaros, Raphael Lenain, Udeepa Meepegama, Stefano Cappa, Dag Aarsland, and Jack Weston. 2021. Evaluation of a speech-based AI system for early detection of Alzheimer's disease remotely via smartphones. *medRxiv*.

Lara Gauder, Leonardo Pepino, Luciana Ferrer, and Pablo Riera. 2021. Alzheimer Disease Recognition Using Speech-Based Embeddings From Pre-Trained Models. In *Proc. INTERSPEECH 2021*, pages 3795–3799.

Praveen Kumar Badimala Giridhara, Chinmaya Mishra, Reddy Kumar Modam Venkataramana, Syed Saqib Bukhari, and Andreas Dengel. 2019. A Study of Various Text Augmentation Techniques for Relation Classification in Free Text. *ICPRAM*, 3:5.

Emmanuel A Jammeh, B Carroll Camille, W Pearson Stephen, Javier Escudero, Athanasios Anastasiou, Peng Zhao, Todd Chenore, John Zajicek, and Emmanuel Ifeachor. 2018. Machine-learning based identification of undiagnosed dementia in primary care: a feasibility study. *BJGP Open*, page bjgpopen18X101589.

Rafael Zequeira Jiménez, Babak Naderi, and Sebastian Möller. 2020. Effect of environmental noise in speech quality assessment studies using crowdsourcing. In *2020 Twelfth International Conference on Quality of Multimedia Experience (QoMEX)*, pages 1–6. IEEE.

Lampros C Kourtis, Oliver B Regele, Justin M Wright, and Graham B Jones. 2019. Digital biomarkers for Alzheimer's disease: the mobile/wearable devices opportunity. *NPJ digital medicine*, 2(1):1–9.

Michał Koziarski and Bogusław Cyganek. 2017. Image recognition with deep neural networks in presence of noise–dealing with and taking advantage of distortions. *Integrated Computer-Aided Engineering*, 24(4):337–349.

Saturnino Luz, Fasih Haider, Sofia de la Fuente, Davida Fromm, and Brian MacWhinney. 2021. Detecting cognitive decline using speech only: The ADReSSo Challenge. *arXiv preprint arXiv:2104.09356*.

Israel Martínez-Nicolás, Thide E Llorente, Francisco Martínez-Sánchez, and Juan José G Meilán. 2021. Ten years of research on automatic voice and speech analysis of people with alzheimer's disease and mild cognitive impairment: a systematic review article. *Frontiers in Psychology*, 12:620251.

Marie Mc Carthy and P Schueler. 2019. Can Digital Technology Advance the Development of Treatments for Alzheimer's Disease?

Julien Meyer, Laure Dentel, and Fanny Meunier. 2013. Speech recognition in natural background noise. *PloS one*, 8(11):e79279.

Babak Naderi, Sebastian Möller, and Gabriel Mittag. 2018. Speech quality assessment in crowdsourcing: Influence of environmental noise. *44. Deutsche Jahrestagung für Akustik (DAGA)*, pages 229–302.

Jekaterina Novikova. 2021. Robustness and Sensitivity of BERT Models Predicting Alzheimer's Disease from Text. In *Proceedings of the Seventh Workshop on Noisy User-generated Text (W-NUT 2021)*, pages 334–339.

Jekaterina Novikova, Aparna Balagopalan, Ksenia Shkaruta, and Frank Rudzicz. 2019. Lexical features are more vulnerable, syntactic features have more predictive power. In *Proceedings of the 5th Workshop on Noisy User-generated Text (W-NUT 2019)*, pages 431–443.

Babafemi O Odelowo and David V Anderson. 2017. A noise prediction and time-domain subtraction approach to deep neural network based speech enhancement. In *2017 16th IEEE International Conference on Machine Learning and Applications (ICMLA)*, pages 372–377. IEEE.

Raghavendra Pappagari, Jaejin Cho, Sonal Joshi, Laureano Moro-Velázquez, Piotr Żelasko, Jesús Villalba, and Najim Dehak. 2021. Automatic Detection and Assessment of Alzheimer Disease Using Speech and Language Technologies in Low-Resource Scenarios. In *Proc. INTERSPEECH 2021*, pages 3825–3829.

Karol J Piczak. 2015. ESC: Dataset for environmental sound classification. In *Proceedings of the 23rd ACM international conference on Multimedia*, pages 1015–1018.

Gokul Prabhakaran, Rajbir Bakshi, et al. 2018. Analysis of Structure and Cost in a Longitudinal Study of Alzheimer's Disease. *Journal of Health Care Finance*.

Martin Prince, Adelina Comas-Herrera, Martin Knapp, Maëlenn Guerchet, and Maria Karagiannidou. 2016. World Alzheimer report 2016: improving healthcare for people living with dementia: coverage, quality and costs now and in the future. *Alzheimer's disease International (ADI)*.

Jessica Robin, John E Harrison, Liam D Kaufman, Frank Rudzicz, William Simpson, and Maria Yancheva. 2020. Evaluation of speech-based digital biomarkers: review and recommendations. *Digital Biomarkers*, 4(3):99–108.

Jessica Robin, Mengdan Xu, Liam D Kaufman, and William Simpson. 2021. Using digital speech assessments to detect early signs of cognitive impairment. *Frontiers in digital health*, 3:749758.

Morteza Rohanian, Julian Hough, and Matthew Purver. 2021. Alzheimer's Dementia Recognition Using Acoustic, Lexical, Disfluency and Speech Pause Features Robust to Noisy Inputs. *arXiv preprint arXiv:2106.15684*.

Antoine Slegers, Renee-Pier Filiou, Maxime Montembeault, and Simona Maria Brambati. 2018. Connected speech features from picture description in alzheimer's disease: a systematic review. *Journal of Alzheimer's Disease*, 65(2):519–542.

Cristiano Rafael Steffens, Lucas Ricardo Vieira Messias, Paulo Lilles Jorge Drews, and Silvia Silva da Costa Botelho. 2019. Can exposure, noise and compression affect image recognition? an assessment of the impacts on state-of-the-art convnets. In *2019 Latin American Robotics Symposium (LARS), 2019 Brazilian Symposium on Robotics (SBR) and 2019 Workshop on Robotics in Education (WRE)*, pages 61–66. IEEE.

B Vellas and P Aisen. 2021. New hope for alzheimer's disease.

Sudip Vhaduri, Theodore Van Kessel, Bongjun Ko, David Wood, Shiqiang Wang, and Thomas Brunschwiler. 2019. Nocturnal cough and snore detection in noisy environments using smartphone-microphones. In *2019 IEEE international conference on healthcare informatics (ICHI)*, pages 1–7. IEEE.

Wei Xue, Catia Cucchiarini, Roeland van Hout, and Helmer Strik. 2019. Acoustic correlates of speech intelligibility: the usability of the egemaps feature set for atypical speech. In *Workshop on Speech and Language Technology in Education*.

Guochang Zhang, Libiao Yu, Chunliang Wang, and Jianqiang Wei. 2022. Multi-scale temporal frequency convolutional network with axial attention for speech enhancement. In *ICASSP 2022-2022 IEEE International Conference on Acoustics, Speech and Signal Processing (ICASSP)*, pages 9122–9126. IEEE.

Luke Zhou, Kathleen C Fraser, and Frank Rudzicz. 2016. Speech Recognition in Alzheimer's Disease and in its Assessment. In *INTERSPEECH 2016*, pages 1948–1952.

Zining Zhu, Jekaterina Novikova, and Frank Rudzicz. 2018. Semi-supervised classification by reaching consensus among modalities. In *NeurIPS Workshop on Interpretability and Robustness in Audio, Speech, and Language IRASL*.

Zining Zhu, Jekaterina Novikova, and Frank Rudzicz. 2019. Detecting cognitive impairments by agreeing on interpretations of linguistic features. In *NAACL 2019, 17th Annual Conference of the North American Chapter of the Association for Computational Linguistics*, arXiv preprint arXiv:1808.06570.

Exploring Multimodal Features and Fusion Strategies for Analyzing Disaster Tweets

Raj Ratn Pranesh
Pennsylvania State University
rrp5338@psu.edu

Abstract

Social media platforms, such as Twitter, often provide firsthand news during the outbreak of a crisis. It is essential to process these facts quickly to plan response efforts in a manner that minimizes loss. In this paper, we present an analysis of various multimodal feature fusion techniques to analyze and classify disaster tweets into multiple crisis events via transfer learning. In our study, we utilized three image models pre-trained on ImageNet dataset and three fine-tuned language models to learn the visual and textual features of the data and combine them to make predictions. We have presented a systematic analysis of multiple intra-modal and cross-modal fusion strategies and their effect on the performance of the multimodal disaster classification system. In our experiment, we used 8,242 disaster tweets, each comprised of image and text data with five disaster event classes. The results show that the multimodal with transformer-attention mechanism and factorized bilinear pooling (FBP)(Zhang et al., 2019) for intra-modal and cross-modal feature fusion respectively achieved the best performance.

1 Introduction

The sudden breakout of crisis events, like natural disasters, creates high-stakes circumstances that are coupled with great uncertainty as well as the need to make quick decisions, often with limited official newscasts. Research in recent years has uncovered the importance of social media communication in disaster situations and shown that information broadcast via social media can improve situational awareness during an emergency (Vieweg et al., 2010). Social media has proven to be an active communication channel, especially during crisis events such as natural disasters including earthquakes, floods, and typhoons ((Hughes and Palen, 2009), (Imran et al., 2016)) or other emergencies such as accidents. These events spur a sudden surge of attention followed by reactive actions from both the general public and the media. The quick detection and analysis of such events are critical to swiftly disseminate information and, more importantly, prepare the relief team. Such situational awareness and tactical information enables the team effectively estimate early damage and launch relief efforts accordingly.

An automated system for crisis-related information retrieval from social media is imperative to rapidly and systematically classify disasters. Information regarding crises is best sourced from the social media site Twitter, which is a real-time, open, and public communication platform. The development of a system requires the extraction of relevant tweets to then classify them into different types of information: affected individuals, infrastructural damages, casualties, donations, caution, or advice. However, because the messages generated during a disaster vary greatly in value and since Twitter is a highly diverse platform, an automatic system needs to filter out messages that are irrelevant and do not contribute to situational awareness. As a result, we designed a system for detecting informative messages that classifies them to decide the type of information to extract (e.g., donation offers, casualty reports).

Information on social media mainly consists of textual messages and images. Past research has mainly focused on using textual content to aid disaster response. However, recent studies have revealed that images shared on social media during a disaster event can also help the relief team in several ways. For example, (Nguyen et al., 2017) incorporated images shared on Twitter to assess the severity of infrastructure damage in their work. Similarly, (Jing et al., 2016) investigated the usefulness of images and text for their study on flood and flood aid. Our work follows this method of taking into account both texts and images.

Previous works (Ofli et al., 2020), (Agarwal

Proceedings of the 2022 COLING Workshop: The 8th Workshop on Noisy User-generated Text (W-NUT 2022), pages 62–68

et al., 2020), (Kumar et al., 2020), (Abavisani et al., 2020) have proposed a multimodal system for analyzing disaster tweets that utilizes feature fusion. However, not much exploration has been done for the enhancement of the extracted visual, textual and their combined multimodal feature representation. In this paper, we present an analysis of various multimodal fusion strategies for intra-modal fusion and cross-modal fusion. We investigate relation-attention, self-attention, and transformer-attention for intra-modal fusion. For the cross-modal fusion, we explore three methods, namely, Factorized Bilinear Pooling (Zhang et al., 2019), Compact Bilinear Gated Pooling (Kiela et al., 2018) and Compact Bilinear Pooling (Fukui et al., 2016). Along with this, we evaluate state-of-the-art models which were three pretrained image models (VGG19 (Simonyan and Zisserman, 2014), ResNet-50 (He et al., 2016) and AlexNet) and three pretrained language models (BERT (Devlin et al., 2018), RoBERTa (Liu et al., 2019) and ALBERT (Lan et al., 2019)) for the disaster tweet analysis and classification task. In our analysis, we utilize multimodal CrisisMMD (Alam et al., 2018) dataset. We found that the ResNet-50 outperformed other image models and among the textual models RoBERTa achieved the best performance. We further utilize these two models for the evaluation of intra-modal and cross-modal fusion strategies.

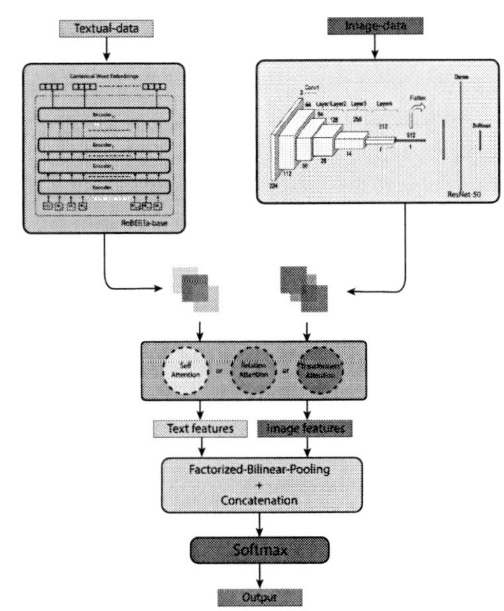

Figure 1: Feature fusion pipeline with textual sub-model (RoBERTa) and visual sub-model (ResNet-50)

2 Methodology

2.0.1 Textual feature extractor:

We employed three pretrained language models, namely, BERT-base (Devlin et al., 2018), RoBERTa-base (Liu et al., 2019) and ALBERT-base (Lan et al., 2019) to extract a high quality text feature vector. We finetuned them with a custom classification head with updatable weights. The averaged pool of sequential output from 12 encoding layers of each model was used as the custom classifier head's input. Once the model was finetuned, each of the language models was fed with a sequence of text inputs (reprocessed tweets) which then went through all of the stacked encoding layers, thereby extracting essential features from the context.

2.0.2 Visual Feature Extractor:

For image feature extraction, we use three image models, namely, VGG19 (Simonyan and Zisserman, 2014), ResNet-50 and AlexNet pretrained on Imagenet-21k (Deng et al., 2009). Each of the pre-trained image models was supplied with a preprocessed image; a visual representation was then extracted from the final finetuned FC layer of each model. The output is a vector of the dimension of 4096, 1000, 1000 for VGG19, ResNet-50 and AlexNet respectively.

2.1 Multimodal fusion

2.1.1 Intra-modal feature fusion

We have developed functions using different attention-based methods, namely, self-attention, relation-attention and transformer-attention methods. These functions can convert a variable number of features into a fixed dimension feature. For an "n" number of features, we denote the i_{th} feature as f_i where $i \in [1, n]$. We applied fusion techniques as follows:

- $Self-attention$: For each feature we apply a 1-dimensional fully connected layer $W^0_{d\times 1}$ and a sigmoid function σ, resulting to the weight a_i of the i_th feature f_i^T as follows:

$$\alpha_i = \sigma(f_i^T \cdot W^0_{d\times 1}) \quad (1)$$

We combined these weights from self-attention (Vaswani et al., 2017) for every feature into a global representation f_s as follows:

$$f_s = \frac{\sum_{i=1}^{n} \alpha_i f_i}{\sum_{i=1}^{n} \alpha_i} \quad (2)$$

- $Relation - attention$: The function derives the relationship between the features and generates relevant features. Since f_s holds global representation of these features, we use sample concatenation of each feature and global representation to shape the global-local relation[f_i:f_s]. Next, we apply the 1-dimensional fully connected layers $W^1_{d/times1}$ with the sigmoid function σ. For relation-attention weight β of i_th feature $[f_i : f_s]^T$ is computed as:

$$\beta_i = \sigma([f_i : f_s]^T \cdot W^1_{d/times1}) \quad (3)$$

Using aggregated weights from self-attention function and relation-attention function, we combine all the features to get a new feature f_r:

$$f_r = \frac{\sum_{i=1}^{n} \alpha_i \beta_i [f_i : f_s]}{\sum_{i=1}^{n} \alpha_i \beta_i} \quad (4)$$

- $Transformer - attention$: Based on the works in (Zhang et al., 2019) and (Yang et al., 2016), we compute the attention weight as follows:

$$f_i' = W^2_{m \times d} \cdot f_i + b\gamma_i \quad (5)$$

$$= exp(u^t_{d \times 1} \cdot tanh(f_i')) \quad (6)$$

To reshape the the dimension of feature f_i, we feed it through a $w \times d$ dimensional FC layer 6. The weight of i_{th} feature f_i is processed through the tanh function which is then fed to the exp function along with dot product of $u^t_{d \times 1}$. We pass the output from the exp function to a 1-dimensional FC layer stated in 6. From the transformers attention we formulate all the features into a single feature f_i, as

$$f_s = \frac{\sum_{i=1}^{n} \gamma_i f_i}{\sum_{i=1}^{n} \gamma_i} \quad (7)$$

2.1.2 Cross-modal feature fusion

- $FactorizedBilinearPooling(FBP)$ (Zhang et al., 2019): The two feature vectors obtained via different modalities are fused together by applying FBP function.

- $CompactBilinearPooling(CBP)$: Originally proposed (Fukui et al., 2016) for VQA task, we modified this feature fusion technique for the classification task.

- $CompactBilinearGatedPooling(CBGP)$: With an additional attention gate applied on top of the compact bilinear pooling module, we adopted the CBGP (Kiela et al., 2018) fusion technique for the cross-modal feature fusion.

3 Dataset

We have used the CrisisMMD (Alam et al., 2018) dataset for training and testing our model. Each text and image pair in the dataset have two annotations: (task_1) humanitarian categories (eight classes), (task_2) informative vs. not-informative (two classes). Since the number of labels across different classes was uneven, following (Ofli et al., 2020), we compressed the number of humanitarian categories to five- namely, (i) *Not-humanitarian* (4312), (ii) *other_relevant_information* (1764), (iii) *rescue_volunteering_or_donation_effort* (1195), (iv) *infrastructure_and_utility_damage* (842) and (v) *affected_individuals* (129). In the CrisisMMD dataset, tweet text and image in a pair were annotated separately, as a result, few pairs had a different label for text and it's associated image. We removed those pairs and performed the experiment only those data who have the same label for text and image. Finally, we have 8,242 pairs and split the data in 70%:15%:15% ratio for training (5770), development (1236), and test (1236) sets. For the informative and not-informative, we had 7875 (train), 1687 (development) and 1688 (test).

4 Experiment

4.1 Exploring Visual feature

In the visual modal, we compared three image models, namely: AlexNet (Krizhevsky et al., 2012),ResNet-50 (He et al., 2016) and VGG19 (Simonyan and Zisserman, 2014); pretrained on large ImageNet (Deng et al., 2009) dataset. In the visual unimodal for each of the image model, the extracted feature vector was passed through two consecutive fully connected layers of dimension 512 and 256. The feature vector was then passed into a batch normalization layer and dropout layer(with dropout probability = 0.4), followed by a 5-dimensional dense layer with a softmax activation function in order to make the final class prediction of the disaster event. Relu activation function and L2 regularization of 0.01 was applied at each dense layer. All of the image models were trained on the training dataset(learning rate = 1e-4) using Adam (Kingma and Ba, 2014) optimizer and with cross-entropy as the loss function. The model's hyperparameter fine-tuning was done on the validation set. We also conducted an evaluation of three models over the test dataset. As shown in table 1, out of all three image models, ResNet-50 achieved the best F1 score of 68.35 as compared to ResNet-50 (He et al., 2016) and AlexNet. This shows that the ResNet-50 was able to understand the image feature more clearly and generate better image representation. The reason behind this could be the residual module based ResNet-50's deeper architecture which lacks in VGG19 and AlexNet models.

Model	Precision	Recall	F1-score
AlexNet	74.42	56.74	64.38
VGG19	76.39	55.01	63.96
ResNet-50	79.23	60.11	68.35

Table 1: Performance of image unimodal on task_1

4.2 Exploring Textual feature

Similar to the visual modal, the textual modal utilizes transfer-learning for learning the textual data representation. For the textual unimodal, we applied the bidirectional transformers with the self-attention mechanism to extract resourceful features from text in the disaster tweets. In our analysis, we use ALBERT-base (Lan et al., 2019), BERT-base (Devlin et al., 2018) and RoBERTa-base (Liu et al., 2019) pretrained language models. These models are mainly known for their pretrained weights over different domain data. For our task, we fine-tuned all of the models on the disaster dataset. As we discussed above, the input text sequence was structured, tokenized and pre-processed according to the language model's input format. From each of the language models, we extracted the $[CLS]$ (for BERT and ALBERT) or $< s >$ (for RoBERTa) which represents the entire input sentence and is used as the aggregate sequence representation for classification tasks. Similar to the visual unimodal, the classification token was then passed through a series of the fully connected layer of size 512 and 256. This was followed by a batch normalization layer, dropout layer(dropout probability = 0.4), and a 5-dimensional dense layer with a softmax activation function. All the dense layer in the model has a relu activation function and L2 regularization of 0.01. All of the models were trained with the learning rate of 1e-4, using Adam (Kingma and Ba, 2014) as optimizer and cross-entropy as the loss function. On analyzing the performance of all the three models on the test data, we observed (table 2) that the performance of RoBERTa-base unimodal was the most optimal. BERT and ALBERT achieved the F1 score of 72.92 and 71.23 respectively.

Model	Precision	Recall	F1-score
ALBERT-base	77.34	66.02	71.23
BERT-base	79.34	67.47	72.92
RoBERTa-base	85.36	66.2	74.56

Table 2: Performance of Text Unimodal on task_1

4.3 Exploring Fusion Strategies

Feature extraction: We extracted the feature maps from the preprocessed visual and textual data and utilized them for the intra-modal fusion. For a given 3 dimension feature map, the size is represented as $H \times W \times C$, where H and W represented the height and width of the feature map, respectively. The number of channel in the feature map was represented as C. For the intra-modal fusion process, we sliced the feature map into n vectors such that $n = H \times W$. Therefore, n number of C-dimensional vectors were obtained. For the image data, we extracted the feature map from the layer before the final average polling layer of the ResNet-50. For the RoBERTa model, instead of using classification token, we extracted the vector sequence consisting of each input token's vector representation. The size of each output token sequence was 768 x 42 (max_length). This vector was split into 768 feature vector (42-dimensional) before intra-modal fusion.

Intra-modal Fusion: As we discussed above in the section *Multimodal Fusion*, we utilized 3 intra-modal attention fusion methods: relation-attention, self-attention, and transformer-attention. Both the visual and textual feature vector were subjected to each of the attention methods before performing the cross-modal fusion. The n split feature vectors from each of the visual and textual modalities, when passes through the attention layer, condenses to form respective unique representations which are then use for the cross-modal fusion.

Cross-modal Fusion: For the cross-modal fusion, we investigated 3 methods: factorized bilinear pooling, compact bilinear pooling and compact bilinear gated pooling. The visual and textual feature vector generated after the intra-modal fusion is then subjected to cross-modal fusion to produce a combined multimodal representation. The multimodal vector is then passed through a classification layer of size 5 with a softmax activation function to make predictions. The model is trained on a batch size of 64 with cross-entropy loss function and Adam (Kingma and Ba, 2014) optimizer for training the model. During the training of the model, we use an initial learning rate of 1e-5, two callback API-early-stopping conditions and reduce the learning rate on the plateau (reducing factor = 0.5, patience = 5).

Visual / Textual	Self attention	Relation attention	Transformers attention
Self-attention	78.7%	79.4%	81.7%
Relation-attention	79.9%	81.1%	82.2%
Transformers-attention	80.0%	81.2%	85.1%

Table 3: Multimodal performance (macro F1 %) on task_1 with FBP

Visual / Textual	Self attention	Relation attention	Transformers attention
Self-attention	82.8%	83.1%	84.9%
Relation-attention	81.8%	84.3%	85.1%
Transformers-attention	82.1%	85.2%	89.5%

Table 4: Multimodal performance (macro F1 %) on task_2 with FBP

5 Results

In this section, we discuss and analyze the multimodal performance with various fusion techniques. Table 3 and 4 show the Macro F1-score of FBP fusion methods on task_1 and task_2 respectively. We have shown the result of the **best cross-model fusion method**: **FBP** applied with various intra-model fusion methods.

For task_2, we observed that by using the FBP (Zhang et al., 2019) and Transformer attention layer in the pipeline, the performance of multimodal was remarkably better (around **12%**) than the other cross layer fusion methods (CBP and CBGP). We also noticed that in either of the cross-modal fusion method, the transformer attention intra-modal fusion performed the best. For task_1 (refer 3) and task_2 (refer 4), FBP with transformers-attention based multimodal model gave the best result of 85.1% and 89.5% respectively. We can also see that models having transformer-attention combined with relation-attention outperformed the model with transformer-attention and self-attention.

Coming to the multimodal baseline (Ofli et al., 2020) and (Abavisani et al., 2020), our model outperform it by **7.99%** and **1.10%** on the task_1 and for task_2 it is **5.92%** and **0.78%**. The reason behind the superior performance of our model lies behind the underlying feature representation generated by the pre-trained language and image models. Moreover, we were able to capture intra-modality information using attention mechanism which produced a denser feature representation before the cross-modal fusion. Therefore using transfer learning and attention-based fusion techniques, we were able to blend together with powerful language and image models and build a more robust multimodal.

6 Conclusion

In this paper, we present an extensive analysis of multiple feature fusion strategies for developing a multi-modal framework for detecting and classifying tweets into various crisis events accurately based on the textual and visual features. In our study, we compared various image and language models and found that the ResNet and RoBERTa outperformed the other models. We also presented a comparative study of various fusion methods; through that, we can conclude that the selection of effective intra-modal and cross-modal method plays a crucial role in developing a more accurate and efficient multimodal framework for classifying the events for faster relief efforts. We observed that the transformer-attention mechanism outperformed the other intra-modal fusion methods. We also showed that by using factorized bilinear pooling, the multimodal feature representation can be improved. The results of the experiments show that one application of the multimodal framework can be the identification and filtration of disaster-related information available on social media platforms.

References

Mahdi Abavisani, Liwei Wu, Shengli Hu, Joel Tetreault, and Alejandro Jaimes. 2020. Multimodal categorization of crisis events in social media. In *Proceedings of the IEEE/CVF Conference on Computer Vision and Pattern Recognition*, pages 14679–14689.

Mansi Agarwal, Maitree Leekha, Ramit Sawhney, and Rajiv Ratn Shah. 2020. Crisis-dias: Towards multimodal damage analysis-deployment, challenges and assessment. In *Proceedings of the AAAI Conference on Artificial Intelligence*, volume 34, pages 346–353.

Firoj Alam, Ferda Ofli, and Muhammad Imran. 2018. Crisismmd: Multimodal twitter datasets from natural disasters. In *Twelfth International AAAI Conference on Web and Social Media*.

Jia Deng, Wei Dong, Richard Socher, Li-Jia Li, Kai Li, and Li Fei-Fei. 2009. Imagenet: A large-scale hierarchical image database. In *2009 IEEE conference on computer vision and pattern recognition*, pages 248–255. Ieee.

Jacob Devlin, Ming-Wei Chang, Kenton Lee, and Kristina Toutanova. 2018. Bert: Pre-training of deep bidirectional transformers for language understanding. *arXiv preprint arXiv:1810.04805*.

Akira Fukui, Dong Huk Park, Daylen Yang, Anna Rohrbach, Trevor Darrell, and Marcus Rohrbach. 2016. Multimodal compact bilinear pooling for visual question answering and visual grounding. *arXiv preprint arXiv:1606.01847*.

Kaiming He, Xiangyu Zhang, Shaoqing Ren, and Jian Sun. 2016. Deep residual learning for image recognition. In *Proceedings of the IEEE conference on computer vision and pattern recognition*, pages 770–778.

Amanda Lee Hughes and Leysia Palen. 2009. Twitter adoption and use in mass convergence and emergency events. *International journal of emergency management*, 6(3-4):248–260.

Muhammad Imran, Prasenjit Mitra, and Carlos Castillo. 2016. Twitter as a lifeline: Human-annotated twitter corpora for nlp of crisis-related messages. *arXiv preprint arXiv:1605.05894*.

Min Jing, Bryan W Scotney, Sonya A Coleman, Martin T McGinnity, Xiubo Zhang, Stephen Kelly, Khurshid Ahmad, Antje Schlaf, Sabine Gründer-Fahrer, and Gerhard Heyer. 2016. Integration of text and image analysis for flood event image recognition. In *2016 27th Irish Signals and Systems Conference (ISSC)*, pages 1–6. IEEE.

Douwe Kiela, Edouard Grave, Armand Joulin, and Tomas Mikolov. 2018. Efficient large-scale multimodal classification. In *Proceedings of the AAAI Conference on Artificial Intelligence*, volume 32.

Diederik P Kingma and Jimmy Ba. 2014. Adam: A method for stochastic optimization. *arXiv preprint arXiv:1412.6980*.

Alex Krizhevsky, Ilya Sutskever, and Geoffrey E Hinton. 2012. Imagenet classification with deep convolutional neural networks. In *Advances in neural information processing systems*, pages 1097–1105.

Abhinav Kumar, Jyoti Prakash Singh, Yogesh K Dwivedi, and Nripendra P Rana. 2020. A deep multimodal neural network for informative twitter content classification during emergencies. *Annals of Operations Research*, pages 1–32.

Zhenzhong Lan, Mingda Chen, Sebastian Goodman, Kevin Gimpel, Piyush Sharma, and Radu Soricut. 2019. Albert: A lite bert for self-supervised learning of language representations. *arXiv preprint arXiv:1909.11942*.

Yinhan Liu, Myle Ott, Naman Goyal, Jingfei Du, Mandar Joshi, Danqi Chen, Omer Levy, Mike Lewis, Luke Zettlemoyer, and Veselin Stoyanov. 2019. Roberta: A robustly optimized bert pretraining approach. *arXiv preprint arXiv:1907.11692*.

Dat T Nguyen, Ferda Ofli, Muhammad Imran, and Prasenjit Mitra. 2017. Damage assessment from social media imagery data during disasters. In *Proceedings of the 2017 IEEE/ACM International Conference on Advances in Social Networks Analysis and Mining 2017*, pages 569–576.

Ferda Ofli, Firoj Alam, and Muhammad Imran. 2020. Analysis of social media data using multimodal deep learning for disaster response. *arXiv preprint arXiv:2004.11838*.

Karen Simonyan and Andrew Zisserman. 2014. Very deep convolutional networks for large-scale image recognition. *arXiv preprint arXiv:1409.1556*.

Ashish Vaswani, Noam Shazeer, Niki Parmar, Jakob Uszkoreit, Llion Jones, Aidan N Gomez, Łukasz Kaiser, and Illia Polosukhin. 2017. Attention is all you need. *Advances in neural information processing systems*, 30.

Sarah Vieweg, Amanda L Hughes, Kate Starbird, and Leysia Palen. 2010. Microblogging during two natural hazards events: what twitter may contribute to situational awareness. In *Proceedings of the SIGCHI conference on human factors in computing systems*, pages 1079–1088.

Zichao Yang, Diyi Yang, Chris Dyer, Xiaodong He, Alex Smola, and Eduard Hovy. 2016. Hierarchical attention networks for document classification. In *Proceedings of the 2016 conference of the North American chapter of the association for computational linguistics: human language technologies*, pages 1480–1489.

Yuanyuan Zhang, Zi-Rui Wang, and Jun Du. 2019. Deep fusion: An attention guided factorized bilinear pooling for audio-video emotion recognition. In *2019 International Joint Conference on Neural Networks (IJCNN)*, pages 1–8. IEEE.

NTULM: Enriching Social Media Text Representations with Non-Textual Units

Jinning Li[1,2§], **Shubhanshu Mishra**[1§], **Ahmed El-Kishky**[1], **Sneha Mehta**[1], **Vivek Kulkarni**[1]
[1] Twitter, Inc.
[2] University of Illinois at Urbana-Champaign
jinning4@illinois.edu
{smishra, aelkishky, snehamehta, vkulkarni}@twitter.com

Abstract

On social media, additional context is often present in the form of annotations and meta-data such as the post's author, mentions, Hashtags, and hyperlinks. We refer to these annotations as Non-Textual Units (NTUs). We posit that NTUs provide social context beyond their textual semantics and leveraging these units can enrich social media text representations. In this work we construct an NTU-centric social heterogeneous network to co-embed NTUs. We then principally integrate these NTU embeddings into a large pretrained language model by fine-tuning with these additional units. This adds context to noisy short-text social media. Experiments show that utilizing NTU-augmented text representations significantly outperforms existing text-only baselines by 2-5% relative points on many downstream tasks highlighting the importance of context to social media NLP. We also highlight that including NTU context into the initial layers of language model alongside text is better than using it after the text embedding is generated. Our work leads to the generation of holistic general purpose social media content embedding.

1 Introduction

Understanding the social context is crucial to the semantic understanding of a social media post (Nguyen et al., 2016; Kulkarni et al., 2021; Mishra and Diesner, 2018; Hovy, 2015). This is especially true for short-text social media such as Twitter where the textual content available for semantic understanding is inherently limited. As such, pretrained language models that ignore non-textual context can demonstrate sub-optimal performance when utilized for social-media NLP.

Fortunately, on social media, there are many available non-textual units (NTUs), which provide social contexts for any written text. For example, the author of a post provides a social prior as to the content written by that author. Additionally, the author may annotate their post with meta-data such as Hashtags, user mentions, or URLs and other media. These units can frame the content of a post by providing social context, a stance, or additional supporting material.

Previous research has investigated augmenting pretrained language model representations with additional signals. These include enrichments by incorporating image features (Sun et al., 2020), better-segmented Hashtags (Maddela et al., 2019), URL understanding (Yasunaga et al., 2022), or temporal-spatial contexts (Kulkarni et al., 2021).

However, these existing works are type-specific and require a specialized technique to integrate just one type of non-textual signal (e.g., requiring an image encoder to extract image features). We claim that this added complexity makes it difficult to incorporate different non-textual signals and effectively train a joint model.

In this paper, our NTU enriched Language Model (`NTULM`) can easily, without loss of generality, train and integrate graph embeddings (El-Kishky et al., 2022a) for *multiple* types of NTUs. `NTULM` can do this through the use of heterogeneous information network embeddings of NTUs. This allows us to not only co-embed multiple NTU types, but also incorporate a variety of interaction types as edges in our network (e.g., *authoring* posts, *favoriting* Hashtags, and *co-mentioning* users). This general embedding framework is simple and does not require specialized feature encoders for different NTU types. After obtaining the NTU knowledge embeddings, `NTULM` deeply integrates them with the language model at the token level and simply applies the default attention mechanism used in the BERT encoder. To ensure our alignment with (Kulkarni et al., 2021) which allows only inclusion of a single context embedding to BERT, we take the average of NTU embed-

§Equal Contribution. Corresponding Author: smishra@twitter.com

Proceedings of the 2022 COLING Workshop: The 8th Workshop on Noisy User-generated Text (W-NUT 2022), pages 69–82

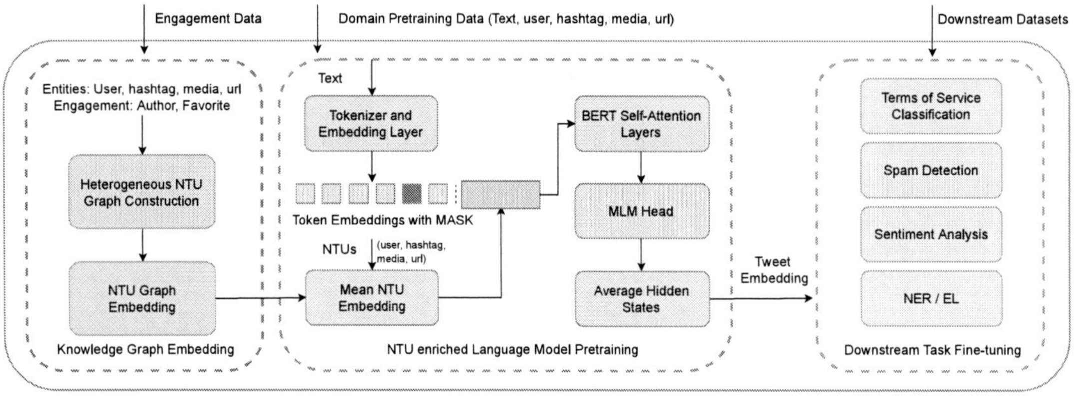

Figure 1: The framework of `NTULM` model. In the Knowledge Graph Embedding module, we use the engagement data to build the heterogeneous graph and train large-scale NTU embeddings. In the NTU enriched LM pre-training, we incorporate the mean NTU embedding at the end of the sequence. We compute the tweet embedding as the average of the last hidden states and use it for multiple downstream tasks.

dings and attach the unified embedding at the end of token embedding sequence. The framework of `NTULM` is shown in Figure 1.

To ensure high coverage of the NTU vocabulary across tweets, we construct a large-scale heterogeneous NTU graph ensuring high overlap with all tweets. With the scalability of our graph embeddings, we can rapidly embed NTUs ensuring high coverage across tweets.

We state and analyze the problem in Section 2, followed by our proposed solution involving NTU embedding and BERT integration in Section 3. In Section 4 we evaluate our proposed solution compared to text-only baselines. We go over related works in Section 6 and conclude in Section 8.

2 Task Formulation

In this section, we formulate the task of enriching pretrained language models with additional NTU embeddings.

2.1 Non-Textual Units (NTUs)

Social media posts are composed of textual content and non-textual units (NTUs) which provide additional context to the text. These include: the author of a post, any mentioned users, annotated topics via Hashtags, shared URLs, etc. While some of these units are encoded textually within a post, their meaning is not fully encapsulated by their textual semantics. Instead, this meaning can be better derived by understanding the social community that engages with the NTUs. Take for example the Hashtag $nlproc$ which is used by the Natural Language Processing community; this differs from nlp which is used by the natural language processing community *and* the Neuro-linguistic programming community. While both Hashtags contain the subword `nlp`, the real meaning is dependent on the social context they occur (e.g., from the author and social Hashtag embedding). This problem is more difficult with user mentions which convey no linguistic information in their textual form but can be more informative if mentions are considered by the social graph context of the user mentioned. We represent these NTUs using the heterogeneous social graph where each NTU is a node, and multi-typed edges represent their relation to other NTUs.

2.2 Integrating NTUs in Language Models

We extend the work introduced by LMSOC (Kulkarni et al., 2021), which demonstrates that the integration of temporal and geographical context in Tweet texts leads to better performance on cloze tasks. Similar to LMSOC, we take a base language model and integrate the NTU information in this model as additional context. Our goal is that each token in the text should not just be contextualized by other tokens in the text but also by the NTUs associated with the text. This approach is generic and we describe the exact choice of language model and NTU integration in detail later.

We improve on LMSOC by: (i) learning richer representations for NTUs using Heterogeneous Information Network embedding approaches (El-Kishky et al., 2022c), (ii) usage of social engagement signals, (iii) utilizing multiple tweet contexts via multiple NTU embeddings, (iv) assessing the performance of these models on a wide variety of downstream Tweet classification tasks.

Finally, we propose a holistic and end-to-end pipeline for training models with NTUs.

3 NTU enriched Language Model

The framework of `NTULM` is shown in Figure 1. In this section, We first introduce how we learn high-quality NTU embeddings by embedding an NTU-centric heterogenous social graph. We then describe how we principally integrate these NTU embeddings in a standard BERT-style language model yielding Tweet embeddings that utilize both text and NTU information.

We will use the Tweet in Table 1 as an example for the following sections.

Author: $user1$
Tweet: Our paper was accepted at $@WNUT$ with $@user2$ $@user3$ $\#nlproc$ $\#socialmedia$
Favorited by: $user4$, $user5$

Table 1: Example tweet with engagement data of author, mentions, Hashtags, and favorites

3.1 NTU Graph Construction and Embedding

We seek to understand NTUs based on the social context in which they're engaged and construct a dense NTU representation such that similar NTUs are close in this dense embedding space.

Constructing Heterogeneous Network: We start by constructing a large-scale heterogeneous graph $\mathcal{G}$ which models engagement between users and a set of NTU-observed Tweets (any language from 2018 till 2022). This heterogeneous graph consists of nodes and edges where multiple edges of different types can exist between a pair of nodes. For this work, we focus on users and Hashtags as NTUs, because they are the most accessible NTUs and are available or retrievable on most datasets. We construct the graph by taking a sample of Tweets, extracting the mention users, Hashtags, and the Tweet author. We also include a list of users who have favorited the Tweet. This leads to a graph where the nodes are either users or Hashtags. We include an edge between a user and a Hashtag if the user has either *favorited* a Tweet with the Hashtag, *authored* a Tweet with the Hashtag, or is *co-mentioned* with a Hashtag. One example of constructed graph is provided in Figure 2. Our choice of edges is based on the easy availability of the user Hashtag data via the Twitter API.

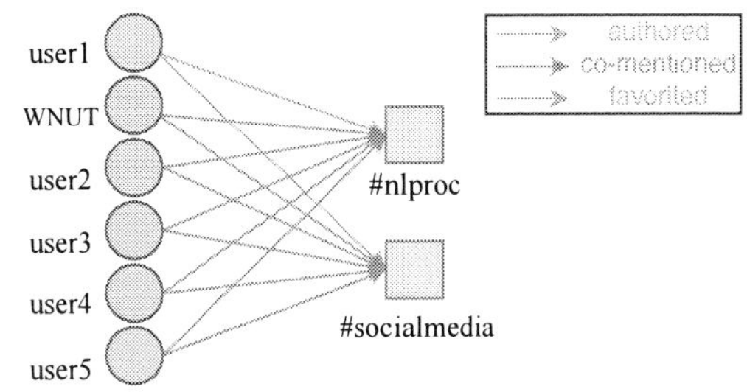

Figure 2: Graph construction with the example data in Table 1 for training `NTULM` user-Hashtag embeddings.

We construct this graph using data from January 1st, 2018 to July 1st, 2022. This leads to a graph with 60M Hashtags, 255M users, 5B authorship edges, 3B favorite edges, and 0.9B co-mention edges. We then learn heterogeneous graph embeddings by following the approach outlined in TwHIN (El-Kishky et al., 2022c). This gives us a set of embeddings for Users and Hashtags which exist in the same embedding space.

Heterogeneous Graph Embedding: We learn embedding vectors by applying a similar scheme to TransE (Bordes et al., 2013). For a pair of nodes in the graph (u_i), (v_j), we denote their embeddings as $\mathbf{u_i}$ and $\mathbf{v_j}$ respectively. We denote an edge as a triplet $e = (u_i, r_k, v_j)$ which consists of head and tail nodes (u_i, v_j) connected by a specific relation (r_k). We score these triplets with a scoring function of the form $f(\mathbf{u_i}, \mathbf{r_k}, \mathbf{v_j})$ where $\mathbf{r_k}$ is the relation embedding. Our training objective seeks to learn $\mathbf{e}$ parameters that maximize a log-likelihood constructed from the scoring function for $e \in \mathcal{G}$ and minimize for $e \notin \mathcal{G}$.

For simplicity, we apply a simple dot product comparison between node representations. For an edge $e = (u_i, r_k, v_j)$, this operation is defined by:

$$f(e) = f(u_i, r_k, v_j) = \mathbf{u_i}^{\intercal}(\mathbf{v_j} + \mathbf{r_k}) \quad (1)$$

As seen in Equation 1, we co-embed all nodes in $\mathcal{G}$ by translating the tail node by the specific relation vector and scoring their respective embedded representations via dot product. The task is then formulated as an edge (or link) prediction task. We consume the input graph $\mathcal{G}$ as a set of (node, relation, node) triplets of the form (u, r, v) which represent a link between nodes in the graph. The embedding training objective is to find node and relation representations that are useful for predicting which nodes are linked via that specific relation. While a softmax is a natural formulation to edge prediction, it is impractical due to the cost of computing the normalization over a large vocabulary of nodes. Following previous methods (Mikolov et al., 2013; Goldberg and Levy, 2014), negative sampling, a simplification of noise-contrastive estimation, can be used to learn the parameters. We therefore maximize the following negative sampling objective,

$$\arg\max_{\mathbf{u},\mathbf{r},\mathbf{v}} \sum_{e\in\mathcal{G}} [\log\sigma(f(e)) + \sum_{e'\in N(e)} \log\sigma(-f(e'))] \quad (2)$$

where: $N(u,r,v) = \{(u,r,v') : v' \in \mathcal{I}\} \cup \{(u',r,v) : u' \in \mathcal{U}\}$. Equation 2 represents the log-likelihood of predicting a binary "real" or "fake" label for the set of edges in the network (real) along with a set of the "fake" negatively sampled edges. To maximize the objective, we learn $\mathbf{u}$, $\mathbf{r}$, and $\mathbf{v}$ parameters to differentiate positive edges from negative, unobserved edges. Negative edges are sampled by corrupting positive edges via replacing either the user or item in an edge pair with a negatively sampled user or item. As user-item interaction graphs are very sparse, randomly corrupting an edge in the graph is very likely to be a 'negative' edge absent from the graph.

3.2 Enriching Language Model with NTU Embeddings

In this section, we explain how we integrate these embeddings into a language model. We build on the LMSOC framework (Kulkarni et al., 2021) to append NTU embeddings into the MLM model. However, unlike LMSOC, which has only one context embedding, we now may have multiple NTU embeddings for a given Tweet. Taking the example above, the NTUs for the Tweet are $user1$, $WNUT$, $user2$, $user3$, $user4$, $user5$, $\#nlproc$, $\#socialmedia$. For our experiments we only limit ourselves to author and hashtag NTUs, i.e. $user1$, $\#nlproc$, $\#socialmedia$. This leads to a choice we have to make for integrating these NTU embeddings into the Tweet text. For this work we simply utilize the average of the NTU embeddings to keep it aligned with the LMSOC framework. In future we also plan to experiment with the social contexts used in LMSOC.

Our final NTU embedding for the Tweet becomes the average embeddings of all NTUs in the Tweet. Let us denote it by e_{ntu}. We concatenate this embedding to the BERT's subword embedding. For NTUs not present in our NTU embeddings we use the average embedding of all the NTUs in our embedding table as a placeholder embedding. We found using the average as opposed to a zero embedding was much more beneficial for downstream task improvements. Furthermore, for Tweets which have no NTUs we also use the average NTU embedding as a placeholder embedding. Given a Tweet text, we tokenize it using the language model tokenizer into a list of subwords, we extract the subword embeddings from the model to get a list of subword embeddings. Lets call these subword embeddings $[s_0, s_1, s_2, ..., s_n]$.

Since, e_{ntu} and s_i are of different embedding sizes, we use a linear layer to project e_{ntu} in the space of s_i and get s_{ntu}. This linear layer is jointly trained during MLM fine-tuning. We do not add a position embedding to the NTU and we do not add a type embedding to the NTU. Finally, we get a new list of embeddings of the Tweet i.e. $S = [s_0, s_1, s_2, ..., s_n, s_{ntu}]$. We feed these embedding to the next layers of a pre-trained Language model. We call this model a NTU enriched Language Model (`NTULM`).

The above model is then trained using the Masked Language Modeling (MLM) task similar to BERT model (Devlin et al., 2018). We use the same setup for training via the MLM objective by masking 15% of the tokens. This translates to the model learning to predict the missing words by using the NTU's context.

While our approach is agnostic to the choice of encoder, for all our experiments we train based on a `bert-base-uncased` model using the HuggingFace Transformers library.[1] We train the models till convergence for a max of 15 epochs on a dataset of 1M English Tweets (see appendix B).

3.3 NTU-enriched Text Embeddings

Once the above model is trained, we use it in downstream tasks. Traditionally pre-trained language models are utilized in downstream tasks is by fine-tuning. However, this setup is not suitable for low-cost inference where multiple downstream models utilize the Tweet features, as doing inference on the full large-scale language model is expensive and doing inference of multiple BERT models is prohibitive. Furthermore, having a single Tweet embedding for all downstream tasks trades off accuracy for computing cost and allows the usage of

[1] `https://huggingface.co/bert-base-uncased`

caching of these Tweet embeddings for multiple downstream tasks. Motivated by this we generate fixed-size Tweet embedding which integrates Text and NTU information. We compare it with a text-only Tweet embedding. We refer to these embeddings as $\texttt{embed}_{ntulm}$ embeddings. Given input embeddings $S = [s_0, s_1, s_2, ..., s_n, s_{ntu}]$ we pass it through a language model which outputs $Z = [z_0, z_1, z_2, ..., z_n, z_{ntu}]$ embeddings. Our `NTULM` embedding is the average of z_i embeddings, i.e. $\texttt{embed}_{ntulm} = \frac{\sum_i z_i}{size(Z)}$. We feed these embedding as input to the downstream models and add a set of MLP layers on top to get the final prediction for each downstream model discussed in the experiments below. Note, that during downstream task training the `NTULM` is frozen and not updated.

4 Experiments

We conduct experiments on a variety of datasets and downstream tasks to highlight the utility of `NTULM`. Additionally, we perform an ablation to measure the contribution of each type of NTU to the overall `NTULM` performance.

4.1 Downstream Datasets

In order to evaluate the performance of our models, we select the following downstream datasets. We choose classification datasets for all our evaluations. The statistics about our datasets can be found in Table 5 in appendix.

Topic Prediction We use a dataset of Tweets annotated with Topics as described in (Kulkarni et al., 2022). This dataset consists of each Tweet annotated with a set of topics. The task is defined as: given a topic-based Tweet, retrieve tweets from the same topic. The final evaluation is based on Mean Average Precision (MAP).

Hashtag Prediction We use a dataset of 1M Tweets with Hashtags. The Hashtag prediction task is formulated as removing a single Hashtag from the Tweet and trying to predict using the remaining information in a multi-class classification task. For this task, we consider the top 1000 Hashtags as prediction classes and remove them from the Tweets containing these Hashtags. We use an equal number of Tweets for each Hashtag for our training and test sets. We evaluate the performance of `NTULM` and baselines using Recall @ 10.

SemEval Sentiment We use the SemEval Sentiment dataset from 2017. This dataset is released in the form of Tweet Ids and labels. We hydrate the Tweet ids using the public Twitter Academic API and fetch the author, Hashtags, and Tweet text from the API response. Because of the deletion of many Tweet ids we can not compare our results with previous baselines hence our only comparison is with the BERT-based baseline we consider. We use the macro F1 score as well. The SemEval dataset consists of three tasks. Task A consists of multi-class sentiment classification where given a Tweet we need to predict the label among positive, negative, and neutral. Task BD consists of topic-based sentiment prediction using only two classes positive, and negative. Task CE consists of Tweet quantification where we need to predict sentiment across a 5-point scale. For topic-based sentiment, we concatenate the topic keyword at the end of the Tweet text to convert it into a text-based classification problem. SemEval comes in data split across years from 2013 to 2017. We evaluate our models on train test splits from each year to assess the temporal stability of our model. We mark yearly evaluation as SemEval 1 and aggregate task evaluation as SemEval 2 in our results.

SocialMediaIE Social Media IE (Mishra, 2021, 2019, 2020) (SMIE) is a collection of datasets specific for evaluation of Information Extraction Systems for Social Media. It consists of datasets of classification and sequence tagging tasks (Mishra, 2019). We utilize the classification tasks from Social Media IE and use them for our evaluation. We use the macro-F1 score for each task. Similar to SemEval this dataset is also released as a set of Tweet IDs and labels, hence we hydrate it using the same approach as SemEval dataset.

TweetEval TweetEval (Barbieri et al., 2020) was released as a benchmark of classification tasks for Tweets. It consists of anonymized Tweet texts without Tweet Ids. The Tweet text has been anonymized by removing user mentions. This limits us to only use Hashtag-based NTUs for this dataset but we include this dataset to highlight the utility of our approach on this standard benchmark.

4.2 MLM Fine-tuning

We start by fine-tuning the BERT and `NTULM` models on 1M Tweet data randomly sampled from latest English tweets posted between 2022-06-01 and 2022-06-15. We experiment with training using different contexts. We only consider the inclusion

Model	NTUs	Perplexity bits	Topic MAP	TweetEval mean F1	SemEval 1 mean F1	SemEval 2 mean F1	Hashtag Recall@10	SMIE mean F1
BERT	-	4.425	0.327	0.577	0.527	0.515	0.689	0.548
NTULM	**author**	4.412	0.325	0.579	0.527	**0.548**	0.693	0.548
NTULM	**Hashtag**	4.391	0.339	0.586	0.534	0.545	0.711	0.539
NTULM	**author+Hashtag**	**4.344**	**0.343**	**0.590**	**0.534**	0.545	**0.720**	**0.549**

Table 2: NTULM compared with BERT (MLM fine-tuned, section 4.2). We report the perplexity, mean average precision (MAP) in Topic, Recall@10 in Hashtag Prediction, and mean F1 score in the rest.

of author and Hashtag contexts as they are the highest coverage contexts across all the datasets. User mentions are few and, in most datasets, they are anonymized. In MLM fine-tuning, we keep all the hyperparameters of NTULM model the same as the BERT baselines.

4.3 Downstream Task Evaluation

For each task we feed the unified NTULM embedding $embed_{\text{NTULM}}$ into a 2-layer perceptron (MLP) with the final layer being a softmax over possible labels. For topic classification, we use a sigmoid activation for multiple labels. We use the task-specific evaluation to compare the model. We report aggregate improvement on each dataset using the average of metrics for each task in the dataset. Often we report the percentage gains over the BERT model, i.e. $\frac{score_{\text{NTULM}} - score_{BERT}}{score_{BERT}} * 100$, this is positive when NTULM is better than BERT. It denotes the percentage NTULM is better or worse than the BERT model. Absolute scores are in table 3. In the experiments of downstream tasks, we keep MLP architectures and hyper-parameters the same for NTULM and baselines.

5 Evaluation Results

5.1 Perplexity Experiments

As highlighted in Table 2 we find that the MLM perplexity (lower is better) of all the NTULM models is much better than the perplexity of the BERT-based model. In terms of percentage change, NTULM (author+Hashtag) has about 2% gain in perplexity than the BERT model. This highlights that using contextual information helps improve the MLM task performance. This result is aligned with the findings of LMSOC (Kulkarni et al., 2021) that also found that using temporal and geographic context leads to better language modeling. Our work highlights that the graph context of authors and Hashtags encodes additional information which

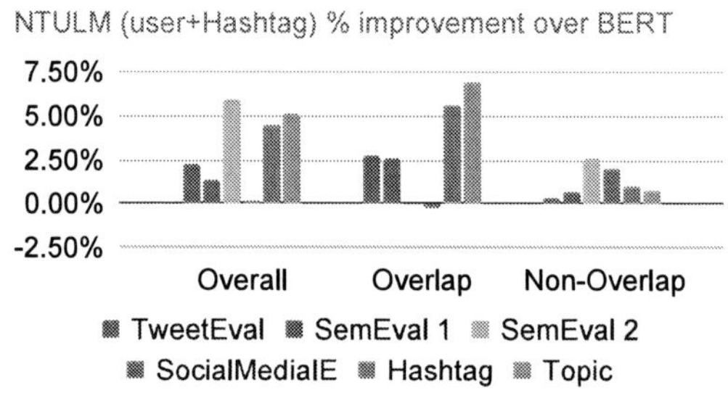

Figure 3: NTULM versus BERT (MLM fine-tuned see section 4.2) on Tweets with and without NTU overlap with NTU embeddings. See Table 4 for details.

can help in better modeling of the text. We also observe that the Hashtag and author information alone is helpful in lowering the perplexity of the model with Hashtags being more effective. This is also aligned with the usage of Hashtags. Authors on Twitter often use Hashtags to supply topical or community information to a Tweet. Hence, using a Hashtag's graph information improves the model's prediction of the masked words.

5.2 Downstream Classification

Now we look at how the NTULM model performs across various downstream tasks. As highlighted in Table 2 (detailed numbers in Table 3), we see that enriching text with NTU information from author+Hashtag always leads to significant performance improvement over BERT fine-tuned using MLM pre-training on the same dataset as NTULM as explained in section 4.2. Specifically, the author+Hashtag NTULM model is 5% better than BERT on Topic prediction, 2% better on TweetEval, 6% better on SemEval 1, 4.5% better on SemEval 2, and 0.2% better on SocialMediaIE.

Furthermore, we assess how the model's performance changes compared to BERT for Tweets which have NTUs overlapping (Overlap) with our NTU embeddings versus those which do not have

Dataset	Sub-Dataset or Metric	BERT	NTULM user	NTULM hashtag	NTULM user+hashtag	BERT post-concat	Best
Topic	**topic**	32.65%	32.49%	33.91%	34.32%	**38.76%**	BERT-post-concat
Hashtag	**recall@10**	68.88%	69.26%	71.09%	71.99%	**72.23%**	BERT-post-concat
TweetEval	**emoji**	18.02%	18.10%	18.44%	18.55%	**19.07%**	BERT-post-concat
TweetEval	**emotion**	**67.70%**	67.65%	66.61%	67.31%	67.60%	BERT
TweetEval	**hate**	**59.50%**	58.59%	56.87%	58.16%	57.83%	BERT
TweetEval	**irony**	60.37%	62.03%	**66.67%**	66.17%	58.88%	NTULM (hashtag)
TweetEval	**offensive**	72.51%	72.73%	**73.71%**	73.63%	71.52%	NTULM (hashtag)
TweetEval	**sentiment**	60.66%	61.40%	60.66%	**61.43%**	58.65%	NTULM (user+hashtag)
TweetEval	**stance**	64.88%	65.11%	67.48%	**67.56%**	66.89%	NTULM (user+hashtag)
SemEval 1	**2013-A**	67.75%	67.61%	67.94%	**68.38%**	67.54%	NTULM (user+hashtag)
SemEval 1	**2014-A**	26.80%	26.06%	**27.96%**	26.91%	27.48%	NTULM (hashtag)
SemEval 1	**2015-A**	53.70%	53.73%	**54.63%**	54.63%	53.31%	NTULM (hashtag)
SemEval 1	**2015-BD**	41.17%	41.36%	40.45%	41.08%	**41.61%**	BERT-post-concat
SemEval 1	**2016-A**	51.38%	52.52%	53.01%	**53.70%**	51.50%	NTULM (user+hashtag)
SemEval 1	**2016-BD**	92.60%	92.65%	**92.71%**	92.56%	92.58%	NTULM (hashtag)
SemEval 1	**2016-CE**	35.58%	35.20%	**36.86%**	36.74%	35.25%	NTULM (hashtag)
SemEval 2	**task-A**	48.02%	47.91%	47.54%	**49.72%**	48.71%	NTULM (user+hashtag)
SemEval 2	**task-BD**	71.56%	71.92%	71.95%	**72.59%**	71.33%	NTULM (user+hashtag)
SemEval 2	**task-CE**	34.83%	34.69%	**34.95%**	33.92%	34.71%	NTULM (hashtag)
SMIE	**abusive 1**	55.84%	**56.27%**	55.08%	55.69%	54.04%	NTULM (user)
SMIE	**abusive 2**	47.36%	47.04%	44.82%	**48.00%**	37.01%	NTULM (user+hashtag)
SMIE	**sentiment 1**	**76.01%**	74.52%	74.73%	75.14%	73.93%	BERT
SMIE	**sentiment 2**	61.86%	**62.20%**	61.70%	61.92%	61.61%	NTULM (user)
SMIE	**sentiment 3**	58.69%	58.73%	**58.80%**	58.43%	58.70%	NTULM (hashtag)
SMIE	**sentiment 4**	53.78%	54.75%	55.68%	56.48%	**57.23%**	BERT-post-concat
SMIE	**sentiment 5**	**60.22%**	59.65%	59.86%	59.77%	57.99%	BERT
SMIE	**sentiment 6**	59.66%	59.58%	**60.15%**	59.81%	59.43%	NTULM (hashtag)
SMIE	**uncertainity 1**	55.37%	55.81%	51.52%	56.00%	**57.14%**	BERT-post-concat
SMIE	**uncertainity 2**	19.03%	19.05%	16.80%	17.63%	**19.11%**	BERT-post-concat

Table 3: Absolute metrics across all tasks and their subtasks. **Best score** and Second best score. SMIE=SocialMediaIE, BERTC=BERT-post-concat with user+Hashtag NTUs, BERT=BERT (MLM fine-tuned, section 4.2).

Dataset	Overall		Overlap		Non-Overlap	
	NTULM	BERTC	NTULM	BERTC	NTULM	BERTC
TweetEval	2.27%	-0.80%	2.73%	-3.33%	0.31%	0.65%
SemEval 1	1.36%	0.08%	2.59%	0.21%	0.65%	0.02%
SemEval 2	5.93%	0.22%	-0.07%	0.58%	2.62%	0.07%
SocialMediaIE	0.20%	-2.12%	-0.27%	-4.12%	1.98%	-22.22%
Hashtag	4.51%	4.87%	5.61%	7.46%	1.01%	-3.37%
Topic	5.10%	18.72%	6.92%	34.72%	0.71%	-4.17%

Table 4: % improvement over BERT (MLM fine-tuned see section 4.2) by using user+Hashtag NTUs in NTULM versus BERT-post-concat (BERTC) across datasets, and split across overlapping and non-overlapping subsets.

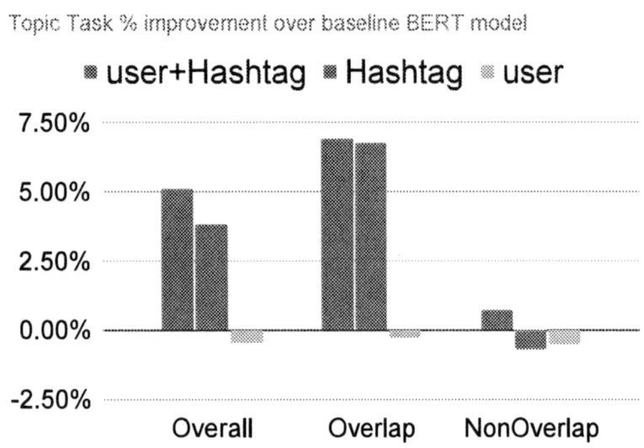

Figure 4: Performance on Tweets with and without NTU overlap with NTU embeddings on Topic prediction task. BERT is MLM fine-tuned see section 4.2.

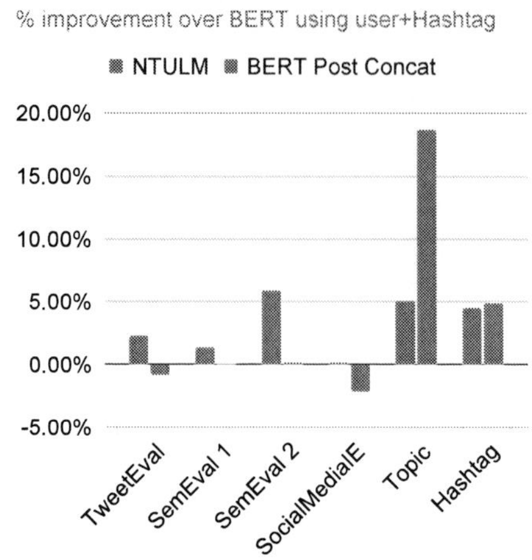

Figure 5: NTULM versus BERT-post-concat as measured in improvement over BERT (MLM fine-tuned see section 4.2) across tasks.

Tweets overlapping with the NTU embeddings (Non-overlap). Our focus here is that for Tweets with NTU overlap we should see significant improvement wherease for Tweets without NTU overlap we should not change our performance compared to BERT as we are back to the text-only setting. As highlighted in Figure 3 and Figure 4 we see that the improvement over BERT on the overlap case is higher than the overall improvement for the author+Hashtag NTULM across most tasks. Furthermore, in the no-overlap case, we do not see any significant loss in performance, in fact author+Hashtag is slightly better compared to BERT (0.7%). This highlights that the NTU contexts are really helping in the downstream tasks whenever the NTUs are available.

5.3 Case-study: Concatenation vs Attention

Next, we consider the setting of concatenating the NTU embeddings to BERT embeddings. This is a simple setting where the language model is not able to generate a Text specific embedding based on NTUs. This is a simple baseline which is often adopted when integrating signals from multiple sources. We name this model BERT-post-concat and compare it with our best model NTULM (author+Hashtag). Here again we compare these models against the BERT model which only uses text and was was MLM fine-tuned as explained in section 4.2.

Figure 5 (detailed numbers in Table 3) highlights that using the NTULM approach is much better than BERT-post-concat for most tasks, except for topic and Hashtag prediction. For Hashtag dataset NTULM is only 0.34% worse in relative performance compared to BERT-post-concat. However, in the topic prediction task NTULM is -11.5% worse. We hypothesize that the improved performance of BERT-post-concat is a result of the direct relevance of Hashtag embeddings to the dowstream task of Topic and Hashtag relevance as NTULM's frozen embedding dilutes this information. We confirm this by inspecting the performance (see Table 4) of BERT-post-concat on the overlapping and non-overlapping slices of the data, where BERT post-concat is better than NTULM on the overlapping slice of the data but is worse than NTULM and even BERT on the non-overlapping slice. This highlights that BERT post-concat is overfitting to the NTU signal in the data which is not the case with NTULM. We reason that fine-tuning NTULM for the downstream task may address this issue and plan to explore this in a future work given that the focus of this work is to generate high quality general purpose Tweet embeddings. Furthermore, for TweetEval and SocialMediaIE BERT post-concat performs even worse than BERT. This can be attributed to the indirect relevance of author and Hashtag identity to the downstream tasks in these datasets which the BERT-post-concat cannot capture.

6 Related Work

Knowledge Graph and Language Models: Previous work has investigated language models with knowledge graphs. KI-BERT (Faldu et al., 2021) extracts and computes the embedding of concepts and ambiguous entities from text and appends them to the end of the sentence to enrich a language model. K-BERT (Liu et al., 2020) uses an external knowledge graph to build a sentence tree and integrates the knowledge graph before the embedding layer of BERT. KEPLER (Wang et al., 2021) incorporates knowledge embedding of text entities as an auxiliary objective alongside the traditional MLM objective for BERT. While these models have shown improvements on some domain-specific tasks, they only consider the textual entities from the text itself, which limits their performance in modeling language with rich contextual information (e.g. social networks). Different from existing works, the `NTULM` framework can incorporate the contextual information of multi-type non-textual units and therefore has a better performance in understanding contexts. There are also some existing works that use social contexts to enrich the language model, such as LMSOC (Kulkarni et al., 2021). However, instead of considering the non-text units such as author, Hashtag, URL, and mention, LMSOC only considers time and location. In addition, LMSOC only supports incorporating one type of social context, which limits its performance on texts with rich contexts.

Representation Learning of Social Graph: Learning the representation of social entities such as tweets and users has been a popular research topic over the past few years. InfoVGAE (Li et al., 2022) constructs a bipartite heterogeneous graph and designs an orthogonal latent space to learn explainable user and tweet embeddings. In kNN-Embed (El-Kishky et al., 2022b), a bi-partite Twitter follow graph is embedded for account suggestion. TIMME (Xiao et al., 2020) uses multi-task learning of link prediction and entity classification to jointly learn the representation of tweets. SEM (Pougué-Biyong et al., 2022) creates a topical Twitter agreement graph and embeds nodes via a random-walk approach to detect user stances on given topics. (Zhang et al., 2022) proposes a second-order continuous GNN to improve the social network embeddings. Most of these models do not consider textual information of social graph. Only the interaction data is applied to learn the representation of social entities, which limits their performance on downstream tasks.

Language Model for Social Networks: Many existing works have explored the training of language models in the social network domain. Tweet2vec (Vosoughi et al., 2016) proposes a character-level CNN-LSTM encoder-decoder to improve the tweet embeddings. DICE (Naseem and Musial, 2019) leverages contextual text to address polysemy and improve the tweet embedding quality. TweeTIME (Tabassum et al., 2016) proposes a minimally supervised method to address the time recognition problem from Twitter texts. TweetBERT (Qudar and Mago, 2020) models are trained on the domain-specific data of tweet texts and outperform traditional BERT models. However, most of these language model does not take NTUs into consideration and cannot benefit from the interaction and engagement data.

7 Limitations

One major limitation of our work is the averaging of heterogenous embeddings. This approach works because the embeddings trained using TransE lie in the same space but is less expressive as we are not including explicit information around which type of NTU an embedding is coming from. In future we plan to address this by including type specific embedding transformation before doing an averaging. However, given the results, this naive averaging of user+Hashtag still works well across tasks it shows the utility of our approach. Next, our training data is relatively small and less diverse with only 1M Tweets as budgetary and computational constraints influenced our experimental setup. In this paper, our goal has been to demonstrate the effectiveness of our approach paving the way for future work that scales up the training and uses a much larger and more diverse dataset. Finally, our results are on English specific datasets and models. While the utilization of NTU embeddings make our approach language agnostic, in future we plan to demonstrate its impact across multiple languages.

8 Conclusion

In this paper we introduced NTU enriched Language Model (`NTULM`), a method of enriching a pretrained BERT model by adding graph embeddings of non-textual units. We experimentally demonstrate that including NTU representations alongside text yields superior representations vs a text-only language model. On several downstream tasks, we show significant improvment using `NTULM` representations compared to BERT-based sentence embeddings.

References

Francesco Barbieri, Jose Camacho-Collados, Luis Espinosa Anke, and Leonardo Neves. 2020. TweetEval: Unified benchmark and comparative evaluation for tweet classification. In *Findings of the Association for Computational Linguistics: EMNLP 2020*, pages 1644–1650, Online. Association for Computational Linguistics.

Antoine Bordes, Nicolas Usunier, Alberto Garcia-Duran, Jason Weston, and Oksana Yakhnenko. 2013. Translating embeddings for modeling multi-relational data. *Advances in neural information processing systems*, 26.

Jacob Devlin, Ming-Wei Chang, Kenton Lee, and Kristina Toutanova. 2018. Bert: Pre-training of deep bidirectional transformers for language understanding. *arXiv preprint arXiv:1810.04805*.

Ahmed El-Kishky, Michael Bronstein, Ying Xiao, and Aria Haghighi. 2022a. Graph-based representation learning for web-scale recommender systems. In *Proceedings of the 28th ACM SIGKDD Conference on Knowledge Discovery and Data Mining*, pages 4784–4785.

Ahmed El-Kishky, Thomas Markovich, Kenny Leung, Frank Portman, and Aria Haghighi. 2022b. knn-embed: Locally smoothed embedding mixtures for multi-interest candidate retrieval. *arXiv preprint arXiv:2205.06205*.

Ahmed El-Kishky, Thomas Markovich, Serim Park, Chetan Verma, Baekjin Kim, Ramy Eskander, Yury Malkov, Frank Portman, Sofía Samaniego, Ying Xiao, and Aria Haghighi. 2022c. Twhin: Embedding the twitter heterogeneous information network for personalized recommendation.

Keyur Faldu, Amit Sheth, Prashant Kikani, and Hemang Akbari. 2021. Ki-bert: Infusing knowledge context for better language and domain understanding. *arXiv preprint arXiv:2104.08145*.

Yoav Goldberg and Omer Levy. 2014. word2vec explained: deriving mikolov et al.'s negative-sampling word-embedding method. *CoRR*, abs/1402.3722.

Dirk Hovy. 2015. Demographic factors improve classification performance. In *Proceedings of the 53rd Annual Meeting of the Association for Computational Linguistics and the 7th International Joint Conference on Natural Language Processing (Volume 1: Long Papers)*, pages 752–762, Beijing, China. Association for Computational Linguistics.

Vivek Kulkarni, Kenny Leung, and Aria Haghighi. 2022. CTM - a model for large-scale multi-view tweet topic classification. In *Proceedings of the 2022 Conference of the North American Chapter of the Association for Computational Linguistics: Human Language Technologies: Industry Track*, pages 247–258, Hybrid: Seattle, Washington + Online. Association for Computational Linguistics.

Vivek Kulkarni, Shubhanshu Mishra, and Aria Haghighi. 2021. LMSOC: An approach for socially sensitive pretraining. In *Findings of the Association for Computational Linguistics: EMNLP 2021*, pages 2967–2975, Punta Cana, Dominican Republic. Association for Computational Linguistics.

Jinning Li, Huajie Shao, Dachun Sun, Ruijie Wang, Yuchen Yan, Jinyang Li, Shengzhong Liu, Hanghang Tong, and Tarek Abdelzaher. 2022. Unsupervised belief representation learning with information-theoretic variational graph auto-encoders. In *Proceedings of the 45th International ACM SIGIR Conference on Research and Development in Information Retrieval*, SIGIR '22, page 1728–1738, New York, NY, USA. Association for Computing Machinery.

Weijie Liu, Peng Zhou, Zhe Zhao, Zhiruo Wang, Qi Ju, Haotang Deng, and Ping Wang. 2020. K-bert: Enabling language representation with knowledge graph. In *Proceedings of the AAAI Conference on Artificial Intelligence*, volume 34, pages 2901–2908.

Mounica Maddela, Wei Xu, and Daniel Preoţiuc-Pietro. 2019. Multi-task pairwise neural ranking for hashtag segmentation. *arXiv preprint arXiv:1906.00790*.

Tomas Mikolov, Ilya Sutskever, Kai Chen, Greg S Corrado, and Jeff Dean. 2013. Distributed Representations of Words and Phrases and their Compositionality. In *Advances in Neural Information Processing Systems*, volume 26. Curran Associates, Inc.

Shubhanshu Mishra. 2019. Multi-dataset-multi-task neural sequence tagging for information extraction from tweets. In *Proceedings of the 30th ACM Conference on Hypertext and Social Media*, HT '19, page 283–284, New York, NY, USA. Association for Computing Machinery.

Shubhanshu Mishra. 2020. *Information extraction from digital social trace data with applications to social media and scholarly communication data*. Ph.D. thesis, University of Illinois at Urbana-Champaign.

Shubhanshu Mishra. 2021. Information extraction from digital social trace data with applications to social media and scholarly communication data. *SIGWEB Newsl.*, (Spring).

Shubhanshu Mishra and Jana Diesner. 2018. Detecting the correlation between sentiment and user-level as well as text-level meta-data from benchmark corpora. In *Proceedings of the 29th on Hypertext and Social Media*, HT '18, page 2–10, New York, NY, USA. Association for Computing Machinery.

Usman Naseem and Katarzyna Musial. 2019. Dice: Deep intelligent contextual embedding for twitter sentiment analysis. In *2019 International conference on document analysis and recognition (ICDAR)*, pages 953–958. IEEE.

Dong Nguyen, A Seza Doğruöz, Carolyn P Rosé, and Franciska De Jong. 2016. Computational sociolinguistics: A survey. *Computational linguistics*, 42(3):537–593.

John Pougué-Biyong, Akshay Gupta, Aria Haghighi, and Ahmed El-Kishky. 2022. Learning stance embeddings from signed social graphs. *arXiv preprint arXiv:2201.11675*.

Mohiuddin Md Abdul Qudar and Vijay Mago. 2020. Tweetbert: a pretrained language representation model for twitter text analysis. *arXiv preprint arXiv:2010.11091*.

Lin Sun, Jiquan Wang, Yindu Su, Fangsheng Weng, Yuxuan Sun, Zengwei Zheng, and Yuanyi Chen. 2020. Riva: a pre-trained tweet multimodal model based on text-image relation for multimodal ner. In *Proceedings of the 28th International Conference on Computational Linguistics*, pages 1852–1862.

Jeniya Tabassum, Alan Ritter, and Wei Xu. 2016. Tweetime: A minimally supervised method for recognizing and normalizing time expressions in twitter. *arXiv preprint arXiv:1608.02904*.

Soroush Vosoughi, Prashanth Vijayaraghavan, and Deb Roy. 2016. Tweet2vec: Learning tweet embeddings using character-level cnn-lstm encoder-decoder. In *Proceedings of the 39th International ACM SIGIR conference on Research and Development in Information Retrieval*, pages 1041–1044.

Xiaozhi Wang, Tianyu Gao, Zhaocheng Zhu, Zhengyan Zhang, Zhiyuan Liu, Juanzi Li, and Jian Tang. 2021. Kepler: A unified model for knowledge embedding and pre-trained language representation. *Transactions of the Association for Computational Linguistics*, 9:176–194.

Zhiping Xiao, Weiping Song, Haoyan Xu, Zhicheng Ren, and Yizhou Sun. 2020. Timme: Twitter ideology-detection via multi-task multi-relational embedding. In *KDD*, pages 2258–2268.

Michihiro Yasunaga, Jure Leskovec, and Percy Liang. 2022. Linkbert: Pretraining language models with document links. *arXiv preprint arXiv:2203.15827*.

Yanfu Zhang, Shangqian Gao, Jian Pei, and Heng Huang. 2022. Improving social network embedding via new second-order continuous graph neural networks. In *Proceedings of the 28th ACM SIGKDD Conference on Knowledge Discovery and Data Mining*, KDD '22, page 2515–2523, New York, NY, USA. Association for Computing Machinery.

A Appendix: Dataset Statistics

Here we provide the statistics of our datasets for downstream evaluation experiments in Table 5.

			Hashtag				User			
dataset	**task split**	**Tweets**	**NTUs**	**>1 NTUs**	**>1 ∈ E**	**∈ E**	**NTUs**	**>1 NTUs**	**>1 ∈ E**	**∈ E**
TweetEval	emoji train	45,000	28,251	46.37%	42.82%	92%	0	0.00%	0.00%	0%
TweetEval	emoji test	50,000	30,989	43.10%	39.68%	92%	0	0.00%	0.00%	0%
TweetEval	emotion train	3,257	1,652	43.94%	43.14%	98%	0	0.00%	0.00%	0%
TweetEval	emotion test	1,421	1,071	47.29%	46.94%	99%	0	0.00%	0.00%	0%
TweetEval	hate train	9,000	2,375	25.69%	25.10%	98%	0	0.00%	0.00%	0%
TweetEval	hate test	2,970	1,615	50.20%	49.70%	99%	0	0.00%	0.00%	0%
TweetEval	irony train	2,862	2,132	38.36%	36.09%	94%	0	0.00%	0.00%	0%
TweetEval	irony test	784	857	72.19%	71.30%	99%	0	0.00%	0.00%	0%
TweetEval	offensive train	11,916	1,937	14.40%	14.10%	98%	0	0.00%	0.00%	0%
TweetEval	offensive test	860	1,276	73.26%	71.28%	97%	0	0.00%	0.00%	0%
TweetEval	sentiment train	45,615	6,956	18.35%	16.63%	91%	0	0.00%	0.00%	0%
TweetEval	sentiment test	12,284	3,933	39.14%	37.63%	96%	0	0.00%	0.00%	0%
TweetEval	stance 1 train	587	455	95.91%	95.91%	100%	0	0.00%	0.00%	0%
TweetEval	stance 1 test	280	277	100.00%	100.00%	100%	0	0.00%	0.00%	0%
TweetEval	stance 2 train	461	423	100.00%	100.00%	100%	0	0.00%	0.00%	0%
TweetEval	stance 2 test	220	251	100.00%	100.00%	100%	0	0.00%	0.00%	0%
TweetEval	stance 3 train	355	416	100.00%	100.00%	100%	0	0.00%	0.00%	0%
TweetEval	stance 3 test	169	201	100.00%	100.00%	100%	0	0.00%	0.00%	0%
TweetEval	stance 4 train	597	353	100.00%	100.00%	100%	0	0.00%	0.00%	0%
TweetEval	stance 4 test	285	198	100.00%	100.00%	100%	0	0.00%	0.00%	0%
TweetEval	stance 5 train	620	407	97.10%	97.10%	100%	0	0.00%	0.00%	0%
TweetEval	stance 5 test	295	201	100.00%	100.00%	100%	0	0.00%	0.00%	0%
Topic	topic train	100,000	57,873	38.59%	38.25%	99%	89,091	100.00%	14.05%	14%
Topic	topic test	20,000	17,122	38.26%	37.90%	99%	19,006	100.00%	14.19%	14%
Hashtag	hashtag train	899,606	282,603	70.92%	70.49%	99%	392,751	100.00%	9.76%	10%
Hashtag	hashtag test	100,372	64,939	70.64%	70.23%	99%	67,903	100.00%	9.65%	10%
SemEval	2013-A train	7,110	1,599	20.03%	17.86%	89%	9,069	100.00%	23.52%	24%
SemEval	2013-A test	2,284	573	20.53%	18.13%	88%	2,814	100.00%	24.87%	25%
SemEval	2014-A train	30	14	100.00%	96.67%	97%	49	100.00%	16.67%	17%
SemEval	2014-A test	1,253	254	16.12%	13.89%	86%	1,563	100.00%	26.18%	26%
SemEval	2015-A train	318	71	22.33%	20.75%	93%	412	100.00%	20.75%	21%
SemEval	2015-A test	1,461	329	20.88%	19.37%	93%	1,887	100.00%	21.15%	21%
SemEval	2015-BD train	316	71	22.47%	20.89%	93%	408	100.00%	20.57%	21%
SemEval	2015-BD test	1,454	333	21.05%	19.46%	92%	1,887	100.00%	21.18%	21%
SemEval	2016-A train	6,180	1,230	17.52%	15.95%	91%	7,775	100.00%	21.13%	21%
SemEval	2016-A test	12,754	1,932	19.53%	17.88%	92%	14,822	100.00%	20.31%	20%
SemEval	2016-BD train	4,404	977	18.35%	16.53%	90%	5,586	100.00%	22.48%	22%
SemEval	2016-BD test	6,494	1,079	19.16%	17.51%	91%	7,776	100.00%	21.40%	21%
SemEval	2016-CE train	6,180	1,230	17.52%	15.95%	91%	7,775	100.00%	21.13%	21%
SemEval	2016-CE test	12,754	1,932	19.53%	17.88%	92%	14,822	100.00%	20.31%	20%
SemEval	task-A train	31,019	5,296	19.32%	17.50%	91%	37,154	100.00%	21.82%	22%
SemEval	task-A test	4,609	1,483	28.77%	26.93%	94%	5,919	100.00%	17.40%	17%
SemEval	task-BD train	11,675	2,143	19.08%	17.40%	91%	14,245	100.00%	21.72%	22%
SemEval	task-BD test	2,324	656	26.25%	24.44%	93%	3,234	100.00%	16.70%	17%

Table 5 continued from previous page

dataset	task	split	Tweets	Hashtag NTUs	Hashtag >1 NTUs	Hashtag >1 ∈ E	Hashtag ∈ E	User NTUs	User >1 NTUs	User >1 ∈ E	User ∈ E
SemEval	task-CE	train	18,887	3,009	18.88%	17.25%	91%	22,223	100.00%	20.59%	21%
SemEval	task-CE	test	4,606	1,485	28.90%	27.05%	94%	5,914	100.00%	17.41%	17%
SMIE	abusive 1	train	32,997	11,177	30.06%	27.98%	93%	48,619	100.00%	23.81%	24%
SMIE	abusive 1	test	9,070	3,619	29.49%	27.67%	94%	14,272	100.00%	23.24%	23%
SMIE	abusive 2	train	8,859	1,015	36.12%	35.22%	98%	4,109	100.00%	21.01%	21%
SMIE	abusive 2	test	2,442	377	37.84%	36.45%	96%	1,602	100.00%	20.64%	21%
SMIE	sentiment 1	train	6,543	999	15.77%	13.48%	85%	4,269	100.00%	27.31%	27%
SMIE	sentiment 1	test	1,813	378	15.00%	12.58%	84%	1,607	100.00%	27.74%	28%
SMIE	sentiment 2	train	20,679	4,430	18.48%	16.18%	88%	30,566	100.00%	28.58%	29%
SMIE	sentiment 2	test	5,719	1,398	18.57%	16.49%	89%	8,566	100.00%	28.66%	29%
SMIE	sentiment 3	train	3,601	775	100.00%	100.00%	100%	3,829	100.00%	15.16%	15%
SMIE	sentiment 3	test	1,007	299	99.90%	99.90%	100%	1,276	100.00%	14.60%	15%
SMIE	sentiment 4	train	558	194	98.75%	98.03%	99%	491	100.00%	21.15%	21%
SMIE	sentiment 4	test	557	161	99.64%	99.64%	100%	522	100.00%	15.26%	15%
SMIE	sentiment 5	train	1,575	27	95.11%	95.05%	100%	720	100.00%	23.94%	24%
SMIE	sentiment 5	test	444	17	97.52%	97.52%	100%	317	100.00%	22.75%	23%
SMIE	sentiment 6	train	9,616	2,052	19.21%	17.34%	90%	12,165	100.00%	22.56%	23%
SMIE	sentiment 6	test	17,347	2,879	19.66%	17.89%	91%	20,456	100.00%	21.05%	21%
SMIE	uncertainity 1	train	1,058	389	57.84%	56.71%	98%	1,390	100.00%	30.62%	31%
SMIE	uncertainity 1	test	314	128	59.55%	58.28%	98%	402	100.00%	25.80%	26%
SMIE	uncertainity 2	train	534	206	44.76%	43.07%	96%	620	100.00%	19.29%	19%
SMIE	uncertainity 2	test	145	65	36.55%	36.55%	100%	187	100.00%	15.86%	16%

Table 5: **Downstream Data Statistics**: **NTUs** means unique NTUs in the dataset, **>1 NTUs** means % Tweets with more than 1 NTU, **>1 ∈ E** is % Tweets with more than 1 NTU which exist in our Embeddings E, and **∈ E** is % Tweets having an NTU in E only across Tweets with an NTU. SMIE = SocialMediaIE.

B Training Details

All models were trained on NVIDIA A100 GPUs. Our context embedding size was 200. Models were trained for maximum of 15 epochs, using eary stopping via the eval dataset. We used the `adam_hf` optimizer in HuggingFace library [2] with default learning rate of `5e-5`.

Downstream models were trained with an 2 layer MLP on top of BERT or `NTULM` embeddings. MLP hidden layer has weight matrix of size $768 * 768$ with a $tanh$ activation. Final layer has size $768 * num\_classes$.

NTU embeddings were trained on 8 NVIDIA A100 GPUs using the following config: dimension=200, learning rate=0.05, epochs=10, batch size=100,000, batch negatives=500, uniform negatives=500, num partitions=1.

[2] `https://huggingface.co/docs/transformers/main_classes/trainer#transformers.TrainingArguments.optim`

Robust Candidate Generation for Entity Linking on Short Social Media Texts

Liam Hebert
University of Waterloo
l2hebert@uwaterloo.ca

Raheleh Makki
Twitter
rmakki@twitter.com

Shubhanshu Mishra
Twitter
smishra@twitter.com

Hamidreza Saghir
Twitter
hsaghir@twitter.com

Anusha Kamath
Twitter
akamath@twitter.com

Yuval Merhav
Twitter
ymerhav@twitter.com

Abstract

Entity Linking (EL) is the gateway into Knowledge Bases. Recent advances in EL utilize dense retrieval approaches for Candidate Generation, which addresses some of the shortcomings of the Lookup based approach of matching NER mentions against pre-computed dictionaries. In this work, we show that in the domain of Tweets, such methods suffer as users often include informal spelling, limited context, and lack of specificity, among other issues. We investigate these challenges on a large and recent Tweets benchmark for EL, empirically evaluate lookup and dense retrieval approaches, and demonstrate a hybrid solution using long contextual representation from Wikipedia is necessary to achieve considerable gains over previous work, achieving 0.93 recall.

1 Introduction

Entity Linking (EL) is the task of linking mentions to their corresponding entities in a Knowledge Base (KB) such as Wikidata. EL is commonly formulated in three sequential steps: Named Entity Recognition (NER), where mentions are identified, Candidate Generation, where a list of possible entity candidates is generated, and Entity Disambiguation, where a final candidate is selected.

Earlier EL works relied on alias tables (dictionary from strings to possible Wikidata entities; often associated with a score) and key-word based retrieval methods (Spitkovsky and Chang, 2012; Logeswaran et al., 2019; Pershina et al., 2015). However, these approaches suffer on noisy text, such as short-form Tweets. An example of a difficult Tweet would be "***Liam** is a gr8 ML Researcher*" where the desired span to link would be "Liam". Here, an alias-based approach would only retrieve entities based on the span "Liam", of which there are 8,350 different Wikidata entities containing that name. Without the context of "gr8 ML Researcher", it quickly becomes unfeasible to find the correct candidate. Furthermore, alias based approaches are also heavily dependent on the spans retrieved, where the retrieved span must be exactly present in the alias table in order to be found (Spitkovsky and Chang, 2012; Logeswaran et al., 2019; Pershina et al., 2015). This presents a challenge due to the difficulties of NER systems on noisy social media text (Lample et al., 2016; Mishra et al., 2020).

More recently, BERT-based dense entity retrieval approaches have shown to produce SOTA results on news datasets such as TACKBP-2010 and Mewsli-9 (Wu et al., 2020; FitzGerald et al., 2021; Botha et al., 2020). Dense retrieval approaches rely on relevant context around the mention, which is abundant in long and clean documents such as news, but often absent or brief in noisy and short user-generated text, such as that found on Twitter.

Prior works that focus on social media linking, such as Tweeki (Harandizadeh and Singh, 2020), used small, annotated datasets and did not study the more recent dense retrieval approaches.

Recently, Twitter researchers released an end-to-end entity linking benchmark for Tweets called TweetNERD. It is the largest and most temporally diverse open-sourced dataset benchmark on Tweets (Mishra et al., 2022). Excited by the availability of this benchmark, we study the application of recent linking methods on this large and noisy user generated data. We empirically evaluate sparse and dense retrieval approaches on this data and describe the challenges and design choices of building a robust linking system for Tweets.

Our main contributions are as follows: **(A)** To the best of our knowledge, we are the first study to compare dense retrieval, sparse retrieval, and lookup based approaches for Entity Linking in a social media setting, which makes our work relevant for the research community interested in processing noisy user generated text. **(B)** We assess the robustness of dense retrieval techniques in the presence of span detection errors coming from NER

Proceedings of the 2022 COLING Workshop: The 8th Workshop on Noisy User-generated Text (W-NUT 2022), pages 83–89

systems for social media text. This is a common problem for social media datasets as the top NER F1 score for social media datasets is significantly lower than other domains (Strauss et al., 2016). **(C)** We assess the impact of using short Wikidata entity descriptions against the longer Wikipedia descriptions for representing candidates, and highlight the significant loss in performance from using shorter descriptions for social media text. This is relevant as many recent dense retrieval methods for generic Entity Linking have proposed using short descriptions from Wikidata for candidate representations. **(D)** Our analysis is the first to explore sparse and dense retrieval on the largest and most temporally diverse Entity Linking dataset for Tweets called TweetNERD (Mishra et al., 2022). **(E)** Finally, through quantitative and qualitative analysis, we assert the complimentary nature of candidates generated by lookup and dense retrieval based approaches. This asserts the validity of our hybrid approach towards candidate generation and is reflected in significant performance improvement by using hybrid candidate generation for Entity Linking.

2 Methodology

2.1 Knowledge Base

To represent our KB, we followed prior work and retrieved a July 2022 download of English Wikipedia[1] (Wu et al., 2020; De Cao et al., 2020). However, Wikipedia also includes miscellaneous pages or pages that refer to multiple entities, such as disambiguation pages and "list of" pages. An example of such a page is "List of Birds of Canada" [2], which describes 696 distinct birds, each with their own respective Wikipedia page. To detect these pages, we retrieve the "instance of" category of each entity from Wikidata, which classifies each Wikipedia entity into distinct categories. Using this information, we reduce the entity set from 56.8M to 6.5M Wikidata entities.

2.2 Span Detection

We observe the performance of our systems utilizing the Gold Spans provided by TweetNERD (Table 1) and compare that to using NER-based spans that reflect a more realistic use-case. The NER model is trained on Tweets from TweetNERD and is similar to the models described in Lample et al. (2016); Mishra et al. (2020).

2.3 Candidate Generation

2.3.1 Dense Retrieval

Our dense retrieval approach retrieves candidates based on the similarity of tweet and entity embeddings. This is done by utilizing two separate language models to encode the semantic content of Tweets and Entities respectively. Our approach is motivated by Wu et al. (2020), which utilized a similar strategy on a clean news corpus. Given a Tweet t with mention span s and entity e^i, we create dense embeddings as

$$T^s = BERT_T([CLS]\ t_l^s\ [M_1]\ span^s\ [M_2]\ t_r^s) \tag{1}$$

$$E^i = BERT_E([CLS]\ title^i\ [M_3]\ desc^i) \tag{2}$$

where $BERT_T$ and $BERT_E$ are two separate language models, t_l^s and t_r^s refer to the text to the left and right of the desired mention span s, and $title^i$ and $desc^i$ are the Wikipedia title and first ten sentences of the respective entity page. Finally, $[M_1]$, $[M_2]$, $[M_3]$ are special tokens to denote the separation of each of the fields in the input.

Given these dense embeddings, we rank the pairing of entities e to Tweet t by computing the dot product between their corresponding CLS representations. During inference, we pre-compute the embeddings for every entity in our knowledge base and index them using fast k nearest neighbour search provided by FAISS (Johnson et al., 2021). We refer to this approach as Dense.

2.3.2 Sparse Retrieval

We utilize a traditional lookup-based approach for finding candidates as used by many prior works (Harandizadeh and Singh, 2020). Specifically, we map surface forms to Wikipedia page candidates from the English Wikipedia parse of DBPedia Spotlight and rank candidates given $p(entity|surfaceForm)$. We also include Wikidata aliases and labels as both have been found previously to be beneficial for identifying named entities (Mishra and Diesner, 2016; Singh et al., 2012; Mendes et al., 2011) and entity candidates in text (Mendes et al., 2011; Mishra et al., 2022; Singh et al., 2012). We refer to this approach as Lookup.

[1] This was the latest version at the time of writing

[2] https://en.wikipedia.org/wiki/List_of_birds_of_Canada

Table 1: Candidate Generation using Gold Spans (R@16)

Data Split	Dense	Lookup	BM25	Hybrid
Academic	0.783	0.741	0.221	**0.916**
OOD	0.772	0.847	0.556	**0.933**
Overall	0.779	0.717	0.362	**0.930**

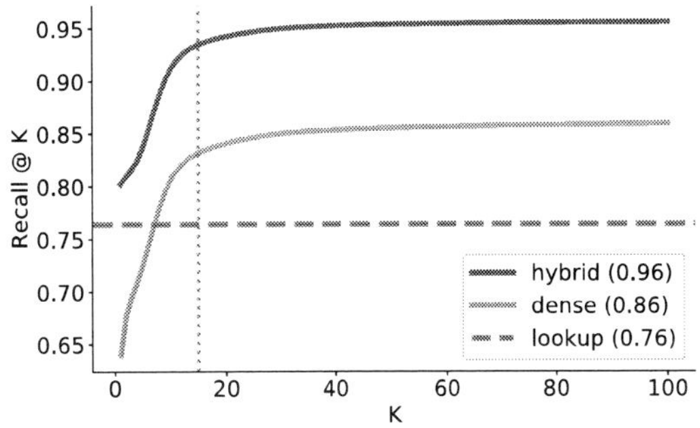

Figure 1: Recall @ K of Dense, Lookup and Hybrid using Gold Spans

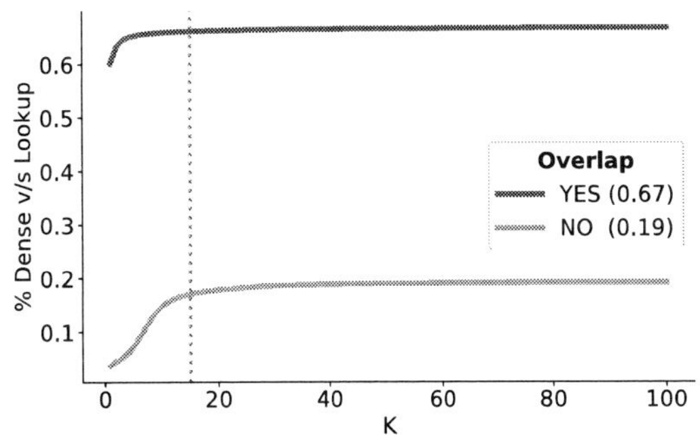

Figure 2: Overlap and Distinction of Dense v/s Lookup using Gold Spans

3 Results

3.1 Experimental Setup

We use TweetNERD for training and evaluation. It consists of 340K+ Tweets linked to entities in Wikidata (Mishra et al., 2022). We follow the authors' setup and evaluate on TweetNERD-Academic and TweetNERD-OOD (out of domain), while the rest of the data is used for training. For Dense retrieval we use pre-trained BLINK[3] encoders which are trained on Wikipedia text and FAISS (Johnson et al., 2021) for indexing candidate embeddings. We compare that to a Lookup based system (Section 2.3.2) and a BM25 baseline (Yang et al., 2018). For BM25, we utilize Wikipedia abstracts as candidate documents and mention spans as queries.

In all experiments, we limit our retrieved candidates set for Dense and BM25 to the top 16 entities due to observed diminishing returns (Figure 1). For Lookup, we retrieve all exact match candidates since they are not explicitly ranked. As a result, the performance of Lookup reflects an upper-bound of the performance of that method. The average number of retrieved Lookup candidates is 19 while the median of 4, reflecting the long tail distribution of retrieved candidates per span.

3.2 Candidate Generation

We begin by evaluating the impact of dense retrieval on Candidate Generation. Since we constrain our dense retrieval methods to 16 candidates, we measure Recall @16 of our various systems.

3.2.1 Gold Spans

We first observe the performance of our systems utilizing the Gold Spans provided by TweetNERD (Table 1). Contrasting Lookup and Dense, we can see that Dense outperforms on the Academic split by 4 points whereas Lookup outperforms on the Out-of-Domain split by 7.5 points. In addition, we see that our trivial BM25 baseline falls significantly behind with 0.221 recall on the Academic set and 0.556 on the OOD set.

Upon further investigation, we find that Dense and Lookup methods produce mutually exclusive results. On the Academic dataset, we find that Dense retrieved 7719 unique correct candidates whereas lookup retrieved 5268 unique correct candidates (Table 2 and Table 3). Leveraging these differences and inspired by van Hulst et al. (2020), we take the union of both methods as a Hybrid approach. This approach yielded a significant **+17.5 recall** increase over Lookup and **+13.3 recall** increase over Dense on the Academic split. In Figure 1, we show the change in Recall for all approaches as K increases. We can see that the benefit of retrieving more Dense candidates plateaus after 16

Table 2: Unique Correct Candidates using Gold Spans

Data Split	Dense	Lookup	BM25
Academic	**7,719**	5,268	1,043
OOD	1,055	**2,664**	1,495
Overall	**8,774**	7,932	2,538

[3]https://github.com/facebookresearch/BLINK

Table 3: Candidate Overlap Across Lookup, Dense and BM25 using Gold Spans

Lookup	Dense	BM25	counts	prop
Y	Y	Y	16,310	0.30
Y	Y	N	19,810	0.36
Y	N	Y	2,190	0.04
Y	N	N	3,566	0.06
N	Y	Y	1,079	0.02
N	Y	N	8,298	0.15
N	N	Y	361	0.01
N	N	N	3,386	0.06

Table 4: Candidate Generation using NER Spans (R@16)

Data Split	Dense	Lookup	BM25	Hybrid
Academic	<u>0.761</u>	0.613	0.164	**0.880**
OOD	0.754	<u>0.757</u>	0.440	**0.903**
Overall	<u>0.759</u>	0.715	0.245	**0.887**

candidates. However, we also find that candidates retrieved by Lookup and Dense continue to be mutually exclusive despite the larger candidate set (Figure 2). This illustrates that the performance plateau is not due to overlap in candidate sets but rather that both methods produce vastly different candidates. We investigate these differences in Section 3.2.3.

3.2.2 NER Spans

Next, to reflect a real-life use-case, we investigate performance of our system on NER spans. Here, we annotate each Tweet using the NER service described in Section 2.2. We capture the recall performance of our systems by evaluating the set of all retrieved candidates against the set of gold entities (Table 4). Here, we can see the benefits of Dense retrieval where Dense achieved similar performance on NER spans as utilizing gold spans. This is contrasted by Lookup, which realized a significant drop in performance. This is likely due to inaccuracies in our NER system, which can return spans that do not have exact entries in our pre-computed table.

Table 5: Unique Correct Candidates using NER Spans

Data Split	Dense	Lookup	BM25
Academic	**8,362**	4,711	983
OOD	1,263	**2,448**	1,496
Overall	**9,625**	7,159	2,479

We also see a continuing trend of complementary results between Dense retrieval and Lookup. Here, Dense and Unique retrieved 8362 and 4711 unique correct entities on the Academic set, respectively (Table 5). By combining the retrieved candidates from both sets, we can increase the performance of Lookup by $\approx$ **26.7 points** on all splits.

3.2.3 Qualitative Analysis

During our experiments, we found significant differences between the candidates retrieved by Dense retrieval and Lookup retrieval. We find that these differences can largely be categorized into span ambiguity, spelling, and the presence of context.

An example of a TweetNERD Tweet requiring context due to span ambiguity would be *"Wiz and **Amber**, Rihanna and Chris, Beyonce and jay-z #grammyscouples"* where the desired span is the word "Amber".

In our results, we found that Lookup returned many entities containing the name "Amber", such as "AMBER Alert" (Q1202607) and "Amber, Rajasthan, India" (Q8197166), but not the correct entity "Amber Rose" (Q290856). To the reader, it is clear upon reading the entire Tweet that the meaning does not concern a rescue service or city, but rather celebrities who have dated someone named "Wiz". This is contrasted by Dense retrieval, which returned the correct entity, but also similar entities such as celebrity "Amber Benson" (Q456862). Furthermore, we can see in the Wikipedia entity description of Amber Rose that she had been married to Wiz Khalifa, information that would not be present in the lookup table.

However, the presence of context can also be detrimental and misleading when taken literally. An example of such a TweetNERD Tweet would be *"No one here remembers The Marine and the **12 Rounds**."* where the desired span is "12 Rounds".

In this case, Dense retrieval returned incorrect candidates such as "12 Gauge Shotgun" (Q2933934), instead of "12 Rounds" the movie (Q245187). However, this was mitigated by Lookup, which accurately found the correct entity. We hypothesize that the context of "Marines" combined with "12 Rounds" misleads the Dense model to retrieve entities related to weaponry, instead of matching the literal title as Lookup did.

4 Conclusion

In this work, we have evaluated the usage of sparse and dense retrieval techniques towards candidate generation on social media text. In our qualitative and quantitative experimentation, we have highlighted the complementary strengths of both methods. Combined, our hybrid approach achieves significant improvements on TweetNERD, a large temporally diverse dataset for entity linking on Tweets. We also demonstrate the improvements that dense retrieval translates to improved downstream entity linking performance using both gold and NER based spans.

There are also a few directions for future work. First, in this work we focused on the Candidate Generation step for Entity Linking. While we report preliminary results for the Entity Disambiguation step in Appendix Section A, future work could explore efficient ways to disambiguate the candidates retrieved from our hybrid approach. Second, future work could expand our evaluation beyond the English Tweets found in TweetNERD and develop a multi-lingual solution. Third, it is important to note that there are significant linguistic differences between the formal text found on Wikipedia and informal speech on Twitter. Recent work has explored leveraging mentions as entity descriptions, which could be applied to Twitter text to bridge this gap (FitzGerald et al., 2021).

Overall, our work highlights the best practices for improving entity linking on short and noisy social media text. We hope this work inspires future entity linking efforts on this challenging domain.

References

Jan A Botha, Zifei Shan, and Dan Gillick. 2020. Entity linking in 100 languages. In *Proceedings of the 2020 Conference on Empirical Methods in Natural Language Processing (EMNLP)*, pages 7833–7845.

Nicola De Cao, Gautier Izacard, Sebastian Riedel, and Fabio Petroni. 2020. Autoregressive entity retrieval. In *International Conference on Learning Representations*.

Nicholas FitzGerald, Dan Bikel, Jan Botha, Daniel Gillick, Tom Kwiatkowski, and Andrew McCallum. 2021. MOLEMAN: Mention-only linking of entities with a mention annotation network. In *Proceedings of the 59th Annual Meeting of the Association for Computational Linguistics and the 11th International Joint Conference on Natural Language Processing (Volume 2: Short Papers)*, pages 278–285, Online. Association for Computational Linguistics.

Bahareh Harandizadeh and Sameer Singh. 2020. Tweeki: Linking named entities on twitter to a knowledge graph. In *Proceedings of the Sixth Workshop on Noisy User-generated Text (W-NUT 2020)*.

J. Johnson, M. Douze, and H. Jegou. 2021. Billion-scale similarity search with gpus.

Nikolaos Kolitsas, Octavian-Eugen Ganea, and Thomas Hofmann. 2018. End-to-end neural entity linking. In *Proceedings of the 22nd Conference on Computational Natural Language Learning*, pages 519–529, Brussels, Belgium. Association for Computational Linguistics.

Guillaume Lample, Miguel Ballesteros, Sandeep Subramanian, Kazuya Kawakami, and Chris Dyer. 2016. Neural architectures for named entity recognition. In *Proceedings of the 2016 Conference of the North American Chapter of the Association for Computational Linguistics: Human Language Technologies*, pages 260–270, San Diego, California. Association for Computational Linguistics.

Lajanugen Logeswaran, Ming-Wei Chang, Kenton Lee, Kristina Toutanova, Jacob Devlin, and Honglak Lee. 2019. Zero-shot entity linking by reading entity descriptions. In *Proceedings of the 57th Annual Meeting of the Association for Computational Linguistics*, pages 3449–3460.

Pablo N. Mendes, Max Jakob, Andres Garcia-Silva, and Christian Bizer. 2011. Dbpedia spotlight: Shedding light on the web of documents. In *Proceedings of the 7th International Conference on Semantic Systems (I-Semantics)*.

Shubhanshu Mishra and Jana Diesner. 2016. Semi-supervised named entity recognition in noisy-text. In *Proceedings of the 2nd Workshop on Noisy User-generated Text (WNUT)*, pages 203–212, Osaka, Japan. The COLING 2016 Organizing Committee.

Shubhanshu Mishra, Sijun He, and Luca Belli. 2020. Assessing demographic bias in named entity recognition. In *Proceedings of the AKBC Workshop on Bias in Automatic Knowledge Graph Construction, 2020*. arXiv.

Shubhanshu Mishra, Aman Saini, Raheleh Makki, Sneha Mehta, Aria Haghighi, and Ali Mollahosseini. 2022. TweetNERD - End to End Entity Linking Benchmark for Tweets.

Maria Pershina, Yifan He, and Ralph Grishman. 2015. Personalized page rank for named entity disambiguation. In *Proceedings of the 2015 Conference of the North American Chapter of the Association for Computational Linguistics: Human Language Technologies*, pages 238–243.

Sameer Singh, Amarnag Subramanya, Fernando Pereira, and Andrew McCallum. 2012. Wikilinks: A large-scale cross-document coreference corpus labeled via links to Wikipedia. Technical Report UM-CS-2012-015.

Valentin I. Spitkovsky and Angel X. Chang. 2012. A cross-lingual dictionary for English Wikipedia concepts. In *Proceedings of the Eighth International Conference on Language Resources and Evaluation (LREC'12)*, pages 3168–3175, Istanbul, Turkey. European Language Resources Association (ELRA).

Benjamin Strauss, Bethany Toma, Alan Ritter, Marie-Catherine De Marneffe, and Wei Xu. 2016. Results of the wnut16 named entity recognition shared task. In *Proceedings of the 2nd Workshop on Noisy User-generated Text (WNUT)*, pages 138–144.

Johannes M van Hulst, Faegheh Hasibi, Koen Dercksen, Krisztian Balog, and Arjen P de Vries. 2020. Rel: An entity linker standing on the shoulders of giants. In *Proceedings of the 43rd International ACM SIGIR Conference on Research and Development in Information Retrieval*, pages 2197–2200.

Ledell Wu, Fabio Petroni, Martin Josifoski, Sebastian Riedel, and Luke Zettlemoyer. 2020. Scalable zero-shot entity linking with dense entity retrieval. In *Proceedings of the 2020 Conference on Empirical Methods in Natural Language Processing (EMNLP)*, pages 6397–6407.

Peilin Yang, Hui Fang, and Jimmy Lin. 2018. Anserini: Reproducible ranking baselines using lucene. *J. Data and Information Quality*, 10(4).

A Entity Disambiguation

To evaluate end-to-end EL performance, we conduct preliminary experiments by training a disambiguation model using the candidate set retrieved from our retrieval methods. Once we generate entity candidates, we score each <Mention, Entity> pair for each Tweet using common mention-entity Lookup based features (e.g., mention count per entity), entity only based features (e.g., Wikipedia page rank), and contextual mention-entity features generated by comparing the mention embedding in the text against the candidate entity description embedding. We train our model to identify the correct entity for each span among the retrieved candidates. Our architecture and features are like the ones described in Kolitsas et al. (2018) with the major difference being the usage of a BERT based encoder instead of BiLSTM.

While our focus is candidate generation, reporting end-to-end performance is important since improvement in candidate generation does not necessarily translate to end-to-end improvement. Dense, unlike Lookup, can retrieve the right candidate even when the mention span is missing due to NER errors, however our disambiguation system currently still requires a span in order to link a mention.

Dataset Split	Dense	Lookup
Academic	**0.617**	0.566
OOD	**0.605**	0.568
Overall	**0.610**	0.567

Table 6: F1 of Entity Disambiguation using NER Spans

Description	Recall	Precision	F1
Lookup			
Short	0.484	**0.686**	0.567
Long	0.543	0.628	0.582
Dense			
Short	0.299	0.249	0.272
Long	**0.613**	0.607	**0.610**

Table 7: Ablation Experiments on Entity Disambiguation

Table 6 shows the F1 score of our disambiguation model using candidates retrieved by our proposed methods. Our results demonstrate that the increased recall brought by Dense candidates have translated into increased end-to-end F1 on all splits when compared to Lookup, achieving a 0.04 F1 gain. Furthermore, we can see the largest difference on the Academic split, where Dense achieved 0.051 higher F1 then our lookup-based approach.

B Ablation Study

A core part of our methodology is how we represent entities. In our proposed approach, we utilize Wikipedia descriptions, which provide a verbose but rich description of entities. We refer to these descriptions as "Long" descriptions. To evaluate the impact of these descriptions on Dense and Lookup retrieval, we conduct an ablation study where we evaluate utilizing Wikidata descriptions. These descriptions are much shorter and terse, often never exceeding 5-6 words. An example of such a description would be "species of bird", which is shared by 23 828 different bird entities [4]. We refer to these Wikidata descriptions as "Short" descriptions.

The results of our ablation study can be seen in Table 7. While we see an overall improvement when utilizing Long descriptions, the most significant impact can be seen on dense retrieval, where

[4]https://www.wikidata.org/w/index.php?search=species+of+bird

we see a leap of F1 performance from 0.272 to 0.610. Furthermore, we can also see that Lookup can still perform well when utilizing Short descriptions, achieving our highest precision result.

There are a few reasons for these results. Due to the k-nearest neighbour nature of Dense retrieval, entities that are retrieved by this method are often very semantically similar. This was demonstrated in Section 3.2.3, where Dense retrieval returned a list of actors when trying to link to an actor mention. However, since short descriptions are often shared between related entities ("species of bird"), often the same description would appear in the retrieved list. This is contrasted by Lookup, where the list of retrieved entities is related only by mentioned name. As a result, the entities are typically much more diverse (AMBER Alert vs Amber Rose) and thus easier to disambiguate with shorter descriptions.

TransPOS: Transformers for Consolidating Different POS Tagset Datasets

Alex Li[1], Ilyas Bankole-Hameed[1], Ranadeep Singh[1], Gabriel Shen Han Ng[1], Akshat Gupta[2]
[1]Carnegie Mellon University, [2]JPMorgan AI Research, New York, USA
{alexli2, ibankole, ranadees, hsng}@andrew.cmu.edu
akshat.x.gupta@jpmorgan.com

Abstract

In hope of expanding training data, researchers often want to merge two or more datasets that are created using different labeling schemes. This paper considers two datasets that label part-of-speech (POS) tags under different tagging schemes and leverage the supervised labels of one dataset to help generate labels for the other dataset. This paper further discusses the theoretical difficulties of this approach and proposes a novel supervised architecture employing Transformers to tackle the problem of consolidating two completely disjoint datasets. The results diverge from initial expectations and discourage exploration into the use of disjoint labels to consolidate datasets with different labels.

1 Introduction

There has been an explosion in the availability and variety of labeled datasets in almost every domain. Unfortunately, Artificial Intelligence (AI) practitioners and researchers often find themselves unable to make use of labeled datasets for tasks related but not identical to their tasks. This is primarily due to different labeling schemes where a trivial mapping to merge the datasets into one larger dataset does not exist. In this paper, we explore the possibility of consolidating datasets that were curated for the same task with different labeling schemes. To make this easy to apply to any pair of datasets, we consider a very interesting scenario in which we attempt to make a model that can understand both datasets without ever actually seeing any examples that have labels from both of them.

There are several domains and application areas to which our technique can be applied to, and frankly might be the only option. For example: When creating a data set to detect people, objects, and vehicles in an urban environment, we may want to supplement our existing data set with the popular Cityscapes dataset (Cordts et al., 2016), but struggle to directly apply those labels to the merged dataset due to a few minor differences in the label scheme, such as a smaller or larger label set. There could also be some information partially correlated with the existing dataset's labels; perhaps in our dataset we have to distinguish between standing and sitting people. Cityscapes does not distinguish between these, so is it possible to use the label information (about where humans are) to get high-quality segmentation under our desired labeling scheme?

The focus of this paper comes from part-of-speech (POS) tagging. Although some tags are common to all datasets, different datasets may have different conventions for how to deal with more uncommon parts of speech, like modal verbs, particles, or even when to treat something as a noun. These problems are exacerbated in informal contexts. We provide a novel design for a supervised model that can translate labels from one dataset into another labeled dataset *without requiring any shared examples*. After analyzing results, we reconsider the situations under which it is possible to squeeze out extra performance from these labels, and show that it is unlikely for any kind of architecture to use label information to perform better than an equivalent model that does not, unless the architecture has access to shared examples or metadata about the meaning of the labels.

1.1 Related Work

The problem of dissimilar POS tagsets has historically been approached in two significant ways:

1. Supervised Learning: (Shen, 2007) proposed a supervised POS tagger with 97.3% accuracy for the English language;

2. Create Dictionary Mapping: (Petrov et al., 2011) proposed a Universal POS tagset to map 25 different treebank tagsets to 12 universal POS tags.

Proceedings of the 2022 COLING Workshop: The 8th Workshop on Noisy User-generated Text (W-NUT 2022), pages 90–95

There has also been a significant amount of progress in creating POS tags for languages other than English leveraging both supervised and unsupervised methods (Das and Petrov, 2011).

Our work can be seen as a type of Multitask Learning (Caruana, 1998) as we are learning from two related datasets that have been labeled independently and differently. A common technique is to create a model for each task (Collobert and Weston, 2008), and enforce weight sharing between their lower layers to allow shared low-level domain knowledge. A key distinction between our methodology and Multitask Learning is that our test time goal also makes use of labels from the other task. We use the actual predictions of the model rather than the more common idea of using the predicted logits or encoded representation from a previous layer.

This problem can also be considered as a type of Domain Adaptation Technique. However, many domain adaptation algorithms ((Daumé, 2009)) assume some shared examples between the source and target domains, so we cannot apply it in our case. Those algorithms that do not make this assumption have never to our knowlege tried to use the labels that are in the target distribution but are not the source distribution labels.

2 Setting

Let Σ be the set of unicode characters. In our setting, we have two datasets that map from the space of sentences of unicode characters $X = \bigcup \Sigma^n$ to part-of-speech tags. However, the two datasets use different labeling schemes: the first may use the standard Universal POS tagset Y while the second uses a proprietary POS tagset Z. Each sentence in the first dataset has a label for each word in $\bigcup_{n=0}^{\infty} Y = \mathbf{Y}$, while each sentence in the second has a label in $\bigcup_{n=0}^{\infty} Z = \mathbf{Z}$.

Then we can name the two datasets as $\mathcal{D}_Y = \{(x_y^{(i)}, y^{(i)}) \in (X, \mathbf{Y})\}_i$ and $\mathcal{D}_Z = \{(x_z^{(i)}, z^{(i)}) \in (X, \mathbf{Z})\}_i$. Presumably, $\mathbf{Y}$ and $\mathbf{Z}$ are very highly correlated, since they are both POS tags for a sentence, just defined with slightly different rules. We would like to expand the dataset $\mathcal{D}_Y$ to include the sentences and labels of $\mathcal{D}_Z$, but unfortunately the labels are incompatible. However, we expect that we can still get useful information from the labels $\mathbf{Z}$. Therefore, our goal is to build a predictor function $f_Y : (X, \mathbf{Z}) \to \mathbf{Y}$ that combines both the text and the information of the annotated $\mathcal{D}_Z$ to predict what the translated label would be in the tagset $\mathbf{Y}$. Similarly, we consider the construction of $f_Z : (X, \mathbf{Y}) \to \mathbf{Z}$.

Here are the two obvious baselines that could be used to construct f_Y:

1. **Direct Map** We could use domain knowledge to directly design a mapping from each label $Z \to Y$. If $|Z| < |Y|$, Y is not a deterministic predictor of Z and this introduces noise into the system. If $|Z| > |Y|$, converting to Y will result in a loss of information.

2. **Supervised Model** We could train a model on $\mathcal{D}_Y$ to build a function $X \to \mathbf{Y}$.

Note that while the second baseline is trained with data, the first baseline is completely based on human understanding of the relationship between labels. Thus, while we can naturally train a model to match the performance of the **Supervised Model**, it is much less obvious how we can train a model to gain the performance advantage given by the **Direct Map** method.

Now we consider the design of our model intended to use information about both X and $\mathbf{Z}$ to perform better than either approach.

3 Model

In our method, we will transform our input X into an embedding space E using a transformer's encoder $Enc : X \to E$ and two GRU decoder functions, one for each type of label $\mathbf{Y}$ and $\mathbf{Z}$. $D_Y : (E, \mathbf{Z}) \to \mathbf{Y}$ and $D_Z : (E, \mathbf{Y}) \to \mathbf{Z}$. Then to infer a label Z for a given training sample (x_y, y), we can compute $D_Z(Enc(x_y), y)$. See Figure 1 for a visualization.

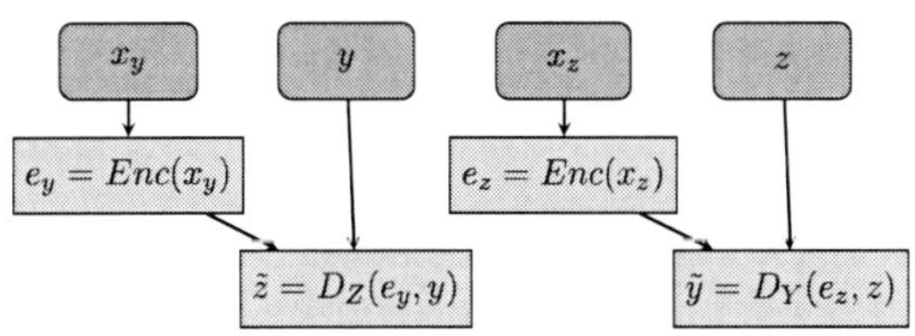

Figure 1: When evaluating the model, we use y and z as inputs!

However, the setup used for validation will not work for training the model. Ideally, we would like to make a loss function that penalizes the predicted value of z from being far from the true z corresponding to x_y, but we do not have any access to the true z! We only have pairs (x, y) and (x, z),

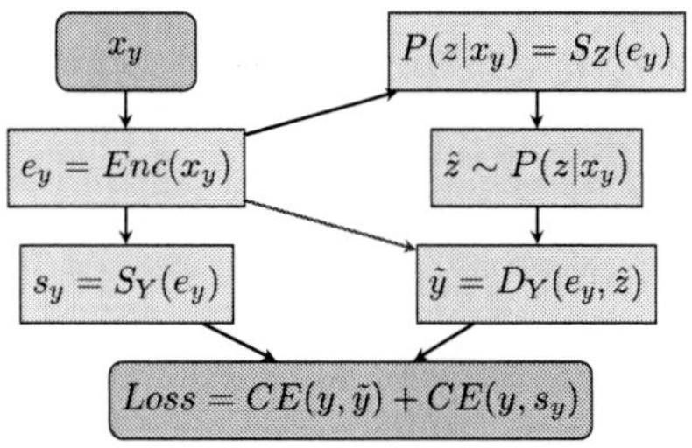

Figure 2: To train the model with the Y dataset, we simulate having Z labels by sampling from the logits of a normal supervised model S_Z. At the same time, we train a model S_Y for the other dataset. Heavy dropout is applied at the location of the blue arrow.

not (x, y, z). One way to fix this is to first predict $\hat{z}$ using (x, y) and then use that as a surrogate for true z. To do this, we can create a supervised model S_Z that takes in the encoded variables $Enc(x_y)$ and outputs a prediction for the label z, which we can then input into the decoder D_Z. However, the careful reader will notice a flaw in this strategy: While D_Z takes the input as one-hot labels at inference time, it takes input as logits at training time. To reconcile this difference, we treat the softmax of the predicted logits as a probability distribution, from which we sample our true predicted label $\hat{z}$.

The entire training process with the inputs $\mathcal{D}_Y$ is shown in Figure 2, and the model for $\mathcal{D}_Z$ is made the same way, but with the y / z inputs flipped. In our implementation, each mini-batch contains some examples from both datasets. To reduce the complexity of the model, we use the same base encoder model weights for S_Y, S_Z, D_Y, and D_Z, though in principal they could be different or only partially shared.

The inquisitive reader may wonder why we use S_Z to predict labels z instead of reusing labels D_Z along with ground truth labels y. In this case, we will have given the label that we want to predict as an input to the model, and so the model can simply learn to predict the input! For example, suppose that in our model, rather than sampling $\hat{z} \sim S_Z(e_y)$, we reused the decoder weights to get $\hat{z} := D_Z(e_y, y)$, then predicted $\tilde{y} = D_Y(e_y, \hat{z})$ (and similarly on the other side). Then, the model can simply learn to ignore the first argument of D_Y and D_Z and instead learn that $D_Y(-, z)$ and $D_Z(-, y)$ are inverses to each other. In this setup, it will perfectly predict all the training data, but it will be completely useless in practice. We actually tried this setup and found that the model would

Text	Ark Label
New	Adjective
FC	Proper noun
Menu	Proper noun
Utility	Proper noun
2.0	numeral
#apple	Proper noun
http://t.co/VftFt2c	URL or email address

Text	Tweebank Label
@USER2082	A
good	ADJ
night	NOUN
I	PRON
Love	VERB
You	PRON
:)	SYM
http://t.co/VftFt2c	U

Table 1: Example tweets from Ark and Tweebank

actually achieve performance competitive with the supervised model for a few epochs (perhaps due to regularization like dropout), but after training long enough, it learns the cheat and arrives at 0 training error and very high validation error. Now, during training, y and z are completely derived from x. So, in principle, D_Y and D_Z may learn to ignore noisy outputs y and z and make predictions based solely on x. To prevent this, we enforce a very heavy dropout of 0.85 on the first term before passing it as input.

The model and training code can be found in out Github repository[1] in the footnote.

4 Datasets

In this project, we consider two datasets:

1. ARK-Twitter Kevin Gimpel (2011), which contains 34k tokens from tweets sampled primarily on Oct 27, 2010.

2. Tweebank dataset Yijia Liu et al. (2018) which maintains 840 tweets from Tweebank v1, 2500 examples from twitter stream from February 2016 to July 2016.

The Tweebank dataset used UD annotation conventions, while the ARK data set used the Stanford POS Tagger trained in WSJ.

However; these two datasets have a data contamination problem: there are 210 identical shared

[1]`https://github.com/Alex7Li/TransPOS`

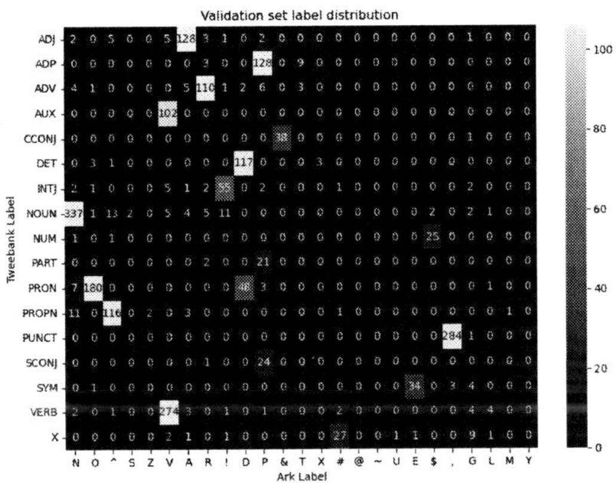

Figure 3: Distribution of validation labels.

tweets. In our case, however, this served as the perfect validation set for our model.

Looking at the distribution of the labels in this validation set (Figure 3), we see that the ambiguity between the meanings of the labels will limit the performance of a direct mapping.

5 Experiments

GPT-2	Tweebank Acc	Ark Acc
supervised model	**89.53%**	89.92%
our model	**89.53%**	**90.17%**
supervisor only	86.96%	88.29%
no label input	88.09%	88.59%
Bertweet-large	**Tweebank Acc**	**Ark Acc**
supervised model	**94.31%**	95.02%
our model	94.26%	94.97%
supervisor only	**94.31%**	**95.09%**
no label input	94.22%	94.97%
direct map	88.31%	89.97%

Table 2: Accuracy (Acc) with Bertweet-large model baseline

The first baseline was created by making a 'direct map' between the labels. We looked at the validation set and chose the map that gave the highest possible score.

The second 'supervised model' baseline was a normal transformer model; we train on the train split of one dataset and evaluate on the validation split of that same dataset.

Then, for 'our model', we trained with the described architecture, using the transformers BERTweet (Nguyen (2020)), and GPT-2 (Radford et al. (2019)) a GPT-2 model and a Bertweet model with the described architecture with dropout $.85$. After the training was complete, we evaluated the accuracy using the method described above to compute our model accuracy.

To see if our model was really learning from the y labels, we used of the supervised model heads $S_Y \circ Enc$ and $S_Z \circ Enc$ to get the 'supervisor only' accuracy. This architecture is exactly the same as the baseline, but differences arise in the accuracy because the training process is not the same (in particular, there is very high x dropout).

Finally, we considered the accuracy of the full pipeline when there with 'no label input': instead of providing the z labels for the first dataset while predicting the y labels of the second, we just took the z labels that the model predicted and sampled from that distribution as we do at training time.

6 Results

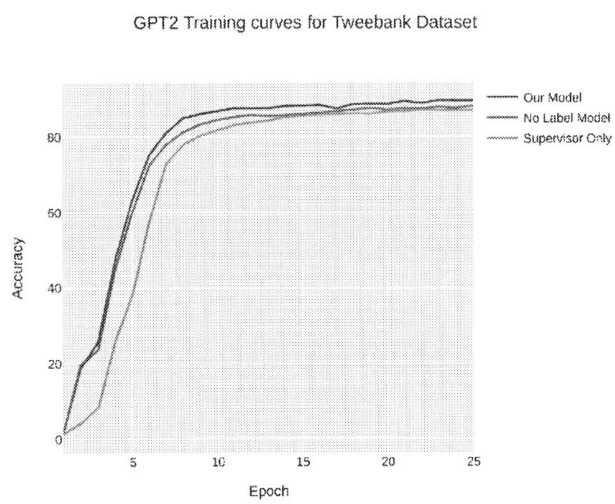

Figure 4: GPT-2 Validation accuracy

We trained the model with both the GPT-2 as our encoder and the Bertweet model as our encoder. All models were trained for 25 epochs, and we report the accuracy at the final epoch in Table 2.

In both cases, our accuracy does not exceed the baseline. Although the Bertweet model appears to gain nothing from the z labels, the GPT-2 model appears to be using the z labels to effectively improve performance as indicated in Figure 4. Since the score of the model improves when we give it the z labels, we can say that it is actually learning to use the joint probability distribution of the y and z labels.

Our approach can only be useful when the correlation between the labels of both datasets provides information that the correlation between the encoder output and the true labels does not. One possible explanation for our inability to beat the baseline model is because the label information was not sufficient or because the baseline model was already too strong. However, using the weaker GPT-2 model as a baseline did not show any improvement.

Although there are a multitude of different ideas for model designs that use the y labels, it is important to first try and understand why this model struggled in this regime. From our results, it seems it will be difficult to design an architecture that can effectively learn from the label information of another dataset without using any shared examples.

To emphasize that this problem will be hard for any architecture, let us consider a toy example of this problem where we no longer have any X data and are just given a set of **Y** POS tokens and **Z** POS tokens. In this case, the the y and z labels are still very correlated, but since it is impossible for a model to predict the price from an integer id, our model will not be able to learn about and make use of the high covariance between labels. As we have given the model two unrelated sets of labels, no matter what model you use, it will be impossible to relate them with anything other than the statistical properties of the **Y** and **Z** distributions. This does not seem too informative in general, since it will be difficult to find the correct relationship between two sets with no shared examples, though the fact that POS is a multi-label prediction problem means that you might be able to get a bit out of it. Still, even trying to make the label distributions similar is not easy as the labels are not in the same space.

In our model, we consider pairs of predicted y and true z data, which ultimately cannot give any more information than the already known relationship between encoder outputs and true labels. The hope was that replacing the predicted label y with the true label y would allow for a final gain in accuracy, but that was not the case in our experiments. There is a difficult tension to balance: When trusting the predicted y label too much, the decoder will not be able to perform well on the training dataset because the predicted label is often wrong. But when we do not trust the label, we cannot do well at evaluation time.

The toy example indicates that the only other way to gain new information would be relating the statistical properties of the distribution. However, it is not clear how to learn this information or how helpful it would be. Therefore, using label information for a separate dataset appears very unlikely to improve performance.

A counterpoint to this argument is the performance gap between *our model* and the *no label input* model. This is especially clear in the early stages of GPT-2 training. In Figure 4, we plot the three accuracies when training GPT-2. Here, using the ground truth labels for the y dataset gives a better score on the z dataset than using the model predictions for y. Thus, it seems that we can conclude that it is possible for the model to learn the joint distribution $P(Y, Z)$ and use that information effectively. However, the problem is that the only information about $P(Y, Z)$ that the model is capable of learning is what can be deduced from $P(X, Y)$ and $P(X, Z)$. In trying to predict Z, it can really only use the information that was learned from $P(X, Z)$, which is already contained in any normal supervised model. The fact that the model performance never surpasses the supervised model is evidence toward the argument that the replacement policy will not help to improve model performance in general.

7 Conclusion

The task of consolidating datasets with different labels and no shared examples is a hard problem. The experiments did not provide any improvement over the baseline of only using the x variables. This was surprising, as the correlation between the y and z labels is quite large. However, this may be due to an intrinsic difficulty with the setting (no shared examples) rather than the model design.

8 Future Work

Future work of consolidating datasets without shared examples should focus on using semi-supervised learning with other x labels or supporting the other dataset labels with metadata.

Another possible direction would be to use the architecture in this paper together with a subset of shared examples between the datasets. Our approach can be easily modified to deal with labels that are sometimes missing instead of all the time. Such a modification could shine in (potentially multi-label) environments with that require frequent missing value imputation.

References

Rich Caruana. 1998. Multitask learning. In Sebastian Thrun and Lorien Y. Pratt, editors, *Learning to Learn*, pages 95–133. Springer.

Ronan Collobert and Jason Weston. 2008. A unified architecture for natural language processing: Deep neural networks with multitask learning. In *Proceedings of the 25th international conference on Machine learning*, pages 160–167.

Marius Cordts, Mohamed Omran, Sebastian Ramos, Timo Rehfeld, Markus Enzweiler, Rodrigo Benenson, Uwe Franke, Stefan Roth, and Bernt Schiele. 2016. The cityscapes dataset for semantic urban scene understanding.

Dipanjan Das and Slav Petrov. 2011. Unsupervised part-of-speech tagging with bilingual graph-based projections. In *Proceedings of the 49th Annual Meeting of the Association for Computational Linguistics (ACL '11)*, page Best Paper Award.

Hal Daumé. 2009. Frustratingly easy domain adaptation.

Brendan O'Connor Kevin Gimpel, Nathan Schneider. 2011. Part-of-speech tagging for twitter: Annotation, features, and experiments. In *Part-of-Speech Tagging for Twitter: Annotation, Features, and Experiments*.

Dat Quoc Nguyen. 2020. Bertweet the first large-scale pretrained language model for english tweets. *VinAi*, 1.

Slav Petrov, Dipanjan Das, and Ryan T. McDonald. 2011. A universal part-of-speech tagset. *CoRR*, abs/1104.2086.

Alec Radford, Jeff Wu, Rewon Child, David Luan, Dario Amodei, and Ilya Sutskever. 2019. Language models are unsupervised multitask learners. *CoRR*.

Libin Shen. 2007. Guided learning for bidirectional sequence classification.

Yi Zhu Yijia Liu, Wanxiang Che, and Bing Qin. 2018. Parsing tweets into universal dependencies. In *Parsing Tweets into Universal Dependencies*.

An Effective, Performant Named Entity Recognition System for Noisy Business Telephone Conversation Transcripts

Xue-Yong Fu, Cheng Chen, Md Tahmid Rahman Laskar,
Shashi Bhushan TN, Simon Corston-Oliver
Dialpad Canada Inc.
Vancouver, BC, Canada
{xue-yong,cchen,tahmid.rahman}@dialpad.com
{sbhushan,scorston-oliver}@dialpad.com

Abstract

We present a simple yet effective method to train a named entity recognition (NER) model that operates on business telephone conversation transcripts that contain noise due to the nature of spoken conversation and artifacts of automatic speech recognition. We first fine-tune LUKE, a state-of-the-art Named Entity Recognition (NER) model, on a limited amount of transcripts, then use it as the teacher model to teach a smaller DistilBERT-based student model using a large amount of weakly labeled data and a small amount of human-annotated data. The model achieves high accuracy while also satisfying the practical constraints for inclusion in a commercial telephony product: realtime performance when deployed on cost-effective CPUs rather than GPUs.

1 Introduction

We describe a named entity recognition (NER) system that identifies entities mentioned in English business telephone conversations. The input to the NER system is transcripts produced by an automatic speech recognition (ASR) system. These transcripts are inherently noisy due to the nature of spoken communication and due to the limitations of the ASR system. The transcripts contain dysfluencies, false starts, filled pauses, they lack punctuation information and have incomplete information about case.

Because there was no pre-existing annotated data set publicly available that matched the characteristics of the ASR transcripts in the domain of business telephone conversations (Li et al., 2020), the NER model is required to be trained on a large dataset containing telephone conversations to effectively detect named entities in such noisy data. Moreover, the NER model needs to provide real-time functionality in a commercial communication-as-a-service (CaaS) product such as displaying information related to the named entities to a customer support agent during a call with a customer. The deployed system was therefore required to be fast (less than 200ms inference time) but economical (able to operate on CPU, rather than more expensive GPUs).

To address the above issues, in this paper, we present a simple yet effective method, *distill-then-fine-tune*, to transfer knowledge from a large and complex model to a small and simple model while reaching a similar performance as the large model. More specifically, we fine-tune a state-of-the-art NER model, LUKE (Yamada et al., 2020), on our limited amount of noisy telephone conversations and predict the labels of a large amount of unlabeled conversations, denoted as distillation data. The smaller model is then trained on the distillation data using pseudo-labels. We conduct extensive experiments with our proposed approach and observe that our distilled model achieves 75x inference speed boost while reserving 99.09% F1 score of its teacher. This makes our proposed approach very effective in limited budget scenarios as it does not require the annotation of a huge amount of noisy data that would otherwise be required to fine-tune simpler transformers on downstream tasks.

2 Related Work

NER is often framed as a sequence labeling problem (Huang et al., 2015; Akbik et al., 2018) where a model is used to predict the entity type of each token. Previously, various models based on the recurrent neural network architecture have been widely used for this task. In recent years, pre-trained language models have been employed to perform the NER task where a new prediction layer is added into the pre-trained model to fine-tune for sequence labeling (Devlin et al., 2019).

More recently, (Yamada et al., 2020) proposed a new approach to provide the contextualized representations of words and entities based on a bidirectional transformer. In their proposed model, LUKE, they treat words and entities in a given context

Proceedings of the 2022 COLING Workshop: The 8th Workshop on Noisy User-generated Text (W-NUT 2022), pages 96–100

Type	Utterances	Person	Prod/Org	Location
Train	16124	4852	4443	4135
Dev	2292	682	627	629
Test	4497	1382	1274	1151

Table 1: Labeled in-domain dataset class distribution. The numbers under each entity type represent number of utterances containing the specific type.

as independent tokens, and output the contextualized representations of them. The LUKE model achieved impressive performance in various entity-related tasks. However, this model is inherently slow due to its complex architecture and so it is not applicable for usage in production environments in a limited computational budget scenario.

In scenarios where the computational budget is limited, using a smaller model that can mimic the behaviour of the large model can be used. Knowledge distillation (Hinton et al., 2015) is one such technique where a large model is compressed into a small model. One prominent approach for Knowledge Distillation that has been used in recent years is the work of (Tang et al., 2019), where they proposed a task specific knowledge distillation method to show that using an additional unlabeled transfer dataset can augment the training set for more effective knowledge transfer. However, most prior work that leveraged such knowledge distillation techniques focused on typed input, whereas the amount of work that leveraged knowledge distillation for noisy texts (e.g., telephone conversation transcripts) is very limited (Gou et al., 2021). Motivated by the advantages of knowledge distillation, in this work, we also leverage knowledge distillation to address the computational issues that occur while utilizing large state-of-the-art language models in a limited computational environment, while minimizing the amount of noisy data that must be human-annotated for use during fine-tuning.

3 Datasets

In this section, we first introduce the in-domain training data (noisy human-to-human conversations) that we sampled and annotated to train the teacher model. Then, we describe the data used for knowledge distillation of the student model.

3.1 In-domain Data Annotation

Since our in-domain dataset is sampled from transcripts produced by an ASR system, the dataset does not contain any punctuation marks and only contains partial casing information. This makes the property of our dataset fundamentally different from the data that most pre-trained models are trained on. This also makes the task more difficult since upper-cased words are a very strong hint of a token being a named entity (Mayhew et al., 2019).

For data annotation, we sampled 26,000 utterances from telephone conversation transcripts and had them annotated by Appen[1]. Four types of named entities were labeled by the annotators: *person name*, *product or organization*, *geopolitical location*, and *none*. The detailed statistic of this dataset labeled by Appen is shown in Table 1.

3.2 In-domain Distillation Data

Our goal is to reduce the amount of human annotated data in the training set. For this purpose, we perform knowledge distillation that transfers knowledge from a large and complex teacher model to a small and simple student model. Since the student model is expected to be much simpler than the teacher model, it requires a large amount of labeled training data. In addition, due to the sparsity of named entities, the model cannot learn too much from randomly sampled utterances where most of them may not contain any named entities. We address this issue by using the spaCy[2] NER model to select utterances that are highly likely to contain at least one named entity of a type we are interested in. Specifically, we only used four entity types relevant to this study from the spaCy model: PERSON, ORG, GPE, PRODUCT. This sampling method produced 483,766 unlabeled utterances from business telephone conversation transcripts and largely increased the information density in the data. However, annotating this huge amount of unlabeled data would be a prohibitively costly process. To tackle this problem, we use the trained teacher model to predict the labels of these utterances. In this way, the teacher model provides the pseudo-labels of a large unlabeled noisy dataset to alleviate the need of human annotation for such data. We use this large noisy speech data with pseudo-labels as the distillation data to train the student model. The statistics of this dataset is listed in Table 2.

4 Our Proposed Approach

In this section, we first describe the architectures of the teacher and student models. We then de-

[1] `https://appen.com/`, accessed on January 4, 2022.
[2] `https://spacy.io/api/entityrecognizer`

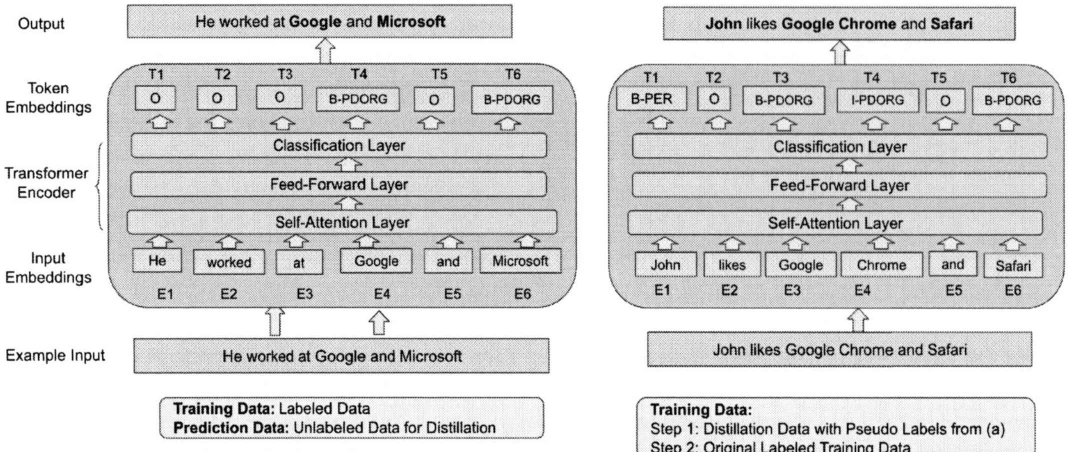

(a) Stage 1: Fine Tuning Teacher on Labeled Data

(b) Stage 2: Two-Step Fine Tuning of Student on the Distillation Data (step 1) and the Training data (step 2)

Figure 1: Our knowledge distillation approach: (a) first, fine-tune the teacher model (LUKE) on the labeled dataset, and generate the pseudo-labels of a huge amount of unlabeled data for distillation. (b) Next, fine-tune the student model (DistilBERT) in two steps, **step 1:** on the distillation data having pseudo-labels that were generated in the previous step, and **step 2:** on the original labeled training data where the teacher model was also trained. Here, 'PDORG' denotes 'PROD/ORG', while 'Bold' font in the output layer denotes the entities tagged by the model.

Type	**# Examples**
Positive utterances	347,412
Negative utterances	136,354
Utterances containing *Person* tags	179,495
Utterances containing *Prod/Org* tags	97,857
Utterances containing *Location* tags	138,989

Table 2: Pseudo-labeled distillation data class distribution. "Positive utterances" are those that contain any of the 3 entity types, and "Negative utterances" are those that do not contain any of the 3 entity types. Here, '#' denotes 'Total number of'.

scribe our proposed knowledge distillation method, *distill-then-fine-tune*, that can be broken down into four steps: i) fine-tune the teacher model on the in-domain data, ii) sample distillation data from unlabeled examples, iii) perform distillation, and iv) fine-tune the student model. An overview of our proposed approach is illustrated in Figure 1.

Model Architecture: We use LUKE, a bidirectional transformer, that was pre-trained by (Yamada et al., 2020) on Wikipedia data to learn contextualized representations of words and entities. In LUKE, the input representation of a token (word or entity) is computed using three types of embedding: token embedding, position embedding, and entity type embedding. Token embedding, which is decomposed into two small matrices, represents the corresponding token. Position embedding represents the position of a token in a word sequence, while the entity type embedding represents whether the token is an entity. To further leverage the entity type embedding, an entity-aware self attention mechanism is used to handle interactions between entities in a given word sequence. Since LUKE is a large model that contains approximately 483M parameters (355M on its encoder and 128M for entity embeddings), we use it as the teacher to teach a student model.

For the student model, we adapt the DistilBERT (Sanh et al., 2019) model, a 6-layer bidirectional transformer encoder that was pre-trained for the language modeling task by Sanh et al. (2019). The DistilBERT model was initialized from its teacher BERT model by taking one layer out of two. It was pre-trained on the same corpus as BERT while using both the distillation loss and the masked language modelling loss. It contains approximately 66M parameters (approximately one seventh the size of the teacher model), making it more economical to deployment in a production environment with limited resources.

Distillation Method: Our goal is to build an NER system that can detect named entities in business conversations, but the LUKE model that we employ as a teacher model was pre-trained on written text, which is very different from noisy transcribed human-to-human conversations. To adapt

Model	F1 Score	Inference Time
LUKE_{ft}	86.07	2980ms
$\text{DistilBERT}_{\text{ft}}$	83.08	40ms
$\text{DistilBERT}_{\text{dtft}}$	85.29	40ms

Table 3: Performance of our proposed $\text{DistilBERT}_{\text{dtft}}$ models (fine-tuned on a large amount of distillation data and a small amount of in-domain human-annotated data) compared to the LUKE_{ft} and $\text{DistilBERT}_{\text{ft}}$ models that were fine-tuned only on the in-domain human-annotated data. Inference time is measured on a 2.20Ghz Intel Xeon CPU with sixteen virtual cores.

to the domain of business conversations, we first fine-tune the LUKE model on 16,124 in-domain human-annotated examples (see Section 3.1 for details). The resulting model is called LUKE_{ft}. The LUKE_{ft} model serves as the teacher that generates pseudo-labels for the distillation data (see Section 3.2 for details).

Next, we use a two-step fine-tuning approach for the student model (Fu et al., 2021; Laskar et al., 2022c). The student model is initialized with the pre-trained DistilBERT model. For step 1, we fine-tune the student model on the distillation data with pseudo-labels generated by the teacher. During the training stage, we use the cross entropy loss defined below.

$$L_{CE} = -\frac{1}{N}\sum_{n=1}^{N}\log\frac{e^{\hat{y}_{n,y_n}}}{\sum_{c=1}^{C} e^{\hat{y}_{n,c}}} \quad (1)$$

Here, N is the number of samples in a batch, and C denotes the number of classes. $\hat{y}_{n,c}$ is the logit of the c-th class in the n-th example, and $\hat{y}_{n,y_n}$ is the logit of the gold class in the n-th example.

For the final distillation step, we fine-tune the student model further on the in-domain human-annotated data. The resulting child model is termed **$\text{DistilBERT}_{\text{dtft}}$**.

5 Experiments

In this section, we describe our experimental settings and results.

5.1 Experimental Settings

Below, we discuss the baseline models and the training parameters used in our experiments.

Baselines: To compare the performance with our proposed model, we use the following baselines, ***(i)*** ***LUKE_{ft}***: The pre-trained LUKE model fine-tuned on our human-annotated in-domain training data, and ***(ii)*** ***DistilBERT_{ft}***: Similar to the other baseline, it was fine-tuned only on our human-annotated in-domain training data.

Training Parameters: For the teacher model, LUKE_{ft}, we set the batch size to 2, learning rate to 5×10^{-5}, and the number of epochs to 3. For the student DistilBERT model, we set the batch size to 32 and the learning rate to 5×10^{-5}, and the number of epochs to 5.

5.2 Results and Analyses

From Table 3, we see that the LUKE_{ft} model (fine-tuned on in-domain human-annotated data) achieves the highest F1 score, 86.07%, but with an inference time of 2980ms it is not practical for realtime applications.

The $\text{DistilBERT}_{\text{ft}}$ model (also fine-tuned only on the in-domain human-annotated data), with an inference time of 40ms is suitable for realtime application, but loses almost three percentage points of accuracy, reducing to an F1 score of 83.08%.

Our proposed **$\text{DistilBERT}_{\text{dtft}}$** model, which leverages two stage of fine-tuning (uses the large distillation data on stage 1 of fine-tuning and the human-annotated data on stage 2 of fine-tuning) brings the F1 score back to within 1% of the LUKE_{ft} model. Since **$\text{DistilBERT}_{\text{dtft}}$** model has the same model architecture and the same number of parameters as the $\text{DistilBERT}_{\text{ft}}$ model, its inference time is identical: 40ms, i.e. 75x faster than LUKE_{ft}. This makes **$\text{DistilBERT}_{\text{dtft}}$** model applicable for production deployment as it achieves an improved F1 score with high efficiency while requiring less computational resources due to its small size.

6 Conclusion

In this paper, we introduce the *distill-then-fine-tune* method for entity recognition on real world noisy data to deploy our NER model in a limited budget production environment. By generating pseudo-labels using a large teacher model pre-trained on typed text while fine-tuned on noisy speech text to train a smaller student model, we make the student model 75x times faster while reserving 99.09% of its accuracy. These findings demonstrate that our proposed approach is very effective in limited budget scenarios to alleviate the need of human labeling of a large amount of noisy data. In the future, we will explore how to apply knowledge distillation to other tasks (Laskar et al., 2022a,b; Khasanova et al., 2022) containing noisy data.

Ethics Statement

The data used in this research is comprised of individual sentences that do not contain sensitive, personal, or identifying information. Each machine-sampled utterance is labelled by annotators before the utterance is used as part of the training dataset. While annotator demographics are unknown and therefore may introduce potential bias in the labelled dataset, the annotators are required to pass a screening test before completing any labels used in these experiments, thereby mitigating this unknown to some extent. Future work should nonetheless strive to improve training data further in this regard.

References

Alan Akbik, Duncan Blythe, and Roland Vollgraf. 2018. Contextual string embeddings for sequence labeling. In *Proceedings of the 27th International Conference on Computational Linguistics, COLING 2018, Santa Fe, New Mexico, USA, August 20-26, 2018*, pages 1638–1649. Association for Computational Linguistics.

Jacob Devlin, Ming-Wei Chang, Kenton Lee, and Kristina Toutanova. 2019. BERT: Pre-training of deep bidirectional transformers for language understanding. In *Proceedings of the 2019 Conference of the North American Chapter of the Association for Computational Linguistics: Human Language Technologies, Volume 1 (Long and Short Papers)*, Minneapolis, Minnesota. Association for Computational Linguistics.

Xue-Yong Fu, Cheng Chen, Md Tahmid Rahman Laskar, Shashi Bhushan, and Simon Corston-Oliver. 2021. Improving punctuation restoration for speech transcripts via external data. In *Proceedings of the Seventh Workshop on Noisy User-generated Text (W-NUT 2021)*, pages 168–174, Online. Association for Computational Linguistics.

Jianping Gou, Baosheng Yu, Stephen J Maybank, and Dacheng Tao. 2021. Knowledge distillation: A survey. *International Journal of Computer Vision*, 129(6):1789–1819.

Geoffrey E. Hinton, Oriol Vinyals, and Jeffrey Dean. 2015. Distilling the knowledge in a neural network. *CoRR*, abs/1503.02531.

Zhiheng Huang, Wei Xu, and Kai Yu. 2015. Bidirectional LSTM-CRF models for sequence tagging. *CoRR*, abs/1508.01991.

Elena Khasanova, Pooja Hiranandani, Shayna Gardiner, Cheng Chen, Simon Corston-Oliver, and Xue-Yong Fu. 2022. Developing a production system for Purpose of Call detection in business phone conversations. In *Proceedings of the 2022 Conference of the North American Chapter of the Association for Computational Linguistics: Human Language Technologies: Industry Track*, pages 259–267, Hybrid: Seattle, Washington + Online. Association for Computational Linguistics.

Md Tahmid Rahman Laskar, Cheng Chen, Jonathan Johnston, Xue-Yong Fu, Shashi Bhushan TN, and Simon Corston-Oliver. 2022a. An auto encoder-based dimensionality reduction technique for efficient entity linking in business phone conversations. In *Proceedings of the 45th International ACM SIGIR Conference on Research and Development in Information Retrieval*, pages 3363–3367.

Md Tahmid Rahman Laskar, Cheng Chen, Aliaksandr Martsinovich, Jonathan Johnston, Xue-Yong Fu, Shashi Bhushan Tn, and Simon Corston-Oliver. 2022b. BLINK with Elasticsearch for efficient entity linking in business conversations. In *Proceedings of the 2022 Conference of the North American Chapter of the Association for Computational Linguistics: Human Language Technologies: Industry Track*, pages 344–352, Hybrid: Seattle, Washington + Online. Association for Computational Linguistics.

Md Tahmid Rahman Laskar, Enamul Hoque, and Jimmy Xiangji Huang. 2022c. Domain adaptation with pre-trained transformers for query-focused abstractive text summarization. *Computational Linguistics*, 48(2):279–320.

Jing Li, Aixin Sun, Jianglei Han, and Chenliang Li. 2020. A survey on deep learning for named entity recognition. *IEEE Transactions on Knowledge and Data Engineering*, 34(1):50–70.

Stephen Mayhew, Tatiana Tsygankova, and Dan Roth. 2019. ner and pos when nothing is capitalized. In *Proceedings of the 2019 Conference on Empirical Methods in Natural Language Processing and the 9th International Joint Conference on Natural Language Processing, EMNLP-IJCNLP 2019, Hong Kong, China, November 3-7, 2019*, pages 6255–6260. Association for Computational Linguistics.

Victor Sanh, Lysandre Debut, Julien Chaumond, and Thomas Wolf. 2019. Distilbert, a distilled version of BERT: smaller, faster, cheaper and lighter. *CoRR*, abs/1910.01108.

Raphael Tang, Yao Lu, Linqing Liu, Lili Mou, Olga Vechtomova, and Jimmy Lin. 2019. Distilling task-specific knowledge from BERT into simple neural networks. *CoRR*, abs/1903.12136.

Ikuya Yamada, Akari Asai, Hiroyuki Shindo, Hideaki Takeda, and Yuji Matsumoto. 2020. LUKE: deep contextualized entity representations with entity-aware self-attention. In *Proceedings of the 2020 Conference on Empirical Methods in Natural Language Processing, EMNLP 2020, Online, November 16-20, 2020*, pages 6442–6454. Association for Computational Linguistics.

Leveraging Semantic and Sentiment Knowledge for User-Generated Text Sentiment Classification

Jawad Khan, Niaz Ahmad, Youngmoon Lee
Hanyang University
{jkhanbk1,niazahamd89,youngmoonlee}
@hanyang.ac.kr

Aftab Alam
Hamad Bin Khalifa University
afalam@hbku.edu.qa

Abstract

Sentiment analysis is essential to process and understand unstructured user-generated content for better data analytics and decision making. State-of-the-art techniques suffer from a high dimensional feature space because of noisy and irrelevant features from the noisy user-generated text. Our goal is to mitigate such problems using DNN-based text classification and popular word embeddings (Glove, fastText, and BERT) in conjunction with statistical filter feature selection (mRMR and PCA) to select relevant sentiment features and pick out unessential/irrelevant ones. We propose an effective way of integrating the traditional feature construction methods with the DNN-based methods to improve the performance of sentiment classification. We evaluate our model on three real-world benchmark datasets demonstrating that our proposed method improves the classification performance of several existing methods.

1 Introduction

Sentiment analysis is used to classify user-generated review/comments into positive and negative classes, and widely applied to various domains such as businesses and organizations, politics, health, education, etc. Existing proposals for text sentiment analysis can be mainly divided into lexicon-based and corpus-based approaches. Sentiment lexicons may ignore important domain-specific sentiment words incurring concerns with word coverage. Unlike lexicon-based approach, corpus-based approaches requires careful consideration of sentiment clues behind sentiment words, that is crucial for determining a text's sentiment orientation.

We propose an effective method for improving sentence-level classification performance by integrating the traditional feature construction method with the DNN-based method, while considering semantics, context and sentiment clue. First, we parse the review sentences and employ linguistic rules to identify mixed opinionated sentences. Then the POS tags are assigned to the sentiment bearing words: adjectives, adverbs, verbs, and nouns by Stanford POS tagger. Next we leverage the integrated wide coverage sentiment lexicon (WCSL) (Khan and Lee) as the semantic and sentiment information to identify and extract sentiment bearing words. After that, we employ statistical features reduction algorithms namely mRMR (Ding and Peng) and PCA (Wold et al.) for optimum features selection. Further we process the optimum sentiment features and convert them to word vector by employing word embedding methods (e.g., Glove, fastText, and BERT). Finally, we apply a CNN classifier to process the word vector/vector embedding and predict the sentiment class of each sentence.

Our main contribution is summarized as follow: (1) We use semantic and sentiment knowledge, linguistic rules, and integrated WCSL to identify and extract the sentiment features in the sentence. (2) We reduce the dimensionality of feature space by employing the mRMR and PCA statistical filter algorithms to filter out redundant features and select the optimum sentiment features. (3) The experimental results of our proposed method using three real word benchmark domain datasets show that the suggested sentiment analysis model improves the performance of several previous baseline methods significantly.

2 Related Work

Many traditional feature-based machine learning methods have been largely used for textual sentiment classification (Tripathy et al., 2016; Yousefpour et al., 2017; Chang et al., 2020). These approaches have employed Bag of Words, high order n-grams, Part of speech (POS) patterns and linguistic patterns for sentiment features representation and sentiment classification. While traditional feature-based selection approaches might lower the

Proceedings of the 2022 COLING Workshop: The 8th Workshop on Noisy User-generated Text (W-NUT 2022), pages 101–105

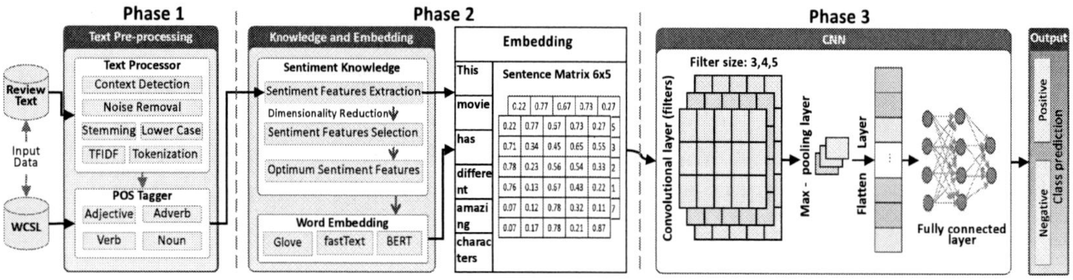

Figure 1: Proposed framework consists of three phases: text pre-processing, knowledge and embedding, and CNN.

dimensionality of textual data to improve classification performance, classifiers still face sparsity issues due to a lack of adequate data representation strategies. **Word embeddings**: Word2vec, Glove, fastText, and BERT (Zhang and Wallace, 2015; Mikolov et al., 2017; Kenton and Toutanova) are alternative approaches recently used for the dense representation of words of the text of analysis.

Deep neural network (DNN) models: CNN, BiLSTM, and BiGRU with word embeddings have achieved tremendous results in textual sentiment analysis (Kim; Rezaeinia et al., 2017; Lei et al.; Huang et al.; Khasanah, 2021). However, according to recent studies, DNN-based methods select some irrelevant and redundant features and also ignore the sentiment clue behind each sentiment word which affects its performance in terms of classification accuracy (Rezaeinia et al., 2017; Ayinde et al.; Denil et al., 2013). Although traditional feature-based methods have benefits in interpretability and time complexity, DNN-based methods outperform classic feature-based methods.

3 Methodology

Our proposed effective method for sentiment classification is composed of three main phases: (1) text pre-processing (2) knowledge and embedding (3) CNN architecture. The overall framework of our proposed method is shown in Figure 1.

3.1 Text Pre-processing

We employ the text pre-processing method to create the initial feature space. The review dataset is loaded first, followed by sentence parser and tokenizer. The noise removal and text transformer module is then used to remove noisy text (e.g., stop words, URLs, numeric symbols, etc.), and convert the text to lowercase respectively. Next the POS tagger is employed to assigns POS tags to the likely words such as adjectives, adverbs, verbs and nouns. Furthermore, these words are searched in the integrated WCSL to identify and extract the sentiment words. We also employ linguistic rules following the work of (Appel et al., 2016; Khan et al., 2021) to identify the context of text sentiment and discriminate synonyms from antonyms. Linguistic rules provide help to the context-based sentiment analysis that comprises differing viewpoints. For example, in the statement "the filmmaker is well-known but the film is dull" linguistic norms only consider the clause after "but" whereas the clause preceding "but" is omitted. It comprises certain words that can change the polarity of a statement, such as "but" "despite" "while" "unless" and so on.

3.2 Sentiment Knowledge and Embedding

We leverage semantic and sentiment knowledge using integrated wide coverage sentiment lexicons to identify, extract and select the relevant sentiment features for word embedding and sentiment classification (Khan and Lee).

Integrated Wide Coverage Sentiment Lexicons In literature different sentiment lexicons (Khan et al., 2021) such as AFFIN, OL, SO-CAL, WordNet-Affect, GI SentiSense, MPQA Subjectivity Lexicon, NRC Hashtag Sentiment Lexicon, SenticNet5, and SentiWordNet with different sizes have been built. There is no one-size-fits-all general sentiment lexicon that can be utilized for sentiment analysis. We standardize them by assigning scores, +1, -1, 0 to positive, negative, and neutral words respectively. Then for integration, we take the average of the sentiment score of the overlapping words, which produces a huge sentiment lexicon with more sentiment words that we called WCSL. In this study sentiment words in the review sentences are matched against integrated WCSL and then used for sentiment classification.

Sentiment Features Extraction For reliable model learning, it's crucial to identify and extract the right features. Specifically, we employ Stanford POS tagger (Toutanvoa and Manning) to assign POS tags to the content words such as adjectives, adverbs, verbs, and nouns and then identify the sentiment orientation of these words/features in the integrated WCSL.

Sentiment Features Selection We utilize two statistical filter-based algorithms namely minimum redundancy-maximum relevance (mRMR) and Principal component analysis (PCA) for feature reduction and selection. We use the mRMR and PCA feature selection techniques to reduce the feature space and select the subset of most acceptable top k high ranked features.

3.3 Word Embedding

We employ popular word embedding methods (Glove, fastText and BERT) to convert words into real-valued, low-dimensional vectors and extract useful syntactic and semantic information from them. The BERT-generated word vector has better quality features. In this study, we utilize these embedding algorithms for vectorization and sentiment classification.

3.4 CNN Architecture

We train our proposed system employing the CNN model, which is made up of four layers.

Input layer In this layer the tokenized input sentence is represented in our model by the matrix $D \in R^{m \times d_i}$, where d_i is the word embedding vector dimension of each word and m is the number of words in the sentence. Each sentence is padded with a zero vector to ensure that all the review sentences are the same size. The embedding matrix for each word in the sentence D is expressed in the embedding layer as:

$$M_e = \{V_{t_1}, V_{t_2}, ..., V_{k_i}, ..., V_{k_m}\}, \quad (1)$$

where V_{t_i} is the word vector and V_{k_i} is the placeholder for it in the embedding space.

Convolutional Layer The second layer is convolution layer and it is applied to the word embedding matrix M_e attained in the preceding layer. Assume that the convolution kernel $K^c \in R^{h \times l}$ has the following properties: c represents the number of convolution kernels, l indicates the length of the convolution kernel, and h represents the width of the convolution kernel. For the input matrix $D \in R^{m \times d_i}$, the feature map is created $P = \{p_1, p_2, ..., p_{n-h}\} \in R^{m-h+1}$ by repeatedly applying a convolution kernel R to perform convolution operation. Over the convolution output, the ReLU activation is applied.

Max-pooling Layer The max-pooling layer is the third layer, and it is applied to each feature map and takes the maximum value $\hat{c} = max\{c\}$(Collobert et al.). The max-pooling procedure is used in this study to save the most significant features (Kalchbrenner et al., 2014). These features are then concatenated and sent to the fully connected layer which is the final layer

Fully-connected Layer The main goal of a fully connected layer is to use the outputs of the convolution and pooling layer to processes and classify them into a label. A sigmoid function is utilized to get the final output. The probability distribution on the label is the output.

4 Experiments

Experimental Setup We tested our system using three real-world benchmark datasets: (1) Movie Reviews (MR) (Pang and Lee, 2005), (2) Stanford Sentiment Treebank (SST-2) datasets (Socher et al.), (3) Customer Review datasets (CR) (Hu and Liu). MR composed of 5331 positive and 5331 negative review samples. SST-2 contains positive and negative sentences, there are 9,613 single sentences in the dataset, which were obtained from movie reviews. CR consists of 14 products extracted from Amazon (Hu and Liu). SST-2 have standard training–test splits. MR and CR do not have such a standard split, we apply 10-fold cross validation, which is consistent with previous research (Huang et al.) on the dataset. We hold out 10 % of the training data for MR and CR for development purposes (e.g. for early stopping), we adopt classification accuracy as an evaluation measure. We generate 300-dimensional word vectors for GloVe and fastText embedding. The BERT-BASE model case version (network layers L = 12, hidden layer dimension H = 768, attention=12, total number of parameters surpass 110 M, Learning rate for Adam = 2e-5) was utilized as the pre-trained BERT model for word vectorization. We employed wide coverage sentiment lexicon (WCSL) for sentiment information extraction from review texts. We used mRMR and PCA filter-based feature selection algorithm for top k optimum feature selection. Top 2000 features of MR, 1500 features of SST-2, and 1000 features of CR dataset are feed to each channel in CNN. The dropout rate for each network's layer is 0.5, and

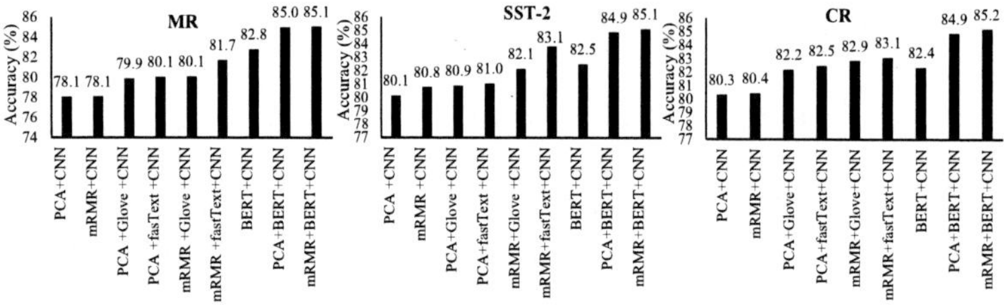

Figure 2: Ablation results of each component of (PCA, mRMR, Glove, fastText, BERT, and CNN) for different datasets (MR, SST-2, CR).

Table 1: Comparative Study

Model	Dataset	Accuracy
Rezaeinia *et al.* 2017	MR	79.80
Lei *et al.* 2018	MR	84.30
Huan *et al.* 2020	MR	79.45
Khasanah *et al.* 2021	MR	80.00
Our model	MR	85.12
Rezaeinia *et al.* 2017	SST-2	83.70
Huan *et al.* 2020	SST-2	84.34
Khasanah *et al.* 2021	SST-2	83.90
Our model	SST-2	85.10
Rezaeinia *et al.* 2017	CR	83.70
Our model	CR	85.20

the layers activation function is Rectified Linear Unit (ReLU). The sigmoid is used for the probability of class label in the fully connected layer. The proposed model and the other baseline models are implemented using the Rapidminer Studio (visual workflow designer) and tensorflow Keras library (High-level neural networks) in python. In our proposed model, the filter sizes of convolution1, convolution2, and convolution3 are 3,4, and 5, respectively, with 100 feature maps. The dropout rate is 0.5, l_2 constraint is (s) 3, mini-batch size is 5, and the layers activation function is Rectified Linear Unit (ReLU). The sigmoid is used for the probability of class label. We used the paired t-test ($P<0.05$) to calculate the evaluation measures of proposed model.

Experimental Results The ablation results of our proposed approach in terms of accuracy for each component with and without embeddings, with different feature selection methods is shown in Figure 2. From Figure 2, we can observe that selecting and representing relevant sentiment feature in a real valued vector/dense representation boost classification performance.We compare our approach with state-of-the-art DL approaches (Rezaeinia et al., 2017; Lei et al.; Huang et al.; Khasanah, 2021) that employed CNN-based model, multi-head attention convolutional network, and DNN models with fastText embedding respectively for sentence-level sentiment classification as shown in Table 1.

Model Analysis We explore the performance of our semantic and sentiment-aware CNN model. From Table 1, it is clear that our proposed model outperform baseline models on three benchmark datasets significantly. There are five reason why the proposed model achieves the best and comparable results. The first reason is that during text pre-processing, noisy and irrelevant features are removed from the text. The extraction and selection of relevant sentiment features is the second reason. The third reason is to classify mixed-opinionated texts using linguistic rules and semantic information. The integration of WCSL for sentiment features identification is the fourth reason. The fifth reason is the dense representation of sentiment features in a real valued vector, and fine tuning the proposed semantic and sentiment aware sentiment analysis model.

5 Conclusion

We propose an effective way of integrating the traditional feature construction method with the deep learning method to improve the overall performance of sentiment classification. To this end, we leverage semantic and sentiment knowledge using integrated WCSL to extract and select the relevant sentiment features for word embedding and sentiment classification. By employing mRMR and PCA filter-based algorithms and pre-trained embedding models (Glove, fastText, and BERT) to select optimum sentiment features and consider the semantics and context of words, we can filter out irrelevant and redundant features and reduce the dimensionality of feature space. In-depth experiments with three benchmark domain datasets demonstrate the effectiveness of the proposed model.

Acknowledgement

This work was supported by the research fund of Hanyang University (HY-2021-0372, HY-2022-0010, HY-2023)

References

Orestes Appel, Francisco Chiclana, Jenny Carter, and Hamido Fujita. 2016. A hybrid approach to the sentiment analysis problem at the sentence level. *Knowledge-Based Systems*, 108:110–124.

Babajide O Ayinde, Tamer Inanc, and Jacek M Zurada.

On correlation of features extracted by deep neural networks. In *IJCNN*.

Jing-Rong Chang, Hsin-Ying Liang, Long-Sheng Chen, and Chia-Wei Chang. 2020. Novel feature selection approaches for improving the performance of sentiment classification. *Journal of Ambient Intelligence and Humanized Computing*, pages 1–14.

Ronan Collobert, Jason Weston, Léon Bottou, Michael Karlen, Koray Kavukcuoglu, and Pavel Kuksa. Natural language processing (almost) from scratch. *Journal of machine learning research*, 12.

Misha Denil, Babak Shakibi, Laurent Dinh, Marc'Aurelio Ranzato, and Nando De Freitas. 2013. Predicting parameters in deep learning. *arXiv preprint arXiv:1306.0543*.

Chris Ding and Hanchuan Peng. Minimum redundancy feature selection from microarray gene expression data. *Journal of bioinformatics and computational biology*, 3.

Minqing Hu and Bing Liu. Mining and summarizing customer reviews. In *SIGKDD*.

Hui Huang, Yueyuan Jin, and Ruonan Rao. Sentiment-aware transformer using joint training. In *ICTAI*.

Nal Kalchbrenner, Edward Grefenstette, and Phil Blunsom. 2014. A convolutional neural network for modelling sentences. *arXiv preprint arXiv:1404.2188*.

Jacob Devlin Ming-Wei Chang Kenton and Lee Kristina Toutanova. Bert: Pre-training of deep bidirectional transformers for language understanding. In *naacL*.

Jawad Khan, Aftab Alam, and Young-Koo Lee. 2021. Intelligent hybrid feature selection for textual sentiment classification. *IEEE Access*.

Jawad Khan and Young-Koo Lee. Lessa: A unified framework based on lexicons and semi-supervised learning approaches for textual sentiment classification. *Applied Sciences*, 9.

Isnaini Nurul Khasanah. 2021. Sentiment classification using fasttext embedding and deep learning model. *Procedia Computer Science*, 189:343–350.

Yoon Kim. Convolutional neural networks for sentence classification. In *EMNLP*.

Zeyang Lei, Yujiu Yang, and Min Yang. Saan: a sentiment-aware attention network for sentiment analysis. In *SIGIR*.

Tomas Mikolov, Edouard Grave, Piotr Bojanowski, Christian Puhrsch, and Armand Joulin. 2017. Advances in pre-training distributed word representations. *arXiv preprint arXiv:1712.09405*.

Bo Pang and Lillian Lee. 2005. Seeing stars: Exploiting class relationships for sentiment categorization with respect to rating scales. *arXiv preprint cs/0506075*.

Seyed Mahdi Rezaeinia, Ali Ghodsi, and Rouhollah Rahmani. 2017. Improving the accuracy of pre-trained word embeddings for sentiment analysis. *arXiv preprint arXiv:1711.08609*.

Richard Socher, Alex Perelygin, Jean Wu, Jason Chuang, Christopher D Manning, Andrew Y Ng, and Christopher Potts. Recursive deep models for semantic compositionality over a sentiment treebank. In *Proceedings of the 2013 conference on empirical methods in natural language processing*.

Kristina Toutanvoa and Christopher D Manning. Enriching the knowledge sources used in a maximum entropy part-of-speech tagger. In *SIGDAT*.

Abinash Tripathy, Ankit Agrawal, and Santanu Kumar Rath. 2016. Classification of sentiment reviews using n-gram machine learning approach. *Expert Systems with Applications*, 57:117–126.

Svante Wold, Kim Esbensen, and Paul Geladi. Principal component analysis. *Chemometrics and intelligent laboratory systems*, 2.

Alireza Yousefpour, Roliana Ibrahim, and Haza Nuzly Abdel Hamed. 2017. Ordinal-based and frequency-based integration of feature selection methods for sentiment analysis. *Expert Systems with Applications*, 75:80–93.

Ye Zhang and Byron Wallace. 2015. A sensitivity analysis of (and practitioners' guide to) convolutional neural networks for sentence classification. *arXiv preprint arXiv:1510.03820*.

An Emotional Journey: Detecting Emotion Trajectories in Dutch Customer Service Dialogues

Sofie Labat[◇*] **Amir Hadifar**[♣*] **Thomas Demeester**[♣] **Véronique Hoste**[◇]
[◇]LT3, Language and Translation Technology Team, Ghent University, Belgium
[♣]T2K, Text-to-Knowledge Research Group, IDLab, Ghent University - imec, Belgium
{sofie.labat, amir.hadifar, thomas.demeester, veronique.hoste}@ugent.be

Abstract

The ability to track fine-grained emotions in customer service dialogues has many real-world applications, but has not been studied extensively. This paper measures the potential of prediction models on that task, based on a real-world dataset of Dutch Twitter conversations in the domain of customer service. We find that modeling emotion trajectories has a small, but measurable benefit compared to predictions based on isolated turns. The models used in our study are shown to generalize well to different companies and economic sectors.[1]

1 Introduction

While emotion recognition in conversations (ERC) has recently become a popular task in NLP (Poria et al., 2019b), its application potential to real-life business-related settings remains understudied. Our research focuses on applying ERC to the domain of customer service (CS), as it can be used to model customer satisfaction, reduce churns, prioritize clients, and detect emotional shifts in clients throughout CS interactions. Since the provision of customer service is gaining ground in both public and private chat channels, timely delivering high-quality assistance is crucial in mitigating the effects of negative word-of-mouth (van Noort and Willemsen, 2012) and creating relational bonds between customers and brands (Deloitte Digital, 2020).

As emotion recognition is often implemented on 'artificial', open-domain conversations (Busso et al., 2008; Li et al., 2017), we worked on real-world, domain-specific data that is more imbalanced and noisy. Moreover, we are the firsts to tackle the ERC task in Dutch dialogues. To these ends, we annotated *emotion layers* in a Dutch subset of 9,489 conversations from the Twitter corpus introduced by Hadifar et al. (2021), which we called EmoTwiCS ('Emotions in CS interactions on Twitter') (Labat et al., 2022b).[2] These emotion layers function as building blocks for *emotion trajectories*, a term emphasizing that emotions are dynamic attributes that can shift at each customer turn in the conversation.

We report classification effectiveness for six prediction tasks (focusing on cause, response strategies, subjectivity, valence, arousal, and emotion clusters). Besides subjectivity prediction which is applied to the conversation level, the five other tasks are run on isolated turns. To investigate the portability of our trained models to future data and other companies or sectors, we introduce three well-chosen train-test segmentation scenarios. We then zoom in on emotions and hypothesize that they follow a trajectory throughout conversations, whereby the operator tries to help the customer, thus deflecting negative emotions. To investigate whether knowledge about recurring emotion transitions may be useful for emotion prediction, we apply a Conditional Random Field (CRF; Lafferty et al., 2001) to the sequence of user turn encodings from a conversation, to make a joint prediction for the emotions in the conversation. We observe a weak, but consistently positive effect with respect to the isolated turn baselines in support of that premise.

2 Related work

Although emotion detection has often been applied to tweets (Mohammad et al., 2018) and chat logs (Ma et al., 2005), the context-aware detection of emotions throughout conversations is a relatively recent development in NLP. State-of-the-art results for emotion detection on isolated texts are achieved by fine-tuning large pretrained language

[*]Both authors contributed equally.

[1]Dataset and code are available at https://github.com/SofieLabat/EmoTwiCS-data and https://github.com/hadifar/DutchEmotionDetection, respectively.

[2]We refer to Labat et al. (2022b) for a detailed inter-annotator study and data analysis on EmoTwiCS.

Proceedings of the 2022 COLING Workshop: The 8th Workshop on Noisy User-generated Text (W-NUT 2022), pages 106–112

models. For Dutch, there currently exist two such models named BERTje (de Vries et al., 2019) and RobBERT (Delobelle et al., 2020), although cross-lingual language models such as XLM (Conneau et al., 2019) can also be applied to Dutch texts.

In contrast to these 'vanilla' emotion detection systems, recent work on ERC models additional information such as the conversational context, the temporal order of turns, and interlocutor-specific attributes (Poria et al., 2019b). There exist two approaches for ERC: we either view it as a sequence labeling task, or we predict emotions for a turn given the previous (and, in some variants, future) utterances. The latter approach was first addressed by recurrence-based models such as LSTMs (Poria et al., 2017), conversational memory networks (Hazarika et al., 2018), and attentive RNNs (Majumder et al., 2019). Afterwards, graph-based (Ghosal et al., 2019; Shen et al., 2021) and knowledge-enriched transformer models (Zhong et al., 2019; Zhu et al., 2021) were also investigated. The sequence labeling approach was introduced by Wang et al. (2020) who used information about the emotional consistency in conversations. His model combines a global context encoder (transformer) with an individual context encoder (LSTM) into a CRF layer to jointly predict emotions for all utterances. Guibon et al. (2021) implemented ERC in a few-shot learning sequence labeling problem. In our second experimental setup, we also tackle emotion detection as a sequence labeling task.

All but the two previously mentioned models are trained on publicly released datasets in English containing open-domain conversations (Busso et al., 2008; Poria et al., 2019a). There is only one small Dutch dataset (Vaassen et al., 2012) with 11 conversations and emotions rated on Leary's Rose (Leary, 1957), a dimensional framework with two axes representing the degree of control and agreeableness. For ERC, the corpus is less suitable given its small size, low agreement, fixed events, and uncommon emotion model. Unlike standard sentiment analysis, the fine-grained task of ERC has not yet become commonplace in CS departments. To our knowledge, there exist only a few papers that apply ERC to CS (Herzig et al., 2016; Maslowski et al., 2017; Mundra et al., 2017; Guibon et al., 2021).

3 Experimental setup

After describing the EmoTwiCS corpus along with its prediction tasks (Section 3.1), our data segmentation strategies are introduced (Section 3.2), followed by the models and their implementation details (Section 3.3).

3.1 EmoTwiCS task descriptions

We rely on a newly annotated corpus of emotion layers called EmoTwiCS. The corpus contains 9,489 Dutch Twitter dialogues in the domain of customer service that were collected for three economic sectors: telecommunication, public transportation, and airline industry. The conversations were annotated for four emotion layers: conversation characteristics, cause, response strategies, and customer emotions. Figure 1 illustrates how the layers and sublayers are annotated on a conversation, while the remainder of this section provides more details about each of them.

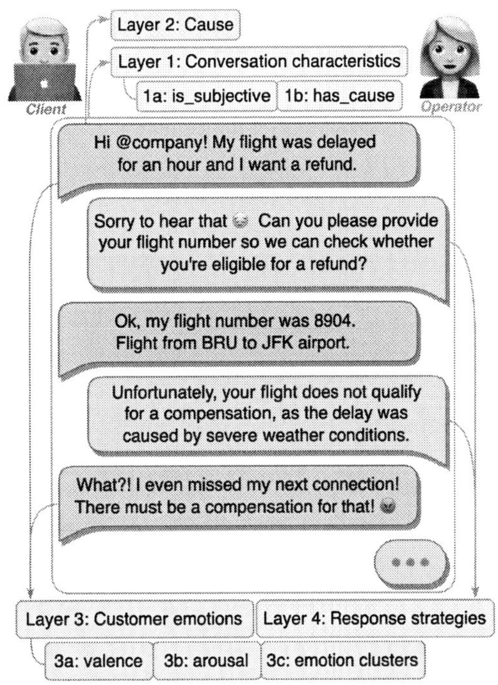

Figure 1: An English mock-up conversation to illustrate how conversations are annotated in the EmoTwiCS corpus along four emotion layers (conversation characteristics, cause, emotions, and response strategies).

Experiments were conducted for the following classification tasks on our emotion layers:

Subjectivity – Detect whether the conversation is subjective, which is the case if at least one customer turn contains emotions. The task involves classifying the concatenation of all customer turns.

Cause – Recognize the event that triggered customers to start a conversation, as a multi-class classification problem with eight classes (see Appendix, Table 3). Since 99% of all causes reside in the first customer turn, we use that as our model's input.

Response strategies – Recognize one or more response strategies operators applied in their responses. This is a multi-label prediction task over eight response strategies (see Table 3). Response strategies have only been annotated for subjective conversations, but cannot be assumed absent in objective ones. We therefore restrict the prediction task to subjective conversations only, and we use single operator turns as input to our models.

Valence/Arousal – Given a customer turn, predict its valence/arousal score (integer from 1 to 5). While valence represents the sentiment of an emotional state ranging from very negative to very positive, arousal stands for the amount of activation an emotion elicits and ranges from calm to excited. We implement both as multi-class tasks.

Emotion clusters – Given a customer turn, predict the emotion clusters that it contains.[3] While annotators could assign multiple labels to a single turn, we find that only 6.5% of the customer turns received two or more annotations. We therefore convert the task from a multi-label to a multi-class detection task by assigning an order of importance to the labels.[4] To validate our heuristic, an external annotator extracted the most prominent emotions from 100 customer turns with multiple emotion annotations. We find that the annotator and our heuristic agree in 78% of the cases.

3.2 Data segmentation

To investigate the out-of-domain transferability of our models on the different prediction tasks, we work with three train-test segmentation strategies. The size of the different splits is given in Table 4 in the Appendix.

Temporal split – 80-20 train-test split based on the chronological order of the first tweet in each conversation, stratified over companies. This way, we want to demonstrate that prediction systems trained on past data generalize well to unseen, future data. The split is also used for the in-context classification experiments (see Section 4.2).

Company splits – As telecom is the most frequent sector in EmoTwiCS, we split the six companies within this sector into three train-test splits, with each four companies for training and two for testing. Averaging the prediction results over these splits gives an idea of the transferability of our models to new companies within the same sector.

Sector splits – Given that EmoTwiCS has data for three economic sectors, we create three corresponding train-test splits in which we train on two economic sectors and evaluate on the third one. Cross-validation over these splits will demonstrate the transfer potential of our models to new sectors.

3.3 Models and implementation details

For the experiments on isolated tweets, we select the following models: majority class baseline, Support Vector Machines (SVM; Cortes and Vapnik, 1995) with tf-idf features, BERTje (de Vries et al., 2019), RobBERT (Delobelle et al., 2020), and XLM (Conneau et al., 2019). For all pretrained transformer models, we use their publicly available 'base' versions and place a single feedforward layer on top to predict the classes. We only tune the learning rate and number of epochs on 15% of the train data for the temporal setup, and reuse the same hyperparameters for the company and sector setups. For the second set of experiments, we put a CRF layer on top of RobBERT to predict the emotion trajectories of conversations (Lample et al., 2016). Given a conversation and its sequence of turns, we first extract the turn embeddings by using the [CLS] token representations from the last layer of the pretrained language model, which are then given to a classifier to estimate emotion cluster probabilities. These probabilities are subsequently fed into a CRF layer to maximize valid emotion sequence predictions.

4 Results and Discussion

We present the results of our models for six classification tasks on isolated tweets across the different train-test setups in Section 4.1. In Section 4.2, we focus on the emotion trajectories, and cast the detection of emotion clusters as a context-aware sequence labeling task.The presented metrics are micro and weighted F1 scores (Table 1), as well as accuracy (Fig. 2) and individual class F1 (Table 2) for emotion trajectories.

4.1 Experiments on isolated tweets

The results of our experiments for the six classification tasks are shown in Table 1, while the standard

[3]We use the term *clusters* to remain consistent with the EmoTwiCS data description paper. In that paper, 28 emotion labels were grouped into 9 emotion clusters.

[4]Heuristic: Anger > Annoyance > Disappointment > Nervousness > Gratitude > Relief > Joy > Desire > Neutral.

Setup	Model	Subjectivity $\mathbf{F1}_{micro}$	Cause $\mathbf{F1}_{w}$	Cause $\mathbf{F1}_{micro}$	Response strat. $\mathbf{F1}_{w}$	Response strat. $\mathbf{F1}_{micro}$	Valence $\mathbf{F1}_{w}$	Valence $\mathbf{F1}_{micro}$	Arousal $\mathbf{F1}_{w}$	Arousal $\mathbf{F1}_{micro}$	Emotion clusters $\mathbf{F1}_{w}$	Emotion clusters $\mathbf{F1}_{micro}$
Temporal	Majority-class	55.4	29.6	46.6	23.2	41.1	38.2	54.3	48.7	63.0	34.9	51.4
	SVM (tf-idf)	75.4	62.7	64.5	79.8	80.5	58.7	61.8	67.4	69.4	66.5	68.3
	BERTje	82.0	70.0	70.4	**87.6**	**87.7**	65.6	65.2	74.2	74.9	71.6	72.0
	RobBERT	**83.4**	**71.1**	**71.7**	86.9	87.1	67.8	67.7	74.0	74.6	**72.8**	**73.7**
	XLM	83.4	70.9	71.6	87.5	87.6	**68.1**	**68.0**	**74.4**	**75.2**	72.7	73.4
Company	RobBERT	**83.0**	71.1	71.4	**84.4**	**84.8**	**66.7**	**67.0**	**73.1**	**74.5**	**71.2**	**72.7**
	XLM	76.3	**71.3**	**71.5**	80.9	81.9	65.7	66.4	72.8	74.1	68.4	71.4
Sector	RobBERT	**83.0**	61.6	**64.0**	**84.6**	**85.4**	65.6	65.7	**73.9**	**74.7**	**71.6**	**72.9**
	XLM	72.90	**63.3**	63.4	81.5	83.5	**65.8**	**66.0**	72.8	73.7	70.6	72.0

Table 1: Results for subjectivity, cause, response strategies, valence, arousal, and emotion clusters classification.

deviations on the results of the company and sector setups are reported in Table 5. In the temporal setup of Table 1, we see that the fine-tuned language models outperform the majority class and SVM baselines by a large margin. Upon comparing the two Dutch language models RobBERT and BERTje, we find that RobBERT outperforms BERTje on four tasks (subjectivity, cause, valence, and emotion clusters). Moreover, the multi-lingual XLM model also achieves good results: it is the best baseline for valence and arousal prediction, but achieves second-to-best scores on all other tasks. As for the company and sector setups, we report scores for the two best-performing systems from the temporal setup. We observe that the results for two latter setups are less than, but still very comparable to the temporal experiments. Our models thus generalize well to other companies within the same domain, and to other economic sectors. This generalizability across sectors is significantly less outspoken for cause detection, which illustrates that cause classes are often linked to a specific domain (e.g., *delay* for public transportation vs. *breakdown* for telecom).

4.2 Modeling emotion trajectories

We hypothesize that emotions follow recurring trajectories that reflect the attempts of the CS operator to mitigate negative customer emotions. This motivated our reformulation of the emotion clustering task as a sequence labeling task (see also Wang et al., 2020; Guibon et al., 2021), modeled with a CRF to make joint predictions for emotion clusters in the conversation. As we work with joint predictions, we test our hypothesis on the subset of subjective conversations with at least two customer turns. We focus on subjective conversations, as these contain a varied distribution of emotion clusters. Figure 2 plots the results of our experiment across the conversations with a given number of customer turns. We notice a weak, yet consistent trend in which the CRF model slightly outperforms the isolated turn predictions. There is no clear indication that this effect is stronger for longer conversations, although that is hard to measure due to the low number of longer conversations. The improved results of the CRF model are thus an indication that there is some signal in modelling the sequence of emotions, although not statistically significant, given the size of the test set.

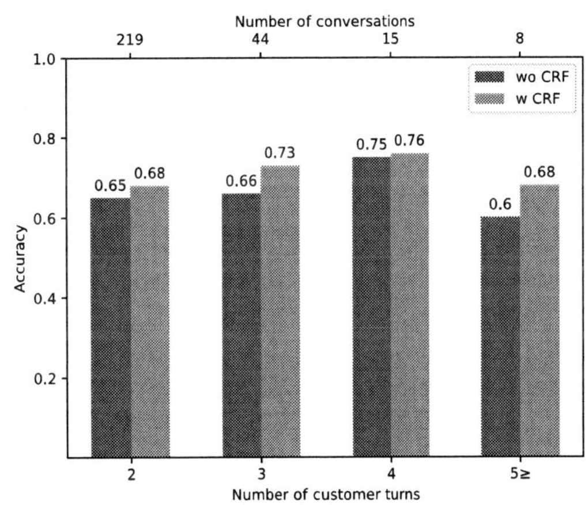

Figure 2: Emotion accuracy for all test conversations with at least two customer turns, calculated on the temporal setup, for the RobBERT baseline without CRF (wo CRF) vs. the one with the CRF (w CRF).

We further investigate the models' performance on individual emotion clusters in Table 2. We find that for some classes there is too little support leading to very low scores (e.g., Relief, Nervousness, and Desire). The F1 scores of both systems are generally higher for classes with more support. Nevertheless, the CRF model outperforms the baseline by a large margin on classes with lesser support (e.g., Anger, Disappointment, and Joy). Note that the high scores for Gratitude may be due to the rather standard lexicalization of it in the corpus.

Classes	w CRF	wo CRF	Support
Anger	0.40	0.04	45
Annoyance	0.53	0.58	182
Desire	0.11	0.0	17
Disappointment	0.45	0.0	36
Gratitude	0.92	0.90	123
Joy	0.51	0.32	35
Nervousness	0.00	0.00	11
Neutral	0.73	0.73	230
Relief	0.00	0.00	8

Table 2: Results (F1) for individual emotion clusters.

5 Conclusion

We presented the first experiments on a newly collected corpus of Dutch Twitter conversations annotated along four emotion layers. For our experiments on isolated tweets, we find that the best performance is obtained by fine-tuning pretrained language models such as RobBERT and XLM. We show that these two models transfer well across (i) time, (ii) companies within the same sectors, and (iii) across sectors. We also demonstrate that the detection of emotion clusters slightly benefits from knowledge about frequently occurring emotion trajectories, especially for classes with lower levels of support. In future research, we will extend our approach to model emotion trajectories for the purpose of real-time prediction (e.g., in chatbots), thus having access to past utterances only. We will also investigate emotion trajectories in longer conversations (e.g., on data collected through Wizard of Oz experiments (Labat et al., 2022a)) and focus on joint prediction tasks such as emotion-cause or emotion-response strategy extraction.

6 Acknowledgements

This research received funding from the Research Foundation Flanders with grant number 1S96322N and from the Flemish Government under the Research Program Artificial Intelligence (174U01222). We would like to thank the anonymous reviewers for their constructive feedback.

References

Carlos Busso, Murtaza Bulut, Chi-Chun Lee, Ebrahim (Abe) Kazemzadeh, Emily Mower Provost, Samuel Kim, Jeannette N. Chang, Sungbok Lee, and Shrikanth S. Narayanan. 2008. IEMOCAP: interactive emotional dyadic motion capture database. *Language Resources and Evaluation*, 42:335–359.

Alexis Conneau, Kartikay Khandelwal, Naman Goyal, Vishrav Chaudhary, Guillaume Wenzek, Francisco Guzmán, Edouard Grave, Myle Ott, Luke Zettlemoyer, and Veselin Stoyanov. 2019. Unsupervised cross-lingual representation learning at scale. *CoRR*, abs/1911.02116.

Corinna Cortes and Vladimir Vapnik. 1995. Support-vector networks. *Machine learning*, 20(3):273–297.

Wietse de Vries, Andreas van Cranenburgh, Arianna Bisazza, Tommaso Caselli, Gertjan van Noord, and Malvina Nissim. 2019. BERTje: A Dutch BERT Model. *arXiv preprint arXiv:1912.09582*.

Pieter Delobelle, Thomas Winters, and Bettina Berendt. 2020. RobBERT: a Dutch RoBERTa-based Language Model. In *Proceedings of EMNLP 2020*.

Deloitte Digital. 2020. Creating human connection at enterprise scale: What our research suggests about turning brands into bonds.

Deepanway Ghosal, Navonil Majumder, Soujanya Poria, Niyati Chhaya, and Alexander Gelbukh. 2019. DialogueGCN: A Graph Convolutional Neural Network for Emotion Recognition in Conversation. In *Proceedings of EMNLP-IJCNLP 2019*.

Gaël Guibon, Matthieu Labeau, Hélène Flamein, Luce Lefeuvre, and Chloé Clavel. 2021. Few-Shot Emotion Recognition in Conversation with Sequential Prototypical Networks. In *Proceedings of EMNLP 2021*.

Amir Hadifar, Sofie Labat, Véronique Hoste, Chris Develder, and Thomas Demeester. 2021. A Million Tweets Are Worth a Few Points: Tuning Transformers for Customer Service Tasks. In *Proceedings of NAACL 2021*.

Devamanyu Hazarika, Soujanya Poria, Amir Zadeh, Erik Cambria, Louis-Philippe Morency, and Roger Zimmermann. 2018. Conversational Memory Network for Emotion Recognition in Dyadic Dialogue Videos. In *Proceedings of NAACL*.

Jonathan Herzig, Guy Feigenblat, Michal Shmueli-Scheuer, David Konopnicki, Anat Rafaeli, Daniel Altman, and David Spivak. 2016. Classifying Emotions in Customer Support Dialogues in Social Media. In *Proceedings of SIGDIAL 2016*.

Sofie Labat, Naomi Ackaert, Thomas Demeester, and Véronique Hoste. 2022a. Variation in the Expression and Annotation of Emotions: a Wizard of Oz Pilot Study. In *Proceedings of the 1st Workshop on Perspectivist Approaches to NLP @LREC 2022*.

Sofie Labat, Thomas Demeester, and Véronique Hoste. 2022b. EmoTwiCS: a corpus for modelling emotion trajectories in Dutch customer service dialogues on Twitter. *Language Resources and Evaluation*. Accepted.

John D. Lafferty, Andrew McCallum, and Fernando C. N. Pereira. 2001. Conditional Random Fields: Probabilistic Models for Segmenting and Labeling Sequence Data. In *Proceedings of ICML 2001*.

Guillaume Lample, Miguel Ballesteros, Sandeep Subramanian, Kazuya Kawakami, and Chris Dyer. 2016. Neural Architectures for Named Entity Recognition. *arXiv preprint arXiv:1603.01360*.

Timothy Leary. 1957. *Interpersonal Diagnosis of Personality: A Functional Theory and Methodology for Personality Evaluation*.

Yanran Li, Hui Su, Xiaoyu Shen, Wenjie Li, Ziqiang Cao, and Shuzi Niu. 2017. DailyDialog: A Manually Labelled Multi-turn Dialogue Dataset. In *Proceedings of IJCNLP 2017*.

Chunling Ma, Helmut Prendinger, and Mitsuru Ishizuka. 2005. Emotion Estimation and Reasoning Based on Affective Textual Interaction. In *Proceedings of ACII 2005*.

Navonil Majumder, Soujanya Poria, Devamanyu Hazarika, Rada Mihalcea, Alexander Gelbukh, and Erik Cambria. 2019. DialogueRNN: An Attentive RNN for Emotion Detection in Conversations. In *Proceedings of AAAI 2019*.

Irina Maslowski, Delphine Lagarde, and Chloé Clavel. 2017. In-the-wild chatbot corpus: from opinion analysis to interaction problem detection. In *Proceedings of ICNLSSP 2017*.

Saif Mohammad, Felipe Bravo-Marquez, Mohammad Salameh, and Svetlana Kiritchenko. 2018. SemEval-2018 Task 1: Affect in Tweets. In *Proceedings of SemEval 2018*.

Shreshtha Mundra, Anirban Sen, Manjira Sinha, Sandya Mannarswamy, Sandipan Dandapat, and Shourya Roy. 2017. Fine-Grained Emotion Detection in Contact Center Chat Utterances. In *Proceedings of PAKDD 2017*.

Soujanya Poria, Erik Cambria, Devamanyu Hazarika, Navonil Majumder, Amir Zadeh, and Louis-Philippe Morency. 2017. Context-Dependent Sentiment Analysis in User-Generated Videos. In *Proceedings of ACL*.

Soujanya Poria, Devamanyu Hazarika, Navonil Majumder, Gautam Naik, Erik Cambria, and Rada Mihalcea. 2019a. MELD: A Multimodal Multi-Party Dataset for Emotion Recognition in Conversations. In *Proceedings of ACL 2019*.

Soujanya Poria, Navonil Majumder, Rada Mihalcea, and E. Hovy. 2019b. Emotion Recognition in Conversation: Research Challenges, Datasets, and Recent Advances. *IEEE Access*, 7:100943–100953.

Weizhou Shen, Siyue Wu, Yunyi Yang, and Xiaojun Quan. 2021. Directed Acyclic Graph Network for Conversational Emotion Recognition. In *Proceedings of ACL-IJCNLP 2021*.

Frederik Vaassen, Jeroen Wauters, Frederik Van Broeckhoven, Maarten Van Overveldt, Walter Daelemans, and Koen Eneman. 2012. deLearyous: Training Interpersonal Communication Skills Using Unconstrained Text Input. In *Proceedings of ECGBL 2012*.

Guda van Noort and Lotte M. Willemsen. 2012. Online Damage Control: The Effects of Proactive Versus Reactive Webcare Interventions in Consumer-generated and Brand-generated Platforms. *Journal of Interactive Marketing*, 26(3):131–140.

Yan Wang, Jiayu Zhang, Jun Ma, Shaojun Wang, and Jing Xiao. 2020. Contextualized Emotion Recognition in Conversation as Sequence Tagging. In *Proceedings of SIGDIAL 2020*.

Peixiang Zhong, Di Wang, and Chunyan Miao. 2019. Knowledge-Enriched Transformer for Emotion Detection in Textual Conversations. In *Proceedings of EMNLP-IJCNLP 2019*.

Lixing Zhu, Gabriele Pergola, Lin Gui, Deyu Zhou, and Yulan He. 2021. Topic-Driven and Knowledge-Aware Transformer for Dialogue Emotion Detection. In *Proceedings of ACL 2021*.

Appendix

Task	Label set
Cause	employee service; product quality; delays and cancellations; breakdowns; product information; digital design inadequacies; environmental and consumer health; no cause / other.
Resp.	apology; cheerfulness; empathy; gratitude; explanation; help offline; request information; other
Emotion	anger; annoyance; desire; disappointment; gratitude; joy; nervousness; neutral; relief

Table 3: Label sets for the tasks cause, response strategies (Resp.), and emotion clusters.

	Subj-Cause		Response strat.		Cust. emotions	
Setup	**Train**	**Test**	**Train**	**Test**	**Train**	**Test**
Temporal	7,587	1,902	6,477	1,489	10,272	2,443
Comp. 1	3,795	1,852	3,002	1,739	4,970	2,571
Comp. 2	3,670	1,977	2,962	1,779	4,802	2,739
Comp. 3	3,829	1,818	3,518	1,223	5,310	2,231
Sector 1	3,842	5,647	3,225	4,741	5,174	7,541
Sector 2	6,727	2,762	5,650	2,316	8,962	3,753
Sector 3	8,409	1,080	7,057	909	11,294	1,421

Table 4: Number of train-test instances for the classification tasks across the different segmentation strategies (temporal, company, sector). Subjectivity and cause are grouped together as they have the same number of train-test instances. The tag 'customer emotions' stands for valence, arousal and emotion clusters which are also grouped together for the same reason.

		Subjectivity	Cause		Response strat.		Valence		Arousal		Emotion clusters	
Setup	**Model**	s $\mathbf{F1}_{micro}$	s $\mathbf{F1}_w$	s $\mathbf{F1}_{micro}$	s $\mathbf{F1}_w$	s $\mathbf{F1}_{micro}$	s $\mathbf{F1}_w$	s $\mathbf{F1}_{micro}$	s $\mathbf{F1}_w$	s $\mathbf{F1}_{micro}$	s $\mathbf{F1}_w$	s $\mathbf{F1}_{micro}$
Company	RobBERT	0.6	1.5	1.8	0.4	0.3	1.1	1.3	1.8	1.8	1.9	1.8
	XLM	9.7	2.0	1.8	1.2	1.2	1.4	1.4	2.1	2.1	2.5	2.2
Sector	RobBERT	1.4	3.2	2.1	4.4	4.3	1.1	1.2	1.6	1.8	1.9	1.9
	XLM	16.5	4.5	4.9	9.7	7.6	1.0	1.0	1.6	1.9	2.5	2.2

Table 5: Standard deviation (s) on the average performance reported in Table 1. Standard deviation is reported for those setups that have several train-test splits (viz., company and sector setups).

Supervised and Unsupervised Evaluation of Synthetic Code-Switching

Evgeny Orlov
HSE University, Moscow, Russia
emorlov@edu.hse.ru

Ekaterina Artemova
HSE University, Moscow, Russia
Huawei Noah's Ark lab, Moscow, Russia
elartemova@hse.ru

Abstract

Code-switching (CS) is a phenomenon of mixing words and phrases from multiple languages within a single sentence or conversation. The ever-growing amount of CS communication among multilingual speakers in social media has highlighted the need to adapt existing NLP products for CS speakers and lead to a rising interest in solving CS NLP tasks. A large number of contemporary approaches use synthetic CS data for training. As previous work has shown the positive effect of pretraining on high-quality CS data, the task of evaluating synthetic CS becomes crucial. In this paper, we address the task of evaluating synthetic CS in two settings. In supervised setting, we apply Hinglish finetuned models to solve the *quality rating prediction* task of HinglishEval competition and establish a new SOTA. In unsupervised setting, we employ the method of acceptability measures with the same models. We find that in both settings, models finetuned on CS data consistently outperform their original counterparts.

1 Introduction

Code-switching (CS) is a phenomenon of mixing words and phrases from multiple languages within a single sentence or conversation[1]. It is common for multilingual speakers and happens across various language pairs across the globe, such as Spanish-English (Spanglish) and Hindi-English (Hinglish). Various studies (Baldauf, 2004) have predicted the high growth in the number of CS speakers, which would surpass the number of native speakers in various globally popular languages (e.g., English).

The advent of social media has highlighted the amount of CS communication and lead to a further increase of the number of multilingual speakers who use this pattern. This availability of CS data and the understanding that existing NLP products need to be adapted for the ever-growing number of CS speakers has resulted into a rising interest in various CS NLP tasks. Work has been done in such tasks as LID (Shekhar et al., 2020; Singh et al., 2018a; Ramanarayanan et al., 2019; Barman et al., 2014; Gundapu and Mamidi, 2020), POS tagging (Singh et al., 2018b; Vyas et al., 2014; Pratapa et al., 2018b), NER (Singh et al., 2018a; Priyadharshini et al., 2020; Winata et al., 2019a), word normalisation (Singh et al., 2018c; Parikh and Solorio, 2021), sentiment analysis (Patwa et al., 2020; Joshi et al., 2016), NLI (Khanuja et al., 2020a), machine translation (Srivastava and Singh, 2020; Dhar et al., 2018) and QA (Chandu et al., 2019; Thara et al., 2020).

Various studies have shown that CS data may pose a challenge for contemporary multilingual models (Birshert and Artemova, 2021). Finetuning on CS data can alleviate this problem (e.g. Ansari et al., 2021). As social media can be noisy and not readily available to build a large scale corpus, various techniques of generating synthetic CS have been proposed (see Section 2). However, it was shown that the performance of the models crucially depends on the quality of CS text used for pretraining (Santy et al., 2021). This creates the task of synthetic CS evaluation which is the main focus of current paper.

CS evaluation methods range from computing intrinsic text metrics to measuring downstream task performance depending on the CS data used for pretraining and human evaluation (see Section 2). Srivastava and Singh (2021a) show that most CS evaluation metrics fail to capture the linguistic diversity which leads to poorly estimating the quality of CS text. Thus, human evaluation remains as a reliable method. Srivastava and Singh (2021b) propose HinGE, a dataset of Hinglish sentences with human quality ratings and organise HinglishE-

[1] Some works make a distinction and refer to intrasentential (within a single sentence) code alternation as "code-mixing" (CM) and intersentential (at or above the sentence level) as "code-switching" (CS). It is also common, however, to use the term "CS" for both cases. Intrasentential code alternation is the focus of this paper and we refer to it as "CS".

Proceedings of the 2022 COLING Workshop: The 8th Workshop on Noisy User-generated Text (W-NUT 2022), pages 113–123

val shared task based on it (Srivastava and Singh, 2021c). In our paper, we address HinglishEval *quality rating prediction* task with Hinglish models proposed in Nayak and Joshi (2022). Moreover, we add an unsupervised setting of the task. Our main contributions are:

- We perform a series of experiments on unsupervised CS evaluation, employing the method of acceptability measures (Lau et al., 2015). To our knowledge, this is the first such attempt.
- We perform a series of experiments on supervised CS evaluation and establish a new SOTA for HinglishEval *quality rating prediction* task.
- We find that models finetuned on CS data consistently outperform their original counterparts.

2 Related works

Generating synthetic CS As large amounts of real-world CS data may be difficult to extract, various generating methods have been proposed. Simplistic methods include re-writing of some words in the target script (Gautam et al., 2021) and various rule-based algorithms used as baselines in the literature (e.g., Tarunesh et al., 2021; Srivastava and Singh, 2021b). The vast majority of methods utilize machine translation engines (Singh et al., 2019), parallel datasets (Jawahar et al., 2021; Gautam et al., 2021; Gupta et al., 2021; Winata et al., 2019b) or bilingual lexicons (Tan and Joty, 2021) to replace the segment of the input text with its translations. Bilingual lexicons may be induced from the parallel corpus with the help of soft alignment, produced by attention mechanisms (Lee and Li, 2020; Liu et al., 2020). Pointer networks can be used to select segments for further replacement (Gupta et al., 2020; Winata et al., 2019b). If natural CS data is available, such segments can be identified with a sequence labeling model (Gupta et al., 2021). A number of works employ popular architectures like VAE (Samanta et al., 2019) and GANs (Garg et al., 2018; Chang et al., 2019). Other methods produce synthetic CS text that grammatically adheres to a linguistic theory of code-switching. Pratapa et al. (2018a) leverage the equivalence constraint (EC) theory (Poplack, 1980), while Rizvi et al. (2021) use EC and Matrix-language (Carol, 1993) theories.

Evaluating synthetic CS Despite the practical need of synthetic CS datasets, the task of evaluating synthetic CS remains relatively understudied. Some evaluation techniques involve estimating intrinsic text properties, such as code-switching ratio and length distribution. One of the most popular metrics is code-mixing index (CMI) (Das and Gambäck, 2014; Gambäck and Das, 2016), which accounts for code-switching ratio and the number of switches in a sentence. We defer to Srivastava and Singh (2021a) for a detailed overview of other metrics used for evaluating CS NLG.

Further, extrinsic measures can be used, like the perplexity of external language model. For example, Nayak and Joshi (2022) propose a finetuned Hinglish GPT model and suggest using it for evaluation. Also, downstream task performance can be measured, depending on the CS data used for augmentation (Samanta et al., 2019; Santy et al., 2021). Downstream tasks are organised into benchmarks such as GLUECoS (Khanuja et al., 2020b) and LinCE (Aguilar et al., 2020) which comprise data for popular language pairs like English-Hindi and English-Spanish.

Finally, human evaluators can be employed to assess the quality of the generated CS. There are examples of such evaluation studies in the literature which are usually performed to prove the quality of the proposed CS generation method (Bhat et al., 2016; Tarunesh et al., 2021). However, these studies are of low scale and do not result into substantial datasets which can be used in further research. In this context, HinGE dataset (Srivastava and Singh, 2021b) is unique being the largest collection of synthetic CS with human ratings to date. It is described in detail in Section 3.1. Based on HinGE, HinglishEval competition was organised (Srivastava and Singh, 2021c; see Section 3.1.1), where the task is to model the annotators' opinion on CS sentences.

Language models for CS Along with the development of language models (LMs), work has been done to adapt them for CS data. Chan et al. (2009) compare different n-gram LMs, Vu et al. (2012) suggest to improve language modeling by generating artificial CS text. A number of works propose LMs that incorporate a syntactic constraint (Li and Fung, 2012, 2014; Pratapa et al., 2018a). Another line of papers introduce LMs where the output layer is factorized into languages, and POS tags are added to the input (Adel et al., 2013a,b, 2014, 2015; Sreeram and Sinha, 2017).

With the advent of Transformers (Vaswani et al., 2017), work has shifted to applying popular architectures to CS data. Pires et al. (2019) show that m-BERT can achieve promising results in Hinglish downstream tasks when Hindi parts are written in Devanagari even in a zero-shot setup. The same, however, does not apply to romanized Hinglish, as m-BERT was pretrained on Devanagari Hindi. Both GLUECoS (Khanuja et al., 2020b) and LinCE (Aguilar et al., 2020) benchmarks provide m-BERT baselines for their leaderboards. Ansari et al. (2021) show that BERT models produce better results in CS LID when pretrained on CS sentences rather than on multiple monolingual corpora. Santy et al. (2021) find that finetuning m-BERT on natural CS data gives the best performance improvement compared to any synthetic CS. Nayak and Joshi (2022) present the first large-scale (52.93M sentences) corpus of real Hinglish CS scraped from Twitter and a line of Transformer models finetuned on it. The corpus and the models are described in detail in Section 4.1.

Acceptability measures Lau et al. (2015) present the task of unsupervised prediction of speakers' acceptability judgements and propose *acceptability measures* as a method to translate LM's probability into acceptability scores. Acceptability measures are variants of the sentence's log probability, devised to normalise sentence length and low frequency words (see Section 4.2 for additional details and equations). The effectiveness of an acceptability measure is evaluated by computing its Pearson correlation with human acceptability scores. Lau et al. (2020) further experiment with Transformer LMs and investigate the dependence of acceptability measures' scores on whether the context of the sentence is provided.

3 Data

3.1 HinGE

HinGE is a dataset of synthetic Hinglish sentences with human quality ratings proposed in Srivastava and Singh (2021b). The dataset consists of firstly, parallel English and Hindi sentences. Second, two synthetic Hinglish sentences are generated from each pair of parallel sentences by two rule-based code-mixed text generation (CMTG) algorithms:

- Word-aligned CMTG (WAC): Noun and adjective tokens are aligned between the parallel sentences. The aligned Hindi token is replaced with the corresponding English token.
- Phrase-aligned CMTG (PAC): Key-phrases of length up to three tokens are aligned between the parallel sentences. The aligned Hindi phrase is replaced with the corresponding English phrase.

For both algorithms, the Hindi parts are then transliterated into the Roman script.

Third, an average of two human quality ratings on a scale of `1-10` is assigned to each synthetic Hinglish sentence. Refer to Table 1 for class balance information.

Label	# sentences	Binary label	# sentences
1	0	0	2279
2	9		
3	61		
4	250		
5	394		
6	633		
7	932		
8	960	1	1673
9	587		
10	126		
Total #	3952		

Table 1: Hinge All classes statistics

Fourth, annotators' disagreement is given, which is calculated as the absolute difference between the human quality ratings and ranges `0-9`. Finally, for each pair of parallel sentences, at least two human-generated Hinglish sentences are provided. Figure 1 demonstrates an example of the described fields of the dataset.

Overall, HinGE contains 1976 parallel Hindi–English, 3952 synthetic CS and 4803 human-generated CS sentences. All synthetic CS sentences have human scores assigned to them, and HinGE is the largest such dataset to date. We refer to the synthetic part of the dataset as *Hinge All.*

3.1.1 HinglishEval competition

The authors also organized HinglishEval shared task based on the HinGE dataset (Srivastava and Singh, 2021c), which includes two subtasks: *quality rating prediction* and *annotators' disagreement prediction*. Both are classification tasks, but are evaluated with MSE in addition to weighted F1-score. Besides, Cohen's Kappa (CK) is computed for *quality rating prediction*. The dataset is split in the ratio 70:10:20 with 2766, 395 and 791 synthetic CS sentences in train, validation, and test, respectively. We refer to this dataset as *HinglishEval.*

English	Hindi	Human-generated Hinglish	WAC	PAC
The reward of goodness shall be nothing but goodness.	अच्छाई का बदला अच्छाई के सिवा और क्या हो सकता है?	The reward of achai shall be nothing but achai. Goodness ka badla goodness ke siva aur kya ho sakta hai. Achai ka badla shall be nothing but achai.	reward ka badla reward ke nothing aur kya ho sakta hai **Rating1**: 7 **Rating2**: 4	reward of goodness goodness ke siva aur kya ho sakta hai **Rating1**: 9 **Rating2**: 7

Figure 1: Example pair of parallel sentences with corresponding human-generated and synthetic CS from HinGE dataset. Picture from Srivastava and Singh (2021b).

For both tasks, the participants can use all the data in HinGE, including the English, Hindi and human-generated Hinglish sentences. Participants are also asked to implicitly answer questions about the reasons influencing the quality of synthetic CS. We seek to answer some of these in our work.

3.2 TCS

The dataset we refer to as *TCS* is a collection of 750 Hinglish sentences with human scores from Tarunesh et al. (2021). It contains Hinglish sentences from five sources (250 sentences each): human-generated CS, two rule-based algorithms, and supervised and unsupervised versions of the Transformer-based generation method proposed in Tarunesh et al. (2021). Each Hinglish sentence is provided with an average of three human scores on a scale of `1-5` under three heads: "Syntactic correctness","Semantic correctness" and "Naturalness". For our experiments, we also take the average of these three scores under the name of "Mean human score".

The original TCS sentences have their Hindi parts in Devanagari script, and we refer to this dataset as *TCS Devanagari.* We also transliterate the sentences into Roman script using `indic-transliteration` library[2] with ITRANS scheme[3] and refer to this dataset as *TCS transliterated.*

4 Experimental setup

4.1 Models

This subsection describes the LMs we experiment with in this work. All of them are taken from the Hugging Face Hub[4]. First, we employ a line of popular Transformers architectures: **BERT** (Devlin et al., 2018); **CoLA BERT**, a BERT model trained on CoLA dataset (Warstadt et al., 2019) and released by Morris et al. (2020); **XLM-RoBERTa** (Conneau et al., 2019); **m-BERT** (Devlin et al., 2018); **GPT-2** (Radford et al., 2019); and **mGPT** (Shliazhko et al., 2022).

Further, we employ Hinglish LMs introduced in Nayak and Joshi (2022). All of them are trained on L3Cube-HingCorpus proposed in the same paper. L3Cube-HingCorpus was collected as follows. First, CS sentences were filtered from continuously scraped tweets using a shallow subword-based LSTM LID classifier which was iteratively improved as the dataset increased. Then a BERT LID classifier was finetuned on the resulting 44455 sentences and was further used to collect the main corpus. The final dataset contains 52.93M sentences (1.04B tokens) of natural Hinglish CS. A Devanagari version of the dataset was created using an in-house transliteration model. Here we list the finetuned Hinglilsh models with their original counterparts in parentheses: **HingBERT** (BERT), **HingMBERT** (m-BERT), **HingRoBERTa** (XLM-RoBERTa), **HingGPT** (GPT-2). There are also two mixed versions of the models, which are pretrained on both Devanagari and roman scripts (**HingMBERT-mixed** and **HingRoBERTa-mixed**), and a model which is trained completely on Devanagari script (**HingGPT-devanagari**).

4.2 Unsupervised approach

We employ the concept of acceptability measures proposed in Lau et al. (2015) to assess the quality of CS in both TCS datasets and Hinge All. Table 2 presents equations for different acceptability measures. Of all the methods, we compute only *LP*, *MeanLP*, and *PenLP*, as *NormLP* and *SLOR* require an additional unigram LM. It should not be oversignificant, however, because for considered models (BERT and GPT-2) the best performance

[2] `https://github.com/indic-transliteration/indic_transliteration_py`

[3] ITRANS scheme showed the best performance scores among others in our preliminary experiments. See `https://www.aczoom.com/itrans/`

[4] `https://huggingface.co/models`

Acc. Measure	Equation
LP	$\log P(s)$
MeanLP	$\dfrac{\log P(s)}{\lvert s\rvert}$
PenLP	$\dfrac{\log P(s)}{((5+\lvert s\rvert)/(5+1))^{\alpha}}$
NormLP	$-\dfrac{\log P(s)}{\log P_{\text{u}}(s)}$
SLOR	$\dfrac{\log P(s)-\log P_{\text{u}}(s)}{\lvert s\rvert}$

Table 2: Acceptability measures for predicting the acceptability of a sentence. $P(s)$ is the sentence probability, computed by a LM; $P_{\text{u}}(s)$ is the sentence probability estimated by a unigram LM; and $\alpha = 0.8$.

was mostly achieved by *PenLP* in the original paper (Lau et al., 2020). To compute the acceptability measures of considered Transformer models, we rely on the code from Lau et al. (2020). To evaluate the effectiveness of each acceptability measure, we compute its Pearson correlation with human acceptability scores in our datasets.

4.3 Supervised approach

We also run our models in a supervised setting on HinglishEval data, particularly the *quality rating prediction* task. As the original 10-way classification task has proved to be quite difficult in our preliminary experiments and the results of the competition, we add two simplified versions of it:

- *Binary classification*: We binarize the labels (`1-7` are converted to `0` and `8-10` to `1`[5]) and perform binary classification. Classes numbers are given in Table 1.
- *Regression*: We perform regression on the original labels. MSE is computed with the models' initial predictions, while the predictions for F1-score and CK are rounded.

All models are trained for 5 epochs with a learning rate of $2e{-}5$, batch size of 32. The best model is then chosen with validation F1-score. For all models, we repeat training 10 times with 10 different seeds (0–9, respectively). We report mean and standard deviation of all metrics over 10 runs.

5 Results

5.1 Unsupervised approach

Acceptability measures' performance on TCS Devanagari and TCS transliterated is given in Tables 3 and 4, respectively. For both versions of TCS, among the three scales, the highest correlations are achieved with *Mean syntactic correctness* score, which may indicate that syntax structure is the easiest for the models to grasp.

For TCS Devanagari, predictably, a substantial advantage is on the side of the models which were exposed to Devanagari during pretraining (mBERT, mGPT, HingMBERT-mixed, and HingGPT-devanagari). The best *Mean human score* correlations are shared by HingMBERT-mixed and notably mGPT which was not pretrained on any CS data.

For TCS transliterated, multilingual models cannot rely on their Devanagari knowledge. HingBERT is a clear leader, as it was exposed to romanized Hinglish during pretraining. Overall, the correlations of Hinglish models are lower than on TCS Devanagari. A possible explanation could be that the transliteration scheme we used to transliterate TCS differs from the way Hinglish is written on social media, whose data was used to finetune Hinglish models.

Acceptability measures' performance on Hinge All is given in Table 5. Here, the best correlations are also predictably achieved by the models which were finetuned on Hinglish CS data.

Comparing different acceptability measures with each other, we observe that unnormalized *LP* works quite well, but is usually outperformed by *PenLP*. In general, however, unidirectional (GPT-like) models benefit more from normalization. These observations support the findings of Lau et al. (2020). In general, we note that CS finetuned models consistently perform better than their original counterparts.

5.2 Supervised approach

Table 6 shows the results of 10-class classification on HinglishEval data. To be consistent with the participants of HinglishEval competition, we report both validation and test results and round the scores to thousandths. Here, HingMBERT-mixed achieves the best score and beats current SOTA (0.261) as reported in HinglishEval leaderboard[6]. It outperforms HingMBERT, although all Hindi data in HinGE is romanized.

Although the best model for regression (see Table 7) is still chosen based on F1-score, this kind of

[5]We choose the boundary so that the classes are of relative sizes.

[6]`https://codalab.lisn.upsaclay.fr/competitions/1688`

model	Mean syntactic correctness			Mean semantic correctness			Mean naturalness			Mean human score		
	LP	*MeanLP*	*PenLP*	*LP*	*MeanLP*	*PenLP*	*LP*	*MeanLP*	*PenLP*	*LP*	*MeanLP*	*PenLP*
BERT	0.08	0.03	0.1	0.07	0.03	0.09	0.05	0.04	0.08	0.07	0.04	0.09
m-BERT uncased	0.33	0.13	0.28	0.31	0.12	0.26	0.28	0.12	0.25	0.31	0.13	0.26
m-BERT cased	0.28	0.15	0.26	0.26	0.14	0.24	0.24	0.14	0.24	0.26	0.15	0.25
GPT-2	0.09	0.16	0.31	0.08	0.16	0.29	0.06	0.16	0.28	0.08	0.16	0.3
mGPT	0.35	0.21	**0.41**	0.33	0.2	**0.39**	0.3	0.2	**0.37**	0.33	0.2	**0.39**
HingBERT	0	-0.08	-0.04	0	-0.07	-0.04	-0.02	-0.07	-0.06	-0.01	-0.08	-0.05
HingMBERT	0.08	-0.07	0.02	0.08	-0.07	0.02	0.07	-0.05	0.02	0.07	-0.06	0.02
HingMBERT mixed	**0.41**	0.28	0.39	**0.39**	0.27	0.37	**0.37**	0.27	0.36	**0.39**	0.28	0.37
HingGPT	-0.02	-0.18	-0.06	-0.03	-0.18	-0.06	-0.04	-0.19	-0.07	-0.03	-0.19	-0.07
HingGPT-devanagari	0.2	**0.31**	0.26	0.19	**0.3**	0.25	0.17	**0.29**	0.23	0.19	**0.3**	0.25

Table 3: Acceptability measures' correlations on TCS Devanagari

model	Mean syntactic correctness			Mean semantic correctness			Mean naturalness			Mean human score		
	LP	*MeanLP*	*PenLP*	*LP*	*MeanLP*	*PenLP*	*LP*	*MeanLP*	*PenLP*	*LP*	*MeanLP*	*PenLP*
BERT	0.03	-0.02	0.01	0.02	-0.03	0	0.01	0	0	0.02	-0.02	0
m-BERT uncased	0.02	-0.05	-0.01	0.01	-0.06	-0.02	0	-0.04	-0.01	0.01	-0.05	-0.01
m-BERT cased	0.01	-0.09	-0.04	0	-0.1	-0.05	0	-0.07	-0.04	0	-0.09	-0.05
GPT-2	0.03	0	0.04	0.02	0	0.02	0	0.01	0.02	0.02	0	0.02
mGPT	0.05	0.02	0.06	0.04	0.02	0.05	0.02	0.04	0.05	0.03	0.03	0.05
HingBERT	**0.18**	**0.2**	**0.22**	**0.16**	**0.18**	**0.2**	**0.16**	**0.21**	**0.22**	**0.17**	**0.2**	**0.22**
HingMBERT	0.15	0.12	0.19	0.13	0.11	0.17	0.13	0.13	0.18	0.14	0.12	0.18
HingMBERT mixed	0.16	0.13	0.2	0.14	0.12	0.18	0.14	0.14	0.2	0.15	0.13	0.2
HingGPT	0.07	0.02	0.07	0.06	0.01	0.06	0.04	0.04	0.06	0.06	0.02	0.07
HingGPT-devanagari	0.05	0.05	0.05	0.04	0.03	0.04	0.02	0.02	0.03	0.04	0.03	0.04

Table 4: Acceptability measures' correlations on TCS transliterated

model	*LP*	*MeanLP*	*PenLP*
BERT	0.19	-0.04	0.15
m-BERT uncased	0.19	-0.07	0.14
m-BERT cased	0.19	-0.08	0.14
GPT-2	0.19	-0.06	0.2
mGPT	0.2	-0.06	0.21
HingBERT	0.22	0.08	0.2
HingMBERT	0.22	0.1	0.21
HingMBERT mixed	**0.23**	0.1	0.21
HingGPT	0.2	0.1	**0.25**
HingGPT-devanagari	0.18	**0.11**	0.19

Table 5: Acceptability measures' correlations on Hinge All

problem statement allows to reduce the MSE score as compared to 10-class classification. A low MSE, however, does not lead to a higher F1-score. The best F1-scores are achieved by HingMBERT and HingRoBERTa, but are insufficient to overcome the level of 10-class classification.

Binarizaton of the problem (see Table 8) allows to significantly raise the F1-scores. The best result here is achieved by HingMBERT-mixed. We observe that CoLA BERT performs better than BERT base model, which may indicate transfer learning from English acceptability task.

We note that similarly with unsupervised setting, CS models consistently outperform their original counterparts in all supervised problem statements.

6 Discussion

Our experiments show that both in unsupervised and supervised setups, models pretrained on Hinglish data consistently outperform their original counterparts. This goes in line with previous studies which have shown that pretraining on CS data yields better results than monolingual pretraining (Santy et al., 2021; Ansari et al., 2021).

On HinglishEval 10-class classification, our HingMBERT-mixed establishes new SOTA, surpassing the m-BERT baseline from Srivastava and Singh (2021c) which was trained solely on Hinglish sentences from Hinge. Moreover, our Hinglish models trained solely on Hinglish sentences produce scores competitive with the participants of HinglishEval shared task which use all available information from HinGE (original Hindi and English sentences and annotators' disagreement; Furniturewala et al., 2022; Guha et al., 2022; Kodali et al., 2022; Singh, 2022).

6.1 Error analysis

In this subsection, we look for sources of errors of our best performing model, HingMBERT-mixed. We analyze its predictions on the test subset of HinglishEval 10-class classification. We put three

model	Val			Test		
	F1	CK	MSE	F1	CK	MSE
BERT	0.232±0.013	0.069±0.015	2.812±0.146	0.238±0.011	0.082±0.014	2.778±0.215
CoLA BERT	0.238±0.014	0.081±0.014	2.774±0.274	0.225±0.019	0.065±0.016	2.76±0.327
m-BERT uncased	0.255±0.016	0.102±0.013	2.867±0.193	0.238±0.016	0.086±0.014	2.826±0.115
m-BERT cased	0.245±0.015	0.08±0.02	2.944±0.215	0.237±0.013	0.078±0.017	2.878±0.149
XLMRoBERTa	0.229±0.014	0.081±0.02	2.957±0.187	0.203±0.013	0.045±0.016	2.878±0.194
GPT-2	0.216±0.013	0.056±0.018	3.182±0.173	0.204±0.017	0.036±0.022	3.175±0.243
HingBERT	0.253±0.005	0.106±0.007	2.689±0.123	0.248±0.012	0.101±0.015	2.839±0.134
HingMBERT	**0.262±0.015**	**0.11±0.015**	2.663±0.213	0.253±0.019	0.1±0.02	2.613±0.182
HingMBERT-mixed	0.253±0.014	0.1±0.02	**2.627±0.23**	**0.267±0.01**	**0.119±0.011**	**2.526±0.184**
HingRoBERTa	0.245±0.012	0.099±0.015	2.682±0.102	0.251±0.024	0.109±0.027	2.734±0.16
HingGPT	0.237±0.009	0.066±0.01	3.116±0.15	0.25±0.014	0.087±0.016	3.031±0.199
HingGPT-devanagari	0.209±0.006	0.051±0.008	3.29±0.141	0.196±0.016	0.037±0.018	3.195±0.154
m-BERT baseline	0.202	0.003	2.797	0.256	0.092	2.628

Table 6: 10-class classification results on HinglishEval. m-BERT baseline from Srivastava and Singh (2021c)

model	Val			Test		
	F1	CK	MSE	F1	CK	MSE
BERT	0.222±0.011	0.063±0.014	2.371±0.086	0.218±0.013	0.055±0.018	2.219±0.123
CoLA BERT	0.219±0.008	0.059±0.012	2.364±0.078	0.222±0.018	0.056±0.018	2.226±0.058
m-BERT uncased	0.223±0.011	0.06±0.016	2.341±0.065	0.215±0.009	0.051±0.015	2.213±0.079
m-BERT cased	0.217±0.006	0.049±0.011	2.391±0.08	0.215±0.008	0.05±0.011	**2.205±0.035**
XLMRoBERTa	0.189±0.007	0.019±0.012	2.453±0.05	0.197±0.009	0.033±0.011	2.396±0.063
GPT-2	0.211±0.012	0.042±0.015	2.411±0.077	0.22±0.013	0.053±0.011	2.246±0.054
HingBERT	0.232±0.016	0.069±0.016	2.359±0.14	0.244±0.016	0.081±0.018	2.331±0.149
HingMBERT	**0.239±0.024**	**0.083±0.028**	2.401±0.088	**0.25±0.014**	**0.093±0.015**	2.37±0.092
HingMBERT-mixed	0.226±0.03	0.066±0.037	2.437±0.146	0.235±0.025	0.075±0.026	2.388±0.154
HingRoBERTa	0.236±0.013	0.08±0.012	**2.276±0.133**	**0.25±0.02**	0.092±0.017	2.276±0.128
HingGPT	0.247±0.008	0.076±0.009	2.389±0.1	0.256±0.007	0.086±0.01	2.278±0.095
HingGPT-devanagari	0.194±0.008	0.027±0.014	2.625±0.188	0.191±0.014	0.027±0.014	2.545±0.228

Table 7: Regression results on HinglishEval

model	Val			Test		
	F1	CK	MSE	F1	CK	MSE
BERT	0.639±0.011	0.253±0.023	0.357±0.013	0.662±0.011	0.304±0.021	0.333±0.011
CoLA BERT	0.633±0.007	0.246±0.018	0.365±0.008	0.673±0.013	0.329±0.026	0.325±0.014
m-BERT uncased	0.646±0.011	0.27±0.025	0.353±0.011	0.648±0.01	0.278±0.022	0.348±0.01
m-BERT cased	0.626±0.015	0.23±0.031	0.371±0.016	0.637±0.01	0.254±0.021	0.359±0.01
XLMRoBERTa	0.623±0.025	0.222±0.058	0.371±0.019	0.639±0.015	0.258±0.036	0.356±0.013
GPT-2	0.612±0.02	0.211±0.041	0.388±0.022	0.619±0.016	0.228±0.026	0.379±0.019
HingBERT	0.665±0.007	0.324±0.02	0.336±0.007	0.648±0.015	0.287±0.026	0.353±0.016
HingMBERT	0.682±0.011	0.354±0.021	0.318±0.012	0.672±0.015	0.333±0.24	0.327±0.016
HingMBERT-mixed	0.682±0.008	0.353±0.014	0.318±0.009	**0.681±0.008**	**0.352±0.019**	**0.319±0.008**
HingRoBERTa	**0.689±0.013**	**0.369±0.026**	**0.312±0.013**	0.668±0.011	0.323±0.021	0.332±0.011
HingGPT	0.642±0.009	0.269±0.02	0.358±0.009	0.643±0.011	0.269±0.022	0.355±0.012
HingGPT-devanagari	0.574±0.01	0.116±0.021	0.42±0.011	0.609±0.008	0.193±0.017	0.383±0.012

Table 8: Binary classification results on HinglishEval

factor	mean		statistically significant
	correct	incorrect	
sentence length	17.0	19.2	✗
Hindi fraction	0.63	0.67	✓
# of switch points	5.5	6.1	✗

Table 9: Error source factors for HinglishEval 10-class classification, model is HingMBERT-mixed

factors under consideration: sentence length in words, fraction of Hindi words in a sentence and number of code switches within a sentence. To compute the latter two values, we annotate HinGE test subset with HingBERT-LID model proposed in Nayak and Joshi (2022). We compare the mean value of the factors depending on the correctness of model's prediction (see Table 9). We find that the mean of all three factors is greater for incorrect predictions, which means that the model tends to consistently make mistakes on more complex sentences. However, computing the t-test shows that only the difference in fraction of Hindi words is statistically significant. These results can be seen as an answer to the questions about the reasons influencing the quality of synthetic CS posed in (Srivastava and Singh, 2021c), e.g. "Does the dominance of a language (English or Hindi) present in the Hinglish sentence impact the rating provided by the humans?".

7 Conclusion and further work

In this paper, we address the task of evaluating synthetic CS in supervised and unsupervised approaches. In supervised setting, we solve HinglishEval *quality rating prediction* task with a line of finetuned Hinglish Transformer models and establish a new SOTA. In unsupervised setting, we apply the method of acceptablity measures to evaluate the synthetic CS sentences in HinGE dataset. We find that Hinglish finetuned models consistently outperform their original versions.

Several further work directions open up based on this work. First, it is promising to directly compare the unsupervised and supervised approaches presented in this paper, possibly applying the semi-supervised method of Warstadt et al. (2019) for acceptability measures. Second, it is of interest to continue the analysis presented in Section 6.1 with various CS metrics, thus repeating the study of Srivastava and Singh (2021a) on a larger scale.

8 Acknowledgements

We thank the anonymous reviewers for their valuable comments and remarks. This research was supported in part through computational resources of HPC facilities at HSE University (Kostenetskiy et al., 2021).

References

Heike Adel, Katrin Kirchhoff, Dominic Telaar, Ngoc Thang Vu, Tim Schlippe, and Tanja Schultz. 2014. Features for factored language models for code-Switching speech. In *Proc. 4th Workshop on Spoken Language Technologies for Under-Resourced Languages (SLTU 2014)*, pages 32–38.

Heike Adel, Ngoc Thang Vu, Katrin Kirchhoff, Dominic Telaar, and Tanja Schultz. 2015. Syntactic and semantic features for code-switching factored language models. *IEEE/ACM transactions on audio, speech, and language Processing*, 23(3):431–440. Publisher: IEEE.

Heike Adel, Ngoc Thang Vu, Franziska Kraus, Tim Schlippe, Haizhou Li, and Tanja Schultz. 2013a. Recurrent Neural Network Language Modeling for Code Switching Conversational Speech. In *The 38th International Conference on Acoustics, Speech, and Signal Processing*.

Heike Adel, Ngoc Thang Vu, and Tanja Schultz. 2013b. Combination of Recurrent Neural Networks and Factored Language Models for Code-Switching Language Modeling. In *Proceedings of the 51st Annual Meeting of the Association for Computational Linguistics (Volume 2: Short Papers)*, pages 206–211, Sofia, Bulgaria. Association for Computational Linguistics.

Gustavo Aguilar, Sudipta Kar, and Thamar Solorio. 2020. LinCE: A Centralized Benchmark for Linguistic Code-switching Evaluation. In *Proceedings of the 12th Language Resources and Evaluation Conference*, pages 1803–1813, Marseille, France. European Language Resources Association.

Mohd Zeeshan Ansari, M. M. Sufyan Beg, Tanvir Ahmad, Mohd Jazib Khan, and Ghazali Wasim. 2021. Language Identification of Hindi-English tweets using code-mixed BERT. ArXiv:2107.01202 [cs].

Scott Baldauf. 2004. A Hindi-English jumble, spoken by 350 million. *Christian Science Monitor*.

Utsab Barman, Amitava Das, Joachim Wagner, and Jennifer Foster. 2014. Code mixing: A challenge for language identification in the language of social media. In *Proceedings of the first workshop on computational approaches to code switching*, pages 13–23.

Gayatri Bhat, Monojit Choudhury, and Kalika Bali. 2016. Grammatical Constraints on Intra-sentential

Code-Switching: From Theories to Working Models. ArXiv:1612.04538 [cs].

Alexey Birshert and Ekaterina Artemova. 2021. Call Larisa Ivanovna: Code-Switching Fools Multilingual NLU Models. ArXiv:2109.14350 [cs].

Myers-Scotton Carol. 1993. Duelling languages: Grammatical structure in codeswitching.

Joyce Y. C. Chan, Houwei Cao, P. C. Ching, and Tan Lee. 2009. Automatic Recognition of Cantonese-English Code-Mixing Speech. In *International Journal of Computational Linguistics & Chinese Language Processing, Volume 14, Number 3, September 2009*.

Khyathi Chandu, Ekaterina Loginova, Vishal Gupta, Josef van Genabith, Günter Neumann, Manoj Chinnakotla, Eric Nyberg, and Alan W Black. 2019. Code-mixed question answering challenge: Crowd-sourcing data and techniques. In *Third Workshop on Computational Approaches to Linguistic Code-Switching*, pages 29–38. Association for Computational Linguistics (ACL).

Ching-Ting Chang, Shun-Po Chuang, and Hung-Yi Lee. 2019. Code-switching Sentence Generation by Generative Adversarial Networks and its Application to Data Augmentation. *arXiv:1811.02356 [cs]*. ArXiv: 1811.02356.

Alexis Conneau, Kartikay Khandelwal, Naman Goyal, Vishrav Chaudhary, Guillaume Wenzek, Francisco Guzmán, Edouard Grave, Myle Ott, Luke Zettlemoyer, and Veselin Stoyanov. 2019. Unsupervised Cross-lingual Representation Learning at Scale. *CoRR*, abs/1911.02116. ArXiv: 1911.02116.

Amitava Das and Björn Gambäck. 2014. Identifying Languages at the Word Level in Code-Mixed Indian Social Media Text. In *Proceedings of the 11th International Conference on Natural Language Processing*, pages 378–387, Goa, India. NLP Association of India.

Jacob Devlin, Ming-Wei Chang, Kenton Lee, and Kristina Toutanova. 2018. BERT: Pre-training of Deep Bidirectional Transformers for Language Understanding. *CoRR*, abs/1810.04805. _eprint: 1810.04805.

Mrinal Dhar, Vaibhav Kumar, and Manish Shrivastava. 2018. Enabling code-mixed translation: Parallel corpus creation and mt augmentation approach. In *Proceedings of the First Workshop on Linguistic Resources for Natural Language Processing*, pages 131–140.

Shaz Furniturewala, Vijay Kumari, Amulya Ratna Dash, Hriday Kedia, and Yashvardhan Sharma. 2022. BITS Pilani at HinglishEval: Quality Evaluation for Code-Mixed Hinglish Text Using Transformers. *arXiv preprint arXiv:2206.08680*.

Björn Gambäck and Amitava Das. 2016. Comparing the Level of Code-Switching in Corpora. In *Proceedings of the Tenth International Conference on Language Resources and Evaluation (LREC'16)*, pages 1850–1855, Portorož, Slovenia. European Language Resources Association (ELRA).

Saurabh Garg, Tanmay Parekh, and Preethi Jyothi. 2018. Code-switched language models using dual rnns and same-source pretraining. *arXiv preprint arXiv:1809.01962*.

Devansh Gautam, Prashant Kodali, Kshitij Gupta, Anmol Goel, Manish Shrivastava, and Ponnurangam Kumaraguru. 2021. CoMeT: Towards Code-Mixed Translation Using Parallel Monolingual Sentences. pages 47–55.

Prantik Guha, Rudra Dhar, and Dipankar Das. 2022. JU_nlp at HinglishEval: Quality Evaluation of the Low-Resource Code-Mixed Hinglish Text. *arXiv preprint arXiv:2206.08053*.

Sunil Gundapu and Radhika Mamidi. 2020. Word level language identification in english telugu code mixed data. *arXiv preprint arXiv:2010.04482*.

Abhirut Gupta, Aditya Vavre, and Sunita Sarawagi. 2021. Training data augmentation for code-mixed translation. In *Proceedings of the 2021 Conference of the North American Chapter of the Association for Computational Linguistics: Human Language Technologies*, pages 5760–5766.

Deepak Gupta, Asif Ekbal, and Pushpak Bhattacharyya. 2020. A Semi-supervised Approach to Generate the Code-Mixed Text using Pre-trained Encoder and Transfer Learning. In *Findings of the Association for Computational Linguistics: EMNLP 2020*, pages 2267–2280, Online. Association for Computational Linguistics.

Ganesh Jawahar, El Moatez Billah Nagoudi, Muhammad Abdul-Mageed, and Laks VS Lakshmanan. 2021. Exploring text-to-text transformers for english to hinglish machine translation with synthetic code-mixing. *arXiv preprint arXiv:2105.08807*.

Aditya Joshi, Ameya Prabhu, Manish Shrivastava, and Vasudeva Varma. 2016. Towards sub-word level compositions for sentiment analysis of hindi-english code mixed text. In *Proceedings of COLING 2016, the 26th International Conference on Computational Linguistics: Technical Papers*, pages 2482–2491.

Simran Khanuja, Sandipan Dandapat, Sunayana Sitaram, and Monojit Choudhury. 2020a. A new dataset for natural language inference from code-mixed conversations. *arXiv preprint arXiv:2004.05051*.

Simran Khanuja, Sandipan Dandapat, Anirudh Srinivasan, Sunayana Sitaram, and Monojit Choudhury. 2020b. GLUECoS : An Evaluation Benchmark for Code-Switched NLP. *arXiv:2004.12376 [cs]*. ArXiv: 2004.12376.

Prashant Kodali, Tanmay Sachan, Akshay Goindani, Anmol Goel, Naman Ahuja, Manish Shrivastava, and Ponnurangam Kumaraguru. 2022. PreCogIIITH at HinglishEval: Leveraging Code-Mixing Metrics & Language Model Embeddings To Estimate Code-Mix Quality. *arXiv preprint arXiv:2206.07988*.

P. S. Kostenetskiy, R. A. Chulkevich, and V. I. Kozyrev. 2021. HPC Resources of the Higher School of Economics. *Journal of Physics: Conference Series*, 1740(1):012050. Publisher: IOP Publishing.

Jey Han Lau, Carlos Armendariz, Shalom Lappin, Matthew Purver, and Chang Shu. 2020. How Furiously Can Colorless Green Ideas Sleep? Sentence Acceptability in Context. *Transactions of the Association for Computational Linguistics*, 8:296–310.

Jey Han Lau, Alexander Clark, and Shalom Lappin. 2015. Unsupervised Prediction of Acceptability Judgements. In *Proceedings of the 53rd Annual Meeting of the Association for Computational Linguistics and the 7th International Joint Conference on Natural Language Processing (Volume 1: Long Papers)*, pages 1618–1628, Beijing, China. Association for Computational Linguistics.

Grandee Lee and Haizhou Li. 2020. Modeling code-switch languages using bilingual parallel corpus. In *Proceedings of the 58th Annual Meeting of the Association for Computational Linguistics*, pages 860–870.

Ying Li and Pascale Fung. 2012. Code-Switch Language Model with Inversion Constraints for Mixed Language Speech Recognition. In *Proceedings of COLING 2012*, pages 1671–1680, Mumbai, India. The COLING 2012 Organizing Committee.

Ying Li and Pascale Fung. 2014. Language Modeling with Functional Head Constraint for Code Switching Speech Recognition. In *Proceedings of the 2014 Conference on Empirical Methods in Natural Language Processing (EMNLP)*, pages 907–916, Doha, Qatar. Association for Computational Linguistics.

Zihan Liu, Genta Indra Winata, Zhaojiang Lin, Peng Xu, and Pascale Fung. 2020. Attention-informed mixed-language training for zero-shot cross-lingual task-oriented dialogue systems. In *Proceedings of the AAAI Conference on Artificial Intelligence*, volume 34, pages 8433–8440. Issue: 05.

John X. Morris, Eli Lifland, Jin Yong Yoo, Jake Grigsby, Di Jin, and Yanjun Qi. 2020. TextAttack: A Framework for Adversarial Attacks, Data Augmentation, and Adversarial Training in NLP. ArXiv:2005.05909 [cs].

Ravindra Nayak and Raviraj Joshi. 2022. L3Cube-HingCorpus and HingBERT: A Code Mixed Hindi-English Dataset and BERT Language Models. ArXiv:2204.08398 [cs].

Dwija Parikh and Thamar Solorio. 2021. Normalization and back-transliteration for code-switched data. In *Proceedings of the Fifth Workshop on Computational Approaches to Linguistic Code-Switching*, pages 119–124.

Parth Patwa, Gustavo Aguilar, Sudipta Kar, Suraj Pandey, Srinivas PYKL, Björn Gambäck, Tanmoy Chakraborty, Thamar Solorio, and Amitava Das. 2020. SemEval-2020 Task 9: Overview of Sentiment Analysis of Code-Mixed Tweets. In *Proceedings of the Fourteenth Workshop on Semantic Evaluation*, pages 774–790, Barcelona (online). International Committee for Computational Linguistics.

Telmo Pires, Eva Schlinger, and Dan Garrette. 2019. How Multilingual is Multilingual BERT? In *Proceedings of the 57th Annual Meeting of the Association for Computational Linguistics*, pages 4996–5001, Florence, Italy. Association for Computational Linguistics.

Shana Poplack. 1980. Sometimes I'll start a sentence in Spanish Y TERMINO EN ESPAÑOL: toward a typology of code-switching. 18(7-8):581–618. Publisher: De Gruyter Mouton Section: Linguistics.

Adithya Pratapa, Gayatri Bhat, Monojit Choudhury, Sunayana Sitaram, Sandipan Dandapat, and Kalika Bali. 2018a. Language Modeling for Code-Mixing: The Role of Linguistic Theory based Synthetic Data. In *Proceedings of the 56th Annual Meeting of the Association for Computational Linguistics (Volume 1: Long Papers)*, pages 1543–1553, Melbourne, Australia. Association for Computational Linguistics.

Adithya Pratapa, Monojit Choudhury, and Sunayana Sitaram. 2018b. Word embeddings for code-mixed language processing. In *Proceedings of the 2018 conference on empirical methods in natural language processing*, pages 3067–3072.

Ruba Priyadharshini, Bharathi Raja Chakravarthi, Mani Vegupatti, and John P McCrae. 2020. Named entity recognition for code-mixed Indian corpus using meta embedding. In *2020 6th international conference on advanced computing and communication systems (ICACCS)*, pages 68–72. IEEE.

Alec Radford, Jeff Wu, Rewon Child, David Luan, Dario Amodei, and Ilya Sutskever. 2019. Language Models are Unsupervised Multitask Learners.

Vikram Ramanarayanan, Robert Pugh, Yao Qian, and David Suendermann-Oeft. 2019. Automatic turn-level language identification for code-switched spanish–english dialog. In *9th International Workshop on Spoken Dialogue System Technology*, pages 51–61. Springer.

Mohd Sanad Zaki Rizvi, Anirudh Srinivasan, Tanuja Ganu, Monojit Choudhury, and Sunayana Sitaram. 2021. GCM: A Toolkit for Generating Synthetic Code-mixed Text. In *Proceedings of the 16th Conference of the European Chapter of the Association for Computational Linguistics: System Demonstrations*, pages 205–211, Online. Association for Computational Linguistics.

Bidisha Samanta, Sharmila Reddy, Hussain Jagirdar, Niloy Ganguly, and Soumen Chakrabarti. 2019. A Deep Generative Model for Code-Switched Text. *arXiv:1906.08972 [cs]*. ArXiv: 1906.08972.

Sebastin Santy, Anirudh Srinivasan, and Monojit Choudhury. 2021. BERTologiCoMix: How does Code-Mixing interact with Multilingual BERT?

Shashi Shekhar, Dilip Kumar Sharma, and MM Sufyan Beg. 2020. Language identification framework in code-mixed social media text based on quantum LSTM—the word belongs to which language? *Modern Physics Letters B*, 34(06):2050086. Publisher: World Scientific.

Oleh Shliazhko, Alena Fenogenova, Maria Tikhonova, Vladislav Mikhailov, Anastasia Kozlova, and Tatiana Shavrina. 2022. mGPT: Few-Shot Learners Go Multilingual.

Jasdeep Singh, Bryan McCann, Nitish Shirish Keskar, Caiming Xiong, and Richard Socher. 2019. Xlda: Cross-lingual data augmentation for natural language inference and question answering. *arXiv preprint arXiv:1905.11471*.

Kushagra Singh, Indira Sen, and Ponnurangam Kumaraguru. 2018a. Language identification and named entity recognition in hinglish code mixed tweets. In *Proceedings of ACL 2018, Student Research Workshop*, pages 52–58.

Kushagra Singh, Indira Sen, and Ponnurangam Kumaraguru. 2018b. A Twitter corpus for Hindi-English code mixed POS tagging. In *Proceedings of the sixth international workshop on natural language processing for social media*, pages 12–17.

Nikhil Singh. 2022. niksss at HinglishEval: Language-agnostic BERT-based Contextual Embeddings with Catboost for Quality Evaluation of the Low-Resource Synthetically Generated Code-Mixed Hinglish Text.

Rajat Singh, Nurendra Choudhary, and Manish Shrivastava. 2018c. Automatic normalization of word variations in code-mixed social media text. *arXiv preprint arXiv:1804.00804*.

Ganji Sreeram and Rohit Sinha. 2017. Language modeling for code-switched data: Challenges and approaches. *arXiv preprint arXiv:1711.03541*.

Vivek Srivastava and Mayank Singh. 2020. PHINC: A parallel Hinglish social media code-mixed corpus for machine translation. *arXiv preprint arXiv:2004.09447*.

Vivek Srivastava and Mayank Singh. 2021a. Challenges and Limitations with the Metrics Measuring the Complexity of Code-Mixed Text. Technical Report arXiv:2106.10123, arXiv. ArXiv:2106.10123 [cs] type: article.

Vivek Srivastava and Mayank Singh. 2021b. HinGE: A Dataset for Generation and Evaluation of Code-Mixed Hinglish Text. Technical Report arXiv:2107.03760, arXiv. ArXiv:2107.03760 [cs] type: article.

Vivek Srivastava and Mayank Singh. 2021c. Quality Evaluation of the Low-Resource Synthetically Generated Code-Mixed Hinglish Text. Technical Report arXiv:2108.01861, arXiv. ArXiv:2108.01861 [cs] type: article.

Samson Tan and Shafiq Joty. 2021. Code-mixing on sesame street: Dawn of the adversarial polyglots. *arXiv preprint arXiv:2103.09593*.

Ishan Tarunesh, Syamantak Kumar, and Preethi Jyothi. 2021. From Machine Translation to Code-Switching: Generating High-Quality Code-Switched Text. Technical Report arXiv:2107.06483, arXiv. ArXiv:2107.06483 [cs] type: article.

S Thara, E Sampath, Phanindra Reddy, and others. 2020. Code mixed question answering challenge using deep learning methods. In *2020 5th International Conference on Communication and Electronics Systems (ICCES)*, pages 1331–1337. IEEE.

Ashish Vaswani, Noam Shazeer, Niki Parmar, Jakob Uszkoreit, Llion Jones, Aidan N. Gomez, Lukasz Kaiser, and Illia Polosukhin. 2017. Attention Is All You Need. *CoRR*, abs/1706.03762. ArXiv: 1706.03762.

Ngoc Thang Vu, Dau-Cheng Lyu, Jochen Weiner, Dominic Telaar, Tim Schlippe, Fabian Blaicher, Eng-Siong Chng, Tanja Schultz, and Haizhou Li. 2012. A first speech recognition system for Mandarin-English code-switch conversational speech. In *2012 IEEE International Conference on Acoustics, Speech and Signal Processing (ICASSP)*, pages 4889–4892. ISSN: 2379-190X.

Yogarshi Vyas, Spandana Gella, Jatin Sharma, Kalika Bali, and Monojit Choudhury. 2014. Pos tagging of english-hindi code-mixed social media content. In *Proceedings of the 2014 conference on empirical methods in natural language processing (EMNLP)*, pages 974–979.

Alex Warstadt, Amanpreet Singh, and Samuel R. Bowman. 2019. Neural Network Acceptability Judgments. *arXiv:1805.12471 [cs]*. ArXiv: 1805.12471.

Genta Indra Winata, Zhaojiang Lin, and Pascale Fung. 2019a. Learning multilingual meta-embeddings for code-switching named entity recognition. In *Proceedings of the 4th Workshop on Representation Learning for NLP (RepL4NLP-2019)*, pages 181–186.

Genta Indra Winata, Andrea Madotto, Chien-Sheng Wu, and Pascale Fung. 2019b. Code-Switched Language Models Using Neural Based Synthetic Data from Parallel Sentences. *arXiv:1909.08582 [cs]*. ArXiv: 1909.08582.

ArabGend: Gender Analysis and Inference on Arabic Twitter

Hamdy Mubarak, Shammur Absar Chowdhury and Firoj Alam
Qatar Computing Research Institute, HBKU, Qatar
{hmubarak, shchowdhury, fialam}@hbku.edu.qa

Abstract

Gender analysis of Twitter can reveal important socio-cultural differences between male and female users. There has been a significant effort to analyze and automatically infer gender in the past for most widely spoken languages' content, however, to our knowledge very limited work has been done for Arabic. In this paper, we perform an extensive analysis of differences between male and female users in the Arabic Twitter-sphere. We study differences in user engagement, topics of interest, and the gender gap in professions. Along with gender analysis, we also propose a method to infer gender by utilizing usernames, profile pictures, tweets, and networks of friends. In order to do so, we manually annotated gender and locations for ∼167K Twitter accounts associated with ∼92K user location, which we make publicly available.[1] Our proposed gender inference method achieves an F1 score of 82.1% (47.3% higher than the majority baseline). We also developed a demo and made it publicly available[2].

1 Introduction

Demographic information (e.g., age, gender) has proven to be useful in many different decision-making processes such as, from business decisions (e.g., personalized online advertising), forensic investigation to policy-making purposes (Li et al., 2016; Volkova et al., 2013; Mukherjee and Liu, 2010; Soler and Wanner, 2016). For example, social media platforms and e-commerce sites are using customers' gender and other demographic attributes for targeted advertising (Tuan et al., 2019). In the past decade, there have been extensive research efforts to automatically infer demographic attributes of the social media users using their social media footprints (e.g., users' posts, names, and other attributes) (Chen et al., 2015; Volkova et al., 2015). In addition, to evaluate the performance of the model's fairness for different tasks it is important to have such attributes (Chakraborty et al., 2021; Wang et al., 2019). Given that such attributes are often removed from the original source for privacy and ethical reasons, however, having such attributes through inference is a possible way to evaluate the model's fairness.

Major research efforts for such attributes inference are mostly done for English, and very little effort has been given to non-English languages (Chakraborty et al., 2021). The research for Arabic demographic inference such as gender is relatively rare for social media users, specifically on Twitter's content. With approximately 164 million monthly active users, Twitter is one of the most popular social media platforms in the Arab region (Abdelali et al., 2021). The large volume of tweets produced represents the social and cultural characteristics of the region. Even though there is a large number of Twitter users, however, usage of Twitter differs in volume, topics, and engagement depending on the users' gender role. Another important factor is that social media users often provide misleading demographic information (e.g., name, age, location and marital status), which is highlighted in a survey conducted in the Arab region (Salem, 2017). Hence, self-declared information might not be always reliable. Though some studies argue that the proportion of such misleading self-reported information is relatively lower (Herring and Stoerger, 2014). While the availability of Twitter data and its large user base provides opportunities to understand such information, however, for privacy reasons, Twitter does not share users' gender information (Mueller and Stumme, 2016). Such factors stress the need to have automatic methods for gender inference, and here our focus is Twitter-sphere for the Arabic region. In addition, there is a gap in the literature in a thorough analysis of Arabic Twitter (e.g., linguistic content) for gender, even

[1] https://alt.qcri.org/resources/ArabGend.zip

[2] https://asad.qcri.org/

Proceedings of the 2022 COLING Workshop: The 8th Workshop on Noisy User-generated Text (W-NUT 2022), pages 124–135

though Arabic is a morphologically rich language where linguistic markers are present to distinguish genders in many cases (see Section 3.1).

To address the gap of gender analysis and automatic inference, in this paper, we perform an extensive analysis of Arabic Twitter data where we identify key distinguishing properties of male/female authorship. We experiment with different features to identify the gender of Twitter users. We examine the usage of friendship networks, profile pictures, and textual information such as usernames, user descriptions, and tweets to classify gender. The contributions of our work are as follows:

- We developed a new dataset of ~167K Twitter accounts that are manually annotated for their gender and location, which we make publicly available for research purposes.
- We show differences between the two genders from different angles such as presence on Twitter in different Arab countries, language usage, etc.
- We show signs of gender gaps in the labor market which align with some official reports.
- We study automatic gender identification of tweets, user accounts, and user descriptions. We also study how profile pictures and networks of friends can influence results.
- Using our models we developed a demo, which is publicly available.

2 Related Work

Gender inference is a well-studied problem in English. Liu and Ruths (2013) present a dataset of 13K gender-labeled Twitter users and propose the use of first names as features for gender inference. Screen_names, full names, user descriptions, and tweets have also been used as features for gender inference (Burger et al., 2011). Rao et al. (2010) use stacked SVMs for identifying gender and other latent attributes of Twitter users. Semi-supervised methods that exploit social networks have also been used for gender classification (Li et al., 2016).

Gender inference has also received attention for a few other languages. Sakaki et al. (2014) combine the output of text processor and image processor to infer the gender of Japanese Twitter users. Taniguchi et al. (2015) propose a hybrid method that uses logistic regression to combine text and image features. Ciot et al. (2013) label 1000 users for gender in each of the following languages: Japanese, Indonesian, Turkish, and French. The authors use Support Vector Machines (SVMs) for classification. Sezerer et al. (2019) present a dataset consisting of 5.5K Twitter users labeled for their gender. Tuan et al. (2019) proposes clustering-based approaches for demographic analysis to support advertising campaigns. Very recently Liu et al. (2021) provided a large-scale study that investigate different inference techniques (e.g., classic machine learning to deep learning models) using Twitter data. The authors highlight that a simpler model performs well to infer age, however, sophisticated models (e.g., sentence embeddings) are important for gender.

For Arabic, on the other hand, work is relatively less explored. Malmasi (2014) use first names to classify the gender of Arabic, German, Iranian and Japanese names. ElSayed and Farouk (2020) uses neural networks to differentiate male and female authors of tweets in Egyptian dialect. Hussein et al. (2019) use classic machine learning classifiers such as Logistic Regression and Random Forest classifiers to identify gender in Egyptian tweets. Habash et al. (2019) use deep learning for gender identification and uses Machine Translation for reinflection. Bsir and Zrigui (2018) use the gated recurrent unit (GRU) for gender identification in Facebook and Twitter posts. Zaghouani and Charfi (2018) collect a corpus of 2.4M multi-dialectal tweets from 1600 accounts that are tagged for gender, age, and language. Wang et al. (2019) propose a new multilingual (32 different languages), multimodal, multi-attribute deep learning system for inferring different demographic attributes.

Our work differs from previous work on gender analysis and inference for Arabic in a number of ways *(i)* it uses a much bigger dataset for male and female users; *(ii)* it has no bias towards a specific country as it covers users from all Arab countries; *(iii)* it uses a generic method for collecting users and their names as opposed to starting with a specific list of names, which can be skewed towards some countries or cultures; *(iv)* in addition to gender inference, we perform a thorough analysis of gender differences in their profile descriptions, topics of interest, the profession gender gap among other things.

3 Dataset

3.1 Background

In Arabic, typically nouns and adjectives have gender markers such as Taa Marbouta letter "ة" as a feminine (f) suffix, and in case of absence, they can be considered as masculine (m). There are special cases where a word can have the feminine marker and it's gender is unknown (e.g., داعية - religious scholar (m and f)). Also, there are some cases where words are feminine without explicit gender markers (e.g., بنت ، أنثى - female, girl). Except for some special cases, converting gender from masculine to feminine can be done by appending the Taa Marbouta suffix "ة", e.g., words like مديرة ، شاعرة (manager(f), poet(f)) are the feminine forms of مدير ، شاعر (manager(m), poet(m)) in order.

It's widely observed that many Arabic users on Twitter describe themselves in the description field in their profiles. This description expresses several identity features such as nationality (NAT), profession or job (PROF), interest (INT), social role (SOC), religion (RELIG), and ideology (IDEO) among others. We provide a few examples in Table 1.

Description	Translation	Class
عراقي وأفتخر	Iraqi (m) and proud	NAT
مواطنة سعودية	Saudi citizen (f)	NAT
طبيبة أسنان	Dentist (f)	PROF
طالب دكتوراه	PhD student (m)	PROF
عاشقة الطبيعة	Nature lover (f)	INT
مهتم بأخبار التقنية	Interested (m) in IT news	INT
زوجة وأم	Wife and mother	SOC
شاب متفائل	Optimistic young man	SOC
مسلم وأفتخر	Muslim (m) and proud	RELIG
مسيحية عربية	Arab Christian (f)	RELIG
سياسي معارض	Opposition politician (m)	IDEO
ليبرالية أحب بلدي	Liberal (f), love my country	IDEO

Table 1: Examples of user description with gender (m/f) and identity label (class).

3.2 Data Collection

For the data collection, we used Twitter API to crawl Arabic tweets using a language tag to Arabic ("lang:ar"), back in January 2018. We collected data in two phases. *First*, we collected 4.35M tweets (*termed as former set*), which covers tweets

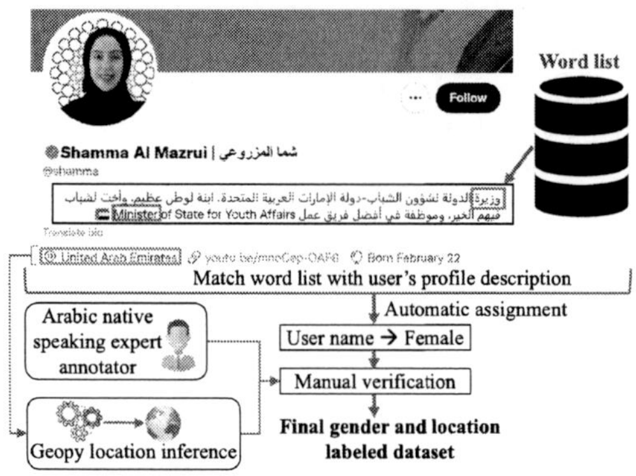

Figure 1: Our pipeline to develop **ArabGend** – labeling gender and location.

from 2008 to January 2018.[3] Using this dataset we developed a word list using a gender marker (see Section 3.3.1). In the *second* phase, we collected additional 100M millions tweets (*termed as later set*), dated from 2018 to 2020, to develop final annotated dataset (see Section 3.3.2). The purpose of the *former set* of tweets was to create a gender marker word list, the purpose of the *later set* of tweets was to create a large annotated dataset with gender and location labels. We used such an approach to avoid any biases that may appear due to the word list selection.

3.3 Annotation

3.3.1 Creating Word List with Gender Info

For the annotation, we first created a word list of gender markers. In order to do that we first extracted all profile information of users who posted these tweets. From the user's profile description, we obtained a list of all the first words that users used to describe themselves.[4] We obtained a unique list of 10K words. We then excluded words that appeared only once, which resulted in a list of ~2,500 words out of 10K. We used the publicly available Farasa tool (Darwish and Mubarak, 2016) to initially detect the gender of each word in the list. Then, a native speaker revised gender information and provided both the masculine and feminine word forms and their different writings to have better coverage. For example, for the feminine form "محامية - lawyer (f)", the masculine form and its different writings "محام ، محامى ، محامي - lawyer (m)" was also added if they did not appear in the word

[3]Note that our data collection might not consist of all of the tweets posted on Twitter during this period, which is because Twitter's free API has a limit.

[4]the First word is a very strong signal in identity description and can be mapped to gender.

list. The final gender marker word list contains 713 words, in which 56% of them indicate masculine and 44% indicate feminine gender.[5] The list can be found in our publicly released dataset.

3.3.2 Gender and Location Annotation

For gender and location annotation, we first collected another set of 100M tweets, *the later set*, which dated from 2018 to 2020.

Gender: We annotated 100M tweets with gender and location information in several steps. We used the word list, discussed in the previous section, and matched the words at the beginning of each user's profile description. The matching approach resulted to assign a gender label to ∼167K users. We could not able to assign the gender label for the rest of the users due to the mismatch between our created word list, and the empty user's profile description. We then manually revised the assigned gender labels of these 167K users by a native Arabic-speaking expert annotator. In Figure 1, we present *ArabGend* development pipeline that demonstrates how the user profile appears, how we used profile description with the word list to the assign gender marker and location information to assign a specific location. Note that we developed the *word list*, highlighted in blue, at the first phase of our dataset development, as discussed in Section 3.3.1. In this profile, user location is clearly visible, however, this is not always the case for which location inference is needed.

Location: Out of these 167K users we extracted 28K unique locations, which are then mapped into Arab countries with geographic location information using *GeoPy toolkit*.[6] Similar to gender annotation, the output of GeoPy is then manually revised by the same annotator. The annotation process resulted in identifying the countries for 92K users (55.08% of all users) out of 167K users. We could not identify the rest of user locations as they were either empty (38%) or cannot be mapped to a specific country (6.92%).

Removing Ambiguous and Inappropriate Accounts The manual annotation process consists of another step to remove ambiguous, inappropriate (e.g., adult and spam) accounts. Typically Arabic words are written without diacritics, which causes ambiguity in many cases, e.g., the word مدرسة can be interpreted as Teacher (f) or School. As we are interested in collecting personal accounts using their profile description, therefore, we excluded organizations' accounts from our data collection. Also, there are some titles that can be used to describe males and females, which we removed. For example, دكتور ، مدير (Doctor, Manager) are used for both genders.

To filter adult and spam accounts we used the publicly available APIs from ASAD system (Hassan et al., 2021). It is a social media analysis toolkit consisting of eight modules to classify dialects, sentiment, emotion, news category, offensiveness, hate speech, adult content, and spam in Arabic tweets.[7] Based on the classified output from ASAD and a manual inspection during the annotation process, we removed *inappropriate* accounts. We use the term *appropriateness* to refer to the labels non-adult and spam content in the rest of the paper. In this phase, after filtering non-personal and inappropriate accounts, we ended up with 167K users (80% are males and 20% are females).

3.3.3 Annotation quality

To assess the quality of the annotation, we manually annotated 500 users' accounts. We selected a random sample of 500 users and then manually assigned gender labels by checking their accounts on the Twitter platform. Agreement with manual annotation was ∼99%. Similarly, for location, we randomly selected another sample of 500 unique user locations and checked their mappings to countries. The accuracy was 98%, which indicates annotation quality is very high for gender and location labels. Note that, Twitter user locations are typically noisy, and mapping them to countries is not always trivial.

Accounts	Count	User Loc.
Male	133,192 (80.0%)	75,539 (81.5%)
Female	33,348 (20.0%)	17,115 (18.5%)
Total	166,540 (100%)	92,654 (56.0%)

Table 2: Statistics of the dataset.

3.3.4 Statistics

In Table 2, we report number of final male and female accounts and percentage of successful map-

[5] Words like شخص ، كاهن ، زول (person, priest, man) have no corresponding feminine words.

[6] https://pypi.org/project/geopy/, It is a python client for several geocoding web services including Nominatim (https://nominatim.org), which uses OpenStreetMap data to find location.

[7] https://asad.qcri.org

User Name	Description	User Loc.	G	C
صفية الشحي (Safia Alshehi)	إعلامية - كاتبة (journalist (f) and writer (f))	UAE - Dubai	F	AE
Ahmed Azhar	إنسان بسيط جدا (very simple person (m))	جدة (Jeddah)	M	SA

Table 3: Annotation: Description was mapped to Gender (G), and User Loc. was mapped to Country (C).

pings of user locations to countries for both genders. According to a report from the World Bank in 2015,[8] the gender gap in Middle East and North Africa region can reach to 34% in internet usage. This gap comes second after the largest gender gap in Sub-Saharan Africa region (45%). Further, while 52% of females (91M) have mobile phones, this ratio increases to 56% for males with additional 8M male users. These factors can explain the less presence of female users on Twitter as shown in our study. In Table 3, we present some annotation examples from our dataset. We use ISO 3166-1 alpha-2 for country codes.[9]

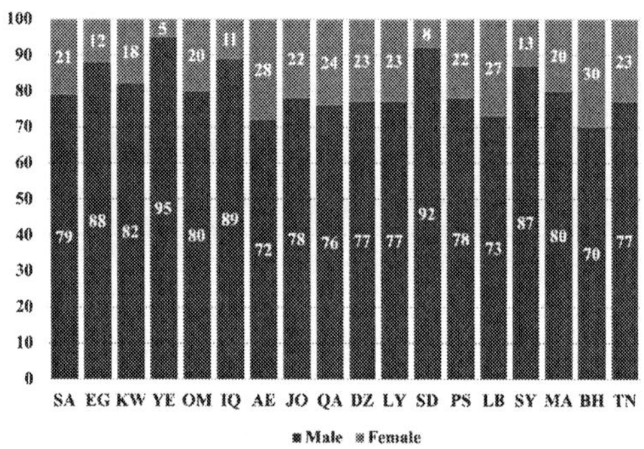

Figure 2: Gender distribution in Arab countries.

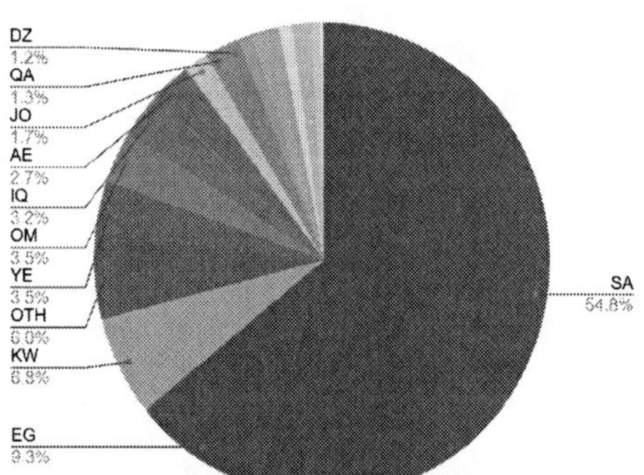

Figure 3: Country distribution of Twitter accounts.

4 Analysis

4.1 Gender and Location Distribution

In Figure 2, we present gender distribution of Twitter users in Arab countries. We observe that the top three countries that have higher percentages of female users. For BH (Bahrain), AE (United Arab Emirates) and LB (Lebanon) are 30%, 28% and 27%, respectively. The lowest percentages of female users from YE (Yemen), SD (Sudan) and IQ (Iraq) are 5%, 8% and 11%, respectively.

In Figure 3, we present country distribution of all accounts in our dataset. We observe that more than half of Twitter users are from SA (Saudi Arabia) and 70% of accounts are from Gulf region (SA, KW, OM, AE, QA and BH) followed by accounts from EG, YE, etc. Distributions are very similar to what was reported in a previous study to collect dialectal tweets in a different time span and using a different approach (Mubarak and Darwish, 2014).

We mapped user locations to OTHER (OTH) for the countries that are outside Arab World. They represent 6% of all user locations. Top five countries that are outside Arab World include US, GB, TR, DE and FR in order. In addition, we found that the dataset has 1,495 verified accounts, out of which 90% are male and 10% are female. Such numbers represent 1% and 0.45% verified male and female accounts, respectively.

4.2 User Engagement

We extracted the date of joining on Twitter for all accounts to study their engagement with Twitter. As shown in Figure 4 (in appendix), we can see that many accounts joined Twitter between 2010 and 2012, then the number of users who joined Twitter between 2013 and 2018 was almost stable for male and female accounts. Starting from 2019, there was an increasing number of users. We notice that there is a slightly increasing number of female accounts who join Twitter over time, however, Twitter was always dominated by male accounts and the gap between the two genders seems to increase in the future as shown in the cumulative chart in Figure 5 (in Appendix).

4.3 User Connections

Figure 6 shows an average number of followers and followees (friends) of male and female accounts in our dataset. We can see that on average, female accounts tend to attract more followers than males (more than double). Further, females have ~30%

[8] https://blogs.worldbank.org/ar/arabvoices/ten-facts-about-women-arab-world

[9] https://en.wikipedia.org/wiki/List_of_ISO_3166_country_codes

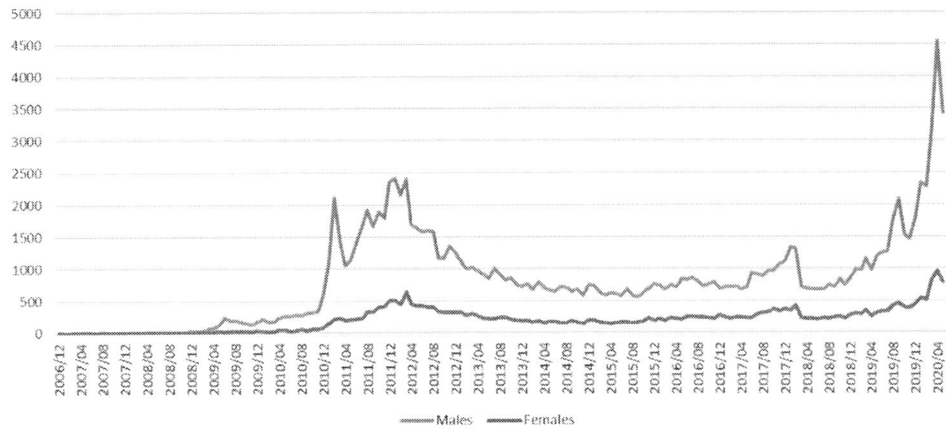

Figure 4: Distribution of Twitter joining date

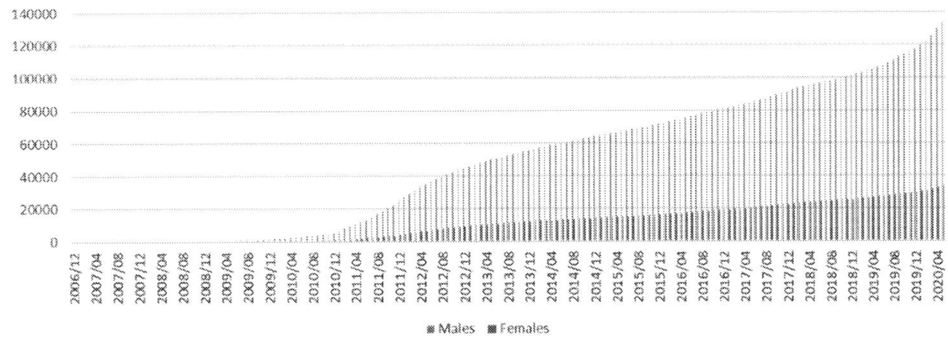

Figure 5: Accounts distribution over time

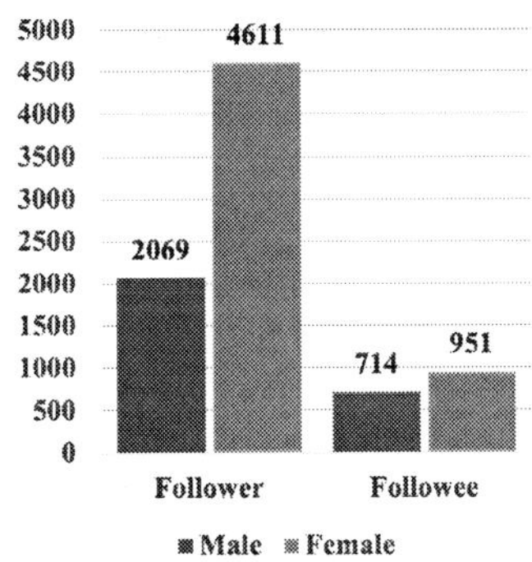

Figure 6: Followers and followees distribution.

more friends than males, which may indicate that females prefer to have a larger community and friends than males on Twitter.

4.4 Person Names

A person's name is a very important feature in identifying gender. To understand the demographics of Twitter users, prior studies have been using a seed list of names to collect male and female accounts. Mislove et al. (2011) used the most common 1000 male and female names in the US to collect Twitter user information. Such an approach, i.e., using a pre-specified list of person names, can create bias in the resulting data collection. In our study, we attempted to follow a different approach to avoid such a bias. We created *initial* dataset to create word list, and used a different set (i.e., the *later* 100M) to create the final list. We further normalized the names by removing diacritics, mapping Alif shapes, Taa Marbouta and Alif Maqsoura letters to plain Alif, Haa, and Yaa letters respectively, and mapping decorated letters to normal letters.

From the obtained lists, we can extracted names that are used for both genders when they are written in Arabic (e.g., شمس ، صباح ، نور - Nour, Sabah, Shams), or due to transliteration ambiguity, e.g., the names علاء(m) and آلاء(f) both are transliterated to "Alaa", also أمجد(m) and أمجاد(f) have the same transliteration "Amjad".

In Figure 7 we show the most common male and female names are written in English. Mostly, they have similar distribution as their Arabic counterparts with different ways of transliteration.

4.5 Interests According to User Description

In Figure 8 we present most common words used in user's profile description for males and fe-

(a) Male names **(b) Female names**

Figure 7: Common Arabic names (in English).

males in order. This gives an indication about jobs and interests for both genders. We can see that females tend to describe their social role (e.g., بنت، أم، فتاة، صديقة - daughter, mother, girl, friend) more than males. For comparison, while more than 1000 female accounts describe themselves first as أم (mother), less than 200 accounts describe themselves as أب (father). We can also see that a good portion of Twitter users is young (e.g., طالب، فتاة، خريجة - student, young woman, graduate) as opposed to few accounts who describe themselves as متقاعد (retired). From our analysis, we observed that self-description can be used to predict the age group of Twitter users. We leave this for future work.

(a) Male accounts **(b) Female accounts**

Figure 8: Description of male and female accounts. The top five for males are: engineer, student, lover, interested (in), and teacher. The top five for females are: student, graduate, teacher, girl, and mother.

4.6 Topics of Interest

In Figures 9 we present the common distinguishing words in tweets written by male and female accounts in our dataset. We computed the valence score discussed in (Conover et al., 2011; Chowdhury et al., 2020) with a threshold of 0.5 to obtain these words.

While tweets from males have many words related to politics (e.g., اليمن، الإخوان - Yemen, Muslim Brotherhood) and sports (e.g., الدوري، الهلال - league, Hilal club), tweets from females have many words related to family and society (e.g., أمي، أبناء، زميلات - my mother, children, colleagues) and feelings (e.g., قلبي، شعور، حبيبتي - my heart, feeling, my love).

4.7 Gender Gap in Professions

We can observe from Figure 8 that the most frequent profession for males was مهندس (engineer) while it was معلمة (teacher) for females. In Table 4, we report the distribution of some professions for male and female accounts in different domains. We observe that the Sport domain is overwhelmingly dominated by males, and other domains (e.g., Management, Software, Health, etc.) have less representation of females (percentages are from 9% to 20%). The best domain that has a good representation of females is the Translation domain with a percentage of 36%.

According to the World Bank's report in June 2020,[10] the labor force participation rate of females in the Middle East and North Africa region is around 20% with a slight improvement from 17.4% in 1990. Our study supports this report by showing that females are less represented in many job domains, and participation rates can be roughly quantified in different sectors of job markets. The same report also mentions that only 11% of females hold managerial positions compared to the world average of 27%.[11] The ratio of female managers to all managers in our dataset is 9% based on the self-description of the profile.

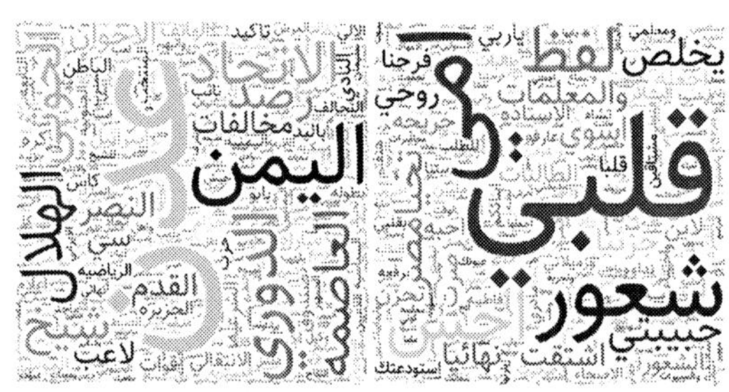

(a) Male tweets **(b) Female tweets**

Figure 9: Most common words.

5 Experiments

For the classification experiments, we focused only on the gender inference and leave the location in-

[10] https://data.worldbank.org/indicator/SL.TLF.CACT.FE.ZS?locations=ZQ

[11] www.dw.com/ar/, shorturl.at/vLOQT

Prof.	Translation	G	Freq.	%	Domain
لاعب	player	m	1,096	98	Sport
لاعبة		f	19	2	
مهندس	engineer	m	6,619	94	Engineering
مهندسة		f	404	6	
مدير	manager	m	2,982	91	Management
مديرة		f	286	9	
مبرمج	programmer	m	153	91	Software
مبرمجة		f	16	9	
محاسب	accountant	m	580	90	Finance
محاسبة		f	61	10	
طبيب	doctor	m	2,265	80	Health
طبيبة		f	577	20	
مترجم	translator	m	177	64	Translation
مترجمة		f	98	36	

Table 4: Profession gaps examples.

ference study as for a future study. We measure the performance of the classification models using accuracy (Acc), macro-averaged precision (P), recall (R) and F1 score. We use macro-averaged F1 score as a primary metric for comparison in our discussion.

5.1 Datasets

We used two datasets for training to provide a comparative study. We used our developed *ArabGend* dataset only for training. We also used *ARAP* dataset (Zaghouani and Charfi, 2018), which consists of 1,600 Twitter accounts labeled for their gender along with country and language. We used half of the *ARAP* dataset for training, and half for the evaluation. Hence, in our experiments, models are evaluated using the half of the *ARAP* dataset, which we considered as our test set.

5.2 Classification Models and Features

We used Support Vector Machincs (SVMs) as our classifier. Our choice of SVM was influenced by a reasonable accuracy and a system deployment in a low computational resource setting. As features, we used character n-gram vectors weighted by term-frequency-inverse document term frequency (tf-idf). We experimented with different n-gram ranges. Only character [2-5] n-gram results are reported in this paper since they yielded the best results.

In addition, we also varied different types of input to the classifiers. We experimented with *(i)* a single tweet from each user, *(ii)* aggregate all tweets from a user, *(iii)* usernames of the Twitter users. We also experimented by balancing the *ArabGend* training set, to have equal number males and females, to understand the affect on the performance of the classifiers. Since ARAP dataset is balanced in terms of gender, hence, we do not apply any sampling to balance the data any further. Since there was not any significant improvement in performance after balancing to equal distribution, therefore, we do not report that results.

5.3 Results

In Table 5, we report the classification results on ARAP test set. From the results, we observed that for both ARAP data and *ArabGend* data, best results are obtained when usernames are used as opposed to aggregation of tweets or user descriptions. In general, aggregating tweets do not improve results in general by a significant margin. The usernames in the *ArabGend* dataset have a significant performance improvement over all other settings, resulting in an F1 score of 82.1.

Train Data	Features	Acc.	P	R	F1
Majority Baseline		53.3	26.7	50.0	34.8
	Usernames	67.2	67.1	66.8	66.8
ARAP (Baseline)	Description	58.2	58.5	58.5	58.2
	Tweets	69.8	70.9	70.4	69.7
	All Features	59.9	65.3	61.6	57.9
	Usernames	**82.4**	**82.7**	**82.0**	**82.1**
ArabGend	Description	64.1	65.4	62.7	61.8
	Tweets	63.1	62.9	62.9	62.9
	All Features	78.0	80.2	77.1	77.1

Table 5: Performance on ARAP test data

5.4 Additional Experiments

Predicting Gender from Profile Images To evaluate the efficiency of profile image based gender detection model we used Gender-and-Age-Detection model (Levi and Hassner, 2015) on ARAP test set. It uses deep learning to identify the gender and age of a person from face image, which was trained on ~27K images from Flickr (Adience dataset) (Levi and Hassner, 2015).[12]

For comparison, we manually annotated the same ARAP test set for gender prediction using profile images and the accuracy was 81%. This shows that profile image can be one of the powerful features to predict gender. It is worth to mention that 87% of the package errors are due to misclassification of female users as males. We plan to use profile images with textual features in future.

[12]Accuracy of this model is 64%. Some images are hard for gender prediction, e.g., flag, natural scene, incomplete face, kid image, cartoon, mixed, etc.

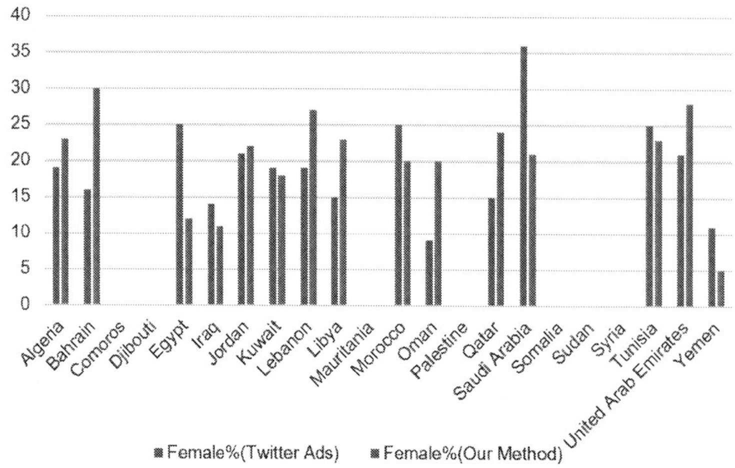

Figure 10: Distribution of female accounts

Predicting Gender from Friends Network Homophily (meaning love of the same) is a tendency in social groups for similar people to be connected together (McPherson et al., 2001). Homophily has predictive power in social media (Bischoff, 2012). We anticipated that female users on Twitter tend to have more female friends than male users and vice versa. To experiment this assumption, we collected a list of up to 100 friends for all accounts in the ARAP test set, and from their usernames, we used our classifier to predict their gender. We experimented with different thresholds on ratio of predicted male to predicted female friends to decide gender of our target users. The best results were obtained when 1/3 of friends of an account are predicted as females. In these cases, we propagated the label "female" to the account and propagated "male" otherwise. By doing so, we could achieve 56% accuracy. This shows that gender distribution of friends network has limited impact on determining gender of a user.

We also explored if information about friend's gender can improve the performance of the model from the earlier section. We adopt the following procedure: if the classifier is not confident that the instance is male, we apply the threshold technique above and take the classifier's predicted label otherwise. By doing this, we were able to improve the performance from 82.1% to 82.9% indicating that friend's gender might be helpful in cases where the classifier is not confident. However, obtaining a list of friends for all accounts needs a significant amount of time. This limits the usage of friends' gender in cases where fast response is needed.

Comparison with Twitter Ads API Advertisers on Twitter can target their campaigns based on geolocation, gender, language, and age. Twitter uses the gender provided by people in their profiles, and extends it to other people based on account likeness. We used Twitter Ads API to get total number of users in all Arab countries and their gender distribution. Figure 10 shows distribution of female users as obtained from Twitter Ads and our method. Although there are some differences between the two methods, the average percentages of female users are similar (19% using Twitter Ads vs. 20% using our method). This can show that our method is close to Twitter Ads for gender prediction of users although Twitter has much larger information to use. Note that Twitter Ads results (also our method) may have limitations in terms of accuracy.

6 Conclusion

In this paper, we have presented *ArabGend*, a new dataset of Twitter users labeled for their gender and location. To the best of our knowledge, this is the largest Arabic dataset for gender based analysis. We analyzed the characteristics of the users from a gender perspective. We identified key differences between male and female accounts on Arabic Twitter such as user connections, topics of interest, etc. We also studied the gender gap in professions and argued that results obtained from our dataset are aligned with recent reports from the World Bank and Twitter Ads information. We also showed that our dataset yields the best inference results on a publicly available test set. In the future, we plan to enhance our data collection method by considering gender markers in the whole user description and other profile fields.

Ethical Concern and Social Impact

User Privacy For privacy protection and compliance with Twitter rules, we make sure that Twitter account handles and tweets are fully anonymized. We share tweets by their IDs, and we share a list of names written in Arabic and English as first names only.

Biases and Limitations Any biases found in our dataset are unintentional, and we do not intend to cause harm to any group or individual. In our study, we tried to remove biases in data collection by providing all forms of male and female description words. But, because Twitter is widely used in some regions (e.g., Gulf) and less used in other regions (e.g., Maghreb), we acknowledge that our statistics and results may be less accurate for some Arab countries in the real world. However, they give rough estimates about the actual presence of users from those countries on Twitter. The bias in our data, for example towards a particular gender, is unintentional and is a true representation of users on Twitter as obtained also from Twitter Ads. Gender label (male/female) is extracted from the data and might not be a true representative of the users' choice.

Further, we heavily depend on users' self-disclosure (first words only) which covers a small portion of Twitter users. Therefore, the statistics presented in our paper provides an estimate of the whole picture. In the future, we plan to consider better methods for data collection with greater diversity and coverage.

References

Ahmed Abdelali, Hamdy Mubarak, Younes Samih, Sabit Hassan, and Kareem Darwish. 2021. QADI: Arabic dialect identification in the wild. In *Proceedings of the Sixth Arabic Natural Language Processing Workshop*, Kyiv, Ukraine (Virtual). Association for Computational Linguistics.

Kerstin Bischoff. 2012. We love rock'n'roll: analyzing and predicting friendship links in last. fm. In *Proceedings of the 4th Annual ACM Web Science Conference*, pages 47–56.

Bassem Bsir and Mounir Zrigui. 2018. Enhancing deep learning gender identification with gated recurrent units architecture in social text. *Computacion y Sistemas*, 22:757–766.

John D. Burger, John Henderson, George Kim, and Guido Zarrella. 2011. Discriminating gender on Twitter. In *Proceedings of the 2011 Conference on Empirical Methods in Natural Language Processing*, EMNLP '11, pages 1301–1309, Edinburgh, Scotland, UK. Association for Computational Linguistics.

Joymallya Chakraborty, Suvodeep Majumder, and Tim Menzies. 2021. Bias in machine learning software: why? how? what to do? In *Proceedings of the 29th ACM Joint Meeting on European Software Engineering Conference and Symposium on the Foundations of Software Engineering*, pages 429–440.

Xin Chen, Yu Wang, Eugene Agichtein, and Fusheng Wang. 2015. A comparative study of demographic attribute inference in twitter. In *Proceedings of the International AAAI Conference on Web and Social Media*, 1, pages 590–593, California, USA. AAAI.

Shammur Absar Chowdhury, Hamdy Mubarak, Ahmed Abdelali, Soon-gyo Jung, Bernard J. Jansen, and Joni Salminen. 2020. A multi-platform Arabic news comment dataset for offensive language detection. In *Proceedings of the 12th Language Resources and Evaluation Conference*, pages 6203–6212, Marseille, France. European Language Resources Association.

Morgane Ciot, Morgan Sonderegger, and Derek Ruths. 2013. Gender inference of Twitter users in non-English contexts. In *Proceedings of the 2013 Conference on Empirical Methods in Natural Language Processing*, pages 1136–1145. Association for Computational Linguistics.

Michael Conover, Jacob Ratkiewicz, Matthew Francisco, Bruno Gonçalves, Filippo Menczer, and Alessandro Flammini. 2011. Political polarization on twitter. In *Proceedings of the International AAAI Conference on Web and Social Media*, pages 89–96, Barcelona, Spain. AAAI.

Kareem Darwish and Hamdy Mubarak. 2016. Farasa: A new fast and accurate Arabic word segmenter. In *Proceedings of the Tenth International Conference on Language Resources and Evaluation*, LREC'16, pages 1070–1074, Portorož, Slovenia. European Language Resources Association (ELRA).

Shereen ElSayed and Mona Farouk. 2020. Gender identification for egyptian arabic dialect in twitter using deep learning models. *Egyptian Informatics Journal*, 21(3):159–167.

Nizar Habash, Houda Bouamor, and Christine Chung. 2019. Automatic gender identification and reinflection in Arabic. In *Proceedings of the First Workshop on Gender Bias in Natural Language Processing*, pages 155–165. Association for Computational Linguistics.

Sabit Hassan, Hamdy Mubarak, Ahmed Abdelali, and Kareem Darwish. 2021. ASAD: Arabic social media analytics and unDerstanding. In *Proceedings of the 16th Conference of the European Chapter of the Association for Computational Linguistics: System Demonstrations*, pages 113–118, Online. Association for Computational Linguistics.

Susan C Herring and Sharon Stoerger. 2014. Gender and (a) nonymity in computer-mediated communication. *The handbook of language, gender, and sexuality*, 2:567–586.

Shereen Hussein, Mona Farouk, and ElSayed Hemayed. 2019. Gender identification of egyptian dialect in twitter. *Egyptian Informatics Journal*, 20(2):109–116.

Gil Levi and Tal Hassner. 2015. Age and gender classification using convolutional neural networks. In *Proceedings of the IEEE conference on computer vision and pattern recognition workshops*, pages 34–42.

Shoushan Li, Bin Dai, Zhengxian Gong, and Guodong Zhou. 2016. Semi-supervised gender classification with joint textual and social modeling. In *Proceedings of COLING 2016, the 26th International Conference on Computational Linguistics: Technical Papers*, pages 2092–2100. The COLING 2016 Organizing Committee.

W. Liu and D. Ruths. 2013. What's in a name? using first names as features for gender inference in twitter. In *AAAI Spring Symposium: Analyzing Microtext*.

Yaguang Liu, Lisa Singh, and Zeina Mneimneh. 2021. A comparative analysis of classic and deep learning models for inferring gender and age of twitter users. In *Proceedings of the International Conference on Deep Learning Theory and Applications*.

Shervin Malmasi. 2014. A data-driven approach to studying given names and their gender and ethnicity associations. In *Proceedings of the Australasian Language Technology Association Workshop*, pages 145–149.

Miller McPherson, Lynn Smith-Lovin, and James M Cook. 2001. Birds of a feather: Homophily in social networks. *Annual review of sociology*, 27(1):415–444.

Alan Mislove, Sune Lehmann, Yong-Yeol Ahn, Jukka-Pekka Onnela, and James Rosenquist. 2011. Understanding the demographics of twitter users. In *Proceedings of the International AAAI Conference on Web and Social Media*, Barcelona, Spain. AAAI.

Hamdy Mubarak and Kareem Darwish. 2014. Using twitter to collect a multi-dialectal corpus of arabic. In *Proceedings of the EMNLP 2014 Workshop on Arabic Natural Language Processing (ANLP)*, pages 1–7.

Juergen Mueller and Gerd Stumme. 2016. Gender inference using statistical name characteristics in twitter. In *Proceedings of the The 3rd Multidisciplinary International Social Networks Conference on SocialInformatics 2016, Data Science 2016*, pages 1–8.

Arjun Mukherjee and Bing Liu. 2010. Improving gender classification of blog authors. In *Proceedings of the 2010 Conference on Empirical Methods in Natural Language Processing*, pages 207–217. Association for Computational Linguistics.

Delip Rao, David Yarowsky, Abhishek Shreevats, and Manaswi Gupta. 2010. Classifying latent user attributes in twitter. In *Proceedings of the 2nd International Workshop on Search and Mining User-Generated Contents*, SMUC '10, page 37–44, New York, NY, USA. Association for Computing Machinery.

Shigeyuki Sakaki, Yasuhide Miura, Xiaojun Ma, Keigo Hattori, and Tomoko Ohkuma. 2014. Twitter user gender inference using combined analysis of text and image processing. In *Proceedings of the Third Workshop on Vision and Language*, pages 54–61, Dublin, Ireland. Association for Computational Linguistics.

Fadi Salem. 2017. Social media and the internet of things. *The Arab Social Media Report*.

Erhan Sezerer, Ozan Polatbilek, and Selma Tekir. 2019. A Turkish dataset for gender identification of Twitter users. In *Proceedings of the 13th Linguistic Annotation Workshop*, pages 203–207. Association for Computational Linguistics.

Juan Soler and Leo Wanner. 2016. A semi-supervised approach for gender identification. In *Proceedings of the Tenth International Conference on Language Resources and Evaluation*, pages 1282–1287. European Language Resources Association (ELRA).

Tomoki Taniguchi, Shigeyuki Sakaki, Ryosuke Shigenaka, Yukihiro Tsuboshita, and Tomoko Ohkuma. 2015. A weighted combination of text and image classifiers for user gender inference. In *Proceedings of the Fourth Workshop on Vision and Language*, pages 87–93. Association for Computational Linguistics.

Tran Anh Tuan, Tien-Dung Cao, and Tram Truong-Huu. 2019. Dirac: A hybrid approach to customer demographics analysis for advertising campaigns. In *2019 6th NAFOSTED Conference on Information and Computer Science (NICS)*, pages 256–261.

Svitlana Volkova, Yoram Bachrach, Michael Armstrong, and Vijay Sharma. 2015. Inferring latent user properties from texts published in social media. In *Twenty-Ninth AAAI Conference on Artificial Intelligence*.

Svitlana Volkova, Theresa Wilson, and David Yarowsky. 2013. Exploring demographic language variations to improve multilingual sentiment analysis in social media. In *Proceedings of the 2013 Conference on Empirical Methods in Natural Language Processing*, pages 1815–1827. Association for Computational Linguistics.

Zijian Wang, Scott Hale, David Ifeoluwa Adelani, Przemyslaw Grabowicz, Timo Hartman, Fabian Flöck, and David Jurgens. 2019. Demographic inference and representative population estimates from multilingual social media data. In *The world wide web conference*, pages 2056–2067.

Wajdi Zaghouani and Anis Charfi. 2018. Arap-tweet: A large multi-dialect Twitter corpus for gender, age and language variety identification. In *Proceedings of the Eleventh International Conference on Language Resources and Evaluation (LREC 2018)*, Miyazaki, Japan. European Language Resources Association (ELRA).

Appendix

A Demo

Using the developed model, we also built a demo that takes a person's name written in Arabic or

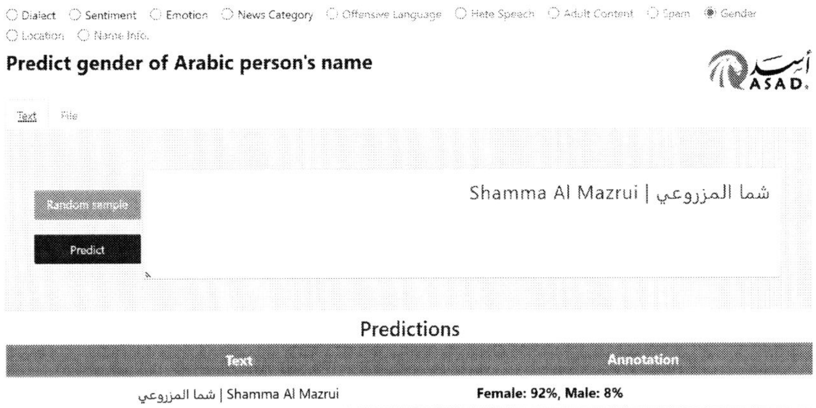

Figure 11: Demo interface for gender inference using our proposed models.

English and predicts a gender label with probabilities. The demo can be accessed using the link: `https://asad.qcri.org/demo` (part of ASAD tools (Hassan et al., 2021)). A screenshot of the demo is presented in Figure 11.

Automatic Identification of 5C Vaccine Behaviour on Social Media

Ajay Hemanth Sampath Kumar **Aminath Shausan**
Gianluca Demartini **Afshin Rahimi**
The University of Queensland
{a.sampathkumar,a.shausan,g.demartini,a.rahimi}@uq.edu.au

Abstract

Monitoring vaccine behaviour through social media can guide health policy. We present a new dataset of 9471 tweets posted in Australia from 2020 to 2022, annotated with sentiment toward vaccines and also 5C, the five types of behaviour toward vaccines, a scheme commonly used in health psychology literature. We benchmark our dataset using BERT and Gradient Boosting Machine and show that jointly training both sentiment and 5C tasks (F1=48) outperforms individual training (F1=39) in this highly imbalanced data. Our sentiment analysis indicates close correlation between the sentiments and prominent events during the pandemic. We hope that our dataset and benchmark models will inform further work in online monitoring of vaccine behaviour. The dataset and benchmark methods are accessible online.[1]

1 Introduction

The development of effective and safe vaccines has been shown as one of the most successful means to mitigate the spread of COVID-19 disease around the globe. As with any other vaccination program, COVID-19 intervention in any country depends on public acceptance and vaccine uptake. This has to be done by a large proportion of society to attain herd immunity, which is estimated to range from 67% to 95% (Mills et al., 2020; Randolph and Barreiro, 2020; Anderson et al., 2020). However, vaccine hesitancy has been identified as one of the top 10 challenges to global health by the World Health Organization in 2019 (World Health Organization, 2019 January [cited 14 August 2022]).

Vaccine hesitancy refers to the delay in acceptance or refusal of vaccination by the public despite the availability of vaccination services (MacDonald et al., 2015). This behaviour has been significantly prominent towards COVID-19 vaccines as they differ from previous vaccines in many respects: accelerated development, novel techniques used, potential side effects, uncertainty regarding the size and extent of their effectiveness, and limited production compared to the demand (Dubé and MacDonald, 2020).

Australia began its mass vaccination program in late February 2021 but was initially hampered by low vaccine uptake due to mistrust of vaccine effectiveness and the government, the blood clotting syndrome (TTS) associated with the AstraZeneca product, shipment delays, and misinformation (Kaufman et al., 2022b). Despite the fact that the present uptake is high ($>$ 90% two doses for over 16 years), the coverage varies across age, jurisdictions, and the number of doses (Australian Government: Department of Health and Aged Care, 2022 August [cited 14 August 2022]). High coverage is primarily driven by travel desires (and travel vaccination requirements) and the need to mitigate risk. As new variants of SARS-CoV-2 are emerging and existing immunity waning in a short period of time, it is likely that people will need to get multiple booster doses. Consequently, identifying immediate and future public behaviour toward vaccination is important for public health authorities to combat possible challenges to reaching and maintaining herd immunity.

The 5C model provides five measures (Confidence, Complacency, Constraints, Calculation and Collective Responsibility) for assessing an individual's psychological reasoning towards vaccination (Betsch et al., 2018, 2020). *Confidence* associates the trust in vaccine effectiveness, safety, and the system that delivers it. People with low confidence mistrust the healthcare system, fall for misinformation, believe in conspiracies, and doubt the benefit of vaccines. *Complacency* exists when vaccination is viewed as a low priority or when vaccine-preventable diseases are not of a concern.

[1] https://github.com/ajayhemanth/5C-Twitter

Proceedings of the 2022 COLING Workshop: The 8th Workshop on Noisy User-generated Text (W-NUT 2022), pages 136–146

High complacency correlates with low uptake of a vaccine. *Constraints* refer to the structural and psychological barriers to getting vaccinated. For example, geographical constraints in accessibility, limited language, and health literacy, and cost may postulate high constraints. *Calculation* defines the engagement in extensive information searching, which may lead to lower vaccination willingness arising with exposure to a high volume of anti-vaccination content. *Collective responsibility* asserts an individual's willingness to protect others by getting vaccinated and contributes to herd immunity. See Table 1 for a summary of the description of the 5C model.

Most works in identifying vaccine behaviour use surveys that are costly, time-consuming, and don't scale to a large population. The use of social media for expressing vaccine-related opinion provides a great opportunity to use online social monitoring tools to guide health policy-making for vaccine adoption. There are few recent studies that adapt the 5C scheme for online health monitoring. Greyling and Rossouw (2022) focus on the analysis of tweets rather than building predictive models, Fues Wahl et al. (2022)'s uses 1794 tweets from Scandinavian users and manually categorise them into the 5C categories, and Boucher et al. (2021) focuses on the vaccine trials and uses unsupervised methods.

Our contributions are as follows: 1) we provide the first large-scale vaccine behaviour dataset in English, annotated with both 5c and sentiment; 2) we present two benchmark models and show the challenges of 5C predictive models given the highly imbalanced data; and 3) we analyse the data showing that changes in 5C distribution is not uniform across regions, indicating opportunities for targeted health messaging. We make the dataset and benchmarks available hoping to impact future work in online vaccine behaviour monitoring based on the 5C framework.

2 Related work

The 5C model has been widely applied to examine COVID-19 vaccination behaviour. In 2020, Kwok et al. (2021a) estimated Hong Kong nurses' intention to receive COVID-19 vaccine using the 5C model and examines the correlation of their vaccine behaviour to previous influenza vaccination. Thunström et al. (2021) applied the 5C scale to investigate psychological reasoning behind the previous uptake of measles and flu vaccines by adults in the United States and their intention to get COVID-19 vaccination for themselves and their children. Wismans et al. (2021) studied the psychological drivers of vaccination intention in university students across the Netherlands, Belgium and Portugal, using the 5C model. Gallant et al. (2021) implemented the 5C model to investigate older adults' vaccination behaviour in the United Kingdom over the first year of the pandemic. Lindholt et al. (2021) examined the levels and predictors of acceptance of an approved COVID-19 vaccine in eight Western countries by utilizing the 5C model. Rustagi et al. (2022) applied the 5C model to identify vaccine hesitancy among chronic disease patients availing care in a primary health facility in India.

Previous studies examined COVID-19 vaccination behavior utilizing traditional surveys (Seale et al., 2021; Trent et al., 2022; Rhodes et al., 2021; Edwards et al., 2021; Dodd et al., 2021; Kaufman et al., 2022a; Kwok et al., 2021a; Thunström et al., 2021; Sherman et al., 2021; Wismans et al., 2021; Paul et al., 2021; Sallam, 2021; Akarsu et al., 2021; Fisher et al., 2020; Freeman et al., 2020; Ward et al., 2020; Lazarus et al., 2021). However, such surveys are often costly in their design and implementation, time-consuming, produces limited data and represent comparatively short-term situation. Recently, Twitter has been increasingly applied in research concerning public attitude towards vaccination due to its advantages of availability of a large amount of real-time posts without any costs, ease of access and public searching facility. In spite of these advantages, there remains a gap in Australia for Twitter-based COVID-19 vaccination research. We found just one study (Kwok et al., 2021b), conducted during 2020, which addresses Australian public opinion towards COVID-19 vaccine solely from Australian Twitter users. Sentiment analysis of this study has shown that the majority of people expressed positive emotions towards vaccine with trust and anticipation as the most prominent behaviors associated with it, while fear being the top negative emotion.

An investigation of Twitter posts from 10 countries, including Australia, has revealed that more information about vaccines' safety and the expected side effects may increase public positive attitudes towards vaccination Greyling and Rossouw (2022). Similarly, sentiment analysis from 4 million tweets

Label	Behavior	Description
C1	Confidence	Trust in safety and effectiveness of vaccines and health system
C2	Constraints	Structural and psychological barriers
C3	Complacency	Not perceiving diseases as high risk
C4	Calculation	Engagement in extensive information searching
C5	Collective responsibility	Willingness to protect others

Table 1: Description of 5C categories. Collective Responsibility and Responsibility (Resp.) are used interchangeably in this work.

across several nations, including Australia, has found the prevalence of vaccine hesitancy and objections outweighs vaccine interests (Yousefinaghani et al., 2021). Various other studies have assessed COVID-19 vaccination behavior using Twitter data from a specific country or a particular region. These include, studies based on posts from the United States (Jang et al., 2021; Engel-Rebitzer et al., 2021; Germani and Biller-Andorno, 2021), the United Kingdom (Hussain et al., 2021), Japan (Niu et al., 2022b,a), China (Gao et al., 2021; Wang et al., 2020), Canada (Griffith et al., 2021), Africa (Gbashi et al., 2021). Other studies address COVID-19 vaccination behaviour at a global scale (Chopra et al., 2021; Lyu et al., 2021; Xue et al., 2020).

Along with sentiment analysis, some studies have implemented the 5C model to examine COVID-19 vaccination emotions as well as attitudes towards other vaccines in tweets. Greyling and Rossouw (2022) constructed a multiple linear regression model to examine positive attitudes towards vaccines across ten countries. In their model, among other methods, the positive 5C categories were applied to identify the covariates. Boucher et al. (2021) applied a topic modeling approach to investigate the mistrust in Covid-19 vaccination based on English and French tweets. They then used the 5C scale to categorize the topics and found that all mistrusts fell into the Confidence category. Fues Wahl et al. (2022) applied the 5C model to map relevant predictors for several vaccination behaviours in Scandinavian Twitter users. Similar to our work, they manually labelled each tweet according to the 5C scale. However, unlike our dataset, their dataset was multi-labeled, as each tweet was assumed to have multiple 5C categories. They did not, however, include Covid-19 vaccination as a specific vaccination category in their analysis.

3 Method

3.1 Dataset

We made use of the Twitter API to collect $60,000$ COVID-19 vaccine-related tweets restricted to Australia from 01 February 2020 to 30 October 2021, using keywords: *vax, vaccine, vaccinate, vaccination, jab, pfizer, astrazeneca*. We selected a weighted sample of $20,000$ tweets with weights proportional to the total number of tweets within the time frame of a week and annotated each tweet first based on its sentiment towards vaccination and then its associated 5C category if the tweet contains either a positive or negative stance. We note that some tweets do not provide a clear positive or negative stance and thus have been categorized accordingly if the stance is totally irrelevant to the topic of vaccination, or if the stance concerns vaccination, but does not belong to either the positive or negative category. We excluded tweets from the last two categories in our analysis. We labeled each tweet based on the most prominent 5C behaviour. Thus, our dataset has the structure of binary categories in terms of.tweet's sentiment and multi-class categories with regard to 5C vaccine behaviour. Table 2 depicts a sample of labeled tweets. The final dataset consists of 9471 annotated tweets. The study has received clearance by the authors' organisation's human research ethics committee.

We note that, in the original 5C model (Betsch et al., 2018) much of the description was made for the negative aspects of the model, hence we made some discretion for labeling positive 5C categories, as, based on the tweet texts, these categories were not clearly identified. For example, tweets which mentioned only about taking vaccine without any further explanations (like 'got my first vaccine !!!') were labeled as positive Confidence. Tweets which talked about getting vaccine as a compulsory action (like 'no jab no job') were labeled as positive Constraints. Similarly, tweets which supported vac-

Label	Sample Tweet (rephrased for privacy reasons)
+ Complacency	It takes just one COVID infected person to start a Pandemic. Please vaccinate.
+ Complacency Resp.	Difficult to wear mask but we have to. Vaccinate, not just for yourself but for others too.
+ Calculation	Vaccines don't prevent infections, they prevent severe disease and hospitalisation.
+ Constraints	no jab no job. That's how it should be.
- Complacency	99% of people recover from COVID, vaccines shouldn't be mandated.
- Confidence	A vaccine that might kill you for various reasons while big pharma benefits.
- Calculation	myocarditis risks is higher in teenage boys, we shouldn't rush into vaccinating them.
- Constraint	AZ age limit should be 60, not 50

Table 2: A sample of eight tweets (rephrased for privacy reasons) and their labels. + and - refer to the positive and negative sentiments towards COVID-19 vaccination, respectively. The five C categories are also shown (see Table 1 for definition).

cine based on data as well as personal experience (like 'I took AZ vaccine 1 week ago, and there is no symptoms of blood clot') were categorized as positive Calculations. To check the validity of the annotations, we compared annotation agreements between two researchers from the team who independently labeled a random sample of 200 tweets. Using the Cohen's kappa (Cohen, 1960; McHugh, 2012) statistic, we found a strong (κ = 0.95) level of agreement between the researchers with regards to the sentiment labels (see Table 3 for contingency table), and a strong (κ = 0.88) agreement for the 5C labels (see Table 4 for contingency table). All 200 tweets have been used in the sentiment label comparison while only those tweets which both annotators agreed as positive and negative have been included in the 5C label comparison.

A/B	InSuff	Neg	Pos	X
Insuff	19	0	2	0
Neg	0	68	0	0
Pos	1	0	82	1
X	0	2	1	24

Table 3: Summary of annotation agreements between two researchers for a random sample of 200 tweets. Labels indicate positive (Pos), negative (Neg), irrelevant (Insuff) and inconclusive (X) stance towards vaccination.

3.2 Data Analysis

Overall, people expressed significantly high negative emotions in the Constraints category, similar levels of positive and negative emotions in the Complacency category and have been otherwise always positive towards vaccination depicting high Confidence and Calculation behaviours (Figure 1). The most eminent concerns regarding negative emotions have been related to the constraints caused by vaccine roll out, Pfizer vaccine, aged care facilities, and the government and its leader (Table 5). On the other hand AstraZeneca and Pfizer vaccines and COVID vaccine in general lead among positive topics, with high calculations and confidence associated with them (Table 5). A high number of tweets with the Positive Calculation category relate to the tweets in support of AstraZeneca with their own experience as evidence to disprove the tweets associating blood clot issues with that vaccine. This causes AstraZeneca to be a dominant unigram in both positive and negative instances.

A/B	C1	C2	C3	C4	C5
C1	75	0	2	1	1
C2	0	27	1	1	2
C3	0	0	4	0	1
C4	0	0	0	4	0
C5	0	1	0	0	17

Table 4: Annotation agreement table for 5C (See Table1 for the definition of C1-C5).

As the pandemic prevailed from 2020 to 2022, negative attitudes towards vaccination continuously varied in terms of prevalence and corresponding 5C reasoning. During 2020, the prevalence of negative stances has been relatively stable apart from the peaks around August and December, and the

Label	Bigrams
Constraints	vaccine rollout, scott morrison, aged care
Confidence	az vaccine, catching measles, pfizer vaccine
Complacency	COVID19 vaccine, blood clots, cold flu
Calculation	blood clots, sore arm, az vaccine
Collective Resp.	aged care, stay safe, vaccine hub
Positive	az vaccine, pfizer vaccine, sore arm
Negative	vaccine rollout, az vaccine, scott morrison

Table 5: Top 3 most frequent bigrams categorized by their sentiment and 5C classes.

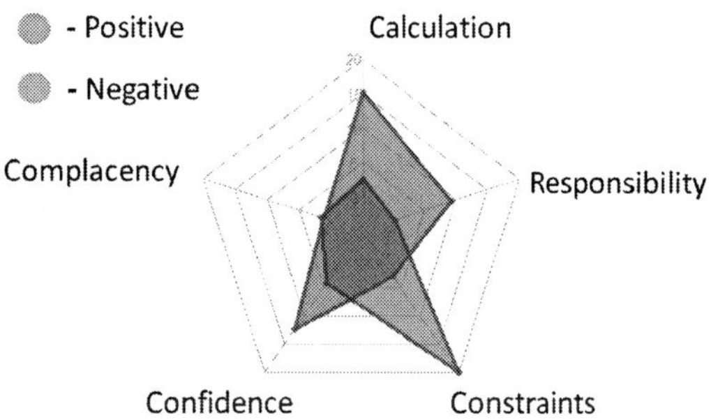

Figure 1: Distribution of positive and negative 5C.

shallow dips between the end of May to the end of July and in September (Figure 2 (left)). The shallow period from the end of May 2020 to the end of July 2020 coincides with the event of high approval towards the government for proactively closing the border, implementing lockdown, releasing super funds. Negative stances have been stable from early 2021 until around the end of March, and peaked during April, possibly due to the panic caused by the blood clot from AstraZeneca vaccine. Multiple peaks have then appeared with prominent ones occurring in July, August and December 2021 (Figure 2 (right)). The peaks in July and August correlate with the public outrage caused by the shortage of vaccine doses, the continuous emergence of blood clotting incidences from AstraZeneca vaccine, and the government ignoring to use the offer of Pfizer vaccine from that company. Consequently, the peak in December 2021 correlates to high displeasure towards the government at that time.

From the beginning of 2020 until around November that year, people voiced strong lack of confidence with regard to vaccination, but has then changed to the constraints from December 2021 onward until September 2021 where the notion has turned back to lack of confidence. Collective responsibility has not been consequential much to negative emotions except during April 2020 to March 2020 (Figure 2 (left)). This may be due to the fact that people resisting to lockdowns around April 2020, pointing their right to freedom. Such emotions have reduced after June 2020, with many deaths due to Covid occurring during April 2020. High level of negative confidence seen from October 2020 to the end of that year may be related to the events of the development of vaccines and people being doubtful of their effectiveness due to some vaccinated people in other countries getting re-infected. The emergence of negative Complacency and Collective responsibility from February 2021 to March 2021 may happen because of public resistance to the government's allocated vaccine, pointing out their right to choose the vaccine type. High level of negative Constraints emotion depicted from April 2021 onward may be a consequence of combination of several factors: shortage of vaccine, fear of blood clotting from the AstraZeneca vaccine, the failure of government to secure Pfizer vaccine when it was first available.

The bulk of opinions about vaccination has been arising from people residing in Sydney and Melbourne, the most populated two cities in Australia (Australian Bureau of Statistics, 2022 August [cited 24 August 2022](b)), with Melbourne slightly dominating in terms of negative stances and people from both cities displaying quite similar levels of positive emotions (Figure 3). Both cities have shown identical behavior in terms of the 5C scale, with negative attitudes attributed mostly to lack of confidence and calculative behaviour, while positive attitudes related mostly to constraints, collective responsibility and confidence behaviour. The prevalence of tweets and people's variable emotions in Melbourne and Sydney towards vaccination may also be related to long lockdown periods in Victoria and New South Wales where these two cities are located, respectively (Australian Bureau of Statistics, 2022 August [cited 24 August

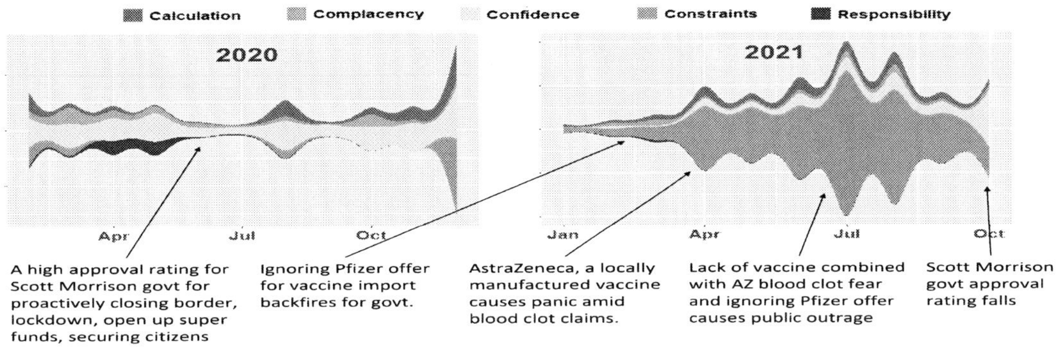

Figure 2: Changes of negative sentiment 5C's through 2020 and 2021 aligned with major COVID-related events. The description of the events are from: Statista (2020 August [cited 24 August 2022]); 9News (2021 August [cited 24 August 2022]); BBC News (2021 August [cited 24 August 2022](a),A); Reuters (2022 August [cited 24 August 2022]).

2022](a)).

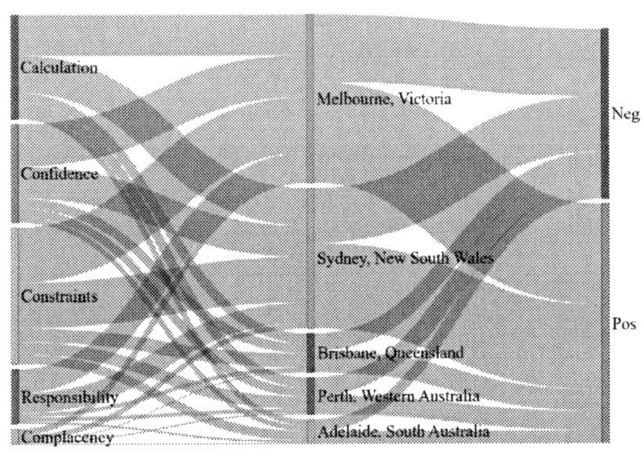

Figure 3: Distribution of positive and negative 5Cs based on location.

3.3 Vaccine behaviour identification

We perform three predictive modeling tasks in our analysis: (1) predicting the sentiment of tweets, (2) predicting the 5C vaccination behaviour in tweets, (3) predicting the combined sentiment and 5C categories in tweets:

Task 1 - Sentiment Identification: The first task is a binary classification problem to identify regardless of the type of behaviour if the post expresses positive or negative attitude towards vaccination. This task is framed as a binary classification problem.

Task 2 - 5C Categorisation: In task 2 our goal is to identify one of the 5C categories from the tweet content regardless of its sentiment. This task is useful to practitioners where there is no sentiment expressed, however, one of the 5C vaccine behaviours are expressed through posts. For example, a vaccine researcher might be expressing scientific data regarding the risks versus benefits of a vaccine in certain population groups without necessarily expressing an opinion. This task is formulated as a multi-class classification trained using categorical cross-entropy loss.

Task 3 - Combined Sentiment and 5C Categorisation : In this task, we categorise a post into one of the ten categories resulting from the two sentiments and the five vaccine behaviour types (10 classes). We formulate this task as a multi-class problem. To identify if the information in the sentiment and the vaccine attitudes are complementary, we compare the results with a model where Task 1 and 2 are trained separately but the results are combined after prediction.

For our benchmark models, we use BERT (Devlin et al., 2018) using the base-uncased English version. To make sure the results are reasonable, we compare Task 3 with a Gradient Boosting Machine (GBM) (Hastie et al., 2009) baseline using TF-IDF features. Prior to fitting the models, we pre-processed the tweet texts by removing stop words (only for GBM), tokenizing sentences and encoding the words to integers. We then randomly partitioned the dataset into train/test/validation sets in the ratio $7:1:2$.

GBM, in Task 3, is a tree-based ML model which sequentially fits new models to enhance the accuracy of the estimated response variable supervised learning tasks such as the classification problems we address here. For each predictive modeling task, we use 50 trees, each with a maximum depth of

Label	P%	R%	F1%
+Sentiment	90	87	**88**
-Sentiment	81	84	82
Confidence	48	55	51
Constraints	79	79	**79**
Complacency	25	18	21
Calculation	61	60	60
Collective Resp.	62	52	57
Combined at prediction	39	39	39

Table 6: Performance of BERT in predicting the sentiment (task 1), 5C categories (task 2) and combined sentiment and 5C during prediction.

A/B	C1	C2	C3	C4	C5
C1	297	84	39	166	70
C2	33	482	11	26	30
C3	2	5	3	1	1
C4	86	19	12	274	27
C5	44	24	7	14	138

Table 7: Confusion matrix for predicting the 5C categories (task 2).

Label	P%	R%	F1%
-Confidence	49	44	46
-Constraints	78	83	**80**
-Complacency	26	29	27
-Calculation	49	40	44
-Responsibility	20	13	16
+Confidence	47	51	49
+Constraint	33	28	30
+Complacency	7	10	8
+Calculation	61	57	**59**
+Collective Resp.	62	57	**59**

Table 8: Performance of BERT in predicting the combined sentiment and 5C categories (task 3).

15 and the minimum number of observations at each leaf node being also 15. The learning rate and column sample rate have been set to 0.1 and 0.4, respectively. We use grid search with 1 to 70 trees, having maximum tree depth in the range 3 to 7, with column sample rate of 0.4 to 1 and minimum rows from 1 to 100 to search for the best parameters in GBM using cross-validation. For BERT, we use the default parameters of the pre-trained model. Additionally, the number of nodes in the output layer equals the total number of classes to be predicted, the activation function of the output layer is "softmax", with the loss function being "categorical cross-entropy".

We evaluate the performance of the models using the precision, recall and F1 scores which are commonly applied measures in classification problems. Because of the imbalanced nature of our problem, we use macro-averaged F1 to evaluate across multiple classes.

4 Results

Our results assert that the largest F1 value corresponds to positive sentiments (88%) from the sentiment task (task 1) and the Constraint class (79%) in predicting the 5C task (task 2) (Table 6). Our results further show that BERT has correctly predicted the 5C categories 1191 times (Table 7).

For the combined sentiment and 5C prediction task (task 3), our prediction depicts that the negative Constraints (80%) and positive Calculation and Collective Responsibility categories (59% for both) have the highest F1 measure (Table 8). BERT has performed quite variably in predicting individual class in all three tasks due to the imbalanced nature of our dataset across the classes. This can be visualized from Figure 4, in which we can see that classes with lower proportions have been less likely predicted. As such, we fitted a GBM model to predict the combined sentiment and 5C task, and found that, overall, BERT performed better than GBM (F1 score of 48%).

We stress that GBM uses boosting, so it oversamples difficult instances, for example, less frequent ones, and thus can handle class imbalance in an indirect way to some extent. However, both GBM and BERT were to be affected by the class imbalance. When the weights of the low-frequency categories were increased to fix this issue, they reduced the accuracy of other categories, and hence we did not implement class weights in the models.

5 Conclusion

We presented the first large dataset for online monitoring vaccination behaviour in Australia, which is annotated by public sentiments towards vaccination and their psychological reasoning by the 5C scale. Our analysis has shown a close correlation between the sentiments of the tweets and the prominent events during the pandemic. Our analysis of vaccination behaviour from this dataset showed

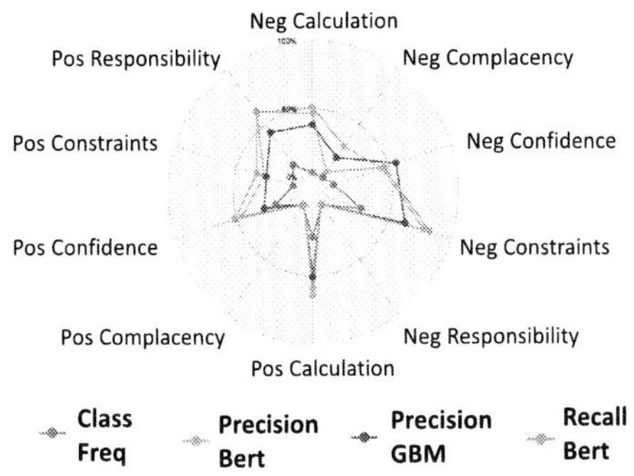

Figure 4: Comparison of precision and recall scores from the sentiment and 5C prediction task (task 3) with the distribution of 5C categories.

Model	P%	R%	F1%
BERT	53	38	**48**
GBM	36	28	32

Table 9: Comparison of the two benchmark methods for the combined sentiment and 5C tweet classification task.

large amount of negative emotions towards vaccination due to the constraints related to vaccine rollout caused by its shortage, delay in securing Pfizer vaccine when it was available, administering vaccination to aged care facilities, and the government's handling of the vaccination program.

Using this dataset, we predicted the sentiments towards vaccination, the 5C behaviour and the combined sentiment and 5C behaviour using BERT. All these predictive tasks are based on classification models, and showed variable performance across classes due to the imbalance proportion of data across classes. We compared performance of BERT with GBM in predicting the combined sentiment and the 5C categories and found that BERT has performed better than GBM.

Our work provides a proof of concept in the application of 5C scales to monitor vaccination behaviour using social media and can be extended to other domains such as Facebook and Google Trends.

6 Acknowledgements

This work is funded by The University of Queensland's AI4Pandemic group whose focus is the application of data science, machine learning, statistical learning, applied mathematics, and computation for managing pandemics both at the epidemic and clinical level. We are thankful for their support and hope that this work contributes to the aims of the group.

References

9News. 2021 August [cited 24 August 2022]. Labor accuses Morrison government of turning its back on Pfizer representatives in June 2020.

Büşra Akarsu, Dilara Canbay Özdemir, Duygu Ayhan Baser, Hilal Aksoy, İzzet Fidancı, and Mustafa Cankurtaran. 2021. While studies on COVID-19 vaccine is ongoing, the public's thoughts and attitudes to the future COVID-19 vaccine. *International journal of clinical practice*, 75(4):e13891.

Roy M Anderson, Carolin Vegvari, James Truscott, and Benjamin S Collyer. 2020. Challenges in creating herd immunity to sars-cov-2 infection by mass vaccination. *The Lancet*, 396(10263):1614–1616.

Australian Bureau of Statistics. 2022 August [cited 24 August 2022](a). Impact of lockdowns on household consumption - insights from alternative data sources.

Australian Bureau of Statistics. 2022 August [cited 24 August 2022](b). Regional population Statistics about the population for Australia's capital cities and regions.

Australian Government: Department of Health and Aged Care. 2022 August [cited 14 August 2022]. COVID-19 vaccination daily rollout update.

BBC News. 2021 August [cited 24 August 2022](a). Covid: Trigger of rare blood clots with AstraZeneca jab found by scientists.

BBC News. 2021 August [cited 24 August 2022](b). What's gone wrong with Australia's vaccine rollout?

Cornelia Betsch, Katrine Bach Habersaat, Sergei Deshevoi, Dorothee Heinemeier, Nikolay Briko, Natalia Kostenko, Janusz Kocik, Robert Böhm, Ingo Zettler, Charles Shey Wiysonge, et al. 2020. Sample study protocol for adapting and translating the 5c scale to assess the psychological antecedents of vaccination. *BMJ open*, 10(3):e034869.

Cornelia Betsch, Philipp Schmid, Dorothee Heinemeier, Lars Korn, Cindy Holtmann, and Robert Böhm. 2018. Beyond confidence: Development of a measure assessing the 5c psychological antecedents of vaccination. *PloS one*, 13(12):e0208601.

Jean-Christophe Boucher, Kirsten Cornelson, Jamie L Benham, Madison M Fullerton, Theresa Tang, Cora Constantinescu, Mehdi Mourali, Robert J Oxoby, Deborah A Marshall, Hadi Hemmati, et al. 2021. Analyzing social media to explore the attitudes and behaviors following the announcement of successful covid-19 vaccine trials: infodemiology study. *JMIR infodemiology*, 1(1):e28800.

Harshita Chopra, Aniket Vashishtha, Ridam Pal, Ananya Tyagi, Tavpritesh Sethi, et al. 2021. Mining trends of covid-19 vaccine beliefs on twitter with lexical embeddings. *arXiv preprint arXiv:2104.01131*.

Jacob Cohen. 1960. A coefficient of agreement for nominal scales. *Educational and psychological measurement*, 20(1):37–46.

Jacob Devlin, Ming-Wei Chang, Kenton Lee, and Kristina Toutanova. 2018. Bert: Pre-training of deep bidirectional transformers for language understanding. *arXiv preprint arXiv:1810.04805*.

Rachael H Dodd, Erin Cvejic, Carissa Bonner, Kristen Pickles, Kirsten J McCaffery, Julie Ayre, Carys Batcup, Tessa Copp, Samuel Cornell, Thomas Dakin, et al. 2021. Willingness to vaccinate against COVID-19 in Australia. *The Lancet Infectious Diseases*, 21(3):318–319.

Eve Dubé and Noni E MacDonald. 2020. How can a global pandemic affect vaccine hesitancy? *Expert review of vaccines*, 19(10):899–901.

Ben Edwards, Nicholas Biddle, Matthew Gray, and Kate Sollis. 2021. Covid-19 vaccine hesitancy and resistance: Correlates in a nationally representative longitudinal survey of the australian population. *PloS one*, 16(3):e0248892.

Eden Engel-Rebitzer, Daniel Camargo Stokes, Alison Buttenheim, Jonathan Purtle, and Zachary F Meisel. 2021. Changes in legislator vaccine-engagement on twitter before and after the arrival of the covid-19 pandemic. *Human vaccines & immunotherapeutics*, 17(9):2868–2872.

Kimberly A Fisher, Sarah J Bloomstone, Jeremy Walder, Sybil Crawford, Hassan Fouayzi, and Kathleen M Mazor. 2020. Attitudes toward a potential SARS-CoV-2 vaccine: a survey of US adults. *Annals of internal medicine*, 173(12):964–973.

Daniel Freeman, Bao S Loe, Andrew Chadwick, Cristian Vaccari, Felicity Waite, Laina Rosebrock, Lucy Jenner, Ariane Petit, Stephan Lewandowsky, Samantha Vanderslott, et al. 2020. Covid-19 vaccine hesitancy in the uk: the oxford coronavirus explanations, attitudes, and narratives survey (oceans) ii. *Psychological medicine*, pages 1–15.

H Fues Wahl, B Wikman Erlandson, C Sahlin, M Nyaku, and G Bencina. 2022. Analysis of vaccine messages on social media (twitter) in scandinavia. *Human vaccines & immunotherapeutics*, 18(1):2026711.

Allyson J Gallant, Louise A Brown Nicholls, Susan Rasmussen, Nicola Cogan, David Young, and Lynn Williams. 2021. Changes in attitudes to vaccination as a result of the covid-19 pandemic: A longitudinal study of older adults in the uk. *PloS one*, 16(12):e0261844.

Hao Gao, Qingting Zhao, Chuanlin Ning, Difan Guo, Jing Wu, and Lina Li. 2021. Does the covid-19 vaccine still work that "most of the confirmed cases had been vaccinated"? a content analysis of vaccine effectiveness discussion on sina weibo during the outbreak of covid-19 in nanjing. *International Journal of Environmental Research and Public Health*, 19(1):241.

Sefater Gbashi, Oluwafemi Ayodeji Adebo, Wesley Doorsamy, Patrick Berka Njobeh, et al. 2021. Systematic delineation of media polarity on covid-19 vaccines in africa: computational linguistic modeling study. *JMIR medical informatics*, 9(3):e22916.

Federico Germani and Nikola Biller-Andorno. 2021. The anti-vaccination infodemic on social media: A behavioral analysis. *PloS one*, 16(3):e0247642.

Talita Greyling and Stephanié Rossouw. 2022. Positive attitudes towards covid-19 vaccines: A cross-country analysis. *PloS one*, 17(3):e0264994.

Janessa Griffith, Husayn Marani, Helen Monkman, et al. 2021. Covid-19 vaccine hesitancy in canada: Content analysis of tweets using the theoretical domains framework. *Journal of medical Internet research*, 23(4):e26874.

Trevor Hastie, Robert Tibshirani, Jerome H Friedman, and Jerome H Friedman. 2009. *The elements of statistical learning: data mining, inference, and prediction*, volume 2. Springer.

Amir Hussain, Ahsen Tahir, Zain Hussain, Zakariya Sheikh, Mandar Gogate, Kia Dashtipour, Azhar Ali, Aziz Sheikh, et al. 2021. Artificial intelligence–enabled analysis of public attitudes on facebook and twitter toward covid-19 vaccines in the united kingdom and the united states: Observational study. *Journal of medical Internet research*, 23(4):e26627.

Hyeju Jang, Emily Rempel, David Roth, Giuseppe Carenini, Naveed Zafar Janjua, et al. 2021. Tracking covid-19 discourse on twitter in north america: Infodemiology study using topic modeling and aspect-based sentiment analysis. *Journal of medical Internet research*, 23(2):e25431.

Jessica Kaufman, Kathleen L Bagot, Jane Tuckerman, Ruby Biezen, Jane Oliver, Carol Jos, Darren Suryawijaya Ong, Jo-Anne Manski-Nankervis, Holly Seale, Lena Sanci, et al. 2022a. Qualitative exploration of intentions, concerns and information needs of vaccine-hesitant adults initially prioritised to receive COVID-19 vaccines in Australia. *Australian and New Zealand Journal of Public Health*, 46(1):16–24.

Jessica Kaufman, Jane Tuckerman, and Margie Danchin. 2022b. Overcoming covid-19 vaccine hesitancy: can australia reach the last 20 percent? *Expert Review of Vaccines*, 21(2):159–161.

Kin On Kwok, Kin-Kit Li, Wan In Wei, Arthur Tang, Samuel Yeung Shan Wong, and Shui Shan Lee. 2021a. Influenza vaccine uptake, covid-19 vaccination intention and vaccine hesitancy among nurses:

A survey. *International journal of nursing studies*, 114:103854.

Stephen Wai Hang Kwok, Sai Kumar Vadde, and Guanjin Wang. 2021b. Tweet topics and sentiments relating to COVID-19 vaccination among Australian Twitter users: machine learning analysis. *Journal of medical Internet research*, 23(5):e26953.

Jeffrey V Lazarus, Scott C Ratzan, Adam Palayew, Lawrence O Gostin, Heidi J Larson, Kenneth Rabin, Spencer Kimball, and Ayman El-Mohandes. 2021. A global survey of potential acceptance of a COVID-19 vaccine. *Nature medicine*, 27(2):225–228.

Marie Fly Lindholt, Frederik Jørgensen, Alexander Bor, and Michael Bang Petersen. 2021. Public acceptance of covid-19 vaccines: cross-national evidence on levels and individual-level predictors using observational data. *BMJ open*, 11(6):e048172.

Joanne Chen Lyu, Eileen Le Han, and Garving K Luli. 2021. Covid-19 vaccine–related discussion on twitter: topic modeling and sentiment analysis. *Journal of medical Internet research*, 23(6):e24435.

Noni E MacDonald et al. 2015. Vaccine hesitancy: Definition, scope and determinants. *Vaccine*, 33(34):4161–4164.

Mary L McHugh. 2012. Interrater reliability: the kappa statistic. *Biochemia medica*, 22(3):276–282.

M Mills, C Rahal, D Brazel, J Yan, and S Gieysztor. 2020. COVID-19 vaccine deployment: behaviour, ethics, misinformation and policy strategies. *London: The Royal Society & The British Academy*.

Qian Niu, Junyu Liu, Masaya Kato, Tomoki Aoyama, and Momoko Nagai-Tanima. 2022a. Fear of infection and sufficient vaccine reservation information might drive rapid coronavirus disease 2019 vaccination in japan: Evidence from twitter analysis. *medRxiv*.

Qian Niu, Junyu Liu, Masaya Kato, Yuki Shinohara, Natsuki Matsumura, Tomoki Aoyama, Momoko Nagai-Tanima, et al. 2022b. Public opinion and sentiment before and at the beginning of covid-19 vaccinations in japan: Twitter analysis. *JMIR infodemiology*, 2(1):e32335.

Elise Paul, Andrew Steptoe, and Daisy Fancourt. 2021. Attitudes towards vaccines and intention to vaccinate against COVID-19: Implications for public health communications. *The Lancet Regional Health-Europe*, 1:100012.

Haley E Randolph and Luis B Barreiro. 2020. Herd immunity: understanding covid-19. *Immunity*, 52(5):737–741.

Reuters. 2022 August [cited 24 August 2022]. Australia PM's ratings tumble to lowest levels in nearly two years, poll shows.

Anthea Rhodes, Monsurul Hoq, Mary-Anne Measey, and Margie Danchin. 2021. Intention to vaccinate against covid-19 in australia. *The Lancet Infectious Diseases*, 21(5):e110.

Neeti Rustagi, Yachana Choudhary, Shahir Asfahan, Kunal Deokar, Abhishek Jaiswal, Prasanna Thirunavukkarasu, Nitesh Kumar, and Pankaja Raghav. 2022. Identifying psychological antecedents and predictors of vaccine hesitancy through machine learning: A cross sectional study among chronic disease patients of deprived urban neighbourhood, india. *Monaldi Archives for Chest Disease*.

Malik Sallam. 2021. COVID-19 vaccine hesitancy worldwide: a concise systematic review of vaccine acceptance rates. *Vaccines*, 9(2):160.

Holly Seale, Anita E Heywood, Julie Leask, Meru Sheel, David N Durrheim, Katarzyna Bolsewicz, and Rajneesh Kaur. 2021. Examining Australian public perceptions and behaviors towards a future COVID-19 vaccine. *BMC Infectious Diseases*, 21(1):1–9.

Susan M Sherman, Louise E Smith, Julius Sim, Richard Amlôt, Megan Cutts, Hannah Dasch, G James Rubin, and Nick Sevdalis. 2021. COVID-19 vaccination intention in the UK: results from the COVID-19 vaccination acceptability study (CoVAccS), a nationally representative cross-sectional survey. *Human vaccines & immunotherapeutics*, 17(6):1612–1621.

Statista. 2020 August [cited 24 August 2022]. COVID-19 and Leader Approval Ratings.

Linda Thunström, Madison Ashworth, David Finnoff, and Stephen C Newbold. 2021. Hesitancy toward a covid-19 vaccine. *Ecohealth*, 18(1):44–60.

Mallory Trent, Holly Seale, Abrar Ahmad Chughtai, Daniel Salmon, and C Raina MacIntyre. 2022. Trust in government, intention to vaccinate and covid-19 vaccine hesitancy: A comparative survey of five large cities in the united states, united kingdom, and australia. *Vaccine*, 40(17):2498–2505.

Junze Wang, Ying Zhou, Wei Zhang, Richard Evans, Chengyan Zhu, et al. 2020. Concerns expressed by chinese social media users during the covid-19 pandemic: content analysis of sina weibo microblogging data. *Journal of medical Internet research*, 22(11):e22152.

Jeremy K Ward, Caroline Alleaume, Patrick Peretti-Watel, Valérie Seror, Sébastien Cortaredona, Odile Launay, Jocelyn Raude, Pierre Verger, François Beck, Stéphane Legleye, et al. 2020. The French public's attitudes to a future COVID-19 vaccine: The politicization of a public health issue. *Social science & medicine*, 265:113414.

Annelot Wismans, Roy Thurik, Rui Baptista, Marcus Dejardin, Frank Janssen, and Ingmar Franken. 2021. Psychological characteristics and the mediating role of the 5c model in explaining students' covid-19 vaccination intention. *PloS one*, 16(8):e0255382.

World Health Organization. 2019 January [cited 14 August 2022]. Ten threats to global health in 2019.

Jia Xue, Junxiang Chen, Ran Hu, Chen Chen, Chengda Zheng, Yue Su, and Tingshao Zhu. 2020. Twitter discussions and emotions about the covid-19 pandemic: Machine learning approach.

Samira Yousefinaghani, Rozita Dara, Samira Mubareka, Andrew Papadopoulos, and Shayan Sharif. 2021. An analysis of COVID-19 vaccine sentiments and opinions on Twitter. *International Journal of Infectious Diseases*, 108:256–262.

Automatic Extraction of Structured Mineral Drillhole Results from Unstructured Mining Company Reports

Adam Dimeski and **Afshin Rahimi**
School of Information Technology and Electrical Engineering
The University of Queensland
a.dimeski@uqconnect.edu.au a.rahimi@uq.edu.au

Abstract

Aggregate mining exploration results can help companies and governments to optimise and police mining permits and operations, a necessity for transition to a renewable energy future, however, these results are buried in unstructured text. We present a novel dataset from 23 Australian mining company reports, framing the extraction of structured drillhole information as a sequence labelling task. Our two benchmark models based on Bi-LSTM-CRF and BERT, show their effectiveness in this task with a F_1 score of 77% and 87%, respectively. Our dataset and benchmarks are accessible online.[1]

1 Introduction

Mineral exploration involves drilling for core samples to assess their mineral composition. These assays are published in annual reports and other public announcements such as press releases. Often these results are presented in a semi-consistent non-tabular form. There is an industry demand for up-to-date mineral exploration results given that aggregate mineral composition information across a region or country can guide and optimise mineral exploration, however, current solutions involve manual collection of data directly from public company resources, which is expensive, time-intensive, and out-of-date (Riganti et al., 2015). This has become more important as the transition from fossil fuels to renewable energy has accelerated the demand for minerals such as lithium, nickel and rare earth metals. An assay report contains "drillhole sentences" which are phrases containing a unique drillhole code, depth, material, type and material percentage. See the example in Figure 1 from a mining company press release. The results are buried in long reports that contain images and natural language text with varying nomenclature, format and placement in the report across companies, geologists and mineral sectors, making their automatic extraction by regular expressions very challenging. The format of the drillhole sentences

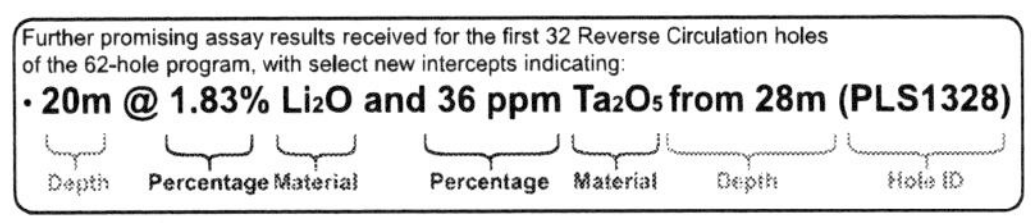

Figure 1: Excerpt from Pilbara Minerals ASX Announcement Pilbara Minerals (2021)

presents an opportunity to apply natural language processing techniques to automatically extract drillhole data. In this paper, we assess the performance of neural network models in extracting structured information about drillhole mineral exploration results. To the best of our knowledge, this work is the first to focus on extracting drillhole results from unstructured text, acknowledging prior work on extracting other geological information such as rick types Holden et al. (2019).

Our contributions are: a) developing a novel dataset for structured drillhole result extraction from 23 public Australian Stock Exchange (ASX) listed mining companies involved in mineral exploration.; b) formulating the extraction task as sequence labelling and presenting two benchmarks: a bidirectional LSTM network with a conditional random field layer (BI-LSTM-CRF) (Lample et al., 2016) and BERT (Devlin et al., 2019), showing that both perform fairly well; and c) performing error analysis and identifying major error types to guide future work.

2 Related Work

In this section, we provide insight into previous work performed on extracting geological data from reports and an overview of neural network models for sequence labelling tasks.

[1]Link to the dataset

Proceedings of the 2022 COLING Workshop: The 8th Workshop on Noisy User-generated Text (W-NUT 2022), pages 147–153

2.1 Geological NLP

Various NLP approaches have been used to extract geological data from reports. GeoDocA is a search portal developed to search for geological terms in reports, research papers and geology results (Holden et al., 2019). GeoDocA performs part-of-speech tagging using a POS tagger from Manning et al. (2014). Although GeoDocA implements a non-neural network machine learning approach, compared to other research GeoDocA's results are most similar to the drillhole data we have extracted from public Australian mining company reports; and use a more textually similar corpus.

Consoli et al. (2020) applies a Bi-LSTM-CRF model to perform POS tagging on Portuguese geoscience literature, however, its objective was to compare different methods of word embedding. They made use of an existing corpus, GeoCorpus-2 and its predecessor from Amaral (2017) tagging rock types and numeric data such as age and period. Consoli et al. (2020) achieved a F_1 from 53.71% up to 84.63% while Amaral (2017) achieved an F_1 score of 54.33%. Challenges in developing NLP models for mining report extraction include the availability of text corpus that contains useful geological terms, and industry-level terminology as shown in Tessarollo and Rademaker (2020).

2.2 Deep Learning for Sequence Labelling

Various neural network models have been used for NLP. LSTM models and their variations have proven to be robust against newer models in natural language tasks including sequence labelling(Melis et al., 2017). Newer models are being developed to better handle more complex language structure, more recently with transformers-based models such as BERT (Devlin et al., 2018). Drillhole sentences are in a structured format, contained in unstructured text. The Bi-LSTM-CRF and BERT benchmark models used to perform sequence labelling on the drillhole sentence implement model tuning for structured data in their loss functions. BERT make use of the cross-entropy loss function to tune the model weights to sentence structure while the Bi-LSTM-CRF model uses an individual CRF layer on top of the Bi-LSTM layers that is tuned to sentence structure. One of the key performance distinctions transformers have shown is being able to better recognise sentence-level context of words, beyond just feature-based models Ghaddar et al. (2021), hence the addition of a CRF layer to a base LSTM model (Lample et al., 2016).

3 Data

The dataset consists of 50 reports from 23 ASX-listed mining exploration companies. The selection criteria for reports, extraction and segmentation of text from the PDF files and the annotation process are reported in this section. Additionally, to test the generalisation ability of the models, the dataset is split into training, dev and test sets based on a) random; b) material; and c) company, to find out if the benchmark models will be able to generalise across materials and companies.

3.1 Selecting Reports

We chose 40 publicly listed mineral companies on the Australian Stock Exchange (ASX). The selection involved sorting the mining companies according to their market capitalisation and randomly selecting 7, 7, and 6 companies from the top, middle, and bottom bins, respectively. In addition, we also included the last 20 mining companies recently listed on the ASX to include more variety in terms of formatting and materials. Annual reports dating back to 2014 were collected from the websites of these companies. Reports and companies without any drillhole results were excluded. The final corpus includes 50 reports from 23 companies which covers a variety of drillhole result formats, materials, localities, and company maturity.

3.2 Preprocessing

The 50 reports included in the corpus are in PDF format. We extracted the text using a PDF parser. Due to the inherent nature of automated PDF extraction, it introduced conversion artefacts into the extracted text resulting in the fragmentation of sentences. To split the extracted text into sentences for the sequence labelling annotation task, we used a rule-based tokeniser that splits sentences after common punctuations and new line characters. Initially, we used the Punkt sentence tokeniser Kiss and Strunk (2006), however, it yielded highly irregular sentence lengths and split drillhole sentences apart as a result of the quality of text extracted from the PDF files. The rule-based sentence tokeniser, however, worked fairly well in comparison. The corpus contained over 20,000 sentences with the majority being of a consistent length.

Set	Hole ID	Material	Percentage	Depth	Extra	Outside	Sentence Count
Train	51%	56%	56%	53%	51%	53%	17.2K
Dev	19%	16%	15%	17%	20%	15%	2.2K
Test	31%	28%	29%	30%	29%	32%	3.3K
Count	1.2K	1.4K	1.9K	2.4K	3.7K	667K	22.7K

Table 1: Tag split among each set shown as a percentage of the total count

3.3 Annotation

Annotation of the dataset was performed on the dataset text files using the IOB sequence tagging format by the author of this work. Four tags were chosen to extract the material: hole id, percentage, material, and depth. A fifth tag was included for words commonly used in drillhole sentences such as "from" and "to" when referring to the hole depth. The tagging schema is shown in Table 2.

Tag	Category	Example
H	Hole ID	PLS1328
M	Material	Li2O
P	Percentage	0.23%
D	Depth	3m
E	Extra	from
O	Outside	This

Table 2: IOB Tags

Due to the varying types of drillhole sentence formats, a set of rules was adopted to have consistent annotation of the data. The most significant rules:

- *Sentence Length:* A drillhole sentences must be separated by punctuation or words tagged as outside.
- *Non-numerical values:* Non-numeral depths and percentage were included.
- *Hole ID Format:* Drillhole sentences that use a location instead of a hole ID were not included unless directly adjacent to a hole ID.
- *Punctuation:* Punctuation that is involved with the direct indication the start of a drillhole sentence was tagged with the extra tag.
- *Filler Words:* Words that are used inside a drillhole sentence are tagged as extra when are used to refer to depth, material, percentage or Hole ID tags.

One of the challenges faced with tagging the dataset was the similarity of drillhole sentences to other geological sentences in the reports. For example, within a piece of text a part of a drillhole result might be mentioned without referring to a specific drillhole. We decided to tag these sentences even if they weren't associated with a hole ID to improve the performance of the model as these sentences also contain material, depth, and percentage attributes. For downstream applications, it will be easy to ignore such information as they are not accompanied by a drillhole ID.

3.4 Annotation Quality

In total, the entire corpus contained over 680K words with 10.8K words being tagged as part of a drillhole sentence (not tagged as outside) resulting in a highly imbalanced dataset. The corpus contained a total of 22.7K sentences. Resource constraints meant that the compiling and annotation of the dataset was a result of a single annotator. Therefore, annotation quality could not be assessed with an inter-annotator agreement. Some analysis of the annotation can be inferred from the error analysis, however the results of the Bi-LSTM-CRF and BERT models will based on a dataset with some annotation inconsistencies.

3.5 Dataset Split

The format, placement in text, and materials vary between reports. For example, a company might use the drillhole ID in parenthesis at the end of a drillhole sentence while another company might use the drillhole ID at the front of a sentence followed by a colon. Similarly, the same material might have various names depending on the type of nomenclature the geologist use. To find out if a model trained on a specific variety of data will generalise on unseen data we split the dataset into training, dev and test sets based on a) random split; b) material; and c) company. The split based on material and company was performed in a way that materials and companies in the dev and test sets were disjoint from the training set, however, Gold, 'au', was the most common material tag, accounting for 80% of all material tags, this was assumed to be in all the material datasets. Table 1 shows the proportion of each tag in each set. The percentage

	Bi-LSTM-CRF			BERT		
Dataset	**P** (%)	**R** (%)	$\mathbf{F_1}$(%)	**P** (%)	**R** (%)	$\mathbf{F_1}$(%)
Random	91 ± 2	67 ± 11	77 ± 7	91 ± 2	78 ± 4	84 ± 2
Material	86 ± 2	75 ± 3	81 ± 3	87 ± 1	87 ± 1	87 ± 1
Company	89 ± 4	69 ± 12	77 ± 7	87 ± 1	87 ± 1	87 ± 1

Table 3: Test set results evaluated over the three split methods averaged over runs with five different seeds for the two benchmarks, Bi-LSTM-CRF and BERT. Evaluation measures, **P** (Precision), **R** (Recall) and $\mathbf{F_1}$ scores show standard deviation values. For detailed tag-specific results see appendix.

of tags among the training, dev, and test sets were consistent across the three datasets.

4 Method

To measure the generalisation ability of a sequence labeling task trained on our dataset we used two benchmarks, both evaluated by precision, recall, and f1 using seqeval library (Nakayama, 2018).

Bi-LSTM-CRF: We use the Bi-LSTM-CRF model proposed in Lample et al. (2016) for the sequence labeling task of identifying drillhole result segments. This model uses both word and character embeddings which is suitable for our task which involves chemical formulas and numerical tokens that might only be captured through character information. The character and word embeddings are concatenated and fed to a Bi-LSTM to capture sequential and contextual information. The resulting final hidden states of the two directions are concatenated and fed into a Conditional Random Field layer that models the conditional probability of the tags.

BERT: We use BERT (Devlin et al., 2019) to find out the effect of pre-training on massive amounts of text on the performance of our task given the relatively small training set and the ability of the pre-trained transformers to transfer knowledge across tasks in low-resource settings. Due to the computational demands, we only experiment with the base (uncased) version of BERT which is lighter compared to BERT-Large in terms of the model size. Given that BERT does not take into account the characters, it is interesting to find out if it can outperform Bi-LSTM-CRF which uses character information.

4.1 Model Parameters

The Bi-LSTM-CRF model uses a default batch size of 32 sentences and embedding size of 256. Tuning of the learning rate was done by applying the "LR Range Test" Smith (2015). A learning rate value of 0.008 was set for the random and material split datasets and a learning rate of 0.005 for the company split dataset. The BERT model uses transformers library with a maximum sequence length of 512 and a default learning rate of 5e-5 for all dataset splits.

5 Results

Evaluation results are shown in Table 3. Overall, both Bi-LSTM-CRF and BERT perform well with an F1 score of 78% and 86%, respectively. Recall is considerably lower than precision for both models which is the result of the class imbalance in the training set, having a large number of outside tags. BERT outperforms Bi-LSTM-CRF substantially in terms of recall across the three dataset splits, demonstrating better adaptation to various drillhole sentence structures, contexts and nomenclature used in the mining reports. The standard deviation of Bi-LSTM-CRF across the three dataset splits and the three evaluation measures was much higher than BERT, indicating that BERT, as expected, is more robust to variation in language use. In terms of splits, while Bi-LSTM-CRF shows variation across the three datasets, BERT is able to consistently generalise to unseen examples from various companies and materials.

Upon further inspection of tag-specific results (shown in appendix), the recall of Bi-LSTM-CRF is 38% which is substantially lower than that of BERT with a recall of 66%. The identification of drillhole is an essential component of extracting the structured drillhole results from reports as it can uniquely identify a drillhole across several reports.

5.1 Error Analysis

Given the lower computational demands of the Bi-LSTM-CRF model, error analysis was performed on the model to identify the types of errors the model makes. The most frequent errors can be categorised into five classes:

- *Context:* variability and inconsistency in context.
- *Annotation:* ambiguity in annotation.
- *UNK*: unseen words during training.
- *Split tag:* a tag split across multiple tokens.
- *Not O:* Correct tag is O, however, the model predicts otherwise.

The error type counts are shown in Table 4. Overall, the context and UNK errors are the most frequent error types that can be addressed by creating noisy data e.g. replacing unseen materials in various sentences to create noisy supervision or to increase annotation.

Split	Random	Material	Company
Error	**Count**	**Count**	**Count**
Context	1157	1053	617
Annotation	83	289	218
UNK	408	386	254
Split Tag	22	238	83
Not O	113	471	306
Total	1249	1345	883

Table 4: Error type counts for the three dataset splits for Bi-LSTM-CRF

6 Conclusion

We present our work in creating a novel dataset for extracting structured drillhole results from unstructured mining exploration reports. We formulate this task as sequence labeling and show that while both our two benchmarks Bi-LSTM-CRF and BERT perform well with an F1 score of 77% and 87%, respectively, BERT substantially outperforms Bi-LSTM-CRF and is more robust to variation in language and format. We performed error analysis on the Bi-LSTM-CRF predictions and identified context variation and unseen tokens in training data to be the most frequent error types. Our error analysis indicates improvement pathways for the Bi-LSTM-CRF model which is more efficient for use in most common computing settings.

References

Daniela Oliveira Ferreira do Amaral. 2017. *Reconhecimento de entidades nomeadas na ?rea da geologia : bacias sedimentares brasileiras*. Ph.D. thesis. Escola Polit?cnica.

Bernardo Consoli, Joaquim Santos, Diogo Gomes, Fabio Cordeiro, Renata Vieira, and Viviane Moreira. 2020. Embeddings for named entity recognition in geoscience Portuguese literature. In *Proceedings of the 12th Language Resources and Evaluation Conference*, pages 4625–4630, Marseille, France. European Language Resources Association.

Jacob Devlin, Ming-Wei Chang, Kenton Lee, and Kristina Toutanova. 2018. BERT: pre-training of deep bidirectional transformers for language understanding. *CoRR*, abs/1810.04805.

Jacob Devlin, Ming-Wei Chang, Kenton Lee, and Kristina Toutanova. 2019. BERT: pre-training of deep bidirectional transformers for language understanding. In *Proceedings of the 2019 Conference of the North American Chapter of the Association for Computational Linguistics: Human Language Technologies, NAACL-HLT 2019, Minneapolis, MN, USA, June 2-7, 2019, Volume 1 (Long and Short Papers)*, pages 4171–4186. Association for Computational Linguistics.

Abbas Ghaddar, Philippe Langlais, Ahmad Rashid, and Mehdi Rezagholizadeh. 2021. Context-aware Adversarial Training for Name Regularity Bias in Named Entity Recognition. *Transactions of the Association for Computational Linguistics*, 9:586–604.

Eun-Jung Holden, Wei Liu, Tom Horrocks, Rui Wang, Daniel Wedge, Paul Duuring, and Trevor Beardsmore. 2019. Geodoca – fast analysis of geological content in mineral exploration reports: A text mining approach. *Ore Geology Reviews*, 111:102919.

Tibor Kiss and Jan Strunk. 2006. Unsupervised multilingual sentence boundary detection. *Computational Linguistics*, 32:485–525.

Guillaume Lample, Miguel Ballesteros, Sandeep Subramanian, Kazuya Kawakami, and Chris Dyer. 2016. Neural architectures for named entity recognition. In *NAACL HLT 2016, The 2016 Conference of the North American Chapter of the Association for Computational Linguistics: Human Language Technologies, San Diego California, USA, June 12-17, 2016*, pages 260–270. The Association for Computational Linguistics.

Christopher D. Manning, Mihai Surdeanu, John Bauer, Jenny Finkel, Steven J. Bethard, and David McClosky. 2014. The Stanford CoreNLP natural language processing toolkit. In *Association for Computational Linguistics (ACL) System Demonstrations*, pages 55–60.

Gábor Melis, Chris Dyer, and Phil Blunsom. 2017. On the state of the art of evaluation in neural language models. *CoRR*, abs/1707.05589.

Hiroki Nakayama. 2018. seqeval: A python framework for sequence labeling evaluation. Software available from https://github.com/chakki-works/seqeval.

Pilbara Minerals. 2021. *Further Exceptional Drilling Results at Pilgangoora*.

Angela Riganti, Terence R Farrell, Margaret J Ellis, Felicia Irimies, Colin D Strickland, Sarah K Martin, and Darren J Wallace. 2015. 125 years of legacy data at the geological survey of western australia: Capture and delivery. *GeoResJ*, 6:175–194.

Leslie N. Smith. 2015. No more pesky learning rate guessing games. *CoRR*, abs/1506.01186.

Alexandre Tessarollo and Alexandre Rademaker. 2020. Inclusion of lithological terms (rocks and minerals) in the open Wordnet for English. In *Proceedings of the LREC 2020 Workshop on Multimodal Wordnets (MMW2020)*, pages 33–38, Marseille, France. The European Language Resources Association (ELRA).

A Detailed Results

Bi-LSTM-CRF									
Dataset	Random Split			Material Split			ASX Split		
Tag	**P (%)**	**R (%)**	**F_1 (%)**	**P (%)**	**R (%)**	**F_1 (%)**	**P (%)**	**R (%)**	**F_1 (%)**
Depth	89 ± 2	70 ± 14	78 ± 9	85 ± 3	81 ± 2	83 ±2	82 ± 1	69 ± 5	74 ± 3
Extra	91 ± 2	70 ± 10	79 ± 6	86 ± 3	76 ± 3	81 ± 1	91 ± 3	63 ± 6	74 ± 3
Hole ID	88 ± 12	39 ± 4	53 ± 4	82 ± 10	37 ± 8	50 ± 8	84 ± 7	39 ± 6	53 ± 4
Material	95 ± 1	71 ± 12	81 ± 8	90 ± 2	78 ± 3	84 ± 1	92 ± 1	54 ± 4	68 ± 3
Percentage	93 ± 4	70 ± 14	79 ± 11	86 ± 3	76 ± 3	80± 1	92 ± 1	60 ± 5	73 ± 3
Total	91 ± 2	67 ± 11	77 ± 7	86 ± 2	75 ± 3	81 ± 3	89 ± 4	69 ± 12	77 ± 7
BERT									
Depth	92 ± 2	83 ± 4	87 ± 2	87 ± 2	92 ± 2	89 ± 1	87 ± 2	92 ± 2	89 ± 1
Extra	91 ± 3	78 ± 5	84 ± 3	84 ± 1	89 ± 2	86 ± 1	84 ± 1	89 ± 2	86 ± 1
Hole ID	86 ± 6	62 ± 7	71 ± 4	88 ± 2	68 ± 9	76 ± 5	89 ± 2	68 ± 9	76 ± 5
Material	96 ± 2	82 ± 4	87 ± 1	92 ± 1	83 ± 2	87 ± 1	92 ± 1	83 ± 2	87 ± 1
Percentage	92 ± 3	80 ± 2	86 ± 2	88 ± 1	88 ± 2	88 ± 1	88 ± 1	88 ± 2	88 ± 1
Total	91 ± 2	78 ± 4	84 ± 2	87 ± 1	87 ± 1	87 ± 1	87 ± 1	87 ± 1	87 ± 1

Table 5: Test set results evaluated over the three split methods averaged over runs with five different seeds for the two benchmarks, Bi-LSTM-CRF and BERT. Evaluation measures, **P** (Precision), **R** (Recall) and **F_1** scores show standard deviation values.

It was shown that the variation of the F_1 score was higher between datasets for the Bi-LSTM-CRF model than the BERT model. Additionally, the variation of the F_1 score for different seeds was also higher for the Bi-LSTM-CRF model compared to the BERT model.

B Detailed Error Analysis

Bi-LSTM-CRF Error Analysis

Code	Description	Random	Material	ASX
		Dataset Split		
1	Probability of O is greatest	1138	874	577
2	Not O prediction. Followed default context when other context is required	24	177	92
3	Unknown word is a specific depth/material/percentage	408	386	254
5	General Lack/incorrect of Context	596	265	212
5.1	Spurious Tag	201	292	192
5.2	Slightly Dissimilar context	336	319	121
6	Correct, but tagged as O because depth was not a number	9	11	10
7	Error caused by split tag	280	238	83
9	Correct but not associated with drillhole	49	240	170
10	Error caused by previous error in sequence	23	76	225
C	Fully Correct	25	38	38
NO	Predicted tag was not O	113	471	306
Total		1249	1345	883

Table 6: Detailed Error Results for Bi-LSTM-CRF results

Error analysis was performed on the results for the Bi-LSTM-CRF model. Using a predefined error schema in Table 6, a rules-based error tagger was implemented to sort the errors into category types. The errors were further manually assessed for their correct error type and further categorised into error subtypes. The majority of errors were due to context errors, which were further defined into subcategories; spurious tags are tags that have been tagged outside of the drillhole sentence and the similar context subcategory was for incorrect tags that are in an uncommon or irregular form of drillhole sentence.

Errors that were as a result of incorrect annotation and the model made a correct prediction made up to 5% of all errors. In total, up to 23% of errors were due to inconsistent/incorrect annotation and the model made the correct prediction.

"Kanglish alli names!" Named Entity Recognition for Kannada-English Code-Mixed Social Media Data

Sumukh S and **Manish Shrivastava**
Language Technologies Research Centre (LTRC)
International Institute of Information Technology, Hyderabad, India (IIIT-H)
sumukhs@research.iiit.ac.in
m.shrivastava@iiit.ac.in

Abstract

Code-mixing (CM) is a frequently observed phenomenon on social media platforms in multilingual societies such as India. While the increase in code-mixed content on these platforms provides good amount of data for studying various aspects of code-mixing, the lack of automated text analysis tools makes such studies difficult. To overcome the same, tools such as language identifiers and parts of-speech (POS) taggers for analysing code-mixed data have been developed. One such tool is Named Entity Recognition (NER), an important Natural Language Processing (NLP) task, which is not only a subtask of Information Extraction, but is also needed for downstream NLP tasks such as semantic role labeling. While entity extraction from social media data is generally difficult due to its informal nature, code-mixed data further complicates the problem due to its informal, unstructured and incomplete information. In this work, we present the first ever corpus for Kannada-English code-mixed social media data with the corresponding named entity tags for NER. We provide strong baselines with machine learning classification models such as CRF, Bi-LSTM, and Bi-LSTM-CRF on our corpus with word, character, and lexical features.

1 Introduction

With the rising popularity of social media platforms such as Twitter, Facebook and Reddit, the volume of texts on these platforms has also grown significantly. Twitter alone has over 500 million test posts (tweets) per day[1]. India, a country with over 300 million multilingual speakers, has over 23 million users on Twitter as of January 2022[2], and code-switching can be observed heavily on this social media platform (Rijhwani et al., 2017).

Code-switching or code-mixing[3] occurs when "lexical items and/or grammatical features from two languages appear in one sentence"(Muysken, 2000). Multilingual society speakers often tend to switch back and forth between languages when speaking or writing, mostly in informal settings. It is of great interest to linguists because of its relationship with emotional expression (Rudra et al., 2016) and identity. However, research efforts are often hindered by the lack of automated NLP tools to analyse massive amounts of code-mixed data (Rudra et al., 2016).

Named Entity Recognition (NER) is the foundation for many tasks related to Information Extraction. When exploring text corpora, being able to explore and browse them by the people and places mentioned in those texts becomes an essential feature.

Below is an example of a code-mixed Kannada-English tweet which has also been translated into English. Named entities have been tagged along with the language tags (*Ka*-Kannada, *En*-English, *NE*-Named Entity, *Univ*-Universal).

> **T1:** Saanu/*Person/NE* next/*Other/En* month/*Other/En* Gujarat/*Location/NE* visit/*Other/En* madtale/*Other/Ka* #excited/*Other/En* :D/*Other/Univ*
>
> **Translation:** *Saanu will visit Gujarat next month #excited :D*

Kannada is a Dravidian language spoken majorly in the Indian state of Karnataka with over 56 million native and second-language (L2) speakers worldwide. Kannada is also one of the six languages designated as a classical language of India by the Indian Government. In code-mixed Kannada-English data, the mixing can happen at phrase, word, syntactic and morphological levels

[1] https://www.internetlivestats.com/twitter-statistics/

[2] https://www.statista.com/statistics/242606/number-of-active-twitter-users-in-selected-countries/

[3] The terms "code-mixing" and "code-switching" are used interchangeably by many researchers, and we also use these terms interchangeably

Proceedings of the 2022 COLING Workshop: The 8th Workshop on Noisy User-generated Text (W-NUT 2022), pages 154–161

too (Appidi et al., 2020). This adds to the fact that the data from Twitter is already difficult to analyse given its short length, high language variation, grammatical errors, unorthodox capitalisation, and frequent use of emoticons, abbreviations and hashtags.

There are widely known solutions for NER on monolingual data of high-resource languages like English (Jiang et al., 2022) and low-resource languages like Kannada (Pallavi et al., 2018, Amarappa and Sathyanarayana, 2015), but the same is not true for CM data. NER for code-mixed social media data in low-resource languages has been explored only recently (details in section 2).

In this paper, we have tried to address this problem for Kannada-English code-mixed social media data by creating the first ever corpus with named entity tags and providing strong baselines for the task of NER.

The structure of the paper is as follows. In Section 2, we review the related work. In Section 3, we discuss the annotation methodology and challenges involved. In Section 4, we describe the steps involved in corpus creation and data statistics. In Section 5, we describe our baseline systems. In Section 6, we present the results of the experiments conducted. Finally, in section 7, we conclude the paper and discuss the future prospects.

2 Background and Related Work

A lot of work has been done in Named Entity Recognition (NER) for resource rich language and newswire data such as such as English (Finkel et al., 2005), German (Tjong Kim Sang and De Meulder, 2003), and Spanish (Copara Zea et al., 2016). However, the noisy data from social media platforms like Twitter are different from traditional textual resources due to slacker grammatical structure, spelling variations, abbreviations and more (Ritter et al., 2011). NER for monolingual tweets was explored in Ritter et al. (2011) and Li et al. (2012).

Bali et al. (2014) analysed Facebook posts generated from Hindi-English bilingual users and confirmed the presence of significant code mixing in them. Sharma et al. (2016) addressed the problem of shallow parsing of Hindi-English code-mixed social media text and developed a system for Hindi-English code-mixed text that can identify the language of the words, normalise them to their standard forms, assign them their POS tag and segment into chunks. Bhargava et al. (2016) proposed a hybrid model for NER on Hindi-English and Tamil-English CM dataset.

Appidi et al. (2020) reported a work on annotating CM Kannada-English data collected from Twitter and creating POS tags for this corpus. Singh et al. (2018a) presented an automatic NER of Hindi-English CM data while Singh et al. (2018b) and Srirangam et al. (2019) have presented a corpus for NER in Hindi-English and Telugu-English CM data respectively. For Kannada-English CM data, Sowmya Lakshmi and Shambhavi (2017) have proposed an automatic word-level Language Identification (LID) system for sentences from social media posts.

To the best of our knowledge, the corpus created for this paper is the first ever Kannada-English code-mixed social media corpus with Named Entity tags.

3 Annotation Methodology

We label the tags with the present three Named Entity tags 'Person', 'Organisation', 'Location', which using the BIO standard become six NE tags. B-Tag refers to beginning of a named entity and I-Tag refers to the intermediate of the entity, if the name is split into multiple tokens. We use the 'Other' tag for for tokens that don't lie in any of the six NE tags.

'Per' tag refers to the 'Person' entity which is the name of a person, twitter handles and common nick names of people.

The 'Org' tag refers to 'Organisation' entity which is the name of a socio-political organisation like 'Bharatiya Janatha Party', 'BJP', 'JDS'; institutions like 'RBI' and 'Canara bank'; social media companies like 'Youtube', 'Twitter', 'Facebook', 'WhatsApp', 'Google', etc.

'Loc' tag refers to the location named entity which is assigned to the names of places for eg. 'Mysore', 'Shimoga', '#Bengaluru', etc.

The following is an instance of annotation with these tags-

> **T2:** Tomorrow/*Other* ,/*Other* Chandu/*B-Per* Reddy/*I-Per* avru/*Other* Mysore/*B-Loc* alliro/*Other* NVIDIA/*B-Org* Graphics/*I-Org* office/*Other* visit/*Other* madtaare/*Other* !/*Other*
>
> **Translation:** *Tomorrow, Chandu Reddy will visit NVIDIA Graphics office in Mysore!*

The ones which does not lie in any of the mentioned tags are assigned 'Other' tag.

3.1 Challenges

Following are the challenges with annotating Kannada-English code-mixed social media data-

- Word-level/morpheme-level code mixing between Kannada and English makes the problem harder as a CM word is a combination of two words from different languages. This is very common for the mixing of a noun from English language or a named entity and prepositions from Kannada language.

  For example, "*companyge*" is used as a single word in code-mixed Kannada-English sentence which roughly translates (depending on context) to "*to the company*" in English.

  Another common occurrence is the addition of "*-galu*" to indicate plural form of words in Kanglish. For example - "*cargalu*" for "cars", "*companygalu*" for "companies", "*bookgalu*" for "books", etc.

- Users tend to use colloquial words/slang on social media and have their own preference of native words. For example, *baralilla* is a Kannada word and it can be written as *brlilla, barlilla*, etc.

- Misspelled words are very common on social media. For example, a word like *tonight* could be written as *tonight, tonite, tonihgt, ton8, etc.,* which posed a significant challenge while building spelling agnostic models.

4 Corpus and statistics

4.1 Data collection

Data collection is a vital step while dealing with any problem with any neural-network based approaches (Roh et al., 2021). As there are only a few sources for code-mixed low-resource language data, this would be challenging as it is difficult to build supervised models.

The corpus that we created from Twitter[4] for Kannada-English code-mixed tweets contains tweets from December 2020 to August 2022. We used hashtags related to city names where Kannada is widely spoken, politics, movies, events, and trending hashtags in collecting the corpus. We also manually identified some of the Twitter account that posted often with code mixing between Kannada and English languages.

Label	Count of tokens
Kannada	20,380
English	19,701
Named Entities	8,096
Universal	5,208
Total number of tokens	53,385
Avg. tweet length	14.2
Total tweets	3,759

Table 1: Corpus statistics

Tag	Count of tokens
B-Per	3,729
I-Per	787
B-Org	1,338
I-Org	750
B-Loc	1,137
I-Loc	355

Table 2: NER tag statistics

Using the twitter API, we retrieved around 222,124 tweets. The following types of tweets were identified and removed-

- Tweets having only English or only Kannada.
- Tweets having only URLs, emojis or hashtags.
- Tweets with less than 5 tokens.

After manually filtering the data with the steps mentioned above, we were left with 3,759 code-mixed Kannada-English tweets. We tokenized these sentences and removed URLs from the same in an effort to reduce the noise.

4.2 Data statistics

The corpus has a total of 53,385 tokens which were tagged for the 7 tags mentioned in the Section 3. The corpus statistics and the tag statistics can be seen in Table 1 and Table 2 respectively.

The corpus will be made available online for public use at the earliest.

4.3 Inter Annotator Agreement

Annotation of the dataset for NE tags in the tweets was carried out by 2 human annotators having linguistic background and proficiency in both Kannada and English based on the methodology in Section 3. In order to validate the quality of annotation,

[4]http://twitter.com/

Tag	Cohen Kappa score
B-Per	0.97
I-Per	0.96
B-Org	0.97
I-Org	0.91
B-Loc	0.96
I-Loc	0.94

Table 3: Inter Annotator Agreement

we calculated the inter annotator agreement (IAA) between the 2 annotation sets of 3,759 code-mixed tweets having 53,385 tokens using Cohen's Kappa (Cohen, 1960). Table 3 shows the results of agreement analysis. We find that the agreement is significantly high. Furthermore, the agreement of 'I-Loc' and 'I-Org' annotation are relatively lower than that of 'I-Per', and this is because of the presence of uncommon/confusing words in these entities.

Disagreements about the tags were resolved through discussions between the annotators to reach a mutual agreement.

5 Experiments

In this section, we present the experiments using different combinations of features and systems. In order to determine the effect of each feature and parameters of the model we performed several experiments using some set of features at once and all at a time simultaneously changing the parameters of the model, like criterion ('Information gain', 'gini') and maximum depth of the tree for decision tree model, regularization parameters and algorithms of optimization like 'L2 regularization', 'Avg. Perceptron' and 'Passive Aggressive' for CRF. Optimization algorithms and loss functions in LSTM. We used 5 fold cross validation in order to validate our classification models. We used 'scikit-learn' and 'keras' libraries in Python for the implementation of the above algorithms.

The training, validation, and testing for all our experiments were 60%, 10%, and 30% of the total data, respectively.

5.1 Conditional Random Field (CRF)

Conditional Random Fields (CRFs) are a class of statistical modelling methods applied in machine learning that takes neighboring sample context into account for tasks like classification. In NER using the BIO standard annotation, I-Org cannot follow I-Per(Tjong Kim Sang and Veenstra, 1999). Since here we are focusing on sentence level and not individual positions, CRFs are suitable and produce better performance measures for NER task.

5.2 Random Forests

Random Forest is a classifier that fits a number of decision trees on various subsets of the dataset and uses averaging to improve the predictive accuracy and control over-fitting (Pedregosa et al., 2011).

On our corpus, a random forest with a max depth of 32, with Gini index as the criterion yielded the best results.

5.3 BiLSTM

Long Short Term Memory (LSTM) is a special kind of RNN architecture that is well suited for classification and making predictions based on time series data. LSTMs are capable of capturing only past information. In order to overcome this limitation Bidirectional LSTMs are proposed where two LSTM networks run in forward and backward directions capturing the context in either directions.

The best result that we came through on our corpus was with a BiLSTM using 'softmax' as activation function, 'adam' as optimizer and 'sparse categorical cross-entropy' for our loss function along with random initialisations of embedding vectors.

5.4 BiLSTM-CRF

The BiLSTM-CRF is a combination of bidirectional LSTM and CRF (Huang et al., 2015;Lample et al., 2016). The BiLSTM model can be combined with CRF to enhance recognition accuracy. This combined model of BiLSTM-CRF inherits the ability to learn past and future context features from the BiLSTM model and use sentence-level tags to predict possible tags using the CRF layer. BiLSTM-CRF has been proved to be a powerful model for sequence labeling tasks like NER (Panchendrarajan and Amaresan, 2018).

After hyperparameter tuning, we found that '*softmax*' as activation function, '*rmsprop*' for optimiser, '*categorical cross-entropy*' as loss function and random initialisations of embedding vectors yielded the best results on our corpus.

5.5 Features

The features to our machine learning models consist of lexical, word-level and character features such as char N-Grams of size 2 and 3 in order to capture the information from emojis, mentions, suffixes in social media like '#', '@', numbers in the string, numbers, punctuation. Features from adjacent tokens are used as contextual features.

1. **Capitalization:** In social media, people tend to use capital letters to refer to the names of persons, organizations and persons; at times, they write the entire name in capitals(von Däniken and Cieliebak, 2017)to give particular importance or to denote aggression. This gives rise to a couple of binary features. One feature is to indicate if the beginning letter of a word is capitalized, and the other is to indicate if the entire word is capitalized.

2. **Mentions and Hashtags:** People use '@' mentions to refer to persons or organizations, they use '#' hashtags in order to make something notable or to make a topic trending. Thus the presence of these two gives a reasonable probability for the word being a named entity which counts under proper nouns.

   Take the following sentence for example - "*@rakshit nim movies andre tumba ishta, namma #Sandalwood industry improve maadi!*".

   The token "*@rakshit*" is referring to a person (B-Per tag) and "*#Sandalwood*" is the name of the Kannada film industry (B-Org tag). They are identified by the symbols @ and #. It is important to note that not all hashtags will be a named entity, so we need to understand the word context to correctly classify.

3. **Word N-Grams:** Bag of words has been the standard for languages other than English (Jahangir et al., 2012) in tasks like NER. Thus, we use adjacent words as a feature vector to train our model as our word N-Grams. These are also called contextual features. We used trigrams in the paper.

4. **Character N-Grams:** Character N-Grams are proven to be efficient in the task of classification of text and are language-independent (Majumder et al., 2002). They are helpful when there are misspellings in the text (Cavnar and Trenkle, 1994;Huffman, 1995;Lodhi et al.). Group of chars can help in capturing the semantic information. Character N-Grams are especially helpful in cases like code mixed language where there is free use of words, which vary significantly from the standard Kannada-English words.

Tag	RF	CRF	BiLSTM	BiL-CRF
B-Per	0.32	0.82	0.81	0.84
B-Org	0.70	0.63	0.65	0.63
B-Loc	0.37	0.70	0.82	0.81
I-Per	0.35	0.55	0.57	0.62
I-Org	0.23	0.52	0.46	0.55
I-Loc	0.30	0.46	0.41	0.45
Other	0.95	0.97	0.96	0.97
Wtd avg	0.89	0.93	0.92	0.94

Table 4: F1-scores for CRF, BiLSTM and BiLSTM-CRF respectively with the weighted average at the end.

Feature removed	Precision	Recall	F1
Capitalisation	0.74	0.53	0.61
Mentions, hashtags	0.72	0.57	0.63
Char n-gram	0.65	0.41	0.50
Word n-Gram	0.62	0.44	0.51
Common symbols	0.75	0.48	0.58
Numbers in String	0.78	0.56	0.65

Table 5: Weighted average scores when a specific feature is removed for the BiLSTM-CRF model.

5. **Common Symbols:** It is observed that currency symbols as well as brackets like '(', '[', etc. symbols in general are followed by numbers or some mention not of importance. Hence, these are a good indicator for the words following or before to not being an NE.

6. **Numbers in String:** In social media content, users often express legitimate vocabulary words in alphanumeric form for saving typing effort, to shorten message length, or to express their style. Examples include words like 'n8' ('night'), 'b4' ('before'), etc. We observed by analyzing the corpus that alphanumeric words generally are not NEs, therefore, serves as a good indicator for negative examples.

6 Results and Discussion

Table 4 captures performance of all models for our dataset. Our best model is the BiLSTM-CRF which achieved a weighted average F1-score of 0.94 with '*softmax*' activation function, '*rmsprop*' optimiser, '*categorical cross-entropy*' loss function and random initialisations of embedding vectors. As BiLSTM-CRF can efficiently use both past and future input features from BiLSTM and sentence level tags from CRF, we see that the accuracy is enhanced.

Word	Truth	Predicted
Banashankari	B-Loc	B-Loc
alliro	Other	Other
BESCOM	B-Org	B-Org
kacheeri	Other	Other
alli	Other	Other
work	Other	Other
siktu	Other	Other
Bharat	B-Per	B-Loc
annavrige	Other	Other

Table 6: BiLSTM-CRF example (T1) prediction

Word	Truth	Predicted
Javalli	B-Loc	B-Loc
village	Other	Other
alli	Other	Other
Jnanadeepa	B-Org	B-Org
School	I-Org	I-Org
sersudvi	Other	Other
nan	Other	Other
maga	Other	Other
Suhas	B-Per	B-Per
puttanige	Other	I-Per

Table 7: BiLSTM-CRF example (T2) prediction

Table 5 shows results of our abalation study after removing each particular feature. We can see that the N-grams features have the most impact on our F1-scores, and this is understandable as char n-grams are helpful when there are misspellings and capturing semantic information when there is free use of words which vary significantly from standard word of Kannada and English words.

On analysing some of the results from the model, we see that the intermediate tags of location and organisation is lower than that of a name. This can be explained with the fact that there are uncommon/confusing words in the oraganisation and location names. For example, the word "*Bhaarath*", one of the names for the country India, is "B-Loc" while the words "*Bharat*" and "*Bhaarti*" are common first names in India which are tagged as "B-Per". Furthermore, there are confusing words like "*Bali*" which is a city in Indonesia, but in Kannada, it means "*near*". This can be seen in the example provided in Table 6 where the word "*Bharat*" is referring to a person with that name while our model is predicting that the word is a location, referring to the country India.

We tested a random tweet with the BiLSTM-CRF model that we trained, and here is the model predicted tags along with the ground truth tags in the Table 7. We noticed that the I-Per is predicted incorrectly for the Kannada word *puttanige* (an endearment word for kids) as this word is very similar to some of the common last names in southern part of India such as *Puttanna* and *Puttagere*. The low scores for intermediate tags (*I-per, I-Org* and *I-Loc*) can be attributed to these reasons along with the "noisiness" of the social media data which tends to have misspelled words and colloquial forms of words. This gets more difficult with Kannada-English code-mixed data as mixing happens at word-level, mostly for Kannada language prepositions and named entities or English language nouns (Section 3.1).

7 Conclusion and future work

The following are our contributions in this paper.

1. An annotated code-mixed Kannada-English corpus for named entity recognition, which to the best of our knowledge, is the first corpus. The corpus will be made available online soon along with the models.

2. Introducing and addressing Named Entity Recognition (NER) of Kannada-English code-mixed data as a research problem.

3. We have experimented with the machine learning models Random Forest, CRF, BiLSTM and BiLSTM-CRF on our corpus and achieved an F1-score of 0.89, 0.93, 0.93 and 0.94 respectively, which looks good considering the complexity of the task and the amount of research done in this new domain for low resource languages.

As part of future work, we plan to explore downstream tasks like semantic labelling and entity-specific sentiment analysis which makes use of NER for code-mixed data. The size of the corpus can be increased to include more data from varied topics.

8 Acknowledgements

We would like to thank our annotators for their hard work and dedication. We would also like to thank the anonymous reviewers, Prashant Kodali, and Mohsin Mustafa for their valuable feedback.

References

S. Amarappa and S. V. Sathyanarayana. 2015. Kannada named entity recognition and classification (nerc) based on multinomial naïve bayes (mnb) classifier. *CoRR*, abs/1509.04385.

Abhinav Reddy Appidi, Vamshi Krishna Srirangam, Darsi Suhas, and Manish Shrivastava. 2020. Creation of corpus and analysis in code-mixed Kannada-English social media data for POS tagging. In *Proceedings of the 17th International Conference on Natural Language Processing (ICON)*, pages 101–107, Indian Institute of Technology Patna, Patna, India. NLP Association of India (NLPAI).

Kalika Bali, Jatin Sharma, Monojit Choudhury, and Yogarshi Vyas. 2014. "I am borrowing ya mixing ?" an analysis of English-Hindi code mixing in Facebook. In *Proceedings of the First Workshop on Computational Approaches to Code Switching*, pages 116–126, Doha, Qatar. Association for Computational Linguistics.

Rupal Bhargava, Bapiraju Vamsi Tadikonda, and Yashvardhan Sharma. 2016. Named entity recognition for code mixing in indian languages using hybrid approach. In *FIRE*.

William B. Cavnar and John M. Trenkle. 1994. N-gram-based text categorization. In *In Proceedings of SDAIR-94, 3rd Annual Symposium on Document Analysis and Information Retrieval*, pages 161–175.

Jacob Cohen. 1960. A coefficient of agreement for nominal scales. *Educational and Psychological Measurement*, 20:37 – 46.

Jenny Linet Copara Zea, Jose Eduardo Ochoa Luna, Camilo Thorne, and Goran Glavaš. 2016. Spanish NER with word representations and conditional random fields. In *Proceedings of the Sixth Named Entity Workshop*, pages 34–40, Berlin, Germany. Association for Computational Linguistics.

Jenny Rose Finkel, Trond Grenager, and Christopher D Manning. 2005. Incorporating non-local information into information extraction systems by gibbs sampling. In *Proceedings of the 43rd annual meeting of the association for computational linguistics (ACL'05)*, pages 363–370.

Zhiheng Huang, Wei Xu, and Kai Yu. 2015. Bidirectional lstm-crf models for sequence tagging. *arXiv preprint arXiv:1508.01991*.

Stephen Huffman. 1995. Acquaintance: Language-independent document categorization by n-grams. In *TREC*.

Faryal Jahangir, Waqas Anwar, Usama Ijaz Bajwa, and Xuan Wang. 2012. N-gram and gazetteer list based named entity recognition for Urdu: A scarce resourced language. In *Proceedings of the 10th Workshop on Asian Language Resources*, pages 95–104, Mumbai, India. The COLING 2012 Organizing Committee.

Hang Jiang, Yining Hua, Doug Beeferman, and Deb Roy. 2022. Annotating the tweebank corpus on named entity recognition and building NLP models for social media analysis. *CoRR*, abs/2201.07281.

Guillaume Lample, Miguel Ballesteros, Sandeep Subramanian, Kazuya Kawakami, and Chris Dyer. 2016. Neural architectures for named entity recognition. In *Proceedings of the 2016 Conference of the North American Chapter of the Association for Computational Linguistics: Human Language Technologies*, pages 260–270, San Diego, California. Association for Computational Linguistics.

Chenliang Li, Jianshu Weng, Qi He, Yuxia Yao, Anwitaman Datta, Aixin Sun, and Bu-Sung Lee. 2012. Twiner: Named entity recognition in targeted twitter stream. In *Proceedings of the 35th International ACM SIGIR Conference on Research and Development in Information Retrieval*, SIGIR '12, page 721–730, New York, NY, USA. Association for Computing Machinery.

Huma Lodhi, Craig Saunders, John Shawe-Taylor, Nello Cristianini, and Chris Watkins. Text classification using string kernels.

P Majumder, M Mitra, and B. B. Chaudhuri. 2002. N-gram: a language independent approach to ir and nlp.

Pieter Muysken. 2000. *Bilingual speech*.

K. P. Pallavi, L. Sobha, and M. M. Ramya. 2018. Named entity recognition for kannada using gazetteers list with conditional random fields. *Journal of Computer Science*, 14(5):645–653.

Rrubaa Panchendrarajan and Aravindh Amaresan. 2018. Bidirectional lstm-crf for named entity recognition. In *Proceedings of the 32nd Pacific Asia Conference on Language, Information and Computation*.

Fabian Pedregosa, Gaël Varoquaux, Alexandre Gramfort, Vincent Michel, Bertrand Thirion, Olivier Grisel, Mathieu Blondel, Peter Prettenhofer, Ron Weiss, Vincent Dubourg, et al. 2011. Scikit-learn: Machine learning in python. *the Journal of machine Learning research*, 12:2825–2830.

Shruti Rijhwani, Royal Sequiera, Monojit Choudhury, Kalika Bali, and Chandra Shekhar Maddila. 2017. Estimating code-switching on Twitter with a novel generalized word-level language detection technique. In *Proceedings of the 55th Annual Meeting of the Association for Computational Linguistics (Volume 1: Long Papers)*, pages 1971–1982, Vancouver, Canada. Association for Computational Linguistics.

Alan Ritter, Sam Clark, Mausam, and Oren Etzioni. 2011. Named entity recognition in tweets: An experimental study. In *Proceedings of the 2011 Conference on Empirical Methods in Natural Language Processing*, pages 1524–1534, Edinburgh, Scotland, UK. Association for Computational Linguistics.

Yuji Roh, Geon Heo, and Steven Euijong Whang. 2021. A survey on data collection for machine learning: A big data - ai integration perspective. *IEEE Transactions on Knowledge and Data Engineering*, 33(4):1328–1347.

Koustav Rudra, Shruti Rijhwani, Rafiya Begum, Kalika Bali, Monojit Choudhury, and Niloy Ganguly. 2016. Understanding language preference for expression of opinion and sentiment: What do Hindi-English speakers do on Twitter? In *Proceedings of the 2016 Conference on Empirical Methods in Natural Language Processing*, pages 1131–1141, Austin, Texas. Association for Computational Linguistics.

Arnav Sharma, Sakshi Gupta, Raveesh Motlani, Piyush Bansal, Manish Shrivastava, Radhika Mamidi, and Dipti M. Sharma. 2016. Shallow parsing pipeline - Hindi-English code-mixed social media text. In *Proceedings of the 2016 Conference of the North American Chapter of the Association for Computational Linguistics: Human Language Technologies*, pages 1340–1345, San Diego, California. Association for Computational Linguistics.

Kushagra Singh, Indira Sen, and Ponnurangam Kumaraguru. 2018a. Language identification and named entity recognition in Hinglish code mixed tweets. In *Proceedings of ACL 2018, Student Research Workshop*, pages 52–58, Melbourne, Australia. Association for Computational Linguistics.

Vinay Singh, Deepanshu Vijay, Syed Sarfaraz Akhtar, and Manish Shrivastava. 2018b. Named entity recognition for Hindi-English code-mixed social media text. In *Proceedings of the Seventh Named Entities Workshop*, pages 27–35, Melbourne, Australia. Association for Computational Linguistics.

B S Sowmya Lakshmi and B R Shambhavi. 2017. An automatic language identification system for code-mixed english-kannada social media text. In *2017 2nd International Conference on Computational Systems and Information Technology for Sustainable Solution (CSITSS)*, pages 1–5.

Vamshi Krishna Srirangam, Appidi Abhinav Reddy, Vinay Singh, and Manish Shrivastava. 2019. Corpus creation and analysis for named entity recognition in Telugu-English code-mixed social media data. In *Proceedings of the 57th Annual Meeting of the Association for Computational Linguistics: Student Research Workshop*, pages 183–189, Florence, Italy. Association for Computational Linguistics.

Erik F. Tjong Kim Sang and Fien De Meulder. 2003. Introduction to the CoNLL-2003 shared task: Language-independent named entity recognition. In *Proceedings of the Seventh Conference on Natural Language Learning at HLT-NAACL 2003*, pages 142–147.

Erik F. Tjong Kim Sang and Jorn Veenstra. 1999. Representing text chunks. In *Ninth Conference of the European Chapter of the Association for Computational Linguistics*, pages 173–179, Bergen, Norway. Association for Computational Linguistics.

Pius von Däniken and Mark Cieliebak. 2017. Transfer learning and sentence level features for named entity recognition on tweets. In *Proceedings of the 3rd Workshop on Noisy User-generated Text*, pages 166–171, Copenhagen, Denmark. Association for Computational Linguistics.

Span Extraction Aided Improved Code-mixed Sentiment Classification

Ramaneswaran S
Vellore Institute of Technology
s.ramaneswaran2000@gmail.com

Sean Benhur
PSG College of Arts & Science
seanbenhur@gmail.com

Sreyan Ghosh
University of Maryland, College Park
sreyang@umd.edu

Abstract

Sentiment classification is a fundamental NLP task of detecting the sentiment polarity of a given text. In this paper we show how solving sentiment span extraction as an auxiliary task can help improve final sentiment classification performance in a low-resource code-mixed setup. To be precise, we don't solve a simple multi-task learning objective, but rather design a unified transformer framework that exploits the bidirectional connection between the two tasks simultaneously. To facilitate research in this direction we release gold-standard human-annotated sentiment span extraction dataset for Tamil-english code-switched texts. Extensive experiments and strong baselines show that our proposed approach outperforms sentiment and span prediction by 1.27% and 2.78% respectively when compared to the best performing MTL baseline. We also establish the generalizability of our approach on the Twitter Sentiment Extraction dataset. We make our code and data publicly available on GitHub [1].

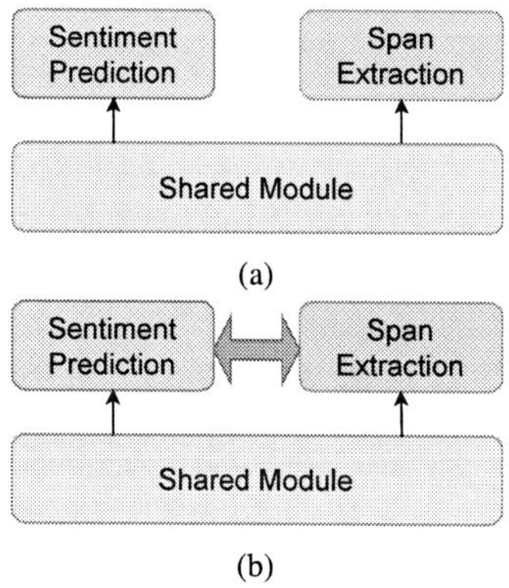

Figure 1: (a) Multi-task learning setup with parameter-sharing and joint learning of sentiment prediction and span extraction tasks (b) Our approach which establishes bi-directional connection to explicitly model the mutual interactions between the tasks

1 Introduction

With the rapid growth of social media networks and the democratization of internet technology, massive amounts of text-based user-generated content is being produced everyday. It is essential to understand the opinion and sentiment of users from these textual posts. In the past decade the NLP research community has made several advancements in the field of language based sentiment analysis. However most of these advances are in high-resource languages like English. In contrast there are limited resources for sentiment analysis for Indian languages.

In the context of the Indian sub-continent, the user-generated content on social media is unique because is not in any one particular language, rather a single utterance may consist of words, phrases and phonemes from multiple different languages. This phenomenon is code-mixing and is widely observed in multi-lingual communities such as India. Although recent advances have been made in developing sentiment analysis text corpora and methods for Indian languages such as Hindi and Bengali there has been little progress for truly low-resourced languages such as Tamil, a Dravidian language which is spoken by well over 70 million people worldwide. (Chakravarthi et al., 2020) is a seminal work on creating corpora for sentiment classification of Tamil-English code-mixed text.

While sentiment classification is well researched; sentiment span extraction on the other hand (Lai et al., 2020) is a rather new NLP task which involves the extraction of supporting phrases from text in the form of a sequence of contiguous words, which reflect the sentiment of the sentence. These support phrases can be used to further perform fine-grained analysis of the sentiment to understand the opinion and feelings of the user. Similar approach has also been applied to toxicity analysis from text (Ghosh and Kumar, 2021).

[1] https://github.com/ramaneswaran/code mixed_sentiment_span_extraction

Proceedings of the 2022 COLING Workshop: The 8th Workshop on Noisy User-generated Text (W-NUT 2022), pages 162–170

In this paper we present our hypothesis that solving sentiment span extraction as an additional task can help the model learn better semantic representations of the text which in-turn will improve sentiment classification. We explore this hypothesis for code-mixed Tamil texts. Firstly we develop a novel Tamil-English code-mixed sentiment extraction dataset to support the task of sentiment span extraction. We obtain this dataset by extending the DravidianCodemix dataset (Chakravarthi et al., 2022) by adding gold-standard human-annotated sentiment span labels to it. To the best of our knowledge this is the first code-mixed sentiment span extraction dataset. The proposed dataset will facilitate further research in this direction and helps improve sentiment classification performance in a low-resource setting in a language spoken by millions around the globe where annotated data is scarce.

Secondly we experiment with various single-task learning and multi-task learning models to evaluate our hypothesis. Further inspired from (Qin et al., 2021) we explore a methodology based on transformer architecture which explicitly models the interactions between the two tasks of sentiment prediction and sentiment span extraction in a unified framework (Refer to Fig. 1b . Extensive experiments and ablation study establish the efficacy of this proposed approach, we also demonstrate that this model generalizes well to a similar English dataset for sentiment analysis. To the best of our knowledge, we are the first to explore the modelling of the two tasks together for improving performance on sentiment classification. Moreover, our framework performs better than the generic multi-task learning setup which acts as one of our baselines.

To summarize, the following are our main contributions

- We propose a novel dataset consisting of 2152 user-generated comments along with gold-standard human-annotated sentiment-span labels.

- We propose a unified sentiment prediction and span extraction framework based on transformer architecture

- Through empirical analysis we establish our proposed method's superiority over strong baselines.

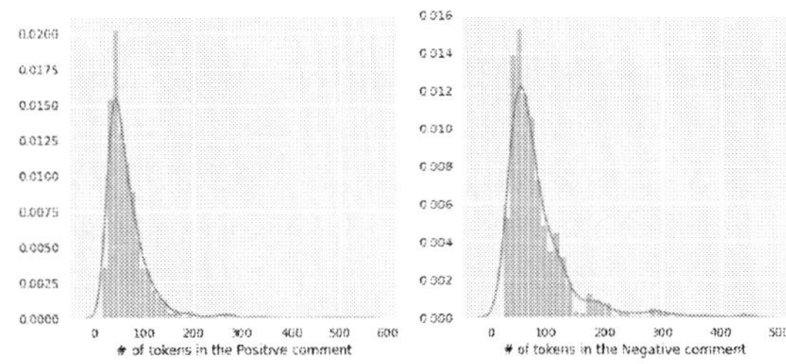

Figure 2: Length of the Positive and Negative comments

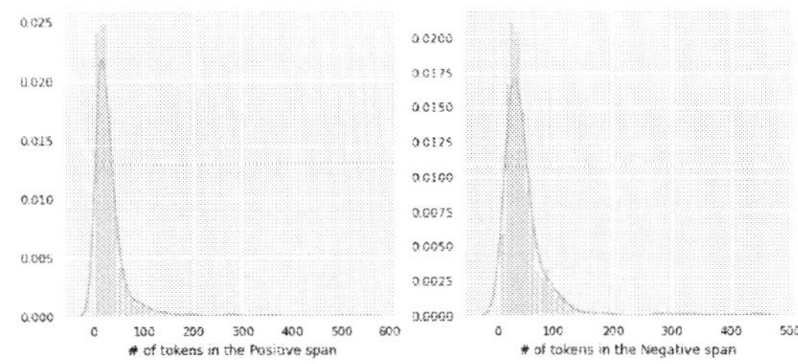

Figure 3: Length of the Positive and Negative spans

- We demonstrate the generalizability of our proposed approach to similar sentiment classification datasets.

2 Related Work

2.1 Sentiment Classification

Sentiment analysis and sentiment classification are widely explored problems in the area of Natural Language Processing. Detecting sentiments in texts helps in identifying its polarity which in turn helps understanding people's opinion.This has been widely employed in e-commerce sites (Agarap, 2018; Hoang et al., 2019) and social media networks (Samuels and Mcgonical, 2020; Aho and Ullman, 1972). With the growing number of users and user-generated content, social media networks are considered a rich data source for this task. Sentiment classification in social media is also critical in tackling mental health problems of its users (Saifullah et al., 2021).

Although most of the advances in sentiment analysis have been in high-resource languages there has been a growing interest and recent progress in low resource and codemixed sentiment analysis. (Patwa et al., 2020) used Twitter to extract the text from users and construct a codemixed corpus for Spanglish and Hinglish. (Kaur et al., 2019) used Youtube to extract hinglish comments from cooking videos and use that to analyze the polarity of the viewers. DravidianCodemix (Chakravarthi et al., 2022) is a recent work that developed sentiment classification corpora for truly low-resourced dravidian languages such as Tamil. As emphasized in (Chakravarthi et al., 2022) it takes lot of effort to obtain and annotate code-mixed sentiment data hence there is a need to make effort to explore and utilize the potential in existing resources.

2.1.1 Sentiment Span Extraction

Sentiment span extraction itself has been less explored in literature.(Pavlopoulos et al., 2021) released dataset of 10k samples for English language.Kaggle hosted a competition for sentiment extraction, the data released from the competition, Sentiment Text Extraction [2] consists of English tweets labelled under three categories- Positive, Negative and Neutral. The task here was to extract the span given the sentiment of the text as input.

2.1.2 MultiTask Learning

MultiTask Learning (Caruana, 1993) have been used for in Machine Learning across the task in Natural Language Processing and Computer Vision, It originates from the idea of learning multiple tasks helps the model to exploit the predictive features of one task to the other task helping in gaining the perfomance. (Barnes et al., 2021) used Multi Task Learning with Attention and LSTM layers for the task of improving the sentiment detection model by using an additional auxillary task of Negation detection. MultiTask Learning also has been widely used in conversational dialogue systems for the task of jointly training the Intent Detection and Slot Tagging tasks. (S et al., 2022) used a Jointly trained pretrained transformers model for the task of Intent Detection and Slot Tagging for Tamil Conversational Dialogues.

3 Dataset

3.1 Data Collection

We extend the DravidianCodemix dataset (Chakravarthi et al., 2022) by adding gold-standard human-annotated sentiment span labels to it. The dataset consists of code-mixed YouTube comments in Tamil-English, Malayalam-English and Kannada-English for the tasks of Sentiment Detection and Offensive Language Identification. It is annotated in a five class setting with classes, Positive state, Negative state, Neutral state and Mixed Feelings.

[2]https://www.kaggle.com/competitions/tweet-sentiment-extraction/

# of unique tokens in a comment	11322
# of unique tokens in a substring	8267
# of unique native Tamil tokens	3435
# of unique romanized Tamil tokens	7885
Avg # of tokens in positive comment	67.07
Avg # of tokens in positive span	32.56
Avg # of tokens in negative comment	82.75
Avg # of tokens in negative span	46.78

Table 1: Corpus analysis of our proposed dataset

Since our goal is to build sentiment span extraction dataset for Tamil-English, we only use the Tamil-English subset. We randomly sample 4935 comments from the Tamil-English subset for the annotation. We only use the comments that were labelled as Positive, Negative and Neutral and discard other labels for the annotation purposes

3.2 Human Annotation

The proposed dataset was completely annotated by human experts who are native speakers of Tamil and who are fluent in English. We hired three annotators who are master's student and native Tamil speaker. We explained the concept of Positive, Negative and Neutral sentiments and provided examples for each. We also explained the concept of code-mixing, based on our interactions with the annotators we found that they also use code-mixing in their daily conversations. We didn't collect any information of annotators other than their education details and known languages. Since YouTube comments may contain comments that are profane in nature, we inform annotators that the comments contain words that are profane, offensive and vulgar in nature. The annotators are given the liberty to withdraw from the annotation, if they feel the necessity.

To aid the annotation effort, we created a custom tool that provides the annotators with an easy to-use interface for annotation. Each annotator was assigned random batches of comments and they worked independently in their own schedule. The annotators were asked to follow the annotation guidelines given below.

- Extract the phrases from the comment which support the sentiment expressed.

- If the comment does not express any sentiment, do not highlight any span.

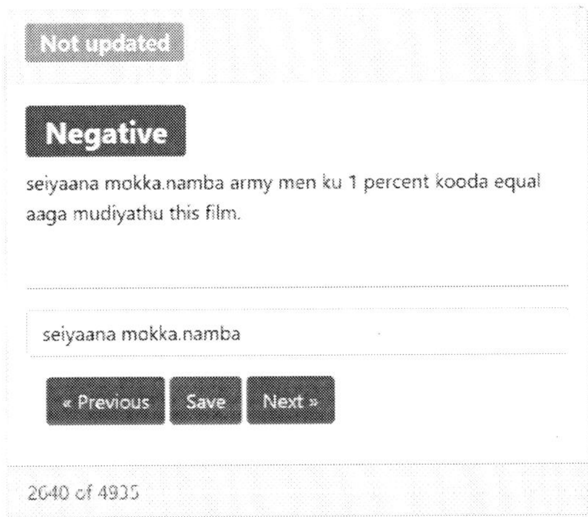

Figure 4: Interface of the annotation tool used during annotation

- If the entire comment expresses a single sentiment, highlight the whole comment
- If there are any emoji characters that expresses the sentiment, highlight that emoji as a span

Dry Run: We first conducted a dry run to ensure the uniformity in annotation and to check whether the spans are annotated correctly. We took a subset of 100 comments and asked the three annotators to annotate each of the comment independently. After this annotation, we computed the Cohen's for annotated tokens. The Inter-Annotater agreement k value is 0.60

Final Run: The annotations obtained in the dry run were evaluated and the annotators were given feedback on mistakes they made and any doubts they had. Once the annotators were confident that they understood the annotation process we proceeded with the final annotation. At the end of annotation we got 2152 samples. The majority of the 3 annotations were then used as the final annotation. At the end of the annotation and after removing wrong samples, we got 2152 samples. We took the majority of the three annotations as our final annotation.

3.3 Corpus Analysis

Table 1 contains the summary statistics of the dataset. From the table we can infer that the average length of the Negative comments is higher than the average length of the Positive comment. The dataset consists of comments written both on native script and roman script comments labelled as Positive, Negative and Neutral. The final dataset consists of 875 Positive, 679 Negative and 598 Neutral comments. Due to the codemixing nature of the dataset, it consists of Tamil comments written in both Native script and Roman script. We used the langid[3] framework to find the original language of the word based on the nature of the script and found there are 7885 unique English tokens and 3435 unique Tamil tokens. We can also note that, there are some comments that is written entirely on English and some comments that are written entirely on Tamil. The dataset was split into Train, Dev and Test sets in the ratio of 80:10:10. Our dataset is released as CSV files.

4 Proposed Approach

In this section we describe our proposed approach. It takes as input a piece of text x and predicts the sentiment of the x and the span within x that display this sentiment.

Fig 5 depicts the architecture of the proposed model. It consists of a text encoder that provides contextual representation of x at both sentence and word level. It then uses a Task Interaction Module (TIM) to learn the interactions between the two tasks of sentiment classification and sentiment span extraction.

4.1 Text Encoder

Given a piece of text x consisting of n tokens $[x_1, x_2, ...x_n]$ we encode it using a transformer based text encoder. We use the word-level representations $H = [h_1, h_2, ...h_n]$ obtained from the last hidden layer.

4.2 Task Interaction Module

The Task Interaction Module (TIM) is utilized to learn the inter-dependencies between the task of sentiment classification and sentiment span extraction.

Each encoder block in TIM consists of the following two components; a label attention layer that produces explicit sentiment and span representations; a co-attention mechanism to model the mutual interactions between the two tasks.

4.2.1 Label Attention Layer

We utilize label attention over the sentiment and span labels to produce explicit sentiment and span representations. These representations are then fed

[3]https://github.com/saffsd/langid.py

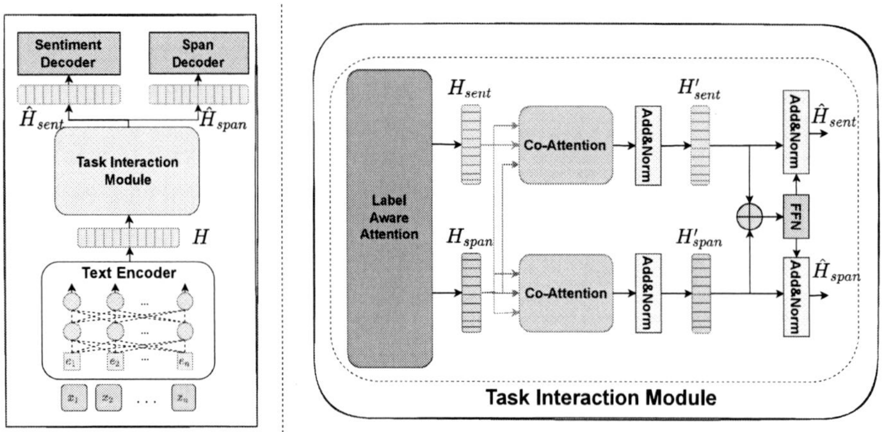

Figure 5: The architecture of our proposed model (left). It uses a transformer based Task Interaction Module (left) to explicitly model the mutual interactions between the two tasks.

into the co-attention layer to capture the mutual interactions. We use the parameters of the fully-connected sentiment and span decoders as sentiment and span embeddings matrices ($W^{sent} \in R^{d\times 3}$ and $W^{span} \in R^{d\times 2}$); as they can be considered to be label distribution in a sense.

We use $H \in R^{n\times d}$ and $W^v \in R^{n\times|v|}$ ($v \in$ sent or span) to obtain the explicit representation H_v as follows

$$A = softmax(HW^v) \quad (1)$$

$$H_v = H + AW^v \quad (2)$$

Here $sent$ represents sentiment and $span$ represents span. We finally obtain the explicit sentiment and span representations H_{sent} and H_{span}, which capture the sentiment and span semantic information respectively.

4.2.2 Co-Attention Layer

H_{sent} and H_{span} are next passed through a co-attention mechanism to model the mutual interactions between the two tasks of sentiment and span prediction. Through this mechanism we get sentiment representations updated with guidance from span representation and vice versa. This establishes a bi-directional connection between the two tasks.

We use linear projections on H_{sent} and H_{span} to generate the query (Q_{sent} , Q_{span}),key (K_{sent} , K_{span}) and value (V_{sent} , V_{span}) vectors respectively.

To incorporate span information in sentiment representation it is necessary to align sentiment with its closely related spans. We use Q_{sent} as query and K_{span}, V_{span} as key and value vectors respectively. We then get span-aware sentiment representation H'_{sent} as follows

$$C_{sent} = softmax\left(\frac{Q_{sent}K^T_{span}}{\sqrt{d_k}}\right) V_{span} \quad (3)$$

$$H'_{sent} = LayerNorm(H_{sent} + c_{sent}) \quad (4)$$

In a similar fashion we obtain sentiment-guided span representation by treating K_{sent}, V_{sent} as key and value vectors and Q_{span} as query vector. Through the co-attention layer we obtain H'_{sent} and H'_{span} which can be considered to be span-guided sentiment representation and sentiment-guided span representation respectively.

We extend the feed-forward network layer from a vanilla transformer encoder block to implicitly fuse sentiment and span information. We concatenate H'_{sent} and H'_{span} to combine the sentiment and span information.

$$H_{ss} = H'_{sent} + H'_{span} \quad (5)$$

Then we follow (Zhang and Wang, 2016) to use word features for each token, which is formulated as

$$h_{(f,t)} = h^{t-1}_{ss} h^t_{ss} h^{t+1}_{ss} \quad (6)$$

Finally we use feed-forward networks to fuse the

Type	Sentiment Classification					Span Prediction		
	Text Encoder	**Accuracy**	**F1**	**Precision**	**Recall**	**F1**	**Exact Match**	**Jaccard Sim.**
STL	BERT	59.72%	55.85%	57.16%	57.52%	52.16%	8.33%	50.84%
	MBERT	62.96%	61.3%	61.97%	61.28%	54.51%	7.41%	45.68%
	MURIL	63.01%	61.87%	62.24%	62.84%	54.81%	8.33%	50.12%
MTL	BERT	61.11%	59.93%	60.14%	59.90%	53.01%	8.80%	51.32%
	MBERT	62.96%	62.22%	62.97%	62.12%	57.80%	9.72%	49.64%
	MURIL †	63.43%	62.85%	65.22%	63.05%	57.23%	8.33%	49.25%
OURS	BERT	61.57%	62.19%	64.27%	62.34%	53.81%	9.72%	52.37%
	MBERT	64.81%	62.80%	64.02%	63.16%	58.83%	9.72%	50.39%
	MURIL *	**65.74%**	**64.12%**	**67.41%**	**64.28%**	**59.94%**	**11.11%**	**52.43%**
$\Delta_{(\star-\dagger)\times 100}(\%)$		↑ 2.31%	↑ 1.27%	↑ 3.39%	↑ 1.23%	↑ 2.71%	↑ 2.78%	↑ 3.18%

Table 2: Comparison of different approaches on our dataset. The last row shows the absolute improvement of our approach over the MTL approach with the MURIL as text encoder.

sentiment and span information.

$$FFN(H_{(f,t)}) = max(0, H_{(f,t)}W_1 + b + 1)W_2 + b_2 \quad (7)$$

$$\hat{H}_{sent} = LayerNorm(H'_{sent} + FFN(H_{(f,t)}) \quad (8)$$

$$\hat{H}_{span} = LayerNorm(H'_{span} + FFN(H_{(f,t)}) \quad (9)$$

Here $H_{(f,t)} = (h^1_{(f,t)}, h^2_{(f,t)} ... h^t_{(f,t)})$; $\hat{H_{sent}}$ and $\hat{H_{span}}$ are the final updated sentiment and span representations that align the corresponding span and sentiment features respectively.

4.2.3 Decoder For Sentiment And Span Prediction

We utilize two decoder heads to get the final predictions, one head each for sentiment prediction and sentiment span extraction task respectively.

Sentiment Prediction We apply max-pooling operation on $\hat{H}_{sent}$ to obtain sentence representation c which is used for sentiment prediction.

$$\hat{y}^{sent} = softmax(W^{sent}c + b_{sent}) \quad (10)$$

Span Classification We pass $\hat{H}_{span}$ through feed-forward networks to obtain the start and end position as follows

$$\hat{y}^{span} = softmax(W^{span}\hat{H}_{span} + b_{span}) \quad (11)$$

5 Experimental Results

In this section we present the results (averaged over 5 independent runs) on our test set and perform comparative analysis followed qualitative and error analysis. For comparison we use the following standard metrics - accuracy, macro averaged F1 score, precision, recall for sentiment prediction task and F1 score, exact match and jaccard similarity for the span prediction task.

5.1 Baselines And Compared Methods

We compare our approach with single-task learning (STL) architectures and multi-task learning (MTL) architectures.

1. **Single-Task Learning** In this setup we separately train two transformer based text encoders, one for sentiment prediction and one for span extraction.

2. **Multi-Task Learning** In this setup we train a transformer based text encoder jointly for sentiment prediction and span extraction

In both STL and MTL setup we use the pooled representation corresponding to the [CLS] token as sentence representation for sentiment prediction and use the token level representations from the last hidden layer for span extraction.

Text Encoders We experiment with three text encoders. The first one is the BERT(Devlin et al., 2018) base model, since the dataset is codemixed we also experiment with MBERT and MURIL(Khanuja et al., 2021) which are multilingual models based on BERT architecture. Both MBERT and MURIL are trained on english and Tamil text corpus and specifically MURIL is trained on a romanized Tamil corpus.

5.2 Main Results

Table 2 depicts the results obtained via different approaches and text encoders on our dataset.

Sentiment Classification					Span Extraction		
Text Encoder	Accuracy	F1	Precision	Recall	F1	Exact Match	Jaccard Sim.
No Label Attention	62.50%	62.36%	64.36%	62.57%	54.11%	9.26%	52.95%
Self Attention Mechanism	64.35%	62.83%	63.41%	62.83%	54.76%	11.11%	53.56%
Sentiment To Span Connection	64.22%	60.88%	64.22%	61.37%	50.20%	9.26%	49.36%
Span To Sentiment Connection	64.43%	61.06%	61.39%	61.28%	53.24%	9.72%	51.30%

Table 3: Each key component in the proposed approach contributes to overall performance. Replacing or removing a component results in a drop in performance.

Type	Sentiment Classification					Span Extraction		
	Text Encoder	Accuracy	F1	Precision	Recall	F1	Exact Match	Jaccard Sim.
STL	BERT	75.01%	75.41%	75.85%	74.91%	48.48%	16.62%	44.58%
MTL	BERT †	76.47%	76.61%	78.92%	75.63%	49.97%	19.07%	45.70%
OURS	**BERT** *	**78.33%**	**78.63%**	**78.97%**	**78.36%**	**54.86%**	**20.16%**	**50.76%**
$\Delta_{(\star-\dagger)\times 100}(\%)$		$\uparrow$ 1.86%	$\uparrow$ 2.02%	$\uparrow$ 0.06%	$\uparrow$ 2.73%	$\uparrow$ 4.89%	$\uparrow$ 1.09%	$\uparrow$ 5.06%

Table 4: Comparison of different approaches on the Twitter Sentiment Extraction dataset. The last row shows the absolute improvement of our approach over the MTL approach.

We experiment with three different text encoders, we observe that among these MURIL performs better than MBERT and BERT in both STL and MTL setup, moreover when MURIL is used as text encoder in our approach it acheives the best performance for our dataset.

We observe that models trained in MTL setup perform better than STL models for all the text encoders across all the metrics, this indicates that jointly learning the tasks of sentiment prediction and span extraction can mutually enhance performance.

MTL can be seen as considering the mutual-interaction between the two tasks via parameter sharing and joint optimization, however our approach out-performs MTL setup with their respective text encoders. Moreover when compared to the best MTL setup which is MTL MURIL, our approach with MURIL text encoder performs better.

5.3 Ablation Study

In this section we study the efficacy of the key components present in our approach. Table 3 shows the sentiment prediction and span prediction results using our approach on our dataset. We modify the key components in our proposed approach to investigate their contribution to the performance.

We drop the label attention layer and replace H_{sent} and H_{span} with H. From Table 3 we observe that this leads to a drop in performance. This demonstrates the usefulness of using label information to generate explicit sentiment and span representations.

We replace the co-attention mechanism in TIM with the vanilla self-attention mechanism. This change means that there is no explicit interaction between the two tasks. From Table 3 we notice that this leads to a drop in performance justifying the use co-attention mechanism. While self-attention only implicitly models the interaction between the sentiment and span tasks, co-attention can explicitly consider the cross-impact between the two.

We restrict the bi-directional flow of information so that the information can either from from sentiment to span or span to sentiment. We implement this by using only one type of information representation as queries to attend to the other information. In table we refer to this as Sentiment To Span and Span To Sentiment. From Table 3 we observe that such a unidirectional flow of information leads to a performance drop. We can conclude that modelling the mutual interaction between the sentiment prediction and span prediction task can enhance the performance in a mutual way.

5.4 Generalizability

In this section we establish the generalizability of our proposed approach by experimenting on the Twitter Sentiment Extraction dataset from Kaggle. The original task for this dataset is to extract the sentiment span given the sentiment, however we repurpose it for our task of joint sentiment prediction and span extraction. Since the span labels are not present in the test set, we split the original train set into a 80/20 split and perform our testing on the unseen 20 split while the training and validation is done on the 80 split.

Table 4 shows the results of STL, MTL and our

proposed appoach on the dataset. We observe that MTL setup performs better that the STL setup indicating that jointly optimizing for the two tasks of sentiment prediction and span extraction is mutually beneficial. Our approach shows improvement over the MTL setup across all the metrics thus demonstrating the capability of our proposed model to generalize to other sentiment prediction datasets.

6 Conclusion and Future Work

In this work we explore the use of sentiment span cues towards improving code-mixed sentiment prediction. We first curate a novel manually annotated dataset to support code-mixed sentiment span extraction. We then propose a novel methodology based on transformer architecture to explicitly model the the mutual interactions between sentiment prediction and sentiment span extraction tasks. Empirical evaluation along with an extensive ablation study suggests the efficacy of our proposed model and its design choices. We also establish the generalizability of the proposed model by demonstrating its performance on the Twitter Sentiment Extraction dataset.

References

Abien Fred Agarap. 2018. Statistical analysis on e-commerce reviews, with sentiment classification using bidirectional recurrent neural network (rnn).

Alfred V. Aho and Jeffrey D. Ullman. 1972. *The Theory of Parsing, Translation and Compiling*, volume 1. Prentice-Hall, Englewood Cliffs, NJ.

Jeremy Barnes, Erik Velldal, and Lilja Øvrelid. 2021. Improving sentiment analysis with multi-task learning of negation. *Natural Language Engineering*, 27(2):249–269.

Richard Caruana. 1993. Multitask learning: A knowledge-based source of inductive bias. In *Proceedings of the Tenth International Conference on Machine Learning*, pages 41–48. Morgan Kaufmann.

Bharathi Raja Chakravarthi, Vigneshwaran Muralidaran, Ruba Priyadharshini, and John Philip McCrae. 2020. Corpus creation for sentiment analysis in code-mixed Tamil-English text. In *Proceedings of the 1st Joint Workshop on Spoken Language Technologies for Under-resourced languages (SLTU) and Collaboration and Computing for Under-Resourced Languages (CCURL)*, pages 202–210, Marseille, France. European Language Resources association.

Bharathi Raja Chakravarthi, Ruba Priyadharshini, Vigneshwaran Muralidaran, Navya Jose, Shardul Suryawanshi, Elizabeth Sherly, and John P. McCrae. 2022. Dravidiancodemix: Sentiment analysis and offensive language identification dataset for dravidian languages in code-mixed text. *ArXiv*, abs/2106.09460.

Jacob Devlin, Ming-Wei Chang, Kenton Lee, and Kristina Toutanova. 2018. BERT: pre-training of deep bidirectional transformers for language understanding. *CoRR*, abs/1810.04805.

Sreyan Ghosh and Sonal Kumar. 2021. Cisco at semeval-2021 task 5: What's toxic?: Leveraging transformers for multiple toxic span extraction from online comments. *arXiv preprint arXiv:2105.13959*.

Suong N. Hoang, Linh V. Nguyen, Tai Huynh, and Vuong T. Pham. 2019. An efficient model for sentiment analysis of electronic product reviews in vietnamese.

Gagandeep Kaur, Abhishek Kaushik, and Shubham Sharma. 2019. Cooking is creating emotion: A study on hinglish sentiments of youtube cookery channels using semi-supervised approach. *Big Data and Cognitive Computing*, 3(3).

Simran Khanuja, Diksha Bansal, Sarvesh Mehtani, Savya Khosla, Atreyee Dey, Balaji Gopalan, Dilip Kumar Margam, Pooja Aggarwal, Rajiv Teja Nagipogu, Shachi Dave, Shruti Gupta, Subhash Chandra Bose Gali, Vish Subramanian, and Partha Talukdar. 2021. Muril: Multilingual representations for indian languages.

Shanrou Lai, Zichen Yu, and Hanyue Wang. 2020. Text sentiment support phrases extraction based on roberta. In *2020 2nd International Conference on Applied Machine Learning (ICAML)*, pages 232–237.

Parth Patwa, Gustavo Aguilar, Sudipta Kar, Suraj Pandey, Srinivas PYKL, Björn Gambäck, Tanmoy Chakraborty, Thamar Solorio, and Amitava Das. 2020. SemEval-2020 task 9: Overview of sentiment analysis of code-mixed tweets. In *Proceedings of the Fourteenth Workshop on Semantic Evaluation*, pages 774–790, Barcelona (online). International Committee for Computational Linguistics.

John Pavlopoulos, Jeffrey Sorensen, Léo Laugier, and Ion Androutsopoulos. 2021. SemEval-2021 task 5: Toxic spans detection. In *Proceedings of the 15th International Workshop on Semantic Evaluation (SemEval-2021)*, pages 59–69, Online. Association for Computational Linguistics.

Libo Qin, Tailu Liu, Wanxiang Che, Bingbing Kang, Sendong Zhao, and Ting Liu. 2021. A co-interactive transformer for joint slot filling and intent detection. In *ICASSP 2021-2021 IEEE International Conference on Acoustics, Speech and Signal Processing (ICASSP)*, pages 8193–8197. IEEE.

Ramaneswaran S, Sanchit Vijay, and Kathiravan Srinivasan. 2022. TamilATIS: Dataset for task-oriented dialog in Tamil. In *Proceedings of the Second Workshop on Speech and Language Technologies for Dravidian Languages*, pages 25–32, Dublin, Ireland. Association for Computational Linguistics.

Shoffan Saifullah, Yuli Fauziyah, and Agus Sasmito Aribowo. 2021. Comparison of machine learning for sentiment analysis in detecting anxiety based on social media data. *Jurnal Informatika*, 15(1):45.

Antony Samuels and John Mcgonical. 2020. Sentiment analysis on social media content.

Xiaodong Zhang and Houfeng Wang. 2016. A joint model of intent determination and slot filling for spoken language understanding. In *Proceedings of the Twenty-Fifth International Joint Conference on Artificial Intelligence*, IJCAI'16, page 2993–2999. AAAI Press.

AdBERT: An Effective Few Shot Learning Framework for Aligning Tweets to Superbowl Advertisements

Debarati Das[1], **Roopana Chenchu**[1], **Maral Abdollahi**[2], **Jisu Huh**[2] and **Jaideep Srivastava**[1]
Department of Computer Science, University of Minnesota, Twin Cities[1]
Hubbard School of Journalism and Mass Communication, University of Minnesota, Twin Cities[2]
{das00015,vuppa007,abdol022,jhuh,srivasta}@umn.edu

Abstract

The tremendous increase in social media usage for sharing Television (TV) experiences has provided a unique opportunity in the Public Health and Marketing sectors to understand viewer engagement and attitudes through viewer-generated content on social media. However, this opportunity also comes with associated technical challenges. Specifically, given a televised event and related tweets about this event, we need methods to effectively align these tweets and the corresponding event. In this paper, we consider the specific ecosystem of the Superbowl 2020 and map viewer tweets to advertisements they are referring to. Our proposed model, AdBERT, is an effective few-shot learning framework that is able to handle the technical challenges of establishing ad-relatedness, class imbalance as well as the scarcity of labeled data. As part of this study, we have curated and developed two datasets that can prove to be useful for Social TV research: 1) dataset of ad-related tweets and 2) dataset of ad descriptions of Superbowl advertisements. Explaining connections to Sentence-BERT, we describe the advantages of AdBERT that allow us to make the most out of a challenging and interesting dataset which we will open-source along with the models developed in this paper.

1 Introduction

The joint consumption of television programming and social media participation has become increasingly popular, leading to the rise of Social TV ecosystems (Proulx and Shepatin, 2012; Benton and Hill, 2012; Cesar and Geerts, 2011). Twitter has become an integral outlet for TV viewers, with a whopping 85% of users tweeting while watching television programming (Midha, 2014). Marketers, television networks, and social media platforms have explored this rising potential of Social TV ecosystems. For example, Twitter and content providers on television networks collaborated recently (Crook, 2016) to create social TV experiences, and companies such as Nielson (Talkwalker, 2020) are investing in technologies to quantify and analyze social TV audiences.

Figure 1: Mapping the the tweets referring to advertisements telecast during the Superbowl event. For e.g., the tweet mentioning *#diversity* and *#inclusivity* is mapped to the advertisement by `Olay` featuring the hashtag *#makespaceforwomen*.

Social TV research is still in its infancy stage (Liaukonyte et al., 2015). However, a few studies (Diakopoulos and Shamma, 2010; Fossen and Schweidel, 2017) have already explored the impact of television on social media word of mouth (WOM) and "impactful" factors (celebrity presence) that influence the volume of social media WOM. Similarly, identifying "attention-grabbing" moments in media (e.g., the performance of the speaker during the presidential debate or a funny ad during the Superbowl), can help gauge the reaction of the viewers'. Hence, it becomes necessary to build tools that capture these "attention-grabbing" moments and analyze the subsequent responses. These tools are not only necessary for program recall and re-contextualization (Wang, 2006), but also for the design of more personalized recommendations in the future. (Pyo et al., 2014).

With a large amount of social buzz generated online, analyzing the responses of the viewers towards televised events has now become much easier as opposed to earlier slow and costly methods that involved surveying the viewers. However, this also comes with its technical challenges. For instance, given a televised event and an associated set of social media posts, an approach that effectively maps the posts to the parts of the event they are referring to (Figure 1) is necessary. This raises two follow-up questions: (a) discretely atomizing the event into segments and (b) identify if the tweet focuses on a specific event segment or the event as a whole. For ex-

Proceedings of the 2022 COLING Workshop: The 8th Workshop on Noisy User-generated Text (W-NUT 2022), pages 171–179

ample, tweets can be related to the commercials during the break or the game as a whole during the Superbowl broadcast. Therefore, a method that can align the tweets and their related televised events is an essential building block toward answering fundamental questions regarding the event's influence on the viewer's social TV activity. Machine learning based methods towards this end have attempted event segmentation (Galley et al., 2003); however, they analyze events and tweets independently. This is a big drawback as the event influences the viewer's response; hence there is a need to *jointly* model tweets ad televised content information.

Our research study considers the specific social TV advertising ecosystem during the high-stakes Super Bowl sporting event. In this event, since the ads telecast and audience responses are on different media channels (i.e. TV and Twitter, respectively) over a fixed time, we view the problem as a closed system consisting of two interacting sets - the set of stimuli (advertisements) and the set of responses (tweets). Our research focuses on modelling the function that maps these two sets to each other.

$$\forall a \in A \;\; \text{(Set of all ads)}$$
$$\forall t \in T \;\; \text{(Set of all tweets)}$$

Estimate a function $f : T \to A$ where the mapping is 1-1.

Tweet to Ad mapping is non-trivial problem as the viewer's tweet could be about multiple aspects of the advertisement, such as its creative elements or the brand making the advertisement. For example, if we consider the tweet,*"The pepsi ad was so amazing"*, this is a simplistic case as it is easy to map that the viewer is talking about the advertisement by `Pepsi`. However, in the case of another tweet, *"Mc hammer is still making money with songs low key"*, it is not easy to understand that this tweet is even ad-related (MC Hammer is a celebrity who featured in the `Cheetos` Advertisement). Moreover, we are trying to capture ad-related tweets against the general noise of the Superbowl-related tweets. In this setting, WOM is much less for ad-related tweets (limited representation) and the viewers are also likely to talk about some ads more than others (class imbalance).

Our mapping methodology **AdBERT** is an effective few-shot learning framework that establishes semantic relatedness between an advertisement and a tweet under the constraints of class imbalance and limited class representation. Once this mapping is established, it can be used as an essential building block in an audience engineering pipeline that can help incorporate a feedback loop to an advertisement and aid in downstream tasks such as ad-engagement measurement and sentiment analysis. As a by-product of our experiments, we also developed a manually annotated rich dataset of ad-related tweets and a manually annotated dataset of Superbowl ad descriptions, which can be used for further research in social TV literature.

2 Related Work

With the rise of social TV technologies, research has been done to examine how media multitasking affects viewers' response to advertisements and how advertisers can leverage this behaviour (Hu et al., 2017). (Lewis and Reiley, 2014) find a sudden increase in online searches for brands shown during Superbowl commercials immediately after the ad is telecast. While the aligning of real-time social media responses to TV advertising has been explored in recent years (Hill et al., 2012), their methods to map the tweets to the advertisement is based on the underlying assumption that a person tweets about an advertisement as soon as they see it, which need not be true (Murphy et al., 2006). Our proposed method relies on content mapping, which would *capture tweets about an advertisement irrespective of its time of airing.*

Though (Hu, 2021) consider the primacy effect, their topic-model based approach method cannot be applied to televised segments for which no transcripts are readily available. Advertisements broadcast on TV are usually tiny time segments for which auto-generated transcripts are not meaningful, as they could be theme songs or even a catchphrase. However, even this kind of short TV content is impactful enough to generate significant WOM. Our approach to solving this correspondence problem with its unique challenges draws inspiration from some previous research works (Devlin et al., 2018; Chang et al., 2019; Thakur et al., 2020) which use different encoders for pairwise sentence scoring tasks and (Reimers and Gurevych, 2019) which inspires the idea for joint learning. Our approach aligns tweets with their corresponding TV advertisement through *jointly learning from both the advertisement information and the tweets.*

3 Superbowl 2020 Dataset

Ad Name	Ad Description
`Audi`	Maisie Williams, Frozen, etron, sportback, traffic, letitgo
`Doritos`	Sam Elliott, Lil Nas X, Old Town Road, cowboy, cool ranch dancer, billy ray cyrus, wild west, wild-wildwest, makeyourmove
`Weather Tech`	pets, golden retriever, dog

Table 1: Subset of the created ad information dataset, that contains descriptive phrases or words describing each advertisement in the Superbowl 2020.

3.1 Data Collection

To validate our idea computationally, our objective was to collect a data set that would provide us with a high density of advertisement-related tweets. This meant that a timed sporting event where a lot of advertisements are shown to consumers (who happen to respond to these advertisements) would be perfect for our study. Hence, the Super Bowl 2020 event was chosen as a use case because it is a high-stakes national sports event in the

US watched by a massive audience. This event attracts multiple advertisers who spend millions of dollars to place their ads during this game to attract consumers' eyeballs and spark social media conversations about their ads and brands.

We collected tweets using the Twitter streaming API via the AIDR (Imran et al., 2014) tool from the start of the broadcast (Feb 2nd, 5:30 PM CST) to the end of the day. For this purpose, we used a set of event-related keywords (#superbowlads, Superbowl 2020 etc.) and brand-related keywords (Nike, Pepsi, Olay, etc.). While the data was being collected, the search terms on AIDR were modified in real-time to include words and catchphrases ad-specific to the Super Bowl. The underlying idea is that the audience could be reacting to the brand's message (e.g. *#makespaceforwomen* is a catchphrase of the commercial broadcast by `Olay`) or specific elements of the commercial (e.g. celebrity *Katie Couric* was present in the `Olay` commercial). This was done to ensure that most tweets mentioning ad-specific features were collected. This collection is preferable to scraping user responses to online advertisements as such a method would be bottle-necked by fewer responses to each advertisement.

3.2 Data Preparation

Firstly, we create an **ad information dataset**, a subset of which is shown in Table 1. To create this dataset, three authors watched all of the Superbowl advertisements and made lists of phrases describing unique elements (celebrity, hashtag, tagline, etc.) they noticed in each ad. These lists were then combined to create a comprehensive set of phrases that describe each advertisement from the "annotator's point of view". These ad-related phrases are intended to be unique with respect to each advertisement, to differentiate ads as best possible and are agreed upon by all three authors.

Secondly, we prepare the **tweet-ads dataset**. As most of the originally collected data (around 1.1 million tweets) were event-related tweets, we had to first filter the general Superbowl-related noise to capture the candidate ad-related tweets to be used as training data. After removing the Twitter-specific symbols and artifacts during the initial tweet pre-processing stages, we remove retweets and duplicate tweets to retain only original tweets made by users. To narrow down on candidate tweets that are possibly ad-related, we developed some heuristics (e.g. checking for the presence of brand names). Another heuristic relied on the ad information dataset collected (mentioned above) and checked for the presence of a high degree of overlap between ad-related information and the tweet by using the Jaccard Index measure (Niwattanakul et al., 2013). For example, some of the phrases that describe the brand `Olay` in the ad information dataset are *{Olay, #makespaceforwomen, Katie Couric, Lilly Singh}*. This kind of Jaccard-based heuristic could capture candidate tweets mentioning any of these ad-related features.

A random sample of these candidate tweets was chosen for manual labeling. The tweets were labeled such that each tweet was assigned to the advertisement it referred to or labeled as "none" if the tweet was Superbowl related. Tweets mentioning multiple ads were disregarded in the sample.

For this annotation task, three authors went through a common training session, where it was agreed that the annotation would be based on the common ad information dataset (Table 1) as well as their own personal notes on viewing the commercial. This annotation task involves matching the tweets to the nearest advertisement given the mention of specific elements in the tweet. Since the advertisements are quite different in terms of these elements, the degree of subjectivity in this task is low and we did not require multiple annotations per tweet. The only advertisements which were similar were the ones from a common brand, and for these cases, we combined the advertisements to represent one ad class. Statistics of the resulting tweet-ads dataset are given in Table 2.

Collected no of tweet samples	1114931
No of candidate ad-related tweets (post filtering)	111652
No of tweet samples - training	4656
No of tweet samples - test	1165
No of ad categories	61

Table 2: Statistics about the Superbowl 2020 ad-tweets dataset

4 Main Technical Challenges

A tweet could be a response to either the advertisement's creative elements (for example, a cute retriever in the `WeatherTech` ad) or the advertisement as a whole. Therefore, **detecting the ad-relatedness** requires a holistic understanding of the advertisement's content.

Identifying ad-relatedness can be viewed through a *semantic relatedness* lens such that we try to establish a relationship between the tweet and the advertisement description. However, the short length of tweets and their characteristic lingo adds to the complexities of identifying semantic-relatedness. While the tweet is a short sentence, the ad description is a comma-separated list of key phrases or words. Hence a semantic gap exists between the twitter lingo and the advertisement descriptions ("audience-annotator" gap.)

Identifying ad-relatedness can also be seen through the lens of *multi-class classification*, which involves scoring a set of candidate labels given an input context. The Superbowl Dataset shows the unique characteristic of **class imbalance** with 15 popular or controversial commercials having high representation in the dataset and we call these -"majority classes". For example, the `Hulu` advertisement featured Superbowl superstar

Tom Brady and was a viral ad and hence, a "majority" class. Our threshold for a majority class is that the number of samples for that class should be at least 40. 46 other commercials exist in our data with lesser than 40 samples for the model to train on and understand patterns in these cases. We call these classes - "minority classes". Each class in our training data also suffered from **limited representation**, with the average number of samples in a majority class being 122 and in a minority class being 17.

5 Experiments

From a *semantic relatedness perspective*, we can try to map the text and ad information into a common feature space wherein a dot product, cosine or (parameterized) non-linear function is typically used to measure their similarity.

SentenceBERT (Reimers and Gurevych, 2019) is a bi-encoder model, which applies BERT independently on the two inputs, followed by mean pooling on the output to create separate fixed-sized sentence embeddings. As the representations are separate, the bi-encoders is able to cache the encoded candidates and reuse these representations for each input resulting in faster prediction times than cross-encoders. However, The tweets and ad description information in our dataset are not in the same vector space because the tweet has a sentence structure, while the advertisement information is a set of key phrases describing the ad from the annotator's point of view.

Therefore we consider the *multi-classification perspective* where we can try to score a set of candidate ad descriptions given an input tweet. This kind of multi-class classification can be done via Classical Machine Learning approaches (Debole and Sebastiani, 2004) such as **Logistic Regression** and **Multilayer Perceptron (MLP)** with TF-IDF vectorization of features. In these approaches, words characteristic to an ad are given greater weight than words that frequently appear across all the ads. Our implementation of the MLP has 12 hidden layers each with dimension of 6000. The model is trained for categorical entropy loss with a batch size of 20 and number of epochs as 50.

Deep learning based methods like **BERT** (Devlin et al., 2018) uses a cross-encoder (Wolf et al., 2019; Vig and Ramea, 2019) where a special SEP token separates the input and label candidate and multi-head attention is applied over all input tokens. In our implementation of BERT for multi-class classification, we fine-tune (Sun et al., 2019) the pre-trained 'Bert-base-uncased' model with 12 layers from Transformers library (Wolf et al., 2019) to identify if a tweet can be identified as related to a Super Bowl commercial or not. If the tweet is "Superbowl event related" and does not relate to any ad, it is categorized as a 'none' class. Else, the tweet is classified as 'ad-related'. For all the tweets classified as ad-related, we compute the embeddings from BERT and run a softmax on similarity scores to identify the ad class. The model is trained on 4656 tweets and 61 classes. We use a batch size of 32, a learning rate of 2e-5 and the number of epochs as 4. We also use the epsilon parameter *eps* with a value 1e-8 to prevent any division by zero in the implementation.

In our implementation of SentenceBERT, we fine-tune the pre-trained "nq-distilbert-base-v1" model using the joint learning setup described in Section 6 and using cosine similarity loss. We use number of epochs as 30, warmup_steps as 100 and evaluation_steps as 500. During test time, we compute the maximum cosine similarity of the input tweet against all of the ad descriptions to get the ad class assigned to the tweet, but with the embeddings obtained from the fine-tuned SentenceBERT model.

6 AdBERT : Proposed Joint Learning Approach

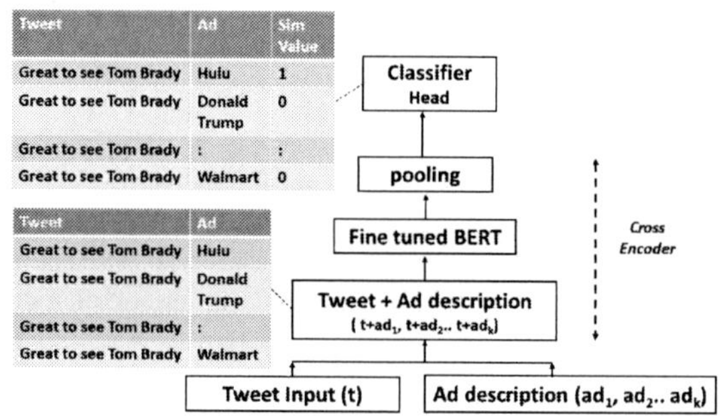

Figure 2: AdBERT Architecture

Our AdBERT approach frames the multi-class classification problem of mapping a tweet to its respective advertisement as a binary classification and semantic relatedness task. As we faced a problem of a limited labeled dataset, we required a better training signal from our dataset. In order to solve this problem, we use an approach utilizing class verbalizers as seen in similar research works for few shot learning (Aly et al., 2021; Pappas and Henderson, 2019; Obamuyide and Vlachos, 2018). In our case study, we propose learning from both the tweet as well as the textual descriptions of each ad class, which is a part of our ad information dataset (Table 1). This means that instead of using label IDs as we did in earlier experiments with BERT, we concatenate tweet text with contextual descriptions about the ad labels. The key phrases of the ad description are concatenated together into a single sequence, which is the contextual description of the ad.

Specifically, the input to the model is a *<tweet, ad-description>* pair, and the output is either 1 (if the tweet is related to the ad in the included ad-description) or 0 (otherwise). Therefore, given N tweets and K ad cat-

	#classes	Without Ad Information								
		LogReg			MLP			BERT		
		Pr.	Rec.	F1	Pr.	Rec.	F1	Pr.	Rec.	F1
Majority	15	0.88	0.84	0.85	0.94	0.76	0.84	0.59	0.72	0.64
Minority	46	0.66	0.52	0.58	0.55	0.36	0.43	0.60	0.49	0.53

Table 3: Given a multi-classification setting where the input is tweet information and the output is ad class, this table reports the weighted average Precision, Recall and F1 score metrics of each model, grouped by majority and minority classes.

egories, the AdBERT model would be trained on NK instances. For each tweet in the original dataset, $K-1$ tweet-ad pairs correspond to negative combinations, and one pair corresponds to the positive class label. The hyperparameters for training remain the same as that used in our experiments with BERT. This architecture is illustrated in Figure 2.

This kind of joint learning training strategy is able to handle the **class imbalance** problem, as the model also learns from the "negative" combinations. The training strategy we describe makes no assumptions about the number of ad categories and is easily extensible. Including new ad categories or adapting to newer ad themes would only require a modification in the ad descriptions with little to no fine-tuning of the classifier architecture. We also do not need to handle explicitly the "not ad-related" case here, as tweets not referring to any ad are automatically classified as 0 in all cases.

The cross encoder in AdBERT takes as input to the network both the tweet and the ad description separated by a SEP token and multi-head attention, is applied across all tokens of the inputs. Compared to a bi-encoder, the cross-encoder offloads the similarity computation to the self-attention matrices and hence is able to better learn to identify ad-relatedness. This implies that both inputs are compared simultaneously and helps solve the **ad-relatedness** problem.

The problem task reformulation we suggest, where we append the label information to the tweet and assist the cross encoder, also solves the **limited representation** problem, thus allowing our model to behave as an effective few-shot learning framework.

7 Results and Discussion

7.1 Quantitative Analysis

We implement the Logistic Regression, MLP and BERT models described in Section 5, where the only input to the model is the tweet information, and the output is the ad class. Table 3 reports the weighted average precision, recall and F1 score metrics of each model, grouped by the majority and minority classes for this multi-classification setting. In the second round of experiments, we implement our benchmarks but supplemented with ad information as per the joint learning strategy described in Section 6. Table 4 reports the metrics of each model, grouped by the majority and minority classes for this setting. Our model, **AdBERT** is a joint learning strategy using a modification of BERT, where the model learns from both the tweet and the ad descriptions.

In our models, we argue that recall is the more important performance metric than precision, given our focus on identifying all true ads. This is because, in the context of Twitter, ad mentions are rare with less than 1% of all tweets even mentioning ad names, with our dataset further highlighting that. For these reasons, we argue that while precision is relevant, it is not critical since false positive ads can be filtered out in downstream tasks, so there is limited harm in falsely identifying ads while there is significance in correctly identifying ads which may not be readily identified using current methods.

In the setting where there is no ad information (Table 3), we observe that Logistic Regression (0.84 Recall) and MLP (0.76 Recall) do well when it comes to prediction of the majority classes. This must imply that there are inherent data patterns in the tweets that can be captured just using TF-IDF features. However, with minority classes both models do quite poorly (0.52 Recall for LogReg and 0.36 Recall for MLP) and cannot handle the class imbalance or limited representation problem. BERT in the multi-class classification setting is comparable (0.72 Recall) to the classical machine learning models with the majority classes.

In the setting where we include ad information (Table 4), we see that the performance of the classical machine learning models goes down as expected. Classical models are known to be sensitive to class imbalance (Atla et al., 2011; Mirylenka et al., 2017; Santiago et al., 2012; Cervantes et al., 2017) and with the joint learning strategy, there is an increase in the size of training data and class imbalance and noise become more pronounced.

In the earlier experiment with BERT, we used just the tweet input, so the cross-encoder in BERT could not be completely harnessed to map the relationship between the tweet and the ad labels. Therefore, the joint learning strategy of **AdBERT** shows very high performance across all metrics across both majority and minority classes. **AdBERT** also does much better than SentenceBERT in the joint learning setting with our data (Recall of 0.75 vs 0.41 for minority classes). This is because the cross-encoder offloads the similarity

	#classes	LogReg_JL Pr.	LogReg_JL Rec.	LogReg_JL F1	MLP_JL Pr.	MLP_JL Rec.	MLP_JL F1	SentenceBERT Pr.	SentenceBERT Rec.	SentenceBERT F1	AdBERT Pr.	AdBERT Rec.	AdBERT F1
		With Ad Information											
Majority	15	0.66	0.32	0.43	0.67	0.34	0.45	0.65	0.73	0.68	**0.91**	**0.91**	**0.91**
Minority	46	0.42	0.23	0.29	0.36	0.15	0.21	0.39	0.41	0.39	**0.74**	**0.75**	**0.74**

Table 4: Given a binary classification setting where the input is tweet information concatenated with ad description and the output is 1 (ad-related) or 0 (not-ad-related), this table reports the weighted average Precision, Recall and F1 score metrics of each model, grouped by majority and minority classes. AdBERT outperforms all other baselines.

computation to the self-attention matrices in all the layers and can better identify ad-relatedness as compared to the bi-encoder of SentenceBERT. Bi-encoder based methods usually achieve lower performance than the cross-encoders method and require a large amount of training data. The reason is cross-encoders can compare both inputs simultaneously, while the bi-encoders have to independently map inputs to a meaningful vector space which requires a sufficient amount of training examples for fine-tuning. The cross-encoder approach is typically not computationally feasible, but it is in this scenario, as the number of ad labels is much less than the number of tweets.

7.2 Qualititative Analysis

This section discusses the different types of tweet-to-ad correspondence we observed in our Superbowl 2020 Dataset and how AdBERT handles them.

When tweet mentions the advertiser's product : In many cases, the tweet responses directly mention the advertising brand or the product of the advertiser. Consider an example tweet, *"pepsi is totally copying #nooriginality"*. AdBERT is easily able to establish this kind of mapping, with the tweet directly mentioning `Pepsi` in its response. TF-IDF based models would also be effective for these cases.

When a tweet is about advertisement's creative elements : Sometimes the tweets are motivated by the creative elements in the commercial, such as a celebrity's presence. In these cases, the tweet content is not enough to map the tweet to the correct advertisement, and additional commercial-related information is necessary to establish context for the mapping. Consider the tweet, *"gotta let it go doritos right away"* to which our model gives `Doritos` a score of 0.98 F1 and `Audi` a score of 0.95 F1. This happens because the `Audi` commercial featured actor Maisie Williams singing "Let it Go", and this aspect of the commercial is learned from the ad information (Table 1). As a result of the combined contextual BERT embeddings of the tweet response and ad information, `Doritos` has a higher probability, and the tweet is eventually mapped to the `Doritos` commercial.

Consider another tweet, *"@google almost got canine cancer! who is one actual sucker for golden retrievers?"*. Our model maps this tweet to the commercial for `Weather Tech`, which featured a golden retriever. Although the word 'google' exists in the sentence, context is given preference over mere word matching, and the AdBERT classifier correctly identifies the appropriate ad mapping.

These examples justify the poor results of TF-IDF based models and establish the need for context-rich models like AdBERT for effective mapping.

When a tweet is about multiple commercials: In our test dataset, we observed several tweets mentioning multiple commercials. For example, the tweet, *"who is the cool ranch doritos with lil nasx or ellen"* is referring to two advertisements : `Doritos` featuring celebrity Lil Nas X, and `Amazon Alexa` featuring celebrity Ellen Degeneres. AdBERT is able to understand that most of this tweet is about the `Doritos` ad and gives it a score of 0.98 F1 vs `Amazon alexa` with 0.67 F1. This is because of the combined learning from ad information input and tweet content input.

When a tweet is about similar commercials : AdBERT demonstrates a certain degree of confusion when the tweet is about similar commercials (when you cannot distinguish based on brand or commercial content). This is evident in the case of the tweet, *"good on you michelob"*. Our model assigns similar scores to commercials `Michelob 6 for 6-pack` (0.87) and `Michelob lite` (0.98) for this tweet. This is probably because the tweet only mentions the brand name, and there is no further information to narrow it down. Similarly, tweets corresponding to `Bud light seltzer` and `Tide bud knight` show a degree of overlap in classification. This is perhaps because both ads are associated with the word 'bud'.

Table 5 describes the true annotated label vs the model predicted ad label for some examples from our tweet-ads dataset and further illustrates the impact of including ad information for joint learning. The ad information that is appended jointly with the tweet text, describes creative elements in the advertisements (such as a celebrities, taglines, etc.) even while the tweet might not have any direct reference to the ad class. For example, *"post malone absolutely best ad so far"* cannot be mapped to an ad category without additional context that the celebrity Post Malone was present in the `Budlight-seltzer` ad. Table 5 also illustrates how multiple minority category advertisements were mapped accurately by AdBERT.

Tweet text	True ad class	Predicted ad class	Predicted Ad category	Ad information
post malone absolutely best ad so far	BudLight Seltzer	BudLight Seltzer	Majority	bud light bud light seltzer post malone anheuser-busch inbev hard seltzer postmalone budlightbud-weiser alcohol
john cena with a super bowl wrap i'm ready to let it go man	Michelob	Michelob	Minority	anheuserbusch inbev mich-elob ultrabeer jimmy fal-lon working gym john cena usain bolt brooks koepka kerri walsh jen-nings worth enjoy low carbs jimmyfallon usain-bolt workingout gymbody alcohol
so far companies have spent millions dollars in ads starring people like molly ringwald	Avocados-from-Mexico	Avocados-from-Mexico	Minority	molly ringwald avocados mexico avonetwork avo-carriermollyringwald food
mc hammer still making money with songs low key	Cheetos	Cheetos	Minority	mc hammer cant touch popcorn cheetos cheetos thing cheetle cant-touchthismchammer food
arya stark nostalgic that frozen winter is never coming	Audi	None	Majority	maisie williams frozen etron sportback traffic letitgo
someone please explain josh jacobs win?	None	Kia	Minority	josh jacobs running back kia seltosraiders give ev-erything joshjacobs kiasel-tos car

Table 5: This table describes the true ad class vs the predicted ad class for some tweets from our tweet-ads dataset. We can observe that jointly learning ad information and the tweet text, led to more successful mapping of the tweets to their ads in both majority and minority represented ad categories.

As a counter example, consider the tweet, *"Arya stark nostalgic that frozen winter is never coming"*. This tweet refers to the character played by actor Maisie Williams in the popular series, Game Of Thrones. "Arya stark" was not included as a relevant ad-related phrase in our ad information data. Since neither the ad description nor the tweet data captured 'Arya stark' as a feature of the `Audi` ad, this tweet did not get classified correctly.

Similarly, *"Someone please explain josh jacobs win"* is annotated as `None` but the model predicts the ad class `Kia`, because Josh Jacobs is a football player mentioned in the ad information for this ad class. This is an ambiguous tweet as it could be related to Josh Jacob's performance in the Superbowl or his racing against the `Kia` car in the advertisement. Thus, false positives and false negatives in the prediction indicate towards issues with using manually annotated class verbalizers.

8 AdBERT used in Downstream Tasks

Our model serves as an essential part of multiple audience engineering pipelines in a social TV setting. In the research by (Lu et al., 2022), the aim is to examine the influence of the viewer's temporary affective states during Superbowl ad exposure. In order to compute the viewer's affective state, a key step is to be able to understand which advertisement impacted the user's affective state, thereby making them tweet in a specific way. This is done using AdBERT, which proves to be superior than time-based tweet-ad alignment. This is because the advertisements are typically very short (10 to 20s) and the user is more likely to tweet much later (Murphy et al., 2006) than during this brief time period. Similarly, in the work by (Kim et al., 2021), ad-related tweets derived through AdBERT are analyzed for evidence of gender-targeted advertising during the Super Bowl.

9 Limitations and Future work

Since our current AdBERT approach uses a fine-tuned Bert-base-uncased model, using fine-tuned BERTweet (Nguyen et al., 2020), which is a pre-trained language model for English Tweets, seems like a suitable next step. AdBERT uses additional information about the ad classes for joint learning. Three authors manually annotate this information in this research, but manually generated class verbalizers heavily depend on domain specific prior knowledge and finding appropriate label descriptions automatically is a challenging research problem that can be further explored. Similar and multiple advertisement mentioning commercials pose a problem in ad-tweet mapping and can be further disambiguated by considering the tweet's timestamp in addition to the tweet content.

The joint learning strategy described in AdBERT can also be extended to other social TV datasets. For example, in the Social TV ecosystem of Presidential Debates telecast on television, tweets could be mapped to segments of the debates. This could have multiple downstream implications such as viewer stance detection, viewer engagement analysis etc.

10 Conclusion

In this paper, we develop a model, AdBERT, that aligns tweets to the advertisements they refer to in the context of the Social TV ecosystem of Superbowl 2020. This problem is technically challenging because of the difficulties in establishing ad-relatedness of a tweet, class imbalance in the dataset and limited representation for each ad class. We find that framing this multi-class classification problem as a binary classification and semantic relatedness task results in superior F1 performance compared to our baseline models. In the joint learning setting, the model learns from both the input and label information together, leading to better classification even in lesser represented classes. Thus our model generalizes well despite the class imbalance and limited labelling problems in the dataset. AdBERT makes no assumptions about the number of ad categories and is easily extensible. Our model can be highly useful as a step toward incorporating feedback into advertisements and analyzing viewer engagement and attitudes. As a by-product of this research, we also developed a dataset of ad-related tweets and a dataset of ad descriptions of Superbowl ads, which can be used to further Social TV research.

Acknowledgements

We thank Dr. Xinyu Lu (Shanghai International Studies University) and Chandramouli Shama Shastry (Dalhousie University) for multiple enlightening discussions and brainstorming sessions.

References

Rami Aly, Andreas Vlachos, and Ryan McDonald. 2021. Leveraging type descriptions for zero-shot named entity recognition and classification. In *Proceedings of the 59th Annual Meeting of the Association for Computational Linguistics and the 11th International Joint Conference on Natural Language Processing (Volume 1: Long Papers)*, pages 1516–1528.

Abhinav Atla, Rahul Tada, Victor Sheng, and Naveen Singireddy. 2011. Sensitivity of different machine learning algorithms to noise. *Journal of Computing Sciences in Colleges*, 26(5):96–103.

Adrian Benton and Shawndra Hill. 2012. The spoiler effect?: Designing social tv content that promotes ongoing wom. In *Conference on Information Systems and Technology, Arizona*, pages 1–26.

Jair Cervantes, Farid Garcia-Lamont, Lisbeth Rodriguez, Asdrúbal López, José Ruiz Castilla, and Adrian Trueba. 2017. Pso-based method for svm classification on skewed data sets. *Neurocomputing*, 228:187–197.

Pablo Cesar and David Geerts. 2011. Past, present, and future of social tv: A categorization. In *2011 IEEE consumer communications and networking conference (CCNC)*, pages 347–351. IEEE.

Wei-Cheng Chang, Hsiang-Fu Yu, Kai Zhong, Yiming Yang, and Inderjit Dhillon. 2019. X-bert: Extreme multi-label text classification with bert. *arXiv preprint arXiv:1905.02331*.

Jordan Crook. 2016. *Twitter signs deal with NFL to live stream Thursday Night Football*. `https://tinyurl.com/76zjdd42`.

Franca Debole and Fabrizio Sebastiani. 2004. Supervised term weighting for automated text categorization. In *Text mining and its applications*, pages 81–97. Springer.

Jacob Devlin, Ming-Wei Chang, Kenton Lee, and Kristina Toutanova. 2018. Bert: Pre-training of deep bidirectional transformers for language understanding. *arXiv preprint arXiv:1810.04805*.

Nicholas A Diakopoulos and David A Shamma. 2010. Characterizing debate performance via aggregated twitter sentiment. In *Proceedings of the SIGCHI conference on human factors in computing systems*, pages 1195–1198.

Beth L Fossen and David A Schweidel. 2017. Television advertising and online word-of-mouth: An empirical investigation of social tv activity. *Marketing Science*, 36(1):105–123.

Michel Galley, Kathleen McKeown, Eric Fosler-Lussier, and Hongyan Jing. 2003. Discourse segmentation of multi-party conversation. In *Proceedings of the 41st Annual Meeting of the Association for Computational Linguistics*, pages 562–569.

Shawndra Hill, Aman Nalavade, and Adrian Benton. 2012. Social tv: Real-time social media response to tv advertising. In *Proceedings of the Sixth International Workshop on Data Mining for Online Advertising and Internet Economy*, pages 1–9.

Yuheng Hu. 2021. Characterizing social tv activity around televised events: A joint topic model approach. *INFORMS Journal on Computing*, 33(4):1320–1338.

Yuheng Hu, Tingting Nian, and Cheng Chen. 2017. Mood congruence or mood consistency? examining aggregated twitter sentiment towards ads in 2016 super bowl. In *Eleventh International AAAI Conference on Web and Social Media*.

Muhammad Imran, Carlos Castillo, Ji Lucas, Patrick Meier, and Sarah Vieweg. 2014. Aidr: Artificial intelligence for disaster response. In *Proceedings of the 23rd International Conference on World Wide Web*, pages 159–162.

Eunah Kim, Debarati Das, Roopana Chenchu, Mayura Nene, Jisu Huh, and Jaideep Srivastava. 2021. *Consumer Responses to Gender-Targeted Advertising: Computational Research Analyzing the 2020 Super Bowl Commercials*. Presented at the 2021 American Academy of Advertising.

Randall A Lewis and David H Reiley. 2014. Online ads and offline sales: measuring the effect of retail advertising via a controlled experiment on yahoo! *Quantitative Marketing and Economics*, 12(3):235–266.

Jura Liaukonyte, Thales Teixeira, and Kenneth C Wilbur. 2015. Television advertising and online shopping. *Marketing Science*, 34(3):311–330.

Xinyu Lu, Debarati Das, Jisu Huh, and Jaideep Srivastava. 2022. Influence of consumers' temporary affect on ad engagement: A computational research approach. *Journal of Advertising*, 51(3):352–368.

Anjali Midha. 2014. *Study: Exposure to TV Tweets drives consumers to take action - both on and off of Twitter*. https://tinyurl.com/32jcf5u9.

Katsiaryna Mirylenka, George Giannakopoulos, Themis Palpanas, et al. 2017. On classifier behavior in the presence of mislabeling noise. *Data mining and knowledge discovery*, 31(3):661–701.

Jamie Murphy, Charles Hofacker, and Richard Mizerski. 2006. Primacy and recency effects on clicking behavior. *Journal of Computer-Mediated Communication*, 11(2):522–535.

Dat Quoc Nguyen, Thanh Vu, and Anh Tuan Nguyen. 2020. Bertweet: A pre-trained language model for english tweets. *arXiv preprint arXiv:2005.10200*.

Suphakit Niwattanakul, Jatsada Singthongchai, Ekkachai Naenudorn, and Supachanun Wanapu. 2013. Using of jaccard coefficient for keywords similarity. In *Proceedings of the international multiconference of engineers and computer scientists*, volume 1, pages 380–384.

Abiola Obamuyide and Andreas Vlachos. 2018. Zero-shot relation classification as textual entailment. In *Proceedings of the First Workshop on Fact Extraction and VERification (FEVER)*, pages 72–78.

Nikolaos Pappas and James Henderson. 2019. Gile: A generalized input-label embedding for text classification. *Transactions of the Association for Computational Linguistics*, 7:139–155.

Mike Proulx and Stacey Shepatin. 2012. *Social TV: how marketers can reach and engage audiences by connecting television to the web, social media, and mobile*. John Wiley & Sons.

Shinjee Pyo, Eunhui Kim, et al. 2014. Lda-based unified topic modeling for similar tv user grouping and tv program recommendation. *IEEE transactions on cybernetics*, 45(8):1476–1490.

Nils Reimers and Iryna Gurevych. 2019. Sentence-bert: Sentence embeddings using siamese bert-networks. *arXiv preprint arXiv:1908.10084*.

José Hernández Santiago, Jair Cervantes, Asdrúbal López-Chau, and Farid García Lamont. 2012. Enhancing the performance of svm on skewed data sets by exciting support vectors. In *Ibero-American Conference on Artificial Intelligence*, pages 101–110. Springer.

Chi Sun, Xipeng Qiu, Yige Xu, and Xuanjing Huang. 2019. How to fine-tune bert for text classification? In *China National Conference on Chinese Computational Linguistics*, pages 194–206. Springer.

Talkwalker. 2020. *Talkwalker acquires Nielsen Social*. https://tinyurl.com/356pbt4t.

Nandan Thakur, Nils Reimers, Johannes Daxenberger, and Iryna Gurevych. 2020. Augmented sbert: Data augmentation method for improving bi-encoders for pairwise sentence scoring tasks. *arXiv preprint arXiv:2010.08240*.

Jesse Vig and Kalai Ramea. 2019. Comparison of transfer-learning approaches for response selection in multi-turn conversations. In *Workshop on DSTC7*.

Alex Wang. 2006. Advertising engagement: A driver of message involvement on message effects. *Journal of advertising research*, 46(4):355–368.

Thomas Wolf, Victor Sanh, Julien Chaumond, and Clement Delangue. 2019. Transfertransfo: A transfer learning approach for neural network based conversational agents. *arXiv preprint arXiv:1901.08149*.

Increasing Robustness for Cross-domain Dialogue Act Classification on Social Media Data

Marcus Vielsted **Nikolaj Wallenius** **Rob van der Goot**
IT University of Copenhagen
robv@itu.dk

Abstract

Automatically detecting the intent of an utterance is important for various downstream natural language processing tasks. This task is also called Dialogue Act Classification (DAC) and was primarily researched on spoken one-to-one conversations. The rise of social media has made this an interesting data source to explore within DAC, although it comes with some difficulties: non-standard form, variety of language types (across and within platforms), and quickly evolving norms. We therefore investigate the robustness of DAC on social media data in this paper. More concretely, we provide a benchmark that includes cross-domain data splits, as well as a variety of improvements on our transformer-based baseline. Our experiments show that lexical normalization is not beneficial in this setup, balancing the labels through resampling is beneficial in some cases, and incorporating context is crucial for this task and leads to the highest performance improvements (~7 F1 percentage points in-domain and ~20 cross-domain).[1]

1 Introduction

The rise of social media and digital assistants has led to new forms of communication, where an enormous amount of data is available, and automatically understanding this has become an important quest. Automatically identifying the intent of an utterance is therefore highly relevant for automatically interacting with humans (i.e. chatbots), or to analyze people's behaviour online. This task is also called Dialogue Act Classification (DAC). An example of two social media utterances annotated for DAC is shown in Table 1. DAC has traditionally mainly been investigated in the context of one-to-one spoken conversations, which is drastically different from one-to-many written conversations.

Utterance	Label
"We are free tomorrow night, right?"	*propositional question*
"No, the final Grand Prix is on!"	*disagreement*

Table 1: Example utterances annotated for DAC

On top of this, language use on social media is evolving rapidly (Eisenstein, 2013). This makes the automatic processing of this data complex, and the standard setup in Natural Language Processing (NLP), where taking train and test data from the same domain is less relevant. New platforms are created while old ones are abandoned, and each platform comes with its own language norms and varieties. Hence we argue for a setup with two test sets, one in-domain and one cross-domain, and aim to improve the robustness of the current state-of-the-art models in NLP, transformers (Wolf et al., 2020; Devlin et al., 2019).

This leads to our research question: **How can dialogue act classification models be made more robust for in-domain and cross-domain applications on social media data?**, followed by our sub-questions:

- *SQ1: Can lexical normalization improve the robustness of a DAC Model?*
- *SQ2: Can resampling of label distributions improve the robustness of a DAC Model?*
- *SQ3: Can incorporating utterance context improve the robustness of a DAC Model?*

Contributions 1) we provide an annotation schema adapted from the ISO 24617-2:2020 standard, which we modify to better fit the task of annotating social media data 2) we provide DAC-annotated datasets for two domains, one large enough to train on, and one from another

[1]Code/data available on https://github.com/marcusvielsted/DialogueActClassification

Proceedings of the 2022 COLING Workshop: The 8th Workshop on Noisy User-generated Text (W-NUT 2022), pages 180–193

domain/time-span to evaluate for robustness. 3) We evaluate and compare three methods to improve the robustness of DAC models: lexical normalization, label resampling, and exploiting context

2 Related Work

Social Media Despite the prevalence of social media in modern society, little research presently exists on the application of dialogue act classification on social media domains. The task has primarily been researched with a focus on verbal communication. Recently, some work has evaluated a CNN for Twitter data (Saha et al., 2019) and LSTMs on Reddit and Facebook data (Dutta et al., 2019). Unfortunately, these datasets are not publicly available.

Cross-domain In relation to the task of DAC, there has been limited research into model performance when predicting across unseen domains. Given the plurality of social media domains and their differences in communication structure, it is an opportune target for cross-domain classification. Dutta et al. (2019) evaluated cross-domain performance from Reddit to Facebook, reporting a drop of 5 absolute points F1 score, showing that the domains are relatively close. Additionally, cross-domain transfer learning between Human-Human and Human-Machine communication has been tested by Ahmadvand et al. (2019), who managed to outperform a state-of-the-art Hidden Markov Model through the use of transfer learning.

Context While some research into DAC has been applied to a single utterance in isolation of its context, dialogue acts are often context-dependent or context-sensitive (Bothe et al., 2018b). Although merely applying the preceding utterance provides performance improvements, Bothe et al. (2018a) demonstrate that using an utterance-level attention-based bidirectional recurrent neural network to analyze the importance of preceding utterances to classify the current one, provides additional performance. This is underlined by Raheja and Tetreault (2019), who use a conditional random field for sequence labeling of preceding utterances in combination with a self-attention recurrent neural network for text classification to achieve similar performance gains.

Transformer-Based Language Models As is the case for most NLP tasks, transformer-based language models finetuned on the target tasks have recently been shown to outperform previous approaches. This was shown by Duran et al. (2021), who comparatively analyzed six different supervised learning models and ten pre-trained language models on DAC; the best performance was obtained by BERT (Devlin et al., 2019) and RoBERTa (Liu et al., 2019) models.

3 Data

3.1 Datasets

Dialogue acts are commonly annotated on the smallest functional segment of a text that conveys an intended goal. Therefore, in this work, we annotate (multiple) utterances within a single social media post. For instance, while it is possible to encapsulate the following utterance within one single social media post: "Hi! How are you? Did you see the final Grand Prix last night?", should not be interpreted as a single utterance, but rather split up and interpreted as three separate utterances, as it aims to convey three different dialogue acts. Additionally, for all input datasets, we assume that context is provided. Therefore, if the information is not present in a dataset, we enrich the dataset with columns containing these.

We will make use of two social media domains. For in-domain DAC, this project utilized the "NPS Chat Corpus" (Eric Forsyth et al., 2008) as source domain, consisting of 10,567 textual utterances collected through various chat forums in 2006 and thus presents a unique collection of early-day social media data. As social media domains can vary substantially in language and structure, we considered the NPS Chat Corpus to be an interesting source domain for cross-domain application, as we hypothesize that the similarities in utterance structure compared to a modern domain, such as Reddit, would be small. Therefore, we would be able to investigate and evaluate our models against two drastically different social media domains, and test the robustness of a given model.

For our cross-domain target, we compiled a Reddit dataset from the "Reddit Corpus (small)" dataset from "Convokit" (CornellNLP, 2021). Reddit is particularly interesting as subreddits potentially have variances in their use of language, vocabulary, and communication structure. Therefore, we are able to get a broader representation of the social media landscape compared to using other social media domains. By imposing our rules for selecting relevant utterances, see Appendix A, we ended

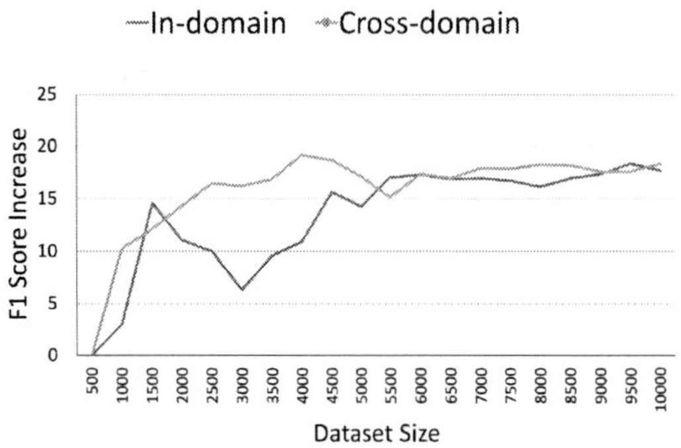

Figure 1: Learning curve of an SVM-based model on the NPS Chat corpus (taken from Wallenius and Vielsted (2021)).

Split	In-domain	Out-of-domain
train	4,800	—
dev	600	853
test	600	852

Table 2: Dataset splits for both in-domain and cross-domain.

up with a dataset consisting of 1,705 unique utterances from 50 unique threads within 37 different sub-reddits. Each thread is comprised of at least 20 consecutive utterances.

In previous research (Wallenius and Vielsted, 2021), it was shown that for a bag-of-words SVM model on the NPS-chat corpus, ~5,000 utterances is sufficient to train a competitive in-domain model (see Figure 1). Hence, we choose to annotate training data of a similar size (4,800 utterances).

Finally, in order to achieve a pure cross-domain setup for our model (i.e. no target domain data seen during development), we utilize a development split from the in-domain dataset for the tuning and model selection of all experiments. As such, the development set from the cross-domain dataset will only be used for the cross-domain model evaluations throughout the experiments. This is done in order to prevent overfitting of the cross-domain model improvement towards a single known cross-domain dataset. As such, this setup prevents over-estimation of performance for testing on additional domains not included in the experiments (Artetxe et al., 2020; Goot, 2021).

3.2 Guidelines

In relation to the task of DAC, various different annotation schemas have been developed, depending on the specific communication format for which a given task is being applied to. One of the first examples of DAC annotation schemas is the SWBD-DAMSL (Dan Jurafsky et al., 1997) intended for use on the Switchboard corpus (Potts, 1998). The Switchboard corpus consists of telephone conversations between two participants, i.e., a 1-1 bidirectional communicative relationship, which is reflected in the corresponding annotation schema.

Additional examples of annotation schemas include the MRDA tag set (Shriberg et al., 2004) created for dialogue annotation of large meetings, and the Posting Act Tagging schema (Wu et al., 2005) for early online chat forums. Though, in the examination of these annotation schemas, we deemed them unfit for this task as they emphasize traditional 1-1 bidirectional conversation formats. The Posting Act Tagging schema initially appeared to better utilized towards unidirectional 1-n social media data, as it was created to support tasks aimed towards earlier online chat forums.

However, having applied this tag-set in previous research, we found it inadequate for capturing many of the nuances of modern unidirectional social media posts and would skew the data towards one specific label. Therefore, the annotation schema utilized for this project has been adapted and modified from the ISO 24617-2:2020 dialogue act annotation standard (ISO 24617-2, 2020) in order to fit the specific task. This is done in an attempt to more accurately capture the nuances and account for the frequent use of unidirectional communication in modern social media data. The ISO 24617-2:2020 standard has specifically been made to address 3 shortcomings made from a previous version of the standard, as well as limitations from other annotation schemas. *"These experiences have brought to light (1) that the standard allowed dialogue act annotations that are slightly inaccurate in some respects, (2) that some applications would benefit from the availability of mechanisms for customizing the set of concepts defined in the standard, and (3) that certain use cases require the representation of functional dialogue act information to be extended with semantic content information."*(ISO 24617-2, 2020). Thus, we have chosen to adapt and modify this standard, as the schema has been designed to account for these limitations by being domain-independent, and encouraging customization and extension as indicated in point (2). This allows us to create an annotation

Label	Example
propositionalQuestion	"r u serious?"
setQuestion	"what list should i put him in?"
choiceQuestion	"shaken or stirred?"
inform	"i wonna chat"
elaborate	"and dr phil said so."
continuer	"I know, but it threw me"
agreement	"i agree"
disagreement	"no, I didnt even look."
correction	"i meant to write the word may."
greeting	"hey ladies"
goodbye	"see u all laters"
positiveExpression	"yay!"
negativeExpression	"ewwwww lol"
offer	"il get you a cheap flight to hell:)?"
suggestion	"We should have a club"
instruct	"shut the fuck up."
acceptAction	"yeah i should toss it"
declineAction	"i don't wanna"
misc	:tongue:

Table 3: Tag-set adapted from ISO24617-2:2020 with examples from NPS Chat Corpus.

schema best suited for the task of labeling social media data. An overview of the resulting label set is shown in Table 3.

Schema Adaptations The primary adaptation involves splitting the generalized `Inform` label into 3 separate labels. The standard definition of the "Inform" label is *"Communicative function of a dialogue act performed by the sender, S, in order to make the information contained in the semantic content available to the addressee, A; S assumes that the information is correct"* (ISO 24617-2, 2020). In addition to this, we wanted to incorporate context into the annotation schema and distinguish between what dialogue act a given utterance is responding to. The two labels `elaborate` and `continuer` were therefore added. These categories are distinguishable from inform in the context of the dialogue act. Both labels imply additional information being added to a given subject, while referencing an object previously mentioned in a conversation. The distinction between the two labels is that `elaborate` implies that a sender is elaborating upon their own previous utterance, whereas, `continuer` implies that a sender is continuing a previous utterance by a different sender. By splitting the `inform` label into 3 we are thus isolating `inform` for instances where the utterance can be read and fully understood without any context, which is a common occurrence in social media data where utterances are often unidirectional. Utterances labeled `inform` will therefore never reference named entities from previous utterances.

Other adaptations to the standard involves generalizing and unifying specific labels to narrow down the total number of labels. This was done in order to ensure that all labels were represented in a dataset. For this purpose, labels encompassed by the "Action-discussion functions" category in the ISO 24617-2 standard (ISO 24617-2, 2020) were reduced to `offer`, `suggestion`, `instruct`, `acceptAction` and `declineAction`. All `accept` and `decline` "Action-discussions functions" labels in the ISO 24617-2 were combined into the two labels, `acceptAction` and `declineAction`. The labels `answer`, `confirm` and `disconfirm` were removed as their functions could be incorporated into `continuer`, `agreement` and `disagreement`. Lastly, "Social-Expression" was incorporated through the labels, `greeting`, `goodbye`, `negativeExpression` and `positiveExpression`, as it is a significant part of communication on social media.

3.3 Annotation

The NPS dataset was annotated with the new tag-set by two annotators. Across 10 iterations with 50 utterances each, they consistently reached a Cohen's κ score of 0.83, which can be interpreted as an "almost perfect" agreement (Cohen, 1960). Given this trend and a stagnation in improvement, the remaining utterances were then annotated individually. The dataset statement (Bender and Friedman, 2018) can be found in Appendix B.

4 Models

4.1 Baseline Model

As this research explores methods to improve DAC performance and robustness for cross-domain social media data rather than reaching optimal scores for one specific domain, hyperparameters were not continuously optimized throughout the experiments. The hyperparameter setup for this project was therefore to establish an optimized baseline model and to freeze the hyperparameters in this configuration throughout the experiments. The method for obtaining the optimized hyperparame-

Hyperparameter	Value	Range
Batch Size	16	[16, 64]
Warmup Steps	125	[75, 125, 250]
Learning Rate	7e-5	[5e-5, 7e-5, 9e-5]
Weight Decay	0.5	[0.1, 0.5]

Table 4: Our hyperparameters test ranges and chosen values.

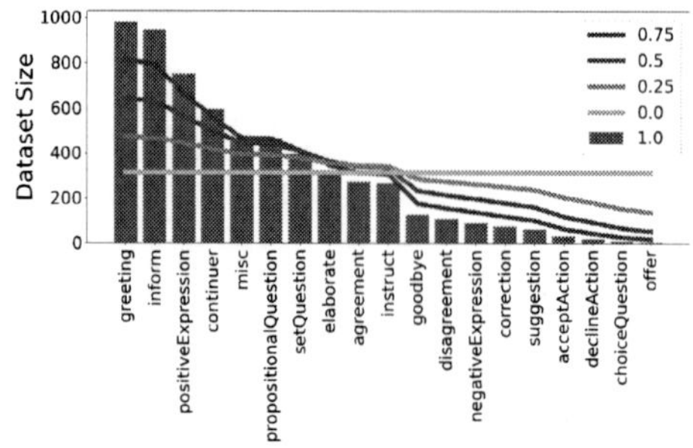

Figure 2: Label resampling of NPS Chat Corpus

ters was a three-step process. Firstly, we used the BERT-base model (Devlin et al., 2019) to find the optimal set of hyperparameters fine-tuned for this specific task. The hyperparameters optimized in this project can be seen in Table 4.

Secondly, having established the optimal hyperparameter values for the BERT-base model, we tested a total of 17 different transformer models (see Appendix C for the full list), to determine the best performing model(s). Lastly, the five best-performing transformer models from the previous test were then re-tested with the same range of hyperparameters as step one, to achieve a single optimal baseline model. By doing this, we could limit the scope of our model fine-tuning to 180 models instead of 612 models. Using this setup, the following five transformer models produced the best results: *"deberta v3 base"*, *"deberta v3 large"* (He et al., 2021), *"bertweet-base"* (Quoc Nguyen et al., 2020), *"bertweet-large"* (Quoc Nguyen et al., 2020), and *"bert-base-uncased"* (Devlin et al., 2019). Doing hyperparameter optimization for the five models, we found *deberta-v3-large* to provide the best performance. However, we selected **deberta-v3-base** as the model for our experiments. This selection was made due to computational restrictions, limiting the number of large models that we would be able to fine-tune and test. To support this selection, the large version was shown to be only slightly better, with an F1 score of 0.325 percentage-points points higher than the base model, which scored **77.11** F1 in-domain and **53.92** F1 cross-domain averaged over five seeds.

4.2 Lexical Normalization

As a result of the informal nature of social media data, utterances often include abbreviations, slang, and misspellings. These language variations already constitute a significant challenge for traditional NLP models trained on chronological text (Baldwin et al., 2013; Eisenstein, 2013). Moreover, language variations potentially pose an even greater challenge for cross-domain application, since it involves two different domains, likely resulting in more Out-Of-Vocabulary (OOV) tokens. Therefore, we hypothesized that applying lexical normalization on both our source and target domains could unify their vocabularies, thus increasing the token overlap and improving our model performance. An example of manually annotated normalization is:

Original: "any ladis wanna chat?"

LexNorm: "any ladies want to chat?"

For this task, we used the lexical normalization tool **MoNoise** (Van Der Goot, 2019), which produces performance on par with the state-of-the-art for English data (van der Goot et al., 2021). We use the publicly available MoNoise model for English, trained on data from Li and Liu (2014), to create parallel datasets for each domain with normalized text. This allows us to continuously test the results of lexical normalization, both in isolation and in combination with methods described in Section 4.

4.3 Multinomial Resampling

For cross-domain applications, we assume that label distributions within the source domain and target domain differ. In order to negate a potential labelling bias towards specific classes, we hypothesized that having more balanced and aligned label distributions between the datasets would improve model robustness. For this purpose, we resampled our datasets with respect to the annotated labels and according to a multinomial distribution. Using a multinomial resampling algorithm, each label is resampled according to the probability of its occurrence in our dataset:

$$\frac{1}{p_i} * \frac{p_i^\alpha}{\sum_i p_i^\alpha}$$

Utterance: I have never used elbow	
Context	Utt. Label
You only scored the goal because you used your elbow	`disagreement`
Did you use your hands or elbows to get up there?	`inform`

Table 5: Impact of differing contexts on dialogue acts. Note that the label column indicates the label of the original utterance

where p_i represents the probability that a random sample corresponds to the label i and α is a hyperparameter, for our sample smoothing function, to determine the proportional degree to resample. $\alpha = 1.0$ corresponds to the pre-existing distribution, and $\alpha = 0.0$ corresponds to an equal distribution for all labels. The effect of α on the training data distribution is visualized in Figure 2.

4.4 Utterance Context

Motivated by the defintion of the task and previous work (Section 2), we hypothesized that integrating context into the model might increase robustness. Table 5 exemplifies this: if isolated from context, it is unclear which label is correct for the utterance. We found three different context elements to be relevant. **context_Label:** the given classification label for the utterance to which a given utterance responds. **context_Text:** the actual utterance text a given utterance is responding to. **context_Sender:** a binary value specifying whether the sender of the context utterance is the same as the sender for a given utterance. This would be the case if a participant responds to their own prior utterance.

These three context elements are concatenated to the text and are separated with the [SEP] token. A total of 15 permutations of the three elements were then combined either pre or post the input text, thus resulting in 30 different context configurations. An additional permutation was added for no context elements (overview in Appendix D).

Gold vs. Predicted Context Label Out of our three context elements described above, context_Text & context_Sender can be easily generated using the utterance_ID. context_Label, however, is not that easily generated: it requires either manual annotation or an iteration of model predictions for the whole dataset. Therefore, our dataset has two different context_Label columns, *Gold* and *Predicted*. The *Gold* labels are used as a baseline to compare the performance for the *Predicted* labels, and are therefore only for analytical importance. The *Gold* labels were manually annotated, when the dataset was annotated. We obtained the *Predicted* labels through a five-fold cross-validation setup on our training data, where we trained on 80% and predicted a label on the remaining 20%. For each fold, we instantiated a new optimized baseline model, see section 4.1, so as to avoid overfitting.

	In-domain	Cross-domain
Base	77.11±1.85	53.92±1.06
+Norm	76.81±0.95	54.02±0.72

Table 6: Average results of lexical normalization in isolation in-domain & cross-domain (dev).

5 Results

All results reported are average macro-F1 scores over 5 random seeds unless mentioned otherwise. As mentioned in Section 3, we always used the in-domain dev-set for model picking, as well as for hyperparameter tuning. We first evaluate each of our proposed improvements (Section 5.1-Section 5.3). Then, we attempt to combine our methods (Section 5.4), and confirm our findings on the test data (Section 5.5). We use Almost Stochastic Order (ASO) for significance testing (Dror et al., 2019) as implemented by Ulmer et al. (2022) over the random seeds, and with an epsilon (ϵ) smaller than 0.5 we reject the null hypothesis.

5.1 Lexical Normalization

As shown in Table 6, we observed a performance decrease in F1 score of .3 percentage points in-domain and a negligible gain of 0.1 percentage points for cross-domain when normalizing the train and dev data. Based on these scores, we conclude that lexical normalization is not beneficial for DAC in our setup. Because the in-domain results show an opposite trend as we hypothesized, namely that normalization is not useful, we do an ASO significance test to confirm whether using the original data is stochastically dominant over using the normalized data. This test resulted in a minimum epsilon of 0.0, and we can thus confirm that normalization leads to lower scores, whereas the cross-domain differences were shown not to be significant.

	In-domain	Cross-domain
Base	77.11±1.85	53.92±1.06
Resample	78.50±1.80	55.54±1.31

Table 7: Scores on the in-domain and cross-domain data when using resampling compared to our baseline (dev). Resampling α is 0.9 and 0.8 respectively.

Setup	#cont.	F1
Baseline In-domain	—	77.11
Gold In-domain	27	85.39
Pred In-domain	27	86.22
Baseline Cross-domain	—	53.92
Gold Cross-domain	14	76.35
Pred Cross-domain	22	76.35

Table 8: Best performing context configuration for all four setups. **The 3 context configs (#cont.) used are:**
27: [Context Sender + Text + Label] Post Input Text
22: [Context Label + Sender + Text] Post Input Text
14: [Context Sender + Label + Text] Pre Input Text.

Feature	In-domain	Cross-domain
Context Conf.	[19, 23, 26, 27, 31]	[11, 19, 22, 23, 31]
Context label	[Gold, Predicted]	[Gold, Predicted]
Resampling α	[.95, .9, .75, .65, .6]	[.95, .9, .85, .7, .4]
Normalization	[+,-]	[+,-]

Table 9: Feature setup for combined models. The exact context configurations can be found in Appendix D, but all of the ones in this table use all three context elements.

In-domain			Cross-domain		
#cont.	α	F1	#cont.	α	F1
27	1.0	86.22	22	0.95	77.17
26	1.0	85.51	11	0.90	76.58
31	1.0	85.48	31	0.70	76.58
23	1.0	85.47	31	0.95	76.48
19	1.0	85.28	31	0.40	76.43

Table 10: The feature values for our best performing models for both our In-domain(ID) and for our Cross-domain(CD). All 10 models are using *predicted context labels* and the *non-normalized* dataset. #cont. refers to the context configuration.

5.2 Multinomial Resampling

For multinomial resampling, the best settings we found where $\alpha = 0.9$ for in-domain and $\alpha = 0.8$ for cross-domain (Section 6.3). Results show a substantial improvement, while keeping standard deviation in a similar range (Table 7). The resampling ratios (α) tested were 0.60, 0.80 and 0.90 for in-domain and 0.80, 0.85, 0.90 and 0.95 for cross-domain. These were selected, as they provided the best results for each domain. Significance tests resulted in a minimum epsilon value of 0.0 for in-domain and 0.02 for cross-domain compared to disabling the resampling ($\alpha = 1.0$), confirming that multinomial resampling is stochastically dominant.

5.3 Context

In Table 8, we report the results for the best permutation of all different elements of context we consider (Section 4.4). Full results can be found in Appendix D. Perhaps surprisingly, the predicted labels perform on par with the gold labels. We hypothesize that a partial explanation for this, is that our model performs very well on the informative labels our models require to learn context. i.e. labels `inform, instruct, offer, suggestion, setQuestion, propositionalQuestion` (see appendix E). We confirmed with an ASO significance test that gold labels are not outperforming predicted labels with an epsilon of 1.0.

5.4 Combining

We evaluated all combinations for the (max.) five setups for each of our robustness proposals, which are summarized in Table 9. Our best performing model reached a performance of 82.09 (in-domain) with the following setup from Table 9: [19, Predicted, 0.95, Original]. This score is lower than our previous highest score, achieved when only using context, see Table 8. On average, the top five feature setups combining resampling and context tested 2.4 percentage points below the same feature setup without resampling. This reduction in score when combining context and resampling could potentially be explained by the two features achieving improvements in similar situations, and are thus not complementary. For the cross-domain experiments, the label resampling still contributes, as the best five combined models (shown in Table 10) outperform the 76.35 reported in Table 8.

5.5 Test Data

On the test data (Table 11), we see that the model slightly overfits on the in-domain dev data (from the lower scores on test), but this does not transfer

Model	In-domain Dev	In-domain Test	Cross-domain Dev	Cross-domain Test
Baseline	77.11	76.27	53.92	55.17
LexNorm	76.81	74.99	54.02	53.35
Resample	78.17	79.09	54.91	55.67
Context	84.42	83.83	75.01	75.18
Best	84.42	83.83	75.70	75.64

Table 11: Development and Test scores for In-Domain & Cross-Domain for selected models.

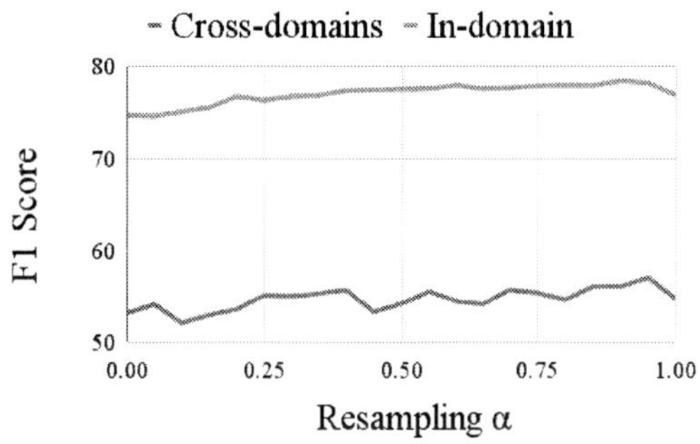

Figure 3: Results of Resampling in isolation in-domain & cross-domain.

to the cross-domain setup (where test>dev). Furthermore, the results align with our observations on the test data: normalization is not useful, resampling benefits performance to some extent, and the context is most crucial for performance. Furthermore, combining context and resampling does not lead to improved performance.

6 Analysis

As our standard deviations were relatively small and to simplify our analyses (and for computational efficiency), all results in this section are obtained over one seed.

6.1 Baseline model

In Appendix E, Figure 6 and 7 we show confusion matrices for both domain's baseline models predictions. As can be seen from these matrices, our baseline models have mostly certain classes with reoccurring mislabeling. These classes with reoccurring mislabeling cover the labels where context is a distinguishing factor, and where the variations of the input text between the labels is often minor. For this reason, it was expected for the baseline to struggle to distinguish between the labels `inform`, `continuer` & `elaborate`, without the addition of context.

The classes with reoccurring mislabeling are most evident for the cross-domain baseline model. We hypothesize that one reason for this could be that the utterance variations within each label between our in-domain train-set and dev-set is smaller compared to the difference between our in-domain train-set and our cross-domain dev-set. Therefore, our in-domain model would more likely have been trained on similar label tendencies as the one present in the in-domain dev-set, compared to our cross-domain model. This argument underlines that social media domains are constantly changing, and confirms the importance of cross-domain evaluation.

6.2 Lexical Normalization

The, perhaps surprisingly, negative results obtained when using lexical normalization can be explained by a variety of reasons: 1) performance of the normalization model, as it is used out-of-domain (it is trained on Twitter), performance might be suboptimal. Upon inspection, we found that the model is too conservative, and many non-standard words are not normalized. 2) removal of information, by normalizing we are essentially removing information, for example: "YOU DID" could be interpreted as a `propositionalQuestion` whereas writing "you did" is more likely to be interpreted as a `continuer`. 3) perhaps word overlap has become less important since modern language models use sub-words.

6.3 Resampling

As the resampling α determines the degree to which the label distribution is normalized, we have tested the full range of resampling ratio (from $\alpha = 0.0$ to $\alpha = 1.0$) in increments of 0.05. From these results, as shown in Figure 3, we were able to identify the trend that a lower resampling ratio (i.e., higher α) provides the biggest performance increase for both in-domain and cross-domain. Focusing on the in-domain line, we see that lower rates consistently perform worse, which can be explained by the fact that the label distribution of the in-domain dev data is similar to the train data, and changing this makes the distribution more distant. On the dev data, there is a slightly increasing trend up to $\alpha = 0.90$. The difference between 1.0 is larger compared to the in-domain line. There is a drop > 0.90 on both dev-sets. As shown in

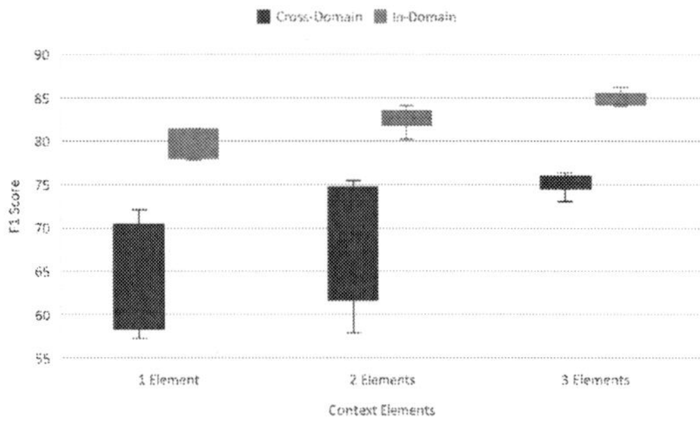

Figure 4: Effect of using different amount of context elements on F1 score.

Figure 2, our dataset has an unequal distribution in label classes, where labels such as `offer` and `choiceQuestion` are much less occurring than `greeting` and `inform`. We hypothesize that with such a label distribution as our NPS dataset, our model does not have enough training data for these rare classes, thus not being able to accurately predict on these. By applying a resampling ratio where one achieves a balance between aligning the training data with the dev-data and increasing the occurrences of rare labels, we get the most out of multinomial resampling.

6.4 Context

The results of all our permutations of using the context are plotted in boxplots in Figure 4. We summarize the results over the number of added elements, and plot quartiles. The trend is clear: more context information leads to higher performance, and in the case of the cross-domain results, all elements are necessary to obtain stable results. When inspecting the individual scores (Appendix D), we can conclude that the text of the previous utterance is the most important context feature.

7 Conclusion

Firstly, we found that lexical normalization does not constitute a stochastically dominant feature for cross-domain applications, but rather had a negative effect on F1 performance. By applying lexical normalization, the performance dropped for both our in-domain data, while staying the same for our cross-domain dataset. Additionally, while it decreased the standard deviation for our in-domain model, it almost doubled the standard deviations for our cross-domain model. We can therefore state that lexical normalization does not improve the robustness nor increase the F1 score of either in-domain or cross-domain DAC model when trained on social media data.

Secondly, we have seen that multinomial resampling is a stochastically dominant feature in isolation with regard to increasing the F1 score for both in-domain and cross-domain. However, for cross-domain applications it increased the standard deviation drastically, while maintaining the same standard deviation for in-domain usage. Used in combination with context for cross-domain applications, we were able to both increase the F1 score marginally, while reducing the standard deviation from 0.92% to 0.42%. We can therefore conclude that multinomial resampling can increase the performance and robustness of a DAC model for cross-domain applications when combined with context as a feature, but should not be included for in-domain models.

Thirdly, we have observed that context has been the most significant contributing factor to the large performance increase of both in-domain and cross-domain models. We have shown that additional context elements in our setup increase robustness and constitutes a stochastically dominant feature compared to fewer context elements. Improving the F1 scores by 7.28 percentage-points for in-domain and 21.23 percentage-points for cross-domain, while also reducing the standard deviation to 0.65% for in-domain and 0.92% cross-domain, we have proved that context can improve the robustness of DAC models for cross-domain as well as in-domain applications.

Acknowledgements

We would like to thank Mike Zhang and the anonymous reviewers for their comments on earlier versions of this paper. We also acknowledge the IT University of Copenhagen HPC for the resources made available for conducting the research reported in this paper.

References

Ali Ahmadvand, Jason Ingyu Choi, and Eugene Agichtein. 2019. Contextual dialogue act classification for open-domain conversational agents. *SIGIR 2019 - Proceedings of the 42nd International ACM SIGIR Conference on Research and Development in Information Retrieval*, pages 1273–1276.

Mikel Artetxe, Sebastian Ruder, Dani Yogatama, Gorka Labaka, and Eneko Agirre. 2020. A call for more rigor in unsupervised cross-lingual learning. In *Proceedings of the 58th Annual Meeting of the Association for Computational Linguistics*, pages 7375–7388, Online. Association for Computational Linguistics.

Timothy Baldwin, Paul Cook, Marco Lui, Andrew MacKinlay, and Li Wang. 2013. How Noisy Social Media Text, How Different Social Media Sources?

Emily M. Bender and Batya Friedman. 2018. Data statements for natural language processing: Toward mitigating system bias and enabling better science. *Transactions of the Association for Computational Linguistics*, 6:587–604.

Chandrakant Bothe, Sven Magg, Cornelius Weber, and Stefan Wermter. 2018a. Conversational Analysis using Utterance-level Attention-based Bidirectional Recurrent Neural Networks. *Proceedings of the Annual Conference of the International Speech Communication Association, INTERSPEECH*, 2018-September:996–1000.

Chandrakant Bothe, Cornelius Weber, Sven Magg, and Stefan Wermter. 2018b. A context-based approach for dialogue act recognition using simple recurrent neural networks. In *Proceedings of the Eleventh International Conference on Language Resources and Evaluation (LREC 2018)*, Miyazaki, Japan. European Language Resources Association (ELRA).

Jacob Cohen. 1960. A Coefficient of Agreement for Nominal Scales. *Educational and Psychological Measurement*, 20(1):37–46.

CornellNLP. 2021. ConvoKit version 2.5.1.

Dan Jurafsky, Liz Shriberg, and Debra Biasca. 1997. Switchboard SWBD-DAMSL Shallow-DiscourseFunction Annotation Coders Manual. *SRI International.*

Jacob Devlin, Ming Wei Chang, Kenton Lee, and Kristina Toutanova. 2019. BERT: Pre-training of Deep Bidirectional Transformers for Language Understanding. *NAACL HLT 2019 - 2019 Conference of the North American Chapter of the Association for Computational Linguistics: Human Language Technologies - Proceedings of the Conference*, 1:4171–4186.

Rotem Dror, Segev Shlomov, and Roi Reichart. 2019. Deep Dominance - How to Properly Compare Deep Neural Models. *ACL 2019 - 57th Annual Meeting of the Association for Computational Linguistics, Proceedings of the Conference*, pages 2773–2785.

Nathan Duran, Steve Battle, Jim Smith, and Nathan Duran. 2021. Sentence encoding for Dialogue Act classification. *Natural Language Engineering*, pages 1–30.

Subhabrata Dutta, Tanmoy Chakraborty, and Dipankar Das. 2019. How Did the Discussion Go: Discourse Act Classification in Social Media Conversations. In *Linking and Mining Heterogeneous and Multi-view Data*, chapter 6, pages 137–160. Springer International Publishing.

Jacob Eisenstein. 2013. What to do about bad language on the internet. In *Proceedings of the 2013 Conference of the North American Chapter of the Association for Computational Linguistics: Human Language Technologies*, pages 359–369. Association for Computational Linguistics.

Eric Forsyth, Jane Lin, and Craig Martell. 2008. The NPS Chat Corpus.

Rob van der Goot. 2021. We Need to Talk About train-dev-test Splits. In *Proceedings of the 2021 Conference on Empirical Methods in Natural Language Processing*, pages 4485–4494. Association for Computational Linguistics.

Pengcheng He, Jianfeng Gao, and Weizhu Chen. 2021. DeBERTaV3: Improving DeBERTa using ELECTRA-Style Pre-Training with Gradient-Disentangled Embedding Sharing.

ISO 24617-2. 2020. ISO 24617-2 - Language resource management - Semantic annotation framework - Part 2: Dialogue acts. *ISO*, pages 1–96.

Chen Li and Yang Liu. 2014. Improving text normalization via unsupervised model and discriminative reranking. In *Proceedings of the ACL 2014 Student Research Workshop*, pages 86–93, Baltimore, Maryland, USA. Association for Computational Linguistics.

Yinhan Liu, Myle Ott, Naman Goyal, Jingfei Du, Mandar Joshi, Danqi Chen, Omer Levy, Mike Lewis, Luke Zettlemoyer, and Veselin Stoyanov. 2019. Roberta: A robustly optimized bert pretraining approach. *arXiv preprint arXiv:1907.11692*.

Christopher Potts. 1998. The Switchboard Dialog Act Corpus.

Dat Quoc Nguyen, Thanh Vu, Anh Tuan Nguyen, and VinAI Research. 2020. BERTweet: A pre-trained language model for English Tweets. In *Proceedings of the 2020 Conference on Empirical Methods in Natural Language Processing: System Demonstrations*, pages 9–14. Association for Computational Linguistics.

Vipul Raheja and Joel Tetreault. 2019. Dialogue Act Classification with Context-Aware Self-Attention. In *Proceedings of the 2019 Conference of the North American Chapter of the Association for Computational Linguistics: Human Language Technologies, Volume 1 (Long and Short Papers)*, volume 1, pages 3727–3733. Association for Computational Linguistics.

Tulika Saha, Sriparna Saha, and Pushpak Bhattacharyya. 2019. Tweet Act Classification : A Deep Learning based Classifier for Recognizing Speech Acts in Twitter. In *2019 International Joint Conference on Neural Networks (IJCNN)*, volume 2019-July. Institute of Electrical and Electronics Engineers Inc.

Elizabeth Shriberg, Raj Dhillon, Sonali Bhagat, Jeremy Ang, and Hannah Carvey. 2004. The ICSI Meeting Recorder Dialog Act (MRDA) Corpus. In *Proceedings of the 5th SIGdial Workshop on Discourse and Dialogue at HLT-NAACL 2004*, pages 97–100. OSD or Non-Service DoD Agency, Association for Computational Linguistics.

Dennis Ulmer, Christian Hardmeier, and Jes Frellsen. 2022. deep-significance-easy and meaningful statistical significance testing in the age of neural networks. *arXiv preprint arXiv:2204.06815*.

Rob Van Der Goot. 2019. MoNoise: A Multi-lingual and Easy-to-use Lexical Normalization Tool. *ACL 2019 - 57th Annual Meeting of the Association for Computational Linguistics, Proceedings of System Demonstrations*, pages 201–206.

Rob van der Goot, Alan Ramponi, Arkaitz Zubiaga, Barbara Plank, Benjamin Muller, Iñaki San Vicente Roncal, Nikola Ljubešić, Özlem Çetinoğlu, Rahmad Mahendra, Talha Çolakoğlu, Timothy Baldwin, Tommaso Caselli, and Wladimir Sidorenko. 2021. MultiLexNorm: A shared task on multilingual lexical normalization. In *Proceedings of the Seventh Workshop on Noisy User-generated Text (W-NUT 2021)*, pages 493–509, Online. Association for Computational Linguistics.

Nikolaj Wallenius and Marcus Lind Vielsted. 2021. Dialogue act classification for social media data.

Thomas Wolf, Lysandre Debut, Victor Sanh, Julien Chaumond, Clement Delangue, Anthony Moi, Pierric Cistac, Tim Rault, Remi Louf, Morgan Funtowicz, Joe Davison, Sam Shleifer, Patrick von Platen, Clara Ma, Yacine Jernite, Julien Plu, Canwen Xu, Teven Le Scao, Sylvain Gugger, Mariama Drame, Quentin Lhoest, and Alexander Rush. 2020. Transformers: State-of-the-art natural language processing. In *Proceedings of the 2020 Conference on Empirical Methods in Natural Language Processing: System Demonstrations*, pages 38–45, Online. Association for Computational Linguistics.

Tianhao Wu, Faisal M. Khan, Todd A. Fisher, Lori A. Shuler, and William M. Pottenger. 2005. Posting Act Tagging Using Transformation-Based Learning. In *Foundations of Data Mining and knowledge Discovery*, pages 319–331. Springer, Berlin, Heidelberg.

Appendix

A Reddit Dataset Creation

"Reddit Corpus (small)" is composed of 297,132 utterances (Posts) from 8,286 conversations (threads) within 100 unique Subreddits. From this starting point, we identified all threads with more than 40 utterances. This limit was set in order to get longer threads with potentially more conversations containing bidirectional communication, which would enable us to better investigate context among utterances. Despite this project splitting each social media post up into multiple different utterances based on its shortest possible functional segments, we still wanted posts with a shorter length, as we hypnotized this would entail a more accurate real world version of singular communicative functions. Furthermore, we hypothesized that relying on shorter posts would balance out the label distribution, as this implies a greater number of different speakers. Therefore, we chose to include all threads where the mean length of posts were between 50 and 150 characters.

Having compiled a list of available treads abiding by the aforementioned rules, we selected 50 random threads, and included the first 20 consecutive utterances from these. This resulted in a total of 1000 posts which, after splitting each post up into its smallest possible communicative function, returns a dataset consisting of 1705 unique utterances from 50 Subreddits.

B Dataset Statement

Following (Bender and Friedman, 2018), the following outlines the data statement:

A. CURATION RATIONALE Collection of text samples from different social media domains. The first part (NPS Chat corpus) was sampled from a variety of platforms in 2006, and the collection of the Reddit samples is a random sample of long threads taken from 100 different Subreddits (more detail in Appendix A)

B. LANGUAGE VARIETY Most of the data is filtered to be English, it is unknown which variety of English is dominant.

C. SPEAKER DEMOGRAPHIC Unknown.

D. ANNOTATOR DEMOGRAPHIC Two software-design master students, both have previous experience with annotating for dialogue act classification. Native language: Danish, but proficient in English.

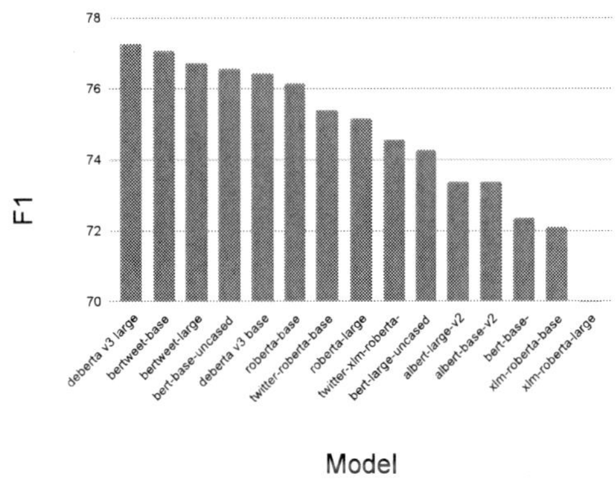

Figure 5: List of all the models used for testing within our project

E. SPEECH SITUATION Online, most probably the old data is typed from a keyboard, whereas the Reddit part of the data might come from a larger variety of devices.

F. TEXT CHARACTERISTICS There could be a variety of noise in the utterances, as well as utterances that contain mainly canonical text. No filtering on style was done.

C Model Selections

Figure 5 show the performance of all of the 17 language models evaluated on the in-domain dev data.

D Context Configurations

Table 12 shows the exact order of each of our context configurations, and their corresponding scores when using gold or predicted context labels for both in-domain and cross-domain. Note that these results are not averaged over 5 random seeds as the results in the main paper, thus the context configurations that do not use context labels still differ between Gold and Pred.

E Confusion matrices

Figure 6 and Figure 7 show the confusion matrices of our baseline model on the In-domain and Cross-domain dev sets.

Id	Context config	Position	# elems.	In-domain Gold	In-domain Pred	Cross-domain Gold	Cross-domain Pred
1	No Context Included		0	76.32	81.41	54.21	52.69
2	Only Context Label	Pre	1	78.02	76.77	58.35	63.54
3	Only Context Sender	Pre	1	79.27	80.84	70.39	69.80
4	Only Context Text	Pre	1	80.72	77.79	60.47	58.72
5	Only Context Label	Post	1	78.76	81.35	60.24	62.12
6	Only Context Sender	Post	1	79.90	79.51	71.37	72.11
7	Only Context Text	Post	1	79.39	78.05	61.76	57.23
8	Context [Label + Sender]	Pre	2	82.50	83.53	72.82	74.01
9	Context [Label + Text]	Pre	2	81.07	82.55	61.11	61.28
10	Context [Label + Sender + Text]	Pre	3	82.93	84.17	74.49	74.41
11	Context [Label + Text + Sender]	Pre	3	83.71	85.28	73.97	75.77
12	Context [Sender + Label]	Pre	2	81.38	83.35	73.17	74.98
13	Context [Sender + Text]	Pre	2	83.73	80.23	75.19	74.71
14	Context [Sender + Label + Text]	Pre	3	83.68	84.09	76.35	74.84
15	Context [Sender + Text + Label]	Pre	3	84.21	84.42	73.77	75.23
16	Context [Text + Sender]	Pre	2	83.86	81.32	75.89	70.99
17	Context [Text + Label]	Pre	2	81.37	82.64	60.97	62.90
18	Context [Text + Sender + Label]	Pre	3	83.19	85.17	75.74	73.07
19	Context [Text + Label + Sender]	Pre	3	83.96	85.28	75.90	76.28
20	Context [Label + Sender]	Post	2	82.54	83.63	71.22	74.33
21	Context [Label + Text]	Post	2	79.83	82.14	59.39	61.33
22	Context [Label + Sender + Text]	Post	3	83.43	84.12	75.07	76.35
23	Context [Label + Text + Sender]	Post	3	84.41	85.47	76.14	75.72
24	Context [Sender + Label]	Post	2	82.05	84.10	75.58	75.45
25	Context [Sender + Text]	Post	2	83.18	81.70	76.02	74.68
26	Context [Sender + Label + Text]	Post	3	83.42	85.51	74.97	74.15
27	Context [Sender + Text + Label]	Post	3	85.40	86.22	73.64	74.99
28	Context [Text + Sender]	Post	2	83.13	82.71	74.59	72.03
29	Context [Text + Label]	Post	2	78.64	82.27	59.28	57.91
30	Context [Text + Sender + Label]	Post	3 3	82.76	84.92	74.08	75.00
31	Context [Text + Label + Sender]	Post	3	83.97	85.48	75.20	76.02

Table 12: Results for all our context configurations (Dev). Position: pre means before the input text, post behind the input text.

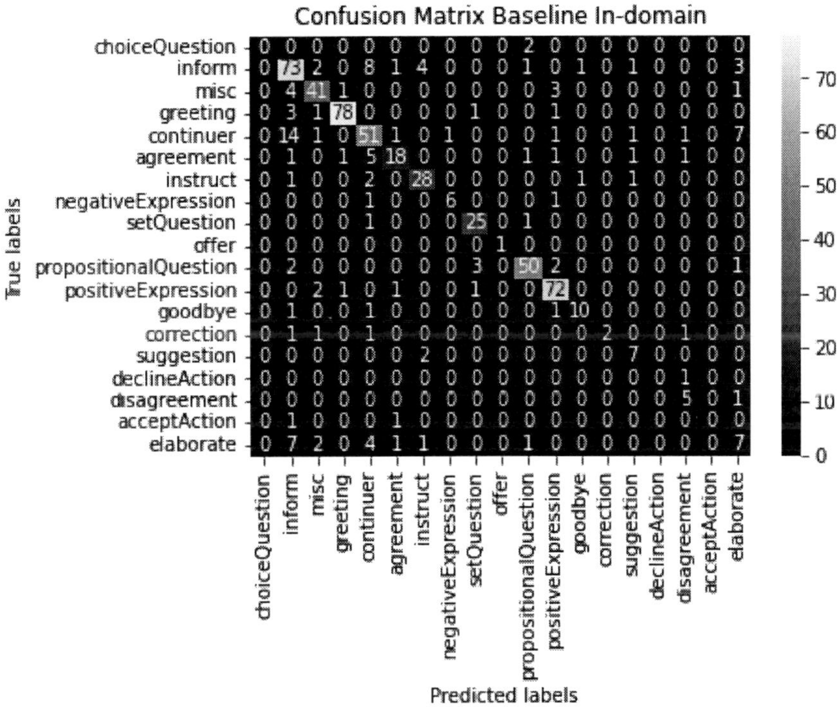

Figure 6: Confusion matrix for our baseline model for In-domain

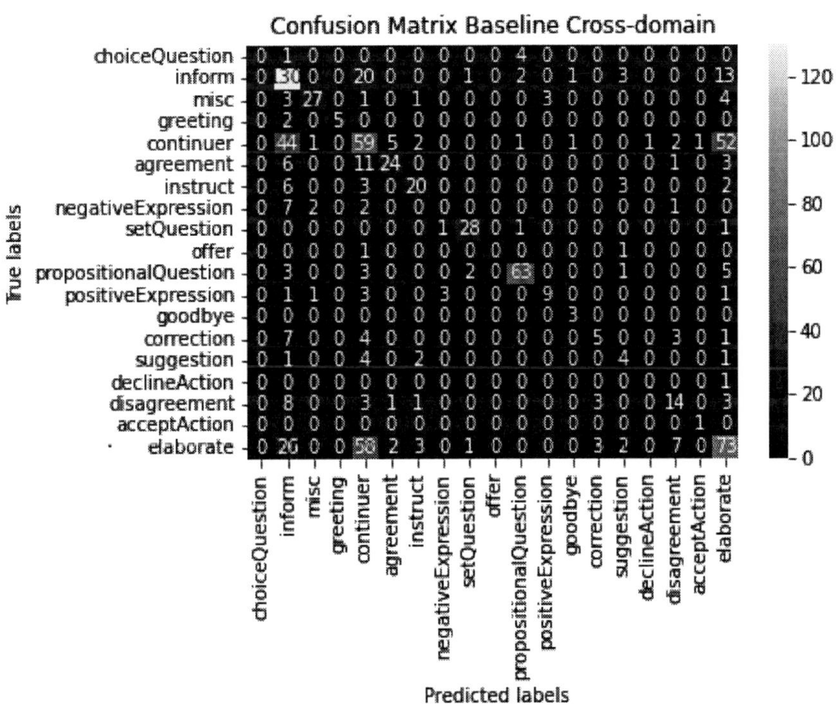

Figure 7: Confusion matrix for our baseline model for Cross-domain

Disfluency Detection for Vietnamese

Mai Hoang Dao[1], Thinh Hung Truong[2], Dat Quoc Nguyen[1]
[1]VinAI Research, Vietnam; [2]The University of Melbourne, Australia
{v.maidh3, v.datnq9}@vinai.io; hungthinht@student.unimelb.edu.au

Abstract

In this paper, we present the first empirical study for Vietnamese disfluency detection. To conduct this study, we first create a disfluency detection dataset for Vietnamese, with manual annotations over two disfluency types. We then empirically perform experiments using strong baseline models, and find that: automatic Vietnamese word segmentation improves the disfluency detection performances of the baselines, and the highest performance results are obtained by fine-tuning pre-trained language models in which the monolingual model PhoBERT for Vietnamese does better than the multilingual model XLM-R.

1 Introduction

Humans do not always exactly predetermine what they intend to say, hence leading to interruptions in natural conversations. This phenomena is informally referred to as *disfluency* (Godfrey and Holliman, 1993; Shriberg, 1994). Disfluencies are highly ubiquitous in human conversations. With the increasing popularity of task-oriented dialogue systems, it is essential to improve the capacity of the systems in dealing with many kinds of distractor sources. Note that a vast majority of spoken language understanding (SLU) models used in the dialogue systems are trained on well-formed input text without disfluencies. However, there is a significant mismatch between the fluent training corpora and the real-world inputs of disfluent utterances/speech transcripts for those models, resulting in serious performance degradation in practical applications. Hence, disfluency detection that identifies (and then removes) disfluencies to produce fluent versions of the disfluent inputs is a crucial component of real-world SLU/dialogue systems.

Almost all benchmark datasets for the disfluency detection task, such as Switchboard (Godfrey and Holliman, 1993), CALLHOME (Canavan et al., 1997) and Child (Tran et al., 2020), are exclusively for English. Therefore, the development of disfluency detection systems has been largely limited to the English language. From a societal, linguistic, machine learning, cultural and normative, and cognitive perspective (Ruder, 2020), it is worth investigating the disfluency detection task for languages other than English, e.g. Vietnamese. In particular, it is interesting to study whether the difference in linguistic characteristics might add difficulties to developing disfluency detection systems to non-English languages, e.g. investigating the influence of Vietnamese word segmentation (Dien et al., 2001) on the Vietnamese disfluency detection task. Despite being the 17th most spoken language in the world (Eberhard et al., 2019) with about 100M speakers, to our best knowledge, there is no previous study as well as no public dataset available for disfluency detection in Vietnamese.

We fill the gap in the literature by conducting the first empirical study for Vietnamese disfluency detection. To conduct this study, we first create a dataset for Vietnamese disfluency detection through two manual phases, including: (i) adding contextual disfluencies into an existing fluent dataset of 5871 utterances (Dao et al., 2021), and (ii) annotating the added disfluencies with two different disfluency types. On our dataset, we then formulate the Vietnamese disfluency detection task as a sequence labeling problem and empirically investigate strong baselines, including BiLSTM-CNN-CRF (Ma and Hovy, 2016) and pre-trained language models XLM-R (Conneau et al., 2020) and PhoBERT (Nguyen and Nguyen, 2020). We find that: (i) automatic Vietnamese word segmentation helps improve disfluency detection performances, and (ii) the highest performance results are obtained by fine-tuning the pre-trained language models, in which the monolingual model PhoBERT outperforms the multilingual model XLM-R. We publicly release our dataset at: `https://github.com/VinAIResearch/PhoDisfluency`.

Proceedings of the 2022 COLING Workshop: The 8th Workshop on Noisy User-generated Text (W-NUT 2022), pages 194–200

2 Related work

Among disfluency detection datasets with manual annotations for English (Godfrey and Holliman, 1993; Canavan et al., 1997; Tran et al., 2020; Ostendorf and Hahn, 2013; Zayats et al., 2014), the Switchboard dataset (Godfrey and Holliman, 1993) is the most commonly used benchmark for developing and evaluating disfluency detection models. The disfluency detection models generally fall into three main categories of approaches based on noisy channel, parsing and sequence tagging. Noisy channel-based disfluency detection models use tree adjoining grammar-based channel models to assign high probabilities to exact copy reparandum words (Johnson and Charniak, 2004; Johnson et al., 2004), and also use language model scores as features to a MaxEnt reranker (Zwarts and Johnson, 2011; Jamshid Lou and Johnson, 2017). Parsing-based models detect disfluencies and the syntactic structure of the sentence utterance simultaneously (Rasooli and Tetreault, 2013; Honnibal and Johnson, 2014; Yoshikawa et al., 2016; Jamshid Lou and Johnson, 2020); however, these models require large annotated training datasets that contain both disfluencies and syntactic structures. Sequence tagging approaches formulate the disfluency detection task as a sequence labeling problem to label individual words by disfluency types or simply fluent/disfluent tags (Ostendorf and Hahn, 2013; Zayats et al., 2014; Jamshid Lou et al., 2018; Bach and Huang, 2019; Rocholl et al., 2021). Among the disfluency detection approaches, the sequence tagging ones that fine-tune pre-trained language models (Devlin et al., 2019) produce the state-of-the-art performances (Bach and Huang, 2019; Rocholl et al., 2021).

3 Our dataset

Our approach to creating a disfluency detection dataset for Vietnamese is first to manually add contextual disfluencies as distractors into an existing fluent dataset. This first phase is inspired by Gupta et al. (2021) who present a disfluent derivative of the question answering dataset SQUAD (Rajpurkar et al., 2016). We choose PhoATIS consisting of 5871 utterance transcripts (Dao et al., 2021) as our base fluent Vietnamese dataset. After adding disfluencies to PhoATIS, we manually annotate disfluent words using disfluency types.

3.1 Disfluency types

A standard annotation of disfluency structure (Shriberg, 1994) includes three annotation types: the Reparandum—to annotate word or words that the speaker intends to be abandoned or corrected by the following words; the (optional) Interregnum—to annotate filled pauses, discourse cue words and the like; and the (optional) Repair—to annotate words that are used to correct the reparandum. For example, in the utterance "cho tôi biết các chuyến bay đến đà nẵng vào ngày 12 mà không ngày 14 tháng sáu" (let me know the flights to da nang on 12th uh no 14th june): "ngày 12" (12th), "mà không" (uh no) and "ngày 14" (14th) can be labeled with types Reparandum, Interregnum and Repair, respectively. Note that as pointed out in (Ostendorf and Hahn, 2013; Zayats et al., 2016), most works on automatic disfluency detection are aimed at cleaning speech transcripts to obtain fluent versions for further processing by removing disfluent Reparandum and Interregnum words. For Vietnamese, we thus annotate data using only two disfluency types Reparandum (denoted by **RM** and illustrated in red text color) and Interregnum (denoted by **IM**, in blue text color).

3.2 Dataset construction

Adding contextual disfluencies: We divide the PhoATIS's training set into 5 non-overlapping and equal subsets and preserve its validation and test sets, resulting in 7 subsets that are used for crafting disfluencies. We employ 7 annotators who are undergraduate students strong in linguistics. Here, each annotator adds disfluent words to all fluent utterances in a subset. The annotators are required to generate a disfluent version of each original fluent utterance, which: (i) is semantically equivalent to the original one; (ii) is natural in terms of human usage, grammatical errors and meaningful distractors (i.e. the added disfluent words exist in real-world circumstances); (iii) contains disfluent words that are corrected by following intent or slot value keywords in the original utterance; (iv) contains both disfluent RM- and IM-type words where possible to obtain a non-trivial dataset.

Annotators are shown example disfluencies as illustrated in Table 1. The annotators are also asked to make sure that when removing all the added words in the disfluent version, we can obtain the exact original utterance. Once the adding process is completed, the first two authors manually verify

Example 1:
mã giá vé [RM: to] [IM: à xin lỗi tôi nhầm ý tôi là] qo nghĩa là gì
what does fare code [RM: to] [IM: uh sorry I really mean] qo stand for

Example 2:
có chuyến bay nào giữa thành phố hồ chí minh và [RM: hà] hà nội với một điểm dừng [RM: ở sân bay] [IM: ừm không] ở đà lạt không
is there a flight between ho chi minh city and [RM: ha] ha noi with a stopover [RM: at airport] [IM: uh no] at da lat

Example 3:
có [RM: sân bay] [IM: í lộn] hãng hàng không nào có các chuyến bay từ điện biên phủ [RM: đến quảng ninh] [IM: à chính xác là] đến quy nhơn khởi hành trước 6 giờ 30 phút sáng không
is there any [RM: airport] [IM: oops] airline that flies from dien bien phu [RM: to quang ninh] [IM: no actually] to quy nhon departing before 6:30 am

Example 4:
tôi muốn biết thông tin về [IM: ờm] chuyến bay từ hạ long [RM: đến] [IM: ờ] [RM: cát bà] [IM: ừm không tôi quên mất đến đâu nhỉ à đúng rồi] đến huế bay vào buổi sáng
i'd like information on [IM: uh] a flight from ha long [RM: to] [IM: uh] [RM: cat ba] [IM: uh no I forget the destination ah actually] to hue a morning flight

Table 1: Disfluent utterance examples with Reparandum (RM) annotations and Interregnum (IM) annotations in our dataset. "hồ chí minh" (ho chi minh), "hà nội" (ha noi), "đà lạt" (da lat), "điện biên phủ" (dien bien phu), "quảng ninh" (quang ninh), "quy nhơn" (quy nhon), "hạ long" (ha long), "cát bà" (cat ba) and "huế" (hue) are cities in Vietnam.

Statistics	Train	Valid.	Test	All
(1) # Utterances	4478	500	893	5871
(2) # Utt. w/ RM & IM	4447	499	891	5837
(3) # RM	4889	811	1049	6749
(4) # IM	5237	843	1135	7215
(5) Avg. Utt. length	22.1	24.1	22.2	22.3
(6) Avg. RM length	2.4	2.3	2.8	2.4
(7) Avg. IM length	2.8	2.6	2.9	2.8

Table 2: Statistics of our dataset. (1): The number of utterances. (2): The number of utterances that contain both RM and IM annotations. (3) and (4) denote the numbers of RM and IM annotations, respectively. (5), (6) and (7) denote the average lengths (i.e. numbers of syllable tokens) of an utterance, an RM annotation and an IM annotation, respectively.

each utterance to ensure that all the requirements are met, discuss ambiguous cases and make further revisions if needed, resulting in a dataset of 5871 disfluent utterances.

Annotation process: Each disfluent utterance is independently annotated by the first two authors who manually annotate disfluent words using the disfluency types RM and IM. We employ Cohen's kappa coefficient score (Cohen, 1960) to measure the inter-annotator agreement between the two annotators, obtaining a substantial agreement score of 0.78. Then the third author hosts and participates in a discussion session with the first two authors to resolve annotation conflicts, resulting in a final gold dataset of 5871 disfluency-annotated utterances. Table 1 shows examples of gold annotated disfluent utterances in our dataset.

Note that when written in Vietnamese texts, the white space is used to mark word boundaries as well as to separate syllables that constitute words. Thus, the utterances in our dataset are presented at the syllable level for convenience in annotating disfluencies (e.g. the examples in Table 1). To obtain a word-level variant of the dataset, we perform automatic Vietnamese word segmentation by using RDRSegmenter (Nguyen et al., 2018; Vu et al., 2018). For example, a 7-syllable written text "sân bay quốc tế Tân Sơn Nhất" (Tan Son Nhat international airport) is word-segmented into 3-word text "sân_bay$_{\text{airport}}$ quốc_tế$_{\text{international}}$ Tân_Sơn_Nhất$_{\text{Tan_Son_Nhat}}$". Here, automatic word segmentation outputs do not affect the span boundaries of disfluency annotations.

3.3 Dataset statistics

Our disfluency detection dataset for Vietnamese contains 5871 disfluency-annotated utterances, thus having a larger number of disfluent regions than Switchboard (2159), CALLHOME (1068), and Child (525). Statistic details of our dataset are reported in Table 2.

3.4 Discussion

Our approach that manually adds contextual disfluencies as distractors into the fluent utterances results in an artificially generated dataset. So our dataset might not correctly or fully reflect real-world scenarios where disfluencies in real-world speech might be more complex than the added contextual disfluencies in our dataset. Note that there is only one public Vietnamese speech dataset with manual transcripts used for automatic speech recognition,[1] however, the transcripts do not contain disfluencies. Thus, we could not annotate disfluencies on a real-world dataset. Our study is an attempt to imitate real-world speech and we will compare the artificially added disfluencies with the real-world disfluencies in future work.

4 Experiments

4.1 Experimental setup

Recall that the sequence labeling approaches fine-tuning pre-trained language models produce the state-of-the-art disfluency detection performances for English (Bach and Huang, 2019; Rocholl et al., 2021). Thus we formulate the Vietnamese disfluency detection task as a sequence labeling problem with the frequently used tagging scheme BIO. On our dataset, we empirically evaluate baselines that obtain competitive or state-of-the-art performances for other Vietnamese sequence labeling tasks (Nguyen and Nguyen, 2020; Dao et al., 2021; Truong et al., 2021), to investigate: (i) the influence of automatic word segmentation on Vietnamese (here, input utterances can be represented in either syllable or word level), and (ii) the effectiveness of pre-trained language models. Our baselines include BiLSTM-CNN-CRF (Ma and Hovy, 2016) and the pre-trained multilingual language model XLM-R (Conneau et al., 2020) and the pre-trained monolingual language model PhoBERT for Vietnamese (Nguyen and Nguyen, 2020). XLM-R and PhoBERT are multilingual and Vietnamese monolingual variants of the pre-trained language model RoBERTa (Liu et al., 2019). XLM-R is pre-trained on a 2.5TB multilingual dataset that contains 137GB of syllable-level Vietnamese texts, while PhoBERT is pre-trained on a 20GB word-level Vietnamese corpus.

We compute the Micro-average F_1 score on the validation set after each epoch, and we apply early stopping if there is no performance improvement after 5 continuous epochs. We select the model checkpoint that obtains the highest F_1 score over the validation set to report the final score on the test set. All our reported scores are the average over 5 runs with 5 different random seeds. See the Appendix for implementation details.

4.2 Main results

Table 3 presents the final F_1 scores (in %) obtained by the baseline models on the test set. We report the standard F_1 score for each different disfluency type and the Micro-average F_1 score for overall measurement. As the filled pauses and discourse markers belong to a closed set of words and phrases and are easier to detect (Johnson and Charniak, 2004), it is not surprising that baseline models produce about 2+% absolute higher scores for the IM type than for the RM type.

The obtained scores are categorized into two comparable settings of using the syllable-level dataset and its automatically-segmented word-level variant for training and evaluation. We find that word-level models outperform their syllable-level counterparts, thus showing the effectiveness of automatic Vietnamese word segmentation in detecting disfluent terms, e.g. BiLSTM-CNN-CRF improves from 91.54 to 92.13. We also find that fine-tuning XLM-R and PhoBERT helps produce substantially better performance scores than BiLSTM-CNN-CRF, thus confirming the effectiveness of pre-trained language models. In addition,

[1] https://institute.vinbigdata.org/en/events/vinbigdata-shares-100-hour-data-for-the-community

	Model	RM	IM	Mic-F_1
Syllable	BiL-CRF	88.17	94.67	91.54
	XLM-R_{base}	94.61	97.70	96.21
	XLM-R_{large}	95.29	97.75	96.57
Word	BiL-CRF	89.44	94.61	92.13
	$PhoBERT_{base}$	**95.61**	97.28	96.48
	$PhoBERT_{large}$	95.34	**98.13**	**96.79**

Table 3: F_1 score (in %) for each disluency type and Micro-average F_1 scores (denoted by Mic-F_1) on the test set. BiL-CRF denotes BiLSTM-CNN-CRF, while **Syllable** and **Word** denote scores obtained when using syllable- and word-level dataset settings, respectively.

	Utterance length	< 20 44%	[20, 30) 44%	⩾30 12%
Syllable	BiL-CRF	92.80	91.44	88.94
	XLM-R_{base}	96.52	96.50	94.74
	XLM-R_{large}	96.47	**97.23**	95.03
Word	BiL-CRF	93.44	92.10	89.20
	$PhoBERT_{base}$	96.35	**97.23**	94.75
	$PhoBERT_{large}$	**96.92**	97.09	**95.67**

Table 4: Mic-F_1 scores (in %) w.r.t. utterance lengths (i.e. the numbers of syllable tokens). The numbers (44%, 44% and 12%) right below length buckets denote the percentages of utterances belonging to the buckets.

PhoBERT does better than XLM-R ("base" versions: 96.48 vs. 96.21; "large" versions: 96.79 vs. 96.57), however, the score differences between PhoBERT and XLM-R are not substantial. It is probably because our utterances are domain-specific and contain disfluencies, while PhoBERT is pre-trained on domain-general and fluent data.

We also present the Micro-average F_1 scores (in %) w.r.t. utterance length buckets on the test set in Table 4. Those obtained scores generally show that the baseline models perform better when the input utterances are shorter than 30 tokens. The longer the input utterances are (i.e. longer than 30 tokens), the more ambiguous their meanings are and the more confused the baselines get.

4.3 Error analysis

To understand the source of error, we conduct an error analysis using the best performing model $PhoBERT_{large}$ that returns a total of 45 incorrect predictions on the validation set (average over the 5 different runs).

The first error group consists of 27/45 instances with inexact disfluency boundaries (i.e. inexact spans) overlapped with gold spans but having correct disfluency labels, while the second error group consists of 4/45 instances with the overlapped inexact spans and incorrect labels. These 27 + 4 = 31 errors are largely caused by the dropping of a reparandum-related term inside the fluent correction part, without affecting the utterance's semantic meaning, however, resulting in contextual ambiguity to the model. For example, in the utterance "tôi muốn biết giá vé hạng thương gia à nhầm phổ thông" (I would like to know the ticket price for the business class oops economy),[2] the whole phrase "hạng thương gia" (business class) is wrongly predicted as a RM while it must only be "thương gia" (business). Here, it is worth noting that the contextual ambiguity is resulted by a dropping of a possibly additional secondary term "hạng" (class) to be coupled "phổ thông" (economy), i.e. "hạng phổ thông" (economy class).

The third group of 2/45 errors with exact spans and incorrect disfluency labels does not provide us with any useful insight. The model also produces the fourth group of 9 errors where gold-annotated disfluent words/phrases are predicted with the label O. The majority of these 9/45 errors are caused by the fact that disfluencies can exist anywhere in a Vietnamese utterance, e.g. IM disfluent words can appear at the end of the utterance. For example, with the utterance "chuyến bay buổi sáng à không tôi đang vội chuyến bay đầu tiên nhé" (morning flight uh no I'm in hurry first flight please), the model could not predict the word "nhé" as an IM. The last error group consists of 3/45 instances where predicted disfluencies are associated with the gold label O. They are general terms such as "sân bay" (airport), "thành phố" (city) and the like, that frequently used in disfluent phrases. Thus, when occurred in the fluent parts of an utterance, these terms are likely predicted as disfluencies, leading to incorrect predictions.

5 Conclusion

In this paper, we have presented the first study for Vietnamese disfluency detection. We create a Vietnamese disfluency detection and empirically conduct experiments on this dataset to compare strong baseline models as well as perform detailed error analysis. Experimental results show that the input representations and the pre-trained language models have positive influences on this Vietnamese disfluency detection task.

[2] Word segmentation is not shown for simplification. Here, we also color the gold annotations.

References

Nguyen Bach and Fei Huang. 2019. Noisy BiLSTM-Based Models for Disfluency Detection. In *Proceedings of INTERSPEECH*, pages 4230–4234.

Alexandra Canavan, David Graff, and George Zipperlen. 1997. CALLHOME American English Speech LDC97S42. Linguistic Data Consortium.

Jacob Cohen. 1960. A Coefficient of Agreement for Nominal Scales. *Educational and Psychological Measurement*, 20(1):37–46.

Alexis Conneau, Kartikay Khandelwal, Naman Goyal, Vishrav Chaudhary, Guillaume Wenzek, Francisco Guzmán, Edouard Grave, Myle Ott, Luke Zettlemoyer, and Veselin Stoyanov. 2020. Unsupervised Cross-lingual Representation Learning at Scale. In *Proceedings of ACL*, pages 8440–8451.

Mai Hoang Dao, Thinh Hung Truong, and Dat Quoc Nguyen. 2021. Intent Detection and Slot Filling for Vietnamese. In *Proceedings of INTERSPEECH*, pages 4698–4702.

Jacob Devlin, Ming-Wei Chang, Kenton Lee, and Kristina Toutanova. 2019. BERT: Pre-training of Deep Bidirectional Transformers for Language Understanding. In *Proceedings of NAACL*, pages 4171–4186.

Dinh Dien, Hoang Kiem, and Nguyen Quang Toan. 2001. Vietnamese Word Segmentation. In *Proceedings of NLPRS*, pages 749–756.

David M. Eberhard, Gary F. Simons, and Charles D. Fennig. 2019. *Ethnologue: Languages of the World, 22nd edition.* SIL International, United States.

John Godfrey and Edward Holliman. 1993. Switchboard-1 Release 2 LDC97S62. *Linguistic Data Consortium.*

Aditya Gupta, Jiacheng Xu, Shyam Upadhyay, Diyi Yang, and Manaal Faruqui. 2021. Disfl-QA: A Benchmark Dataset for Understanding Disfluencies in Question Answering. In *Findings of ACL*, pages 3309–3319.

Matthew Honnibal and Mark Johnson. 2014. Joint Incremental Disfluency Detection and Dependency Parsing. *Transactions of ACL*, 2:131–142.

Paria Jamshid Lou, Peter Anderson, and Mark Johnson. 2018. Disfluency Detection using Auto-Correlational Neural Networks. In *Proceedings of EMNLP*, pages 4610—-4619.

Paria Jamshid Lou and Mark Johnson. 2017. Disfluency Detection using a Noisy Channel Model and a Deep Neural Language Model. In *Proceedings of ACL*, pages 547–553.

Paria Jamshid Lou and Mark Johnson. 2020. Improving Disfluency Detection by Self-Training a Self-Attentive Model. In *Proceedings of ACL*, pages 3754–3763.

Mark Johnson and Eugene Charniak. 2004. A TAG-based noisy-channel model of speech repairs. In *Proceedings of ACL*, pages 33–39.

Mark Johnson, Eugene Charniak, and Matthew Lease. 2004. An improved model for recognizing disfluencies in conversational speech. In *In Proceedings of Rich Transcription Workshop*.

Diederik P. Kingma and Jimmy Ba. 2014. Adam: A Method for Stochastic Optimization. *arXiv preprint*, arXiv:1412.6980.

John D. Lafferty, Andrew McCallum, and Fernando C. N. Pereira. 2001. Conditional Random Fields: Probabilistic Models for Segmenting and Labeling Sequence Data. In *Proceedings of ICML*, pages 282–289.

Yinhan Liu, Myle Ott, Naman Goyal, Jingfei Du, Mandar Joshi, Danqi Chen, Omer Levy, Mike Lewis, Luke Zettlemoyer, and Veselin Stoyanov. 2019. RoBERTa: A Robustly Optimized BERT Pretraining Approach. *arXiv preprint*, arXiv:1907.11692.

Xuezhe Ma and Eduard Hovy. 2016. End-to-end Sequence Labeling via Bi-directional LSTM-CNNs-CRF. In *Proceedings of ACL*, pages 1064–1074.

Anh Tuan Nguyen, Mai Hoang Dao, and Dat Quoc Nguyen. 2020. A Pilot Study of Text-to-SQL Semantic Parsing for Vietnamese. In *Findings of EMNLP*, pages 4079–4085.

Dat Quoc Nguyen and Anh Tuan Nguyen. 2020. PhoBERT: Pre-trained language models for Vietnamese. In *Findings of EMNLP*, pages 1037–1042.

Dat Quoc Nguyen, Dai Quoc Nguyen, Thanh Vu, Mark Dras, and Mark Johnson. 2018. A Fast and Accurate Vietnamese Word Segmenter. In *Proceedings of LREC*, pages 2582–2587.

Mari Ostendorf and Sangyun Hahn. 2013. A sequential repetition model for improved disfluency detection. In *Proceedings of INTERSPEECH*, pages 2624–2628.

Pranav Rajpurkar, Jian Zhang, Konstantin Lopyrev, and Percy Liang. 2016. SQuAD: 100,000+ Questions for Machine Comprehension of Text. In *Proceedings of EMNLP*, pages 2383–2392.

Mohammad Sadegh Rasooli and Joel Tetreault. 2013. Joint Parsing and Disfluency Detection in Linear Time. In *Proceedings of EMNLP*, pages 124–129.

Johann C. Rocholl, Vicky Zayats, Daniel D. Walker, Noah B. Murad, Aaron Schneider, and Daniel J. Liebling. 2021. Disfluency Detection with Unlabeled Data and Small BERT Models. In *Proceedings of INTERSPEECH*, pages 766–770.

Sebastian Ruder. 2020. Why You Should Do NLP Beyond English. https://ruder.io/nlp-beyond-english/.

Elizabeth Shriberg. 1994. *Preliminaries to a Theory of Speech Disfluencies*. Ph.D. thesis, University of California.

Trang Tran, Morgan Tinkler, Gary Yeung, Abeer Alwan, and Mari Ostendorf. 2020. Analysis of Disfluency in Children's Speech. In *Proceedings of INTERSPEECH*, pages 4278–4282.

Thinh Hung Truong, Mai Hoang Dao, and Dat Quoc Nguyen. 2021. COVID-19 Named Entity Recognition for Vietnamese. In *Proceedings of NAACL*, pages 2146–2153.

Thanh Vu, Dat Quoc Nguyen, Dai Quoc Nguyen, Mark Dras, and Mark Johnson. 2018. VnCoreNLP: A Vietnamese Natural Language Processing Toolkit. In *Proceedings of NAACL: Demonstrations*, pages 56–60.

Masashi Yoshikawa, Hiroyuki Shindo, and Yuji Matsumoto. 2016. Joint Transition-based Dependency Parsing and Disfluency Detection for Automatic Speech Recognition Texts. In *Proceedings of EMNLP*, pages 1036–1041.

Vicky Zayats, Mari Ostendorf, and Hannaneh Hajishirzi. 2016. Disfluency Detection Using a Bidirectional LSTM. In *Proceedings of INTERSPEECH*, pages 2523–2527.

Victoria Zayats, Mari Ostendorf, and Hannaneh Hajishirzi. 2014. Multi-domain disfluency and repair detection. In *Proceedings of INTERSPEECH*, pages 2907–2911.

Simon Zwarts and Mark Johnson. 2011. The impact of language models and loss functions on repair disfluency detection. In *Proceedings of ACL*, pages 703–711.

A Appendix

Experimental models

- BiLSTM-CNN-CRF (Ma and Hovy, 2016) represents each input token by concatenating its corresponding pre-trained token embedding and CNN-based character-level token embedding; then concatenated representations of input tokens are fed into a BiLSTM encoder to extract latent feature vectors for the input tokens; each latent feature vector is then linearly transformed before being fed into a linear-chain CRF layer (Lafferty et al., 2001) for disfluency label prediction.

- Fine-tuning XLM-R (Conneau et al., 2020) or PhoBERT (Nguyen and Nguyen, 2020) for disfluency detection is done in a common approach that uses a linear prediction layer on top of its architecture. In other words, we feed the XLM-R- or PhoBERT-based contextualized token embeddings as input for the linear prediction layer, to predict the disfluency label for each token.

Hyper-parameter	**Value**
Optimizer	Adam
Learning rate	0.001
Mini-batch size	36
LSTM hidden state size	200
Number of BiLSTM layers	2
Dropout	[0.25, 0.25]
Character embedding size	50
Filter length, i.e. window size	3
Number of filters	30
W2V embedding dimension	300

Table 5: Hyper-parameters for BiLSTM-CNN-CRF.

For training the baseline BiLSTM-CNN-CRF, we employ the pre-trained 300-dimensional Word2Vec syllable and word embeddings for Vietnamese from (Nguyen et al., 2020). We fix these embeddings during training. Optimal hyper-parameters that we select via performing a grid search for BiLSTM-CNN-CRF are presented in Table 5. We fine-tune XLM-R and PhoBERT for the syllable- and word-level settings, respectively, using the optimizer Adam (Kingma and Ba, 2014) with a fixed learning rate of 5e-5 and a batch size of 32 (Liu et al., 2019). Note that BiLSTM-CNN-CRF is trained for 50 epochs while XLM-R and PhoBERT are fine-tuned for 30 training epochs.

A multi-level approach for hierarchical Ticket Classification

Matteo Marcuzzo * **Alessandro Zangari** *
Digital Strategy Innovation Srl
30175, Venice, Italy
{name.surname}@unive.it

Lorenzo Giudice **Andrea Gasparetto**
Ca' Foscari University of Venice
Department of Management
30121, Venice, Italy
{name.surname}@unive.it

Michele Schiavinato **Andrea Albarelli**
Ca' Foscari University of Venice
Department of Environmental Sciences, Informatics and Statistics
30172, Mestre (VE), Italy
{michele.schiavinato,albarelli}@unive.it

Abstract

The automatic categorization of support tickets is a fundamental tool for modern businesses. Such requests are most commonly composed of concise textual descriptions that are noisy and filled with technical jargon. In this paper, we test the effectiveness of pre-trained LMs for the classification of issues related to software bugs. First, we test several strategies to produce single, ticket-wise representations starting from their BERT-generated word embeddings. Then, we showcase a simple yet effective way to build a multi-level classifier for the categorization of documents with two hierarchically dependent labels. We experiment on a public bugs dataset and compare our results with standard BERT-based and traditional SVM classifiers. Our findings suggest that both embedding strategies and hierarchical label dependencies considerably impact classification accuracy.

1 Introduction

Support tickets and incident reports are a valuable point of contact between customers and service providers (Al-Hawari and Barham, 2021). They are fundamental tools in the management of the relationship between businesses and users, allowing for the swift resolution of issues, thus leading to improved customer satisfaction, productivity, and compliance which Service-Level Agreements (SLAs) (Gupta and Sengupta, 2012). Tickets can be derived from multiple communication channels, most commonly emails, specialized web forms, phone calls, live chats, and social media platforms (Zicari et al., 2021). Help requests are therefore logged as text, which represents the most important source of information to be used for automatic ticket management. Being conversational by nature, tickets describe the issue or request in an often noisy and concise format (Cristian et al., 2019).

As a response to the increasingly high volume of these requests by customers, researchers have proposed the automation of various steps of the ticket resolution pipeline (Fuchs et al., 2022; Ali Zaidi et al., 2022). These include the classification of tickets into broad topic categories (*ticket classification*) (Zicari et al., 2021; Revina et al., 2020), the direct assignment of the issue to an expert capable of resolving it (*expert finding*) (Husain et al., 2019), as well as the direct resolution of tickets in a completely autonomous way (*ticket resolution*) (Zhou et al., 2017). Among these tasks, the accurate classification of incoming tickets within a pre-defined hierarchy of labels is among the most prevalent, as well as one of particular importance to ensure that these requests are dealt with swiftly. Indeed, it is common for support tickets to be framed within a multi-level hierarchy such as the one just mentioned: each level of the hierarchy describes the issue at different levels of specificity.

Contributions This work will explore Ticket Classification (TiC), a sub-task of Text Classification (TC), with the following objectives:

- Verifying the effectiveness of contextualized Language Models (LMs) (Radford et al., 2018; Marcuzzo et al., 2022) on noisy pieces of text from this particular domain;
- Exploring the impact of document embedding strategies on downstream task performance;
- Establishing how much a LM can benefit from the injection of hierarchy information for topical classification within a two-level hierarchy.

Our experiments show that both document summarization strategies and hierarchical information injection can contribute in a major way to TiC accuracy. The code and datasets utilized in this work's experiments are made publicly available online[1].

* Authors contributed equally.

[1] https://gitlab.com/distration/dsi-nlp-publib/-/tree/main/WNUT22

Proceedings of the 2022 COLING Workshop: The 8th Workshop on Noisy User-generated Text (W-NUT 2022), pages 201–214

2 Related work

The task of topical TiC has been explored in recent works, which we briefly outline. Relatedly, we also discuss recent advancements in the broader TC environment, as well as a short mention of dedicated hierarchical TC methods.

Ticket Classification (TiC) In the particular context of TiC, much work has been done towards the application of traditional methods, a popular example being that of Support Vector Machines (SVMs) (Boser et al., 1992) applied on simple word-count-based text representation techniques such as TF-IDF (Jones, 1972). Recent works such as Yang (2021); Revina et al. (2020) have argued for the efficacy of traditional methods, often introducing more advanced text representation techniques such as Word2Vec (Mikolov et al., 2013). There has also been recent interest in the application of Deep Neural Networks, such as Multilayer Perceptrons (Kallis et al., 2019), Convolutional Neural Networks (Zicari et al., 2021; Pistellato et al., 2018), and Recurrent Neural Networks (Mani et al., 2019; Lyubinets et al., 2018).

Text Classification (TC) In the broader environment of Natural Language Processing (NLP), all downstream tasks — including TC — have been recently revolutionized by the introduction of the Transformer architecture (Vaswani et al., 2017). This approach to text representation has allowed for much more meaningful vectorial representations for words, crucially able to discern context. Contextualized LMs based on this architecture are now the staple NLP transfer learning approach, and have showcased massive performance boosts in TC benchmarks. Among others, we focus on the influential Bidirectional Encoder Representations from Transformers (BERT) (Devlin et al., 2019), which we utilize in this work. We refer to Gasparetto et al. (2022a,b) for a thorough description of BERT's architecture. Though succeeded by more refined LMs in recent years, it is still widely studied and utilized. BERT-based LMs have been extensively applied to NLP tasks on user-generated content, such as tweets (Polignano et al., 2019) and user reviews (Lu et al., 2020). Interestingly, recent findings suggest that BERT is quite sensible to the presence of noise in text (*e.g.*, spelling mistakes) (Kumar et al., 2020). On the other hand, other works suggest that BERT is quite resistant to label-noise, and the application of common noise-handling methods can in fact deteriorate BERT's performance (Zhu et al., 2022). With this work, we aim to give practitioners some insights into the usage of BERT for classification in the support ticket classification domain. While an excellent source of noisy user-generated data, we find this context to be understudied at present.

Hierarchical Text Classification As we are discussing datasets whose labels are hierarchical by nature, it would be reasonable to utilize Hierarchical TC approaches. The architecture we propose in this work is partly inspired by these approaches, in particular by the distinction between *flattened classifiers* (Koller and Sahami, 1997), which simplifies the hierarchy by flattening it to a single multiclass or multilabel problem, and *global classifiers*, which build upon these classifiers but integrate hierarchy information within their framework (Labrou and Finin, 1999). Still, we point out that the amount of overlap with hierarchical TC literature is somewhat limited by the fact that the hierarchy in ticketing systems is usually very shallow (two to three levels), while HTC systems usually operate in multilabel environments with very complex hierarchies.

3 The Linux Bugs dataset

To evaluate a TiC scenario, we experiment on a dataset of bugs crawled from the publicly available Linux kernel bug-tracker [2], as inspired by Lyubinets et al. (2018). The resulting *Linux Bugs dataset* contains tickets organized through the hierarchical dependent labels of "product" (*e.g.*, Network, Drivers, etc.) and "component" (*e.g.*, BIOS, scheduler, etc.). Therefore, we utilize the former as main labels and the latter as sub-labels. To be precise, to avoid redundancies, we utilize the flattened labels as sub-labels, such as to differentiate sub-labels that share their name across main categories (*e.g.*, `Network_Other` vs `Drivers_Other`). Moreover, to reduce class imbalance, we discard all labels and sub-labels that appear less than 100 times. More details on the dataset, including an exemplary subset of the resulting hierarchy, reports on the labels' frequency and an example of the content of a ticket can be found in Appendix B.

4 Methods

The aforementioned BERT LM has been one of the most popular contextualized LMs since its inception. Conceptually, BERT is a bidirectional

[2]`https://bugzilla.kernel.org`

Transformer-based neural network, made by stacking multiple encoder blocks. These blocks are entirely based on the self-attention mechanism (Bahdanau et al., 2015), eliminating the sequential bottleneck of previous recurrent models.

BERT models are pre-trained on two specifically devised language modeling tasks that allow the networks to learn semantically and contextually meaningful representations of text. These models can then be fine-tuned on specific tasks quite easily (in the case of classification, by adding a simple linear layer as a classifier) to obtain state-of-the-art performances. In our case, we utilize the models available on HuggingFace (Wolf et al., 2020), which are pre-trained on BookCorpus (Zhu et al., 2015) and English Wikipedia, and have a vocabulary of around 30,500 word segments.

4.1 Document summarization strategies

In terms of text interpretation, BERT first transforms raw text into tokens through the WordPiece sub-word tokenization algorithm (Schuster and Nakajima, 2012). The output is then passed through the stacked encoder blocks, with each layer producing an embedding for each token.

A common approach to classification using BERT is to utilize the `[CLS]` token as a document summary. This special symbol is pre-pended to each sequence of words and is utilized during pre-training on the Next Sentence Prediction binary classification task (NSP). Despite its popularity, several authors suggest that other "summarization strategies" for documents may be preferable (Reimers and Gurevych, 2019). For instance, Tanaka et al. (2019) experiment with the averaging of the individual word embeddings composing the sentences rather than the single `[CLS]` token. They utilize the output of one or more encoder blocks and combine them, highlighting classification improvements when concatenating the output of several layers. Researchers have further hinted at the phenomenon of "layer specialization" within BERT, arguing that each encoding block may focus on the extraction of linguistic features at different levels: syntactic features are mostly extracted in the first blocks, while deeper layers progressively focus on semantic features. They also discuss how information from each layer can be beneficial to downstream tasks, like classification (de Vries et al., 2020; Jawahar et al., 2019; Torsello et al., 2014).

In this work, we explore the impact of different approaches to the creation of a condensed document representation starting from BERT's word vectors. In particular, we test several strategies, including the usage of the `[CLS]` token from the last layer (referred to as *cls last*), but also the concatenation and average of the `[CLS]` tokens of the last h hidden layers, respectively indicated with *cls* $concat_h$ and *cls* avg_h. We also experiment with approaches that do not use such token, such as averaging the embeddings of all words in a document (*avg*), taking the maximum (*max*), or using their normalized sum (*sum nor*). A description of each strategy is given in Appendix A.

4.2 Multi-level classifiers

Our second aim in this work is to design an effective multi-level architecture able to exploit the hierarchical dependency information between labels. The following paragraphs detail the two proposed approaches. Notably, our multi-level classifiers are based on BERT LMs, but may be used with any model capable of producing contextualized word embeddings. In both frameworks, we utilize two separate LMs trained on the categorization of macro-labels (task T1) and on the categorization of flattened sub-labels (T2). A visualization of the approaches is provided in the Appendix (Fig. 1).

ML-BERT The Multi-Level BERT (`ML-BERT`) classifier is a combination of two distinct pre-trained BERT LMs, previously fine-tuned on the prediction of the T1 and T2 tasks, respectively (LM_1, LM_2). In the `ML-BERT` model, the weights of the two base LMs are kept frozen during the fine-tuning procedure — the output of the pre-trained classifiers is discarded. Only the word embeddings produced by each model are utilized; document representations are obtained by using the best-performing summarization strategy among the ones mentioned in Section 4.1. Embeddings from both models are then concatenated into a global ticket representation and passed through a single linear layer with a softmax activation function. Therefore, fine-tuning only requires the learning of the last layer's weights, reducing the computational cost.

Supported-BERT The `Supported-BERT` classifier similarly utilizes a LM previously trained on T1 (LM_1). However, LM_2 is not trained in isolation but instead utilizes the fine-tuned LM_1 as support during its own fine-tuning. As before, the ticket embeddings from the two LMs are concatenated and passed to the output layer. Thus, the difference from the previous setup is that LM_2 is trained directly with the output layer and with external influence, instead of being trained beforehand.

5 Experiments

We report in this section the experiments we conducted to select the most suitable summarization strategy and to determine the effectiveness of the multi-level classifiers. While the core of our experiments was performed on BERT's base pre-trained model (*i.e.*, "bert-base-uncased"), we also report results using a larger BERT LM (*i.e.*, "bert-large-uncased").

5.1 Experimental setup

We describe our experimental settings in this section, adding details on the metrics we choose to use and on how we select the model hyper-parameters.

Metrics We evaluate the models in a multiclass setting, where the ground truth label is the concatenation of the parent and child categories. Therefore, the models must predict a single class for each ticket (*e.g.*, `Networking_IPV4` is the target label for a ticket that belongs to the `Networking` category and `IPV4` sub-category). This approach is widely utilized in the evaluation of global HTC methods, which our approaches can be seen as (Silla and Freitas, 2011). We use standard classification metrics, *i.e.*, accuracy and F_1-score, to measure the performance. Briefly, *accuracy* measures the ratio of correct predictions over the total of number predictions, but can give a skewed representation of imbalanced datasets. F-score is a combination of *precision* and *recall*, which measure a model's correctness and completeness, respectively (Gasparetto et al., 2022a, 2018). We report the F_1-score — the harmonic mean of precision and recall — in its *macro-averaged* version, *i.e.*, considering all class contributions equally.

Hyper-parameter tuning We use a stratified 3-fold CV to split the dataset into training and testing subsets. Before testing BERT's performance with different summarization strategies on the testing split, we tune the learning rate and the number of training epochs on the training split, reserving 20% of it as a validation set. We use the BERT-base model on task T2 using the standard *avg last* strategy with early stopping set on the loss function to determine the optimal number of epochs.

Table 1: Effect of additional processing procedures on the performance of a BERT model on the validation set.

Model	Clean	Weigh	Acc	F_1
	✗	✗	**0.533** [± 0.003]	**0.396** [± 0.005]
BERT	✓	✗	0.503 [± 0.003]	0.374 [± 0.006]
(base)	✗	✓	0.471 [± 0.005]	0.382 [± 0.004]
	✓	✓	0.464 [± 0.007]	0.371 [± 0.008]

* Standard deviation over 3 runs is reported in brackets.

After validation, the BERT-base models are trained for 3 epochs with learning rate set to $2e^{-5}$ and batch size set to 8. The BERT-large models were similarly validated and trained with a learning rate of $1e^{-5}$ for 3 epochs, with batch size set to 8.

Following Lyubinets et al. (2018), we test the impact of a more comprehensive text cleaning procedure that removes most of the stack traces and memory addresses, which are quite frequent in this dataset. Listing 2 in the Appendix showcases an example of a bug report treated with the more aggressive cleaning procedure. Furthermore, because our dataset is imbalanced class-wise, we experiment with weighting classes' contribution to the loss value based on their support. We find that neither the additional preprocessing step nor the weighting scheme improved the performance in terms of F_1 and accuracy scores using the default *avg last* strategy, as can be seen in Table 1. We hypothesize that, even though the representations of pieces of text such as the hexadecimal codes of Listing 1 have low syntactic and semantic value, they still provide discriminative power in the downstream classification task.

To train the multi-level models, we separately train LM_1 and LM_2 on T1 and T2 tasks respectively, and use the same hyperparameters selected for the previous tests. Moreover, we select the best learning rate and number of epochs for the final classifier using the same procedure as described above, obtaining the values of $2e^{-5}$ (2 epochs) and $1e^{-5}$ (3 epochs) for the base and large versions of BERT, respectively.

5.2 Results

In this section, we report test set results obtained with the best hyper-parameters as just described.

Document summarization Results with the different summarization strategies introduced in Section 4.1 using BERT-base on task T2 are reported in Table 2. First off, there is a considerable difference in performance between the pooled and "raw" ver-

Table 2: Test set results* with BERT classifier on T2 comparing summarization strategies on Linux Bugs.

Basis	Strategy	Acc	F_1
	last (p)†	0.518 [± 0.006]	0.354 [± 0.009]
	last	0.566 [± 0.012]	0.446 [± 0.018]
	avg_2	0.531 [± 0.010]	0.393 [± 0.012]
cls	$concat_2$	0.535 [± 0.010]	0.400 [± 0.014]
	$concat_3$	**0.571** [± 0.008]	0.456 [± 0.013]
	$concat_4$	0.568 [± 0.009]	**0.457** [± 0.014]
	$concat_5$	0.565 [± 0.012]	0.456 [± 0.013]
	last	0.525 [± 0.008]	0.387 [± 0.010]
avg	avg_2	0.522 [± 0.005]	0.383 [± 0.013]
	$concat_2$	0.523 [± 0.007]	0.390 [± 0.009]
	last	0.522 [± 0.011]	0.385 [± 0.014]
max	avg_2	0.519 [± 0.007]	0.375 [± 0.013]
	$concat_2$	0.518 [± 0.006]	0.373 [± 0.015]
max_min	*last*	0.522 [± 0.010]	0.377 [± 0.011]
	avg_2	0.522 [± 0.009]	0.374 [± 0.010]
max_avg	*last*	0.516 [± 0.007]	0.381 [± 0.012]
	avg_2	0.519 [± 0.006]	0.379 [± 0.007]
	last	0.406 [± 0.018]	0.171 [± 0.017]
sum_nor	$concat_2$	0.379 [± 0.013]	0.135 [± 0.019]
	$concat_5$	0.388 [± 0.015]	0.135 [± 0.015]

* Standard deviation over 6 runs is reported in brackets.
† Pooled, using *cls pooled* strategy.

Table 3: Test set results* for all models on the T2 task. BERT models utilize the *cls* $concat_3$ strategy.

Model	Acc	F_1
SVM	0.551 [± 0.004]	0.473 [± 0.006]
ML-BERT (base)	0.602 [± 0.010]	**0.500** [± 0.014]
Supp-BERT (base)	**0.611** [± 0.007]	0.485 [± 0.013]
BERT (base)	0.571 [± 0.008]	0.456 [± 0.013]
ML-BERT (large)	0.577 [± 0.008]	0.461 [± 0.006]
Supp-BERT (large)	0.597 [± 0.007]	0.480 [± 0.011]
BERT (large)	0.559 [± 0.008]	0.438 [± 0.011]

* Standard deviation over 6 runs is reported in brackets.

sions of the *cls last* strategy, with the raw `[CLS]` token without pooling achieving considerably better results. Stacking multiple layers further improved the results; tests with *cls* $concat_3$ achieved the best overall performance in terms of accuracy, precision, and recall (though macro-averaging favors *cls* $concat_4$ in terms of F_1 score), confirming that features extracted in other BERT hidden layers can be beneficial to the classification task (see Table 5 in the Appendix).

Multi-level classifiers Table 3 reports the classification performance of both `ML-BERT` and `Supported-BERT` (shortened as `Supp-BERT`), utilizing the previously determined best document summarization strategy (in our case, *cls* $concat_3$).

The smaller `ML-BERT` achieves an improvement of 9.7% macro F_1-score and 5.4% accuracy as compared to the BERT model trained on the flattened hierarchy of labels. `Supported-BERT`'s improvement amounts instead to 6.4% and 7.0% on the same metrics. While `ML-BERT` performed better in terms of macro F_1-score, `Supported-BERT` resulted in the highest accuracy. The larger pre-trained BERT model showcases overall a similar trend, though with lower performance than with the base model in all experiments. Nevertheless, the multi-level models still improved results over the flat T2 classifier: `ML-BERT` (large) achieved 3.1% and 5.2% improvement in macro F_1-score and accuracy respectively, while the performance of `Supported-BERT` improved by 6.8% and 9.5%. In practice, we observed that the larger model did not converge as well as the base one. This is likely to be a consequence of the limited size of our highly skewed dataset, as well as the limited semantic significance of its composing documents (that contain many technical bits of text, like stack traces).

The SVM classifier was trained with a simple one-vs-rest strategy and also performed very well, surprisingly achieving better macro F_1 than the smaller BERT model in the flattened setting. However, all base multi-level models perform better on both metrics. As is also discussed in the literature, BoW features with TF-IDF weighting are suitable representations for noisy text, effectively able to filter out many unimportant words (Das et al., 2021). On the other hand, contextualized LMs such as BERT are meant to exploit sentence structure and word context, which might be insufficiently informative in such environments.

Error analysis Because of time and space limitations, we do not perform an in-depth error analysis of our models in this work. However, a discussion in this regard can be found in Appendix D, in which we also discuss how we would like to address this analysis in future work.

6 Conclusion

In this article, we experimented with contextualized LMs for TiC, and found that different document embedding summarization strategies are a major factor in classification performance. Moreover, we devised two multi-level classification approaches based on LMs, and found further improvement by injecting information from the label hierarchy within the architecture. We hope our work can provide useful insights into the usage of BERT models for classification in a previously understudied domain.

References

Feras Al-Hawari and Hala Barham. 2021. A machine learning based help desk system for it service management. *Journal of King Saud University - Computer and Information Sciences*, 33(6):702–718.

Syed S. Ali Zaidi, Muhammad Moazam Fraz, Muhammad Shahzad, and Sharifullah Khan. 2022. A multiapproach generalized framework for automated solution suggestion of support tickets. *International Journal of Intelligent Systems*, 37(6):3654–3681.

Dzmitry Bahdanau, Kyunghyun Cho, and Yoshua Bengio. 2015. Neural machine translation by jointly learning to align and translate. *arXiv.org*, abs/1409.0473.

Bernhard E. Boser, Isabelle M. Guyon, and Vladimir N. Vapnik. 1992. A training algorithm for optimal margin classifiers. In *Proceedings of the Fifth Annual Workshop on Computational Learning Theory*, pages 144–152. Association for Computing Machinery.

Matei Cristian, Săcărea Christian, and Tolciu Dumitru-Tudor. 2019. A study in the automation of service ticket recognition using natural language processing. In *2019 International Conference on Software, Telecommunications and Computer Networks (SoftCOM)*, pages 1–6.

Mamata Das, Selvakumar Kamalanathan, and PJA Alphonse. 2021. A comparative study on tf-idf feature weighting method and its analysis using unstructured dataset. In *COLINS*, pages 98–107.

Wietse de Vries, Andreas van Cranenburgh, and Malvina Nissim. 2020. What's so special about BERT's layers? a closer look at the NLP pipeline in monolingual and multilingual models. In *Findings of the Association for Computational Linguistics: EMNLP 2020*, pages 4339–4350, Online. Association for Computational Linguistics.

Jacob Devlin, Ming-Wei Chang, Kenton Lee, and Kristina Toutanova. 2019. BERT: Pre-training of deep bidirectional transformers for language understanding. In *Proceedings of the 2019 Conference of the North American Chapter of the Association for Computational Linguistics: Human Language Technologies, Volume 1 (Long and Short Papers)*, pages 4171–4186, Minneapolis, Minnesota. Association for Computational Linguistics.

Simon Fuchs, Clemens Drieschner, and Holger Wittges. 2022. Improving support ticket systems using machine learning: A literature review. In *Proceedings of the 55th Hawaii International Conference on System Sciences*, pages 1893–1902, Honolulu, HI 96822. ScholarSpace.

Andrea Gasparetto, Matteo Marcuzzo, Alessandro Zangari, and Andrea Albarelli. 2022a. A survey on text classification algorithms: From text to predictions. *Information*, 13(2).

Andrea Gasparetto, Dalila Ressi, Filippo Bergamasco, Mara Pistellato, Luca Cosmo, Marco Boschetti, Enrico Ursella, and Andrea Albarelli. 2018. Cross-dataset data augmentation for convolutional neural networks training. In *2018 24th International Conference on Pattern Recognition (ICPR)*, pages 910–915.

Andrea Gasparetto, Alessandro Zangari, Matteo Marcuzzo, and Andrea Albarelli. 2022b. A survey on text classification: Practical perspectives on the italian language. *PLOS ONE*, 17(7):1–46.

Hari S. Gupta and Bikram Sengupta. 2012. Scheduling service tickets in shared delivery. In *Service-Oriented Computing*, pages 79–95, Berlin, Heidelberg. Springer Berlin Heidelberg.

Omayma Husain, Naomie Salim, Rose Alinda Alias, Samah Abdelsalam, and Alzubair Hassan. 2019. Expert finding systems: A systematic review. *Applied Sciences*, 9(20).

Ganesh Jawahar, Benoît Sagot, and Djamé Seddah. 2019. What does BERT learn about the structure of language? In *Proceedings of the 57th Annual Meeting of the Association for Computational Linguistics*, pages 3651–3657, Florence, Italy. Association for Computational Linguistics.

Karen Spärck Jones. 1972. A statistical interpretation of term specificity and its application in retrieval. *J. Doc.*, 28(1):11–21.

Rafael Kallis, Andrea Di Sorbo, Gerardo Canfora, and Sebastiano Panichella. 2019. Ticket tagger: Machine learning driven issue classification. In *2019 IEEE International Conference on Software Maintenance and Evolution (ICSME)*, pages 406–409.

Daphne Koller and Mehran Sahami. 1997. Hierarchically classifying documents using very few words. In *Proceedings of the Fourteenth International Conference on Machine Learning*, ICML '97, page 170–178, San Francisco, CA, USA. Morgan Kaufmann Publishers Inc.

Ankit Kumar, Piyush Makhija, and Anuj Gupta. 2020. Noisy text data: Achilles' heel of BERT. In *Proceedings of the Sixth Workshop on Noisy User-generated Text (W-NUT 2020)*, pages 16–21, Online. Association for Computational Linguistics.

Yannis Labrou and Tim Finin. 1999. Yahoo! as an ontology: Using yahoo! categories to describe documents. In *Proceedings of the Eighth International Conference on Information and Knowledge Management*, CIKM '99, page 180–187, New York, NY, USA. Association for Computing Machinery.

Ilya Loshchilov and Frank Hutter. 2019. Decoupled weight decay regularization. In *International Conference on Learning Representations*, New Orleans, Louisiana, USA.

Zhibin Lu, Pan Du, and Jian-Yun Nie. 2020. Vgcn-bert: Augmenting bert with graph embedding for text classification. In *Advances in Information Retrieval*, pages 369–382, Cham. Springer International Publishing.

Volodymyr Lyubinets, Taras Boiko, and Deon Nicholas. 2018. Automated labeling of bugs and tickets using attention-based mechanisms in recurrent neural networks. In *2018 IEEE Second International Conference on Data Stream Mining & Processing (DSMP)*, pages 271–275.

Senthil Mani, Anush Sankaran, and Rahul Aralikatte. 2019. Deeptriage: Exploring the effectiveness of deep learning for bug triaging. In *Proceedings of the ACM India Joint International Conference on Data Science and Management of Data*, CoDS-COMAD '19, pages 171–179, New York, NY, USA. Association for Computing Machinery.

Matteo Marcuzzo, Alessandro Zangari, Andrea Albarelli, and Andrea Gasparetto. 2022. Recommendation systems: an insight into current development and future research challenges. *IEEE Access*.

Tomas Mikolov, Kai Chen, Greg Corrado, and Jeffrey Dean. 2013. Efficient estimation of word representations in vector space. In *1st International Conference on Learning Representations, ICLR 2013*, volume abs/1301.3781.

Mara Pistellato, Luca Cosmo, Filippo Bergamasco, Andrea Gasparetto, and Andrea Albarelli. 2018. Adaptive albedo compensation for accurate phase-shift coding. In *2018 24th International Conference on Pattern Recognition (ICPR)*, pages 2450–2455.

Marco Polignano, Pierpaolo Basile, Marco de Gemmis, Giovanni Semeraro, and Valerio Basile. 2019. AlBERTo: Italian BERT language understanding model for NLP challenging tasks based on tweets. In *Proceedings of the Sixth Italian Conference on Computational Linguistics, CLiC-it 2019*, volume 2481 of *CEUR Workshop Proceedings*, Bari, Italy.

Alec Radford, Karthik Narasimhan, Tim Salimans, and Ilya Sutskever. 2018. Improving language understanding by generative pre-training.

Nils Reimers and Iryna Gurevych. 2019. Sentence-BERT: Sentence embeddings using Siamese BERT-networks. In *Proceedings of the 2019 Conference on Empirical Methods in Natural Language Processing and the 9th International Joint Conference on Natural Language Processing (EMNLP-IJCNLP)*, pages 3982–3992, Hong Kong, China. Association for Computational Linguistics.

Aleksandra Revina, Krisztian Buza, and Vera G. Meister. 2020. It ticket classification: The simpler, the better. *IEEE Access*, 8:193380–193395.

Mike Schuster and Kaisuke Nakajima. 2012. Japanese and korean voice search. In *2012 IEEE International Conference on Acoustics, Speech and Signal Processing (ICASSP)*, pages 5149–5152.

Carlos N. Silla and Alex A. Freitas. 2011. A survey of hierarchical classification across different application domains. *Data Mining and Knowledge Discovery*, 22(1):31–72.

Hirotaka Tanaka, Hiroyuki Shinnou, Rui Cao, Jing Bai, and Wen Ma. 2019. Document classification by word embeddings of BERT. In *16th International Conference of the Pacific Association for Computational Linguistics, PACLING 2019*, pages 145–154, Hanoi, Vietnam. Springer Singapore.

Ian Tenney, James Wexler, Jasmijn Bastings, Tolga Bolukbasi, Andy Coenen, Sebastian Gehrmann, Ellen Jiang, Mahima Pushkarna, Carey Radebaugh, Emily Reif, and Ann Yuan. 2020. The language interpretability tool: Extensible, interactive visualizations and analysis for NLP models. In *Proceedings of the 2020 Conference on Empirical Methods in Natural Language Processing: System Demonstrations*, pages 107–118, Online. Association for Computational Linguistics.

A. Torsello, A. Gasparetto, L. Rossi, L. Bai, and E.R. Hancock. 2014. Transitive state alignment for the quantum jensen-shannon kernel. *Lect. Notes Comput. Sci.*, 8621:22–31.

Ashish Vaswani, Noam Shazeer, Niki Parmar, Jakob Uszkoreit, Llion Jones, Aidan N. Gomez, Łukasz Kaiser, and Illia Polosukhin. 2017. Attention is all you need. In *Proceedings of the 31st International Conference on Neural Information Processing Systems*, NIPS'17, pages 6000–6010, Red Hook, NY, USA. Curran Associates Inc.

Thomas Wolf, Lysandre Debut, Victor Sanh, Julien Chaumond, Clement Delangue, Anthony Moi, Pierric Cistac, Tim Rault, Remi Louf, Morgan Funtowicz, Joe Davison, Sam Shleifer, Patrick von Platen, Clara Ma, Yacine Jernite, Julien Plu, Canwen Xu, Teven Le Scao, Sylvain Gugger, Mariama Drame, Quentin Lhoest, and Alexander Rush. 2020. Transformers: State-of-the-art natural language processing. In *Proceedings of the 2020 Conference on Empirical Methods in Natural Language Processing: System Demonstrations*, pages 38–45. Association for Computational Linguistics.

Tongshuang Wu, Marco Tulio Ribeiro, Jeffrey Heer, and Daniel Weld. 2019. Errudite: Scalable, reproducible, and testable error analysis. In *Proceedings of the 57th Annual Meeting of the Association for Computational Linguistics*, pages 747–763, Florence, Italy. Association for Computational Linguistics.

Libo Yang. 2021. Fuzzy output support vector machine based incident ticket classification. *IEICE Transactions on Information and Systems*, E104.D(1):146–151.

Jun Yuan, Jesse Vig, and Nazneen Rajani. 2022. Isea: An interactive pipeline for semantic error analysis of nlp models. In *27th International Conference on Intelligent User Interfaces*, IUI '22, pages 878–888,

New York, NY, USA. Association for Computing Machinery.

Wubai Zhou, Wei Xue, Ramesh Baral, Qing Wang, Chunqiu Zeng, Tao Li, Jian Xu, Zheng Liu, Larisa Shwartz, and Genady Ya. Grabarnik. 2017. Star: A system for ticket analysis and resolution. In *Proceedings of the 23rd ACM SIGKDD International Conference on Knowledge Discovery and Data Mining*, KDD '17, pages 2181–2190, New York, NY, USA. Association for Computing Machinery.

Dawei Zhu, Michael A. Hedderich, Fangzhou Zhai, David Adelani, and Dietrich Klakow. 2022. Is BERT robust to label noise? a study on learning with noisy labels in text classification. In *Proceedings of the Third Workshop on Insights from Negative Results in NLP*, pages 62–67, Dublin, Ireland. Association for Computational Linguistics.

Yukun Zhu, Ryan Kiros, Rich Zemel, Ruslan Salakhutdinov, Raquel Urtasun, Antonio Torralba, and Sanja Fidler. 2015. Aligning books and movies: Towards story-like visual explanations by watching movies and reading books. In *2015 IEEE International Conference on Computer Vision (ICCV)*, pages 19–27.

Paolo Zicari, Gianluigi Folino, Massimo Guarascio, and Luigi Pontieri. 2021. Discovering accurate deep learning based predictive models for automatic customer support ticket classification. In *Proceedings of the 36th Annual ACM Symposium on Applied Computing*, SAC '21, pages 1098–1101, New York, NY, USA. Association for Computing Machinery.

A Embedding summarization strategies

Table 4 describes all the summarization strategies tested in this work. The "*cls last* (p)" strategy refers to the one adopted in the original BERT paper, using the `[CLS]` token embedding passed through the NSP prediction layer, with a `tanh` activation, commonly referred to as "pooled" embedding. In contrast, all other *cls* strategies use the un-pooled embedding, meaning that it is used directly as provided by the encoder without additional processing.

Table 5 reports the complete set of performance metrics measured to test the effectiveness of the summarization strategies. In the main article, only the accuracy and F_1-score are reported. All metrics besides accuracy refer to the macro-averaged metrics; metrics are computed separately for each label and then averaged, irrespective of the labels' frequency.

B Details on the Linux Bugs dataset

The preprocessing procedure applied to the Linux Bugs dataset discards bug reports without a valid message text, applies lowercasing to all text, and concatenates the issue title with the message body. The final dataset, after preprocessing, contains 35,050 bug descriptions, 17 first-level labels, and 73 sub-labels. The average number of characters per-ticket is 2,026 and each ticket is labeled with exactly one label and one sub-label. The label hierarchy for a subset of 3 macro-labels is shown in Fig. 2, and histograms with the frequency of labels and sub-labels are shown in Figs. 3 and 4, respectively.

One example of a pre-processed and lowercased bug report is displayed in Listing 1, and the effect of the text cleaning procedure described in Section 5.1 on the same body of text is showcased in Listing 2. As can be seen, these tickets are rich in technical information, like stack traces and error messages, mixed with text written in natural language. Misspellings are also quite frequent, since bugs are often filed by non-native English speakers.

C Other experimental details

All tests are run using PyTorch 1.11.0 and Python 3.10 using an NVIDIA RTX 2080 Ti. We use the AdamW optimizer (Loshchilov and Hutter, 2019) during training.

BERT-large validation The BERT-large models are validated on the T2 task to find the most suitable learning rate (choosing between $1e^{-5}$, $2e^{-\{5,6\}}$) and number of epochs. In this case, we use gradient accumulation to emulate this batch size value, due to the larger model size and computational limitations.

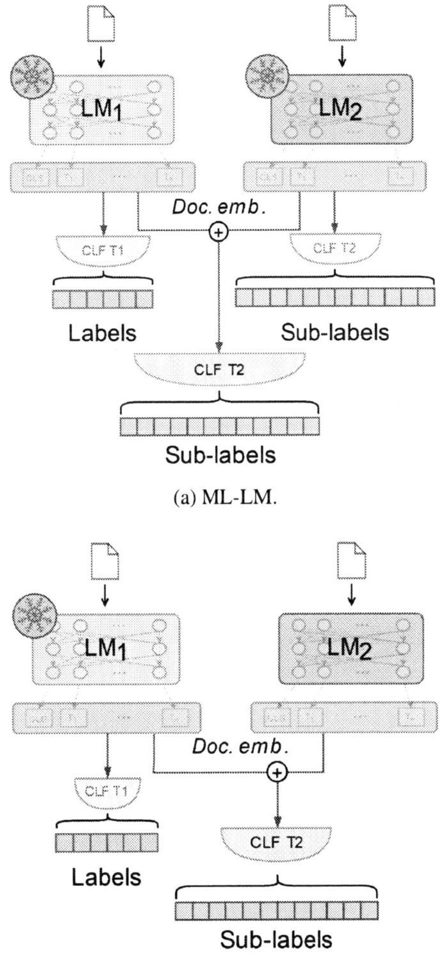

(a) ML-LM.

(b) Supported-LM.

Figure 1: Two-level classification models.

Multi-level validation We search for the best learning rate and number of epochs for the multi-level models separately, as `Supported-LM` contains a trainable LM, while `ML-LM` does not. In the first case, we validate with learning rates $1e^{-5}$ and $2e^{-\{6,5,4\}}$ with both base and large BERT, and use $2e^{-5}$ (2 epochs) and $1e^{-5}$ (3 epochs), respectively, during tests. The classification layer of the `ML-LM` models is validated with learning rates set to $1e^{-\{5,3\}}$ and $2e^{-\{5,4\}}$, and final tests are run with $2e^{-4}$ (1 epoch) and $1e^{-3}$ (1 epoch) respectively for the smaller and larger BERT models.

D Error analysis

We share a brief analysis of the per-class performance of our models (ML-BERT and Supported-BERT) in Table 6. In particular, the table reports per-class metrics of three of the top-performing labels, as well as of three of the worst-performing labels. The average length of tickets in that class (number of characters) and the number of samples of that class present in the test and train splits, respectively, are also displayed. The average ticket length is, in general, a good representative of actual length, as the outliers are few in this dataset, and are usually very long tickets (which will be truncated by the tokenizer in any case). Classes with a higher number of samples usually perform better, though this is not always the case (as exemplified by the Networking_Wireless category). Finally, the worst values of the F_1 score seem to be mostly dominated by low recall, which indicates a high number of false negatives. In this regard, it would be interesting to test different over- and under-sampling techniques, such as to verify whether this can help in the classification of these classes.

An analysis performed through specialized tools could reveal whether these classes are hard to classify because of linguistically-relevant factors, such as the lack of discriminative terms. For instance, it could be argued that certain labels are semantically similar (*e.g.*, Drivers_Network, Drivers_network-wireless, and Networking_Wireless), and might therefore contain semantically similar tickets. We plan to expand this analysis in future work, looking into more refined tools aimed at interpreting the inner workings of LMs, such as Errudite (Wu et al., 2019), the Language Interpretability Tool (LIT) (Tenney et al., 2020) and iSEA (Yuan et al., 2022). For example, the LIT would allow to directly examine individual examples that the model performs poorly upon as well as performing an investigation of the reasoning behind the model's decisions.

Table 4: Summarization strategies for document embeddings.

Basis	Strategy	Emb. size	Description
cls	*last* (p)	d	`[CLS]` embedding from last layer (default strategy)
	last		`[CLS]` embedding from last layer without pooling
	avg_h		Average of the `[CLS]` embeddings (no pooling) from the last h layers
	$concat_h$	$d * h$	Concatenation of the `[CLS]` embeddings from the last h layers
avg	*last*	d	Average of all embeddings* from the last layer
	avg_h		Average of the average of embeddings from the last h layers
	$concat_h$	$d * h$	Concatenation of the average of embeddings from the last h layers
max	*last*	d	Column-wise maximum of all embeddings* from the last layer
	avg_h		Average of the max of embeddings from the last h layers
	$concat_h$	$d * h$	Concatenation of the max of embeddings from the last h layers
max_min	*last*	$d * 2$	Concatenation of the max and min of embeddings from the last layer
	avg_h		As above, but averaging vectors from the last h layers
max_avg	*last*	$d * 2$	Concatenation of the max and avg of embeddings from the last layer
	avg_h		As above, but averaging vectors from the last h layers
sum_nor	*last*	d	Sum of token embeddings divided by its norm (*i.e.*, normalized sum)
	$concat_h$	$d * h$	Like *last* but concatenating the last h layers

* Excluding special symbols (*e.g.* `[CLS]` and padding).

Table 5: Test set results* with BERT classifier on T2 comparing summarization strategies on the Linux Bugs dataset. Best results are outlined in bold.

Basis	Strategy	Acc	F_1	Prec	Rec
cls	*last* (p)†	0.518 [± 0.006]	0.354 [± 0.009]	0.386 [± 0.009]	0.365 [± 0.006]
	last	0.566 [± 0.012]	0.446 [± 0.018]	0.479 [± 0.027]	0.452 [± 0.017]
	avg_2	0.531 [± 0.010]	0.393 [± 0.012]	0.420 [± 0.018]	0.398 [± 0.012]
	$concat_2$	0.535 [± 0.010]	0.400 [± 0.014]	0.426 [± 0.015]	0.401 [± 0.012]
	$concat_3$	**0.571** [± 0.008]	0.456 [± 0.013]	**0.498** [± 0.013]	**0.458** [± 0.015]
	$concat_4$	0.568 [± 0.009]	**0.457** [± 0.014]	0.490 [± 0.013]	0.458 [± 0.017]
	$concat_5$	0.565 [± 0.012]	0.456 [± 0.013]	0.486 [± 0.011]	0.458 [± 0.018]
avg	*last*	0.525 [± 0.008]	0.387 [± 0.010]	0.420 [± 0.015]	0.388 [± 0.010]
	avg_2	0.522 [± 0.005]	0.383 [± 0.013]	0.409 [± 0.021]	0.387 [± 0.010]
	$concat_2$	0.523 [± 0.007]	0.390 [± 0.009]	0.411 [± 0.015]	0.394 [± 0.011]
max	*last*	0.522 [± 0.011]	0.385 [± 0.014]	0.415 [± 0.011]	0.391 [± 0.014]
	avg_2	0.519 [± 0.007]	0.375 [± 0.013]	0.395 [± 0.021]	0.387 [± 0.014]
	$concat_2$	0.518 [± 0.006]	0.373 [± 0.015]	0.401 [± 0.021]	0.383 [± 0.012]
max_min	*last*	0.522 [± 0.010]	0.377 [± 0.011]	0.395 [± 0.019]	0.395 [± 0.010]
	avg_2	0.522 [± 0.009]	0.374 [± 0.010]	0.395 [± 0.019]	0.385 [± 0.011]
max_avg	*last*	0.516 [± 0.007]	0.381 [± 0.012]	0.406 [± 0.017]	0.390 [± 0.012]
	avg_2	0.519 [± 0.006]	0.379 [± 0.007]	0.402 [± 0.011]	0.392 [± 0.007]
sum_nor	*last*	0.406 [± 0.018]	0.171 [± 0.017]	0.192 [± 0.023]	0.206 [± 0.016]
	$concat_2$	0.379 [± 0.013]	0.135 [± 0.019]	0.149 [± 0.022]	0.179 [± 0.021]
	$concat_5$	0.388 [± 0.015]	0.135 [± 0.015]	0.149 [± 0.015]	0.180 [± 0.014]

* Standard deviation over 6 runs is reported in brackets.

† Pooled, using *cls pooled* strategy.

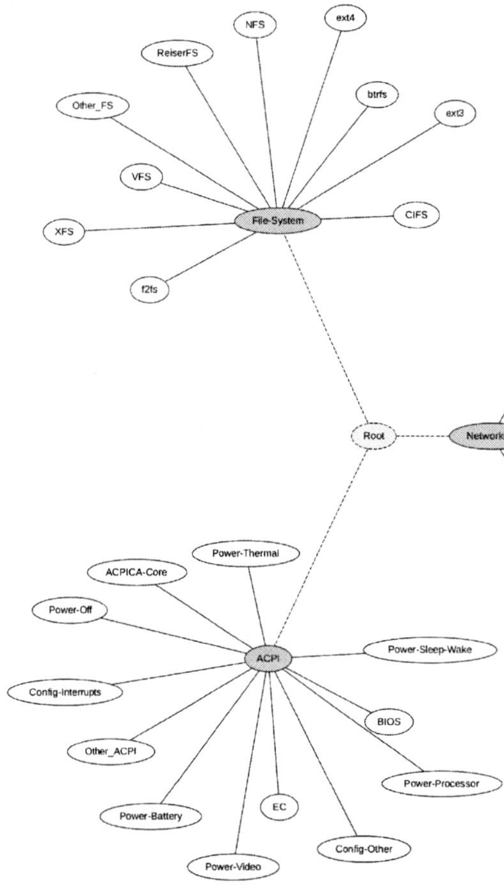

Figure 2: Example of 3 macro-categories (in blue) and their children from the Linux Bugs dataset.

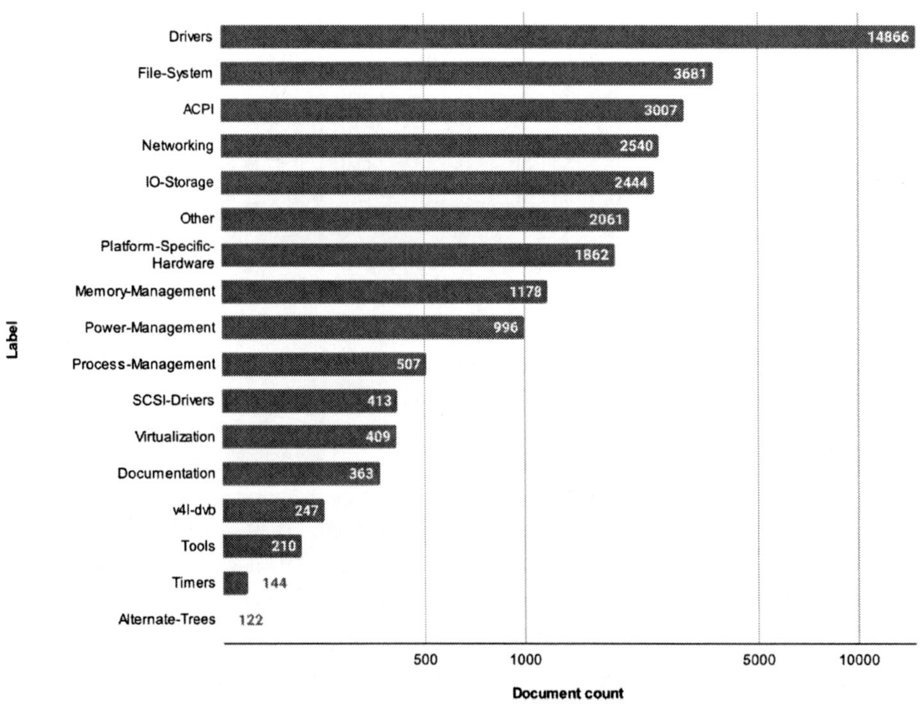

Figure 3: Frequency count of first-level labels in the Linux Bugs dataset.

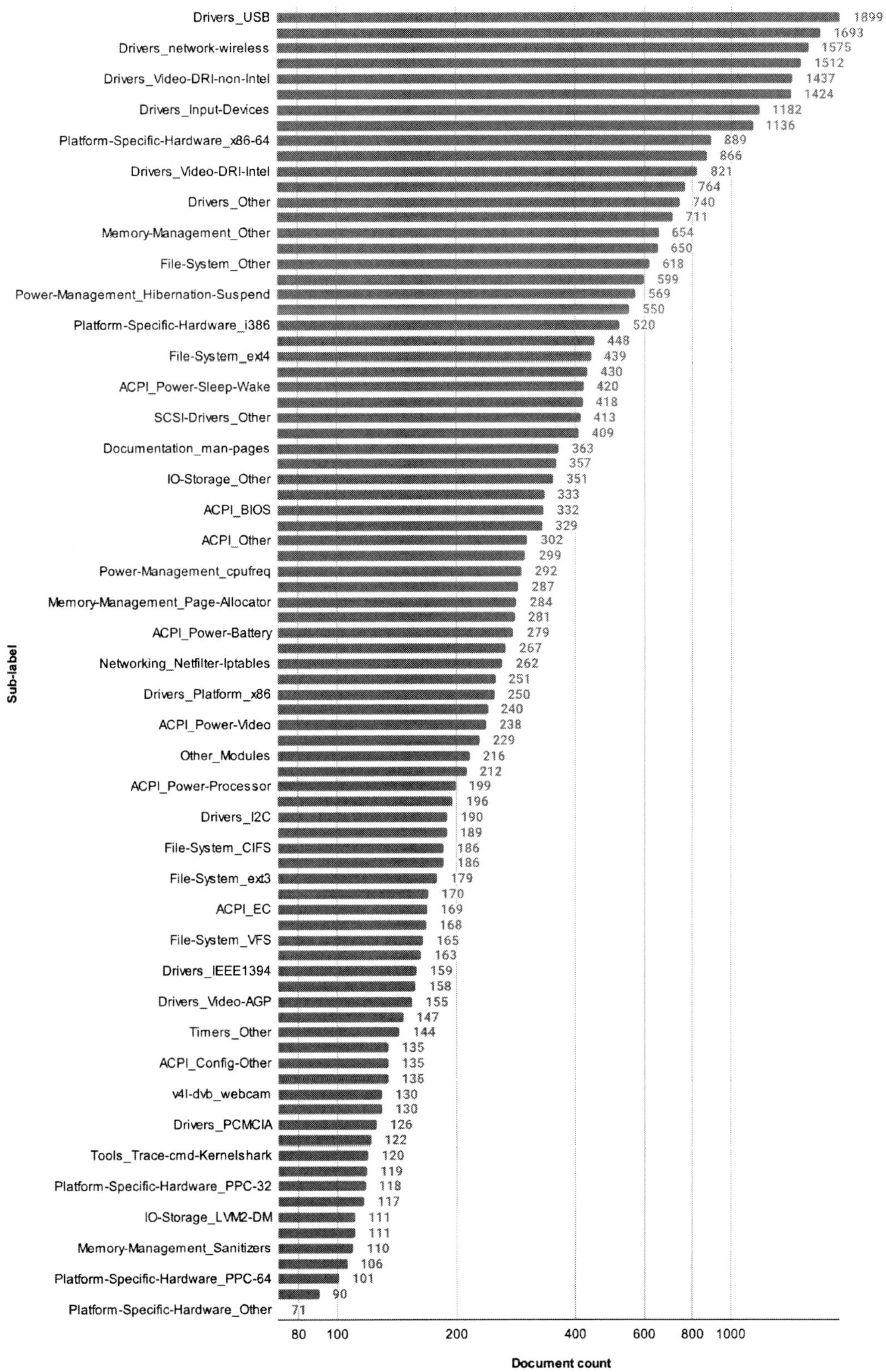

Figure 4: Frequency count of second-level labels in the Linux Bugs dataset, obtained by flattening labels and sub-labels.

Product: Drivers

Component: Network

Title: `kernel crashes after stop network and remove e100.`

Description:
```
exact kernel version:linux-2.5.51 distribution:redhat 8.0+linux2.5.51
hardware environment:intel stl2 mother boar d problem description:  compile
e100 as kernel module, insmod e100 and start the network.  then stop network and
remove e100 together.  then kernel crashes in random places.  for example:  use
command :  insmod e100 /etc/init.d/network start /etc/init.d/network stop; rmmod
e100 then the kernel crashes.  eflags:  00010887 eip is at cascade+0x25/0x60
eax:  defd02b8 ebx:  00000001 ecx:  00000000 edx:  c150a4c0 esi:  c150acd4
edi:  c150acd4 ebp:  c150acd4 esp:  c0559f1c ds:  0068 es:  0068 ss:  0068
process swapper (pid:  0, threadinfo=c0558000 task=c0497f60) stack:  00000000
c0559f94 00000001 c150a4c0 fffffffd 00000000 c012abb2 c150a4c0 c150acd4
c010baf5 00000000 00000000 c0559f94 00000001 c0553d68 fffffffd 00000000 c0125bb5
c150a4c0 00000046 00000000 00000000 c0559f94 c01070c0 call trace:  [<c012abb2>]
__run_timers+0x1b2/0x202 [<c010baf5>] handle_irq_event+0x45/0x70 [<c0125bb5>]
do_softirq+0xc5/0xd0 [<c01070c0>] default_idle+0x0/0x50 [<c0116f3d>]
smp_apic_timer_interrupt+0xcd/0x130 [<c01070c0>] default_idle+0x0/0x50
[<c010a3a6>] apic_timer_interrupt+0x1a/0x20 [<c01070c0>] default_idle+0x0/0x50
[<c01070c0>] default_idle+0x0/0x50 [<c01070ea>] default_idle+0x2a/0x50
[<c010718a>] cpu_idle+0x3a/0x50 [<c0105000>] rest_init+0x0/0x30 code:  0f 0b
6f 01 ba a7 41 c0 8b 18 89 44 24 04 89 3c 24 e8 a5 0c
```

Listing 1: A lowercased ticket from the Linux Bugs dataset; Fields "Product" and "Component" are used as labels and sub-labels respectively.

Product: Drivers

Component: Network

Title: `kernel crashes after stop network and remove e100.`

Description:
```
exact kernel distribution:redhat hardware environment:intel stl2
mother boar d problem description:  compile e100 as kernel module, insmod e100
and start the network.  then stop network and remove e100 together.  then
kernel crashes in random places.  for example:  use command :  insmod e100
/etc/init.d/network start /etc/init.d/network stop; rmmod e100 then the kernel
crashes.  eflags:  eip is at eax:  ebx:  ecx:  edx:  esi:  edi:  ebp:  esp:  ds:
0068 es:  0068 ss:  0068 process swapper (pid:  0, stack:  fffffffd fffffffd
call trace:  code:  0f 0b 6f 01 ba a7 41 c0 8b 18 89 44 24 04 89 3c 24 e8 a5 0c
```

Listing 2: The same ticket from Listing 1, preprocessed with the more aggressive strategy.

Table 6: Label-specific performances and statistics for three of the best performing and three of the worse performing classes. The values are calculated and averaged over the usual 3-fold CV.

Model	Label	F_1	Prec	Recall	Avg ticket len	# in test	# in train
	Drivers_Network	0.958	0.953	0.963	2825.49	379	1008
	Drivers_Hardware-Monitoring	0.891	0.861	0.925	1365.25	62	74
`ML-BERT`	File-System_VFS	0.842	0.789	0.905	2494.28	143	110
(base)	...						
	Tools_Trace-cmd-Kernelshark	0.328	0.436	0.268	1429.63	24	80
	Documentation_man-pages	0.196	0.284	0.163	907.67	41	242
	Networking_Wireless	0.064	0.107	0.074	2406.04	45	434
	Drivers_Network	0.963	0.961	0.965	2825.49	379	1008
	Drivers_Hardware-Monitoring	0.888	0.887	0.892	1365.25	62	74
`Supp-BERT`	File-System_VFS	0.829	0.767	0.902	2494.28	143	110
(base)	...						
	Tools_Trace-cmd-Kernelshark	0.104	0.667	0.057	1429.63	24	80
	Documentation_man-pages	0.225	0.472	0.163	907.67	41	242
	Networking_Wireless	0.079	0.192	0.052	2406.04	45	434

Towards better structured and less noisy Web data: Oscar with Register annotations

Veronika Laippala[•] Anna Salmela[•] Samuel Rönnqvist[•] Alham Fikri Aji[○*]
Li-Hsin Chang[•] Asma Dhifallah[•] Larissa Goulart[‡] Henna Kortelainen[•]
Marc Pàmies[⋆] Deise Prina Dutra[◇] Valtteri Skantsi[•]
Lintang Sutawika[□] Sampo Pyysalo[•]

[•]University of Turku [○]Amazon [‡]Montclair State University
[⋆]Barcelona Supercomputing Center [◇]Universidade Federal de Minas Gerais [□]Datasaur.ai
[•]{mavela,annsaln,saanro}@utu.fi

Abstract

Web-crawled datasets are known to be noisy, as they feature a wide range of language use covering both user-generated and professionally edited content as well as noise originating from the crawling process. This article presents one solution to reduce this noise by using automatic register (genre) identification—whether the texts are, e.g., forum discussions, lyrical or how-to pages. We apply the multilingual register identification model by Rönnqvist et al. (2021) and label the widely used Oscar dataset. Additionally, we evaluate the model against eight new languages, showing that the performance is comparable to previous findings on a restricted set of languages. Finally, we present and apply a machine learning method for further cleaning text files originating from Web crawls from remains of boilerplate and other elements not belonging to the main text of the Web page. The register labeled and cleaned dataset covers 351 million documents in 14 languages and is available at `https://huggingface.co/datasets/TurkuNLP/register_oscar`.

1 Introduction

Massive Web-crawled datasets are widely used in Natural Language Processing (NLP), for instance for training language models (Conneau et al., 2020; Raffel et al., 2019; Xue et al., 2020). However, the challenge with these crawled datasets is that they are typically very noisy. First of all, this noise originates from the lack of structure and metadata—the datasets don't include any information on the origin of the documents. This complicates their use, because language on the Web varies extremely, ranging from toxic language, discussion forums and other user-generated content to professionally-like edited texts. Second, the noisiness comes from the crawling process—despite the cleaning efforts, Web-crawled data still contain remains of boilerplate and other elements not belonging to the main text, such as *click here* or *read more*. All these properties affect the automatic processing of text (Maharjan et al., 2018; Barbaresi, 2021; Kilgarriff, 2007).

The automatic identification of Web genres or registers—whether the documents are, e.g., forum discussions, originally spoken, informative or narrative (Biber and Conrad, 2019)— would offer a solution to reduce the noisiness of Web data and to add metadata on the origin of the documents. However, this has been a challenge. There are no gatekeepers ensuring that the users follow any conventions when writing on the Web, and thus, Web language use has been referred to as a jungle (Sharoff, 2010). The available register datasets, almost entirely focusing on English, have been restricted to only selected and well-defined registers, and they do not generalize to the entire Web (Sharoff et al., 2010; Asheghi et al., 2014; Santini, 2008; Madjarov et al., 2019).

Recently, however, the Corpus of Online Registers of English (CORE) (Egbert et al., 2015) sampled from the unrestricted open Web has allowed the modeling of the full range of registers found in Web-crawled datasets. Furthermore, similarly register-annotated datasets in Finnish, Swedish and French (Laippala et al., 2019; Repo et al., 2021) have extended these possibilities to a multilingual setting (Rönnqvist et al., 2021).

In this paper, we benefit from these advances and present Register Oscar, a version of the widely used Oscar dataset (Ortiz Suárez et al., 2019) to which we have automatically created register labels. Furthermore, we introduce and apply a machine learning method for cleaning text files originating from Web crawls—such as the Oscar documents—to filter out noise left after boilerplate removal.

Register Oscar covers 14 languages. To identify the document registers, we use the multilingual

[*]Work done prior to Amazon.

Proceedings of the 2022 COLING Workshop: The 8th Workshop on Noisy User-generated Text (W-NUT 2022), pages 215–221

register model by Rönnqvist et al. (2021) based on four languages. To evaluate the model on the wider set of languages included in Register Oscar, we present new CORE-style annotated evaluation datasets in eight languages: Arabic, Catalan, Chinese, Hindi, Indonesian, Portuguese, Spanish and Urdu. We find that the zero-shot performance of the model on these culturally and linguistically different languages is 0.70 F1-score, similar to the previously reported zero-shot results.

In sum, our main contributions are:

- We provide automatic register annotations for 351M documents in Oscar in 14 languages, using the register model by Rönnqvist et al. (2021).
- We present new manually annotated register corpora for eight languages and evaluate the register identification model on these.
- We introduce and apply a new machine learning method for cleaning text files from Web crawls.

The register annotations for Oscar are available at `https://huggingface.co/datasets/TurkuNLP/register_oscar`, and the new manually annotated register corpora and the text quality annotations used to train the cleaning system at `https://github.com/TurkuNLP/multilingual-register-labeling`.

2 Data

Oscar (Ortiz Suárez et al., 2019) is our main source of data. We use the version available at `https://huggingface.co/datasets/oscar` in the following 14 languages: Arabic, Basque, Bengali, Catalan, Chinese, English, French, Hindi, Indonesian, Portuguese, Spanish, Swahili, Urdu and Vietnamese. Following the Big Science project[1], the languages were selected so that they represent a variety of language families and geographical locations and include also low-resource languages.

The new manually annotated multilingual register corpora cover eight languages created as a part of the current study, the main objective being to allow for a more extensive evaluation of the register identification model on the Oscar languages. The

Narrative NA
News report / news blog, narrative blog
Opinion OP
Review, opinion blog, advice
Informational Description IN
Description of a thing or a person, research article
Interactive Discussion ID
How-to HI
How-to / instruction, recipe
Informational Persuasion IP
Description with intent to sell
Lyrical LY
Spoken SP
Machine Translated MT

Table 1: Main registers and examples of sub-registers.

newly annotated datasets include culturally and linguistically varied languages. As register is deeply associated with the situational context of the text (Biber, 1988) and, e.g., blogs can have very different characteristics in different cultures, this offers a unique chance to evaluate the robustness of the register model.

The documents for the annotation were randomly sampled from a recent Common Crawl[2] dataset. The annotation was done using a custom annotation tool. Most of the annotators have a background in linguistics or NLP. The annotators were given a detailed tutorial to the register scheme, see `https://turkunlp.org/register-annotation-docs/`.

The annotations of the new datasets follow the hierarchical CORE register scheme consisting of eight main registers, tens of subregisters, and the category Machine Translated, see Table 1. To cover all the documents found in the online jungle, the scheme has been created in a data-driven manner and allows for the annotation of *hybrid* documents simultaneously assigned to several registers (Biber et al., 2020; Egbert et al., 2015). For instance, a lifestyle blog telling about the writer's day and promoting a product would be annotated as both *Narrative* and *Informational Persuasion*.

The newly annotated register corpora are described in Table 2. Their sizes vary, Indonesian being the largest and Arabic the smallest language. Overall, the sizes are relatively small. Therefore, we focus here on the main register level. The register distributions are also very uneven. This was expected, as similar distributions have been found for the four original languages (Laippala et al., 2019; Repo et al., 2021).

The text quality annotations are used to train the

[1] `https://bigscience.huggingface.co/`

[2] `https://commoncrawl.org/`

	HI	ID	IN	IP	LY	NA	OP	SP	HYB	MT	No label	Total
ar	2	3	12	7		32	10		23	3		92
ca	2	2	41	11	2	34	10	2	2	3	2	111
es	6	3	25	27		31	4		3	1		100
hi	3	1	26	12	10	82	6	2	13	5	1	161
id	34	5	153	131	10	239	79	2	504	29	4	1190
pt	24	6	47	101	3	97	23		31		2	334
ur	1	1	13	9	2	94	22		17	1		160
zh	8	5	58	104	1	84	27	1	24	5		317

Table 2: New multilingual register corpora. Hybrids (HYB) are presented as one class. No label refers to documents for which the annotators could not find a suitable register.

Language	Texts	Accepted lines	Rejected lines	Lines total
English	104	3 360	2 812	6 172
Finnish	89	1 797	2 480	4 277
French	1 807	57 345	26 171	83 516
German	112	2 529	925	3 454
Spanish	70	1 536	1 483	3 019
Swedish	2 114	47 302	51 099	98 401
Total	4 296	113 869	84 970	198 839

Table 3: Text quality annotations.

model behind the cleaning pipeline. The method is trained on documents annotated line-by-line as *accept* or *reject* according to if the line was part of the main text or not. The statistics of this dataset are described in Table 3. The documents were retrieved from Common Crawl using the same pipeline as the register annotated documents, and they were preprocessed for boilerplate removal using Trafilatura version 0.3.

3 Methods

The register labeling of the Oscar documents is done using the *master multilingual* model by Rönnqvist et al. (2021). The model is based on a fine-tuned XLM-R (Conneau et al., 2020) using French, Finnish and English data, and is available at `https://github.com/TurkuNLP/multilingual-register-labeling`. To account for hybrid documents (see Section 2), the model is multi-label allowing to predict several registers for one document.

The register model has been reported to achieve an F1-score of 0.77 on a multilingual dataset. Furthermore, it outperforms also monolingual language-specific neural classifiers in these languages (Rönnqvist et al., 2021), and provides much higher performance than earlier systems based on SVMs or statistical techniques that additionally would not allow for the modeling of languages without training data (Laippala et al., 2021; Biber and Egbert, 2016). Therefore, the use of the XLM-R is motivated in the current study despite the computational costs. Finally, we also evaluate the performance of the XLM-R-based register identification model on the new multilingual register corpora.

The cleaning of the Oscar documents from remains of boilerplate and elements not belonging to the main text works on text files and is based on machine learning, unlike boilerplate removal that is typically rule-based and takes html as input.

The pipeline consists of three steps. First, the data is run through a heuristic filtering script with language detection using langdetect to filter out e.g., documents that are less than 75 words long or have a high ratio of digit (> 0.075) or foreign characters (>0.02).

Second, an XLM-R (Conneau et al., 2020) classifier is trained to predict whether a document is machine generated or not, using data from our ongoing register annotation projects where Machine translation and generation is one of the register categories. We optimize learning rate using a grid of rates between 1e-7..9e-5.

Third, we filter out lines, defined as sequences of characters separated by a line break, that do not belong to the main text of the document. This step uses the text quality annotations described in Section 2 and includes two XLM-R models: a bag-of-lines classifier to predict whether a line is main text content or not, and another one with an extra Long Short-Term Memory (LSTM) layer to predict the line quality based on sequences of embeddings retrieved from the first model. We optimize the learning rate within the range of 1e-7..9e-5, and compare the performances of the first model to the entire architecture.

4 Evaluation

4.1 Register model performance on the new languages

Figure 1 presents the performance of the register identification model on the new multilingual register corpora and on English and French already used in the original model development (Rönnqvist et al., 2021). The model performance varies between 0.58 and 0.82 for the new languages, the lowest being for Indonesian and the highest for Urdu. Overall, the total average F1-score on all the evaluation datasets is 0.70.

Model	Accuracy	sd	t-value
Bag-of-lines XLM-R	0.84	0.011	
Sequential XLM-R	0.88	0.002	t(2) = 45

Table 4: Performances of the line-wise cleaning models.

The performance of the model on the new set of languages is somewhat lower than the original performance reported by Rönnqvist et al. (2021), 0.77. However, importantly, the original setting was multilingual with the same languages included in the training and testing, whereas ours is zero-shot. This explains the decrease—similarly, Rönnqvist et al. (2021) report an F1-score of 0.71% on a zero-shot experiment.

4.2 Cleaning pipeline

The classifier predicting whether entire documents are machine generated or not achieved a mean F1-score of 0.98, averaged over three instances (*SD* 0.001).

The performances of the bag-of-lines classifier and the sequence-to-sequence architecture identifying the text quality based on the line-wise annotations are described in Table 4. The results are means over three runs. We can see that while both methods achieve competitive results, the sequence-to-sequence model outperforms the classifier approach by four percentage points. This was to be expected considering that lines featuring actual text and noise are not evenly distributed in a document—instead, there may be long passages of actual text, and then again several lines of noise. The sequence-to-sequence approach can take advantage of this ordering, resulting in a higher performance.

	Texts	Main content lines	Noise lines	Words	Cleaned texts
ar	9.01M	43.5M	901k	2.65B	**3.36M**
bn	1.11M	7.19M	332k	358M	**1.1M**
ca	2.46M	9.43M	235k	556M	**1.22M**
en	304M	2.99B	103M	169B	**214M**
es	56.3M	393M	8.76M	21.3B	**34.6M**
eu	257k	835k	12.6k	37.1M	**112k**
fr	59.4M	360M	9.96M	18.6B	**34.2M**
hi	1.91M	9.03M	370k	630M	**1.13M**
id	9.95M	43.4M	590k	2.1B	**6.23M**
pt	26.9M	162M	2.79M	8.49B	**15.9M**
sw	24.8k	38.7k	1.19k	1.37M	**24.7k**
ur	429k	1.86M	51.9k	162M	**260k**
vi	9.9M	76.5M	2.61M	4.86B	**7.09M**
zh	41.7M	186M	5.99M	24.7B	**31.2M**
Total	524M	4.28B	136M	253B	**351M**

Table 5: Data sizes before and after the cleaning.

4.3 Register Oscar in numbers

Table 5 describes the Oscar dataset we use and the effect of the cleaning pipeline to its size. The word counts represent space-separated tokens except for Arabic and Chinese, where the texts were tokenized with UDPipe (Straka and Straková, 2017). Overall, the filtering reduced the dataset sizes relatively aggressively to ~30-40% of the original. However, for most of the languages, the sizes are still giant—English, French, Spanish, Portuguese and Chinese cover tens of millions of documents, and Arabic, Bengali, Catalan, Hindi, Indonesian and Vietnamese 1-10 million documents. Basque, Swahili and Urdu have only 20,000-260,000 cleaned documents, but their sizes were small already in the uncleaned version. Finally, Figure 2 in Appendix presents the register distributions for each language in the cleaned dataset. For most languages, the distributions follow the training data—Narrative and Informational Description are the most frequent, while Spoken and Lyrical feature a much smaller proportion of the data. E.g., English Lyrical covers 164,105 documents. For some of the lower-resource languages—Bengali, Hindi, Swahili and Urdu—the vast majority of the documents are predicted as Narrative. This can be related to many aspects of the data collection and processing, and will be examined in future work.

5 Conclusions

In this paper, we have presented automatically produced register annotations for the widely used Oscar dataset in 14 languages, and we have evaluated the register identification model against new datasets covering eight languages not included in the original model development. Furthermore, we have described a machine-learning method for cleaning text data originating from Web crawls, and we have applied the method to further clean the documents in the entire dataset.

The evaluation showed that the performance of the register model is comparable to previously reported zero-shot results, although the newly annotated datasets feature linguistically and culturally diverse languages. This suggests that multilingual register identification can be used to provide structure and improve the usability of Web-crawled data, where the content ranges from noisy user-generated text to professionally edited documents. The register annotations automatically produced in this study cover altogether eight

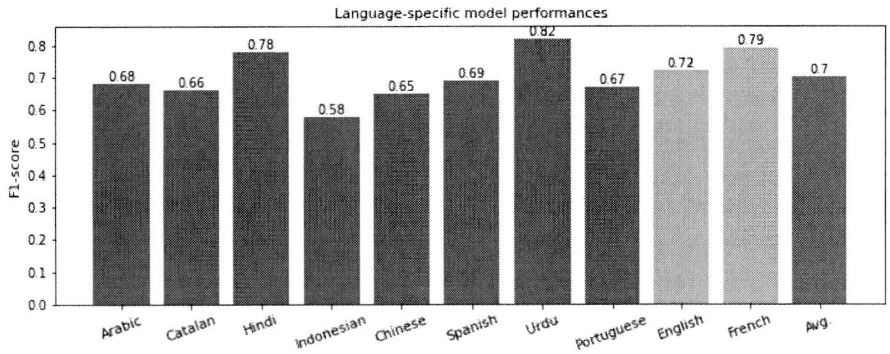

Figure 1: Language-specific performances of the register model.

registers and 351 million documents, available at https://huggingface.co/datasets/TurkuNLP/register_oscar. The new manually annotated register datasets and the text quality annotations used to develop the cleaning pipeline can be found at https://github.com/TurkuNLP/multilingual-register-labeling.

Acknowledgements

We thank the Emil Aaltonen Foundation and Academy of Finland for financial support and the Big Science project for collaboration. We also wish to acknowledge CSC – IT Center for Science, Finland for computational resources.

References

Rezapour Noushin Asheghi, Katja Markert, and Serge Sharoff. 2014. Semi-supervised graph-based genre classification for web pages. In *Proceedings of TextGraphs-9*, pages 39–47.

Adrien Barbaresi. 2021. Trafilatura: A web scraping library and command-line tool for text discovery and extraction. In *Proceedings of the 59th Annual Meeting of the Association for Computational Linguistics and the 11th International Joint Conference on Natural Language Processing: System Demonstrations*, pages 122–131, Online. Association for Computational Linguistics.

Douglas Biber. 1988. *Variation across speech and writing*. Cambridge University Press, Cambridge.

Douglas Biber and Susan Conrad. 2019. *Register, Genre, and Style*. Cambridge University Press, Cambridge.

Douglas Biber and Jesse Egbert. 2016. Using grammatical features for automatic register identification in an unrestricted corpus of documents from the open web. *Journal of Research Design and Statistics in Linguistics and Communication Science*, 2:3–36.

Douglas Biber, Jesse Egbert, and Daniel Keller. 2020. Reconceptualizing register in a continuous situational space. *Corpus Linguistics and Linguistic Theory*, Ahead of print.

Alexis Conneau, Kartikay Khandelwal, Naman Goyal, Vishrav Chaudhary, Guillaume Wenzek, Francisco Guzmán, Edouard Grave, Myle Ott, Luke Zettlemoyer, and Veselin Stoyanov. 2020. Unsupervised cross-lingual representation learning at scale. In *Proceedings of the 58th Annual Meeting of the Association for Computational Linguistics*, pages 8440–8451, Online. Association for Computational Linguistics.

Jesse Egbert, Douglas Biber, and Mark Davies. 2015. Developing a bottom-up, user-based method of web register classification. *Journal of the Association for Information Science and Technology*, 66:1817–1831.

Adam Kilgarriff. 2007. Last Words: Googleology is Bad Science. *Computational Linguistics, Volume 33, Number 1, March 2007.*

Veronika Laippala, Jesse Egbert, Douglas Biber, and Aki-Juhani Kyröläinen. 2021. Exploring the role of lexis and grammar for the stable identification of register in an unrestricted corpus of web documents. *Language resources and evaluation.*

Veronika Laippala, Roosa Kyllönen, Jesse Egbert, Douglas Biber, and Sampo Pyysalo. 2019. Toward multilingual identification of online registers. In *Proceedings of the 22nd Nordic Conference on Computational Linguistics*, pages 292–297, Turku, Finland. Linköping University Electronic Press.

Gjorgji Madjarov, Vedrana Vidulin, Ivica Dimitrovski, and Dragi Kocev. 2019. Web genre classification with methods for structured output prediction. *Information Sciences*, 503:551 – 573.

Suraj Maharjan, Manuel Montes, Fabio A. onzález, and Thamar Solorio. 2018. A genre-aware attention model to improve the likability prediction of books. In *Proceedings of the 2018 Conference on Empirical Methods in Natural Language Processing*, pages

3381–3391. Association for Computational Linguistics.

Pedro Javier Ortiz Suárez, Benoit Sagot, and Laurent Romary. 2019. Asynchronous pipelines for processing huge corpora on medium to low resource infrastructures. Proceedings of the Workshop on Challenges in the Management of Large Corpora (CMLC-7) 2019. Cardiff, 22nd July 2019, pages 9 – 16, Mannheim. Leibniz-Institut für Deutsche Sprache.

Colin Raffel, Noam Shazeer, Adam Roberts, Katherine Lee, Sharan Narang, Michael Matena, Yanqi Zhou, Wei Li, and Peter J. Liu. 2019. Exploring the limits of transfer learning with a unified text-to-text transformer. *CoRR*, abs/1910.10683.

Liina Repo, Valtteri Skantsi, Samuel Rönnqvist, Saara Hellström, Miika Oinonen, Anna Salmela, Douglas Biber, Jesse Egbert, Sampo Pyysalo, and Veronika Laippala. 2021. Beyond the English web: Zero-shot cross-lingual and lightweight monolingual classification of registers. In *Proceedings of the 16th Conference of the European Chapter of the Association for Computational Linguistics: Student Research Workshop*, pages 183–191, Online. Association for Computational Linguistics.

Samuel Rönnqvist, Valtteri Skantsi, Miika Oinonen, and Veronika Laippala. 2021. Multilingual and zero-shot is closing in on monolingual web register classification. In *Proceedings of the 23rd Nordic Conference on Computational Linguistics (NoDaLiDa)*, pages 157–165, Reykjavik, Iceland (Online). Linköping University Electronic Press, Sweden.

Marina Santini. 2008. Zero, single, or multi? genre of web pages through the users' perspective. *Information Processing & Management*, 44(2):702–737.

Serge Sharoff. 2010. In the garden and in the jungle comparing genres in the bnc and internet.

Serge Sharoff, Zhili Wu, and Katja Markert. 2010. The web library of babel: evaluating genre collections. In *Proceedings of the Seventh International Conference on Language Resources and Evaluation (LREC'10)*, Valletta, Malta. European Language Resources Association (ELRA).

Milan Straka and Jana Straková. 2017. Tokenizing, pos tagging, lemmatizing and parsing ud 2.0 with udpipe. In *Proceedings of the CoNLL 2017 Shared Task: Multilingual Parsing from Raw Text to Universal Dependencies*, pages 88–99, Vancouver, Canada. Association for Computational Linguistics.

Linting Xue, Noah Constant, Adam Roberts, Mihir Kale, Rami Al-Rfou, Aditya Siddhant, Aditya Barua, and Colin Raffel. 2020. mt5: A massively multilingual pre-trained text-to-text transformer. *CoRR*, abs/2010.11934.

A Appendix

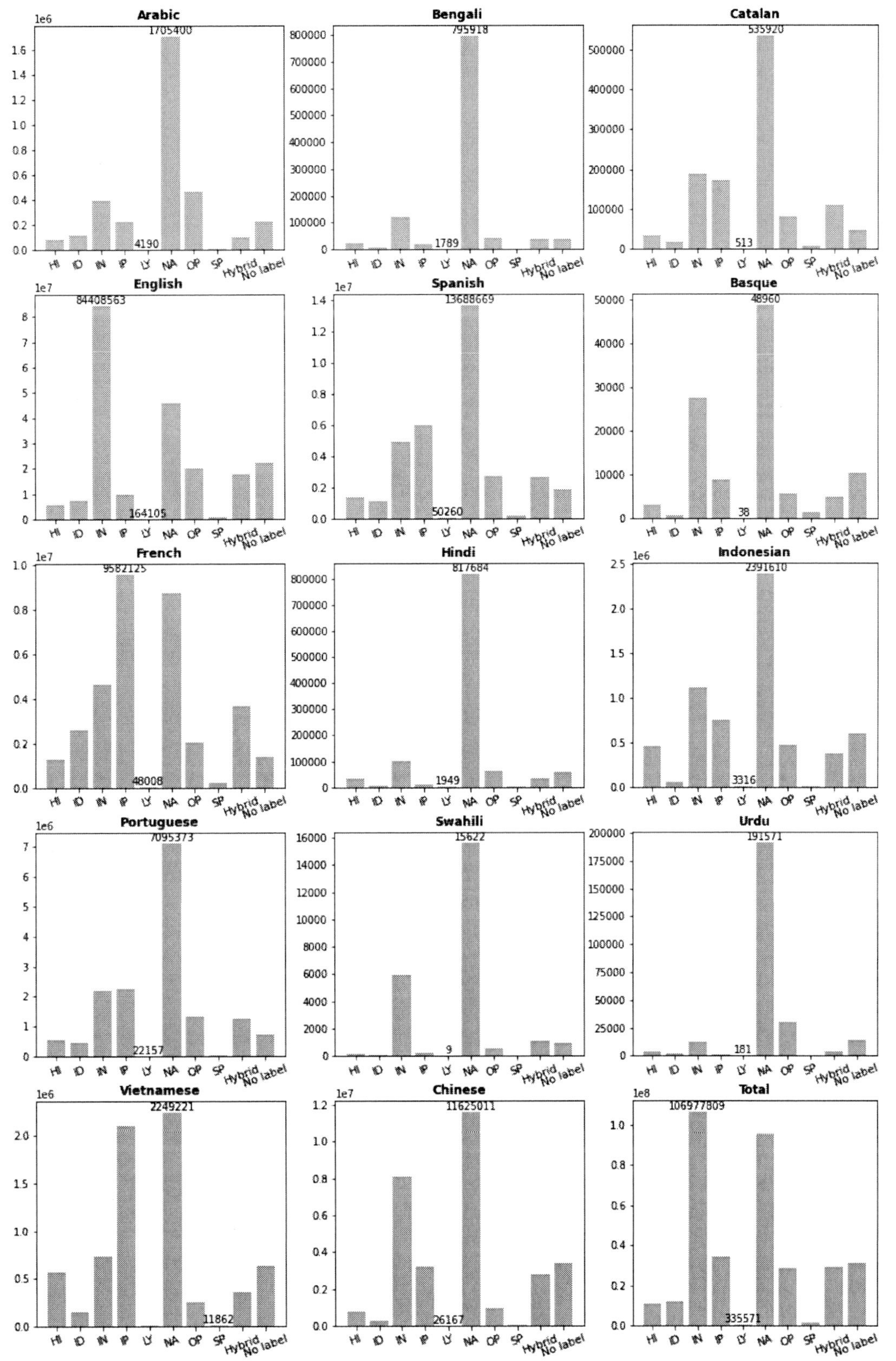

Figure 2: Register distributions per language in the cleaned dataset. The sizes of the largest and the smallest class for each language are indicated. Please note the varying scales of the figures.

True or False? Detecting False Information on Social Media Using Graph Neural Networks

Samyo Rode-Hasinger[1], **Anna Kruspe**[1,2] and **Xiao Xiang Zhu**[1]
[1]Technical University of Munich
[2]Technische Hochschule Nürnberg
{samyo.rode, xiaoxiang.zhu}@tum.de, anna.kruspe@th-nuernberg.de

Abstract

In recent years, false information such as fake news, rumors and conspiracy theories on many relevant issues in society have proliferated. This phenomenon has been significantly amplified by the fast and inexorable spread of misinformation on social media and instant messaging platforms. With this work, we contribute to containing the negative impact on society caused by fake news. We propose a graph neural network approach for detecting false information on Twitter. We leverage the inherent structure of graph-based social media data aggregating information from short text messages (tweets), user profiles and social interactions. We use knowledge from pre-trained language models efficiently, and show that user-defined descriptions of profiles provide useful information for improved prediction performance. The empirical results indicate that our proposed framework significantly outperforms text- and user-based methods on misinformation datasets from two different domains, even in a difficult multilingual setting.

1 Introduction

The spread of misinformation on social media is a growing problem that can hardly be tackled without the help of AI-based detection methods due to the large amount of data and its complexity. This is evident in crisis situations such as the COVID-19 pandemic (Naeem and Boulos, 2021) or Russia's attack on Ukraine where a sheer flood of fake news has exacerbated the situation causing great insecurity and harm among the people.

Previous work has focused primarily on the verification of news content, taking into account user profiles and propagation patterns in social networks. However, in real life scenario, news articles are not always freely available, and matching user-generated content from social media to published articles is often hard to accomplish (Shu et al., 2017). Therefore, we propose a method for automatic fake news detection that is based only on data available on social media. We introduce a unified framework with graph neural networks (GNNs) that leverages short text messages, user profile information and social network properties. As a case study, we train and evaluate our model on mono- and multilingual social media content from Twitter. To this end, we jointly model the heterogeneous graph structure of the data formed by users, retweeters and their tweets, and cast the verification task as a node classification problem. We exploit self-defined profile descriptions from Twitter users and retweeters as well as the tweets' text to create initial user and tweet node features. Unlike previous approaches which use pre-trained word embeddings to encode text features (Monti et al., 2019) or learn word-level features during training (Lu and Li, 2020), we utilize state-of-the-art context-aware multilingual representations from Sentence-BERT (Reimers and Gurevych, 2019). Since we avoid expensive fine-tuning of the text encoders, we make our model efficient and easily applicable. Finally, we train our system in an inductive setting, boosting its capability to reliably predict new unseen instances without the need of re-training.

2 Related Work

Text- or content-based fake news detection models have been greatly enhanced by the advancement of pre-trained language models (Hossain et al., 2020; Kaliyar et al., 2021; Panda and Levitan, 2021; Tziafas et al., 2021). Since GNNs leverage news propagation patterns and user network information, they are particularly suitable for social media data. However, GNNs have only recently been introduced for the detection of false information in social networks.

Monti et al. (2019) collect news stories and Twitter content, and are the first to employ a GNN architecture to model text and user features together with the social network properties for fake news

Proceedings of the 2022 COLING Workshop: The 8th Workshop on Noisy User-generated Text (W-NUT 2022), pages 222–229

detection. Lu and Li (2020) extract user and tweet features, and model user propagation paths with GRU- and CNN-based models. A graph convolutional network (GCN) is used to learn interactions among users who share the same content. Chandra et al. (2020) independently train a text encoder for news content and a graph encoder for modelling the follower-following network of users spreading a new articles. Han et al. (2020) cast fake news detection as a graph classification task, extract features from Twitter's user objects only and use GNNs to compute the dissemination of news content among multiple users. The authors tackle the problem of new, unseen data by using techniques from continual learning. Finally, Dou et al. (2021) propose a GNN-based method for user preference-aware fake news detection which exploits historical user posts for node generation and models propagation patterns of news articles among respective retweeters.

Except for Lu and Li (2020) and Han et al. (2020), the above-mentioned approaches incorporate extensive text content from news articles. We follow the approach of Lu and Li (2020) by addressing the challenge of classifying short and noisy text documents, but instead of applying GNNs to user networks only, we propose a unified way of modelling user interactions and user-created content with a graph-based approach. Moreover, none of the previous works address multilingual aspects of social media messages and user origins. We show that our approach significantly outperforms text- and user-based baselines even in a multilingual setting.

3 Methodology

3.1 Graph Representation

We model Twitter users, their social media posts (tweets), and their interrelations by building a network graph with nodes and edges. We denote the set of user nodes by $\mathcal{U}$ and the set of tweet nodes by $\mathcal{T}$. We establish connections, i.e., graph edges, between users and their tweets e^T and between tweets and users who re-posted (retweeted) a tweet e^R. For a given dataset, we construct a heterogeneous graph $\mathcal{G} = (\mathcal{V}, \mathcal{E})$ with a set of nodes $\mathcal{V} = \{\mathcal{U} \cup \mathcal{T}\}$ and a set of edges $\mathcal{E} = \{e^T \cup e^R\}$. We note that an explicit connection between users and retweeters is not necessary, because these interactions are learned by means of the depth of our network. Likewise, the model can learn relations between tweets from users and retweeters if a tweet-retweeter connection exists.

3.2 Tweet Nodes

Let $t_i \in \mathcal{T} = \{t_1, t_2, ..., t_N\}$ be a tweet in a given dataset of size N. We generate the initial tweet nodes for our network graph by encoding the tweet's text with a pre-trained language model. We preprocess the text by replacing URLs with the 'HTTPURL' token, e-mail addresses with the 'EMAIL' token and user mentions with the '@USER' token. We also convert emojis into their corresponding string shortcodes.[1] We use Sentence-BERT (SBERT) to generate a vector representation $\mathbf{v}_{t_i}$ of each processed tweet $t_i \in \mathcal{T}$. Specifically, we test two multilingual embedding models of different sizes from the SentenceTransformers library[2] trained in a teacher-student setting (Reimers and Gurevych, 2020): 1. `distiluse-base-multilingual-cased-v1` which is based on Multilingual Universal Sentence Encoder (mUSE) (Chidambaram et al., 2019; Yang et al., 2019) and a distilled version of mBERT (Sanh et al., 2019). This model supports 15 languages and has an embedding dimension $d_D = 512$. 2. `paraphrase-multilingual-mpnet-base-v2`, which was trained using `paraphrase-mpnet-base-v2` (Song et al., 2020) as teacher and the base version of XLM-RoBERTa (Conneau et al., 2020) as student model. It supports 50+ languages and has an embedding dimension $d_M = 768$.

3.3 User Nodes

Each tweet t_i is authored or retweeted by a user u_j on Twitter. The set of users in each dataset is defined as $\mathcal{U} = \{u_1, u_2, ..., u_M\}$, where M is the total number of unique users. M includes the number of authors and the number of retweeters. It should be noted that a user u_j can be the author and retweeter of one or more tweets at the same time. To initialize the user nodes in our network graph, we generate a vector representation $\mathbf{v}_{u_j}$ of the user's `description` attribute contained in the user object.[3] Again, we use preprocessing and the two pre-trained multilingual models from SentenceTransformers introduced in Sec. 3.2. To distinguish our systems with different initial tweet and

[1] `https://pypi.org/project/emoji/`

[2] `https://www.sbert.net/`

[3] `https://developer.twitter.com/en/docs/twitter-api/v1/data-dictionary/object-model/user`

user node representations in our experiments, we use the prefixes 'Distiluse-' and 'Mpnet-'.

3.4 Model

Our proposed fake news detection framework has a 2-layer GNN at its core and takes as input the heterogeneous graph described in Sec. 3.1. We initialize the user and the tweet nodes with their corresponding embeddings $\mathbf{v}_u \in \mathbb{R}^d$ and $\mathbf{v}_t \in \mathbb{R}^d$ which we do not fine-tune during training.

Next, we project the embeddings into a lower dimensional space $\mathbf{h}_{v_i} \in \mathbb{R}^{128}$ using a separate fully-connected layer followed by a ReLU activation function for each node type $v_i \in \mathcal{V}$.

For computing the node representations, we implement the GraphSAGE operator (Hamilton et al., 2017) according to the PyTorch Geometric[4] library, add a ReLU non-linearity, and apply it to all edge types specified in $\mathcal{E}$ (Sec. 3.1). One operation step of the GraphSAGE convolution with the mean-based aggregator at layer k is defined as:

$$\mathbf{h}'_v = \text{ReLU}(\mathbf{W}_1^k \mathbf{h}_v + \mathbf{W}_2^k \cdot \text{mean}_{n \in \mathcal{N}(v)} \mathbf{h}_n)$$

where $n \in \mathcal{N}(v)$ is a node in the neighborhood of v, $\mathbf{h}_n$ its hidden representation, and $\mathbf{W}_1^k$ and $\mathbf{W}_2^k$ are the weight matrices at the k-th layer. Additionally, we ℓ_2-normalize the output features of each node and group the features generated by different relations by summation.

We test one variant of our proposed network by replacing the SAGE operator with a graph attention network (GAT) (Veličković et al., 2017). By employing a self-attention mechanism (Vaswani et al., 2017), GAT learns different parameters for different nodes in a neighborhood and has been utilized in previous works (Monti et al., 2019; Chandra et al., 2020).

For the final binary node classification of 'real' and 'fake' tweets, we feed the tweet representations $\mathbf{h}_t \in \mathbb{R}^{128}$ learned by the GNN into a 2-layer feed-forward network with a ReLU non-linearity after the hidden layer and a logistic sigmoid function after the final layer.

4 Experimental Setup

4.1 Datasets

We collect two published fake news datasets which provide social media context: *FakeNewsNet* (Shu et al., 2020), and a multilingual dataset related to COVID-19 (Alam et al., 2021b) which we refer to as *Covid-19-Disinfo*.

FakeNewsNet is a popular dataset for automated fake news detection which contains English news articles from two fact-checking websites together with related content from Twitter. For our study, we use the 'fake' and 'real' tweets compiled from PolitiFact[5] available at the *FakeNewsNet* data repository website.[6] We hydrate the tweet objects via Twitter's API using tweepy.[7] As many tweets have been deleted since the date of the publication of the dataset (Balestrucci and De Nicola, 2020), we end up with a total size of 289,602 'real' and 111,101 'fake' (unique) tweets, which is 72.54% and 67.38% of the original dataset size, respectively. To prevent data leakage and bias during training and evaluation, we remove similar tweet objects from the dataset by normalizing the tweets' text (incl. lowercasing, see Sec. 3.2) and applying exact-duplicate filtering according to Alam et al. (2021a).This results in a total number of 282,643 instances, with 233,071 tweets being annotated as 'real' and 49,572 as 'fake'. In order to counteract the impact of an unbalanced dataset, we randomly sample 49,000 tweets from each class label. Finally, we randomly split all instances into 70% train, 10% validation and 20% test sets.

Covid-19-Disinfo is a multilingual Twitter dataset related to the spread of false information during the COVID-19 pandemic. The dataset was compiled for fine-grained disinformation analysis and contains various independent classification tasks formulated in the form of questions. We choose the binary classification task 'Q2' which is designed for detecting false information. When downloading the tweet objects via the Twitter API, we face similar issues as mentioned above. From the total number of 9,583 tweet IDs (Q2 task) we were able to hydrate only 8,810 unique tweet objects from Twitter, resulting in a predefined train, validation and test split of 6,462, 602 and 1,746 tweet objects, respectively.

We extend *FakeNewsNet* and *Covid-19-Disinfo* with 73,722 and 57,966 unique retweeter objects, respectively. Thus, we obtain a total number of 147,690 unique user objects for *FakeNewsNet* and 62,598 unique user objects for *Covid-19-Disinfo*.

[4] https://github.com/pyg-team/pytorch_geometric

[5] https://www.politifact.com/

[6] https://github.com/KaiDMML/FakeNewsNet

[7] https://www.tweepy.org/

Model	FakeNewsNet	Covid-19-Disinfo
Mpnet-Tweet	.8817 (.0025)	.4101 (.0274)
Distiluse-Tweet	.8618 (.0013)	.3791 (.0243)
Mpnet-Tweet-User	.8696 (.0010)	.4135 (.0192)
Distiluse-Tweet-User	.8650 (.0003)	.3310 (.0228)
Mpnet-GAT	.9241 (.0016)	.4252 (.0193)
Distiluse-GAT	.9351 (.0006)	.3889 (.0325)
Mpnet-SAGE	.9370 (.0008)	**.4868** (.0172)
Distiluse-SAGE	**.9467** (.0015)	.4421 (.0055)

Table 1: Mean F_1 scores ('fake' class) and standard deviation ($\pm$) of 5 runs on the test sets of *FakeNewsNet* (Politifact) and *Covid-19-Disinfo*. **Bold**: Best overall performance for each dataset.

4.2 Baselines

We use two baseline models to compare the performance of our proposed GNN model each with two input feature variations.

Tweet Neural Network. We encode the tweets' text adopting the same embedding models described in Sec. 3.2. We then compute a prediction for each instance with a 3-layer feed-forward network similar to the prediction network in our GNN model. We also use a hidden size of 128, but add the tanh activation function (instead of ReLU) after each layer.[8] We refer to these baselines as 'Distiluse-Tweet' and 'Mpnet-Tweet', depending on the embedding model.

Tweet-User Neural Network. We encode the tweets' text and the `description` attribute of the user objects (see Sec. 3.3). We use two separate 2-layer feed-forward networks to obtain the hidden representations $\mathbf{h}_u$, $\mathbf{h}_t \in \mathbb{R}^{128}$ of user u_j who posted tweet t_i in the dataset. Again, we use the tanh activation function after each layer. Intuitively, the network should learn the interrelation between users and their messages. We compute $\mathbf{h}' = \mathbf{h}_u \oplus \mathbf{h}_t$, where $\oplus$ is the concatenation operator, and use another fully-connected layer for the final prediction. We denote this baseline by 'Tweet-User' prepended by the embedding specifier.

5 Results and Analysis

For each model architecture, we report the mean F_1 of the positive class ('fake') of five runs with different random seeds. The results are listed in Table 1. Overall it can be observed that our proposed GNN model outperforms all baselines on both datasets, except for 'GAT' which is inferior with initial 'Distiluse' features and only marginally better with 'Mpnet' on *Covid-19-Disinfo*. Specifically designed for inductive graph representation learning, the SAGE module is more robust than GAT and can generalize better on unseen test data (Brody et al., 2021).

As for *FakeNewsNet*, Distiluse-SAGE outperforms all baseline architectures, Mpnet-SAGE and our proposed GNNs with the GAT operator. Among the baseline models, additional user information (Tweet-User) only helps with 'Distiluse' embeddings. However, the best results are achieved with 'Mpnet' representations. Since 'Mpnet' embeddings have a larger dimension, i.e., $d_M = 768$ vs. $d_D = 512$, they have the ability to capture more information within shallower networks. Among the GNN architectures initial 'Distiluse' nodes outperform their 'Mpnet' counterparts.

Regarding *Covid-19-Disinfo*, all 'Mpnet' models outperform the 'Distiluse' models. The larger embedding size seems to be useful in scenarios where little training data is available. For our proposed approach, 'Mpnet' embeddings outperform 'Distiluse' representations by roughly 4 percentage points in both setups, i.e., 'GAT' and 'SAGE'. The strongest model, Mpnet-SAGE, is more than 7 percentage points better than the strongest baseline, Mpnet-Tweet-User.

Figure 1: t-SNE (van der Maaten and Hinton, 2008) plot of *Covid-19-Disinfo* tweet embeddings (test set) generated by the baseline Mpnet-Tweet model. Fake tweets are in red.

In general, the results suggest that the *Covid-19-Disinfo* classification task is much harder than the *FakeNewsNet* task. Most likely this is due to the lack of sufficient training and validation data, since we use regularization methods to mitigate overfitting. Other reasons could be the multilingual character of the content and the domain-specific vocabulary which is difficult to capture for the pre-

[8] In our preliminary experiments, the tanh activation function performed slightly better than ReLU.

Figure 2: t-SNE plot of *Covid-19-Disinfo* tweet features (test set) generated by our Mpnet-SAGE encoder. Fake tweets are in red.

Model	FakeNewsNet	Covid-19-Disinfo
SAGE (rnd tweets)	.6594 (.0138)	.2964 (.0318)
SAGE (rnd users)	.9102 (.0016)	.3019 (.0387)
Mpnet-SAGE	–	**.4868** (.0172)
Distiluse-SAGE	**.9467** (.0015)	–

Table 2: Ablation results (mean F_1 scores ('fake' class) and standard deviation ($\pm$)) of best performing models randomizing either tweet or user node features. **Bold**: Best performance without random features.

trained language models. However, the final representations of 'fake' and 'real' tweets generated by our proposed GNN detection framework are more distinct than the baseline features, and, therefore, help to improve detection performance on both datasets (see Figs. 1 and 2).

Although we use publicly available data in a purely observational manner, we point out that our model may learn a 'semantic bias' (Shah et al., 2020) towards user-defined descriptions. Under certain conditions, this bias could lead to questionable results that are not intended.

Ablation Study In order to investigate the effect of the models' input components to the results, we conduct a comparative study with the best performing model on the corresponding dataset. To this end, we either randomize tweet ('SAGE (rnd tweets)') or user ('SAGE (rnd users)') node features while keeping other model settings constant. The results of 5 runs (Table 2) indicate that in the balanced dataset scenario with sufficient examples (*FakeNewsNet*), pre-trained tweet nodes primarily contribute to the performance of Distiluse-SAGE. Yet, both node representations modelled with our proposed GNN lead to the significant performance gain. In the case of the more challenging *Covid-19-Disinfo* dataset, we observe for both model variations a sharp drop in performance to almost equal F_1 scores. This indicates that both input components equally contribute to the performance increase of our proposed model.

6 Conclusion

In this work, we present a simple, yet efficient GNN approach for the detection of fake news on social media. Our model employs pre-trained language models to encode text features of social media messages and user profile descriptions. By jointly modelling the relations between users and their tweets and between users who shared similar content, our GNN architecture outperforms text-based models as well as models which combine text and user features from pre-trained language models. In addition, our model is able to apply its knowledge to unseen data without the need of re-training. We show that our approach has limitations in settings with insufficient training data. But with the right choice of initial node representations, the model still outperforms all baselines. In future work, we will investigate domain-adapted language models for initializing graph nodes. Further, we plan to evaluate our model on similar social media content, such as Reddit (Sakketou et al., 2022).

Acknowledgements

The work is jointly supported by the European Research Council (ERC) under the European Union's Horizon 2020 research and innovation programme (grant agreement No. [ERC-2016-StG-714087], Acronym: *So2Sat*), by the Helmholtz Association through the Helmholtz Excellent Professorship "Data Science in Earth Observation - Big Data Fusion for Urban Research" (grant number: W2-W3-100), and by the German Federal Ministry of Education and Research (BMBF) in the framework of the international future AI lab "AI4EO – Artificial Intelligence for Earth Observation: Reasoning, Uncertainties, Ethics and Beyond" (grant number: 01DD20001). We would like to thank Matthias Häberle and all the anonymous reviewers for their valuable input.

References

Firoj Alam, Hassan Sajjad, Muhammad Imran, and Ferda Ofli. 2021a. Crisisbench: Benchmarking crisis-related social media datasets for humanitarian information processing. *Proceedings of the International AAAI Conference on Web and Social Media*, 15(1):923–932.

Firoj Alam, Shaden Shaar, Fahim Dalvi, Hassan Sajjad, Alex Nikolov, Hamdy Mubarak, Giovanni Da San Martino, Ahmed Abdelali, Nadir Durrani, Kareem Darwish, Abdulaziz Al-Homaid, Wajdi Zaghouani, Tommaso Caselli, Gijs Danoe, Friso Stolk, Britt Bruntink, and Preslav Nakov. 2021b. Fighting the COVID-19 infodemic: Modeling the perspective of journalists, fact-checkers, social media platforms, policy makers, and the society. In *Findings of the Association for Computational Linguistics: EMNLP 2021*, pages 611–649, Punta Cana, Dominican Republic. Association for Computational Linguistics.

Alessandro Balestrucci and Rocco De Nicola. 2020. Credulous users and fake news: a real case study on the propagation in twitter. In *2020 IEEE Conference on Evolving and Adaptive Intelligent Systems (EAIS)*, pages 1–8.

Shaked Brody, Uri Alon, and Eran Yahav. 2021. How attentive are graph attention networks? *ArXiv*, abs/2105.14491.

Shantanu Chandra, Pushkar Mishra, Helen Yannakoudakis, and Ekaterina Shutova. 2020. Graph-based modeling of online communities for fake news detection. *ArXiv*, abs/2008.06274.

Muthu Chidambaram, Yinfei Yang, Daniel Cer, Steve Yuan, Yunhsuan Sung, Brian Strope, and Ray Kurzweil. 2019. Learning cross-lingual sentence representations via a multi-task dual-encoder model. In *Proceedings of the 4th Workshop on Representation Learning for NLP (RepL4NLP-2019)*, pages 250–259, Florence, Italy. Association for Computational Linguistics.

Alexis Conneau, Kartikay Khandelwal, Naman Goyal, Vishrav Chaudhary, Guillaume Wenzek, Francisco Guzmán, Edouard Grave, Myle Ott, Luke Zettlemoyer, and Veselin Stoyanov. 2020. Unsupervised cross-lingual representation learning at scale. In *Proceedings of the 58th Annual Meeting of the Association for Computational Linguistics*, pages 8440–8451, Online. Association for Computational Linguistics.

Yingtong Dou, Kai Shu, Congying Xia, Philip S. Yu, and Lichao Sun. 2021. User preference-aware fake news detection. In *Proceedings of the 44th International ACM SIGIR Conference on Research and Development in Information Retrieval*, SIGIR '21, page 2051–2055, New York, NY, USA. Association for Computing Machinery.

William L. Hamilton, Rex Ying, and Jure Leskovec. 2017. Inductive representation learning on large graphs. In *Proceedings of the 31st International Conference on Neural Information Processing Systems*, NIPS'17, page 1025–1035, Red Hook, NY, USA. Curran Associates Inc.

Yi Han, Shanika Karunasekera, and Christopher Leckie. 2020. Graph neural networks with continual learning for fake news detection from social media. *ArXiv*, abs/2007.03316.

Tamanna Hossain, Robert L. Logan IV, Arjuna Ugarte, Yoshitomo Matsubara, Sean Young, and Sameer Singh. 2020. COVIDLies: Detecting COVID-19 misinformation on social media. In *Proceedings of the 1st Workshop on NLP for COVID-19 (Part 2) at EMNLP 2020*, Online. Association for Computational Linguistics.

Rohit Kumar Kaliyar, Anurag Goswami, and Pratik Narang. 2021. Fakebert: Fake news detection in social media with a bert-based deep learning approach. *Multimedia Tools Appl.*, 80(8):11765–11788.

Diederik P. Kingma and Jimmy Ba. 2014. Adam: A method for stochastic optimization.

Yi-Ju Lu and Cheng-Te Li. 2020. GCAN: Graph-aware co-attention networks for explainable fake news detection on social media. In *Proceedings of the 58th Annual Meeting of the Association for Computational Linguistics*, pages 505–514, Online. Association for Computational Linguistics.

Federico Monti, Fabrizio Frasca, Davide Eynard, Damon Mannion, and Michael M. Bronstein. 2019. Fake news detection on social media using geometric deep learning. *ArXiv*, abs/1902.06673.

Salman Bin Naeem and Maged N Kamel Boulos. 2021. Covid-19 misinformation online and health literacy: A brief overview. *International Journal of Environmental Research and Public Health*, 18.

Subhadarshi Panda and Sarah Ita Levitan. 2021. Detecting multilingual COVID-19 misinformation on social media via contextualized embeddings. In *Proceedings of the Fourth Workshop on NLP for Internet Freedom: Censorship, Disinformation, and Propaganda*, pages 125–129, Online. Association for Computational Linguistics.

Nils Reimers and Iryna Gurevych. 2019. Sentence-BERT: Sentence embeddings using Siamese BERT-networks. In *Proceedings of the 2019 Conference on Empirical Methods in Natural Language Processing and the 9th International Joint Conference on Natural Language Processing (EMNLP-IJCNLP)*, pages 3982–3992, Hong Kong, China. Association for Computational Linguistics.

Nils Reimers and Iryna Gurevych. 2020. Making monolingual sentence embeddings multilingual using knowledge distillation. In *Proceedings of the 2020 Conference on Empirical Methods in Natural Language Processing (EMNLP)*, pages 4512–4525, Online. Association for Computational Linguistics.

Flora Sakketou, Joan Plepi, Riccardo Cervero, Henri Jacques Geiss, Paolo Rosso, and Lucie Flek.

2022. Factoid: A new dataset for identifying misinformation spreaders and political bias. In *Proceedings of the Language Resources and Evaluation Conference*, pages 3231–3241, Marseille, France. European Language Resources Association.

Victor Sanh, Lysandre Debut, Julien Chaumond, and Thomas Wolf. 2019. Distilbert, a distilled version of BERT: smaller, faster, cheaper and lighter. *CoRR*, abs/1910.01108.

Deven Santosh Shah, H. Andrew Schwartz, and Dirk Hovy. 2020. Predictive biases in natural language processing models: A conceptual framework and overview. In *Proceedings of the 58th Annual Meeting of the Association for Computational Linguistics*, pages 5248–5264, Online. Association for Computational Linguistics.

Kai Shu, Deepak Mahudeswaran, Suhang Wang, Dongwon Lee, and Huan Liu. 2020. Fakenewsnet: A data repository with news content, social context, and spatiotemporal information for studying fake news on social media. *Big Data*, 8(3):171–188. PMID: 32491943.

Kai Shu, Amy Sliva, Suhang Wang, Jiliang Tang, and Huan Liu. 2017. Fake news detection on social media: A data mining perspective. *SIGKDD Explor. Newsl.*, 19(1):22–36.

Kaitao Song, Xu Tan, Tao Qin, Jianfeng Lu, and Tie-Yan Liu. 2020. Mpnet: Masked and permuted pre-training for language understanding. In *NeurIPS 2020*. ACM.

Georgios Tziafas, Konstantinos Kogkalidis, and Tommaso Caselli. 2021. Fighting the COVID-19 infodemic with a holistic BERT ensemble. In *Proceedings of the Fourth Workshop on NLP for Internet Freedom: Censorship, Disinformation, and Propaganda*, pages 119–124, Online. Association for Computational Linguistics.

L.J.P. van der Maaten and G.E. Hinton. 2008. Visualizing high-dimensional data using t-sne. *Journal of Machine Learning Research*, 9(nov):2579–2605. Pagination: 27.

Ashish Vaswani, Noam Shazeer, Niki Parmar, Jakob Uszkoreit, Llion Jones, Aidan N. Gomez, Łukasz Kaiser, and Illia Polosukhin. 2017. Attention is all you need. In *Proceedings of the 31st International Conference on Neural Information Processing Systems*, NIPS'17, page 6000–6010, Red Hook, NY, USA. Curran Associates Inc.

Petar Veličković, Guillem Cucurull, Arantxa Casanova, Adriana Romero, Pietro Liò, and Yoshua Bengio. 2017. Graph attention networks.

Yinfei Yang, Daniel Cer, Amin Ahmad, Mandy Guo, Jax Law, Noah Constant, Gustavo Hernández Ábrego, Steve Yuan, Chris Tar, Yun-Hsuan Sung, Brian Strope, and Ray Kurzweil. 2019. Multilingual universal sentence encoder for semantic retrieval. *CoRR*, abs/1907.04307.

A Additional Training Configurations

We use PyTorch[9] and the PyTorch Geometric library to build our models. We train our GNN framework for 300 epochs with early stopping. We optimize with Adam (Kingma and Ba, 2014) setting the learning rate to 0.005 and weight decay to 0.001. For regularization of the whole network, we use dropout with $p = 0.3$ before the first fully-connected layer, after each graph neural network layer, and after the hidden layer in the prediction network.

We train all baseline models for 100 epochs with early stopping and a batchsizc of 64. We set the size of all hidden layers to 128. Again, we optimize with Adam setting the learning rate to 0.005 and weight decay to 0.001. We use dropout with $p = 0.5$ after the first hidden layer for regularization. All experiments are run on NVIDIA GeForce RTX 3090 24 GB GPUs.

[9]https://pytorch.org/

Analyzing the Real Vulnerability of Hate Speech Detection Systems against Targeted Intentional Noise

Piush Aggarwal **Torsten Zesch**
Computational Linguistics
CATALPA - Center of Advanced Technology for Assisted Learning and Predictive Analytics
FernUniversität in Hagen
{piush.aggarwal,torsten.zesch}@fernuni-hagen.de

Abstract

Hate speech detection systems have been shown to be vulnerable against obfuscation attacks, where a potential hater tries to circumvent detection by deliberately introducing noise in their posts. In previous work, noise is often introduced for all words (which is likely overestimating the impact) or single untargeted words (likely underestimating the vulnerability). We perform a user study asking people to select words they would obfuscate in a post. Using this realistic setting, we find that the real vulnerability of hate speech detection systems against deliberately introduced noise is almost as high as when using a whitebox attack and much more severe than when using a non-targeted dictionary. Our results are based on 4 different datasets, 12 different obfuscation strategies, and hate speech detection systems using different paradigms.

1 Introduction

Computer-mediated communication is plagued by toxic and hateful behavior that can cause serious harm (Waldron, 2012; Gelber and McNamara, 2016). Consequently, automatically detecting such behavior has become a major research area (Waseem and Hovy, 2016; Waseem et al., 2017; Kumar et al., 2018; Wiegand et al., 2019; Aggarwal et al., 2019; Kovács et al., 2021).

Whenever there is an automatic system in place to filter out hateful messages, people will try to circumvent it by obfuscating their message. However, there are limits, as the communicative intent has to stay intact. If the intended audience cannot relatively easily understand a message, obfuscation has gone too far. Thus, people will usually only obfuscate a few terms they think will be problematic or could be responsible for filtering out a message (see Table 1). Adding to much noise may render the message unrecognizable even to human readers.

In this paper, we analyze the real vulnerability of state-of-the-art hate speech detection systems against targeted obfuscation. We keep a post recognizable by obfuscating at most one target token per test example. We perform an annotation study to analyze the target selection strategies in real-world setting. We use 12 types of plausible obfuscation strategies and apply them to the targeted tokens. In order to generalize our analysis, we repeat our experiments on multiple hate speech datasets. For future benchmarking, we open-source our code base, trained models, and obfuscated test samples[1].

2 Ethical Considerations

In our research, we are discussing and explaining obfuscation strategies. People could use those strategies to avoid detection and eventually cause even more harm (Prabhumoye et al., 2021). We consider this risk to be small, as people are creative and would have (and almost certainly already have) come up with all of the described strategies.

We decided to release all our code (even the parts obfuscating single words), as we see a clear benefit in researchers reproducing our results and facilitate their own research. This outweighs the risk caused by people using that code to automatically obfuscate their messages.

Law enforcement agencies might use our research to build more robust detection systems. This can be positive, as marginalized groups might not have to deal with being targets of hate speech all the time and might dare again to use their free speech rights without being threatened into silence. However, social media platforms may use deobfuscation to ban words they consider offensive. This might have unintended consequences, e.g. a person called *Richard Gaywood* was not able to use his name as it include the word *gay* and consider to violate community standards (Suzor, 2010).

An even more serious harm are overreaching governments censoring non-hateful expression of

[1] https://github.com/aggarwalpiush/HateSpeechDetection

Proceedings of the 2022 COLING Workshop: The 8th Workshop on Noisy User-generated Text (W-NUT 2022), pages 230–242

Post	Obfuscation Level
`A** h*te sp**ch res**rchers sh**ld b* b**ten t* d**th`	High
`All h*te speech res**rchers should be b**ten to d**th`	Medium
`All hate speech researchers should be b**ten to d**th`	Low

Table 1: Trade-off between level of obfuscation and message understandability.

opinions. Over the last years, the web-based censorship as well as surveillance has significantly increased in some parts of the world (Polyakova and Meserole, 2019). Improved detection models will even more empower such authoritarian regimes and give them the opportunity to increase the severity of surveillance towards its citizens (Sherman, 2020; Wright, 2018), as they can no longer circumvent censorship through obfuscation.

3 Obfuscation Strategies

Obfuscation is the deliberate act of obscuring the intended meaning of communication by adding noise to the message. This can happen in many ways. For example, Gröndahl et al. (2018) show that appending a positive word like *love* can already fool a classifier. Kirk et al. (2022) demonstrate the vulnerability of hate detection models by simple replacements of certain tokens with emojis. Another obfuscation strategy is to paraphrase the whole message or use a metaphorical expression to indirectly express the same point. For example, instead of *All those researchers are stupid as hell* one could write *Those Einsteins are not the sharpest knife in the drawer*. However, this also changes the meaning and presupposes that the intended audience is aware of the possible replacement and able to make the connection. Such a replacement might also change the perceived severity of a toxic comment, e.g. it is possible that people would consider the sentence with *Einstein* as more hateful, as it adds a potential connotation of *Jewish researcher*.

In this paper, we only focus on producing simple obfuscation strategies (Röttger et al., 2020) which are generally observed to be implemented in realistic settings. Table 2 gives examples of all strategies that we consider.

Camel Case While camel casing is usually used to improve the readability of a text (e.g. naming conventions in computer programming), it can also be used to add noise. In our camel-casing strategy, we capitalize every alternate letter (starting from the second letter).

Char Drop While keeping first and last character untouched we either drop a randomly chosen character from the selected token or drop all vowels (Cleary, 1976; Baluch, 1992). We call the later obfuscation as **Vowel Drop**. We ensure preservation of token perception (Baba and Suzuki, 2012; ThambiJose, 2014; Pruthi et al., 2019)). Therefore, we only add the noise to tokens with 3 or more characters.

Char Flip Character shuffling within the boundaries of the word (excluding boundary characters) does not have much effect on word semantics. However, it would be quite easy to get this implemented during the message composition. To generate such noise, we only consider tokens having length more than 3. Excluding first and last, we randomly select two characters and flip them.

Diacritics Some non English languages use extra marks or glyph (such as ^) above or below (or sometimes next to) a letter for explicit enunciation. We use mapping table to generate diacritic version of the input token.

Kebab Instances are created by adding a *dash* (-) between each letter of the word. This looks like meat on a kebab stick, hence the name.

Leetspeak Visual resemblance of alphabets (Simpson et al., 2012) with numbers and mathematical symbols can also be used to obfuscate token. Therefore we exploit leetspeak where we consider commonly used English alphabets namely *a*, *e*, *l*, *o*, *s* and replace with *4*, *3*, *1*, *0*, *5* respectively.

Masking Deliberate introduction of symbols such as mathematical operators are common practice to obfuscate the disputed tokens. We generate masking based obfuscation examples where we randomly choose and replace one letter with * (tokens with two letters are not considered for this obfuscation). To increase the perception of the token, we do not consider first and last letter of the token for the replacement.

Mathspeak Similar to leetspeak, mathspeak replaces characters with mathematical symbols such

Strategy	Example
	researcher
Camel Case	rEsEaRcHeR
Char Drop	researher
Char Flip	resaercher
Diacritics	résearchêr
Kebab	r-e-s-e-a-r-c-h-e-r
Leetspeak	re5earc7er
Masking	resear**er
Mathspeak	ℜesearcher
Phonetic	rɪsɜːtʃə
Spacing	r e s e a r c h e r
Snake	r_e_s_e_a_r_c_h_e_r
Vowel Drop	rsrchr

Table 2: Overview of Obfuscation Strategies.

as *R* with ℜ.

Phonetic In phonetic obfuscation, the token is replaced with a representation of how it is pronounced. For our example *researcher*, this could be a layperson representation like *'ri-sur-chur'* or blending with aspects of mathspeak if using the international phonetic alphabet (IPA) which would result in 'rɪsɜːtʃə'. In this study, we apply IPA representation for obfuscation generation. Though we do not consider this a very practical obfuscation strategy outside of 'Linguistics Twitter', still keep it in our experiments as an extreme case.

Spacing In this case, examples are created by adding *spaces* between each letter of the word.

Snake Instances are created by adding *underscore* (_) mark between each letter of the word.

4 Target Selection

We propose model independent token selection strategies that range from very broad (all tokens) to very specific (the words conveying the hateful intent). Our intention is to provide every possible cases in order to analyse the model robustness in depth. Table 3 illustrates how tokens are chosen based on different target selection strategies. In this section, we describe each of the strategy in detail.

All We obfuscate all tokens with more than 3 characters (obfuscation of shorter words cannot be reliably performed). This is the most aggressive obfuscation strategy that will probably make it unreadable to humans and machines alike.

Random Any A single word (with more than 3 characters) is randomly selected from the message text. We do not obfuscate the first and last word of the text.

Random Content The same strategy as random word, only that selected words have to be either nouns, verbs, adjectives, or adverb.

Dict Fixed We collect a number of lexicons with hateful words from various sources (including Hatebase[2] and published research on lexicons (Bassignana et al., 2018; Wiegand et al., 2018; Chandrasekharan et al., 2017)). For each language we combine all lexicons and remove duplicates. As token (starting from left side) in the input text found match in the dictionary is selected for the obfuscation and the remaining available tokens are ignored.

Dict Whitebox Following (Papernot et al., 2016) hypothesis, we build an in-house lexical dictionary populated with tokens which are important for an LSTM-based hate-speech classification model for hate-labels predictions. We refer these lexicons as whitebox tokens as they are selected based on model internal parameters. To extract such tokens, first we train this model on the existing hate-speech datasets (see Section 4) and apply a hierarchical based explanation method (Jin et al., 2020). To generate explanations, we use the same training instances on which the model was trained as we are only interested in hateful tokens. The explanations are in the form of scores for all possible n-grams available in the training statements which represent contribution of the n-grams towards hate label predictions. Heuristically, we choose all unigrams having threshold value less than or equal to -0.02 (negative polarity leads to hatefulness). For selection, among all the token matches, we consider token with most negative score.

Dict Domain All target selection methods outlined so far, are trying to simulate the real obfuscation process in a rather crude way. When people want to obfuscate single words, they know which are the most problematic ones and focus only on those. However, for our experiments, we do not know which words this would be. We thus performed an annotation study (described next), which resulted in a domain-specific dictionary. We later use this dictionary (like *Dict Whitebox*) to obfuscate exactly one word in each post that people consider as most problematic. Thus, this target selection strategy is much more realistic than the other

[2]https://hatebase.org/

Target Selection	Post
Clean	All hate speech researchers should be beaten to death
Random Content	All hate speech **researchers** should be beaten to death
Random Any	**All** hate speech researchers should be beaten to death
Dict Fixed	All hate speech researchers should be beaten to **death**
Dict Whitebox	All hate speech researchers should be **beaten** to death
Dict Domain	All hate speech researchers should be **beaten** to death
All	**All hate speech researchers should be beaten to death**

Table 3: Overview of target selection strategies. They differ in which and how many tokens will be selected for obfuscation.

ones and will allow us to better estimate the real vulnerability of hate speech detection systems.

4.1 Annotation Study

To gather a domain specific lexicons, we perform an annotation study. We chose a random sample of 100 hate speech statements from the (Davidson et al., 2017) dataset. We recruited three annotators[3] and asked them to think like potential hater and select three tokens from each statements which are most likely to be chosen for obfuscation (see Figure 1) For the annotation study, we used the inception framework (Klie et al., 2018).

Annotators received the following instructions. First, we provided the scenario:

> Imagine you want to spread hate using social media platforms. Sooner, you realize most of these social media platforms are equipped with hate speech detection systems. Now you want to fool these systems by playing with words you used in message. For example: *Researchers should be banished from holy places*
>
> You can play with words such as *banished*
>
> and make it *ban1shed*

Then, we provided the purpose of annotation study:

> This annotation process is intended to perform sociological analysis. We manually labelled the tokens in the social media posts which potentially be obfuscated during the post-compositlon to escape from automatic hate-speech detection process.

Finally, we explained the annotation process:

> For each sentence (total: 100), choose three tokens and annotate with their priority levels. For example:
>
> First_Priority: *banished*
>
> Second_Priority: *Researchers*
>
> Third_Priority: *holy*

[3]university graduates and active social media users.

The study resulted in 455 tokens marked by the annotators. Inter-annotator agreement (taking priority into account) was 0.64 gamma (Mathet et al., 2015). It illustrates that annotators are not only in high agreement for token selection but also for priority.

To generate the domain specific dictionary from the annotations, we assign them with a score. This score represents the polarity of hatred carried by the token relative to other tokens available in the list. We use the scores[4] (Equation 1) to prioritize the token selection strategy during obfuscation process.

$$S_{ti} = \sum_{j=1}^{v_{ti}} \vec{P_{tij}} \cdot \vec{W} \tag{1}$$

To calculate, we create priority vectors (e.g. [1,0,0] for *retard*, [0,0,1] for *stupid*, etc. in Figure 1) for each token (S_{ti}), we take dot product of the priority vector ($\vec{P_{tij}}$) with constant scalar weight vector ($\vec{W}$) $[0.5, 0.33, 0.17]$, summation over token's frequency (v_{ti}) (as single token can have multiple priority vectors depending upon its usage across the statements). The constant weight vector describe the relative amount of preference should be given to each token based on its priority with respect to other token.

5 Experimental Setup

We experiment with all the obfuscation and target selection strategies outlined above. To make sure that our results are not specific to a dataset or detection method, we also use multiple dataset and methods as outlined next.

5.1 Datasets

In order to analyze the vulnerability of available hate speech classifiers, we have used 4 social media hatespeech datasets (see Table 4).

[4]The list of tokens with their scores can be download from the provided github repository

Figure 1: A sample hate statement with top three tokens that are most likely to be obfuscated by a potential hater.

Name	Reference	# posts	tokens	% hate
T1	(Davidson et al., 2017)	24,783	370k	6
T2	(Waseem and Hovy, 2016)	10,588	160k	26
G	(Kennedy et al., 2022)	27,663	590k	12
TF	(Mandl et al., 2019)	7,004	170k	36

Table 4: Specification of datasets use to analyze the real vulnerability against target obfuscations.

- Davidson et al. (2017) (T1) contains Twitter posts labeled with *hate, offensive, not*. It contains a wide range of domains as its collection strategy is based on lexicons provided by *Hatebase.org*.
- Waseem and Hovy (2016) (T2) contains tweets manually tagged with *sexist, racist, not*. Like T1, the tweets were collected but with fewer lexicons.
- Kennedy et al. (2022) (G) contains posts from social media service *gab.ai* with multiple hate-based rhetoric labels.
- Mandl et al. (2019) (TF) contains binary-labeled Tweets and Facebook posts.

For datasets with non-binary labels, we aggregate the labels into two categories namely *hateful* and *not-hateful*. We randomly stratified dataset posts into train, dev and test set in the ratio of 80:10:10 respectively. We apply the proposed obfuscation attacks only on the test set in order to analyse the model robustness against unknown attacks.

5.2 Hate Detection Systems

To generalize our study we train 12 different types of hate detection systems. It include shallow, deep, deep-attention and deep-contextualized based paradigm.

Shallow Models Following Davidson et al. (2017), training shallow machine learning algorithm for hate-speech classification such as support vector machine and logistic regression can be considered as strong baseline. In addition, we use ensemble based classification algorithms such as AdaBoost, Gradient Boosting and Random Forest.

Deep Models Wide range of approaches have been used for hate speech detection. We select a range of reference architectures instead of specific configurations by certain researchers, as we are mainly interested in the relative vulnerability of architectures. Contextualized language model based classification systems such as BERT (Devlin et al., 2019) promise state of the art result in wide domain of downstream tasks. Consequently, for hate-speech classifications, we perform fine-tuning of a variant of BERT called *Distilbert* (Sanh et al., 2019). Textual classification is often considered a time-series problem, where the representation of each token in the text is depends on former and later tokens available in the text. Therefore, we train different variants of LSTM based neural network such as LSTM, BILSTM, CNN with attention networks and CNN-LSTM. Hochreiter and Schmidhuber (1997); Zhou et al. (2016); Brahma (2018); Sainath et al. (2015).

5.3 Model Training

Except *Distilbert*, for training of rest of the systems, we lowercase all postings for each dataset and use the Ark Tokenizer (Gimpel et al., 2011) for word splitting. To extract features, we use word embeddings (Zhang and Luo, 2018; Kshirsagar et al., 2018; Badjatiya et al., 2017). Due to many OOVs in hate speeches, hate speech models adopt character level features (Del Vigna et al., 2017; Warner and Hirschberg, 2012; Lee et al., 2018) where a DNN produces local features around each character of the word and then combines them using a max operation to create a fixed-sized character-level embedding of the word. Char-level embeddings are more likely to encode all variants of a word's morphology closer in the embedded space (Bojanowski et al., 2017). We use n-char fastext embeddings trained on Twitter corpus of 400 Million tweets (Godin, 2019). For shallow models, we apply grid-search algorithm using a dev set on all shallow classifiers (Pedregosa et al., 2011). For all the deep-neural networks, we use the learning rate of 10^{-3} with 16 as batch size. We train each network for 10 epochs with early stopping on dev set accuracy and for 4 patience level. In the case of

Distilbert, we use BERT-base tokenizer and corresponding contextual embeddings for tokenization and feature extraction respectively. We use default hyperparameter settings described in the original *Distilbert* implementation[5]

6 Results

We analyze model vulnerability by looking at the decline in relative performance when they are tested on obfuscated posts. Since we use unbalanced datasets, we estimate the performance using F1 Macro score evaluate on hate-labels.

Target Selection Table 5 shows relative change in F1(Hate) averaged over obfuscation strategies for all systems. We use the broadest as well as the most specific target selections for obfuscations. As expected, model performance is worst when *All* tokens are obfuscated in the test samples. Since this is an unrealistic strategy, we do not consider this effect as real vulnerability. On the other end of the spectrum, random target selection (*Random Content* and *Random Any*) has little effect. It becomes clear that the model are sensitive to specific and meaningful tokens.

Dict Fixed accommodates meaningful lexicons towards hatred and therefore makes systems relatively more vulnerable to it. The T2 dataset is an exception, as it has relatively fewer swear words and hence less number of target tokens are selected. It also indicate that reliance on fixed set of tokens may not be the best solution to generate the obfuscation examples.

An important finding is that a model-dependent dictionary (*Dict Whitebox*) has a large impact on model susceptibility, as does *Dict Domain*. The comparable performance indicate towards the similar ranking order of tokens in both of the dictionaries. To estimate the similarity, we calculate the *Spearmanr Coefficient* (Schober et al., 2018) and find it as 0.421 with $p < 0.005$ which is a moderate correlation. This shows the promising future direction for conducting annotation studies on larger datasets to compile a better manual preferences based dictionary.

Obfuscation Strategies Table 6 shows the average relative change in F1 (Hate) for all our obfuscation strategies, where higher numbers mean that systems are more vulnerable against this strategy. We find that the type of preprocessing might play an important role as e.g. *camelcasing* has almost no effect because lowercasing is performed during preprocessing. In general, models are more vulnerable to strategies that insert characters in a token (like *Kebab* or *Spacing*), than to strategies that remove characters (like *Char Drop* or *Vowel Drop*). This could be linked to the modeling of subwords, but more research is needed in that direction. Strategies that replace characters sometimes have limited applicability, e.g. *Mathspeak* can only be applied for certain characters limiting its effect.

Distilbert To perform deep analysis, we visualize the fine-grained results for our best performing model *Distilbert* (Figure 2 and 3) on T1 dataset. In most cases, we find the model performance in accordance with numbers mention in Table 5 and 6. As expected, the effect of *Random Content* is more prominent compared to *Random Any* which validate the advantages of using limited POS tags. Multiple edit operations make system more vulnerable to *Vowel Drop* than *Char Flip* and *Char Drop* (need only single edit). We also note that for this specific classifier (in contrast to the averaged results discussed above) the *Phonetic* method is even better than *Kebab* and *Spacing*. Please refer Appendix A for fine-grained results of *Distilbert* evaluated on other datasets.

Other Paradigms Other than *Distilbert*, we have evaluated the vulnerability on shallow classifier such as SVM, LogReg, AdaBoost, Gradient Boosting and Random Forest as well as on Deep Networks namely LSTM, BILSTM, CNN with attenion networks, also on CNN-LSTM. We found the order of model's vulnerabilities with respect to obfuscation targets are consistent with *distilbert* which can be interpreted by Tables 5. Table 7 in Appendix B illustrates the performance drop for each system across T1 dataset.

7 Related Work

Although most of the previous studies raise concern about model robustness against obfuscation attacks, the real vulnerability is understudied. Among simple obfuscation strategies, studies (Gröndahl et al., 2018; Röttger et al., 2021; Ebrahimi et al., 2018; Szegedy et al., 2013) introduce syntactic perturbations to validate the robustness of hate detection models. We find overlapping of some of the obfuscation strategies discussed in this paper. Kirk et al.

[5]`https://huggingface.co/docs/transformers/model_doc/distilbert`

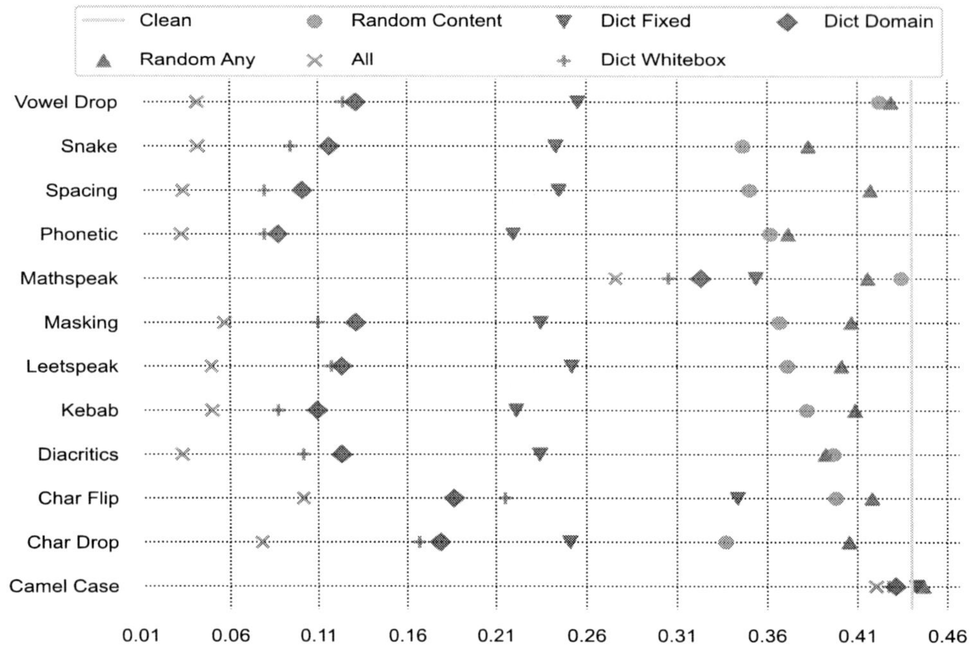

Figure 2: Distilbert's F1 (Hate label) performance on T1 dataset before and after obfuscation on all obfuscation strategies for all target selections. Except *Camel Case*, differences are found to be statistically significant based on McNemar-Test after Bonferroni correction $p < 0.05$.

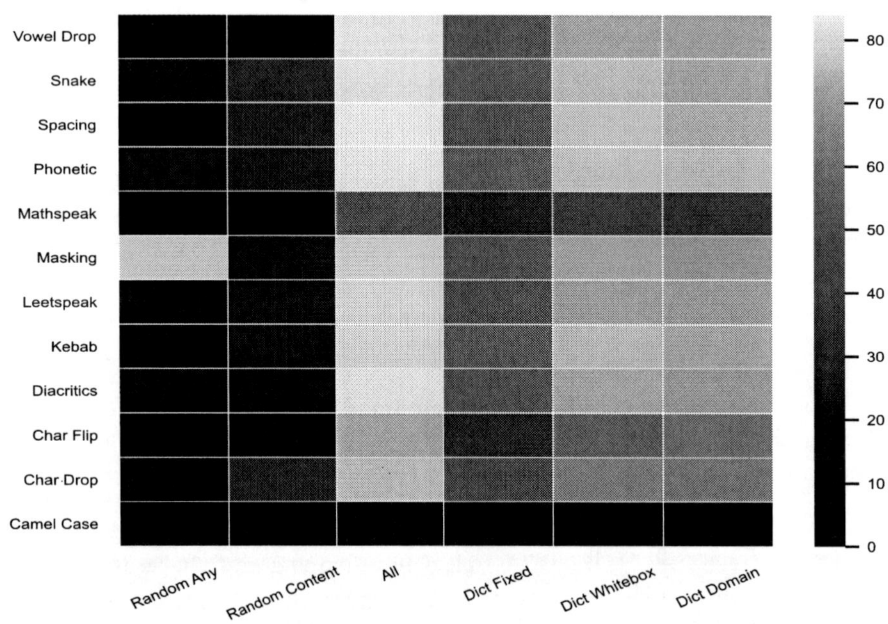

Figure 3: Distilbert's performance decline on T1 dataset based on differences in the True Positives (Hate label) before and after obfuscation on all obfuscation strategies for all target selections.

Target	T1	Datasets T2	TF	G
All	.16	.35	.26	.28
Dict Domain	.13	-	-	-
Dict Whitebox	.13	.13	.16	.10
Dict Fixed	.11	.01	.06	.11
Random Content	.05	.06	.02	.08
Random Any	.03	.05	.02	.07

Table 5: Relative change in F1 (Hate) for different target selection strategies. Results are averaged over obfuscation strategies and detection systems.

Strategy	T1	Datasets T2	TF	G
CamelCase	.01	.02	.03	.04
Char Drop	.12	.11	.09	.13
Char Flip	.09	.11	.13	.13
Diacritics	.12	.11	.14	.14
Kebab	.17	.25	.13	.19
Leetspeak	.12	.11	.06	.11
Masking	.12	.12	.13	.14
Mathspeak	.07	.03	.05	.07
Phonetic	.13	.13	.14	.13
Snake	.12	.12	.14	.14
Spacing	.16	.21	.10	.17
Vowel Drop	.12	.10	.10	.14

Table 6: Relative change in F1 (Hate) for different obfuscation strategies. Results are averaged over target selections and detection systems.

(2022) proposes test-suite contained emoji-based hateful statements and find high vulnerability of text based models. The study also proposes adversarial examples to strengthen the model robustness. Complex obfuscation include *VIPER* (Eger, 2015) which is a probabilistic visual perturber that keep the token recognizable. Target selection has been studied in both model dependent and independent settings. Model dependent targets are either selected by looking at model architecture and its parameters (Goodfellow et al., 2014; Ebrahimi et al., 2018) or solely depend upon model output (Narodytska and Kasiviswanathan, 2017; Papernot et al., 2016; Liu et al., 2017). Among model independent targets, studies consider all the tokens in the message (Gröndahl et al., 2018; Jones et al., 2020; Eger et al., 2019). However, in real time settings, this type of target selection is not observed. In our work, we squeeze target selection to maximum of single token and perform an annotation study, that estimate real vulnerability of the models.

8 Conclusions

Previous work, simulating the obfuscation behavior of haters in a simplified way, is likely to misanalyze the real vulnerability of hate speech detection systems to obfuscation. We have shown that obfuscating all words in a post is a useful lower bound, but a very unrealistic strategy (as the communicative value of the message breaks down). Note that in this work, we deliberately limited ourselves to quite simple lexical modifications. However, detection systems still show a surprising vulnerability against these simple strategies. While it might be possible (and fairly easy) to shield a system against particularly known obfuscation strategies (e.g. by detecting K-e-b-a-b or S_n_a_k_e obfuscation with a regular expression), we need to aim for systems that are also robust against unseen strategies.

As the user study conducted in this paper shows, people have an intuitive understanding of which words are problematic. By obfuscating a single word, someone trying to obfuscate their message can impact the system performance on the same scale as when using a whitebox attack (that has the 'unfair' advantage of having access to the internal workings of the system). We also show that experiments relying on a fixed dictionary of problematic words for obfuscation are likely underestimating the impact of obfuscation on hate speech detection systems.

Acknowledgments

This work was conducted at CATALPA - Center of Advanced Technology for Assisted Learning and Predictive Analytics of the FernUniversität in Hagen, Germany.

References

Piush Aggarwal, Tobias Horsmann, Michael Wojatzki, and Torsten Zesch. 2019. LTL-UDE at SemEval-2019 Task 6: BERT and Two-Vote Classification for Categorizing Offensiveness. In *Proceedings of the International Workshop on Semantic Evaluation (SemEval)*, Minneapolis USA. Association for Computational Linguistics.

Yukino Baba and Hisami Suzuki. 2012. How Are Spelling Errors Generated and Corrected? A Study of Corrected and Uncorrected Spelling Errors Using Keystroke Logs. In *Proceedings of the 50th Annual Meeting of the Association for Computational Linguistics (Volume 2: Short Papers)*, pages 373–377,

Jeju Island, Korea. Association for Computational Linguistics.

Pinkesh Badjatiya, Shashank Gupta, Manish Gupta, and Vasudeva Varma. 2017. Deep Learning for Hate Speech Detection in Tweets. In *Proceedings of the 26th International Conference on World Wide Web Companion*, WWW '17 Companion, page 759–760, Republic and Canton of Geneva, CHE. International World Wide Web Conferences Steering Committee.

Bahman Baluch. 1992. Reading with and without vowels: What are the psychological consequences? *Journal of Social and Evolutionary Systems*, 15(1):95–104.

Elisa Bassignana, Valerio Basile, and Viviana Patti. 2018. Hurtlex: A Multilingual Lexicon of Words to Hurt. In *5th Italian Conference on Computational Linguistics, CLiC-it 2018*, volume 2253, pages 1–6. CEUR-WS.

Piotr Bojanowski, Edouard Grave, Armand Joulin, and Tomas Mikolov. 2017. Enriching Word Vectors with Subword Information. *Transactions of the Association for Computational Linguistics*, 5:135–146.

Siddhartha Brahma. 2018. Improved Sentence Modeling using Suffix Bidirectional LSTM. *arXiv preprint arXiv:1805.07340*.

Eshwar Chandrasekharan, Umashanthi Pavalanathan, Anirudh Srinivasan, Adam Glynn, Jacob Eisenstein, and Eric Gilbert. 2017. You Can't Stay Here: The Efficacy of Reddit's 2015 Ban Examined Through Hate Speech. *Proc. ACM Hum.-Comput. Interact.*, 1(CSCW).

Donna McKee Cleary. 1976. Reading Without Vowels: Some Implications. *Journal of Reading*, 20(1):52–56.

Thomas Davidson, Dana Warmsley, Michael Macy, and Ingmar Weber. 2017. Automated Hate Speech Detection and the Problem of Offensive Language. In *Proceedings of the 11th International AAAI Conference on Web and Social Media*, ICWSM '17, pages 512–515.

Fabio Del Vigna, Andrea Cimino, Felice Dell'Orletta, Marinella Petrocchi, and Maurizio Tesconi. 2017. Hate Me, Hate Me Not: Hate Speech Detection on Facebook. In *ITASEC*.

Jacob Devlin, Ming-Wei Chang, Kenton Lee, and Kristina Toutanova. 2019. BERT: Pre-training of Deep Bidirectional Transformers for Language Understanding. In *Proceedings of the 2019 Conference of the North American Chapter of the Association for Computational Linguistics: Human Language Technologies, Volume 1 (Long and Short Papers)*, pages 4171–4186, Minneapolis, Minnesota. Association for Computational Linguistics.

Javid Ebrahimi, Anyi Rao, Daniel Lowd, and Dejing Dou. 2018. HotFlip: White-box adversarial examples for text classification. In *Proceedings of the 56th Annual Meeting of the Association for Computational Linguistics (Volume 2: Short Papers)*, pages 31–36, Melbourne, Australia. Association for Computational Linguistics.

Steffen Eger. 2015. Multiple many-to-many sequence alignment for combining string-valued variables: A G2P experiment. In *Proceedings of the 53rd Annual Meeting of the Association for Computational Linguistics and the 7th International Joint Conference on Natural Language Processing (Volume 1: Long Papers)*, pages 909–919, Beijing, China. Association for Computational Linguistics.

Steffen Eger, Gözde Gül Şahin, Andreas Rücklé, Ji-Ung Lee, Claudia Schulz, Mohsen Mesgar, Krishnkant Swarnkar, Edwin Simpson, and Iryna Gurevych. 2019. Text processing like humans do: Visually attacking and shielding NLP systems. In *Proceedings of the 2019 Conference of the North American Chapter of the Association for Computational Linguistics: Human Language Technologies, Volume 1 (Long and Short Papers)*, pages 1634–1647, Minneapolis, Minnesota. Association for Computational Linguistics.

Katharine Gelber and Luke McNamara. 2016. Evidencing the harms of hate speech. *Social Identities*, 22(3):324–341.

Kevin Gimpel, Nathan Schneider, Brendan O'Connor, Dipanjan Das, Daniel Mills, Jacob Eisenstein, Michael Heilman, Dani Yogatama, Jeffrey Flanigan, and Noah A. Smith. 2011. Part-of-Speech Tagging for Twitter: Annotation, Features, and Experiments. In *Proceedings of the 49th Annual Meeting of the Association for Computational Linguistics: Human Language Technologies*, pages 42–47. Association for Computational Linguistics.

Fréderic Godin. 2019. *Improving and Interpreting Neural Networks for Word-Level Prediction Tasks in Natural Language Processing*. Ph.D. thesis, Ghent University, Belgium.

Ian J Goodfellow, Jonathon Shlens, and Christian Szegedy. 2014. Explaining and harnessing adversarial examples. *arXiv preprint arXiv:1412.6572*.

Tommi Gröndahl, Luca Pajola, Mika Juuti, Mauro Conti, and N. Asokan. 2018. All You Need is "Love": Evading Hate Speech Detection. In *Proceedings of the 11th ACM Workshop on Artificial Intelligence and Security*, AISec '18, page 2–12, New York, NY, USA. Association for Computing Machinery.

Sepp Hochreiter and Jürgen Schmidhuber. 1997. Long Short-Term Memory. *Neural Comput.*, 9(8):1735–1780.

Xisen Jin, Zhongyu Wei, Junyi Du, Xiangyang Xue, and Xiang Ren. 2020. Towards Hierarchical Importance

Attribution: Explaining Compositional Semantics for Neural Sequence Models. In *International Conference on Learning Representations*.

Erik Jones, Robin Jia, Aditi Raghunathan, and Percy Liang. 2020. Robust Encodings: A Framework for Combating Adversarial Typos. In *Proceedings of the 58th Annual Meeting of the Association for Computational Linguistics*, pages 2752–2765, Online. Association for Computational Linguistics.

Brendan Kennedy, Mohammad Atari, Aida Mostafazadeh Davani, Leigh Yeh, Ali Omrani, Yehsong Kim, Kris Coombs, Shreya Havaldar, Gwenyth Portillo-Wightman, Elaine Gonzalez, Joe Hoover, Aida Azatian, Alyzeh Hussain, Austin Lara, Gabriel Cardenas, Adam Omary, Christina Park, Xin Wang, Clarisa Wijaya, Yong Zhang, Beth Meyerowitz, and Morteza Dehghani. 2022. Introducing the Gab Hate Corpus: defining and applying hate-based rhetoric to social media posts at scale, journal=Language Resources and Evaluation. 56(1):79–108.

Hannah Kirk, Bertie Vidgen, Paul Rottger, Tristan Thrush, and Scott Hale. 2022. Hatemoji: A Test Suite and Adversarially-Generated Dataset for Benchmarking and Detecting Emoji-Based Hate. In *Proceedings of the 2022 Conference of the North American Chapter of the Association for Computational Linguistics: Human Language Technologies*, pages 1352–1368, Seattle, United States. Association for Computational Linguistics.

Jan-Christoph Klie, Michael Bugert, Beto Boullosa, Richard Eckart de Castilho, and Iryna Gurevych. 2018. The INCEpTION Platform: Machine-Assisted and Knowledge-Oriented Interactive Annotation. In *Proceedings of the 27th International Conference on Computational Linguistics: System Demonstrations*, pages 5–9, Santa Fe, New Mexico. Association for Computational Linguistics.

György Kovács, Pedro Alonso, and Rajkumar Saini. 2021. Challenges of Hate Speech Detection in Social Media. *SN Computer Science*, 2(2).

Rohan Kshirsagar, Tyrus Cukuvac, Kathy McKeown, and Susan McGregor. 2018. Predictive Embeddings for Hate Speech Detection on Twitter. In *Proceedings of the 2nd Workshop on Abusive Language Online (ALW2)*, pages 26–32, Brussels, Belgium. Association for Computational Linguistics.

Ritesh Kumar, Atul Kr. Ojha, Shervin Malmasi, and Marcos Zampieri. 2018. Benchmarking aggression identification in social media. In *Proceedings of the First Workshop on Trolling, Aggression and Cyberbullying (TRAC-2018)*, pages 1–11, Santa Fe, New Mexico, USA. Association for Computational Linguistics.

Chanhee Lee, Young-Bum Kim, Dongyub Lee, and Heuiseok Lim. 2018. Character-Level Feature Extraction with Densely Connected Networks. In *Proceedings of the 27th International Conference on Computational Linguistics*, pages 3228–3239, Santa Fe, New Mexico, USA. Association for Computational Linguistics.

Yanpei Liu, Xinyun Chen, Chang Liu, and Dawn Song. 2017. Delving into Transferable Adversarial Examples and Black-box Attacks. In *International Conference on Learning Representations*.

Thomas Mandl, Sandip Modha, Prasenjit Majumder, Daksh Patel, Mohana Dave, Chintak Mandlia, and Aditya Patel. 2019. Overview of the HASOC Track at FIRE 2019: Hate Speech and Offensive Content Identification in Indo-European Languages. In *Proceedings of the 11th Forum for Information Retrieval Evaluation*, FIRE '19, page 14–17, New York, NY, USA. Association for Computing Machinery.

Yann Mathet, Antoine Widlöcher, and Jean-Philippe Métivier. 2015. The Unified and Holistic Method Gamma (γ) for Inter-Annotator Agreement Measure and Alignment. *Computational Linguistics*, 41(3):437–479.

N. Narodytska and S. Kasiviswanathan. 2017. Simple Black-Box Adversarial Attacks on Deep Neural Networks. In *2017 IEEE Conference on Computer Vision and Pattern Recognition Workshops (CVPRW)*, pages 1310–1318.

Nicolas Papernot, Patrick Mcdaniel, and Ian J. Goodfellow. 2016. Transferability in Machine Learning: from Phenomena to Black-Box Attacks using Adversarial Samples. *ArXiv*, abs/1605.07277.

F. Pedregosa, G. Varoquaux, A. Gramfort, V. Michel, B. Thirion, O. Grisel, M. Blondel, P. Prettenhofer, R. Weiss, V. Dubourg, J. Vanderplas, A. Passos, D. Cournapeau, M. Brucher, M. Perrot, and E. Duchesnay. 2011. Scikit-learn: Machine learning in Python. *Journal of Machine Learning Research*, 12:2825–2830.

Alina Polyakova and Chris Meserole. 2019. Exporting digital authoritarianism: The Russian and Chinese models. *Policy Brief, Democracy and Disorder Series*, pages 1–22.

Shrimai Prabhumoye, Brendon Boldt, Ruslan Salakhutdinov, and Alan W Black. 2021. Case Study: Deontological Ethics in NLP. In *Proceedings of the 2021 Conference of the North American Chapter of the Association for Computational Linguistics: Human Language Technologies*, pages 3784–3798, Online. Association for Computational Linguistics.

Danish Pruthi, Bhuwan Dhingra, and Zachary C. Lipton. 2019. Combating Adversarial Misspellings with Robust Word Recognition. In *Proceedings of the 57th Annual Meeting of the Association for Computational Linguistics*, pages 5582–5591, Florence, Italy. Association for Computational Linguistics.

Paul Röttger, Bertie Vidgen, Dong Nguyen, Zeerak Waseem, Helen Margetts, and Janet Pierrehumbert. 2021. HateCheck: Functional tests for hate speech detection models. In *Proceedings of the 59th Annual Meeting of the Association for Computational Linguistics and the 11th International Joint Conference on Natural Language Processing (Volume 1: Long Papers)*, pages 41–58, Online. Association for Computational Linguistics.

Paul Röttger, Bertram Vidgen, Dong Nguyen, Zeerak Waseem, Helen Z. Margetts, and Janet B. Pierrehumbert. 2020. HateCheck: Functional Tests for Hate Speech Detection Models. *CoRR*, abs/2012.15606.

Tara N. Sainath, Oriol Vinyals, Andrew Senior, and Haşim Sak. 2015. Convolutional, Long Short-Term Memory, fully connected Deep Neural Networks. In *2015 IEEE International Conference on Acoustics, Speech and Signal Processing (ICASSP)*, pages 4580–4584.

Victor Sanh, Lysandre Debut, Julien Chaumond, and Thomas Wolf. 2019. DistilBERT, a distilled version of BERT: smaller, faster, cheaper and lighter. *arXiv preprint arXiv:1910.01108*.

Patrick Schober, Christa Boer, and Lothar A. Schwarte. 2018. Correlation coefficients: Appropriate use and interpretation. *Anesthesia & Analgesia*, 126(5).

Justin Sherman. 2020. Digital authoritarianism and the threat to global democracy. *Bulletin of the Atomic Scientists*.

Ian C. Simpson, Petroula Mousikou, Juan Manuel Montoya, and Sylvia Defior. 2012. A letter visual-similarity matrix for Latin-based alphabets. *Behavior Research Methods*, 45(2):431–439.

Nicolas Suzor. 2010. The role of the rule of law in virtual communities. *Berkeley Technology Law Journal*, 25(4):1817–1886.

Christian Szegedy, Wojciech Zaremba, Ilya Sutskever, Joan Bruna, Dumitru Erhan, Ian Goodfellow, and Rob Fergus. 2013. Intriguing properties of neural networks. *arXiv preprint arXiv:1312.6199*.

Franklin .S ThambiJose. 2014. Orthographic errors committed by sophomore students: A linguistic analysis. *Mediterranean Journal of Social Sciences*.

Jeremy Waldron. 2012. *The Harm in Hate Speech*. Harvard University Press.

William Warner and Julia Hirschberg. 2012. Detecting hate speech on the world wide web. In *Proceedings of the Second Workshop on Language in Social Media*, pages 19–26, Montréal, Canada. Association for Computational Linguistics.

Zeerak Waseem, Thomas Davidson, Dana Warmsley, and Ingmar Weber. 2017. Understanding abuse: A typology of abusive language detection subtasks. In *Proceedings of the First Workshop on Abusive Language Online*, pages 78–84, Vancouver, BC, Canada. Association for Computational Linguistics.

Zeerak Waseem and Dirk Hovy. 2016. Hateful Symbols or Hateful People? Predictive Features for Hate Speech Detection on Twitter. In *Proceedings of the NAACL Student Research Workshop*, pages 88–93, San Diego, California. Association for Computational Linguistics.

Michael Wiegand, Josef Ruppenhofer, Anna Schmidt, and Clayton Greenberg. 2018. Inducing a lexicon of abusive words – a feature-based approach. In *Proceedings of the 2018 Conference of the North American Chapter of the Association for Computational Linguistics: Human Language Technologies, Volume 1 (Long Papers)*, pages 1046–1056, New Orleans, Louisiana. Association for Computational Linguistics.

Michael Wiegand, Melanie Siegel, and Josef Ruppenhofer. 2019. Overview of the GermEval 2018 Shared Task on the Identification of Offensive Language. Proceedings of GermEval 2018, 14th Conference on Natural Language Processing (KONVENS 2018), Vienna, Austria – September 21, 2018, pages 1 – 10. Austrian Academy of Sciences, Vienna, Austria.

Nicholas Wright. 2018. How Artificial Intelligence Will Reshape the Global Order. *Foreign Affairs*.

Ziqi Zhang and Lei Luo. 2018. Hate Speech Detection: A Solved Problem? The Challenging Case of Long Tail on Twitter. *Semantic Web*, Accepted.

Xinjie Zhou, Xiaojun Wan, and Jianguo Xiao. 2016. Attention-based LSTM network for cross-lingual sentiment classification. In *Proceedings of the 2016 Conference on Empirical Methods in Natural Language Processing*, pages 247–256, Austin, Texas. Association for Computational Linguistics.

A Fine-Grained Results

Figure 4, 5 and 6 illustrates fine-grained results for *Distilbert* evaluated on T2, G and TF datasets. On all datasets, models are highly susceptible to *Dict Whitebox* which is considered to be expected behavior. We find large influence of static dictionaries (*Dict Fixed*) on G and TF datasets because of the availability of larger amount of obscene tokens which make more target selection. Also *Spacing* and *Kebab* are most sensitive obfuscation strategies.

B System Performance on T1 Dataset

Figure 7 illustrating the performance drop for each hate speech detection systems on applying obfuscation attacks across the targets. We find the consistency in the order of vulnerabilities. We also find that the drop is proportional to model's performance.

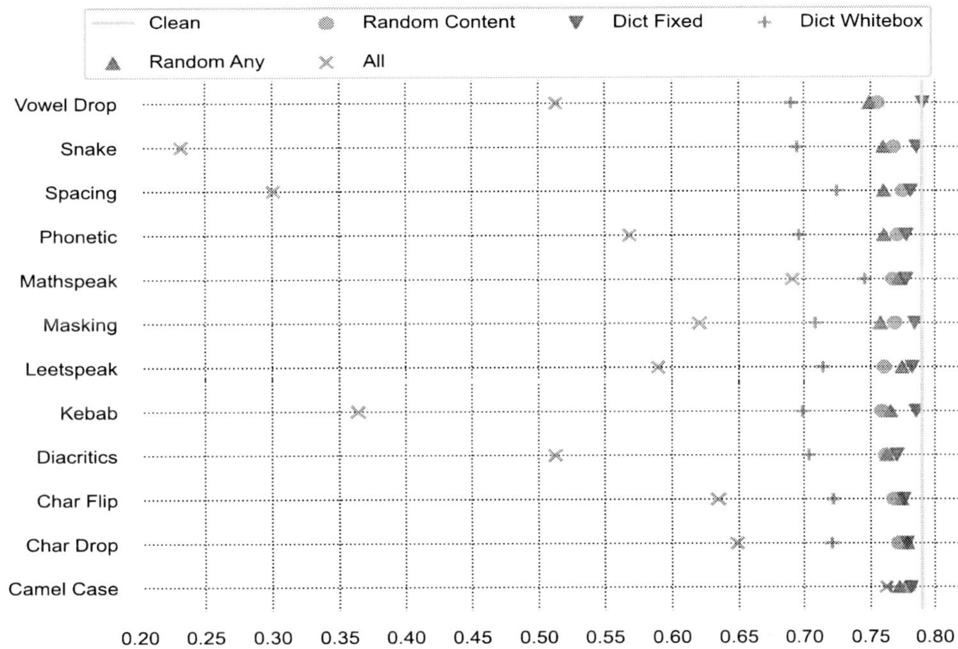

Figure 4: Distilbert's F1 (Hate label) performance on T2 dataset.

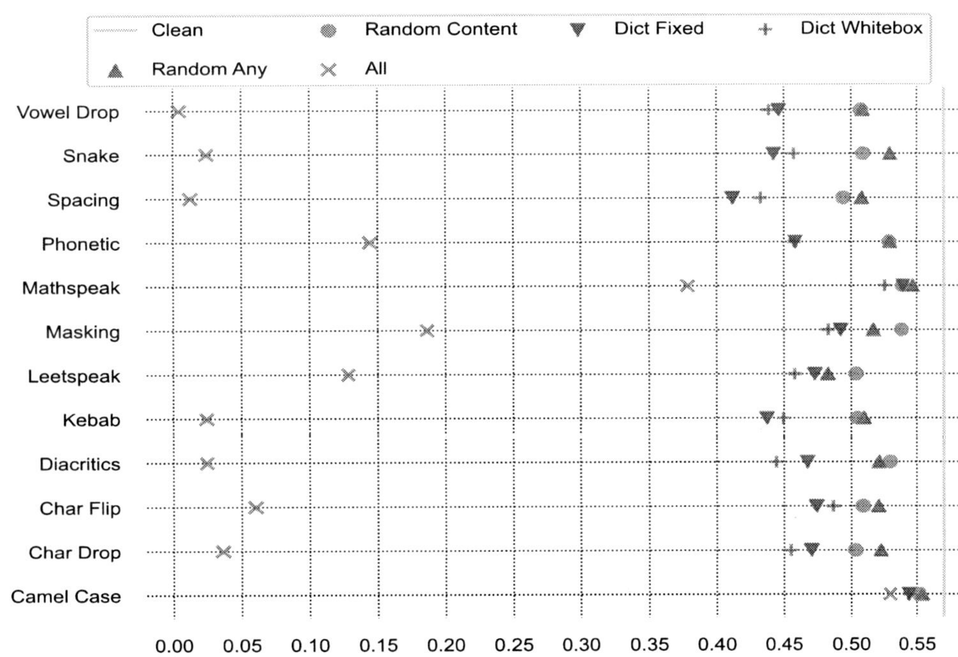

Figure 5: Distilbert's F1 (Hate label) performance on G dataset.

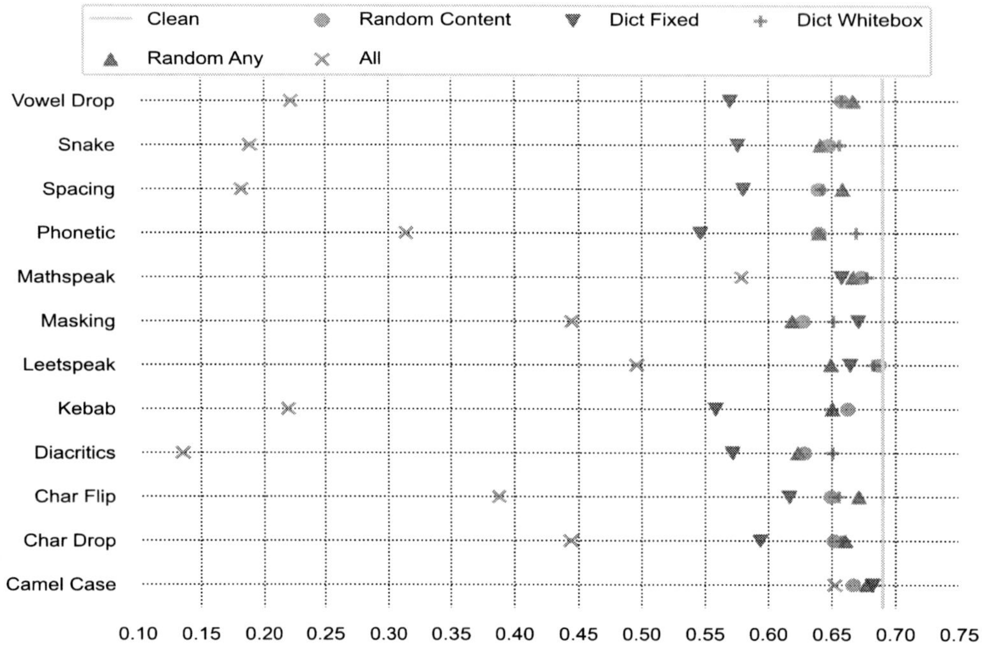

Figure 6: Distilbert's F1 (Hate label) performance on TF dataset.

	Hate Detection Systems									
Target	**Distilbert**	**BILSTM**	**CNN-ATT**	**CNN-LSTM**	**LSTM**	**AdaBoost**	**GradB**	**LogReg**	**RF**	**SVM**
All	.34	.21	.07	.21	.20	.08	.18	.13	.10	.25
Dict Domain	.27	.15	.05	.18	.17	.07	.13	.11	.09	.18
Dict Whitebox	.29	.17	.05	.18	.18	.07	.12	.10	.08	.21
Dict Fixed	.17	.14	.05	.14	.12	.07	.10	.11	.09	.17
Random Content	.06	.06	.03	.07	.04	.03	.05	.05	.04	.08
Random Any	.04	.05	.03	.04	.03	.02	.04	.03	.03	.07

Table 7: Relative change in F1 (Hate) performance for each system estimated on the T1 dataset for different obfuscation strategies. Results are averaged over target selections. GradB, LogReg and RF is abbreviated for *Gradient Boosting*, *Logistic Regression* and *Random Forest* respectively.

Author Index

Association for Computational Linguistics
209 N. Eighth Street
Stroudsburg, Pennsylvania 18360

ISBN 978-1-7138-6200-0

CURRAN ASSOCIATES INC.
proceedings
.com